THE HANDBOOK
TO BIBLE STUDY

THE HANDBOOK TO BIBLE STUDY

With a Guide to the Scofield Study System

Paul S. Karleen

New York   Oxford
OXFORD UNIVERSITY PRESS
1987

Oxford University Press

Oxford   New York   Toronto
Delhi   Bombay   Calcutta   Madras   Karachi
Petaling Jaya   Singapore   Hong Kong   Tokyo
Nairobi   Dar es Salaam   Cape Town
Melbourne   Auckland

and associated companies in
Beirut   Berlin   Ibadan   Nicosia

Published by Oxford University Press, Inc.,
200 Madison Avenue, New York, New York   10016

Oxford is a registered trademark of Oxford University Press

Library of Congress Cataloging-in-Publication Data

Karleen, Paul S.
The handbook to Bible study

"This book is intended as a companion to the New
Scofield Reference Bible"—Pref.
Bibliography: p.
Includes index.
1. Bible—Study—Handbooks, manuals, etc.
2. Scofield reference Bible system—Handbooks, manuals,
etc.   I. Title.
BS600.2.K33   1987   220'.07   87-5569
ISBN 0-19-504987-X

2 4 6 8 9 7 5 3 1

Printed in the United States of America
on acid-free paper

To Joy

Preface

In this computer age it is customary to speak of computing power as a measure of the ability to accomplish complex tasks with ease and speed. Such a description is appropriate for work with the Bible, too. A study or reference Bible offers learning power to any individual who wants to understand God's revelation better.

For over seventy years the Scofield Reference Bible has occupied a leading position among study Bibles. It has enabled countless individuals to see the plan of the Bible and explore its most intricate details.

This book is intended as a companion to *The New Scofield Reference Bible*. Although it can easily and profitably be used with any Bible, many of its features are designed to be used in conjunction with the Scofield.

Several specific goals shaped the writing and final form of this handbook:

1. It is aimed primarily at the average reader and not the Bible scholar, although it is based on scholarly work.

2. If used carefully it can take a new student of the Bible to a place of stability in interpretation.

3. It can function as a concise reference tool.

4. It will open doors to new areas of study, and serve, along with a *New Scofield Reference Bible*, as part of a basic and lifelong study library.

5. It offers treatment of biblical features from the perspective of areas of study not usually applied to works available to the average reader: communications, linguistics, language history, literary criticism, and detailed relations between the testaments.

In order to facilitate study with various Bibles, quotations are given from the Authorized Version (King James) and the New International Version (corresponding to Scofield Reference Bible editions), and the New American Standard Bible, a popular study translation.

Many individuals deserve acknowledgement for their assistance and encouragement. Stephen S. Wilburn, formerly of Oxford University Press, originally conceived the idea for the book. Donald C. Kraus, Bible Editor at Oxford University Press, provided inestimable assistance in the editing process. Hargis V. Thomas, Jr., Bible Marketing Manager, was a continual source of encouragement. Several of my colleagues at Philadelphia College of Bible read portions of the manuscript and offered valuable assistance: Julius Bosco, Gordon Ceperley, Glenn Goss, Samuel Hardman, and Jude Nixon.

I am especially thankful to my wife, Joy, and my children, Daniel, Jessica, and Benjamin, for their support.

If this companion enables its readers to become more ''powerful'' in handling and applying the Scriptures, its purpose will have been fulfilled.

Langhorne, Pennsylvania   P.S.K.
April 1987

Contents

Abbreviations and General Notes   xi
The Names and Order of the Books of the Old and New Testaments   xiii
Alphabetical List of the Books of the Old and New Testaments   xiv

1 Introduction   3

I Backgrounds for Bible Study   9

2 The Nature of the Bible   11
3 How to Study the Bible   37
4 The Language of the Bible   50
5 Interpreting the Bible   73
6 Literary Aspects of the Bible   99
7 Relations Between the Testaments   129
8 Essentials of Biblical Geography   168

II Summary of Bible Doctrine   177

9   Introduction to Bible Doctrine   179
10 The Bible   182
11 God   200
12 The Person of Christ   209
13 The Holy Spirit   225
14 Sin   232

15 Humanity   240
16 Angels   250
17 Salvation   257
18 The Church   283
19 Future Things   296

III Reference   305

20 Quick-Reference Guide to Bible Study Terms   307
21 Outlines of Individual Books of the Bible   368
22 Guide to Old Testament Quotations in the New Testament   404
23 Annotated Bibliography of Basic Books for Bible Study   429

Notes   439
Index   453
Selective Index of Scripture Passages Discussed   466

Abbreviations

Aram.	Aramaic
AV	Authorized Version (= King James Version)
c.	century
cp.	see as a contrasting item
cf.	see as a parallel or similar item
Eng.	English
gen.	generally
Gr.	Greek
Heb.	Hebrew
KJV	King James Version
Lat.	Latin
lg.	language
LXX	Septuagint
Medit.	Mediterranean
NASB	New American Standard Bible
NIV	New International Version
NEB	New English Bible
NSRB	*The New Scofield Reference Bible*
N.T.	New Testament
O.T.	Old Testament
Pss.	Psalms
RSV	Revised Standard Version
Scr.	Scripture

General Notes

The so-called long vowels in Greek, *eta* and *omega,* are represented by *ē* and *ō*.

Translations of biblical passages not otherwise labeled are the author's.

Quotations labeled *AV* are taken from *The New Scofield Reference Bible* and in some cases vary slightly from the standard King James translation. This companion is designed to be used with the New Scofield Study System, as found in *The New Scofield Reference Bible* (published in 1967) and the *Oxford NIV Scofield Study Bible,* (published in 1984). The Scofield annotations in these two study Bibles are identical except for adjustments necessitated by differences between the two translations. In some cases the Scofield Reference Bible (published in 1917) will contain material relevant to the point under discussion. The letters *NSRB* are used to refer to material that is distinctive to *The New Scofield Reference Bible* and the *Oxford NIV Scofield Study Bible,* such as particular numbered maps of Bible lands, changed from the 1917 edition.

The words *see note* direct the reader to a footnote indexed to a particular verse. For example, *see note, 1 Cor. 12:13* directs the reader to the footnote at 1 Cor. 12:13.

The Names and Order of the Books of the Old and New Testaments

THE OLD TESTAMENT

BOOK	ABBR.	CHS.	BOOK	ABBR.	CHS.
Genesis	Gen.	50	Ecclesiastes	Eccl.	12
Exodus	Ex.	40	Song of Songs	Song	8
Leviticus	Lev.	27	Isaiah	Isa.	66
Numbers	Num.	36	Jeremiah	Jer.	52
Deuteronomy	Dt.	34	Lamentations	Lam.	5
Joshua	Josh.	24	Ezekiel	Ezek.	48
Judges	Jud.	21	Daniel	Dan.	12
Ruth		4	Hosea	Hos.	14
1 Samuel	1 Sam.	31	Joel		3
2 Samuel	2 Sam.	24	Amos		9
1 Kings	1 Ki.	22	Obadiah	Obad.	1
2 Kings	2 Ki.	25	Jonah	Jon.	4
1 Chronicles	1 Chr.	29	Micah	Mic.	7
2 Chronicles	2 Chr.	36	Nahum	Nah.	3
Ezra		10	Habakkuk	Hab.	3
Nehemiah	Neh.	13	Zephaniah	Zeph.	3
Esther	Est.	10	Haggai	Hag.	2
Job		42	Zechariah	Zech.	14
Psalms	Ps.	150	Malachi	Mal.	4
Proverbs	Prov.	31			

THE NEW TESTAMENT

BOOK	ABBR.	CHS.	BOOK	ABBR.	CHS.
Matthew	Mt.	28	1 Timothy	1 Tim.	6
Mark	Mk.	16	2 Timothy	2 Tim.	4
Luke	Lk.	24	Titus	Ti.	3
John	Jn.	21	Philemon	Phile.	1
Acts		28	Hebrews	Heb.	13
Romans	Rom.	16	James	Jas.	5
1 Corinthians	1 Cor.	16	1 Peter	1 Pet.	5
2 Corinthians	2 Cor.	13	2 Peter	2 Pet.	3
Galatians	Gal.	6	1 John	1 Jn.	5
Ephesians	Eph.	6	2 John	2 Jn.	1
Philippians	Phil.	4	3 John	3 Jn.	1
Colossians	Col.	4	Jude		1
1 Thessalonians	1 Th.	5	Revelation	Rev.	22
2 Thessalonians	2 Th.	3			

Alphabetical List of the Books of the Old and New Testaments

BOOK	ABBR.	BOOK	ABBR.
Acts		Joel	
Amos		John	Jn.
1 Chronicles	1 Chr.	1 John	1 Jn.
2 Chronicles	2 Chr.	2 John	2 Jn.
Colossians	Col.	3 John	3 Jn.
1 Corinthians	1 Cor.	Jonah	Jon.
2 Corinthians	2 Cor.	Joshua	Josh.
Daniel	Dan.	Jude	
Deuteronomy	Dt.	Judges	Jud.
Ecclesiastes	Eccl.	1 Kings	1 Ki.
Ephesians	Eph.	2 Kings	2 Ki.
Esther	Est.	Lamentations	Lam.
Exodus	Ex.	Leviticus	Lev.
Ezekiel	Ezek.	Luke	Lk.
Ezra		Malachi	Mal.
Galatians	Gal.	Mark	Mk.
Genesis	Gen.	Matthew	Mt.
Habakkuk	Hab.	Micah	Mic.
Haggai	Hag.	Nahum	Nah.
Hebrews	Heb.	Nehemiah	Neh.
Hosea	Hos.	Numbers	Num.
Isaiah	Isa.	Obadiah	Obad.
James	Jas.	1 Peter	1 Pet.
Jeremiah	Jer.	2 Peter	2 Pet.
Job		Philemon	Phile.

BOOK	ABBR.	BOOK	ABBR.
Philippians	Phil.	1 Thessalonians	1 Th.
Proverbs	Prov.	2 Thessalonians	2 Th.
Psalms	Ps.	1 Timothy	1 Tim.
Revelation	Rev.	2 Timothy	2 Tim.
Romans	Rom.	Titus	Ti.
Ruth		Zechariah	Zech.
1 Samuel	1 Sam.	Zephaniah	Zeph.
2 Samuel	2 Sam.		
Song of Songs (called also Canticles and Song of Solomon)	Song		

THE HANDBOOK
TO BIBLE STUDY

1

Introduction

The Scofield Bible occupies a unique place among publications designed to help individuals to understand the Scriptures. Its popularity and usefulness are due both to historical circumstances surrounding its publication and subsequent revision and to several important doctrinal features it embodies. The history of the Scofield Bible is a fascinating story in itself, and can give anyone who uses it greater understanding of what the volume is all about, how to use it, and how to study the Bible in general. This is because the very history of the Scofield Bible is tied to important developments in biblical studies, preaching, and teaching. In a very real sense it arose out of the intense Bible study of an individual, and was designed as an aid to enable others to comprehend the Bible for themselves. As the first study Bible of its kind, it has accomplished this in a way that its first compiler probably never imagined.

Background

Cyrus Ingerson Scofield was born August 19, 1843, in a rural area of Lenawee County, Michigan, southwest of Detroit. After serving in the army of the Confederacy and being awarded the Confederate Cross of Honor, he studied law in the office of a St. Louis firm. When Scofield was twenty-nine, Ulysses S. Grant appointed him United States Attorney for Kansas.

In 1879, while practicing law in St. Louis, he was confronted with the message of the Gospel and received Christ. He immediately began to devote himself to intense study of the Scriptures. There can be no question that through this study God was preparing him for a later work of consolidating a framework for personal Bible study in an easily usable tool.

A number of significant individuals exercised formative influence on Scofield before and during his work on his study Bible. One of the first was Dr. James H. Brookes, a St. Louis pastor and one of the leading Bible expositors of his day. Another was D. L. Moody, whom Scofield had met shortly after his conversion, and whose place he later assumed as pastor of the Congregational Church in Northfield, Massachusetts. These and other great students of the Scriptures helped Scofield to shape his unifying view of the Bible, as well as his passion for seeing it change lives.

After his conversion, Scofield had a continuous involvement with Christian service, first as a worker among railroad men in St. Louis, and later as a pastor in Dallas (1882–1895, 1903) and Northfield, Massachusetts (1895–1903). This fortified an emphasis on *practical* Bible teaching, the kind that results in fruit and Christlikeness. He emphasized Bible study and evangelism, and he was involved in the founding of two important present-day ministries, the Central American Mission (1890), and Philadelphia School of the Bible (with William L. Pettingill in 1914), later Philadelphia College of Bible. His Scofield Bible Correspondence Course, based on his personal Bible study notes, and the highly influential short book *Rightly Dividing the Word of Truth*, actually a product of a Bible class he taught in Dallas, also exemplify his fervent desire to help people to learn to open the Bible for themselves.

In 1903, after resigning from pastoral ministry, Scofield began an intense period of study and writing, both in the United States and in Europe, in order to compile a unified Bible study system that would serve as a vehicle for the great truths of Scripture that he felt were crucial for belief and service. His preparation included research at Oxford and interaction with international scholars. He conceived of a study Bible that would have key features such as chain references, introductions to individual books and to sections of the Bible, a paragraph/outline system, and annotations. Although he was without formal theological training, he proved to be able to capture—in a form that could easily be grasped by the average reader—the great orthodox teachings that had been emphasized during the period of doctrinal awakening about the turn of the century. The result of his work, completed in 1907, was released in 1909 by the New York branch of Oxford University Press as *The Scofield Reference Bible*. Consulting in the preparation of that publication were several leading Bible teachers of the early part of this century, representing diverse ecclesiastical backgrounds—men such as James M. Gray, Dean of Moody Bible Institute, and Arno C. Gaebelein, noted expositor and champion of prophetic truth. Scofield died July 24, 1921, after several years of poor health.

The Study System

No Bible student or teacher should ever claim to be able to present new doctrinal truth or material given from God and on a par with the Bible. But we must acknowledge that God has given gifted individuals to the Body of Christ, and some of their valuable observations about the Bible have been preserved in writing for us. These include such foundational works as editions of the O.T. and N.T. in Heb., Aram., and Gr., compiled from existing manuscripts generally inaccessible to the average person. Many great linguistic studies and historical works relevant to biblical interpretation or to the study of biblical times themselves have been produced and preserved. Some of these works have been done by individuals who had no particular interest in the message of the Bible. Yet God in His providence has kept these in existence for our profit.

Perhaps if he were living C. I. Scofield would be the first to acknowledge that his study system should never be taken as a substitute for the pages of the Bible itself. It is for this very reason that the Scofield Bible is significant. It announces that its purpose is to permit the Bible to speak for itself, by allowing the Bible student to compare parts of the Bible with each other, working from what is more easily understood to what is more difficult. The whole system is designed to open up as much Scripture as possible to the individual. In order to accomplish this, the Scofield Bible not only offers study helps such as cross-references and chain references, but also espouses a theological position that gives a comprehensive picture of the Bible. It is this combination of theological frankness and extensive mechanical helps that makes the Scofield unique.

Can a study Bible take a particular stand and not be biased? Yes, if it seeks to allow the Bible to demonstrate its own teachings. It should be remembered that every translation reflects the theological position of the individual or committee that shaped it. And every work on biblical interpretation espouses some position, with some assumptions. For Scofield there were two overriding guidelines that directed him in his study: (1) that the most accurate understanding of the Bible comes when it is allowed to shed light on itself, and (2) that in the final analysis, all Scripture is to be related to the work of the Lord Jesus Christ. This is in keeping with the biblical principle enunciated in Rev. 19:10: "The testimony of Jesus is the spirit of prophecy" (NASB; see Scofield note).

The resulting stress on orthodox doctrines of the faith and vital prophetic truths, especially the premillennial return of Christ, caused the Scofield study system to be of great value for millions. It enabled them to appropriate for their faith and service a unified biblical message. Bible students could see the Scriptures as a progressive revelation of varying dealings of God with humanity. And they could recognize that although God's purposes at different times in human history might not all have had the same facets, *all* of His acts were ultimately to be related to the cross, and *all* of His blessings for humanity were to be mediated through covenants. This emphasis on dispensations and covenants is indeed a doctrinal distinctive of the Scofield. But it is one that lies at the heart of dispensationalism, the most fruitful approach to the Bible known until now (see ch. 2, The Nature of the Bible). In a real sense the Bible is a history of the making of covenants by God. It encourages us to formulate a theology of covenants. And the understanding that dispensationalism gives as an *approach* to the Bible makes it a significant framework for biblical study. Frank Gaebelein, one of the consulting editors for *The New Scofield Reference Bible,* published in 1967, notes:

> That [Scofield] himself would have equated this particular dispensational system with intimate and absolute truth is doubtful. But that it is a useful tool for comprehending the inspired unfolding of the divine plan for the ages is undeniable, as multitudes of users of this edition of the Bible know.[1]

In other words, then, the very theology of the Scofield is based on the assumption that the best approach to the Bible is one that allows the reader to understand the greatest portion of the Bible. The dispensational framework does this. Many people have attested to the fact that this feature, emphasizing as it does the great network of prophetic truth in the Bible, much of it yet unrealized, opened the Bible to them in a sensible and fruitful way. This has often been in great contrast to teaching they had previously received to the effect that many parts of the Bible could not be understood, were merely repetitive of each other, or were to be taken as nonliteral (see ch. 5, Interpreting the Bible, and ch. 2, The Nature of the Bible).

Finally, it is not without significance that Scofield's emphasis on service in his own life and in the formulation of the annotations has led so many to appreciate the Scofield Bible for its assistance in their own personal walk with God. A presentation of doctrinal understanding of the Bible is incomplete without an accompanying encouragement to lead a fruitful and Christlike life. In the final analysis, sound biblical doctrine actually accomplishes that. It takes the teachings of the Bible as they are intended to be applied to the lives of real people and, by its reasonableness and exaltation of Christ, leads individuals to serve a gracious God. We can see this link between doctrine and practice clearly in such passages as Ti. 2:11, where understanding of God's purposes centered in Christ brings godly living while believers await His return. Correct doctrine leads to correct behavior, but the reverse is never true. Sound interpretation of the Bible is the prerequisite to pleasing God. Scofield knew this, and has helped millions to see it confirmed in their own lives.

History of Publication

The original 1909 edition of *The Scofield Reference Bible* was revised by Scofield and a slightly altered consulting committee, and a new edition was published in 1917. By 1930, *The Scofield Reference Bible* in its two editions had sold one million copies, the first Oxford University Press book to do so. In 1954 Oxford commissioned a group of nine leading evangelical educators to revise and expand the 1917 edition. They were to clarify annotations and integrate into the study system biblical discoveries made since the last publication was prepared. Furthermore, in the interest of enhanced comprehension of the biblical text, changes would be made in the King James translation in order to remove archaic language. These alterations would touch on the occurrence of certain by then obsolete terms (e.g., *corn of wheat*, replaced by *grain of wheat*, in Jn. 12:24), and terms for which new information necessitated changes. The members of the revising committee worked under the leadership of E. Schuyler English, also the editor of *The Pilgrim Study Bible*, another Oxford publication.

The work of the committee yielded an increase in the number of notes from 806 to 1,525; in the number of paragraph subheadings, from 3,040 to 3,500; and in the total number of cross-references, from about 27,000 to about 50,000. The subject chain reference was expanded to include every mention of the particular topic in each chain. It is not surprising that the work of the committee, including the final compiling and editing of contributions by Dr. English, took thirteen years. The product of this extended labor, *The New Scofield Reference Bible* (abbreviated in this handbook as *NSRB*), was published in 1967.

In 1982 Oxford entered into agreement with the Zondervan Corporation to utilize the New International Version translation of the O.T. and N.T., a widely accepted contemporary version executed by a team of evangelical scholars, in a new edition of the Scofield. Consultants from Philadelphia College of Bible worked closely with the editorial staff of Oxford University Press to produce an adaptation of the Scofield material to the NIV translation. This appeared in 1984 as the *Oxford NIV Scofield Study Bible*. In its theological particulars, the NIV/Scofield is identical to *The New Scofield Reference Bible*. Throughout this handbook, references to features of the NSRB apply also to the NIV Scofield.

I

Backgrounds for Bible Study

2

The Nature of the Bible

What Is the Bible?

A Common Name for an Uncommon Document

Although we might be inclined to accord the word *Bible* itself special status, it has quite an ordinary origin. The ancient Greeks called parts of the papyrus plant *bublos* or *biblos*. By a natural process, this term, and other variations of it, was used for the writing material made from such plants, which grew especially along the Nile, and then for joined pieces of that material. Hence, the word we use to describe the written revelation from God was simply, but perhaps very significantly, the ordinary Greek word for book.

It is important for the student of the Bible to think of the object of his study as a book. It is as genuinely a book in nature as *War and Peace* of the *Iliad*. As such, it contains words in human languages—several languages, as a matter of fact. And it uses figures of speech and other devices that we are familiar with. It speaks of historical events and real places, some that we can visit today. It describes real people and is grounded in authentic history, culture, and language.

But as we think further about the Bible, God, and humanity, we are led to the conclusion that, although this is a genuine book, it is absolutely unique among all the books of the world. For it claims to be—and we had better accept that at face value—a revelation from the God of the universe.

It is worthwhile to ponder the process of communication between God and humanity. To begin with, it is possible that a personal God could exist, and yet not communicate at all with humanity. In that case, we would find ourselves forced to agree with the deist, who holds that a personal God is out there somewhere but does not reveal

Himself or intervene in human affairs (see 2 Pet. 3:4–7). Secondly, we might conjecture as to other ways in which God could communicate with us. He could write signals in the sky, or speak so that all on earth could hear him physically. Of course, we do find in the Bible itself that He has spoken with an audible voice at times to individuals, as with Moses on Mt. Sinai. But although there are certainly many ways He could communicate to us, when we stop to think about it, a book is a very natural and effective instrument. There are several reasons why this is so.

To begin with, we know books from ordinary life. Granted, they haven't always been around, but written documents have been in existence now for over four millennia, as far as we know. So it is easy for us to accept a book containing something special from God, especially as compared with smoke signals.

A book is also portable, at least if it is small enough—even ancient scrolls such as the Hebrews used were portable to some degree. That means many people can be exposed to a document. In the case of the Bible, this makes spreading the message relatively easy.

Although God has communicated to many people over the centuries, sometimes face to face, sometimes in dreams and visions, sometimes through overt control of history, we would be at the mercy of oral report for information about such disclosures, if we did not have the advantage of the lasting medium of writing. Thus the Bible makes all other communication from God permanent.

Perhaps most important is the fact that human beings obviously have a facility for communicating with each other by means of that capacity we call language. How natural for God to utilize that same capacity to speak to us! In fact, some writers have asserted that the very reason we have a language capacity is so that God can interact with us.[1] If we stop to think about it, this is quite an amazing thing. The God of the universe uses a channel that seems so terribly ordinary to us—language—to tell us great things we could not otherwise know about Himself and His goodness toward us. (To be sure, some philosophers and theologians have suggested in recent decades that our language is meaningless in talking about the kind of God who must be "out there," so the Bible is inadequate as a help in understanding God. If we believed this we would be adrift on a sea of uncertainty concerning God, and might as well give up the whole matter.) When we have our language in a book from God, we have a very appropriate medium of communication indeed.

And it is this that makes the Bible unique among documents. Although it has some of the same qualities as other books, it has some that no others possess. It claims to be a revelation from God, and backs that up with several qualities. First, it predicts events ahead of time, then records their fulfillment. This is nowhere more prominent than in the book of Daniel, where events concerning the Greek and Roman Empires are unambiguously prophesied in minute detail four hundred years before the fact. No wonder critics of the Bible have worked overtime especially to discredit this particular prophetic book that so clearly supports the supernatural nature of Scripture.

We must also admit—it we are honest about ourselves—that there is no other book that so accurately describes the human condition. Perhaps we could rephrase the familiar adage and say that "nothing knows me like the Book." Sometimes we don't appreciate its piercing insight, but if we are open to the things of God, we come to value it. Incidentally, we should remember that, humanly speaking, one reason the sinner does not come to God is that the Bible exposes his evil deeds (Jn. 3:19–20).

The Bible has also been corroborated in amazing ways with regard to its historical, geographical, prophetic, cultural, and linguistic features by the findings of archaeology, linguistic studies, and other fields. Other books have been so justified, to be sure (except for the prophetic aspect), but none that makes the claims that the Bible does.

The Bible, then, is a unique book, and we must never approach it lightly. We should be thankful that, if we can read and have an appropriate translation, we can scan its pages as easily as those of a newspaper, although we definitely have to expend effort in putting its message together. And we should remember that there is a special spiritual quality about it. Certainly we would not worship it, as followers of Muhammad do the Koran. Only Jehovah deserves our worship—even the revelation He has given does not. (That, by the way, is one reason that we do not possess the original manuscripts of any portions of the O.T. and N.T.) But the Bible certainly merits all our respect.

We must also reckon with the fact that the Bible changes lives—and has changed societies for good on many occasions over the centuries. Every individual, group, or nation that obeys it finds itself on the receiving end of blessing from God. The Psalmist rightly understood the relation between the Bible and behavior, as he expressed it in Ps. 119:165: "Great peace have they who love your law, and nothing can make them stumble" (NIV).

Diversity within Unity

The Bible is actually a collection of books, sixty-six in all. As such, they form the greatest library in the world! It is safe to say that no other single book or set of books has influenced so many people for good as has the Bible.

Within this collection there are several elements of both unity and diversity. With regard to authorship, the Bible is the product of many human authors, some known, some anonymous. They range from the highly educated to the fisherman, from the king to the exiled prophet, from the statesman to the tax collector. Yet, although over forty individuals labored as co-authors with God, every one presents the same God, the same basis of salvation, and the same human needs. While the products of their pens make distinctive contributions, their words all blend into a harmonious unit, pointing at every turn to the unchanging purposes of God centered on providing salvation through the incarnate Lord Jesus Christ.

We can also see that in giving us the Bible God has dealt with humanity progressively. As each book of the sixty-six was penned under the leading of the Holy Spirit, it contributed something new, necessary, and unique. Although some books provided quantum leaps in human understanding of the things of God, and some appeared only to take small steps, each added to the momentum of revelation until God completed His whole disclosure with the final chapters of the book of Revelation. In cumulative fashion, from Genesis to Revelation, God exposed the human condition and unfurled His plan.

The Bible displays diversity in other ways. It was originally written in three languages, with a number of individual words from yet other languages occurring in scattered places. Several cultures are represented, from the earliest attempts at human social grouping in the days immediately after the fall, to the still influential Greek and Roman cultures extending past the N.T. era. The Bible presents a spectrum of literary features, from epic to poetry, drama to narrative. Yet through all of this we can see that there is one God who utilized linguistic, cultural, and literary elements that occur naturally in human life to communicate a unified message centered on the cross. The inscription above the cross is a perfect witness to this kind of unity in diversity, as it comments on the work of Christ in three languages, Gr., Lat. and Aram., each related to a particular culture (see Jn. 19:20).[2]

We should not fail to notice that the Bible is built around several far-reaching contrasts: old and new, temporary and permanent, effective and ineffective (in regard to sacrifices, for instance), shadow and reality, partial and complete, temporal and eternal. One of the best places to see all of these together is in the book of Hebrews. And it is in that book that all of these binary oppositions are resolved and given purpose, for they are all related to the final, perfect, eternally effective work of Christ. The writer to the Hebrews combines many of these contrasts when in describing His sacrifice he says, "For Christ did not enter a man-made sanctuary that was only a copy of the true one; he entered heaven itself, now to appear for us in God's presence" (Heb. 9:24, NIV).

How the Bible Came into Being

Types of Material

As the human authors of the Bible labored with pen and ink, they utilized different sources of material for their compositions. For example, when Moses wrote the Pentateuch, he certainly utilized his own memory of events, but he had to rely on others for information about what he did not witness. Similarly, we know that Luke was present for only a portion of the events he records in the book of Acts. Both were dependent on oral information and, probably especially in the case of Luke, some written information.

Although some theologians have held that all that was not directly accessible to the writers of the Bible was given directly by God, most today would not hold to such an extreme position. In fact Luke, for example, virtually tells us that he did research in preparation for writing his gospel (Lk. 1:1–3; see note at 1:3), and presumably did so also for the second part of his work, the book of Acts. Such a view of human activity in recording Scripture does not in any way lessen the extent of the role of the Holy Spirit in supervising the process. The Spirit could just as easily have led Luke to record the details of an event as provided by an eyewitness or by a written document as He could have given it to him directly. There has been much discussion in recent years about writers' use of oral and written sources—documents especially—in the composition of the Scriptures, particularly the Gospels. The conservative interpreter of the Bible need not fear such concepts concerning sources if he maintains a high view of the accuracy of the Bible and of the clear role of the Holy Spirit.[3]

Disclosure from God

If we look at this from the standpoint of God's activity, we find that the Bible records different kinds of disclosures from God: dreams, visions, direct writing (the tablets of the Law), messages through prophets, the words of Jesus, the Person of Jesus Himself (Heb. 1:1–2), and others. And clearly God led some to record previously unknown data as they wrote. We might well ask if Paul knew all the details about the rapture as recorded in 1 Th. 4 before he took pen in hand. Perhaps he did, but then again God may have given him the specifics as he wrote.

What is clear, though, is that the Bible says of itself that it is all from God. It is both a revelation and a breathed-out document. We usually think of revelation as only the disclosure of what was previously unknown. But that is only part of what is involved. For example, Luke must have known many historical and geographic details before he wrote the book of Acts. However, their precise combination is a kind of revelation, and is guaranteed by a work of the Holy Spirit called *inspiration*. In this sense, then, all of the Bible is a revelation, because both the newly given spiritual material and what was known were shaped by God to form a coherent spiritual message. (See ch. 10, The Bible, under "Revelation" and "Inspiration.")

We desperately need this kind of revelatory activity centered on Scripture, because we are incapable of apprehending spiritual realities directly by ourselves. To be sure, we can know certain things about God from the heavens (Ps. 19:1–6; Rom. 1:19–20) and from our consciences (Rom. 2:15). But we need to know what our spiritual condition is before God, what God is like, and what possibility there is of a remedy for our predicament. The things we can know about God from looking around ourselves or even within—what theologians have called general revelation—are inadequate to help us with our sin problem. The great theologian B. B. Warfield addresses this point:

> Man as finite needs to be told directly by God about the ultimate direction of the course of history. . . .
> . . . Sinful man wants to suppress the truth of God that comes to him. . . . The natural man is at enmity with God. He always seeks to make himself believe that he has not been confronted with God; his forms of worship are ways by which he makes himself believe that God is finite. . . .
> . . . If sinful man is to be saved he must be saved against his will. He hates God. God's work of salvation must be a work into territory that belongs to him by right but that has been usurped by King Diabolus. . . . So an entrance has to be forced . . . And when God by grace makes friends within the enemy country these friends . . . are as much as was Adam in need of supernatural word revelation. And they are . . . to an extent under the influence of the old man within them and so would even when redeemed never be able to interpret mere revelational facts correctly and fully. Hence the necessity of Scripture.[4]

So God has taken some things we know about already—the Roman Empire, the geography of Judea, the elements of poetry, and many more—and combined them with new information in an overall (though limited in certain respects) special revelation of Himself and His purposes for humanity and the universe. God has communicated in ways that meet our spiritual needs totally, and put that message in a book. Old Testament scholar Gleason Archer puts it this way:

> How then can we know God or His will for our lives? Only if He reveals Himself to us! Unless He Himself tells us, we can never know for sure the answers to those questions which matter most to us as human beings. At this point it is important to observe that the Bible presents itself as the written revelation of God. This purports to be a Book in which God gives us the answers to the great questions which concern our soul, and which all the wisdom and science of man are powerless to solve with any degree of certainty.[5]

We should worship Him more because in His wisdom He has spoken in grace to us.

How We Got the Bible

Ancient Writing Practices

To understand the written character of the Bible, we need to know a few things about how ancient writing and copying were practiced. In the twentieth century we are thoroughly conditioned to think of written documents as possessing a high degree of accuracy, due to the printing process, in spite of the fact that almost every book has some errors introduced by the author, editors, or typesetters. We tend to forget that the printing press is a comparatively recent invention. Before that all copying had to be done by hand, with high likelihood of introduction of variations. When we examine the process of producing ancient books and other documents, it is amazing that, given the totally manual nature of the task, there are as few errors as there are.

We do not know the precise dates for the production of any biblical books. Nor do we know exactly how much oral, how much already written, or how much eyewitness material went into each. However, we do know that each original portion of what is now considered canonical Scripture was initially inscribed and subsequently copied by hand. As we might suspect, copying was a laborious process in which scribes attempted to reproduce as perfectly as possible the manuscript before them. Sometimes groups of copiers (during the Christian era, often in monasteries) worked together, writing from dictation by an individual who read the master copy. One of the most famous (but not for N.T. manuscripts) workrooms used for this purpose is in the ruins of the Essene community at Qumran (see ch. 20, Guide to Bible Study Terms).

Although the methodology was simple and primitive by our standards, the pens, inks, and writing surfaces were often quite sophisticated and the subsequent product quite durable and attractive. The fact that we are able to read such documents today, in many cases without any eyestrain at all (if we know the language!) attests to the quality of the materials that were used. In many instances beautiful colored inks have lasted through the centuries. The papyrus and vellum (animal skin) surfaces that were used are usually remarkably well preserved today. The study of ancient writing and copying practices and of the products of such activity is called paleography. This is a fascinating field, and the Bible student interested in pursuing it further is encouraged to consult the works by Ewert and Greenlee listed in ch. 23, Annotated Bibliography.[6]

Determining the Text

Now all of this may seem to be very dry, separated as it is by so many years from our time, especially when we have complete Bibles in abundance. But it is part of a foundational area of biblical study, called *textual criticism*. This science attempts, through guidelines and procedures, to determine the original content of the biblical books. Actually, textual criticism is needed for any hand-copied document where we do not possess the original and where it is important for us to find out what the author wrote. This is absolutely necessary where two or more copies are in disagreement at any point. Such alternate wording is called a *variant*. Because the Bible contains variants and is such an important document, textual criticism is essential to biblical studies. As a matter of fact, it is the most foundational of all endeavors related to Bible study, since it determines the nature of the text we study.

Textual criticism can be defined as the attempt to determine the original words of any literary work for which the original document does not exist. Part of the process involves working backward through variant readings, attempting to determine how changes in the text may have arisen, and deciding what variant has greater claim to originality. It is important to realize that we cannot call a particular variant an error, since we do not know for sure which of two or more alternatives represents the original. However, in order to get anywhere at all, we must assume that one of the variants does correspond to what the author wrote. It is hypothetically possible, of course, that the original at a particular point in the biblical text is not represented. In that case, we would have a text that was not preserved by God during the process of transmission through the ages. It is generally accepted by textual critics that the N.T. text is in such a state of preservation that we have all the material needed to make adequate decisions as to originality. In the case of the O.T., however, there are times when even theologically conservative textual critics are willing to agree that the standard Heb. text and other texts (such as the Septuagint) may not contain satisfactory readings. It should be stressed that the number of such instances is remarkably low, and that textual critics, especially conservative ones, are very reluctant to suggest readings beyond what is contained in manuscript evidence.

Reasons for Confidence

The existence of variants in the text and attempts to piece it together might tend to make one uneasy about the trustworthiness of the Bible. Actually, despite the fact that not all the manuscripts of the Bible are in agreement, there are many reasons for being very confident about the state of the text (a manuscript is simply any hand-copied portion of the Bible, whether a few words or a whole testament). To begin with, as compared with other ancient literature, the existing manuscripts of the Bible come remarkably close in time to their sources. For instance, some N.T. manuscripts have been dated at less than a hundred years from the time of writing of the original they represent. In general, copies of classical works in Gr. and Lat. are much further removed in time from their originals. Also, there are large numbers of manuscripts attesting to the text of the Bible, especially in the case of the N.T., for which there are probably over five thousand Gr. manuscripts alone, not to mention those in other languages, such as Lat. and Gothic. These and other factors should lead us to believe that we can proceed confidently with biblical studies that build upon the work of textual critics.

As with all biblical study, we should keep in mind that anyone who works with the text and expects to put it together accurately must have a high regard for its integrity and inspiration and must allow it to speak for itself. Just as there have been some who have written commentaries and theological studies who do not have a high regard for the text, there have been some who have engaged in textual criticism who have not held to the divine source of the text. However, most textual critics have attempted to be genuinely fair with the text of the Bible. Every Bible student must simply be on guard in this area, as in every other, for teaching and conclusions that are not consistent with a high view of Scripture. Aside from this, the results of textual criticism are indispensable to anyone who seeks to discover the message of the Bible. In fact, without such study down through the ages, we would not have a coherent text to work with in any language.

We must further assume in all of this that God has preserved for us reliable texts of both the O.T. and N.T. Although certainly not all of the textual problems have been resolved, we must believe that God has not led us astray in regard to the words of the text of the Bible. In fact it should always be kept in mind that no variant reading affects a major doctrine. There is always enough information elsewhere for us to determine the full counsel of Scripture on any given teaching.

It is historically and theologically realistic to acknowledge that some textual criticism on the Bible is necessary, and the Bible student should not glibly accept the verdict of those who assert that it isn't. Even those who hold that the type of text underlying the AV is homogeneous, and therefore the mainstream text preserved by God, must face the fact that some textual criticism on that type of text is necessary (see ch. 4, The Language of the Bible, regarding translations).

Some Examples of Textual Criticism

In attempting to determine the original text, modern textual critics use two main lines of evidence. Manuscripts have individual characteristics (handwriting style, a history of circulation and use that may be known, etc.), can often be located as to time and place of writing or use, and can sometimes be grouped with other similar manuscripts. Such features are said to constitute *external evidence*. On the other hand, there are details in the text itself at the point of variant readings. These particulars, such as grammatical elements, similarity to other passages, pronunciation of words in question, etc., are called *internal evidence*. Most textual critics today work with a combination of internal and external evidence in making decisions at particular points in the text.[7]

A description of the whole process is beyond the scope of this book. However, we will look at two examples that are found in some editions of the NSRB. Scribes introduced changes in the texts they were copying for two basic reasons. They may have altered wording intentionally, or may simply have copied incorrectly. The latter class of changes is far more frequent than the former. Intentional changes may have occurred because a scribe knew of a passage parallel to the one he was copying and attempted to bring his text into line with the other, thinking that a scribe before him had erred and caused a divergence between the two texts. Such a change is called a *harmonization*. Another reason was to introduce a particular doctrinal feature that the scribe wished to present. This type of change was, as far as we can tell, very infrequent. Scribes who were very conscious of grammatical niceties such as spelling variations, alternative suffixes, etc., sometimes made alterations in the text, again, in order to reverse what was felt to be a place where an earlier scribe had made an error, since only in the rarest instance would a scribe change what he believed the author wrote.

Some changes introduced by scribes are entirely unintentional, and involve such mundane things as reading and writing the same suffix or other letter sequence twice *(dittography)*, eliminating one of two repeated elements *(haplography)*, misreading letters that looked alike (such as the Heb. equivalents of Eng. *d* and *r;* the Gr. equivalents of Eng. *A, D,* and *L; E* and *S*), or confusing two letters or sequences of letters that sounded similar or alike (such as Gr. omicron and omega), a practice called *homoeoteleuton*.

For example, in Gen. 10:4 some Heb. manuscripts and the Septuagint have, as in 1 Chr. 1:7, *rodanim,* i.e., a reference to the Rhodians of the Aegean Sea. Other Heb. manuscripts have *dodanim.* The AV adopts *dodanim,* while the NIV and NASB opt for *rodanim.* The textual problem is apparently due to the confusion of the Heb. equivalents of Eng. *r* and *d*. The reading *rodanim* is taken by most today to be the better reading, due to the possibility of connection with the Rhodians (see note, Gen. 10:4).

In Eph. 5:9 there are two variant readings, "spirit" *(pneumatos)* and "light" *(phōtos)*. The NSRB, along with the NIV and NASB, regards "light" as the better reading. "Light" could have arisen under the influence of the presence of the same word in the preceding verse, but it is more likely that "spirit" was introduced as an intentional or unintentional harmonization to Gal. 5:22, where "the fruit of the Spirit" occurs (see marginal note in NASB at Eph. 5:9).[8]

The Gathering of Inspired Scripture: The Canon

A question foundational to all Bible study concerns what books we consider to be authoritative in spiritual things. Conservative Protestants view the present sixty-six books of the O.T. and N.T. as forming a complete revelation from God. Yet there are other groups within the broad umbrella of nominal Christendom that hold different views. Further, agreement as to the acceptability and desirability of the sixty-six did not come instantly.

The collected books that are considered (by anyone) to be spiritually authoritative for Christianity are called the *canon*. This is actually a transliteration of a Gr. word that means "rule" or "standard." As employed in reference to the Bible, it denotes the set of writings that are taken as normative under some set of guidelines or principles for evaluating spiritual worth. The existence of a canon is a fact. The questions, then, are what elements went into decisions made many centuries ago, and how guidelines vary for different groups. Practically speaking, the answers to these questions involve a study both of the history of the gathering of books, and of views that we have access to concerning reasons for compiling and approving.

We need to be very clear on what the basic idea of the canon is. If we allow the Bible to speak for itself, we arrive at the fundamental belief that it carries with it its own authority and qualities of excellence, because it is a product of the creative breath of God (2 Tim. 3:16). It stands as an inspired revelation, no matter what human beings think about it. Therefore, determining the extent of accepted and profitable books is not at all a matter of the granting of approval by an individual or an institution, such as a church body, or investing a book with spiritual quality. Rather, it is solely a matter of human beings being led by God to recognize what He had already placed in existence as authoritative revelation, and, conversely, of determining what books did not have their source in God. In other words, the Church did not create Scripture; instead Scripture has primacy and is the basis for the Church. Gleason Archer states:

> The biblical authors indicate very clearly, whenever the matter comes up, that the various books of the Bible were canonical from the moment of their inception, by virtue of the divine authority ("Thus saith the Lord") behind them, and the books received immediate recognition and acceptance by the faithful as soon as they were made aware of the writings.[9]

A place where it is quite easy to see this is in the attitude of our Lord and the N.T. writers toward the Scriptures. Jesus always put Himself under Scripture and often asserted its unalterable authority. Hence, when in Mt. 5:18 He declares, "I tell you the truth, until heaven and earth disappear, not the smallest letter, not the least stroke of a pen, will by any means disappear from the Law until everything is accomplished'' (NIV), He is teaching that the Bible stands on its own and needs no help from human beings to accomplish its ends. To have this quality it must be from God. Jesus is thus putting His stamp of approval on that portion of the O.T. as He quotes it. In 2 Pet. 3:16 Peter puts Paul's writings on a par with the O.T. Scriptures. Thus, probably even before they had been circulated widely, at least some of Paul's books were viewed as authoritative. No councils were needed to give approval.

This brings us to the key factors that must have been used in determining the canon, especially for the N.T.: apostolic source, connection with an apostle, correspondence with known apostolic doctrine, doctrinal harmony with other accepted writings, evidence of divine origin, and spiritual profitability. The last three were evidently determinative in establishing the canon of the O.T.[10]

Evidence for the Old Testament Canon

Our knowledge of the process of recognition of O.T. books is not as extensive as that concerning the determination of the canonicity of N.T. books. The earliest written indications of conscious thoughts of a canon date to the early part of the second c. B.C. Individual books as we know them appear at various times in different combinations, e.g., 1 and 2 Sam. are considered a unit in some systems of division. However, as far as the Heb. text is concerned, records indicate that only a few books were debated as to their canonicity, with records of resolution of questions about some books coming in the first c. A.D.[11] It is significant that the Hebrew canon of apostolic times is identical to the present thirty-nine-book O.T. familiar to Protestants.[12]

Fourteen books form the disputed O.T. Apocrypha, a term meaning "hidden," and here denoting books that are in some way ancillary to others:

Additions to Esther	1 and 2 Maccabees
Baruch	Prayer of Manasses
Bel and the Dragon	Song of the Three Holy Children
Ecclesiasticus	Susanna
1 and 2 Esdras	Tobit
Judith	The Wisdom of Solomon

Today the Roman Catholic Church views most of them as canonical. Some people trace their authoritative nature to the Septuagint, but different manuscripts of that translation contain varying combinations of apocryphal books. Hence, their status was in doubt, especially during the early centuries of the Christian era. They were never included in the Heb. canon, and it is significant that the N.T. writers never clearly quote from any apocryphal book. For these and other reasons, conservative Protestants today deny canonical status to the apocryphal books.

Testimony to the Canon of the New Testament

The earliest testimony to the canonicity of the N.T. lies in the N.T. itself, where, as indicated above, writers give obviously unsolicited affirmation of the spiritual worth of other writings. Some examples are found at 1 Th. 5:27 and 2 Pet. 3:15–16. Apparently, in a very natural process, the early Church used writings in both public and private situations as they appeared, circulated them, compared them with other early Christian writings and the O.T., and assessed their spiritual worth. Many people in the first c. would have known firsthand of the sayings of Jesus, and could compare written documents and the N.T. books with them for accuracy. Perhaps the O.T. canon as a fixed collection formed a model for establishing a set of documents presenting works of God in the new age.

The earliest testimony outside the N.T. appears toward the end of the first c. in the writing of Clement of Rome, where there is apparent reference to Mt., Rom., 1 Cor., Heb., and perhaps other books. Discussion and presentation of opinions continued until the end of the fourth c., when there was widespread unity on the present twenty-seven books as canonical. The process included separation of evidently apostolic books from inferior ones such as 1 and 2 Clement, The Didache, etc. The principles listed above, centering on apostolic connection and spiritual worth, were the overriding criteria.

Subsequent Forms

The missionary nature of Christianity has engendered a unique phenomenon in the history of written documents. Prior to the writing of the N.T., very few ancient works were translated into other languages. The O.T. was translated into Gr., although not to bring the message to other ethnic groups, but because a large segment of the Jewish people had changed their language. However, with the intensive evangelizing thrust of the first few centuries after the apostolic age, the need for adequate translations of both the O.T. and the N.T. became apparent. It is interesting that some of these translations comprise some of the earliest records we have of particular languages, e.g., Gothic and Slavic. As such they are of great value in even nonbiblical linguistic studies.

The wide range and larger number of translations of the Bible provide a significant source of evidence for the nature of early Gr. and Heb. texts, and as such are utilized extensively by textual critics. Close to ten thousand manuscripts in Lat. and other languages (besides Gr. and Heb.) provide information for the process of working back to the autographs (the original manuscripts), and for other aspects of biblical studies. There are many good books on translations of the Bible into English and other languages. The reader should consult ch. 23, Annotated Bibliography, for further information.[13]

People living in every generation owe a great debt to those preceding them who have labored in establishing the canon of Scripture, in attempting to determine the exact nature of the text and in translating it into different languages. Speakers of Eng. have been especially favored by God to possess so many equitable translations of the Bible (see ch. 4, The Language of the Bible, concerning translations).

General Qualities of the Bible

Revelation

God communicated to human beings in many ways over many centuries. This is the meaning of Heb. 1:1. However, we would not know of those disclosures without permanent records. The Bible, then, contains the records of all we need to know about God and His purposes for us. We should discuss two crucial questions here: How do we know that the Bible is from God? and How do we know that God has stopped giving revelation?

The answer to the first question is essentially a matter of faith based on evidence internal and external to the Bible. To begin with, the Bible clearly claims to have a divine origin. In Acts 1:16 Peter ascribes David's words in Pss. 69 and 109 to the Holy Spirit. Paul was conscious in 1 Th. 4:15 that he was reiterating what Jesus (whom he viewed as God) had said, or was giving information provided to him in some way by God. It is likely that the latter is the case, since we do not have a record in the gospels of Jesus' words on the rapture as presented this way (for a definition of *rapture,* see ch. 20, Guide to Bible Study Terms).

In addition to such internal evidence, external corroboration of divine origin has been plentiful over the centuries. History, archaeology, language studies, and changed lives have attested to that source. In the final analysis, however, viewing the Bible as a revelation from God is a matter of faith. We can never prove it. If we could, all the other spiritual systems of humanity would be rendered patently illogical. God has given us a healthy amount of internal and external evidence for faith to operate on. As a matter of fact, this helps us to see what biblical faith is. It begins with a small amount of evidence, but not outright proof. The Spirit of God gives assurance of the appropriateness of that evidence for the life of an individual. God-pleasing faith trusts God on the basis of small amounts of evidence, seeing spiritual realities beyond the evidence of the senses. This is the great message of Heb. 11:1.

How do we know that other existing books do not have spiritual value equal to the Bible? The existence of a canon ratified over fifteen centuries ago by godly individuals, is a strong argument for the uniqueness of the Bible. It is also a matter of record that new works that lay claim to divine authority today are beset with considerable internal inconsistency and historical inaccuracies.[14]

The second question concerns the possibility of further revelation on a par with that contained in canonical Scripture. Although we cannot in theory rule this out, since God can do anything He wishes, the patterns of His activity as recorded in the Bible and the principles associated with them argue against further written revelation. For instance, much N.T. revelation came through the work of prophets during the apostolic age. Ephesians 2:20 describes as foundational the ministry of those with the prophetic gift. The intense revelation of truth from God during the ministry of the Lord Jesus Christ and the apostolic age were clearly part of a time of special dealing by God with humanity, involving dreams, visions, miracles and other signs. The completed inauguration of the present age, which was attested by such signs, argues against further special revelation. That such miraculous activity was fading out even during the latter part of the apostolic age is taught in Heb. 2:2. To be sure, Heb. is considered to be canonical Scripture. But the point is that the overall revelatory activity of God was diminishing when Heb. was written, apparently before 70 A.D. Historical notices concerning the late years of the first century also attest to the fade-out of miraculous activity, associated in the Bible with new revelation. The process of recognizing canonical N.T. books operated on the assumption that God had ceased giving new revelation. That assumption became a dogma with the close of the issue of the canon at the end of the fourth c. in the Western and Eastern Churches.

Divine Oversight and Its Result

If God had given us a revelation of His purposes for us and yet had left it full of inconsistencies and outright errors, we would be left to drift in a sea of spiritual uncertainty. In fact, those who view the Bible as having errors put themselves in that position. But we have to assume that if a truthful God has spoken, He has preserved His words in such a way that we cannot be deceived. Of course, we do not possess the originals of the O.T. or the N.T. And clearly there are contradictions among the existing manuscripts. Yet the Bible's own testimony to its origin is that it is breathed out by God. It teaches us that the God behind it is perfect and would not deceive. Furthermore, we desperately need spiritual help. It must have been designed to meet our needs perfectly. So we are led to conclude that the Bible is trustworthy in every way, and must have been without error as originally penned. For discussion of a recent movement among evangelicals that departs from this position, see ch. 10, The Bible, under "Trustworthiness—Inerrancy and Infallibility."

But some might ask if the present state of biblical manuscripts, not identical to the originals, puts us in a position where we can be led astray. To begin with, as we pointed out above, the variants in biblical manuscripts do not affect any major doctrine (obviously they affect some content). In addition, we must assume that if God went to the trouble (humanly speaking) to give us a significant body of truth, one that we are completely dependent on for knowledge of the spiritual realm, then He must have taken steps to see to it that we would be able to use it reliably. Why did God allow errors to enter during the process of transmission? The answer must be that if we possessed perfect copies, we would venerate them, just as we would any extant originals. As we look at the broad picture, we must conclude that God in His providence provided a trustworthy revelation, caused it to be transmitted to succeeding generations, yet saw to it that the written message would always turn our attention to the God who has revealed, rather than the revelation itself. When we acknowledge the depravity of humanity and its bent always to pervert the things of God that it knows about, that plan appears to be very wise indeed.

Resultant Authority

What we have really been describing in this section is a chain. God has revealed, that revelation has had divine oversight, and the product was without error in the originals. There is one more link in this sequence. Because the Bible is breathed out from God, is spiritually correct, discerning truth from error, darkness from light, and is our only source of spiritual help in written form from God, it can make claims on us that no other source of information can. Although we do not realize it, every human being relies on some source of authority in making decisions in life. We may depend on another person, on experience, on emotions, or on any one or more of many things that we feel are worthwhile. But the fact is that we make decisions, whether we are aware of it or not, on the basis of things that we feel will lead us to reach certain ends, useful or destructive. Our sources can be good or evil, from God or from the Devil.

The Bible clearly claims to possess the only legitimate authority over our lives. If God were present with us visibly, then we would be obligated to obey Him directly— although sinners would still rebel, and will in the last days, according to the Bible's teaching on the millennium (Rev. 20:7–9). But in His absence He has given written instructions for leading a life that pleases Him. And those instructions are valid whether we acknowledge them or not. A person can certainly ignore the Bible and scoff at its teaching on the existence of a Creator/Savior and judgment to come. But we cannot make the rules. The Bible contains the standards for life, and we ignore them at our peril. It is a God-given authority for our lives.[15] And the more we bring ourselves under it, the more we will prosper spiritually:

> Blessed are they whose ways are blameless, who walk according to the law of the Lord. Blessed are they who keep his statutes and seek him with all their heart. (Ps. 119:1–2, NIV)

The Plan of the Bible

We spoke earlier about unity and diversity in the Bible. There is another important kind of unity/diversity feature in the Bible that is often overlooked. It is easy enough to see that there are distinct books from different authors, as well as a dichotomy between two testaments. But the student of the Bible must also notice that God is doing different things with humanity, all, of course, centered on the Person and work of the Lord Jesus Christ. We do not mean by this that there are hidden people on various continents that He is dealing with, as some cults suggest, or that he is working with groups on other planets. The point is this: we can never make sense of the Bible unless we see that there are many segments to God's work within time, segments that for want of a better word some have called *dispensations*.

Dispensationalism

If one mentions the word *dispensationalism* in any group of evangelicals, there are likely to be various responses. What is a dispensationalist? How can you recognize one? Is it someone who carries a Scofield Bible? Is it a person who frequently attends Bible conferences? Once he is identified, can he be labeled immediately as unscholarly, as some might do?

For some, dispensationalism is foolishness. But for others it is a tremendous help in understanding the Bible. This writer believes it is a valid approach, and this section will provide a number of reasons in support of its accuracy and value.

In ch. 5, Interpreting the Bible, we stress that the best system of interpretation is the one that opens up the most Scripture and allows Scripture to be consistent with itself. This type of interpretation is at the heart of dispensationalism. It is really an approach to the Bible, rather than a system of theology. True enough, it includes certain truths regarding the Church, prophecy, and Israel, but it is basically an outlook on the Bible that works on the basis of historic, orthodox tenets of the faith, and attempts to allow the Bible to open itself to the reader. This is clearly the factor that divides it from other conservative systems of interpretation.

There is no question that the Scofield Bible is dispensational in its approach to the Scriptures. For this reason, attacks on dispensationalism go hand in hand with attacks on the Scofield Bible. Because of this situation it will be useful to treat in this section some of the issues involved in the controversy.

God's goal. It is worthwhile to ask if there is some overall thing that God is doing in eternity in relation to the universe and the beings that He has made, both human and angelic. We might, for example, suggest that the bottom line is to provide salvation. Although that is certainly important, it is too one-sided and is simply centered on what we get. If that were all, then God would be just a great benefactor, giving us what we need or want.

We might then say that God's overall purpose is to bring peace on earth, certainly an important and needed goal. There is no doubt that that is part of what He is doing. Yet, once again, if that were His main purpose, He would be seen simply as a supplier of what we are missing or have failed to achieve. Certainly there must be much more, and something that draws attention to God Himself.

Perhaps God's main purpose is to build the Church. This idea has great merit, and would be supported by Jesus' statement to Peter in Mt. 16:18: "Upon this rock I will build my church, and the gates of Hades shall not overpower it" (NASB). And wasn't this the goal of the commission of Acts 1:8 to evangelize? But if we read a little further in Acts, we find that something other than the Church is proclaimed, some kind of glorious day for Israel, as in Acts 3:17–23. For this and many other reasons we would be correct in suspecting that, even though building the Church is an extremely important part of God's plan, there is more.

We could make many other suggestions as to the overall purpose of God in history—and eternity. But one concept that seems to do justice to the Bible as a whole is this: God is working in many ways, at many times, with many groups, in many circumstances, to bring glory to Himself and to show what He is like. Now we can hardly object to any statement of purpose that puts God at the center, and that's as it should be. And when we consider all that we know about God, we find that this way of describing God's goal makes a lot of sense. We must be careful, of course, not to claim that we know all that God is doing. The reverent person always looks for more about God and His ways, and admits that he sees imperfectly. But we would like to put together as much as we can, because God Himself encourages us to find out what He is doing. In fact, that is just what 2 Tim. 2:15 tells us to do—handle all of the Bible very carefully. The Bible commends earnest searching of His purposes (1 Pet. 1:10–12).

This kind of purpose certainly does justice to the character of God. He is unique, the only uncreated being in the universe. Everything comes from Him. But, more important, everything exists for Him. That, by the way, is Paul's point in Rom. 11:33–36. And it is no accident that his doxology comes not in connection with the Church primarily, but with Israel, after an exposition (in chs. 9–11) of the certainty of the future restoration of that nation from disgrace.

When we think more about bringing glory to God in the way that Paul speaks of, by way of contrast we must take note of ourselves and our failure to be like Him. This is what Paul reminds us of in Rom. 3:23: "All have sinned and fall short of the glory of God" (NIV). It would not be unreasonable to find, in connection with God's glory, different tracks and different segments in God's dealings with humanity, especially if God were showing us in various scenes and stages how completely all creatures fail to be like Him. And that is just what the Bible emphasizes. If we look in on humanity where the Bible begins our story, in the Garden, we find that in spite of the perfect environment, our first parents failed. Leaping way ahead, we see that even in an environment where the King Himself is present, the millennial kingdom, human beings will demonstrate their ingrained sinfulness—and by contrast, God's holiness—and rebel under Satan's leadership (Rev. 20:7–8).

This kind of evidence, and much more, leads us to believe that there are indeed segments in the plan that are related to demonstrating the glory of God. Although many people in an initial approach to the Bible see the contrast between old and new across the testaments, and the distinction between law and grace during the time before the cross and after, we miss too much of the Bible if we fail to make other distinctions. The Scofield notes speak of seven major stages in God's dealings with humanity. There are many who agree in general with the concept of multiple stages but who see only five or six, or perhaps even eight. It is important, however, to realize that disclosed to us in the Bible is a great unifying feature, the demonstration of the glory of God and the sinfulness of humanity. The segmentation of history highlights this central purpose, as God deals with various groups under differing regulations and expectations. We would not be wrong in seeing the cross at the heart of all of this, because it is through the Lord Jesus Christ that God most profoundly shows how incompatible His character is with our sinfulness, as He places sin on the sinless One.

The great plan of the Bible, then, is to present a holy and glorious God as One who blesses humanity for His own purposes in spite of our sinfulness, which is demonstrated over and over. The greatest example (but not the only one) of this process is found in His dealings with Israel. It is not difficult to see that God enters into an intimate spiritual relation with Israel, one that Israel alternately cherishes and tramples on. This is beautifully exemplified in the book of Hosea. God is gracious and long-suffering, but will not allow those He showers His love on to spurn Him with impunity. Yet for all this, He will ultimately bless Israel, and when He does they, and the world, will see that He was always right, and any disappointments along the way were introduced entirely by human beings. We must not overlook this special role of Israel in the segmentation of history. For the nation of Israel, first identified as a recipient of special favor in Gen. 12, becomes the arena for a unique work of God to show His character and human sinfulness. He is good to Israel in spite of Israel, and because of that the universe will be amazed (Rom. 11:25–36).

Segments and responsibilities. The N.T. suggests the concept of an ordered period of time in which God is accomplishing certain purposes. In Eph. 1:10 the future rule of Christ is described as an *oikonomia.* (From this passage alone we cannot be sure if this is a future millennial age or the eternal state.) The word here appears to refer to God's establishment of a structured system of life under Christ involving earthly and heavenly beings. It is from the translation of this word in the AV that the term *dispensation* has been borrowed. Eph. 3:2 and 9 appear to use the word in the same way, pointing to the Church Age as one of the segments in God's plan.[16] In some of its uses inside and outside the N.T., the word *oikonomia* describes a situation where individuals are entrusted with management responsibilities. The same word is used in Col. 1:25 of responsibilities given to Paul. It should be noted that the word *oikonomia* is not used of any periods of time or segments in God's program other than the ones in Eph. 1:10 and 3:2, 9. And exactly how much human responsibility is involved there is not said. But it does at least suggest that God structures periods of time with certain purposeful objectives.

Uniqueness of the Church. Progressive revelation is a feature of the biblical text that has implications for many areas of biblical studies. It is not difficult to show that God's revelation was not complete until the book of Revelation was written. But more important, there are some crucial doctrines that unfolded step by step, or relations of people to God that changed. For example, the relation of Adam and Eve to God after the fall was clearly different from what it was before. Different responsibililties were inherent in the two situations. The same is true of Noah before and after the flood (see note, Gen. 1:28).

Of even greater significance is the nature of progressive revelation concerning the Church. Ephesians 1:22–23 is crucial to proper understanding of the place of the Church in God's program for humanity. To begin with, Paul virtually defines the Church as the Body of Christ. This certainly cannot have any connection with any physical aspect of Christ. It must refer to a spiritual entity, in some sense an extension of Christ. On the basis of this very fact alone we have strong warrant for asserting that it must have begun after the death of Christ. And the stress in Eph. 1:15–23 is on the great work done through the display of resurrection-power by God. This contributes to our understanding of the Church as having a post-resurrection beginning. But Eph. 3:6 tells us that the Gospel brings together Jew and Gentile in one body. We would be hard pressed to take these two occurrences of *body* as not equivalent to each other. Hence the Church consists of a union of Jew and Gentile in one entity. That this had never occurred before cannot be disputed. Gentiles could approach God under the law through proselytism, but that could never be described as equal heirship with Jews (see note at Eph. 3:6). Further, the description of this entity as a mystery contributes to the impression that something previously unknown is in view. In the progress of revelation, the existence and nature of the Church was not given before the first century A.D. There are O.T. passages that *allow for* some features of the Church or the present age, but that does not permit the interpreter automatically to assume that the Church is also present as an entity in the O.T. Similarly, although the N.T. describes the Church in language drawn from the O.T. that originally was used for Israel (e.g., Rom. 9:25–26 quoting Hos. 2:23 and 1:10), we are not justified in seeing the Church as a continuation of Israel (see also 1 Pet. 2:9, note).

Also contributing to our understanding of the period of time in which the Church exists is the statement in 1 Cor. 12:13 that "by one Spirit we were all baptized into one body, whether Jews or Greeks, whether slaves or free, and we were all made to drink of one spirit" (NASB). If this is the same "body" as in Eph. 1 and 3, and there is every reason to assume it is, then we know that the Church depends for its existence on the baptizing work of the Spirit of God. This work was clearly portrayed by Christ as yet future in Acts 1:5. Hence we conclude that the Church could not have been present in the O.T. This is one line of evidence that should lead us to maintain a distinction between Israel and the Church (see ch. 18, The Church).

One of the beliefs of the amillennial system, which believes the Church is in the O.T., is that O.T. saints in some way saw Christ as the object of their faith (see ch. 19, Future Things, under "Amillennialism"). By virtue of having the same object of faith as those after the cross, they must have entered the same entity, that is, the Church. The issue here is that we ask exactly what the Bible does and does not say. It clearly does not say that O.T. saints knew very much about the identity of the One who would take away sin. In referring to 1 Pet. 1:10–12, dispensational writer John Feinberg says:

According to verse 11, the Old Testament prophets wanted to know what the Holy Spirit was revealing about the kind of time *(poion kairon)* it would be and the kind of events there would be *(tina)*, when the Holy Spirit informed them of the sufferings of the Messiah. What is obvious from this verse is that Old Testament saints did know about a coming suffering Savior. No one disagrees that such information was available. But it seems erroneous to conclude on the basis of this passage that they knew that Jesus of Nazareth would be that suffering Messiah. In verse 12 we are told that in response to their questions, the prophets learned essentially that the time of fulfillment was not their own time. They were prophesying of things that would occur in the lifetime of others. Certainly, there is no statement to the effect that they were or were not informed that the Messiah would be Jesus of Nazareth. They may have been so informed, but 1 Peter 1:10–12 neither proves nor disproves that. Arguments from silence are consistent with everything and consequently prove nothing.[17]

There are other passages that should be treated in connection with the matter of the object of faith in the O.T., but the point is simply this: one must always ask what the text of Scripture actually says and does not say.[18]

Israel's future. Another feature of the biblical text that the dispensationalist seeks to give equal weight to, along with God's goal in human history, human responsibilities, and the uniqueness of the Church, is the mass of O.T. and N.T. predictions concerning millennial blessings in the land for a restored remnant of Israel. The dispensationalist sees no reason to shift to a figurative meaning for these statements. If they are taken at face value, the normal interpretation would be that they are still not fulfilled and need to be brought to pass in the purposes of God. It is worth noting that some nondispensational premillennialists slight these promises and thus do not feel a need to stress a distinctive future program for Israel (for discussion of this and other millennial positions, see ch. 5, Interpreting the Bible, and ch. 19, Future Things).[19]

Examples of such kingdom predictions are 2 Sam. 7:12–16, which promises an eternal Davidic monarchy; Dan. 2:44, where the description of the kingdom as the successor to four earthly kingdoms argues for its location on earth; Lk. 1:32–33, where Jesus' rule on the Davidic throne is asserted; and Acts 1:3, 6, where one of the key issues during the last discussions between Jesus and His disciples is Israel's kingdom. Concerning the disciples' question in Acts 1:6, we should note carefully that it must have had a physical kingdom as its subject. They knew the kingdom was among them in some way already (see note, Lk. 17:21). They must have been asking about another kind of kingdom, similar to earlier theocracies, to be given to the nation of Israel (not to the world in general). Jesus does not say that the restoration of this kingdom will not come. He simply changes their concept of its timing. The book of Acts never indicates that the promise of restoration of the kingdom has been abrogated. In fact, the book closes in ch. 28 (v. 31) with a description of Paul's presentation of the kingdom. We would be inattentive to Luke's flow of thought if we took the two instances of "kingdom" to be different.

The amillennialist (and some nondispensational premillennialists) grants that the O.T. references were probably understood as pointing to a physical kingdom by those reading the O.T. before the first c. A.D., but asserts that the N.T. indicates that such an interpretation was faulty and that no such actual fulfillment is to be expected. According to this view, the promises were transferred to the Church and exist now as spiritual blessings during this age; hence, such kingdom references cannot be taken at face value.

Amillennialists differ on whether the promises are for those on earth during the present age or for those in the presence of Christ. One wonders if these "blessings," such as the gift of the land (Gen. 15:18), can have any meaning at all under the amillennial view! This should be viewed as extremely unnatural interpretation of the biblical text.

This matter is only one among many that the dispensationalist insists are at issue on the basis of distinctions that the Bible itself makes. It concerns only one of a large number of points in the text where the interpretation of prophecy is involved. The dispensationalist argues that prophecy should not automatically involve a switch by the interpreter to a metaphorical meaning (see. ch. 5, Interpreting the Bible). And, indeed, the amillennialist does not do that at all with prophecies relating to the first advent of Christ. This fact should be a giveaway that such a system of interpretation is biased due to theological presuppositions that cannot be brought under the scrutiny of the data of the text itself.

When the amillennialist states that the Church began with Adam or Abraham, or that the Church is composed of the saved of all ages, or that the kingdom blessings for Israel, indeed any distinctive national future for Israel, have been abrogated, he is giving examples of a failure to test what is held as statements about the Bible by the very words of the Bible itself.

It is significant that many nondispensationalists have admitted that consistent interpretation that does not switch to metaphorical meanings without warrant from the text itself will lead to dispensationalism:

> [This] view of the Church is the inevitable result of the doctrine that Old Testament prophecy must be fulfilled literally to Israel and that the Church is a mystery first revealed to the apostle Paul. The Church thus becomes a parenthesis between the historical kingdom of David and his successors which is long past and the Davidic kingdom of the future. . . . This . . . is a distinguishing feature of Dispensationalism; not that there are dispensations in Biblical history—no one denies that—but that the Church is a parenthetical dispensation which delays or interrupts the fulfilment of God's promises to Israel.[20]

The reader should be aware, also, that the fact that careful formulations of dispensationalism are recent does not make it any less biblical than other systems. After all, such important doctrines as justification by faith and the sole authority of Scripture were for the most part lost to the Church until the Reformation.[21]

Why is this an important area, and why have we spent so much time on it? First of all, we should note that at issue is the matter of fairness to the Word of God, of letting it speak for itself. Second, it is an area where many are fooled and misled. Third, it involves major beliefs regarding the Church, prophecy, Israel, and other topics. As a matter of fact, few doctrines are not touched by this issue. Here is a partial list of areas that dispensationalism is directly connected with:

1. The purpose of God in history
2. The promises made to Israel
3. The identity of Israel and of the Church
4. The second advent of Christ
5. The nature and time of the millennium
6. The nature of the Church in regard to:
   a. Its beginning point
   b. The doctrine of Spirit baptism
   c. The work of the Spirit in this and other ages
   d. The nature of the Body of Christ
   e. The "mystery" character of the Church (see note, Eph. 3:6)
   f. The work of the Spirit in salvation in this age

     g. The relation of the resurrection to the Church
     h. The relation of the Church to the tribulation
   7. The relation of the law to grace in this age
   8. The purpose of the law
   9. The fulfillment of prophecy about events still to come
  10. The relation of the millennium to the eternal state

We must be very careful at this point. Every human being who encounters the text of the Bible is in danger of distorting its message. All of us come to it with presuppositions. They may arise from considered reflection or from casually formulated opinion. Either way, they blind us to the meaning of the text. And we can be guilty of such careless handling of the text in regard to *any* portion or *any* particular topic. All of us must continually go back to the text itself to test our interpretations. We are privileged to have the Spirit of God as a teacher. And we should learn from the successes and failures of those who have preceded us in these endeavors. Above all, we must regard the Bible as a self-interpreting book that God *does* want us to understand, seeking all the while to allow it to give us as much information as the divine Author intended us to have.

Summary of distinctives. The key features of dispensationalism as an approach to the Bible, then, are:

   1. The recognition of God's goal of glorifying Himself in spite of and through sinful humanity and its failures
   2. A consistent approach to O.T. and N.T. prophecies regarding the future of ethnic redeemed Israel
   3. A stress on the N.T. distinction between Israel and the Church

These features distinguish dispensationalism from other conservative approaches to the Bible, including covenant amillennialism and nondispensational premillennialism. Some of the implications of dispensationalism for other areas of interpretation, such as prophecy, are discussed in ch. 19, Future Things, where millennial systems are compared, and in ch. 5, Interpreting the Bible, where consistency in approaching prophecy is discussed (see also the note at Gen. 1:28).

Concise definition. It would be helpful to offer a condensed definition of dispensation at this point. A dispensation is a period of time in which God is dealing with human beings according to certain divine goals and human responsibilities. Such segments, which may have overlapping features, are designed to show His grace and human failure apart from Him. A dispensationalist is one who believes that the Bible sets forth such distinctives and also sees a particular role and time for the Church as the Body of Christ, as well as a unique future for Israel. For a similar definition, see the Scofield note at Gen. 1:28.

Overview of dispensations. Table 2.1 displays features of the dispensational approach to the plan of God. It attempts to represent general dispensational views, and not all dispensationalists would agree on the finer details.

Contribution of Books and Sections to the Plan

The Old Testament. The books of the Bible can be grouped according to their content and their contribution to our understanding of God's plan. The O.T. can be divided into four sections, as follows:

Law	History	Poetry and Wisdom Books	Prophecy
Genesis	Joshua	Job	Isaiah
Exodus	Judges	Psalms	Jeremiah
Leviticus	Ruth	Proverbs	Lamentations
Numbers	1 and 2	Ecclesiastes	Ezekiel
Deuteronomy	Samuel	Song of Songs	Daniel
	1 and 2		Hosea
	Kings		Joel
	1 and 2		Amos
	Chronicles		Obadiah
	Ezra		Jonah
	Nehemiah		Micah
	Esther		Nahum
			Habakkuk
			Zephaniah
			Haggai
			Zechariah
			Malachi

The Pentateuch, the first five books, covers a time period in which a number of dispensations were in effect. Although many people immediately equate the Pentateuch with the law, the historical record in Genesis dealing with the time before the law describes several separable periods. During these God placed human beings under requirements that varied with the particular dispensation. For example, God's relationships with Adam and Eve both before and after the fall differed from those with humanity during the time of Noah and then Abraham (see notes, Gen. 1:28; 3:7; 3:15; 12:17). Each was designed to show man's failure and to highlight God's grace. Beginning with Abraham in Gen. 12, the Pentateuch describes God's choice of one family line to be the recipients of blessing (see note, Gen. 12:2). From that point on, all favor from God would come to or through descendents of Abraham. Thus even Gentiles during the present age have access to God only through the Lord Jesus Christ, one from Abraham's line.

Although in terms of space the majority of the O.T. describes the relations of God with that one people, we should not think that His program with them is the only one in the O.T. or is in itself unitary. Before Abraham God blessed human beings, as in the case of Noah, who was obedient with regard to the knowledge God had given him. And there was basically a two-stage relationship between God and the descendants of Abraham. First, Abraham and his descendants were tested with regard to their response to the promise of land and future blessing. Their reaction was to be that of trusting God concerning those disclosures. It was almost six hundred years later that the law entered, forming a major element in God's relation to that one line (see notes, Gal. 3:10, 24). It is worth noting at this point that God will establish a third kind of testing situation with Israel during the time of the kingdom, during which the physically present King will be the object of obedience. The rebellion at the end will be a clear demonstration of human failure once again (Rev. 20:7–9; see note, 20:10).

The remainder of the O.T., from the giving of the law in Exodus to the last revelation through the prophet Malachi, provides information on the history (mainly through the historical and prophetic books), spiritual life (mainly through the poetry and

TABLE 2.1. Overview of Dispensations

Features	Scripture Duration	Scofield Note	Point of Test	People/ Groups	Time**	Human Failure/ God's Judgment	Key Elements (including some changes and continuities)****
Dispensation:							
Innocence	Gen. 1–3	Gen. 1:28	Fruit of the tree	Adam and Eve	Adam and Eve	Fall/expulsion from Garden	1. Dominion 2. Garden
Conscience	Gen. 4–8	Gen. 3:7	Individual obedience	Various	Adam and Eve to Noah	Widespread sin/the Flood	1. Failure of dominion 3. Blood sacrifice*****
Human Government	Gen. 8–11	Gen. 8:15	Human rule in righteousness	Various	Noah to Abraham	Failure to govern, Babel/confusion of language	4. Animal's fear of people 5. Meat diet 6. No more floods 7. Right to govern/capital punishment
Promise	Gen. 11– Ex. 18	Gen. 12:1	One family to trust God for blessings in the land	Israel (started with Abraham)	Abraham to Moses	Disobedience/ slavery in Egypt	8. Abrahamic Covenant/ blessing on all nations 9. Palestinian covenant (land), rule by patriarchs
Law	Ex. 18– Acts 1	Ex. 19:1	Keep the law	Israel	Moses to the cross	Didn't keep the law/slavery in captivities	10. Law
Church (Grace)*	Acts 2– Rev. 19	Acts 2:1	Live by the Spirit	All saved are in the Church (except during trib.)	Pentecost to millennium***	Unbelief/tribulation period	10. No Mosaic law (Acts 15, Gal.) 11. Church = Body of Christ

Millennium	Rev. 20; Zech. 14, etc.	Rev. 20:4	Response to the visible King	1000 yrs./after second advent	Living Jews and Gentiles plus res-urrected saints of all ages	Rebellion, unbelief/ judgment of unsaved	1. Dominion restored 3. Memorial sacrifices 7. The King governs 8,9. Covenants fulfilled/blessings of land, King, new heart 12. Personal presence of Christ 13. Israel in the land 14. Church ruling and reigning 15. Satan bound
(Eternal State)	Rev. 21,22	None		Eternal	Saved of all ages in the New Jerusalem	None	1. Dominion perfect 2. Garden recalled 12. Personal presence of Christ

*Because of the distinctive display of grace during the present age, some prefer to call it Grace.

**The time indications are not strict in every case, since there are overlaps of features, as seen in the key elements section.

***If the tribulation is considered a separate dispensation, then the dispensation of the Church does not continue to the millennium; of course, the dispensationalist believes that the rapture removes those in the Body of Christ before the tribulation begins.

****Items in this column with the same numbers are part of continuous features.

*****As an example of the overlap of features, blood sacrifices continued through four dispensations, not being removed until the cross.

wisdom books) and divine direction (especially through the prophets) of the people of Abraham's line. If we take the O.T. at face value, we can reach no other conclusion than that God promised unconditionally to bring the nation of Israel to spiritual and physical blessing in the land of Palestine. Because that has not yet occurred since those promises, we conclude that God's program with that people is not yet finished. God has shown, and will show, through Israel that he is glorious and that human beings continually fail. Israel is a divine showcase for this purpose, but it is only one of many found in the Bible, several of which existed before the choice of Israel. That such a large part of the O.T. is devoted to Israel must mean that God wants to show more in and through that people.

The New Testament. We can view the N.T. as having a four-part structure: the Gospels, Acts, the Epistles, and Rev. In the Gospels God through the incarnate Son offered divine favor to Israel, but the nation rejected her Messiah. The book of Acts indicates that God did not continue to invite Israel to blessing in the same way as recorded in the Gospels. That does not mean that blessings have been removed completely from Israel. The book of Romans in particular indicates how Israel will be restored (chs. 9–11). In the meantime, God will save individual Jews and Gentiles out of the mass of humanity during the present age. The Epistles describe that work of God, as well as the removal of the Church (2 Th. 2; 1 Th. 4) so that God can continue that work with His showcase people. And the book of Revelation furnishes a description of the culmination of the ages, during which Israel and the Church will find their proper places.

Interwoven in a beautiful way with God's dispensational dealings with individuals and groups is His provision of salvation through the joining of humanity with deity. As Gen. 3:15 records so early in Scripture, He would raise up one from the offspring of Eve to reverse Satan's victory. With Abraham, the line of earthly and spiritual blessing coincides with the line of the Redeemer. The benefits promised in Gen. 12:3 would come from an individual who Himself was of that line. No outsider would be needed. The remainder of the O.T., along with portraying God's challenges to those of Abraham's line, also catalogued the steps toward the provision within time of a Savior.

In the N.T. the Gospels relate the account of His birth and death, the book of Acts chronicles the initial stages of God's dealings through Christ with a new group, and the Epistles explain the coming of Christ and the principles of the new age during which believers would be part of His Body. But the latter books also describe, along with Rev., how the Body will be removed from the earth and God will resume his dealings with Israel, culminating in the application of the work of Christ to them as a large segment of the nation comes to repentance (Zech. 13:8–9).

The major portion of the O.T., devoted as it is to showing God's patience with Israel and their repeated wandering from Him, serves to highlight that final national regeneration. The tribulation period, described in the prophets, the Gospels, Acts, the Epistles and Rev., will be the point at which God's dispensational and soteriological purposes merge in a startling way. For at that time God will pressure Israel so that their rebellion will be removed and their hearts will be changed. The obstinate people, who failed test after test, will be brought by God to the place of blessing. They will not want to come. Their restoration will be completely God's work. Thus Zech. 12:10, in predicting that renewal, states,

"And I will pour out on the house of David and the inhabitants of Jerusalem a spirit of grace and supplication. They will look on me, the one they have pierced, and they will mourn for him as one mourns for an only child, and grieve bitterly for him as one grieves for a firstborn son.'' (NIV)

Almost three millennia of spiritual failure will be replaced by repentance, but only as God does the turning. He will be glorified as He overcomes human sin. As the final dispensation opens under the auspices of the King Himself, Israel, the showcase for grace, will be a trophy of God alone.

This section is not intended as a detailed and systematic apologetic for dispensationalism. For that, see works in the Annotated Bibliography (ch. 23).[22] See also the section "Introduction" in the NSRB, especially the section "The Plan of the Bible," and in this book ch. 19, Future Things, and ch. 5, Interpreting the Bible.

Biblical Covenants

A series of key divine promises or *covenants* form the backbone of God's dealings with human beings. Because of our inability to secure our own prosperity—spiritual and physical—on the earth, a gracious God has committed Himself to providing what we cannot.

The main biblical covenants are a unifying factor for all events described in the Bible involving God and human beings. Some of them provide the guarantee that yet-future predicted events will occur. For example, the Abrahamic covenant is the basis for all of God's subsequent dealings with Israel, and is expanded in the Palestinian, Davidic, and New covenants, which, respectively, provide for Israel's eternal possession of the land, an eternal kingship, and the conversion of a remnant.

The time in which a covenant is in effect may coincide with a dispensation, as in the case of the Mosaic Covenant. It may cover many dispensations (e.g., the Noahic Covenant, which has been in effect since the flood), or be worked out through several dispensations and climaxed in one (e.g., the Abrahamic, New, Palestinian, and Davidic, which all find their ultimate fulfillment during the kingdom).

The major biblical covenants, along with the location of the Scofield note for each, are:

1. Edenic; Gen. 2:16.
2. Adamic; Gen. 3:15.
3. Noahic; Gen. 9:16.
4. Abrahamic; Gen. 12:2.
5. Mosaic; Ex. 19:5.
6. Palestinian; Dt. 30:3.
7. Davidic; 2 Sam. 7:16.
8. New; Heb. 8:8.

For more information on the major covenants, see the note at Gen. 2:16.

Questions for Further Study

1. Study Gen. 12:7; 13:15; 24:7 and Gal. 3:14–16 and associated notes. The promises to Abraham are made in connection with his "seed" or "offspring." Gal. 3:14–16 applies the promises to one portion of that seed. What is the significance of that in light of the discussion in this chapter concerning the provision of salvation through Israel?

2. What does Rev. 20:7–9 teach concerning the nature of sin and the long-suffering of God? Why does Satan rebel at this time, and what is the outcome, especially in terms of God's work with humanity?

3

How to Study the Bible

Growing as a Student of the Bible

Receiving Direction

Almost 3,000 years ago one who loved God's words penned a reflection on the joy that comes from careful attention to Scripture: "I meditate on your precepts and consider your ways. I delight in your decrees; I will not neglect your word" (Ps. 119:15–16, NIV). The sequences described here are true in every age. Meditation on the commands of God goes hand in hand with contemplation of how God acts. And reveling in the decrees of God leads to obedience. One cannot know God apart from His revealed Scriptures, and rejoicing in God's Word changes behavior. Our happiness in God and usefulness to Him are directly related to our strength in the Scriptures. Yet we grieve God continually by our carelessness with the Book.

But even if we have a thirst to know the Bible better, several questions present themselves immediately. Where do we start in the Bible? How can we establish good study habits? How do we go about making sense of the Bible? How can we interpret it, relate one part to another, identify problems, and get further help? If we are to be successful in understanding Scripture, we must face these initial questions and get ourselves grounded.

This section has the goal of orienting you to lifelong fruitful Bible study, so that you may intelligently meditate on the precepts of God, observe and reflect on God's acts toward us, love the words of God, and be led to humble obedience.

Studying with Goals

The Apostle Paul understood well the value of acting with purpose: "Therefore I do not run like a man running aimlessly; I do not fight like a man beating the air" (1 Cor. 9:26, NIV). The imagery of the Corinthian games has its parellel in the spiritual realm: success depends on moving in the right direction. What kinds of goals might students of the Bible have? They should above all seek to allow the message of the Bible to come through to them; so that the power of the word may continually change their lives. But they should have other immediate and long-range objectives: gaining an overview of the Bible; mastering the teachings found in individual books; putting those separate teachings together into doctrinal understanding; becoming familiar with key words; acquiring an appreciation for the historical, cultural, linguistic, and geographical backgrounds of the Bible; and moving toward using the Bible in serving God. As you read this chapter you should be able to add to the list.

Working Systematically

In his teaching ministry the Apostle Paul left no stone unturned. His house-to-house instructing (Acts 20:20, NIV) is a model of careful service. So, too, must it be with our handling of Scripture. Bible study deserves the very best of our organization. Those who take the most from God's Word are in it regularly—daily. They are consistent in seeking its meaning and its application. Their care extends to being patient and exacting. No one has ever fathomed all there is in the Bible, and it is safe to say that no one ever will. Even the most minute details are worthy of fine attention. Every word has a purpose. No doubt Satan attempts to discourage every soul that desires to feed on the Word. So develop daily persistence. Do not be afraid of hard work. Those who are powerful in the Scriptures have come to be that way in great part through willingness to exert themselves. God rewards systematic, concentrated effort at understanding the Bible. It brings that "delight" which the psalmist enjoyed.

Preparing Spiritually

One of the most serious errors students of the Bible can make is to think that their labors alone determine what they will gain from Scripture. The divine Author of the Book is its ultimate Interpreter. The believer can count on the truth of 1 Cor. 2:12: "Now we have received, not the spirit of the world, but the Spirit who is from God, that we might know the things freely given to us by God" (NASB). Those who know Jesus Christ as Savior have the same Holy Spirit within them to illumine Scripture. Being regenerated is the first requisite to making sense of the Bible.

Further, since God speaks to us through His Word, we should regard every occasion of reading or studying that Word as an encounter with God Himself. The more you expect God to open divine truth to you, the more you must be willing to lay your spiritual state bare before God as you open the Book. And the more clearly you understand it and the more you apply it to your life, the more spiritual needs it will reveal. It is the malleable heart that will glean the most from Scripture.

Although the Bible contains enough to challenge the greatest minds to lifelong study (and even *they* can never exhaust its content!), it is the personal appropriation and ultimate application of its truths which are at issue. Vance Havner understood this when he said:

The storehouse of God's Word was never meant for mere scrutiny, not even primarily for study but for sustenance. It is not simply a collection of fine proverbs and noble teachings for men to admire and quote as they might Shakespeare. It is ration for the soul, resources of and for the spirit, treasure for the inner man. Its goods exhibited upon every page are ours, and we have no business merely moving respectfully amongst them and coming away none the richer.[1]

The conservative Protestant believes that God's authority for faith and practice is mediated through His written Word, not through human institutions or even human systems of understanding that Word. The Bible takes precedence over both tradition and reason in regulating our lives. Any error that Satan would perpetrate upon hapless humanity will always come in some form of distortion or dismissal of Scripture. And Satan's challenge to God's sovereignty—and our challenge, too—always takes the shape of opposing His Word. Calvin sensed this when he remarked, "Adam would never have dared to oppose God's authority unless he had disbelieved in God's Word."[2] As I open the Bible I must be willing to submit to whatever I find there, whether or not it agrees with my notions of how God should act or what He should expect of me. Not to do so is to resist God. Over 250 years ago Johann Albrecht Bengel advised, "Apply yourself wholly to the text; apply the text wholly to thyself."[3]

When confronted with multiple and, especially, competing interpretations of portions of the Bible, some have questioned how God can allow such variations. After all, wouldn't God lead everyone uniformly to the same understanding of Scripture? It is safe to say that human beings will never reach a consensus on the meaning of every part of the Bible—even if they could plumb its depths. Our finiteness and our tendency to see in data only what we have already decided must be there, will see to that. We will always take our presuppositions and prejudices to the text. That does not mean that disagreement is good or desirable. But we should not be alarmed that it occurs.

There is, however, a significant point that arises from all of this about how we should approach the Bible personally. In our Bible study we should prepare ourselves to go to the Bible in a receptive frame of mind; so that we can allow ourselves to be surprised by what it says. It alone carries the power to overcome fallacious interpretation, whether on the part of the believer who has little training, or that of the professional scholars. (Note our Lord's use of this principle in Mt. 22:29 where he said, "You are in error because you do not know the Scriptures . . . " [NIV]). Our task is to remain open to correction—both in understanding and in application. If our study of the Bible only confirms what we already believe, we have not allowed it to speak. British writer Graham Stanton underscores this:

Once the text is given priority and once the interpreter ceases to erect a barrier between himself and the text, he will find that as he seeks to interpret the text, the text will, as it were, interpret him. When this happens, the authority of Scripture is being taken seriously; God's word is not a dead letter to be observed coldly but a Word which speaks to me in my situation.[4]

Establish an attitude of mental and spiritual openness toward God's written Word.

Making the Most of Helps

If the Bible is its own best interpreter, then why bother consulting any other work? Simply because although God gave us the Bible as a whole set of canonical writings,

He did not at the same time give us a book to serve as a key to understanding it. We appreciate God's revelation more if we have to work in order to make sense of it. And the collective labors over the centuries to determine what God meant are of great value to us. Studies that give the historical, linguistic, and cultural background for biblical writings not only serve to connect the Bible with space and time but also provide information that most people do not have the opportunity and training to ferret out. Such written helps, along with interpretations of the Bible itself, are valuable in at least two ways: (1) the student can see where some have gone astray and others have been on target as time tests the views of all, and (2) the illuminating ministry of the Spirit in students of the past is preserved for those living in succeeding generations. We owe a great debt to those lovers of the Book who have attempted in writing to unfold its message for others. The Scofield Bible itself is one such attempt at setting forth in a coherent way the meaning of some of the salient features of Scripture. It is one among many valuable tools.

The one who wishes today to understand the Bible better had more than enough written aids to assist him. Intelligent use of such tools necessitates ongoing acquaintance with available works. Building a library of helpful books is a lifelong process (see ch. 23, Annotated Bibliography).

Preparing for Actual Bible Study

Seeing the Plan of Scripture

In order to work with the Bible, to apply it in a living way, and to avoid confusion, it is essential to grasp its overall plan and general structure. The books of the Bible were written at various times by a spectrum of authors, each of whom took pen in hand for a different purpose. The O.T. is a record of God's creative activity and subsequent work preparatory to providing salvation and blessing the human race through the descendants, and in particular one descendant, of one man, Abraham. It is not, as some have claimed, an account of the awakenings and development of the religious consciousness of humanity, but rather a divinely revealed documentation of God's dealings with people in preparation for the appearance of the God-man, Jesus Christ. The N.T. is the record of that appearance in space and time, at the focal point of all history, and its subsequent impact during the first century. Every book of the sixty-six contributes in some way to these central features of biblical history. For assistance in gaining an overview of Scripture, the Bible student should be sure to read the introductions to the various sections of the Scofield Bible (The Pentateuch, The Historical Books, etc.).

The Bible student should then learn to see how individual parts contribute to God's revelation. Scofield's introductions to specific books are designed to show something of the place of each in God's disclosure. The divisions and subdivisions within each Bible book are important also. For example, the major break keyed by the words "Therefore, I urge you, brothers, in view of God's mercy . . . " (NIV) and by the change of tone and topic in Rom. 12:1, are crucial in understanding Paul's purpose in this book. Although such further segmenting of the Bible into chapters and paragraphs does not stem from the earliest witnesses to its text, the student will see its parts and their relation to each other better by noticing these divisions. The Scofield Bible attempts to provide suggested divisions and titles at important points .n the biblical text.

Being Alert to Backgrounds and Languages

You will not have to proceed very far in your Bible study before you realize that you are encountering social and language features which are strange to you. Modern translations may alleviate part of this problem, but the cultural and linguistic differences between biblical times and any other age and culture will always exist. The gap never goes away. Some ignore it, to their confusion. We are attempting to understand documents that were written *by* people who cannot explain them to us, and *to* people in a different age and society from any other. Simply stated, there is a communication problem.[5]

Many modern translations make serious attempts to bridge that gap. Any translation (in any language) worth its salt seeks to bring to bear on the text of the Bible the latest in historical and linguistic insight in order to transfer the message of distant cultures and language groups into the languages of the day, at the same time preserving the meaning without theological bias. This is a terribly difficult task even for professionals. But the Bible student must have at least a minimum competence in understanding the social and linguistic features across the gap. As far as language is concerned, the NSRB edition, which utilizes the King James translation, contains numerous suggestions that pertain especially to alternatives in translation, as for example at Acts 2:15, where *disciples* is literally *brethren*. The NIV translation annotates (shown with bracketed footnotes, in the *Oxford NIV Scofield Study Bible*) such points, where the translators felt that there was sufficient warrant to offer alternatives. The comparison of several translations will alert the Bible student who is not acquainted with the original languages to further points where renderings differ (see ch. 4, The Language of the Bible). Bible dictionaries and encyclopedias should be the first resource consulted for further study of features of culture and history that lie across the gap.

Asking Questions of the Text

One of the main characteristics you should possess to be fruitful as a Bible student is curiosity. Since you are always to be a prober of the intentions of God as they are expressed in writing, you will be well served by the reporter's interrogative guidelines: "Who? What? When? Where? Why?" Use questions such as these to orient yourself to the text, as well as to expose veins of truth which are buried more deeply. These kinds of questions are particularly appropriate, because the books of the Bible came to us in human history. So, for example, when you are studying Acts 2 and the phenomenon of tongues, it is extremely important to notice that it is the disciples who are speaking (answers "who?"), that they were uttering comprehensible language (answers "what?"), and that this event occurred after our Lord's ascension in connection with the prophecy of Acts 1:8 (answers "when?"). Asking questions of the text of Scripture is really a way of forming hypotheses and allowing it to confirm or reject them. Thus we allow it to speak for itself.

Overviewing Passages

If you were blindfolded and transported to a new location, your first reaction upon removal of the blindfold would probably be to attempt to orient yourself. The best way to get your bearings in studying passages of the Bible is to read the text several times.

This accomplishes several things. First, it provides general familiarity with a piece of Scripture. Second, it leads you to see passages in context. Third, it previews features that will be encountered, for instance, the length of chapters, and the numbers of paragraphs, words, and verses that pose problems and will need work. And fourth, it helps you become more comfortable with the portion you are working on. In fact, even after dealing with specific verses or words, a rereading of the larger passage will often modify your conclusions or stimulate new insights. Be willing to read long stretches of text.

Keeping the Plan of Revelation in View

In successful interpersonal communication, human beings pass oral and written messages back and forth in chunks of differing sizes. But for the message to be received and understood it must have a certain degree of coherence. If such coherence is lacking, the listener or reader will react in one of several ways—by being confused, puzzled, or disturbed, by requesting repetition, or by rejecting the content. Messages used in human communication are marked by complex networks of signals within and beside the basic information, which are put there by the sender to assist the receiver. For example, words or phrases such as *finally, the latter,* and *therefore* do not carry information by themselves, but serve rather to link parts of texts. If we were to imagine a text—or oral message—as an area of terrain to be traversed, then we could say that such words or phrases act as road signs to aid in navigation. These are pieces of information (called *metalinguistic*) that stand beside the message and are designed to help the reader/listener assimilate the other material. There are many other features of a communicative act that tie it together (unless it is intended as nonsense) and enable the receiver to take in as much as the sender intended.

This is no less the case with Scripture. The Bible is a piece of literature—divinely inspired literature, but literature nonetheless. The individual books are literarily disparate—some authors are Jews, at least one is a Gentile, some are highly educated, others apparently not so at all. Yet the Bible possesses cohesive factors. The primary cohesion of the sixty-six lies not in the literary *genre* (to use a current term) or the human setting behind the parts of the Bible, but rather in the overall purpose of God in revelation.

It is the weakness of many who study the Bible, and many who have written on it, that they have seen the trees but not the forest. It is a strength of the dispensational approach to Scripture found in the Scofield Bible that it is able to relate so many of the parts of Scripture to each other. Doing so is valuable because it opens up more of the total message of the Bible to our understanding. So we should always try to see the relation of tree and forest. We must ask continually, "How does *this* part of the Bible fit with the wider purposes of God as revealed elsewhere in the Scriptures?" The structure of the dispensations as presented in the Scofield Bible is an attempt to relate successive stages in God's dealings with us to His overall plan. We cannot discover the broad scheme except through the individual parts, and we should review our understanding of the separate pieces in the light of the whole. Is this circular? Not really. If a number of features of Scripture seem to fit together to form a significant generalization, we should make such a general interpretation. If later discoveries agree with it, it will be further confirmed. But we may have to modify it. In any case, the Bible student can get nowhere by looking only at the segments. How do they fit together? What is God doing through the ages? How does His activity in one age contrast with that in another?

We encounter, for instance, some significant problems in understanding the person and work of the Holy Spirit if we fail to notice that His work is not the same after Pentecost as it is before. The N.T. describes His activity after that point in terms radically different from earlier ones. If we miss this fact, we will fail to appreciate His fundamentally changed relation to people. Furthermore, we should go on to ask why such differences have been placed in the text. The Scofield note at Acts 2:4 explains many of these distinctions.

The overall coherence of God's message lies then in the unity of His purpose in revealing Himself to humanity. Certainly the cross is at the center of divine activity. But beyond that, there are many far-reaching patterns the Bible student must notice. The interplay of such features—God's work toward Israel, the intervention of the Church Age, the duration of covenants, etc.—ties the message together, and, indeed, beyond that, presents a spiritual dimension reflecting the work of a wise and perfect redeeming God. Learn to study the Bible with the aid of its own distinctions and continuities. The message thus becomes infinitely richer.

Recording Discoveries

One of the greatest helps to studying the Bible is developing the habit of writing down results of interaction with the text. These can include observations, reactions, points of difficulty, items for further study, outlines, quotations, cross-references, etc. You should devise your own system for notation and then use it and improve on it. What you have discovered at one sitting can often be a basis for work in the Bible on subsequent occasions.

Becoming Involved in the Process of Bible Study

Learning to be Passage-Oriented

One of the basic reasons for weakness in a knowledge of the Scriptures is the inability to handle *sections* of the Bible. Many preachers are oriented toward topics that are supported or explained by individual verses that the speaker views in isolation. And many people who write on biblical topics treat Scripture as a source book of isolated proof texts. The Bible is a literary and theological *whole*. Each book of the sixty-six is a subunit of that whole. As mentioned above, messages that have a high likelihood of being understood have internal coherence and ongoing clues. Part of that coherence is continuity of the presentation of themes. In Rom., for instance, Paul expounds for eleven chapters the need for and provision of righteousness. It is unlikely that a verse or two from that section could be studied and interpreted correctly without some degree of attention to the surrounding context. And for some issues within Rom. 1–12, we must examine the whole twelve chapters. Not all passages of Scripture involve such lengthy contextual coherence. But all Scripture has some degree of relevant thematic unity. It is up to the Bible student to attempt to discover how much.

There are other equally obvious values of studying whole passages wherever possible. Events and circumstances that concern individuals in biblical history are set in sections of text whose bounds sometimes stretch beyond the appearances of the individuals alone. The circumstances of Peter's life and ministry in the early chapters of Acts are woven into the early history of the Church and the atmosphere of Judaism. We cannot isolate Peter from the wider context in which his account is given.

Perhaps even more important is the safeguard aspect of passage study. As much as anything else, it limits the tendency to take verses and sentences out of context, in part because it is the surrounding material that is most determinative in enabling the interpreter to understand individual parts of sections. Too many of the errors seen in the history of doctrine are due to disregard for contexts. Passages—larger, thematically coherent pieces of Scripture—are a check on our tendency to see only what we want to in the text (see also ch. 5, Interpreting the Bible, where context is approached from a slightly different perspective.)

In the following sections we will present examples of how to study portions of Scripture, making use of the Scofield Bible helps and being as careful as possible to pay attention to the surrounding relevant portions.

Beginning to Work with a Passage

There can be any number of reasons for approaching a passage of Scripture. But when you settle on a particular one there are several important initial steps. You should use the Scofield Bible introductions and outlines to get an overview and read the passage several times. The helps for the book of Ezekiel provide an example. The introduction to the book gives a theme (judgment and glory), the time in history (sixth c. B.C.), the key features of the literary aspects of the book (communications by visions, use of symbolism), and so forth. Such clues become crucial for your understanding even before you reach the second verse of the book. In this case, then, historical, literary, and thematic features are extremely valuable in interpreting the book even at the outset. To be specific, Israel (actually Judah, the southern kingdom) was in captivity in Babylon in the sixth c. B.C. God brought the Babylonians upon Israel beginning in 604 B.C. as a result of her sin, particularly idolatry. But God's glory is prominent throughout the book, and especially in ch. 1. While calamity falls, God is present in His glory as a sovereign over the affairs of earth. For Israel the glory inherent in God's presence is withdrawn (chs. 9–11), but it returns in ch. 43. The interplay of God's glory and His work of chastising His own is a key to the book.

The NSRB paragraph heading at Ezek. 1:1 notes that the first three chapters highlight Ezekiel's call to ministry. His first vision (1:4–28) lies at the heart of that commissioning. Many people have read this chapter and come away confused and bewildered, or have seen here flying saucers or visitations by extraterrestrial beings. Nothing could be more foreign to the text. God's glory (v. 28, "the likeness of the glory of the Lord" [NIV]) appears to Ezekiel, as Israel is in captivity, to encourage primarily him. His call consists in large part of strengthening for a difficult ministry (see also 2:1ff). Approach Ezek. by scanning chs. 1–3, reading them several times if possible, before focusing on ch. 1. You will probably find it helpful to make further titles of your own to describe the contents of the subsections of chs. 1–3, and especially ch. 1.

Zeroing in on Themes and Verses

One textual feature that quickly becomes evident in any portion of Scripture is the interplay among topics, ideas, characters and places—some of the important devices that make a text of any kind interesting. A well-written novel makes constant use of these elements, and so does the literature of the Bible. In Ezek. 1 again there are several instances of such interplay. The first three verses introduce the vision, which extends from v. 4 through v. 28. Thus there are two main parts to this chapter. In turn, the vision appears to have four parts: v. 4, the storm; vv. 5–14, the living creatures; vv. 15–21, the wheels and the living creatures; and vv. 22–28, the expanse and the figure upon the throne. The main topics are the storm, the creatures, the wheels, the expanse, the throne, and the figure upon the throne. There is interaction in several dimensions. The creatures are in the storm, which in turn is in the fire. The creatures are related to each other in various ways (junction, motion, appearance, etc.). They are somehow interconnected with the whole. And as the chapter develops, everything in vv. 4–25 appears to move toward the climax, the vision of "the appearance of the likeness of the glory of the Lord" (NIV). The chapter is constructed literarily in such a way as to emphasize the sight of the representation of God's glory. Verse 25 could be considered the key to the whole chapter. At this point the vision abruptly ceases, and God talks to Ezekiel directly. Hence, before attempting any detailed deciphering of the chapter, you should seek to have a good grasp of the wider context and the structure of the passage itself.

At this point in such a study, you can check some of the Scofield notes. In this passage, the note at 1:4 summarizes some of the key features of the vision, but there is much left for you to do on your own.

Thinking Biographically

It is generally profitable at some stage of study to examine the lives of the characters who appear in a biblical account. Returning to Ezekiel, we quickly discover that we know virtually nothing about him from any source outside of the book that bears his name. However, we know a great deal from within it. If we were to scan the book, noticing where he appears, we could glean a great deal of information about the man himself. The note at 1:3 suggests some of the information that can be found. We would also discover that above all he was obedient and dependent. And since God often took him back to the vision of ch. 1, it appears that the revelation was given in great part to shape his character in preparation for ministry. He needed to know of God's glory and power, but also of His gracious interest in human affairs (the note at 1:4 is helpful with this). Only then could he have the courage to minister to a people whose spiritual insensibility God predicted (ch. 2). Ezekiel's life is interwoven with the book, and vice versa. In this case, then, a biographical study helps to open up the whole book. For more help on this read especially the notes at 2:1; 3:22; 4:1; and 9:3.

Becoming a Concordance User

The most valuable tool for assistance in understanding the Bible is a concordance. It is simply an index to words or phrases in the Bible. Its importance for study springs from the nature of the Bible as a unified book. Since Scripture has one Author, the Holy Spirit, it must throughout be a result of uniform intentions. What is said in one portion is usually related to information somewhere else. Using a concordance gives assent to the principle that Scripture is its own best interpreter.

One could quickly find in a concordance, for example, that the living creatures in

Ezek. 1 are cherubs. They appear in ch. 10 and are connected with ch. 1 in 10:15ff. The Scofield note at 1:5 directs the reader to 10:20, where the explicit identification is made. But where else do cherubs appear in the Bible? An examination of a complete concordance would reveal that they are found in the NIV, for instance, in the following books (eighty-nine times altogether): Gen., Ex., Num., 1 Sam., 2 Sam., 1 Ki., 2 Ki., 1 Chr., 2 Chr., Ps., Isa., Ezek. Study of these passages will reveal that cherubs are seen in Scripture at points where the intimate presence of God is described: the Garden of Eden, the Ark of the Covenant, etc. Their mention in Ezek. 1 contributes to this picture by delineating them as occupied in some way with the glory of God.

Utilizing Cross-References

The marginal references found in the Scofield are similar to a concordance. However, their connection with the verse to which they are keyed is intentionally less precise. A concordance is based on the occurrence of exact words. Hence, the living creatures in ch. 1 can be traced through Scripture only by means of the phrase *living creatures*. We found that in Ezek. 10 they are equated with cherubs, and were able to find out more about them by subsequently using the concordance to locate references to cherubs.

Sometimes the marginal references will be keyed to a particular word, and so will act as a concordance. In many cases, however, they index only related concepts, events or individuals. In Ezek. 1:19 the Scofield Bible has a cross-reference to Rev. 4:7. When we turn there we find similar beings. Yet they differ from the cherubs/living creatures in enough particulars to caution the student against immediate or conclusive identification of the two. In Rev. 4:7 the living creatures have the same facial identity as those in Ezek. 1, but they have six wings each, not four as in Ezek. Use of the marginal reference has led us to a possibly related passage, but we would need to put the exact nature of the relationship between the two passages on a list of areas for further study.

Both a concordance (whether complete or partial) and the marginal references are the first tools that the Bible student should turn to in dealing with any passage. Both foster familiarization with varied portions of Scripture and allow the Bible to interpret itself. Develop the habit of consulting them regularly.

Exploring the Relations Between the Testaments

One of the most important and fascinating features that Bible study uncovers is the relation between the testaments. Augustine's observation has been often quoted: "The Old Testament [is] revealed in the New, the New [is] veiled in the Old."[6] Any use of a concordance or marginal references will quickly reveal that neither of the two main sections of the Bible exists in isolation. And so the O.T. and N.T. cannot be interpreted apart from each other. This is traceable to the continuity of revelation in the plan of God. Heb. 1:1–2 describes the progressive nature of a portion of God's activity. The prophets were channels of disclosure "at many times and in various ways" (Heb. 1:1, NIV). But God's culminative statement to us has come in the Son Himself. And of course His words and works are recorded in the N.T. The O.T. is entirely valid, but incomplete.

Popular, but faulty, views of the relation between the testaments are that the Old is characterized by law and the New by grace, or that the Old moves in the realm of judgment, the New in love. Both analyses are superficial and have missed the point by a wide margin. Aside from the fact that there is law in the N.T. and grace in the O.T., the hues of the complex relation between the testaments are much more varied than such a simplistic analysis would suggest. The relation is that of shadow to light, of prophecy to fulfillment, of partial to complete, of promise to enactment, of anticipation to culmination (as in Heb. 1:1).

All of these relationships, and many more, can be seen in the recurrence of themes (redemption, grace, peace, etc.), in the mutual treatment of key individuals and groups (Israel, Abraham, Adam, etc.), in the fulfillment of prophecy (Mic. 5:2; Mt. 2:5; etc.), in the constants of geography (Palestine) and culture (Judaism), and in the unchanging nature and purposes of God as presented in both divisions of the Bible. But one of the most interesting and frequently occurring links is the phenomenon of the quotation of portions of the O.T. by the writers of the N.T. Such usage may take the form of direct quotations (Mt. 1:23/Isa. 7:14; Rom. 1:17/Hab. 2:4), intentional allusions (1 Cor. 2:9/Isa. 64:4), or casual allusions (Rev. 12:1/Gen. 37:9). Often the dividing line between the last two categories is hard to draw. In any case, the total number of such examples exceeds one thousand.

Why are such quotations of value to the Bible student? To begin with, they reveal the N.T. writers' own views of their Bible, the O.T. Whether they quote from the Septuagint or the Hebrew text, they show a minute acquaintance with the words, contexts and theology of the O.T. Further, they display by such quoting that the O.T. Scriptures were entirely authoritative for their lives.

We should be especially struck by the attitude of the Lord Jesus Christ toward the O.T. He wove the O.T. into what He did, even at crucial times, in an entirely natural way (e.g. Mt. 26:31). He was able to turn immediately to the right passages to express His message (Lk. 4:18). Even in His most trying moments He depended on Scripture. In the temptation in the wilderness He quoted three thoroughly relevant Scriptures from Dt. (8:3; 6:16, and 6:13). And for our Lord to quote Scripture in His agony on the cross demonstrates His familiarity with, respect for, and total trust of the written Word of God (Mt. 27:46, quoting Ps. 22:1). This example demonstrates that He knew how fully He was to live out Scripture because it had binding authority over His life (Mt. 4:4).

Enough has been said to demonstrate that our Lord believed the O.T. was of crucial importance for His finding and following the will of God. The same is true of the writers of the N.T. Their use of the O.T. reveals an acquaintance with it that few today who love the N.T. can match. Lifelong study of the use of the O.T. in the N.T. can foster the same kind of regard for the O.T. as the N.T. figures had. The N.T. use of the O.T. is a mine of instructive material for the student of the Bible.

A further reason for observing carefully the use of the O.T. in the N.T. is for the doctrinal understanding which such care affords. For example, each O.T. quotation in the N.T. has its particular purpose—proof (1 Cor. 1:19/Isa. 29:14), illustration or explanation (Mt. 4:15–16/Isa. 9:1), analogy (Rom. 1:17/Hab. 2:4), etc. The fact that the O.T. can be used in such ways reveals an outlook in the minds of the writers—and in the mind of the Holy Spirit—that the O.T. and N.T. are a theological whole. There is new revelation after the incarnation, but it only serves to amplify, explain, augment, and fulfill—never to contradict—that which was prior, though the old may be superseded. The study of the O.T. quotations and allusions in the N.T. provides ready access to the doctrinal outlooks of the writers.

Then, one should not overlook the simple broadening effect which comes from studying O.T. quotations. The very valuable habit of moving back and forth in Scripture (with contexts, of course) is encouraged by attention to quotations. It is simply the case that a large portion of the N.T. is O.T. material. And further, some books of the N.T. depend on large portions of the O.T. for their interpretation (Rev. on Dan., for instance).

How does a Bible student get at this material? Most N.T. references to the O.T. are keyed in the marginal references (e.g. Eph. 4:8/Ps. 68:18). Studying the N.T. text with one eye on these will invariably lead to encounters with quoted material and its O.T. source. Since it is obvious that it is the intent of the divine Author to reflect such a large part of the O.T. in the N.T., the student of Scripture misses too much if he neglects this key relation between the testaments (see ch. 7, Relations Between The Testaments, for expanded treatment of these topics).

Tracing the Meaning of Particular Words

The Bible carries much of its message in key doctrinal terms: grace, propitiation, salvation, sanctification, and many others. Probing the rich treasury of such individual words often discloses complexities of divine dealings and revelation which cannot be uncovered by other means.

The Scofield Bible assists you in many ways to begin studies of individual terms. Some key words are discussed in the notes, e.g., the Heb. word *kaphar* at Ex. 29:33. Such a note gives places where the concept is elucidated, but where the word itself may not occur (Heb. 9:15, 26; 10:4; Lev. 16:6), locations of other notes (Gen. 4:4; Rom. 3:25), and related words (e.g: *sacrifice*). A glance at the index to the annotations at the back of the Scofield Bible will reveal that the key note on ''propitiation''/*kaphar* is found at Rom. 3:25. Use of the concordance in this instance adds 1 Jn. 2:2 and 4:10 as containing instances of the N.T. word for propitiation.

An initial step in such a study would be to note all the occurrences of such a word, and for this the use of a complete concordance might be needed. Since the same Heb. or Gr. word may be translated in different ways at different places, a search for one translation of a word may not accurately reveal all the relevant passages. In the case of *kaphar,* use of a complete concordance (such as Young's) shows that the AV translates it several ways. The following list gives all the AV variations (but not all the places where it occurs), and the NIV translation in the same verses:

	AV	NIV
1. Gen. 32:20	appease	pacify
2. Ex. 29:36	make atonement	make atonement
3. Lev. 6:30	make reconciliation	make atonement
4. Num. 35:33	cleanse	(make) atonement
5. Dt. 21:8	be merciful	accept . . . atonement
6. 2 Chr. 30:18	pardon	pardon
7. Ps. 65:3	purge away	atone(d) for
8. Ps. 78:38	forgive	atone for
9. Prov. 16:14	be pacified	appease
10. Isa. 28:18	be disannulled	annulled
11. Isa. 47:11	put off	ward off with a ransom

The student now has a partial list of references which involve translation of the word *kaphar*. Only some of these involve cultic, i.e., religious, use of the term, viz., Ex. 29:36; Lev. 6:30; Num. 35:33; and Ps. 65:3. Proverbs 16:14, for example, describes a relation between two individuals in which appeasement or pacification is needed. It can be seen that behind many of these references lies the idea that an act of payment turns away the anger of another. Deuteronomy 21:8 shows this quite clearly in the NIV. Romans 3:25 uses a Gr. word *(hilastērion)* that the Septuagint (the Gr. translation of the O.T.) often used to translate *kaphar*. Paul is apparently thinking of Christ's work as a turning away of God's wrath by the payment that is His blood.

This example cannot be exhaustive, since in the case of *kaphar* the complexities of Heb. and Gr. usage introduce problems that the student using only translations cannot surmount. Here we must bring into play knowledge of the original languages of Scripture. However, the student can consult word-study reference works such as those listed in the Annotated Bibliography in this volume.

Thinking Ahead

In any type of work in the Scriptures, alert students will realize that they continually uncover areas that need further study. Perhaps they notice individual words that arouse their interest, or that a passage appears to lead in directions that lie beyond their immediate concerns. Such areas should be noted as worthy projects for future work. There is always more to learn and profit from! As you put each discovery into words, and write it down if at all possible, such ongoing projects often suggest themselves. This is especially the case when you regularly ask questions about the meaning of what you are reading.

Questions for Further Study

1. Make a list of the reasons you may have right now for Bible study based on your maturity in Christ and your service for Him.

2. Study the Scofield notes given as introduction to the book of Philippians. List all the background features that are relevant to understanding the book.

3. Scan the whole book of Philippians, reading it quickly several times. How might the suggested key verse (1:21) be reflected in the rest of the book?

4. What passages outside of Phil. are of value in understanding the book?

5. What O.T. passages are quoted in the book, if any?

6. What picture of Paul does the book present?

7. How is Phil. 3:6 connected with other passages in the N.T.?

8. Is Epaphroditus (2:25; 4:18) mentioned anywhere else in the N.T.?

9. What picture of Christ does Phil. present?

10. Can you find teaching that the N.T. does not give elsewhere?

11. Where does the word *perfect* occur in the NIV translation of the N.T.? How else is the Gr. word behind it translated? (Use Strong's or Young's concordance.)

4

The Language of the Bible

The Nature of Language

Values of Knowing about Languages in General

The inscripturated revelation from God is the most important document ever put in human language. Yet the three languages in which the original biblical texts were penned were thoroughly natural and human languages. They are only three among thousands of different languages that have existed in human history. As such, insofar as we have data that enable us to study them, we can examine them as we would examine any other human language, and can apply what we have learned about languages in general to the biblical languages as well.

In recent years many discoveries have been made about languages and how they work. In fact, a relatively new field, linguistics, has emerged as a result of efforts to understand how people interact with oral and written communication. Many of the findings of individuals working in this field, who consider themselves as attempting to carry out scientific investigation of language, are relevant for biblical studies. Their work does not concern itself with learning a particular language but with describing and accounting for features of languages in general. Knowledge of some of their conclusions can help the student of the Bible in many ways.

Breaking provincialism based on native language. Human beings tend to think very narrowly about their own language—and culture—in relation to that of others. For instance, we feel that our language is the most "natural" or the "most regular," that other languages are somehow less suited to normal communication, and that languages

50

spoken by groups deemed to be primitive by Western societal standards must be somehow less advanced than ours. Some exposure to the features of language can enable us
to see that all of the above assumptions are incorrect.

Seeing the non-uniqueness of the biblical languages. Heb., Aram., and Gr. were languages used by real people in real-life situations. God chose to employ them as channels
for the communication of the O.T. and N.T., and they must have had properties that
enabled them to carry the divine message effectively (existing and adaptable vocabulary
for theological terms, for instance). But aside from this kind of feature, they were not
supernaturally shaped any more (or less) than all the affairs of men are guided by God's
providential hand.

One sometimes hears it said that "Greek is the most perfect language ever devised," or that "Greek is inflected even more highly than Hebrew or Aramaic, and
hence is capable of great precision."[1] There are several errors here. To begin with,
languages aren't devised: they develop over time. Nor is any of the biblical languages
in any sense "perfect." Language is a remarkable, God-given medium for human interaction. Speakers of any language are able to communicate effectively with each other
concerning any matter which is of interest or importance to them. No language can be
said to be more or less complicated or precise than others. They are all very complex
and all capable—where speakers desire—of great precision. And they are all adaptable
and expandable to meet situations that a language community feels are worth communicating about orally or in writing. Scholars have long recognized that the dialect of Gr.
in which the N.T. and some related early Christian literature were written had a vocabulary containing words that were useful for theological discussion, such as "justify"
(dikaioō) and "love" *(agapē)* (see discussion of Greek below in this ch.). Also, it was
in the providence of God that Gr. was the prevailing language of the Mediterranean
world at the time the N.T. was written. As such it facilitated the missionary nature of
Christianity. But it is still a language with the same general features as other human
languages.

Perhaps the most telling fact standing against such idealistic views of the perfection
of biblical language is that the Bible still must be interpreted. There are a large number
of very puzzling problems in the language of the O.T. and N.T. documents. If Gr. or
Heb. were perfect, we would not have ambiguities at various levels of those languages,
but we do. Eugene Nida and Charles Taber, speaking of both Gr. and Heb., say:

> Greek and Hebrew are simply languages, like any other languages, and they are
> to be understood and analyzed in the same manner as any other ancient tongues.
> They both possess extraordinarily effective means of communication, even as all
> languages do. For example, in the Greek Gospels there are some 700 grammatical
> and lexical ambiguities, but of course, as in most languages, a high percentage of
> these are resolved by the linguistic context.[2]

New Testament Gr. is a *language,* one used in a special way by God, but a language,
nevertheless. And the same is true for Heb.

Improving biblical studies. An awareness of some of the ways languages work is a
significant advantage for the student of the Bible, even if he does not have extensive
knowledge of the languages themselves. He can, for instance, see the fallacies in many
statements that have been made concerning vocabulary and meaning in the text. In
connection with one such error, James Barr stated:

It is probable that a greater awareness . . . of general linguistic method in all its
aspects, and an application of such awareness in biblical interpretation, would have
valuable and important results for theology.[3]

Some understanding of such linguistic principles can help the student of Scripture in
regard to semantics and lexicography (the study of word meanings), translation theory
and practice (see "Translations and Translating" below in this ch.), relations between
the biblical languages, understanding of culture (language is intimately bound up with
culture), and many other areas of Bible study.

A Brief History of the Scientific Study of Language

The present century has seen a great advance in understanding of the phenomenon of
language. This advance was preceded by concentrated efforts in the nineteenth century,
especially in Europe, to understand the historical and genetic relations between major
known languages, especially among those of the Indo-European family (see in the discussion of Greek below). This concentrated study, although it was primarily concerned
with the history of language, provided a knowledge-base for the twentieth-century revolution in language study. Shortly after 1900, the idea that each language consists of its
own structured system began to be accepted. Furthermore, there developed the valuable
distinction between descriptions of language over a period of time (called *diachronic*)
and at a particular point in time (called *synchronic*). Both kinds of investigation are
important, but by and large they can be done separately. The nineteenth c. had seen
mostly diachronic investigation. It is of interest that the remainder of this c. has seen
interest in language develop generally in a fashion parallel to what have often been
viewed (not without controversy) as four *levels* of language—*phonology* (roughly the
sound system), *morphology* (roughly the system of words and minimal meaning units),
syntax (the grouping together of words) and, very recently, *semantics* (the ultimate
meaning of utterances). There are many current competing theories of how language
works, and it is generally acknowledged by those in the field of linguistics that many
features of language are not understood well at all.

General Features of Human Language

Primacy of sound. Many people appear to be under the mistaken impression that the
essence of a language is its written representation. For instance, if the graphemic (spelling) system does not match the sound system well (as in Eng. and French), we tend to
view the language as more complex than others and more difficult to learn. It turns out,
however, that spoken language is more basic than written. This is demonstrated first by
the fact that there are many real and complex languages in the world that have never
been reduced to writing. Nevertheless, they are vehicles well suited for the communication needs of the social groups that use them. Furthermore, in the normal learning
process, children acquire spoken language long before they are able to read or write that
language. Also, change in the sound systems of languages is usually not accompanied
by corresponding change in the graphemic system—hence the lack of correspondence
(cf. *knife* and the varied sounds of *ough* in *thought, though, through,* etc.). The sound
system changes independently of the written. Finally, the fact that writing systems have

been devised late in human history argues for the priority of the sound system over the written form of language.

Perhaps the most important consequence of the primacy of spoken language is that the most effective discussions and descriptions of how language works must deal with the oral characteristics. To facilitate such work, linguists have devised a graphic system (the International Phonetic Alphabet) which attempts to capture all the language sounds that can be produced by the human vocal apparatus.

Language as code. Although human language can be used for aesthetic (as one important feature of poetry, for instance) and other secondary purposes, its primary function is to communicate information. It accomplishes this as *a coded system* that utilizes symbols—sound units in combinations (the graphic representation is *not* the symbol system). The symbols, which occur at different levels of language—individual sounds, sounds in complex constructions—are similar to those in a system such as Morse code, where written letters are represented by sequences of short and long sounds, or, if written, by dots and dashes. In this way, discrete symbols are assigned to pieces of real language information (letters). Such a system makes use of a small stock of building blocks that can be combined in endless ways.

There are, as linguists have pointed out in recent years, many common features that are shared across languages, called *language universals.* Certainly these are due to our being endowed by God with the capacity for communication by speech. We can see them, for example, in the fact that languages use a limited stock of basic sounds and the combinations of these sounds tend to follow certain patterns.

Nevertheless, each language has its own complete and very complex system. Because of such individuality, each language must be described in its own terms, not in terms of the grammar of another language, as is still often done by attempting to impose Gr. or Lat. "categories" on other languages, for example. The relations among elements in the system, not the elements themselves, constitute the essence of the information-carrying property of the language. Thus, it is not important which vowels and consonants a language uses, or how they are combined in words and then sentences (of course, some combinations cannot be pronounced easily or at all). No sounds or combinations are more or less expressive than others. They are abstract in that they bear no intrinsic relation to the items, actions, states, relations, etc., that they "point to," except for a few onomatopoetic terms such as *buzz, hiss,* etc., in Eng., or, for example, *gongusmos,* grumbling, in Gr. The entire system is thus *arbitrary,* arrived at apart from any intrinsic connections between the symbols and what they stand for. The features of a language are also established by *convention,* that is, through tacit agreement by its speakers.

At first glance it seems that some languages are more complicated than others. Perhaps they are in some areas. But usually such evaluations occur when a language is not presented well to learners, or, unfortunately, when there are sociological or other reasons for viewing a language as having a certain mystique, as with the biblical languages. People often say that the case system of Gr. is more refined than parallel portions of the morphology and syntax of other languages. Thus it is argued that God chose it as a superior vessel for the N.T. revelation. It turns out, however, that ancient Gr. simply used cases as one feature of its system. Other languages can and do accomplish the same thing in their respective systems with different mechanisms.

The elements of the system of a language have several important properties. To begin with, they are "reusable." The small stock of sound units can be combined and recombined, and the same is true of the larger units and syllables formed from them, and so on. Moreover, these units can be described in terms of their existence both as sounds and as meaning-related. This is the feature of *duality*. Language units partake of both realms.

An important feature of language that has been stressed in recent years is that of *productivity*. There is no limit to the number of new, previously nonutilized, encodings of messages that can be made. Every human language is capable of creating brand new utterances because of the complexity and flexibility of its system.

It is important to realize that within the system of any language, information is carried at various levels and in different ways. It is a mistake to think that individual words are the primary carriers of "meaning," and that the total meaning of an utterance, that is, a section of the exhibition of real language, is determined by adding the values (as if they could be isolated) of the occurring words. Language systems have *lexical meaning* and *grammatical meaning,* which together carry messages. *Lexical meaning* is the information carried by individual words (or short phrases or compounds). *Grammatical meaning* is the information carried by things such as word order, intonation (variation in pitch in spoken language), case endings, etc.

Most people think that words have fixed meanings that they take with them into utterances. There are actually ranges for most words, which contexts narrow down to one meaning, or a few choices for the hearer/reader to pick from. In addition, because of the great influence of context in determining the meaning of words, we must avoid thinking that words have central or "root" meanings that every use is somehow connected with. An example would be viewing Gr. *logos,* as having some element of the idea of *word* in all its occurrences, even when it is equivalent to Eng. *thing, item,* or *topic.* And because words do not have fixed meanings, a dictionary/lexicon cannot give "official" meanings. A lexicographer can only make generalizations, and usually insufficient ones at that (in principle, the meanings of words are infinitely extendable), from observations of words in contexts. See "Understanding 'Messages' " in ch. 5, Interpreting the Bible, for a discussion of the English word *bank* as an example of how speakers of a language determine meaning.

Linguistic incompatibility. From what has been said so far it should be evident that there can be no one-to-one correspondence of meaning units across languages. For instance, there is no single word in Eng. that can be used to translate each occurrence of the Gr. word *logos* ("word," "item," "matter," "utterance," etc.). Translating languages is not simply a matter of substituting units, whether words or other features of the system. This is often difficult for beginning language students to become accustomed to, but it is crucial for language-based approaches to translation, especially of the Bible. Furthermore, the description presented in the previous section of language as a system has significance for translation theory and practice.

The twentieth c. has seen extensive investigation of the phenomenon of transferring messages from one language to another. Greater awareness of how best to do translating, which people have been doing anyway as long as language barriers have existed, has in part led to attempts to integrate conscious perspective on language as a system into the craft of translation. One of the most evident results has been the shift from the *word* as the translational unit to stretches of *discourse* as units to be considered as wholes. It is generally acknowledged today that a translator is not to be concerned primarily with transferring the *form* of the message but the meaning. Form *may* be important, but only where the source language is consciously playing with its structural features, as in poetry, etc. Even there, preservation of meaning takes priority over preservation of form, by word substitution, retention of word order, etc. (see below under "Principles of Translating" for more discussion of how languages carry information).

Language change. It is not difficult to demonstrate that languages change over time, most rapidly in their vocabulary, less rapidly but sometimes more extensively in their sound system, and less so in other areas. It is, however, very difficult for us to see our own language changing. This is so because our own speech patterns (our *idiolect*) do not change a great deal over our lifetime. Nor do we make conscious comparisons of two or more stages of our language.

But whatever the changes, several principles apply. Changes do not affect a language's usefulness for those it serves. *People* change language for certain reasons, although they are usually not aware of doing so. Intentional change is rare and usually unsuccessful. When languages change they do so to serve their users. If new vocabulary is created, it fills gaps. An example that is quite obvious is the stock of new words arising from the computer revolution—"computerese" terms such as *byte,* a unit of information utilized by a computer. Similarly, the word *access,* previously used only as a noun, has been used in the last ten years or so as a verb in computer jargon, as in "I accessed the information." It is possible that we will see this use in other contexts, as in *"I accessed the teacher,"* meaning "I talked to the teacher," and that such an innovation will spread to the speech of most speakers of English. If vocabulary items fall into total disuse, they are probably not needed anyway. If a language simplifies in one area (e.g., loss of case distinctions in Gr.) it may make up for it in another area (creation of new prepositions and wider range of meanings for existing ones in Gr.). A clear case of language change related to biblical studies is the shift in the range of meanings of *flesh*. In the seventeenth c., and for the translators of the AV, one meaning of *flesh* referred to parts of animals used for human consumption. Since then it has lost that meaning (while retaining others), and so the word *meat* should be used in contemporary translations where biblical words denote edible animal tissue.

Can we say that change constitutes deterioration? Not when language is viewed as a social tool. Societies change and so do their languages. Certainly some language forms are preferred over others by some groups. An educated individual may be come suspect if he uses certain "nonstandard" Eng. features, such as *ain't*. And biblical language (usually that of the King James Version) has for some people a prestige factor in prayer *(e.g., brethren, thou)*. But these are sociological evaluations. Language in itself is neither pure nor corrupt. And change in language does not introduce substandard conditions. Such an evaluation is usually made on the basis of attempts by some segment of society to preserve the status quo.

Economy and redundancy. As complicated as all human languages are, they have one feature that pervades all utterances: they are economical. Speakers will avoid repeating information in uninteresting ways. For instance, if the sentences *John did his homework* and *Mary did her homework* appear in sequence, they will invariably be combined as *John and Mary did their homework*. Such features as using personal pronouns and relative pronouns to replace nouns in Eng. are examples of the many mechanisms for economizing.

Interestingly enough, it is well known that there is a large amount of redundancy in human communication, perhaps as high as fifty per cent.[4] Particular information is usually given in more than one place. In Eng. the *-s/-z* on third person singular verbs *(hit-s, go-z)* duplicates information given by the subject, which must be present in Eng. *He goes, she writes* could be *he go, she write* with no loss of information.

These two features, economy and redundancy, complement each other in that a language will only invoke economy to the point where information can in some way be recovered from context. In other words, redundancy rescues language from economy. And apparently economy limits redundancy that would lead to boredom. In some poetry the writer utilizes extreme economy, sometimes to the point of obscuring the message and making it quite difficult to interpret. Nevertheless, the human mind seems to enjoy this kind of challenge and game playing with language. And so in normal language, economy operates to the point of creating interest and eliminating redundancy that is of no interest or use.

Hebrew and Aramaic

The Language Family

Hebrew and Aramaic are both members of what is called the Semitic family of languages. The name for the family is derived from the name of Noah's oldest son, Shem (Gen. 10:21), since ostensibly most of the speakers of this language family were descended from him, although the term's technical accuracy should not be pressed. Speakers in this family have at various times been found from Africa to the Fertile Crescent and Arabia. Hebrew belongs to a subdivision known as Northwest Semitic, whose member languages are Ugaritic, Phoenician, Moabite, Canaanite, Hebrew, and Aramaic. Other Semitic languages include Akkadian, Arabic, and Ethiopic. Only Heb. and Aram. are found in the O.T. Today Arabic has the greatest number of speakers. Hebrew, as well as Gr. and other western languages, owes a debt to the Phoenicians for their development of a nonsyllabic alphabet. Ugaritic has been extremely valuable in shedding light on its sister language, Heb. Ancient Ugarit was discovered in 1929 at the site of modern Ras Shamra on the Syrian coast, and yielded important finds for O.T. studies. The exact relation of the members of the Northwest Semitic group is unclear. Some of them may have been sister dialects, mutually intelligible variants of the same language. Abraham and his descendents adopted one of them, Heb., as their language sometime after entering Canaan.[5]

Depending on the passage and the translation, the Heb. language is variously referred to in the O.T. as "Hebrew," "the language of Canaan" (Isa. 19:18), or "the Jew's language" (see 2 Ki. 18:28 as an example of translational variation).

Hebrew began to be supplemented by Aram. as the spoken language of the Israelites in the sixth c. B.C. Modern Heb., spoken in Israel today, is a revival of the ancient language, preserved in the Heb. Scriptures and the writings of Jewish scholars down through the centuries.

Some Characteristics of Hebrew

Hebrew is like the other Semitic languages in utilizing a triconsonantal (triliteral) root system, made up of either consonants or consonants and semivowels *(y, r, w)*. Some have attempted to establish the existence of diconsonantal roots. Either root analysis is an abstraction, since the root never appears without associated vowels. It is well known that in the later Heb. spelling system the vowels are usually represented, if at all, by super- or submarkings. Such writing is said to be "pointed." The root situation is really not unlike that inherited in Eng. from Germanic, such as in the verb *sink,* where variants *sank* and *sunk* are formed by varying the vowel and leaving the consonants the same.

Among other notable grammatical features of Heb. is the preference for connecting sentences with coordinating conjunctions (like the English *and*), subordinating constructions being less frequent. This can be seen quite clearly in the AV translation of Gen. 1:3–31, for example. The situation in ancient Gr. is the opposite. Here the tendency is to use complex sentences, that is, sentences within sentences joined by subordinating conjunctions. This is a frequently occurring feature that translators must pay careful attention to. In addition, Heb. often uses nouns to add further information to other nouns, as, for example, *King of glory* (Ps. 24:7,10) instead of *glorious King,* which involves a noun with an adjective.

It is of interest that the writers of the N.T. often import this feature of Heb. syntax into Gr., as in the case of "throne of grace," (Heb. 4:16), which perhaps has as its best Eng. equivalent "throne filled with grace" or something similar. This feature of being influenced by the syntax of Heb., known as the use of Semitisms or Hebraisms, is due in large part to the influence of the grammar of the Septuagint and to the native Semitic speech of many writers of the N.T.

It is often asserted that Heb. is more "pictorial" than other languages, and so is "particularly suited for its task of relating the biography of God's people and His dealings with them."[6] The verdict of modern linguistics is that, in general, what can be said in one language can also be said in another, although it may take more words to do so. Hence, assertions to the effect that Heb. "is a language through which the message is felt rather than merely thought"[7] are not true to the nature of Heb. per se, or Heb. versus Gr.

Similar to this error are assertions that assess the ability of Heb. to be precise: "Hebrew is well-suited for narrative and verse but lacks the precision of Greek."[8] If this were true, we would presumably rarely encounter problems in the N.T. occasioned by features of the language. But this is simply not the case.

Furthermore, one sometimes hears it said that this kind of feature reveals how the Heb. mind worked, that is, for instance, the Hebrews *thought* more pictorially than the Greeks. This assumes that the language of a speech community binds its speakers to think along certain lines. For example, Gleason Archer states:

> Just as truly as the genius of the Greek language imposed its stamp upon the New Testament revelation and the terms in which its message was cast, even so was the genius of the Hebrew language determinative for the expression of the Old Testament message. It made a great deal of difference that Greek was precise in expressing time values, and that Hebrew laid chief emphasis upon mode of action rather than upon tenses.[9]

If this were true, we would have to conclude that the Greeks did not care very much about mode of action (starting, stopping, states, etc.) and the Hebrews did not care as much as the Greeks about when events took place. If they were normal human beings, they cared about both! In addition, one of the implications of such a statement is that, because of such fixed thought forms in Heb., God would be limited in what He could communicate through speakers of Heb. But another generally prevailing verdict of modern linguistics is that people are not forced to think in the categories of their language (i.e. "pictorially," etc.), but rather that people use language and develop forms and "categories" for the things they usually think about in their culture.[10]

Aramaic

Several portions of the O.T. are written in Aram.: Ezra 4:8–6:18; 7:12–16; Jer. 10:11; Dan. 2:46–7:28. The first example in the O.T. of an Aram. word is in Gen. 31:47 (actually two words), where Laban bestows an Aram. name, "Heap of Witness," on the place where Jacob's tribe erected a stone in Gilead. Other Aram. place names appear in the O.T. Speakers of Aram. ranged from Syria to the Euphrates Valley, and the language (actually a group of dialects) was an international trade and diplomacy medium during much of Israel's later history, especially during the tenth to fourth centuries B.C. This is illustrated by the incident found in 2 Ki. 18:17–37, where the Assyrians made demands in Heb., and were then requested to speak in Aram. The international character of Aram. is seen especially in its use in the book of Daniel under the Babylonian and Persian captors. It is especially interesting to note that the words of condemnation given in Dan.—*mene, mene, tekel, uparsin*—are Aram. Aram. is also the language of the Targums, Jewish translations of portions of the O.T. As sister languages, Aram. and Heb. stand in a relationship to each other similar to that of Eng. and Dutch. Aramaic became the dominant language of the Jewish people after the Babylonian captivity, and so was probably their language in N.T. times.

The Septuagint

The origins of this translation (also referred to as the LXX) of the O.T. into Gr. are still debated. It seems likely that at least part of the translation was made in the second or third c. B.C. in Alexandria, Egypt. The pseudonymic Letter of Aristeas (second c. B.C.) asserts that a group of seventy-two rabbis made a translation of the Heb. O.T. for the Gr. ruler of Egypt, Ptolemy Philadelphus. Hence the use of the rounded-off number seventy (Lat. *septuaginta*). Parts of the work may have been done later.[11]

In general, the Gr. of the Septuagint is heavily influenced by the Heb. it attempts to translate. Often it simply imitates Heb. syntax. The style is not consistent, however, thus showing the hand of various translators.

The Septuagint is useful in biblical studies for several reasons. To begin with, it gives information on the meanings of individual Heb. words at the time the translation was made. Hence it is valuable for Heb. lexicography. It is also of great use in textual criticism of the O.T., that is, the establishing of a text as close as possible to the original. The Septuagint is also notable as one of the very first translations made among ancient literature. While we take such a practice as normative, crossing language barriers with documents was actually quite rare in the classical world. In fact, the missionary nature of Christianity provided impetus in the early centuries after the apostolic age for other notable translations from the Septuagint, such as Gothic, Old Church Slavic, Coptic, Ethiopic, Armenian, Arabic, Georgian, and Latin. The Septuagint is still today the O.T. of the Greek Orthodox Church.

Perhaps the most significant place of the Septuagint in ancient times was its function as the O.T. for speakers of Gr. in the early Church. Portions of it were quoted extensively, along with words from the Heb. text, by the writers of the N.T. In particular, Luke, in his Gospel, and the writer to the Hebrews quote from it the most, the latter to the exclusion of the Heb. text of the O.T. (see ch. 7, Relations Between the Testaments).

Greek

Greek is a member of the Indo-European language family, a completely different group from the Semitic family. (A language family is a group of languages descended from a known or posited parent language.) Linguists and historians have posited the existence of speakers of a single language who lived in central Europe until the fourth millennium B.C. Groups within this speech community separated and migrated in three directions—west, east, and south. These groups must have spoken mutually intelligible variants of their language just before their breakup, dialects that subsequently changed sufficiently to establish them as separate languages. In the last 150 years much effort has been expended by linguists in showing the relationships between these languages and trying to establish the nature of the posited parent language, today called Indo-European, of which no written records exist.

There are many correspondences among the daughter languages that incontrovertibly show this common source. The ancient daughter languages were Indo-Iranian, Armenian, Albanian, Balto-Slavic, Greek, Italic, Celtic, Germanic, Hittite or Anatolian, and Tocharian.[12]

Ancient Gr. itself can be divided into subgroups including almost twenty dialects. Among these dialects are Attic (a subdialect of Ionic), Cyprian, Cretan, Thessalian, and Corinthian.[13] The Gr. of the N.T. is a dialect formed mainly from Attic, and has a well-known history (see below). Greek as a whole is distinctive among languages of the world in that it has the longest continuous literary history, from approximately the fifteenth c. B.C. down to the present. Among the Indo-European languages it has the second oldest records, with Sanskrit's datable to the sixteenth c. B.C. One should be careful not to assert that Sanskrit is older than Gr. or Lat., as some do. They existed at the same time as sister languages, which, by definition, are contemporaneous.

While Arabic is the only Semitic language that is spoken today by large numbers of people, the languages of the Indo-European family are spread virtually around the globe. Of the original Indo-Europeans, those speaking descendant languages of what is now called Indo-Iranian traveled the farthest. Today daughter languages in that branch are found as far as Iran and India. The Hittites of the O.T. were speakers of an Indo-European language (see Gen. 15:20; see note at 2 Ki. 7:6). Today the Balto-Slavic group is represented by millions of speakers in Europe and Western Russia. The Germanic family includes as daughter languages German, English, Swedish, Norwegian, Icelandic, Danish, and Dutch. Celtic developed into Gaelic, Welsh, and Breton. Latin, the Italic dialect spoken in the area of Rome, is continued today in such Romance languages as French, Portuguese, Spanish, Italian, Romanian, and Sardinian.

Those who spoke what has been classed as proto-Greek (a parent language behind the dialects) must have begun to enter the Gr. peninsula in the third millennium B.C. They apparently settled that land mass and adjacent islands in waves, so that from early times the Gr. language existed in several subgroups, each with one or more subdialects. The most influential were Ionic and its offshoot, Attic. The former was spoken in the Gr. colonies in Asia Minor, including Ephesus, and many of the islands between the Gr. peninsula and Asia Minor. Attic, which was essentially Ionic with a few innovations, was spoken in the area of Athens. The dialects remained distinct for centuries, in great part because of the geographical separation of Gr. colonies and city-states. However, in general, ancient Gr. is remarkably homogeneous, especially in its syntax and basic vocabulary. This is easily verified, since written records of the dialects exist in sufficient numbers for detailed comparison.[14]

The language of the N.T. has its own unusual, documented history. Such accounting is rare in the realm of language development. When in 337 B.C. Alexander the Great assumed command of the army of his father, Philip II of Macedon, he unwittingly began a process that would lead to the loss of independent existence of most of the individual Gr. dialects. Soldiers of various dialects were thrown together in his army and were most heavily influenced by the Athenian dialect. The resulting new dialect was described by the Greeks as *koine* ("coynay"), i.e., "common" or "shared." (There were other such koine dialects in earlier periods of Gr. history, but none was involved in such far-reaching social changes.) This new form of Gr. came to be the most dominant dialect after the fourth c. B.C., and is today simply called Koine. It is the dialect in which the N.T. and the Septuagint were written. Although some other dialects remained after Alexander's time, this swift and unusual language change had a profound effect on the overall Gr. language picture. The extent of Alexander's conquests added to the geographical influence of this new dialect. In fact, Alexander sought actively to further the spread of Gr. language and culture, and the effects of this have lasted until today. It was from this dialect that Byzantine Gr. and then modern Gr. developed. Koine is also referred to as Hellenistic, from *hellēn,* which in the plural, *hellēnes,* was the name the Greeks used for themselves. The classical dialects were used until the time of Alexander, Koine from 330 B.C. to the sixth c. A.D., Byzantine to the fifteenth c. A.D., and modern Gr. from then to the present. (It should be remembered that such exact divisions are somewhat artificial.) Because of this linguistic continuity a Gr. person living today does not have great difficulty in reading Koine.

Some of the prominent features of Koine, both biblical and nonbiblical, deserve mention. In general, syntax, that is, the ordering and arranging of words in sentences, is simpler than in the earlier classical Gr. First, a smaller variety of sentence-connecting conjunctions was used. Second, classical Gr. frequently embedded one sentence inside another. Such an embedded sentence could serve as the equivalent of a direct object of the main verb in the matrix sentence. For example, in English we embed one sentence inside another in *I knew he was kind,* where *he was kind* functions as a direct object of *knew.* But we also have the alternative *I knew him to be kind,* a sentence that has the same meaning as the first, but that has changed the verb in the embedded sentence to an infinitive. Classical Gr. would have preferred the second type, Koine, the first, although Koine used the other, also. Third, repetition of words, or common parts of words, became more frequent, ostensibly for emphasis, as in Gr. *eiserchetai eis,* where *eis* means "into" and occurs as a free-standing preposition and as a preposition prefixed to a verb. This has the literal Eng. equivalent "he goes into into." Such overuse often defeated the purpose of calling attention to words and became very redundant. It is important that translators of the N.T. be aware of such repetition and not attempt to render it word for word (this example is exaggerated for the purpose of illustration; few translators would fail to translate this particular example correctly).

There existed two socially determined strata in Koine, the literary and the conversational. At times the language of the N.T. varies between the two, with some N.T. documents even showing literary characteristics of classical Gr., such as those found in Lk. and Heb.

Until the present century it had been generally accepted that the N.T. was written in a special, heavenly influenced language. However, it has become increasingly clear in modern study of the language of the N.T. that the Koine of the apostolic writings was essentially the everyday Gr. of the first c. A.D. Large numbers of papyrus fragments discovered in Egypt in the late nineteenth c. have supported this conclusion.

There are, however, a number of linguistic features that are unique to N.T. or Septuagintal Gr. These are certainly due to the particular nature of the message of the O.T. and N.T. Most of these consist of words not attested in known Gr. literary or inscriptional records. Some examples are *akrobustia* ("circumcision"), *antichristos* ("antichrist"), *baptisma* ("baptism"), etc.[15] Also to be found are words that are attested outside biblical literature, but with different meanings. Among these are *baptizō* ("baptize"), *diabolos* ("devil"; outside the N.T. it means "slanderer"), *episkopē* ("overseer"), *dikaioō* ("justify"), and *pisteuō* ("believe"). The latter two words have similar meanings outside biblical literature, but have had new semantic fields opened up to them by the N.T. revelation. Thus *dikaioō* previously could mean "justify," as in a court context, but was never used to describe the theological transaction based on the cross-work of Christ.[16]

In addition to general distinctives of biblical Koine, it is possible to identify characteristics of individual authors. Many of these are useful for the student who has no knowledge of N.T. Gr., since they often are reflected in translations.[17]

It is generally acknowledged that of all the N.T. books the Epistle to the Hebrews displays vocabulary and syntax features closest to those of nonbiblical literary Koine of the first c. and those of earlier classical Gr. Choice of individual words, sentence structure, and overall thematic development evidence the hand of a careful and experienced writer. Its author sometimes employs striking alliteration, as in 1:1, where four key words begin with the letter *p*. The American N.T. scholar Bruce Metzger describes the overall structure of this book as "the longest sustained argument of any book in the New Testament,"[18] and characterizes the author as one "whose work is easily recognized as coming closer to the definite literary style of a master of the Greek language than anything else in the New Testament."[19]

Among other authors showing stylistic and grammatical features similar to those of Hebrews are James, who is also fond of carefully wrought alliteration, and Luke, who demonstrates a particularly extensive vocabulary. The introduction of his two part Gospel-history, Luke-Acts, found in Lk. 1:1–3, is well known as a carefully framed statement of historical methodology, shaped in Gr., that is very similar to that of literary composition of centuries earlier.

Peter, too, in his first epistle, evidences linguistic features similar to those of literary Koine and earlier Gr., especially in his use of the article. Beginning students of N.T. Gr. are often puzzled by his practice of placing the article before long strings of words, often prepositional phrases, turning them into unwieldy nounlike segments, as in 1 Pet. 5:4, where a literal translation would read "you will receive the unfading-of

glory-crown,'' or 3:1, "the-of-the-wives-behavior.'' For the first example the NIV has
"the crown of glory that will never fade away." Obviously a translator must do a great
deal of rearranging in such instances (see below under "Principles of Translating").
Could such classical style and general literary ability be attributed to a fisherman? Perhaps, although some have suggested that, as appears to be indicated in 5:12, Silvanus
was the ultimate polisher of the written words.

An interesting feature that translators must wrestle with is Mark's frequent use of
euthus, "immediately," and *kai,* "and," a feature Metzger describes as part of his
"homely simplicity." [20] Mark repetitively employs *kai* to join sentences and clauses.
To avoid a stilted and boring rendering, translators must be careful to search for expressive but correct alternatives to *immediately* and *and.* An example of the use of
euthus is found at Mk. 1:29, where the AV has "And *forthwith,* when they were come
out of the synagogue" (italics mine), substituting *forthwith* for *euthus* and following the
rest of the Gr. sentence almost word for word. The NIV has rendered this *"As soon as*
they left the synagogue" (italics mine; see also 1:20 and 21).

The use of Gr. in Revelation shows unusual features, including a number of sequences that some have incorrectly labeled as ungrammatical. For example, in 2:7 John
repeats the phrase *to him* ("To him who overcomes I will give *to him* to eat from the
tree of life"). But many of John's supposed "errors" have been found in normal usage
outside the N.T. over the years, as new discoveries have come to light. Further, it is
certainly the case that much of his usage is tailored to the unusual message he has to
present. Such unusual linguistic elements seem often to enhance the message when the
whole is considered.

John's Gospel, on the other hand, has quite a different flavor in terms of language
usage and style, but in this case also the message and the vehicle for it are well matched.
His simple syntax provides a good starting point for beginning students of N.T. Gr. His
frequent linking of sentences with *kai,* "and," is evident in most translations, as in
7:30: ("Then they attempted to take him, *and* no one laid hands on him") where one
would expect *but.* The translator here is faced with the problem of deciding whether
there is enough contrast between the two sentences to warrant translation with an ad-
versative, such as *but, yet,* or *however.* Although the AV and NASB use *and,* the NIV
uses *but.* Since there *is* a contrast here, the NIV translators are justified. Here is just
one example of why translators cannot proceed word by word, but must consider longer
stretches of text in deciding the exact words to use (see below in this ch. under "Principles of Translating").

John also shows great variety in his use of Gr. verbal forms, especially in regard
to those features that can show differences in kinds of action—what some have called
aspect. These have to do with how long or how frequently an action takes place, whether
it is beginning or ending, or whether something is in a state (as in *He is dead*). All
languages must include such distinctions if they are to communicate such information,
and the N.T. is no exception. But John is unusual both among the Gospels and, especially, N.T. narrative literature for his careful switching from form to form to stress
aspect. He makes frequent use of the perfect tense,[21] which often, depending on the
context, describes a state, either of the subject or the object of the sentence it is in. The
most noteworthy is in 19:30, where Jesus' final assessment of His work is described by
the sentence "It is finished," which could also be translated, "It (the work to remove
sin) has been brought to a state of completion." Such uses of the perfect are often
difficult to translate into Eng. Usually the present perfect or past perfect is used. These

consist of a present form of *have* + past participle *(has gone, have eaten)* or past *had* + past participle *(had gone, had eaten)*. But in many instances these miss the mark. There is no simple Eng. equivalent for the Gr. perfect that can be plugged in every time.

Certainly we must mention some of the characteristics of Paul's style and grammatical usage. Perhaps no other writer in the N.T. shows in his language as much of his personality and his own spiritual concerns as the apostle Paul. Well known are his method of question and answer and his frequent (twelve times) use of the Gr. interjection *mē genoito*. The AV uniformly translates this as "God forbid." The NASB renders it as "May it never be." The NIV, however, varies it: Rom. 3:4—"Not at all!" Rom 3:6—"Certainly not!" Rom. 6:2—"By no means!" Also quite evident is his outpouring of emotions (Rom. 9:1–3), giving insight into the intense involvement of the Apostle with his readers and his subject. At times his style is halting and disconnected, as in Eph. 2:1–5, where the first idea is interrupted and not finished for five verses. Another example is Rom. 5:12–21, where vv. 13–18 form an involved parenthesis. On the other hand, the lofty style of 1 Cor. 13 has through the AV translation found a permanent place among great chapters in literature. No less majestic is the powerful confirmation of the security of the believer in Rom. 8:31–39:

> For I am convinced that neither death, nor life, nor angels, nor principalities, nor things present, nor things to come, nor powers, nor height, nor depth, nor any other created thing, shall be able to separate us from the love of God, which is in Christ Jesus our Lord (NASB).

The great variation in style among Paul's epistles has led some critics to disavow Pauline authorship in the case of some books. Yet, although complex issues are involved, this can be explained by such things as span of time between writings, use of amanuenses, etc.[22] Similarly, some have attempted to show that the vocabulary of the Pastoral Epistles (1 and 2 Tim., and Ti.) is so different from that of other writings ascribed to Paul that they could not possibly have been written by him. However, it has been demonstrated that such approaches ignore the presence of normal variables in lexical usage due to factors of time and topic.[23]

Linguistic Interaction in Palestine in the First Century A.D.

General Features

The linguistic situation in Palestine at the time of the appearance of the second Person of the Trinity joined with humanity, was, as we can best assess it today, very complex. The predominant language of international relations was Koine Gr. Latin was the language of the Romans, and was used throughout their military activities. The influence of Lat. on N.T. writings is confined to the use of vocabulary (lexical) items mainly associated with Roman relations with Palestine, such as *census, colonia, flagellum,* etc.[24]

Also, the N.T. tells us (Jn. 19:20) that the Jews in Palestine spoke Heb. For many years it has been debated as to whether this and other statements refer to the classical language of the O.T. or to Aram. Some believe that Heb. was the predominant language of Palestine at the time,[25] but it has long been assumed that Aram. was adopted by the

Jews in captivity in Babylon and was brought back to the land. The linguistic issues are complex, and there is evidence for both positions. The matter is also related to the question of the original language of the Gospels. Some have posited an Aram. original of the Gospels that was subsequently translated into Gr., although this view is not widely held today.

At the very least, one would have to say that many in Palestine, both Jews and Gentiles, were bi- or even trilingual. Paul's bilingualism is apparently demonstrated by a passage such as Acts 22:2. Interacting with different speech communities often presupposed such ability. It may have been that four languages were in current use, Gr., Lat., Heb., and Aram. As to the earliest N.T. records, one N.T. scholar has asserted, "We can be sure that the tradition about Jesus was expressed from the very first in Hebrew, Aramaic, *and Greek.*" [26] However, understanding of the issues is still in an unsettled state.

New Testament Greek and Semitic Influences

Although there is no consensus on the exact nature of the language makeup of Palestine in the N.T. era, one thing that is clear is that the Gr. of the N.T. shows extensive influence from both the Heb. O.T. and its Gr. translation, in syntax, vocabulary, and quotation. In many instances Hebrew language features show up through the Septuagint. Such sequences as *he answered and said* are pure Heb. syntax and usually come directly to the N.T. from the Septuagint. An example is Jn. 1:26, where the AV has "John answered them, saying," the NASB has "John answered them saying," and the NIV has simply "John replied." Another example is Jn. 17:12, where the AV and NASB have "son of perdition," and the NIV has "the one doomed to destruction." It should be remembered that the Septuagint was probably more accessible to first-century Jews than was the Heb. O.T., and N.T. writers would have been steeped in its language. [27] Certainly the N.T. is affected in its choice of particular words by the Septuagint. [28] In many instances Heb. words are "borrowed" into the Koine Gr. of the N.T. via the Septuagint, e.g., *abba* and *pascha*. [29] Why such borrowing? The authors were using familiar words drawn from the language in which the earlier revelation appeared. Perhaps the most obvious effect of the Septuagint and Heb. texts on the language of the N.T. can be seen in the quotations of one or the other of those sources in the N.T. Since a large proportion of the N.T. consists of quotations or substantial allusions, the presence of Heb. words translated into Gr. by the writers, or of material quoted directly from the Septuagint, is extensive (see ch. 7, Relations Between the Testaments).

Translations and Translating

Principles of Translating

Something of the value of accurate translations that can be understood by most people can be seen from the words of Erasmus written over four hundred years ago in 1516:

> I totally disagree with those who are unwilling that the Holy Scriptures, translated into the common tongue, should be read by unlearned. Christ desires His mysteries to be published abroad as widely as possible. I could wish that even all women

should read the Gospel and St. Paul's Epistles, and I would that they might be read and known not merely by the Scots and the Irish but even by the Turks and the Saracens. I wish that the farm worker might sing parts of them at the plough, and that the weaver might hum them at the shuttle, and that the traveller might beguile the weariness of the way be reciting them.[30]

In the same century the martyr William Tyndale wrote in the preface to his translation of the Pentateuch (1538):

I had perceived by experience, how that it is impossible to stablish the lay people in any truth, except the scripture were plainly laid before their eyes in their mother tongue, that they might see the process, order, and the meaning of the text.[31]

Although Bible translation is such a crucial undertaking, until the twentieth c. very little systematic attention was given to the question of how translation of written documents should best be carried out, whether of biblical material or secular. Thus, in the case of the Bible, although actual translation has been practiced for centuries, conscious attempts at formulating guidelines have often been absent.[32] Two things in particular have led the practice of Bible translating to undergo a needed period of methodological self-examination. The first is the development of modern linguistics and the allied field of cultural anthropology. The second is the rise in the twentieth c. of groups such as Wycliffe Bible Translators, and The United Bible Societies, which as part of its work coordinates the worldwide efforts of many translators.

The general task of the Bible translator can be simply stated: to reproduce the meaning of the message contained in a document of a first ("source") language, in a document of a second ("receptor" or "target") language. This may seem too obvious, but some qualifying statements must be made. First, the translator is working with two distinct languages. No two languages have the same structure, not even related languages. For centuries descriptions in grammars of Eng. and other languages were modeled on descriptions of Gr. or Lat., which supposedly possessed standard, ideal structures that were to be discovered in other languages, regardless of whether or not they were historically related to Gr. or Lat. Such an approach masked individual differences among languages (see above in this ch. under "Language as Code"). Since each language has its own structure, its means of communicating information is unique. What one language does with a participle, another may do with a noun. Or, as in the case of Gr., a language may carry a type of information on one occasion with cases and on another with prepositions. This principle of the uniqueness of language structure is hard for most people to grasp.[33] Nevertheless, recognizing this is absolutely foundational to successful translating, especially in regard to the Bible.

The translator must be aware that the meaning of a document (or an utterance) is carried by many linguistic features. In fact, although words seem to be and have long been assumed to be the carriers of meaning, many components in a message carry meaning. The total meaning, that is, content of information to be communicated, does not consist of the meaning (as if there were one) of word 1 + word 2 + word 3 + . . . word n. Words themselves carry information only in connection with other words. And some words, such as *former,* as in *the former and the latter,* only serve to show listeners or readers how to process information. Another example of this directive function is the word *that* in *I know that he is alive.* The first *that* in Eph. 1:18 (NIV) or 1:17 (AV) simply serves to indicate that a sentence (here *He is alive*) is coming that is the direct object of a verb (see above in this ch. under "Greek" for a discussion of such *embedding*).

No two languages carry information in the same places and ways. Although it is true that anything that can be said in one language can be said in another, the means of doing so varies from language to language. Thus if meaning is of primary importance, then all must be subservient to that, and particular features of structure or form will have to be sacrificed if need be.[34]

A translation is of little use if the context is not taken across the language barrier, or if information is lost or distorted. Yet, unfortunately, that is what many translations do, and readers accept it. Nida and Taber show cogently how an accepted translation of a portion of Scripture can actually fail to be acceptable language, in this case, Eng.:

> In addition to being quite misleading a translation may also be so stylistically heavy as to make comprehension almost impossible. For example, in the American Standard Version (1901), 2 Corinthians 3:10 reads, "For verily that which hath been made glorious hath not been made glorious in this respect, by reason of the glory that surpasseth." The words are all English, but the sentence structure is essentially Greek. The New English Bible quite rightly restructures this passage to read, "Indeed, the splendour that once was is now no splendour at all; it is outshone by a splendour greater still."[35]

Nida and Taber point out two problems that can contribute to this: 1) expressions that are likely to be misunderstood, and 2) expressions that are heavy and discourage the reader from attempting to understand the message.[36] Only if the form, such as an acrostic, a clear play on words, or rhyming, is part of the meaning should attempts be made to preserve it.

The difficulty of the task of Bible translating, into Eng. for example, is heightened because the biblical world is removed from the twentieth-century reader by time and custom. The inclination in translating is to regard the worldview of the writer of the first document as the same as that of the reader of the second. However, to do so will lead to a failure to translate *culture*, which is also part of the translator's responsibility. This does not mean he can alter the meaning to suit the new culture.[37] He is always under obligation to preserve the meaning of any part of the divine revelation. But if he does not allow for cultural differences, he actually obscures the meaning. Examples are "children of the bridechamber" (Mk. 2:19, AV) and "heap coals of fire on his head" (Rom. 12:20, AV). Nida and Taber explain:

> The average person unacquainted with Semitic idioms is simply not going to understand that the "children of the bridechamber" are the friends of the bridegroom, or wedding guests, and that "heap coals of fire on his head" means to make a person ashamed of his behavior, and is not a way of torturing people to death.[38]

Although correct translation will usually involve departure from form (syntax, etc.), the translator must be careful to preserve meaning, as exemplified by the following error:

> It has been argued, for example, that in present-day English a natural equivalent of "demon-possessed" would be "mentally distressed." This might be regarded by

some as a natural equivalent, but it is certainly not the "closest equivalent." Moreover, "mentally distressed" is a cultural reinterpretation which does not take seriously the cultural outlook of the people of biblical times.[39]

All of this presupposes, of course, that the translator must know both languages and both cultures well. Learning the source language and culture is difficult because the translator must always force himself to think outside his own culture, and because there may not be enough information from history, archaeology, language studies, etc. He must also be knowledgeable in scriptural doctrine. Further, it may be difficult to understand the culture of the target language (the one he is translating into) because 1) it may be unfamiliar to him, in the case of little-known language cultures, or 2) if he is translating into his own language he may assume knowledge of features of his own culture or he may fail to take into account the subcultures of speakers outside of his own dialect. What may be a natural Eng. structure for him may be unusual for others.

This then brings us to the issue of the target audience. The translator must formulate the cultural and linguistic attributes of his target language and of his readers, and translate in terms of their culture and dialectical patterns. If he doesn't target his audience, his translation may seem odd to those who should be the best consumers. A striking example of proper adjustment to audience is *The Gospels in Scouse,* a British vernacular translation. Here is a portion of Jn. 1:14 from this translation:

> So wot I've bin sayin, like, is this. God's ole attitude to the werld became flesh. All wot God's got ter say about man became a man—Real Man. An de Real Man lived among us. We could see just exackly wot e was like. An e wus terrific! E wus jus filled from top to bottom wid goodness and love an onesty. An you could see e wusn't juss on'y the truth about man. E was also the truth about God. you could. Honest.[40]

This whole task is complicated by theological demands. A translation may be understandable, yet theologically biased. If so, it still fails to reproduce the meaning of the text of the Bible. A case in point is Moffatt's translation of the N.T., which takes theological liberties with the text of the Bible.[41]

Some have criticized this concern for preserving meaning, which Nida and Taber call dynamic equivalence,[42] and have called it paraphrase, implying that it involves loose or careless translation.[43] In technical use, *paraphrase* is applied to translation that is not word for word, i.e., not literal. Translation that is inaccurate is to be avoided, but the burden of proof is on such a critic to show that a rendering that is not word for word is theoretically less accurate.[44]

One way to help the reader to understand the issue of the transfer of meaning is to compare types of translations. Historically, translations into Eng. have tended to be of two types, with one type appearing only recently. The earlier type can be characterized as having two features, word substitution and word count. The first is also called *concordant* translation. Under this method, the translator attempts to find in the target language the most typical equivalent of an individual word in the source language, and use it as often as possible. Thus, for example, the Gr. word *logos* would be rendered "word" in all occurrences, if possible. Of course, such a choice is entirely arbitrary, because *logos* has many other meanings, or, in the case of a translation, other equivalents in the target language. (In Eng. it can be equivalent to *thing, item, topic, utterance,* etc.) Furthermore, although word-substitution translation may operate this way in most instances, it varies the substitution when this is unavoidable, but only then! Hence it is inconsistent, for when the translator feels the message would be highly distorted, the substitution method is rightly abandoned. For example, the AV usually translates *logos* as "word," and switches only when forced to, as in Acts 8:21, where it uses "matter."

The philosophy of word count works hand in hand with that of word substitution. In effect, it assumes that for every string in the source language of *n* words in length, the new document must have *n* words also. Furthermore, they should be kept in the same order. Hence, in a Gr. sentence, whose word order may not, and often does not, match that of Eng. (the verb may be first, or even last), the word-count/word-order translator will usually deviate from that order no more than necessary, and will also render a verb with a verb, a noun with a noun, etc., even when the meaning may be obscured due to the known principle that structure varies from language to language.

The other basic type of translation attempts to preserve information rather than form and salvages the latter only when it is really part of the message. To accomplish this the translator must know his source language very well, and force himself to think continually in terms of global structures in both languages, i.e., contexts, small and large, of the individual portion being translated.

It is an axiom of modern translation theory that a good translation is always longer than its source document.[45] This is because of the many items of *implicit* information that cannot be carried over from one language to another in their original form. The process of making them explicit consumes more space. Thus the most understandable rendering of, say, Rom. 5:1–12 would be a careful Eng. commentary. This is not a translation in the narrow usage of the word, of course, but an interpretive discourse. However, in a sense all translation is interpretation, and one of the criteria for differentiating among interpretations is length.[46] In the narrow sense a translation is a rendering in language *B* from language *A* in approximately the same space. There is no question that a longer rendering, all other things being equal, could give more information. This is one of the reasons why a word-count and word-substitution translation loses information.

Evaluating Translations

The history of the Bible in Eng. is a fascinating and important story. There are many competent accounts available, and to cover the whole field would be beyond the scope of this book.[47] There are, however, two particularly important issues on which the Bible student should be informed. The first is that of the evaluation and use of the AV in the present generation. There are few issues among Bible students that are as emotionally charged or as complex. To what degree does the AV correspond to the originals? Is it a specially blessed translation? Is it somehow more "the Word of God" than others? Does it produce more fruit or disclose more of the will of God? There are a number of factors that should be brought to bear on these questions in order to evaluate them fairly and objectively. Although the issue cannot be covered fully here, the main question is: does the AV communicate the meaning of the Bible, in terms of style, grammar, and theology, better than other translations? Is it, in short, more readable and accurate? This is really the key to evaluating any translation.

It would be helpful at this point to recall some of what was said above concerning language and language change. A language is a social phenomenon, shaped by members of a speech community to best accomplish according to their views the needs of communicating within that community. Languages change, slowly, subtly, but inevitably, and Eng. is no exception. In the more than 350 years since the publication of the AV, Eng. has changed in vocabulary, syntax, and other features of grammar. Much of the 1611 AV is strange and foreign to the late-twentieth-century ear. This factor alone hinders readability. New versions of the AV, which update its seventeenth-century language, are improvements on an important translation.

One must be very careful to acknowledge the deep influence that the AV has had on Western literature and world society. It has been unquestionably the most accepted and widely read Eng. translation. Since the early seventeenth century, phrases from the AV have found their way into all forms of literature in the Eng. language. Its style and sonorous tones in many places are still considered to demonstrate some of the finest Eng. ever written. Nevertheless, many of today's readers find other translations easier to comprehend.

As to the issue of accuracy and fidelity to the Heb., Aram., and Gr. texts, there are two things that need to be mentioned. First, large numbers of discoveries have been made since the seventeenth century that bear upon biblical studies and the process of translation. More is understood today about the original languages, about archaeology, geography, history, and culture, and newer translations have been able to take advantage of this vast body of knowledge. This does not mean that the reader can be seriously misled in using the AV. But there can be a greater quantity of helpful information in new translations.

A second important area of which the Bible student should be aware is the issue of the manuscript source of various translations. Most available Eng. translations have been produced by translators who knew and consulted Heb., Aram., and Gr. manuscripts, or, more typically, published editions. The variation among Hebrew editions of the O.T. is not great. However, the Gr. N.T. displays greater variation among editions. The AV is based in great part on the editions published by Theodore Beza in 1588 and 1598. These are similar to the 1516 edition compiled by Erasmus.[48] An edition published by Beza in 1565 was the basis for one produced by the Elzevir brothers of Leiden in 1633, which came to be called (on the basis of its editors' description of it) the Textus Receptus, or "received text." All of these editions were based in general on manuscripts copied at a later date than many that are available today. All other things being equal, the nearer a manuscript is dated to the original, the more likely it is to reflect the text of the original. There are many qualifications to that kind of statement, and many other important factors (for example, the manuscripts of the Textus Receptus type of edition do contain some variant readings that many contemporary textual critics view as likely to correspond to the original, although some of these are found in older manuscripts, too). Nevertheless, many scholars today feel that the kind of Gr. text underlying the AV reflects the original Gr. N.T. less accurately than that underlying more recent editions, which make greater use of manuscripts copied within a few centuries of the apostolic period. This is not to say that the AV is therefore a bad or misleading translation. It can be safely asserted that no major doctrine is endangered by the type of manuscript variations found in the text used for the AV. It is especially important to realize that one should not argue for the superiority of one translation on the basis of the supposed superiority of a text, Gr. or Heb.

The argument that asserts that the AV is the best Eng. translation because it preserves key doctrines which all others tend to slight is not really valid.[49] In fact the opposite is often true. This kind of argument is often used with more of an emotional basis than a scholarly one. One must be careful of becoming an instant scholar and expert in areas that take many years to master and in which there are complex issues.

Perhaps a helpful assessment would be to say that the AV is one among many important and helpful Eng. translations. It is not "the Word of God" more than another theologically sound translation, for we do not possess the first manuscripts of any of the revealed Word. That is what we would need in order to have the exact "Word of God."

Further, it must be remembered in evaluating or advocating the AV that languages other than Eng. have and need translations. The AV is usable by only a portion of the world's population. It would be fallacious to argue that no translation into another language could have the spiritual impact of the AV.

The original translators of the AV admitted the need for continual refinement and revision of any Bible translation.[50] Changes in biblical scholarship (discovery of manuscripts, new knowledge concerning languages, etc.) and in language itself necessitate this.[51] Bible translation is never finished. The most up-to-date (language-wise) translations today will not be entirely satisfactory for readers a generation or two hence.[52]

How to Choose and Utilize Translations

Evaluating available translations. How does one choose among the available translations in English? The book *So Many Versions?*, by Sakae Kubo and Walter Specht, has an excellent discussion of this question.[53] There are many competing translations available. What are some of the criteria for choosing? We will suggest four factors that should be considered:

1. Accuracy—This criterion can be described in different ways. As discussed above, a translation should aim to have the same effect on new readers as the originals did on the first readers. Put another way, the goal should be to communicate all that the author intended. Of course, it is virtually impossible to capture every feature. We are today historically, linguistically, and culturally removed from the situation of the writers. This is one reason why there will always be a need for further exegesis and new Bible translations.

There are several things a translator must do or possess as a minimum in order to achieve accuracy. First, he must have a high degree of exegetical, linguistic, and literary ability. This will help him in knowing how languages in general are structured.[54] Second, it is imperative that the translator go to the original languages.[55] The practices of the translators in regard to this are usually stated in the preface of each translation. Third, assessment of the needs of the audience must be consciously undertaken, since they are the all-important hearers of the message. Often a translator will have the goal of making a translation suitable for personal study, or for public reading. A translation that is limited to one particular readership or purpose will appear out of place when used for another. J. B. Phillips wrote his first translation for British youth. It received widespread acceptance because it was suited to his audience.[56] On the other hand, the New English Bible, a British translation, often seems too British for many Americans (aside from spelling differences) as when it uses British monetary terms (*two pence*, Lk. 12:6, etc.), or *weeds* for "garments" (Gen. 38:14).[57]

2. Literary quality and style—Attention to these is important for several reasons. First, a translation that is not written smoothly will be tiring to read, and will eventually be neglected. Freshness, vigor, and quality are all required. But a danger in attempting

to be too natural in translation is that of becoming slangy. If a translation is to be used for any type of public reading, it should have literary qualities that make it acceptable to a broad audience. In order to achieve the goal of literary coherence and quality, the NIV, for instance, was edited for style by literary experts after the translators had done their work.[58]

3. Theological neutrality—It is difficult to avoid presuppositions in any scholarly endeavor, even in biblical studies and Bible translating.[59] It is not difficult to see such personal or philosophical factors in the history of interpretation. One cannot help having a starting point, a set of assumptions that give direction to study or translation. But, of course, the important thing in biblical studies or Bible translation is to test all assumptions by the light of Scripture, and avoid the situation described by one theologian: "Every exegesis that is guided by dogmatic prejudices does not hear what the text says, but only lets the latter say what it wants to hear."[60] Such non-neutrality can enter in at various levels, as when the Jerusalem Bible (a Roman Catholic translation) adopts a poorly attested Gr. reading in Jn. 1:13 which allows the verse to read (in support of the virgin birth): "Jesus who was born, not of blood nor of the will of the flesh," versus "those . . . who were born . . ."[61]

One way to minimize the interference of presuppositions in translation work is to channel the process through a committee.[62] Of course, whole committees can be biased in certain directions. Another problem with committees is the tendency toward variation in the quality of work from book to book. Many modern translations have been produced by committees whose composition has intentionally been broad-based. In any case, it is good to attempt to learn the theological positions of translators involved. Often this information is given in a preface, or can be determined in other ways.[63] The student of Scripture has the responsibility, as with all other biblical material, of testing what is presented to him to see if it matches Scripture as best he can understand it from all the translations and helps he has available. This is merely the principle of 1 Cor. 14:29 and 1 Th. 5:21, where the believer is required to evaluate the teaching that comes from others to discern false from true, and then "hold fast" 'to what is valid. Information given in the preface or material published ancillary to a translation will often state the goals or purposes of a translator or translating group.[64] Such information may be of help in evaluating literary or doctrinal positions, also, as when the NEB states in its introduction to the N.T.:

> We have conceived our task to be that of understanding the original as precisely as we could (using all available aids), and then saying again in our own native idiom what we believed the author to be saying in his. . . . In doing our work, we have constantly striven to follow our instructions and render the Greek, as we understand it, into the English of the present day, that is, into the natural vocabulary, construction, and rhythms of contemporary speech.[65]

4. Original language editions utilized—The variation in editions used as the basis of translations, especially of the N.T., has been mentioned above. In general, major doctrines will not be affected. More recent translations, such as the NIV, NASB, and RSV, have used editions of the N.T. supported by the general consensus of scholarship, editions that use manuscripts older than the Textus Receptus type of edition utilizes. However, the committees involved in making such translations have not followed those editions slavishly.[66]

Utilizing translations. At times you may feel, especially if you do not have access to the original languages, that you cannot be sure of anything in the biblical text, since there are so many translations available. Here are some guidelines for taking advantage of Eng. translations of the Bible:

1. Compare renderings—It is often very helpful to study with more than one translation. In the turgid portions of Paul's epistles, for example, translations such as those by Phillips or Way often clarify what is obscure.[67] This comparative process can be even more effective if different types of translations are used, since sometimes quite different perspectives can be found and integrated into understanding of a passage.

2. Learn strengths and weaknesses—After repeated use of a translation, the Bible student can often notice where that translation shines or where it misses the mark. The NIV, for example, will break up long sentences that the AV or NASB leaves in correspondence with those in the original languages. A good example of this is found in Eph. 1:3–14. Such a practice enhances readability.

3. Read widely—One of the greatest hindrances to progress in Bible study is the failure to read extensively and take in new information. Employing various Bible translations can help overcome that weakness. You may have a favorite study Bible, but you should keep other versions at hand for consultation.

4. Be open to new interpretations—As serious Bible students we must always walk a tightrope between two extremes: (1) not accepting new truth given by the illuminating ministry of the Spirit, but stubbornly clinging to the familiar, and (2) seeing, on our own, what is not there in the text. Openness is good if what we see is verifiable by other Scripture. It is destructive if we see, because of excessive prejudice or a hobbyhorse mentality, what is not and never will be in the text. We all ought to be willing to be surprised by what we find in a new translation, and be ready to accept it as valid, if it accords with the rest of the Bible (see ch. 5, Interpreting the Bible).

5. Take advantage of study helps—While the features of study editions of the Bible, such as marginal references, a concordance, etc., are not part of the translation, they do in most instances shed light on the translation. This is true of the Scofield Bible, as for example, at Heb. 1:8, 9. Some notes may be the product of the translators themselves, who after wrestling with thorny problems suggest alternative readings or explanations. The NIV translators' notes appear on each page of that translation, and are found in the *Oxford NIV Scofield Study Bible*.

5

Interpreting the Bible

Becoming an Independent Student of Scripture

The Importance of Having a System

Believe it or not, everyone has a method of interpreting the Bible. But not all methods are equally profitable. Some use the magic finger approach. It consists of acting upon some supposed divine directive, locating a particular verse—usually with the eyes closed—and taking that portion of Scripture as an answer or truth provided by God. We may laugh at that, but often we come quite close to that when we ignore contexts. Then there are those who read the Bible a lot, but never seem to get very far in putting it all together. They can quote at great length, but have difficulty seeing what the passage means. Others follow an extreme devotional approach. They read only what "warms" them at the moment, as if the Bible were intended to make them feel good continually. All of these people have systems of interpreting the Bible, and it is not difficult to see why such methods do not lead to spiritual soundness. As a result of these approaches—which are really partly Bible study methods and partly interpreting methods—many are spiritually weak and discouraged about their prospects of getting anything solid from the Bible. Such practices never lead to a mature ability to handle the Bible with power and fruitfulness.

Methods of interpretation can be haphazard or systematic, and even systematic interpretation can be either profitable, or unprofitable, so that it does violence to the meaning of the Bible. God's desire is that believers come to the place where they are able to read the Bible with understanding, balance, and facility in relating various portions of the Scriptures to each other.

Unfortunately, many people seem to leave this area to others. Can you state why you understand the Bible the way you do? Do you believe it is important to know why you are to understand the Bible in certain ways, or would you rather just accept what someone tells you? What do you do when two Bible teachers are 180 degrees apart on a problem passage—do you become discouraged or just laugh and forget the whole matter? What do you do when you face a spiritual problem? Do you turn to someone else or perhaps try to find a book to help? The best response to such situations is to open the Bible and begin to find out just what it says.

There is one important truth that makes it crucial that every believer pay careful attention to how Scripture is handled. It's this: God intends the Bible to be understood. Now you may say that this is self-evident. In a sense it is. It is also a ground-level assumption about how we relate to God. If He has not made it possible to understand certain things about Him that He has revealed, then we have been left to struggle on our own. But if He really wants us to know Him (and that is a teaching that runs throughout the Bible), and has given us a readable book, then He must intend for us to comprehend it. Eugene Nida and Charles Taber, linguists and Bible translators, have put it this way:

> Writing to be understood might seem to be a truism, but for some persons it is a startling revelation, for many individuals have assumed that the Bible is not a book to be understood. One person, for example, who began to read Today's English Version remarked, "This must not be the Bible; I can understand it."
>
> The Bible is not a collection of cabalistic writings or of Delphic oracles. The writers of the Bible were addressing themselves to concrete historical situations and were speaking to living people confronted with pressing issues. It is not always possible for us to understand precisely what the writers meant, but we do injustice to them to assume that they were intentionally trying to be obscure.[1]

This basic assumption gives us hope that we *can* know the things of God, but it also puts an obligation upon every individual who knows Christ as Savior to dig into the Book in a meaningful way. God has not made His Word obscure. It is difficult in some places, to be sure, but understanding it is not impossible. He has made it complicated enough that we have to *work* to get even a minimal understanding of it.

Let's look at it this way. God has given us only one book. There are some tough spots in it. But there is no accompanying handbook that was given along with that first book to tell us how to interpret it. We are on our own, and we need to make the most of what we have. We will see later in this chapter that the fact that the Bible does not have a divinely given instruction book along with it determines our basic approach to the Bible itself.

The purpose of this chapter is to encourage you to become a balanced interpreter of the Bible. An interpreter can be defined as one who understands the content the author or speaker has put in a communication, whether oral or written. The best Bible interpreter is one who takes from the Scriptures the most information, as the authors intended it, in such a way as to be able to apply it to life (the ability to apply it as intended by the speaker/author is simply the intended outcome of communication, which has the goal of changing something in relation to the hearer/reader). Technically, it is advantageous to speak of assimilating *information,* rather than understanding "meaning." Meaning is the relation of message units to items that are being talked about (e.g., the word *tree* is somehow to be connected with a woody plant). When people communicate, they are involved in the business of imparting new information to others. Determining meaning is only part of the larger process.[2]

The Value of Independence

There are many important reasons why every believer should strive to be an independent, capable interpreter of the Bible:

1. We are dealing with the revealed and inspired Word of God. It exhorts us to pay attention to its message, even to its smallest features. 2 Tim. 2:15–17 reminds us that we are to be diligent, accurate and comprehensive in our approach: "Be diligent to present yourself approved to God as a workman who does not need to be ashamed, handling accurately the word of truth" (v. 15, NASB). In this passage the figure Paul uses is that of a stone mason who cuts blocks of stone straight to fit together correctly. Our handling of the Bible is to be carried out with equal care and precision.

2. Although everyone has a system of interpretation, it is vital to have one that derives the most from Scripture and is consistent with the Bible's own statements about itself.

3. We are removed from the biblical world by over nineteen centuries and many cultural gaps. We must be able to take this into account and overcome it where possible.

4. We are separated from the biblical documents by a language barrier. Anytime there is *translation* of a document, there must added effort to gain proper understanding of the actual message as the writer gave it.

5. Our overall system of theology is shaped by our system of interpretation. If the system is not proper, the theology will not be biblical.

6. In every age there are opponents to the Word of God, and this is no less true today. This makes it all the more imperative that the Word of God be understood and proclaimed accurately.

7. Often we fall into the error of *applying* the words of Scripture to life before we *understand* them. In doing so we put into practice something other than what is intended by God, unless we accidentally do what He intended. Interpretation must always precede application.

8. Down through the ages subtle theological errors have often been based on improper systems of interpretation. In order to be equipped to combat error, the student of Scripture must know why he understands the Bible to say what he believes it does. This is why in Tit. 1:9 we are told the elder must be able to safeguard the truth in the local assembly by handling the Word of God with power.

The Personal Requirements

It is a simple teaching of Scripture that only those who know the Author of the Book can understand spiritual truths and apply them to life. This is enunciated in 1 Cor. 2:11–12, where Paul explains that the Spirit of God communicates with the spirit of the child of God, the one who possesses His Spirit, to teach him those things that can be understood in no other way. Others can certainly comprehend facts about the Bible and see important biblical principles for life. But the veil imposed by sin prevents a person from taking the Bible and relating it successfully to life without the specific ministry of the third Person of the Godhead, the divine Author of Scripture. Furthermore, the believer who is consistently controlled by the Spirit (Eph. 5:18) will be better able to appropriate God's revelation than one who is not (see note, 1 Cor. 2:13).

The verse in 2 Tim. 2:15 quoted above is sometimes applied to the process of formulating correct systems of doctrine, especially in regard to dispensations. But it applies equally to the attitude we should have in approaching the Bible. It contains a command that is well known, often repeated, but too little heeded: handle the Bible carefully! Mark well what it says, but be careful not to go beyond what it says. And, just as important, be sure to see *all* it says. Do not assume anything. Do not take anything for granted. Lay aside any preconceived notions. Do not be bound by tradition, because no system of doctrine, no matter how old or how highly respected, can ever be a substitute for the Word of God. At every point the question every one of us must ask ourselves is, "What does the Scripture say?" (Rom. 4:3, NIV). Then we must be ready to do what it says. Be willing even to be startled by what you discover, and be bold to put it into practice.

Some Lessons from History

Usefulness of the Past

It is valuable for anyone who works in a discipline or field of study to know something of the history of that field. How have earlier researchers, teachers and scholars approached it? What kind of conclusions have been drawn? What kind of evidence have they acknowledged as acceptable? When have they followed lines of investigation that have led to dead ends? Where have they fallen into error that was later corrected by others?

For example, every scientist must know something of the history of science, since in it are found principles for establishing scientific methodology and its use. One can learn about the failures of earlier scientists, as well as their great discoveries. And, if there is enough documentation, one can learn why they succeeded or failed, and follow the methodology that led to positive results. The same is true for the student of the Bible.

Before we turn to look at the history of the interpretation of the Bible, it will be valuable to set forth a working premise that will be developed more fully later in this chapter. It is this: The best system for interpreting the Bible is one that gets the most information from Scripture—that is, one that does not leave gaps, and yet does not make one part contradict or dominate another. Some of the reasons for this premise are: (1) God intends for us to understand Scripture; (2) The Bible does not contradict itself; (3) It is to be read as any other normal book and taken at face value.

One way to learn how important these things are is to see how this premise and reasons for it have been missed by some in the history of the interpretation of Scripture. Simply stated, the Christian should know enough of the history of approaches to the Bible in order to profit by the errors and discoveries of the past. Such understanding will not only help in avoiding errors and guarding against carelessness, but it will also enable us to avoid narrowness in our own interpretation, for we will see that others have discovered truth, too.

Ancient Jewish Interpretation

The beginning of conscious biblical interpretation is usually assigned to the period of Ezra (455 B.C.). In Ezra 7:6 he is described as "a teacher well versed in the Law of Moses" (NIV). Further, in 7:11 he is said to be a priest. He apparently studied the law, taught it, and assisted people in applying it. Many consider Ezra to be the first of the significant Jewish interpreters, as well as the founder of the Jewish school that approached the Scriptures with extreme literal interpretation. In a certain sense their principles were good, as in the case of the rule that a word must be interpreted in light of the sentence it appears in, and sentences, in their contexts.[3] But they often failed to adhere to their own rules and emphasized minor points to the detriment of what was essential. This was due to the skewed belief that even the letters of Scripture had significance. This preoccupation with graphic symbols themselves led to extensive attempts to see word plays and connections. A. Berkeley Mickelsen describes a typical error:

> Unfortunately, although the rabbis did apply these rules, they also utilized such practices as substituting one letter for another, forming new words, assigning a numerical value to words, etc. In Genesis 2:7 the Hebrew word "and he [The Lord] formed" has two yods (smallest Hebrew letter, equivalent to English "y") in the unpointed Hebrew text. In Rabbinic Hebrew the word impulse *(yetzer)* is a noun from the same root as "to form." Hence, the rabbis deduce that because of the two yods in Genesis 2:7—the first letter of the words "to form" and "impulse"—God created two impulses in man, a good impulse and a bad one! This makes us smile, but it at least shows that these interpreters carefully observed what was written. Unfortunately, instead of using their ingenuity to clarify the precise meaning conveyed by the language, they looked for "deeper hidden meanings."[4]

The lesson to be gained from this is to avoid exalting the very letters and words of the Bible, otherwise the result will be that the message is missed. Words, including the letters they are composed of, have meaning only in connection with other words, all of which are found in historical contexts, that is, in real life situations, as recorded in the Bible.

Allegorism

Over the centuries the method of interpretation known as allegorism has appeared in various schools and under different guises. Its common thread, however, is an approach to the text that attempts to look beneath the obvious meaning to a "deeper" or "more real" meaning. Thus a text is interpreted without serious regard for the grammatical elements that are visible on the surface, and apart from its historical connections. Although in this approach a text has more than one meaning, it is the less obvious meaning that is more important, is taken to be intended by God, and often, under this approach, can be understood only by those with special insight. After all (so the approach goes), it *does* take extra wisdom or spirituality to be able to see beyond the surface into what is of greater moment for life.

John Bunyan's *Pilgrim's Progress* is an allegory. However, with Bunyan the surface is to be entertaining, while the subsurface meaning is to be related to life; with the Bible the surface is actually tied to history, etc., and cannot be ignored. We are not to look beneath the surface unless there is warrant for doing so (for example, the tree in

Dan. 4 has evident reference to Nebuchadnezzar's kingdom, and the text actually tells us that). This is not the same as typological interpretation, where both levels are real and important and historical. This will be discussed further in ch. 6, Literary Aspects of the Bible, and ch. 7, Relations Between the Testaments.

Allegorical interpretation was practiced extensively by the Greek philosophers and historians in their treatment of secular and sacred Greek texts. Schools at Alexandria, Egypt, given to the preservation of the Greek classics, exercised profound influence on Jewish interpreters who labored there in the interpretation of O.T. texts.

The most prominent Jewish allegorist was Philo (ca. 20 B.C.–54 A.D.). For him those who could see only literal meaning were at an immature level of understanding. Only those who achieved maturity were able to enter into allegorical interpretation. For example, in Philo's view the biblical account of Abram's journey to Palestine is really intended to portray the story of a stoic philosopher who leaves Chaldea, which signifies "understanding by the senses." Upon becoming Abraham he enters into the condition of being a truly enlightened philosopher. His marriage to Sarah really signifies the philosopher's acquisition of abstract wisdom.[5]

Surprisingly there was overt methodology in this, since for Philo the presence of synonyms in a text was a clue that an allegorical meaning was to be looked for. But it was permissible to explain words while ignoring the punctuation found in sentences.

Allegorism did not remain outside the sphere of Christian interpretation of the biblical texts. Origen of Alexandria and Caesarea, who lived from 185 to 254 A.D., although recognized as one of the great early scholars of the Church, often brought the allegorical approach to texts which did not lend themselves to easy interpretation. Thus he views Jesus' entry into Jerusalem as the entry of the Word of God into the soul.[6] Subsequent interpreters were influenced by allegorical methodology, among them Augustine (354–430). This church father justified such an approach by appeal to 2 Cor. 3:6: "The letter kills, but the Spirit gives life" (NIV). He understood this to mean that the spiritual or allegorical interpretation discovers the real meaning of the Bible; the literal interpretation brings spiritual bondage. Fortunately, Augustine was not consistent in his use of allegorical interpretation.

The Reformers

This brief sketch must omit many details of the history of interpretation through the centuries. There were, however, many who laid foundations for methodology that is used today. And it is with the Reformers that we begin to see the conscious formulations of approaches to Scripture that we often employ today without thinking about their ancestry.

Although Martin Luther (1483–1546) is well known for his battles with Rome, his formulations of fruitful approaches to Scripture were at least as important as, and certainly were part and parcel of, his actions as a reformer. Abandoning earlier approaches that sought multiple meanings in texts, Luther stressed the natural sense of words as indicated by grammar.[7] He assumed that the Bible was understandable and could be approached by all. This went hand in hand with his insistence that each individual must respond to the biblical presentation of justification by faith alone. Thus each believer has the right to interpret the Bible for himself. In so doing he is to be dependent on the Holy Spirit for illumination. Luther also saw that the O.T. is essential for understanding the N.T., and that the Church is based on Scripture, not Scripture on the Church. The teaching of justification by faith is a key to understanding the whole Bible, and those parts that convey that message more clearly are to be used to aid in the interpretation of those that are problematic. Insistence on the value of reading the Scriptures in the original languages bolstered Luther's concern for the grammatical and historical details of the text.[8]

John Calvin (1509–64) continued Luther's emphasis on the centrality of the Christ-event to approaches to the Bible, and likewise rejected allegorical methodology.[9] Although he is perhaps known primarily as a theologian, he wrote many fine commentaries and wrestled with details of interpretation. It is safe to say that he was a good theologian because he knew his Bible well and was a good interpreter. He stressed the importance of grammar and history in approaching texts, as well as the indispensable role of the Holy Spirit in guiding the interpreter. His understanding of progressive revelation was linked with an appreciation of the manner in which the O.T. is unfolded in the N.T. (see ch. 7, Relations Between the Testaments). Later in this chapter we will discuss the relation between theology and interpreting by context. Calvin clearly had an appreciation of this connection, for he attempted to carry out his interpretation on the basis of understanding of the whole book in which a text was found, as well as all of Scripture. This anticipates the contemporary findings of communications and linguistics scholars who describe messages as encodings whose parts can be understood only by referring at least to some degree to the neighboring constituents. In other words, elements of a message are carried in more than one place, and the interpreter must be alert to the appearance of clues coming in various forms and found in various locations (see below under "Understanding 'Messages' ").

In stressing the need to pay attention to grammar, history, and context, individuals such as Calvin and Luther played a significant role in enabling interpreters to approach the Bible with objectivity. Observing these important elements of Scripture, which are present because the Bible is a genuine book, set in real human times, enables us to avoid those aberrations and excesses that cloud the meaning of Scripture. We face the danger, however, of obscuring it ourselves whenever we do not take the necessary steps to interpret according to grammar, history, and context, for then we are free to impose on the text any interpretation that strikes our fancy. Many do that today in a manner that is not far from classical allegorism.

It is safe to say that it is a necessary basic assumption of biblical interpretation that attention to the plain meaning of the text is the door to healthy understanding of the Bible. Many excesses beyond the ones that have been mentioned here have arisen quite easily when this principle has been neglected. The importance of understanding this lesson of history, as well as many others, is expressed in this statement by the nineteenth-century textual critic Alexander Souter: "It can never cease to be of moment to the real lover of Scripture what was thought of its meaning by any patient investigator in any country or in any age."[10] The successful interpreter will (1) avoid exalting the letters or form of Scripture over the meaning of words in contexts and avoid other forms of over-literalism; (2) be dependent on the Holy Spirit and not on a church to lead in understanding the Bible; (3) allow the Bible to speak of Christ, making necessary connections between the O.T. and N.T. with alertness to progressive revelation.

We set forth above a working premise that stresses the need to get the most from Scripture while at the same time not making one part contradict or dominate another. The history of interpretation of the Bible (although our treatment has necessarily been brief) provides us with illustrations of how some have failed to meet this. They have allowed contradictions to stand in the interest of getting information from passages, or have made certain truths dominant over others.

Interpretation and the Nature of the Bible

We can see from another angle the importance of the basic premise if we investigate the character of the Bible as a whole. In a certain sense, what we believe about the Bible helps us to arrive at a useful system of interpretation. Put another way, the manner in which we approach the Bible is determined by what we believe about it.

A Divine Revelation

To begin with, the Bible is a revelation from God, as asserted in such places as Jude 3, which speaks of "the faith that was once for all entrusted to the saints" (NIV), where "faith" refers to the body of revealed truth to which human faith responds (see also 1 Jn. 5:9–12). Such a view of communication by God is echoed in the many occurrences in the O.T. of the phrase "thus saith the Lord." The prophets understood that the words they passed on to others were not from themselves (2 Pet. 1), but were, instead, the product of the creative breath of God (2 Tim. 3:16). Because of this we have to assume that it must be understandable, for God wouldn't waste His time giving us a book we couldn't comprehend (see Nida and Taber's observation quoted above in this ch. under "Importance of Having a System").

   Nor would God mislead us. We can count on the fact that there are no tricks in the Bible. Of course we must be extremely careful not to impress our own ideas (presuppositions) on Scripture. Finite, fallen human beings have been attempting to distort the words of God since Eve heeded the serpent's lie about the judgment of God. And not only is the Bible a revelation from God, but that disclosure has also come in stages (see ch. 7, Relations Between the Testaments). Because of this "progressive revelation" we must be alert, as Luther and Calvin were, to ways in which the N.T. unfolds the O.T. and ways in which the N.T. is contained in the O.T. Connected with this is the need to recognize distinctions in what God is doing at different times in biblical history. The meaning of Pentecost in Acts 2, for instance, and the "mystery" of Eph. 3, cannot be adequately related to other portions of the Bible without an understanding of the progressive unfolding of God's plan for humanity (see ch. 2, The Nature of the Bible).

A Creation of God

A second feature of the Bible that is important for shaping our methods of interpretation is the teaching that it is detailed and exact by virtue of its being breathed out by God. This quality of being associated with the very nature of God, as expressed primarily in 2 Tim. 3:16 (see also 2 Peter 1:20–21), must mean, among other things, that Scripture will not contradict itself. It is not the product of human activity, but of God's creative power, for in Ps. 33:6 the breath of God is what brings the world into existence, and that breath is sufficient to accomplish this all by itself (see note at 2 Tim. 3:16).

   This principle of noncontradiction is far-reaching in its implications. In the final analysis it means that, first, our task of interpretation is guaranteed success, and, second, the Bible will shed light on itself without leading us astray. The breathed-out character of the Bible also sobers us to realize that not only must we not miss the meaning through neglect or distortion, we dare not ignore its application to life.

Another, and very practical, result of this characteristic of Scripture is the need for accurate translations. Each rendering of the O.T. and N.T. in any language should ideally always go back to the original languages as part of the process of exercising the utmost care in transferring the message into a new language.

Further, we must accept the Bible for what it says, at face value. This is the basis of so-called literal interpretation. Because God gave us the very words He desired, then the words must mean what they say. The error of allegorism is apparent when we understand this principle. We will develop the implications below under "Literal Interpretation."

The breathed-out quality of the Bible also encourages our interpretation by context, since all the parts of the message are important. None are accidental and none are misplaced (see ch. 2, The Nature of the Bible, for discussion of textual criticism).

Our Sole Authority

A third characteristic of the Bible that it teaches us about itself is that it has authority over us and is the sole standard for faith and practice. This is found in such passages as 2 Tim. 3:16 and Mk. 12:24. Consequently, we are not allowed to change it, but instead must ourselves be changed by it. We must always be ready to accept it at face value, never softening a message that might strike too close to home.

We are also taught that the Bible is powerful: "The law of the Lord is perfect, reviving the soul. The statutes of the Lord are trustworthy, making wise the simple" (Ps. 19:7–9, NIV). Theologians call this quality animation. The Bible is sufficient in every way for changing the condition of fallen humanity. Our responsibility is to allow it to speak for itself.

Situated in Genuine Experiences

In a slightly different vein we note that the Bible is rooted in culture, history, and language. It was written by real people for real people about real-life situations. The experiences of Paul in prison, of Esther in Persia, and of Ezekiel in Babylon attest clearly enough to this. Consequently we need to know the purpose of each book and its setting. As an example, when we consider the purpose of Phil. we learn that Phil. 4:19 does not give a blank check to anyone who seeks to serve the Lord, but instead promises the one who gives money sacrificially that God will make up his lack. One of the basic purposes for the writing of the book was to notify the Philippians that their gift had been received, a gift that exceeded what their circumstances might have led them to give. Historical, contextual, grammatical, and literary features should never be neglected in the examination of this book that is grounded in the human situation. It is a genuine book in terms of literary qualities, in a sense like any other fine book that we possess, and it asks, among other things, that we treat it as we would any other work that we respect.

Hence, we see that we can best interpret the Bible by allowing for its own nature as ascertained by its statements about itself. It tells us much about how to approach it. It is divine revelation, is a creation of God, is our sole authority, and is situated in real life. It is God's book, and we can trust it as we accept what it says at face value. And because of all of this, we must allow it to interpret itself for us. It has the power, precision, and authority to do so.

Let us return to our premise for a moment. We can see better now why we are to understand as much of the Bible as possible—it is all valuable—and why we must not see one part as contradicting another. But we can confirm this from still another angle.

"Literal Interpretation"

Understanding "Messages"

In everyday communication we determine the meaning of a whole utterance that we hear or a text that we read (and thus gain information) by means of all the clues contained in the message.[11] Interestingly enough, linguists have discovered that it is quite difficult to show just how all the clues are recognized, or even to show what they are. Language is now believed to be much more complex than it was felt to be even a few decades ago. But somehow, by a gift of God, we are able to recognize clues very rapidly, combining in our minds the components of the given message.

In doing this we are constantly making adjustments as information is given, linking new with old, setting parts of the message against what we know of the world, what we know about the speaker, what we believe he shares in common with us, and what he may be assuming.[12] We determine the meanings of smaller components, let us say words, by comparing them with existing information, working back and forth.

For instance, if someone tells me he went to the "bank," I might be puzzled, especially if I know that he often visits a river area and also makes transactions at a financial institution. However, if he later specifies that it was the First National that he went to, I rule out the possibility of his having been near water.[13] Further, if I were told that someone banked in his automobile, I might think of a drive-in teller, but could also reasonably think of navigating a corner on two tires.

This shows that we determine the "meaning" of words or groups of words on the basis of wider stretches of the utterance they occur in. Ultimately the meaning of those parts is determined by the whole.

It is just this kind of process that we must duplicate in working with the text of the Bible. Our task is made difficult by several factors: we are culturally and linguistically removed from the biblical world and biblical texts; we do not know all we would like to know about the language and culture of biblical times; we do not have a guidebook for interpretation. In human communication between speakers of the same language, we usually have little difficulty accurately receiving messages. *How* we do that is not yet understood, and there is a newly developing branch of linguistics and literary analysis that is devoted to the attempt to discover how people understand texts and utterances.[14] In any case, it is generally more difficult to work with a written document than to take in a spoken utterance, and of course it is much more difficult to work with a translated document from which we are removed in time.

However, there is sufficient information in the Bible for us to understand its message, although comprehending it may take a long time. As we approach the text with its clues, we attempt to interpret it in the only way we know how, as a written document, as a book, for we are familiar with books. We try to use all the signals contained in the language of the revelation to determine the meanings of words, groups of words, and ultimately the whole message. But because of our limitations and the inherent problems, we frequently come to points where we do not know which of often several possible meanings to attach to a unit in the text. And so we are forced to try to decide, for instance, whether Jesus is really a door, or a vine, or a shepherd, or what kind of "dining" is meant in Rev. 3:20, or what the word *bound* means in 1 Cor. 7:15 in regard to an abandoned spouse. And there are myriads of other difficulties.

Since we have no divinely given guidebook to assist us, and the text we are dealing with is a book, we begin by approaching it as we would any other written document, looking from individual clues (an article, a conjunction, a verb tense, a case suffix) to larger segments, (phrases and sentences) to macroelements (paragraphs, chapters, books, testaments) and ultimately the whole message.

In communication theory it is axiomatic that as hearers we attempt to maximize the content of the message given to us.[15] We assume that every part is important, and only neglect parts if the speaker/writer seems to ramble through incoherence or laziness in organizing the message. All other things being equal, we assume that all parts contribute to the total message (although some features are more central than others, and not all parts contribute equal amounts of information); that parts will not contradict each other (we ask for repetition or clarification if they seem to); and that the message is a unity. If we did not do these things we would not do very well at all at communicating. Speaker and hearer could not work together. Furthermore, the hearer—or reader, as the case may be—assumes that he can count on any signal unit to be consistent in meaning/content with (1) the overall message, (2) the world of background information shared by speaker and hearer, and (3) the particular circumstances of speaker and hearer at the moment. In normal conversation, when something that is not in keeping with these standards is perceived, we usually ask for a repetition.[16]

In approaching the Bible we can expect to get the most information if we proceed in the same way. We maximize the parts, that is, we do not want to leave anything out, either word, paragraph, chapter, or testament, in working through a particular text. Every part is to be measured against the other to get the meaning of each part, for we are dealing with the phenomenon of language, which carries information as a system.

Further, we cannot allow any part to be inconsistent with another, for our expectation of a normal text is that it will be coherent, that it will not have any conflicts. (Contrast with this the recent assertion by some conservatives to the effect that the Bible may contain errors and is therefore in contradiction with itself. See ch. 2, the Nature of the Bible, and ch. 10, The Bible). And so we freely compare one part with another, adjusting as we go.

We must admit that any generation of Bible interpreters sees what seem to be contradictions, places where the Bible does not seem to be internally consistent, or even externally consistent, as with dates provided by external historical sources. Because of the assumptions given above about the nature of the Bible (a revelation from God who would not deceive) we must refrain from final judgment. Ultimately, the Bible will be seen to be in accord with truth, although along the way we may have to live with a difficulty, or may learn a great deal more about what it says, or even alter our views of what it says.[17]

For example, many years ago some interpreters asserted they had grounds for doubting that Paul wrote the Pastoral Epistles because those books show elements of style that appear to vary from what is called Pauline elsewhere in the N.T. On the basis of such

"discrepancies," a rather large segment of the N.T. was reduced to the status of pseudonymic writing. Now, if the Pastorals claim to be written by the Paul who wrote the
Epistle to the Romans, etc., the assumption has to be be that we are missing some
information, that time will provide what we need to bring, in our thinking, the style of
the Pastorals into harmony with that of other Pauline writings. As a matter of fact, more
recent scholarship has tended to show that assumptions about uniformity put N.T. writers in straitjackets that we would not allow in other kinds of literature. People speak
and write differently on different occasions. Such flexibility is called *register* by linguists.[18] In this case, literary and linguistic conclusions have given clear support to the
assumption of Pauline authorship of the Pastorals.[19]

This kind of process, involving assumptions about the coherence of texts, noncontradiction, and consistency, has been called literal interpretation. Perhaps that is an
unfortunate term, for the same word is used of translation which does the opposite of
what we are describing (see ch. 4, The Language of the Bible). A literal translation
fails to adjust the meanings of words or groups of words to their surroundings, and so
actually loses parts of the message. Perhaps a better term for this kind of interpreting
process would simply be *normal* interpretation, approaching the Bible the way we would
any other book.

Since this approach in normal speech communication seeks to discover the meaning
of words by examining micro- and macroelements, it constantly adjusts on the basis of
information that is perceived to be relevant. With biblical interpretation, of course, we
are not always certain what is relevant to the determination of meaning for particular
points in the text. Yet we have no other way to proceed.

One of the corollaries of all of this, of course, is that we must continually reex-
amine our earlier findings. When we believe that we have reached firm understanding
about the meaning of a word or phrase, we look around to see if that will necessitate
the adjustment of any conclusions we made earlier. The process never ends, unlike face-
to-face communication. We are always obligated to interpret the parts by the whole and
to maximize the parts as meaningful units in the whole message. This, of course, is just
another way of stating our premise above. In this way we open up the most Scripture,
and we do not knowingly allow any part to contradict another.

Figurative Language

The question arises, however, of how to interpret so-called figurative language (see also
ch. 6, Literary Aspects of the Bible). Some, in thinking about the "literal" method,
have been disturbed as to where such language might fit in. But when we view the
communication process as described above, the issue becomes clearer. Figurative language involves variation from the most expected meaning. It is designed to be graphic,
to startle, to alert and to portray in unexpected ways. One writer speaks of this as
creating "new meaning which is not merely decorative but is a new perception of the
relationships within one's world."[20]

An illustration might help here. The phrase *on the horns of* occurs in the following
two sentences:

1. He's working on the horns of his Buick.
2. He's caught on the horns of a dilemma.

In the case of the first, knowledge of the world will lead most readers to take *horns* to refer to automobile parts. In fact, it is likely that this association between the sound or letter sequence *horn* and a noise-producing mechanism is the first we are likely to make. We might subsequently associate it with the appendages found on some animals. But in sentence (1) we are unlikely to think of anything other than a part for a car. However, in the case of sentence (2) the surrounding words and our knowledge of the world immediately clue us to the likelihood that *horns* is not to be associated with noise or animals. Instead, we are to make a leap to a less expected meaning, and this leap is to be made for shock value, at least it was when the expression was initially coined. We are, by the words surrounding *horns* in (2), made to transfer our expectations to an unanticipated meaning.

The question in interpretation is, how do we know when to make that leap? With any message, we are not to make it unless we are forced to. We are to consider the *expected* meaning first, since speakers/writers use figurative language for certain purposes. Stated differently, figurative language is a representation of one thing in terms of another; the issue is when to know that this representation is taking place. For example, the term *lamb* is used in Rev. 5. Are we to take this as the most expected, nontransferred *lamb,* or make the jump to a metaphorical animal? In a certain sense the decision is no different from understanding the meaning of bank 1, bank 2 and bank 3 above (in the section on "Understanding 'Messages' "), where the leaning on two wheels could be viewed as some kind of metaphorical variant of the use involving the side of a river. It is the element of the unexpected that is crucial.[21]

This is all tied in with the issue of probability in messages. We make decisions on meaning on the basis of what we expect to be communicated.[22] Also involved is the matter of how much information individual parts of the message carry. It is axiomatic in modern linguistics that the meaning to be chosen for an individual part, say a word, is normally the one that contributes the least to the message, that is, it is the most expected in the light of what its neighboring words are.[23] Figures of speech are less expected, and so contribute more to the message.

In any linguistic situation our choice of interpreting an element as metaphoric or not is greatly affected by context. This is no less so with the Bible's metaphor. In the example of *horn* above, two speakers of Eng. with roughly equivalent knowledge of American culture would have no difficulty operating successfully as sender and receiver of the two sentences. The second would be taken as metaphorical, the first not. However, in the case of biblical interpretation, we are faced with those time, language, and cultural gaps. In addition, expectations of metaphor vary according to the kind of literature we are reading. Reference to a lamb in connection with Temple sacrifices is likely to be taken (and intended) as a physical animal. However, if a lamb is mentioned in Rev. 22, we are not likely to look for any bleating animal, but instead would be inclined to see a metaphorical reference to Christ as the Lamb, since we know that that soteriological image is prominent elsewhere in the book (chs. 4–5, etc.).

Literary critics tell us that an overused metaphor can quickly lose its surprise/ shock/graphic quality, and then speakers no longer make the transfer. It is then a "dead metaphor." *Bank,* with the meaning "traverse a bend on an incline," is probably such a metaphor and is undoubtedly newer in the English language than the other uses, since it involves a mechanical apparatus, a vehicle. This is how many new meanings enter languages. As one writer points out, "What was novel becomes commonplace, its past is forgotten, and metaphor fades to mere truth."[24]

The Crucial Step

Now we come to a crucial point in the matter of biblical interpretation. We can always run the risk of arbitrarily combining meaning units to get total meaning. We may make that transfer to the analogical—for that is what figures of speech are—without enough warrant to do so. That is exactly what Origen did. He usually attempted to go for the unexpected meaning first, believing that the text required him to go beyond the normal, beyond the expected in light of the total message. It apparently was more interesting to do that. However, it was clearly out of keeping with normal human communication, for we do not expect heavy use of metaphor. A person who does so is often known for using clichés. Too much metaphor ruins the effect.

This issue of when to take certain parts of texts at face value (as expected information), versus metaphorically, is an important one in biblical interpretation today.[25] Particularly involved is the discussion of the kingdom and the return of Christ. The clearest example is the interpretation by some of Rev. 20:4—and surrounding verses— to mean a nebulous period of time rather than the expected thousand physical years. Our first inclination in reading this text as any other is to take the thousand years as referring to a period of time as we know it. But some take the *thousand years* as unexpected information, that is, as metaphorical, and assign it a meaning other than *physical years*. Of course, in doing so, they are taking it figuratively. The question is, is this justified?

The issue becomes particularly important when this is done consistently in patterns. This has often been called in biblical studies spiritualizing or mystical interpretation. In that it is regularly looking for a meaning other than the expected, it can be described with these terms, and is really no different from Origen's allegorical interpretation. Some apply this procedure to passages prophetic of yet future events and those that have to do with the overall plan of God, of which prophecy is a vital, woven-in element. This is the approach of the amillennialist, who believes that the Bible does not teach a literal thousand-year kingdom of Christ on the earth. Suffice it to say here that unusual assumptions are involved in the decision to take such passages metaphorically. We will return to this topic and spell the process out more fully below under "Examples from Prophecy."

What might lead to this approach to the Scriptures, one that is really a portion of a system of interpretation? Does it have validity? To answer this we must turn to another issue, that of the nature of theology. What is theology? How does it relate to interpretation? As we do so, we will also be dealing more explicitly with the issue of presuppositions.

Theology and Interpretation

Theology and Scientific Method

For many people the word *theology* is frightening. Perhaps for some it immediately suggests boredom. But actually it involves some quite ordinary concepts, some of which we have already mentioned.

Let's think for a moment—and this may seem to be off the subject, but it actually isn't—about how a scientist carries out his work (assuming he is a good scientist). He first accepts some body of data as relevant to his work. Then he attempts to organize the data in a reasonable way. Analyzing what he has observed, he asks what explanation might account for all that he has seen. This explanation may be simple or quite detailed, but it should in some way provide a means of tying together all the information. This explanation is really a hypothesis, a guess about how things work. And it is a kind of *interpretation* of the data that has been observed. The scientist then seeks to verify what he has hypothesized. This should be both an attempt to falsify the explanation and to demonstrate its validity.[26] Thus he may devise an experiment in which the goal is to see if constant, repeatable outcomes can be achieved. Or, he may look for more data and see if they fit with his explanation. If they fit, the explanation is retained. If they don't fit, or if the experiment doesn't produce what it was predicted to produce, then the explanation, interpretation, or hypothesis must be reworked. It is either modified, extended by added statements, or discarded.

This process can never stop, since we live in a universe where there are always more data to analyze. Continual refinement may be necessary, and rarely does a scientist come to the point where he feels he has accounted for all the data. Take the flat-earth view. Some may believe that this explanation concerning the shape of the earth and related phenomena is entirely sufficient, and that new data will do nothing to affect their hypothesis. In this case their explanation has passed into the realm of dogma. Most people believe that the earth is spherical. Once that is reasonably well established, it is accepted, and further work concerning the earth's shape and character is based on that. But the scientist must always leave himself open to the possibility that new data may alter some of his views (the earth is slightly flat at the poles!).

In certain respects biblical theology relies on a similar process. The theologian is actually attempting to place an interpretation on the whole field of data that is the Bible. And he may link it with other areas of study and other things in the universe—the stars, passage of time, etc. Since the Bible does not give information in entirely structured, systematic, outlined form, we are obliged to bring order to it. The theologian first makes an initial hypothesis concerning something he has observed, for instance, words about God. He may state that certain verses appear to say that God has three parts associated with Him. Then he must look elsewhere to see if this is verified. He is attempting to prove or disprove what he has guessed as an explanation. He may then find that his guess was not wrong, but that it needs to be modified, for the data (biblical statements) show, as far as he can tell, that the three parts are Persons (as in Ps. 110:1). So he now states that he believes the Bible shows that God consists of three ''parts'' that are Persons. And so he continues, modifying and extending his explanation/interpretation. This process is illustrated in Figure 5.1, where *a, b, c,* and *d* are elements of data, and x, x_1, and x_2 are progressively modified conclusions. New evidence should lead to new or modified conclusions, with the process never stopping.[27]

In all of this, the theologian must work back and forth from little pieces of information to large pieces, from nearby to distant statements, from explicit to implicit, from language to culture to history and back. Each new piece of information must be made to fit reasonably with what has been seen before. As each piece is seen, it must be measured against the hypothesis, the explanation, the interpretation that has been made for all the preceding information. This explanation is really a guess about how it *all* works, about what it all means (although one may work with subparts—the Trinity versus all of God's Person and works, for instance).

This is a very reasonable way to proceed in approaching the Bible, for it actually

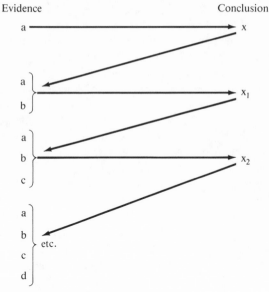

Figure 5.1

views the Bible as a coherent document that can be understood as its parts are interpreted in light of the whole, and vice versa. This really amounts to saying that the Bible
interprets itself, that is, all the different parts are needed in order to provide an explanation for the whole, and the whole, when related to the parts, explains them. That is
why the supreme principle of biblical interpretation is that the Bible is its own best
interpreter. All other principles of interpretation flow from this.[28]

The process of examining small portions of text is usually known as exegesis.
Unfortunately, many have failed to see the intrinsic connection between exegesis and
theology. Theology is nothing more than the summarizing of findings, the making of
explanations of what has been observed. Some have noted in recent years that theology
and exegesis are inseparable. One cannot do one without the other.[29]

This failure to see a necessary connection is due in great part to the error of those
who have actually left the text of Scripture and attempted to do "theology" without
taking the express statements of the Bible seriously. From the perspective of orthodox
Christianity, this is not theology at all. And in practice it often ends up being more
psychology or sociology than study of God and His works.

Let us illustrate this in the following way. Suppose that on the basis of Heb. 2:14,
Col. 2:15, and 1 Jn. 3:8, we hypothesize that the cross-work of Christ was designed to
vanquish Satan. We predict on the basis of this that all cross-work passages will be
satisfied by this explanation (i.e., will have to do with Satan). We do not have to look
very far, however, before we find that they are not. We must then reformulate our
hypothesis in the light of the information given in all the passages.

There is then a necessary circle in which one examines portions of the Bible, makes
a tentative statement about their meaning, looks at other portions, measures them against
what has been seen already, and adjusts the interpretation accordingly. Since we will
never have a perfect understanding of the Bible (an assumption, but, I believe, a valid
one), this process, this circle, must ever continue. Just as the scientist cannot stop, the
theologian cannot stop either.

We can see then that theology properly done, far from being a frightening concept, is just another way of saying that one is gathering information from the Bible as well as other, secondary, sources, making interpretations and reanalyzing previous findings. For biblical interpretation, information given by general revelation, that is, what we know of God and His works through nature, our consciences, etc., is relevant data. This is a reasonable process, for the Bible interpreter is simply approaching the Bible as a document containing communicated information. We are to interpret the Bible just as we would interpret the speech of another person in a conversation. As we mentioned above, however, working with a written document from which we are removed by time and language makes the process much more difficult.

One of the dangers in theology is that of stopping too soon in the cycle. As the scientist must continually look for new data and attempt to falsify his hypotheses, so must the Bible interpreter. Let's take a central doctrine as an example. We may say that we believe that God is infinite, tripersonal, rational, etc. We may be very confident that all the biblical data support this. We may believe it with all our hearts. But we must leave ourselves open to finding out more about Him. We do not expect that we will find anything to contradict what we have concluded about these features of God, in great part because we have traversed the ground often. So with this doctrine we have great confidence that our interpretation is correct and can be built on to formulate other interpretations.

But there are many areas where we are more in doubt. We certainly would like to know more about the nature of the death of Christ, the process of sanctification, the local church and how God intends it to work, God's program for the ages, the relations between the synoptic Gospels, and many other teachings. If we investigate any of these areas, make a generalization, an explanation, and fail to go on to look further, we are in trouble. We must constantly keep looking. Only when all the parts fit together well can we be confident that we have a solid interpretation. Of course there are many doctrinal areas today which are being investigated, in particular the nature of the Bible and prophetic issues. We cannot afford in any of these to stop with a particular interpretation as though it were final. In a sense, if we do that, we are allowing our theology to color unfairly our further examination of pieces of the text of the Bible. In other words, we are allowing our interpretation/explanation to fly in the face of data we haven't looked at yet. Then the process of interpretation breaks down. We could really say that we have allowed our presuppositions to dominate us, since we have not allowed the text to speak for itself.[30] In this case, the process described in Figure 5.1 would be modified as shown in Figure 5.2. Here the conclusion x_1 is accepted as final, and the piece of data c is never investigated.

It should be kept in mind that the text of the Bible is always primary, not our statements about it. We are only attempting to summarize. That summarizing is necessary, but we can never allow it to take on a life of its own. All of us who ever read the Bible, no matter how simple or how scholarly, are in danger of imposing our own views and our own conclusions on it. The theologian, too, must be careful not to do that. He can thus ignore data, misunderstand them, or make them say what he wants them to say. The danger arises from the fact that we come to hold the theological statements as more important than the Bible itself, and, as they take on lives of their own, we pay more attention to them than to the Bible.

When we say, then, that we are to interpret the Bible so as to give each part its due, and should work out all contradictions, we are simply affirming this process of

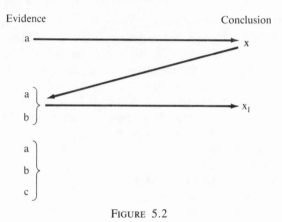

FIGURE 5.2

looking at the parts, then comparing them with the other parts, then making an interpretation, then looking some more, all the while attempting to fit it all together.

This is, of course, just what a person does in a conversation, using all the clues to get the whole message. It would be foolish to ignore some of the information and interpret it so as to allow contradictions, since one should assume that the speaker does not wish to feed him nonsense.

Forced Interpretation

Examples from history. The history of biblical interpretation illustrates where presuppositions lead. In the first half of the nineteenth c., David Friedrich Strauss approached the N.T. text with the presupposition that God would not enter into human affairs, much less perform miracles. Hence he had to devise an alternative to explain the recorded ministry of Christ. The result was an interpretation that viewed the N.T. as mythology.[31]

During the same era, Ferdinand Christian Baur's study of Pauline writings led him to conclude that the N.T. displayed a deep rift between Paul's ministry and the church at Jerusalem. Since he adopted this position, it was a logical outcome that N.T. books that did not display such a problem (including the Gospels and Acts) were to be considered the work of second-century pseudonymous writers. Later scholars have rejected his conclusions concerning such dating.[32]

More recently, in this century Rudolph Bultmann's approach to the N.T. involved existentialist presuppositions that determined much of what he felt the text to be saying. Interestingly enough, he set forth in writing his views on the need to attempt to be aware of one's presuppositions, although he concluded that no interpreter could ever really operate without them.[33]

The history of the interpretation of the book of Dan. displays a pervasive prejudice against its miraculous predictions, especially those in chs. 2, 7, and 11, where details of the Gr. and Roman empires are given, along with extensive description of the intertestamental period (ch. 11). So precise are these prophecies that many have been led to view the book as written in the second c. as a fictional account containing historical references viewed after the fact.[34]

Every interpreter of Scripture comes to it with presuppositions. But an awareness that they exist and to the need always to be open to the text will take us a long way. The British theologian Graham Stanton sums this up forcefully:

> The interpreter must allow his own presuppositions and his own pre-understanding to be modified or even completely reshaped by the text itself. Unless this is allowed to happen, the interpreter will be unable to avoid projecting his own ideas on to the text. [Interpretation] guided rigidly by pre-understanding will be able to establish only what the interpreter already knows. There must be a constant dialogue between the interpreter and the text. The hermeneutical circle is not only unavoidable but desirable. Indeed, one must go still further: the text may well shatter the interpreter's existing pre-understanding and lead him to an unexpectedly new vantage point from which he continues his scrutiny of the text. Once the text is given priority and once the interpreter ceases to erect a barrier between himself and the text, he will find that as he seeks to interpret the text, the text will, as it were, interpret him.[35]

Examples from prophetic interpretation. In ch. 2, The Nature of the Bible, and in the section above in this ch. entitled "The Crucial Step," we introduced the metaphorical methodology of the amillennialist regarding kingdom prophecies. We return to that here, adding insight gained from our discussion of theology in the section "Theology and Scientific Method."

Among evangelical interpreters, views on the fulfillment of prophecy are linked to several generalized positions on the plan of God, especially that portion from the cross to the inauguration of the eternal state. These are the premillennial, amillennial, and postmillennial systems. The Scofield Bible has been for decades an important vehicle for the teaching of the premillennial position, as well as the dispensational (see ch. 19, Future Things, for an overview of millennial positions, and ch. 2, The Nature of the Bible, for a treatment of dispensationalism). We will discuss these systems, particularly the amillennial and premillennial, as illustrations of the principles of interpretation presented so far in this chapter.

To begin with, some distinctions should be drawn. We have already mentioned that the amillennialist asserts that the Bible does not teach that there will be a physical kingdom on the earth over which Christ will reign. Hence, Israel will not experience fulfillment of the O.T. promises of national blessing. The premillennialist believes that there will be a physical kingdom on the earth, involving the fulfillment of national promises to Israel, with Christ present as King. The postmillennialist holds that there will be an earthly kingdom, but without the visible presence of Christ. This view sees Scripture as teaching that Christ will return to earth after the kingdom has been inaugurated by human beings and has run its course. This kingdom is to be equated roughly with some period of blessing in the present age between the two advents of Christ.

How is this relevant to theology and the interpretation of figurative language? This is one area where some have apparently stopped too soon in the process of searching Scripture and rested on their conclusions. The amillennialist has hypothesized as an overall statement about the Bible that the purpose of God is to take out of mankind a people who will be recipients of special blessings, particularly the enjoyment of Him. This sounds very reasonable. However, when it is allowed to reshape the data rather than *being reshaped by* the data of the Bible, then it becomes a prejudice. Such is the case with the amillennialist's understanding of the identity of *Israel* in Rom. 11, for instance. Since God's purpose is not, in their view, to work with separate peoples through history, but rather to establish one people, there is no essential difference between Israel and the Church here, and the future of Israel does not involve national regathering, regeneration, and enjoyment of the land. The land blessings, which from the O.T. alone may reasonably be interpreted as physical, earthly and visible, are viewed by the amillennialist as absorbed by the Church, part of the same people as Israel. Thus, the land and other promises were supposedly never meant to be fulfilled physically. This amounts to a reinterpretation of the O.T. by the N.T.[36]

Now here is where our words above about figurative interpretation come in, as well as the absolute need to allow the whole Bible, with all its parts, to speak. The amillennialist is forced to take many parts of the Bible figuratively, in that "startling" way, because his interpretation of individual portions is prejudiced by his theology, his overall explanation. He comes to Rev. 20:1–7, for instance, which teaches about a time of rule by Christ, and views it as figurative, as something other than a thousand-year period on earth. In the light of the whole passage, this view is very weak, for it at once makes the thousand-year description bear too much weight, taking it as figurative, that is, in the unexpected sense in relation to the context. This is strange, to say the least, especially since *thousand* is mentioned six times, in several different connections! We must underscore the fact that we are all in danger of imposing our own views upon the Bible at any points. But consistently interpreting in this way betrays a flaw in one's approach to the Bible. Hypothesis has been given primacy over the words of the text of the Bible. What one writer calls "forced" exegesis has taken the place of the "normal."[37]

Since we are suggesting that the process of biblical interpretation should be similar to that employed in interpreting any written or oral message, we should point out that the amillennial approach falls prey to two errors. First, it fails to maximize the contribution of the various parts of the message in that it views without warrant different statements or words as saying the same thing: e.g., Israel and the Church are often taken as synonymous in the N.T. Further, many prophecies in the O.T. that speak of Israel's future blessings in the kingdom are taken as describing a spiritual state during the present age, and actually have little meaning at all. They can almost be dismissed. Secondly, this approach overinvokes the switch to the unexpected meaning in that it sees figures too easily, when the surrounding words do not suggest the need for such a switch. In the same passage the amillennialist is once again obligated a second time by his system to switch to the less expected meaning. In Rev. 20:4–5 the text speaks of a living or coming to life. This is predicated of two groups. The normal, expected manner of interpreting these would be to take them to refer to physical resurrection, especially since one's normal expectation in reading this text with its description of ruling would be to take the living to be exiting from the grave, that is, being resurrected bodily, as described in so many other places in the Bible. But the amillennialist takes the "first resurrection" to refer to the new birth of individuals, since it occurs in connection with the thousand years, which for him, of course, is a nebulous period of time, somehow to be connected with the present age (the "after" is a problem for him, too; how can something happen after an unknown period of time?). And the other resurrection applies for him (and this *is* in keeping with the sense of the passage) to the resurrection of the unsaved of all ages at the close of time as we know it.

Nearly a hundred years ago Henry Alford said of this interpretation:

> If in such a passage the first resurrection may be understood to mean *spiritual* rising with Christ, while the second means *literal* rising from the grave;—then there is an

end of all significance in language, and Scripture is wiped out as a definite testimony to any thing. If the first resurrection is spiritual, then so is the second, which I suppose none will be hardy enough to maintain: but if the second is literal, then so is the first, which in common with the whole primitive Church and many of the best modern expositors, I do maintain and receive as an article of faith and hope.[38]

Alford is pointing out in a very eloquent way that the amillennialist shifts *strangely* to a metaphorical interpretation in order to maintain his position. A. Berkeley Mickelsen underscores the need for systematic evaluation of figurative language:

The literal meaning—the customary and socially acknowledged meaning which carries with it the ideas of actual and earthly—must become the base for figurative meanings. Upon this base they depend. If an interpreter declares that a certain expression is figurative, he must give reasons for assigning a figurative meaning. These reasons must rise from an objective study of all factors and must show why the figurative meaning is needed. Sometimes interpreters insist that elements are figurative because their system of eschatology requires it, not because the Scriptures and objective factors demand it. . . . Where there are compelling grounds for figurative meanings, they could be adopted. A careful interpreter will interpret both literally and figuratively because the passage he is interpreting demands these procedures.[39]

This general criticism of unwarranted switch to metaphor also applies to many premillennnialists who are not dispensational, such as George Eldon Ladd. Ladd is very inconsistent concerning the fulfillment of promises to Israel. He admits he had little idea of how Israel's conversion and the millennium are related.[40] The reason is that he allows the N.T. to dominate the O.T. regarding predictions of Israel's restoration:

Dispensationalism forms its eschatology by a literal interpretation of the Old Testament and then fits the New Testament into it. A nondispensational eschatology forms its theology from the explicit teaching of the New Testament.[41]

According to Ladd, since the N.T. does not have a full treatment of the millennium, and the N.T. takes precedence over the O.T., we cannot say much about Israel's restoration.[42] Such is Ladd's basic presupposition (and its outcome). It is not very different from that of the amillennialist. One further result is the confusion of Israel and the Church. Obviously, when the N.T. is allowed to dominate the O.T., then the Church absorbs Israel's promises (Ladd thinks some are fulfilled; he has no consistent way of arriving at this and no reason for assuming the O.T. predictions cannot be fulfilled).[43] A specific example of his methodology is his treatment of Rev. 7. Since he wants to see Scripture as supporting the presence of the Church in the tribulation (which the dispensationalist takes to be a time of special testing for Israel), he takes the individuals in the first part of the ch. to be the Church, not Jews saved out of the tribulation, although the text clearly refers to "Israel" in v. 4.[44]

We have offered only a few of many examples of how the amillennialist and a representative nondispensational premillennialist fall prey to evident inconsistency. One of the important contributions of the Scofield Bible has been its demonstration of a consistent attempt to allow the Bible to speak for itself, especially in this area that concerns the overall purposes of God in history. In fact, it is its display of a willingness on the part of Scofield himself and its editors to relate the parts to the whole, back and forth, that has led many people to appreciate the way it allows insight into the plan of God for humanity. The fulfillment of prophecy surrounding the return of Christ is an integral part of that plan (in fact, its culmination, according to Eph 1:7–9) and cannot be neglected.

We should stress again the warning that we all must be careful of weak points in our armor! But any approach to the Bible worthy of consideration must allow all the parts to speak for themselves and yet not allow contradictions, all the while treating the Bible as we would any message whose parts must be measured against each other to achieve a comprehensive understanding of what the author/speaker intended. This is a key feature of sound interpretation.

Learning to See Whole Messages: The Place of "Context"

General principles. Enough has already been said to indicate the importance of sur-roundings of a section in Bible study. Let us turn to a few examples. If we read 1 Chr. 26:18 by itself we are left hanging: "As for the court to the west, there were four at the road and two at the court itself" (NIV). Some have read Mt. 24:13 by itself and concluded that (in any age) a person must cling to his salvation to the end, and could potentially lose it. And taking Mt. 24:17 by itself and applying it to just any situation in the present age would lead to nonsense: "Let him who is on the housetop not go down to get the things out that are in his house" (NASB). It would be even more dangerous to take Jas. 2:24 by itself, since it would lead us to conclude that works can save. Many have read 1 Jn. 2:27 in isolation and concluded that they could understand the whole Bible on their own without assistance from anyone, ignoring the revelation elsewhere that gifted individuals are given to the Body of Christ to teach others. The problem in all of these is that the reader attempted to interpret a segment of text without reference to the other parts that also existed, parts that the writer intended to be a unit.

We can define context in a document or utterance as the surroundings of a portion of a word, a word, or a group of words. This does not specify the size of the environment. It is all the elements (parts of words or larger) that precede or follow a segment, as well as all that writer/speaker and reader/hearer may consider relevant to their inter-action by means of language, such as knowledge of the world, awareness of possible responses to the message, etc. This is equally true of the biblical text. A biblical context can be a small amount of text, or the whole Bible. Actually, all of the Bible is relevant in some way to every other portion. This definition of context does not tell us how to find what is more or less relevant. There are no fixed rules that help. Interestingly enough, as we mentioned above, linguists are just now beginning to formalize proce-dures for determining what kinds of things are relevant to portions of utterances or texts and how they bear upon stretches of language.

How can the Bible interpreter best pay attention to context? First, one should know the context that is the whole book in which a particular passage is found. In the Scofield Bible, the introductions to each book and the embedded outlines furnish great assistance in seeing books as a whole (see also ch. 21, Outlines of Bible Books).

For example, when the reader realizes that the whole book of Philippians was intended as a thank-you letter to believers who had given money to him, then a verse such as 1:5 can be interpreted with optimum attention paid to surroundings (the whole book). Since the "partnership" of 1:5 includes giving, we learn that supporting a ministry makes us part of it (see above under "Situated in Genuine Experiences").

Second, knowledge of parallel books, that is, those that contain the same material as a book under study, is always helpful. Jude and 2 Pet. appear to speak to common themes and situations, as do Eph. and Col. The marginal references in the Scofield Bible will alert the reader to such correspondences, as will the introductions (see introduction to 2 Pet. and introduction to Eph.). Parallels are quite evident in the synoptic Gospels, where many paragraph headings in the Scofield give cross references to the other gospel accounts.

Third, a simple way to maximize context is to examine what precedes and follows verses or words in question. This alone would solve most of the problems associated with some people's interpretation of those verses listed above. In 1 Jn. 2:27, for instance, we find that John is trying to show his readers that they are in danger of being led astray by false teachers. However, believers are under no obligation whatsoever to pay attention to them, since as God's children they have the Holy Spirit within them to carry out a perfect teaching ministry. Similarly, a superficial reading of Phil. 2:12 might lead a person to conclude that he is ultimately responsible to procure and maintain his own salvation. Looking further will show (from 2:13, for instance) that what is really at issue is cooperation with God in the process of sanctification. And so the verse in question is actually speaking about our practice, and not about our basic position before God (see the parallel truth and the note at 3:12).

A portion of Scripture which explicitly teaches this context principle is 2 Pet. 1:19–21 (see note): "No prophecy of Scripture came about by the prophet's own interpretation. For prophecy never had its origin in the will of man, but men spoke from God as they were carried along by the Holy Spirit" (vv. 20b–21, NIV). The portions of the prophetic message of the O.T. form a unified whole. They have their source in the Holy Spirit Himself (v. 21), and therefore are the product of a single Author. The linguistic assumption here is that an individual author gives a unified message. Hence the interpreter is bound to seek a coherent, unfragmented prophetic message. This is, of course, a warning that many have ignored through the years as they have twisted prophecy to fit their own ends. The Scofield note points out that this passage is probably asserting the need for deriving a unified message from prophecy. These principles must also be true for the whole Bible. It claims to have God as its author (see note, 2 Tim. 3:16). It must be a unified message. Therefore it must be interpreted as a unit. This is the basis for interpretation by context, that is, all the features surrounding a portion under study. So the Bible itself tells us to interpret by context.

The example of our Lord Jesus Christ teaches us to be very careful with contexts. In Lk. 20:27–38 He asserts that in some way "Moses showed that the dead rise" (NIV) when he wrote in Ex. 3:6 that the One who met with him at the burning bush was "the God of Abraham, and the God of Isaac, and the God of Jacob" (NIV). We should ask initially how this statement proves resurrection (a point Jesus was making to counter the Sadducees, who did not believe in bodily resurrection). When we look at Ex. 3, we discover that the main point of the passage is that God is at long last coming to fulfill His covenants to Abraham and his descendents. He made everlasting promises with Abraham, Isaac, and Jacob, promises that He would surely keep. So he reveals himself as the "I am," the self-existent God who has the authority and power to back up His word. The fulfillment of the promises of eternal blessings to Abraham, Isaac, and Jacob—now dead—would depend on an act by that omnipotent God to bring them back to life. The picture is actually quite simple: no resurrection after death—no enjoyment of the covenants. Or we could state this as a logical argument: God made promises of future blessing on earth; God always keeps His promises; to enjoy such blessings one must be alive; those who received the blessings are now physically dead; therefore, there will be a future resurrection of individuals by the power of God.

The point here for our purposes is that our Lord knew the background of the verse He quoted, Ex. 3:6. That background, the context, of that verse was crucial for the argument He was making concerning the reality of bodily resurrection. Since we are in many places exhorted to be like our Lord, we ought to be as careful as He was in paying attention to the contributions of context.

Some examples. We can better appreciate the usefulness of this feature of interpreting the Bible if we examine one book, the Gospel of John, to see how it can be illumined by contextual information, sometimes from within the book itself, sometimes from without.

The character of John's Gospel, in terms of its form and literary aspects, is quite different from that of the first three Gospels. John himself tells us in 20:30–31 why that is so:

> Jesus did many other miraculous signs in the presence of his disciples, which are not recorded in this book. But these are written that you may believe that Jesus is the Christ, the Son of God, and that by believing you may have life in his name. (NIV)

This stated purpose for writing, connected here with Thomas' confession, ought to alert us to distinctive features of the book. John did not write in order to cover every event of Jesus' life. Instead, he was selective, as he states in v. 30. He did not record all the miracles Jesus performed, but highlighted seven acts done in the presence of the disciples. His stated purpose is to move individuals to belief in the Son of God. This is different, for example, from Matthew's goal, which was to present Jesus as King. Consequently, we are not surprised to find the word *believe* used about a hundred times in John's gospel, and the key use of the word *life*. John gives his readers, then, a focused purpose for his writing.

Many Bible books are anonymous, but where the author is known it is of value to be aware of the writer's background, profession, circumstances of writing, age, the place of writing, etc. In the case of John's Gospel, the author is never explicitly identified. However, we do have mention in 21:20 of a "disciple whom Jesus loved." At least this individual must have had intimate knowledge of our Lord's life and ministry. We are also told that he had been sitting next to Jesus at the supper on the eve of Jesus' death. Further, in 20:2 we discover that the same individual was with Peter at the tomb on the resurrection morning. And 20:8 records that "the other disciple . . . saw and believed." Since in Acts 3:1 Peter's companion is John, we are led to believe that the writer of John's gospel and the disciple John are one and the same, especially considering that the author might have been reluctant to mention that he was the "disciple whom Jesus loved." Thus context enables us to reach a likely conclusion as to the identity of the author of this anonymous book (see Introduction to John in the Scofield Bible).

Culture is all the ways, tools, and institutions that a social group uses in its life. These elements contribute to interpretation that pays attention to context. For example, in Jn. 13–17 John portrays the so-called Upper Room Discourse. Something of the nature of that time together can be grasped when we learn that second-story rooms in homes were often larger than lower rooms and were used for group meetings, feasts, or meditation and prayer.

The particular Jewish custom behind the request of Jn. 19:31 stemmed from Dt. 21:22–23. There God pronounced the executed criminal to be a source of pollution for the land if left to hang overnight. Thus, ironically enough, the Jewish leaders feared leaving Jesus on the cross overnight, even though they unwittingly brought judgment on themselves in putting Him there (see Gal. 3:13).

The statement in Jn. 2:6 concerning the presence of six stone water jars containing water for ceremonial washing is puzzling until we realize that water was "purified" by the Jews by letting it sit in jugs. This kind of helpful insight can be found in a Bible dictionary or encyclopedia (such as those listed in ch. 23, Annotated Bibliography).

Closely connected with cultural features in the process of interpretation are historical and archaeological details. The description of our Lord's encounter with Nicodemus becomes much more transparent to us when we know something about the background of the latter. Significantly, the first verse reveals that he was a Pharisee. This made him a member of a Jewish cult that became prominent in the second c. B.C. By the first c. A.D. its members numbered about six thousand. They believed in immortality and resurrection, neither of which the Sadducees held to. They made their interpretations of the law binding on Jews of their day. Thus our Lord's statement in 3:10 has great significance. He identifies Nicodemus as "the teacher in Israel" ("Israel's teacher"— NIV). As such he should have understood the need for a spiritual birth in order to get into the presence of God. But he did not. And if *he* didn't, certainly no one else would. Thus a prominent teacher and Pharisee was leading the people astray. The spiritual bankruptcy of that dominant religious and cultural group is thus highlighted in a very powerful way by our Lord's perception of Nicodemus' dullness.

The apparently unexplained statement in Jn. 4:4 concerning the necessity of Jesus' traveling through Samaria, and the accompanying racially connected statements made by the woman in 4:9–10, are illumined by certain well-known details of Israel's history. In 931 B.C. Jeroboam revolted against Rehoboam. Attempting to keep the twelve tribes divided, he separated his people from Jerusalem and set up independent worship. Samaria, capital of the northern kingdom(Israel/Ephraim) during the divided-kingdom period (see NSRB 6), and scene of part of the ministries of Elijah and Elisha, had been captured by the Assyrians in 721. These conquerors brought in colonists who mixed with the Jewish inhabitants. The descendents were the Samaritans of the N.T. The significant fact in Jn. 4 is John's aside in v. 9, where he explains that the woman's surprise at Jesus' request for a drink is due to the prohibition of social interaction between Jew and Samaritan. Jesus' overriding of this barrier is an important part of His spiritually oriented contact with her. His concern and power to heal spiritual hurt transcend the hostility built up over centuries of separation between once unified peoples.

Contextual elements—authorship, purpose for writing, characteristics of people involved, historical framework, places, customs and objects of culture, economic and political characteristics—all contribute to our understanding of the biblical text. The Bible student should make use of the many published works that shed light on backgrounds to the biblical texts. Among these are Bible dictionaries, introductions to the O.T. and N.T., geographies, atlases, and commentaries.

When we say that a precious jewel is more valuable in an appropriate and attractive setting we are enunciating the principle that surroundings make significant contributions to something that is already valuable. In the case of the Bible, the surroundings are interwoven in such a way that they contribute in incalculable ways to the invaluable biblical text. They cannot be ignored.

6

Literary Aspects of the Bible

A Pervasive Literary Figure

We wouldn't have done it that way. It is sheer incongruity. The God of the universe, the *El*—Strong One—of the O.T., portrayed as a four-footed, fuzzy, hoofed creature? Yet for our benefit in the wisdom of God, we possess in Scripture the complete figure of our Lord Jesus Christ as the Lamb.

There is no mistaking the fact that this characterization has been given to increase our understanding and quicken our response to spiritual realities. In that sense the Lamb is at heart theological, but it belongs also to the category of a literary figure. And it is its potency as a literary figure that gives it its effectiveness. God in His wisdom knew it would be valuable, and so it pervades all of Scripture, from Gen. to Rev.

The existence of the biblical metaphor of our Savior as the Lamb of God should be very instructive to us. It is only one of the countless (but certainly one of the most effective) literary features in the Bible. But unfortunately many readers of Holy Scripture are missing out on this rich mine of revelation. For we either de-emphasize the literary aspects of the Bible, or we miss them through neglect. Perhaps we are aware of the excesses of those of past generations who have viewed the Bible as *only* great literature, and not a genuine revelation from God, so we avoid literary analysis as something less than spiritual.

But the Bible *is* literature and possesses literary qualities. And we simply miss or distort the message of God if we fail to acknowledge this. To illustrate something of how far-reaching just one literary feature can be, we will explore the Lamb figure, one that is doctrinal, cultural, and personal, as well as literary.

The first hint of the role in God's program of an animal with a use related to human spiritual needs is found in Gen. 3:21, where the earliest pair are given coverings that in some way ease their disgrace. The most noteworthy feature of this verse is that God Himself is the provider. Already, then, the death of an animal is tied to both sin and the grace of God. We only need to look a few verses ahead to see an expansion of this embryonic figure. In Gen. 4:4 Abel, a representative righteous human being (Heb. 11:4), is seen bringing a domesticated animal as an acceptable sacrifice to God. An act in bringing this sacrifice is somehow God's act, too, because Abel is slain for thinking God's way.

The Scofield note at Gen. 4:4 explains a few of the features of Christ as the Lamb, pointing out how this figure can show several things at once as it leads in many directions. Yet at the same time it draws many concepts together—theological, cultural, historical, etc. Although we are not told explicitly that Abel brought a lamb, we can be sure that already in the early pages of Scripture this figure is connected with the theological features of sin, guilt, separation from God, provision by God, obedience by a human being in sacrifice, and the need for the sacrifice itself. Often in great literature the connections and interrelations of literary features become very complex—one leads to another, and figure is piled upon figure. Literary analysts acknowledge the difficulty of their chosen task of peeling off the layers and sorting out the components.[1] We will discuss this in the next section. But it is interesting that in Gen. 22 we find two literary figures intertwined. The relation of Abraham to Isaac is portrayed as a parallel to the relation of the Father to the Son. Abraham methodically prepares his son as a sacrifice (see Scofield notes at Gen. 22:6, 9). But a human is not sacrificed; a divinely provided ram is (22:8). Abraham's faith in that provision is significant: he expects God to provide an animal. Now we can see that the provided animal—varied slightly from lamb to ram—is a substitute. In Gen. 3:21 Adam and Eve could not diminish their guilt, but the skins could. Actually we have two beautiful figures intersecting here. In some way the ram is like Christ (we find out later), and in some way Isaac is. Furthermore, here the figures assist each other, for a sacrificed ram is passively obedient, and so is Isaac, both illustrating the willingness of Christ to die in the place of others. (It is this willingness that is highlighted in Isa. 53:7.) The collocation of two figures makes the illustrative material more complex, but also more helpful.

Later in the Bible we find that God underscores the importance of the Lamb figure by institutionalizing it under the law. In Ex. 12 it is linked to another figure—the meal. Here the lamb is slain *and* eaten. It has become a center of national attention (see note at Ex. 12:11 for descriptions of some of the other directions in which this figure points).

Hence, when John the Baptist utters his cry of recognition as recorded in Jn. 1:29, there is already a rich background of figurative and theological revelation to assist in interpreting his words. He is initially tying together the two testaments, bringing the O.T. figures to bear on the incarnation scene. Thus this literary/theological figure serves to give continuity to the progress of revelation. But more important, John the Baptist is making an explicit identification of Jesus with the O.T. Lamb figure/institution. He is saying that all the features pictured in the symbol are to be actualized in a person. As a preparer for Christ, John has the role of introducing the Lamb figure to the N.T. age. As he does so we begin to find out that the sacrificial lamb of the O.T. was planned and full of significance.

It is interesting that John's statement is a prophetic utterance, also: Christ was destined to die the sacrificial death of a lamb. This is part of progressive revelation, but it is also a segment of the step-by-step unfolding of the significance of the Lamb figure. About this, as well as most other features of the divine disclosure of Scripture, God does not tell us everything at once. There is an element of suspense, which creates interest. As we read the O.T., we should ask, "What is going on with this lamb?" The lamb was real and important in the O.T. But it is less important than and points forward to the Person and work of Christ, for in His makeup as the God-man and in His sacrificial role He is lamblike. Peter links both correspondences in 1 Peter 1:18–19 (see ch. 7, Relations Between the Testaments, for discussion of types and the priority of the antitype over the type).

Certainly the most fascinating—and extensive—use of the Lamb figure in the N.T. is found in the book of Revelation. There this feature of the Bible that is literary, doctrinal, cultural, and personal makes a startling appearance in 5:6, where several theological truths are presented at once. John subsequently uses this description to assist in communicating other portions of his message. The lamb, which certainly describes Christ, is (1) in the middle of God's throne, (2) in the center of angelic beings, (3) standing, (4) in a slain condition, i.e., bloody, (5) alive (!), (6) horned, and (7) endowed with sevenfold spirit-sight.

Here is an excellent example of the power of a literary figure to convey compactly large amounts of information in a highly graphic manner. We are not likely to forget this description! This lamb is now seen to be in the very presence of God (we are interpreting now), the center of angelic attention, paradoxically dead but alive (the word translated "slain" is equivalent to Eng. *slaughtered*). He is alive apparently because he was resurrected, and now evidently possesses divine characteristics.

We should also note the intersection of this occurrence of the figure with at least two others here—the Lion and Root of v. 5. Christ is the Root of David (Isa. 11:10) in His lineage and lowliness; He is the Lion (Gen. 49:9) at His second advent, an event made possible because He came first as the Lamb. This last important truth is underscored by the fact that it is the Lamb, i.e., Christ as the slaughtered, resurrected sacrifice, who alone can take the scroll (another figure!) and open its seals. This act apparently describes Jesus' authority to control the events of the tribulation period (chs. 6–19). He has the authority now because He was first the obedient Lamb. He seemed insignificant to most the first time He came. But all will answer to Him as Judge. The Lamb is the Judge because He earned that right by death. Christ as the Lamb is also Conqueror (17:14), Lover of the Church (His bride—see note, 19:7), and the Light, i.e., center and life, of the New Jerusalem (21:22; 22:3). So when John tells us that we will see the face of the Lamb (22:4), we are being told that we will enjoy the presence of the God-man who carried out for us His role as pictured so beautifully in the Lamb figure. It is of course important to notice that John does not refer to Christ, but to the Lamb. It is this God-given literary figure that enhances the precious doctrinal truths of our Savior's Person and work.

Literature and the Bible

The Purposes of God

We have examined, and not in great depth, only one literary figure in the Bible. But this should be instructive enough to alert us to the great value of being careful with the literary aspects of Scripture. The Bible reader simply cannot understand the whole Bible without seeing it as literature. Furthermore, such an approach does not exclude theological study; it enhances it, because doctrine is interwoven with literary features.

Perhaps we can begin to see now *why* God has used literary methods in His revelation. First, He has given human beings the capacity to think in terms of symbols and figures, of transferring of ideas, and of analogies. We do it elsewhere in life and in reading of other literature. He knew we would thus find His revelation easier to understand. Second, His message is enhanced by literary features. Our memories, intellects, and hearts are helped by images, illustrations, and associations. Then, too, we enjoy stories, pictures, and purposeful playing with words. Further, in terms of the text of the Bible itself, we can see that it is unified by literary features, such as the Lamb.

The Nature of Literature

What is literature? To give a simple answer would be difficult.[2] But most literary critics agree that it has at least the following features: it involves interpretive insight into the human condition; its purpose is to communicate; it usually focuses on a significant human experience; it is concentrated and organized; it is aesthetically pleasing and interesting. This excludes purely historical reporting, polemic, and direct teaching.

In the chapter on relations between the testaments, we discuss the role of analogy in the Bible and human experience in general. Analogy is the establishing of an illustrative/informative relation between two or more cases/instances sharing one or more similar features. When we are presented with an analogical relationship, we think about the information it gives and are led to understand more about the reality of which it speaks. Literature is a way of reflecting reality by analogy, utilizing symbolic language. It points to realities beyond itself, and so provides us with a look at the human condition from a standpoint outside ourselves.

In a sense all of language is analogical and symbolic in that it conveys information about things other than itself, and is a representation of reality. Robert Longacre, in his excellent linguist's defense of biblical theism, describes all of language as "a gigantic parable," reflecting spiritual and physical realities. He points out the source of all language/literature/symbol/parable:

> Language . . . is at once a gigantic parable—and indicative of reality as we confront it as human beings. And back of the world of color and the world of language stands the supreme Symbol Maker who in creating intelligent creatures has given them ways to interact in practical poetry with their environment, each other, and Himself . . .
>
> In calling language practical poetry, analogous to the perception of physical color, we must not lose sight of its truth-revelatory nature. The supreme Symbol Maker has given us the parable of language not to veil reality from us but to reveal it to us. In the Judeo-Christian Scriptures the parable of language emerges in various genres and types: in narrative, law-code, oration, poetry, proverbs, parable (narrowly conceived), letters—and, last but not least, in propositional statements scattered through the above. These propositional statements concern God, man, and the universe. While all, even 'literal' propositional statements involve elements of analogy, I have suggested above that such analogy characterizes language as a whole, not just religious language, and analogy is not a synonym for inaccuracy.[3]

The communicative power of literature derives much of its force from our shared stock of analogies. Leland Ryken, in discussing the interpretation of Rev., describes the purpose of literary symbols as communicating in a universal language.[4] Literature is thus analogical, as all language is, and is also written, worked, carefully shaped communication.

The Bible as Literature

The Bible is really an anthology of different types of literature. It is poetry, drama, epic, narrative, even fiction (e.g., the parables). Within this collection, however, is an internal unity. The Bible is homogeneous because of the plan of God, the centrality of Christ, the constant recurrence of key figures (God, human beings, Satan, angels, Israel) and issues (sin, death, life, moral choice, redemption). Within the overall plot (the Fall, and provision of salvation within time) there are many subplots. All of this is overarched by the constant movement of events from eternity to eternity. Furthermore, the whole Book is unified by quotation of the O.T. in the N.T. and other relations between the testaments (see ch. 7, Relations Between the Testaments). But we should notice that these are all *literary* features in this largely literary work.

One of the obvious distinctions of the Bible as literature, however, is the fact that God has not spoken to provide us with pleasurable diversion but to change us through teaching and example. So we should not be surprised to find a didactic intent behind all of biblical literature. For example, the poetry of the Bible does not exist to entertain, but to reveal the experiences of real people as they interacted with God. Similarly, dramatic elements in the Bible (in the book of Esther, for example) have the intent of underscoring the crucial choices people make and the far-reaching issues they are involved in as they walk with God.

Yet while the Bible is all a disclosure from God, it is still revelatory *literature,* and in fact the highest kind of literature we possess, since it has a divine Author, the Holy Spirit, and has the purpose of revealing truth from God. And so, for example, Heb. poetry is in a sense the most important poetry available to us. Because of the high and pervasive literary qualities of Scripture, it can be said that it is no accident that "western literature has been more influenced by the Bible than by any other book."[5]

Examples of Literary Features

In this brief treatment of literary aspects of the Bible, it would be impossible to do more than provide examples of such features. The reader is encouraged to utilize standard reference works on the subject, some of which are listed in ch. 23, Annotated Bibliography.

Structural Features

Plot. Good literature is directional: it possesses movement. Characters interact with each other and circumstances, exert influence, and in turn are influenced, often displaying change. There may be surprise; there must be purpose. A particular viewpoint on life will be present. The book of Habakkuk provides a good biblical example. It opens with a dialogue between God and the prophet, who is questioning God's actions in allowing Babylon to harm Judah. This establishes an initial problem, a tension. How can God love His chosen nation and allow unclean invaders to wreak havoc on it? What has happened to His promises? The tension could be stated more formally: can God's love and promises be compatible with damage from someone outside the covenant relationship? The problem is "worked out" as Habakkuk interacts with God during the progress of the book. The resolution comes as the prophet learns that a good God chastises his people legitimately for their good and uses whatever means he wishes. As stated particularly in 3:17, this means that what God does is right, even though at the time it is painful to his children.

Suspense. This is one of the elements of literature that controls the reader's interest by causing anticipation. One of the features of a sporting event that makes it interesting is the indeterminate outcome. We follow a game or competition with greater interest if we do not have a good idea of who will win. We want to be left hanging, to be in a position of never knowing until the contest is over. This element of suspense keeps us asking, "What's going to happen?"

Genesis 22 provides us with a brief but powerful example of the use of suspense. As the account builds through the accumulation of details, we sense that something unusual is about to happen. Will Abraham actually go through with the commanded sacrifice? Will God really allow him to do it? Along the way the intensity is magnified by small but significant features, such as: 1) it is the promised son who is to be sacrificed; 2) a long trek is necessary, giving Abraham time to back out; 3) Isaac is quite innocent, even to the point of wondering where the sacrifice would come from (v. 7); 4) Isaac is evidently old enough to escape, if he wants to, but instead goes willingly. The suspense has an intense theological purpose, of course. The resolution in vv. 12–14 shows that Abraham's faith had stood the test, and that God Himself would provide the sacrifice. If we look at this as a type, we notice an interesting shift in the figures at v. 12. In the first eleven verses of the account, Abraham is like God, and Isaac like the sacrificed Son. Then, beginning at v. 12, Isaac is like us and the ram is like Christ. This shift coincides with the point of climax and resolution of the suspense.

Dramatization. Conveying of information is made more interesting by dramatization, the practice of showing characters as speaking and acting. The account in Gen. 22 could have been given in pure narrative form, without any recorded speaking by the parties involved. However, conversation and interaction between God and Abraham, on the one hand, and Abraham and Isaac, on the other, heighten the suspense and intensity of the account.

Theme. Accounts with centralized ideas or insight enable the reader to trace the flow of information more readily. Often several themes are interwoven, although if they become too complex, the reader can become confused and might give up. For example, most interpreters take the book of Romans to be an exposition of the righteousness of God. This is announced in 1:16–17, where it is stated in the form of a quotation from Hab. 2:4: "The just [i.e. 'righteous person'] shall live by faith" (AV). Subsequent sections show the need for righteousness (1:18–3:20), its provision (3:21–26), its nature (2:27–4:25), its results (5:1–11), etc. Not all Bible books have such visible thematic structure. The book of James possesses a form that does not lend itself to easy analysis.

Allusion. This is reference to otherwise known figures or information and includes quotation. The Bible constantly quotes itself in order to show the homogeneity of God's revelation, and to assist us in interpretation. Many of the quotations are not spelled out, but simply implied. In Rom. 5:14 Paul alludes to Adam and his experience in the Garden. Adam's experience and position before God are bases for Paul's presentation of the counteracting work of Christ. In a few instances the Bible draws from external writers (e.g., Tit. 1:12).

Figurative Language

This involves use of words in startling and unusual connections. Many instances involve the principle of analogy, where comparisons are made, in this case, to enable the reader to move from the known to the unknown (see more on analogy in ch. 7, Relations Between the Testaments). Figures of speech make the Bible vivid, pictorial, and more familiar, especially when they utilize features that spring from every day life—trees, animals, water, food, heavenly bodies, and others.

Metaphor. Metaphor is description of one thing in terms of another. It involves a shift in usage, such that a word (or phrase) is employed in an unusual and striking connection with another. The phrase *babbling brook* is an example. The term *babbling* is usually reserved for human beings. When we use this metaphor, we are implying that some of the ways in which *babbling* fits with *child*, for instance, fit also with *brook*. However, the usage with *child* is well-established, and the phrase *babbling brook* startles the hearer, although he almost instantly recognizes the possibility of the meaningful use of the two words, transferring some of the elements he knows to be true of a child making meaningless noise, to the sound produced by running water.

Jesus' description of Himself as a "door" (or "gate," depending on the translation; Jn. 10:7) and as "bread" (Jn. 6:48) is metaphorical, utilizing commonly known objects. In the case of the second, the reader almost immediately transfers some of the things he knows about physical bread to Jesus. Since it is quite obvious (at least to most human beings) that Jesus is not made of flour and does not get placed on a table, the reader takes the word *bread* in a metaphorical or transferred sense. Some of the features of physical bread are true of Jesus, some are not. The reader filters out (at least he should) what cannot be transferred, and retains what he can—in this case, the features of providing sustenance and perhaps enjoyment of life.

When to take biblical language metaphorically is a significant problem in interpretation. Some instances of language are obviously metaphorical, as in the above examples. Some are not so at all. Some have occasioned great disagreement (see in ch. 5, Interpreting the Bible, concerning Rev. 20:4). Exactly how human beings recognize metaphor is not known. Much of our perception of metaphor depends on how much we share the speaker/writer's world view and assumptions.[6]

Simile. A simile is an announced comparison, such as "The sun . . . is like a bridegroom" (Ps. 19:4–5, NIV). It is a metaphor that cannot be missed. While "You are a lion's cub, O Judah" (Gen. 49:9, NIV) is a metaphor, "His feet were like bronze" (Rev. 1:15, NIV) is a simile, since it uses the word 'like.'

Metonymy. This is a shortened metaphor, in which the bridging term (such as *babbling* above) is substituted for the second member of the comparison, as would be the case if we addressed the brook directly and called it a babbler. For example, taking the Gen. 49:9 example given under "Simile" above, "You are a cub" is a metaphor, "You are like a cub" is a simile, and directly addressing Judah as a cub, as in "O cub," is a metonymy. In Eph. 2:11 Paul notes that Israel referred to itself as "the circumcision," an obvious connection, since circumcision was a characteristic so closely associated with the nation.

Irony. This is the use of words to mean the opposite of what they usually mean. In 1 Cor. 4:8 Paul uses irony to catch the attention of the Corinthians. When he says, "Already you have become rich! you have become kings—and that without us!" (NIV), he actually means that they do *not* have the qualities he describes. In a sense, irony is metaphor turned 180 degrees, a reverse symbolization.

Personification. When inanimate entities are ascribed qualities of living things we have personification. In Ps. 19 several instances occur: "The heavens declare . . . The skies proclaim . . . Their voice goes out . . . the sun . . . makes its circuit . . ." (NIV). Such use of language is metaphorical, since, in this case, we normally think of people as declaring messages, not heavenly bodies.

Allegory. Allegory is extended, running, metaphor, with two continuous levels of information. Since allegory involves linked figures, it must have its base in narrative. Sometimes allegory is quite contrived and obvious, as in Bunyan's *Pilgrim's Progress.* The surface story may be interesting but it is evident that the reader is to look below the surface for the greater message. Although the surface account in allegory may be plausible or even likely, the distinctive feature of allegory is that "the allegorist is pretending to talk about one series of incidents when he is actually talking about another."[7]

It is crucial that the biblical interpreter recognize the difference between allegorical structure in the Bible and allegorical interpretation. The latter tries to find allegory as part of a method of approaching the text of Scripture. The early centuries of Christian interpretation witnessed extensive use of the allegorical method of interpretation, with subsequent abuse, amounting to disregard of the historical details of the text (see ch. 5, Interpreting the Bible). Some contemporary interpreters, reacting against such excesses, shy away from acknowledging the presence of any intentional allegory in the Bible. From a literary standpoint, however, we are hard pressed not to acknowledge the existence of some biblical allegory. Some obvious examples are the cut-off tree of Dan. 4 (an allegory of the temporary incapacitation of Nebuchadnezzar under the sovereign hand of God) and the vine and the branches of Jn. 15:1–10 (a picture of the sustenance of the believer by Christ). Some feel there are no examples of allegorical interpretation in the N.T., which would show up particularly as the N.T. interpreted the O.T. Paul's description of the relation between the children of Hagar and Sarah, on the one hand, and law and grace, on the other, has been taken by some as one of the few examples of such allegorical interpretation in the N.T.[8] However, we should notice that Paul in no way indicates that the details of Gen. are anything other than historical. It is better to see this passage as an extended type. But this illustrates that the lines separating such figures are difficult to draw.

What is important, however, in approaching passages that seem to contain allegory, is that we attempt to give the words of Scripture their historical and non-metaphorical meaning before resorting to the possibility of figurative interpretation. In other words, the reader should ask what the message must have meant to the original hearers/readers, trying to come under the same worldview and assumptions. When we determine that allegory is present, we should note the points of comparison between the details of the allegory and the real life situations they correspond to, remembering that not every detail in the story can have a counterpart. Often the Bible interprets for us, as in Dan. 4, where Daniel reveals that the tree is king Nebuchadnezzar.

Parable. GENERAL FEATURES. The Bible itself tells us a great deal about what parables are and why they are used. Words that are translated "parable" in the O.T. and N.T. have meanings such as "a dark, mysterious saying" (*paroimia,* as in Jn. 10:6), "a similitude or proverb" (*mashal,* as in Job 27:1), or simply "one thing placed beside another" (*parabolē*). This last term, found about fifty times in the N.T., is used for short and long utterances, as in Lk. 4:23 ("Physician, heal thyself" [AV]) and Mt. 13:3 (the sower and the seed).

As part of the indirect-language segment of divine revelation, parables are given to disclose, while at the same time not spelling out every detail. Drawn as they are from everyday life, they connect the natural realm with the spiritual world and show how the laws of nature correspond to spiritual truths. Parables involve all of the following features: 1) revelation; 2) a picture; 3) a clarification; 4) an example used to illustrate; 5) a short discourse; 6) a comparison.

Some see biblical parables as a type of allegory.[9] Literarily, it is hard to distinguish between the two, since both involve narrative and often hypothetical surface accounts.[10] Some have pointed out that a parable is extended simile, while allegory is extended metaphor.[11] We might say this for parables that use comparative terms such as *like* (e.g., in Mt. 13:24), but others are not so explicit. We could say, however, that in many instances a parable focuses on a single point of comparison, while an allegory presents many points of comparison.[12] See ch. 7, Relations Between the Testaments, for discussion of the relation of parables to other forms of analogical language.

THE KINGDOM PARABLES. The parables of the Lord Jesus Christ comprise some of His most memorable teaching. Although some occur in the earlier stages of His ministry, most are found after evident rejection by Israel. Here the basic quality that all figurative language possesses comes to the fore, and has intense theological significance. Whether metaphor, simile, allegory or parable—all reveal and hide at the same time. They say, but they don't say. With simple metaphor, for example, we are never quite sure exactly how many points of comparison the speaker/writer intends us to pick up. In fact, if we have to explain a metaphor, the effect is lost.

After the rejection of the miracles of the Lord Jesus Christ in Mt. 12, where the Jews accuse Him of working by the power of Satan (while He actually performed them by the Spirit), His communication goes underground. In Mt. 12:38–41 He indicates that the sign aspect of His ministry will change radically. Immediately after this occurs the extensive set of the parables of the kingdom, whose rationale is explicitly given in Mt. 13:15–17. In answer to the disciples' question of why He was speaking in parables (i.e. figurative language), He quotes from Isa. 6, indicating that people with hard hearts could not receive His words. As a judgment on such people in Israel, Jesus turned to the parabolic method, so those not sensitive to Him *could not* understand.

It is crucial to recognize, then, that the majority of Jesus' parables, and especially the kingdom parables, come after this watershed point of rejection, one which led inexorably to the cross. To try to understand the parables that follow this event apart from Jesus' interaction with the Jewish leaders simply leads to confusion. Jesus has initiated a new kind of approach to Israel. The kingdom parables do not talk about the Church or about salvation in general, but are tied to the history of Israel. They begin to unfold "secrets" or "mysteries" of the kingdom (Mt. 13:11). Why? The Gospels present the incarnation of Christ as the appearance of the promised King over Israel (Mt. 2:1–2; Lk. 1:32). With the presence of the King comes the offer of the kingdom (Mk. 1:14–

15). But after Mt. 12 the kingdom assumes a new form. Public offers have ceased. The kingdom is now in abeyance. National blessings for Israel are held up. The new form of the kingdom involves a hidden aspect, a mystery or secret form. The parables are an intrinsic part of Jesus' description and presentation of the kingdom from Mt. 12 on. They reveal only to a select few, and they reveal that the kingdom has a new character.

The kingdom parables thus 1) present a new form of the kingdom, and 2) reveal (by their basic nature) judgment on most of Israel (the wicked and adulterous generation of Mt. 12:39, the one who "does not have," of Mt. 13:12) and the suspension of the predicted earthly kingdom. We should not conclude, however, as so many have, that the Church takes over the vacuum left by the shift in the nature of the kingdom. The parables teach a delay in the coming of the King (e.g., as in the "wheat and weeds" or "wheat and tares" parable of Mt. 13:29–30 and 37–43, where the Son of Man establishes His kingdom at the end of the age). They do not teach that the earthly kingdom will not come. Luke 19:11–27 specifically teaches, in response to the people's conclusion that the kingdom would appear at once, that there would be a delay in the King's return, and the kingdom would come with the King. These parables, then, are really a form of prophecy, and are an integral part of the historical movement in the ministry of Christ and of the theology of the kingdom as part of the plan of God.

INTERPRETING PARABLES. How then do we interpret parables, especially the kingdom parables? Only a few guidelines can be given here. The context is important, and the interpreter should note the setting of each parable. He should ask what point or points they seem to be illustrating or teaching. Sometimes they are explained for us (the sower and the seed, and the wheat and weeds/tares). Sometimes Jesus puts Himself in the parable, so we get an idea of how it relates to Him, as in Mt. 13:37. We should be careful to note what is said and what isn't said in each parable, and to observe who the audience is. We may find relations between two parables. In the case of the sower and the seed and the wheat and weeds/tares, seed is present both times, but does not point to the same thing. We should also expect complex teaching, since most parables have dispensational and spiritual lessons. A parable may teach about Israel in the first c., the form of the kingdom from the first c. until the return of the King (a period in which the Church Age falls), and the nature of the kingdom in the future (as with the wheat and weeds/tares [Mt. 13:43]). At times there are two parallel lessons running throughout a parable, as in Lk. 18:1–8, where there is teaching on prayer that is linked with that on the second advent (v. 8).

While the interpretation of parables is not easy sledding, it offers many rewards. We learn lessons about the Father, the Spirit, and especially the Son (His deity, incarnation, death, absence/return, role as Judge, and tenderness toward the lost). Human beings can see themselves laid bare (self-reliance, refusal to honor God, lack of a forgiving spirit, counterfeit spirituality, and lack of preparedness).

We learn through parables to appreciate the beautiful design of Scripture. Since parables make up the major part of our Lord's recorded words, they comprise a large part of the N.T. They are, of course, found elsewhere, too. They are complex in themselves and in their relation to the rest of Scripture. Their nature as figurative language reminds us that God does not put all the truth within easy grasp. Scripture is complicated, but has design and harmony. When we dig into the parables we see this more clearly.

Since they are difficult to interpret, parables show us that we need to ask God for wisdom and for the teaching ministry of the Spirit as we approach them. We are reminded of the value of comparing Scripture with Scripture (as in the case of the vineyard parable of Mt. 21:33–41, where in the O.T. the vineyard is Israel itself, but in the N.T. it is the kingdom, since the original tenants are rejected [vv. 41–46]). We learn the need to draw aside with God to meditate on such difficult portions of Scripture, and learn the necessity of keeping straight the distinctives God has placed in the Bible (Israel versus the Church, etc.).

The parables are an excellent channel for learning to appreciate God's plan of the ages and understanding the course of history. As we look at them in Mt., we see the sequence of incarnation, presence of the King, offer of the King and kingdom, rejection, postponement and suspension, return and glory, all presented through complex *literary* features. It is unfortunate that many people approach the parables assuming that they apply directly to the Church, and perhaps also (as in the case of the amillennialist) that the physical kingdom has been entirely abrogated. As one writer has said in connection with serious study of the parables:

> There is one prayer especially that covers all the parables. "That I may know Him" will more and more be the longing of our hearts. The study of His portrait, and of the revelation which He gave of Himself in these pictures, will be one means by which the prayer will not only be prompted but answered; and will be instrumental in helping us to obey the exhortation given through the apostle Peter—"Grow in grace, and in the knowledge of our Lord and Saviour Jesus Christ." [13]

The Bible student should consult the many helpful Scofield notes on the parables, especially those in the Gospels. [14]

Types of Literature

A full-length treatment would be needed to do justice to the variety of literary types in Scripture. We can only touch on some prominent ones here.

Narrative

The Bible is unique in literature in that it weaves together historical account and revelational information, using stories as vehicles for spiritual lessons. Two subtypes within the biblical forms of narrative are: 1) heroic narrative, which centers on the experiences of an individual; 2) epic, involving separate episodes centering on individual heroes, with political overtones. Homer's *Odyssey* is an example of secular epic. Probably the only narrative epic in the Bible is the Exodus account. [15]

The story of Joseph forms a classic example of heroic narrative. One of the most difficult things for those who love the Bible to understand is that sensitive and intelligent human writers could participate in the inscripturation process, utilizing highly productive literary effects. The details of Joseph's life as given in Gen. are true to the facts as they occurred. Yet the narrator clearly does not tell us everything that happened to the hero. In his selection and arrangement of details, guided by the Spirit of God, he creates an account that displays literary excellence along with spiritual power. His product is replete with the effective use of literary features such as conflict, suspense, apparent catastrophe, climax, polarization, suffering, and dramatic irony.

The plot is established on the basis of the polarization between Joseph and his brothers, with Jacob in the middle, loving all his sons, but favoring Joseph. Joseph's unusual dreams, first about the sheaves and then the sun, moon, and stars, serve to alienate him from the brothers even more. We should not miss the fact that Joseph is associated with dreams several times, at the beginning of the narrative and then in his dealings with Pharoah. The narrator uses this at prominent points in Joseph's life, in part to show heaven's favor. As the hero proceeds through various trials, the reader cannot miss noticing that he is favored in some way, that, given enough time, circumstances always turn around to cause him to prosper. This is one of the spiritual elements, and, although nothing is said in the Bible to this effect, we cannot help making a comparison between Joseph and Christ, who was also rejected by those close to Him, but will be yet publicly raised up to evident prosperity. Each stage in the narrative underscores Joseph's innocence, wisdom, and favor by God. In fact, he is presented without any flaws—a complete hero.[16]

The climax of the book is actually two-pronged. The narrator resolves the conflict between Joseph and his brothers, and at the same time shows that it is God's providential hand that has controlled the events of the account, as Joseph declares in Gen. 50:20 that the brothers' evil intent was turned to blessing for Jacob's whole clan. Thus, on top of the more obvious emotional resolution operating with the ingredients of family, geography, governments, and acts of nature (the famine), there is a spiritual resolution, disclosing that God was behind everything. A sovereign God used the mistreatment of Joseph by human beings to communicate lessons that could not be taught as effectively in any other way. This narrative, as all biblical narrative, uses its literary charms to point beyond itself to key spiritual issues.

Tragedy

Tragedy usually involves a central figure who is, because of circumstance or decision, brought to misfortune or disaster. In secular literature the world is often pictured as hostile and arrayed against human beings, deterministically forcing individuals to downfall and loss.

There has been considerable discussion as to whether biblical tragedy can have the same elements. Since, in the view of the biblicist, a loving God sovereignly controls the universe, can individuals be subject to deterministic forces? Is there thoroughgoing tragedy where the possibility of redemption or other divine intervention exists? Perhaps it is best to say that the Bible redefines the tragic. True loss in the biblical sense is failing to appropriate the things of God, to avail oneself of general and special revelation, to accept God's offer of grace. There are clearly many aspects of life that we cannot understand as we are in them, and that cannot be explained by steadied reflection over time—the problem of evil, the existence of sin, etc. But there is enough biblical information to put us on the right track, and it is the ignoring of what has been revealed that makes for biblical tragedy.

David's life provides an example of misery that occurred during the life of one who was never destined for ultimate tragedy. His sins committed in relation to Bathsheba and Uriah resulted in a life altered from what it could have been. Yet there was no question that he could be restored and would face joy in the presence of God after death.

Judas, however, made decisions that would result in eternal misery. His account is tragic not in the secular sense of his being the victim of forces in life that he could not control, but in the sense that he was so long in the presence of God Himself and yet still put his own interests first. In this vein, Ryken points out the basic difference between secular and biblical tragedy:

> Perhaps the distinction between biblical and nonbiblical tragedy can be summed up by saying that in nonbiblical tragedy the tragic hero is, above all, the sympathetic tragic victim, while in biblical tragedy he is the unsympathetic sinner. The appropriate response in the first case is, Isn't it too bad that all this happened to the tragic hero? The appropriate response to biblical tragedy is, Isn't it too bad that he disobeyed God, when it might have been otherwise?[17]

Poetry

See the extensive treatment below under ''Poetic Literature in the Bible.''

Allegory

See the treatment above in this ch., where allegory is approached as figurative language, ch. 5, Interpreting the Bible, and ch. 7, Relations Between the Testaments.

Wisdom Literature

In Prov., Eccl., and Jas. we encounter literature that is characterized especially by reflection on life by one who has observed it at length and is passing on valuable conclusions. In the first two books, there is extensive or even exclusive use of short, powerful sayings—proverbs, aphorisms and maxims—but such are not absolutely necessary to identify portions of the text as wisdom literature. To take just one of these books, one of the reasons Jas. is difficult to outline is because it contains a number of topics, many of which are wisdom-related. The presentation is often punctuated by short sayings, such as 1:19–20: ''My dear brothers, take note of this: Everyone should be quick to listen, slow to speak and slow to become angry, for man's anger does not bring about the righteous life that God desires''(NIV).

Gospel

As a historical and literary form, the works of Matthew, Mark, Luke, and John are unique among human writings (although, to be sure, they had their first-century imitators). Although they contain biographical elements, they have overriding spiritual goals. Each of the four writers approaches the life of the Lord Jesus Christ from a different standpoint, as dictated by the overall purpose for writing. For example, one of Matthew's overriding goals is to present Jesus as King in relation to Israel. He selects only those elements of Jesus' life and ministry that further that theme. But the Gospels are not only selective biography. As literary works that skillfully utilize a large number of literary features (parable, narrative, dialogue, conflict, suspense, climax, etc.), they show the hands of master craftsmen. As such they have stood the test of time, humanly speaking, and are examples of the world's greatest literature. For more on the distinctives of the Gospels, see ''The Four Gospels'' in the NSRB.

Epistle

Although the epistles of the N.T. were almost certainly penned originally as genuine correspondence from the apostles to historical groups of individuals, they contain distinctive and powerful literary elements. As with the gospels, they have spiritual goals that are far beyond the usual role of a letter as simply conveying information. Thus even the short book of Philemon, while clearly written in response to a particular occasion, exhibits important spiritual lessons interwoven with the particular occasion for writing, in this case, the return of a runaway slave. Here, as so often in the epistles, the emotions, spiritual concerns, personal habits, and love for those ministered to come through in a compact literary piece that informs, teaches, and stirs the heart at the same time. For more on the doctrinal emphases of the epistles, see "The Epistles of Paul" in the NSRB.

Apocalyptic

This type of literature, usually prophetic, opens vistas into the spiritual realm by means of visions, and striking and unusual descriptions. Several nonbiblical Jewish apocalyptic works exist, such as First Enoch, the Assumption of Moses and the Apocalypse of Baruch. In addition, the N.T. period gave rise to apocalyptic writings, e.g., the Apocalypse of Paul and the Apocalypse of Ezra. In the Bible, portions of Isa., Ezek., Dan., Joel, and Zech. are apocalyptic. Among other things, they make use of symbolism (especially based on animals and other features of nature), numerology, angelic activity and intervention, and recurring conflicts between good and evil individuals and forces (see below in this ch. on literary features of Rev.).

Poetic Literature in the Bible

The Form of Biblical Poetry

Although there are poetic elements throughout the Bible, those books classed particularly as poetic are Job, Ps., Prov., Eccl., and Song. Hebrew poetry is known for its feature of parallelism of thought (although this is not present everywhere). People familiar with Eng. poetry expect the Bible to display rhyme and rhythm. Although Heb. poetry does possess some metrical features, the distinctive feature lies in the placing of ideas in relation to each other. This can consist of parallelism that is synonymous (where the two lines essentially repeat the same idea), contrastive (where the two lines give opposite ideas), or progressive (where the first line is advanced in some way by the second). These are illustrated by the following (there are other patterns):

a. *Synonymous*
   "I have chosen the way of truth;
     I have set my heart on your laws." (Ps. 119:30, NIV)
b. *Contrastive*
   "For the LORD watches over the way of the righteous,
     but the way of the wicked will perish." (Ps. 1:6, NIV)

c. Progressive

"I have hidden your word in my heart
    that I might not sin against you." (Ps. 119:11, NIV)

It is worth noting that all of these are preservable in the process of translation, unlike rhyme and meter.[18]

The Nature of Poetry

What is poetry? To begin with, it is the most concentrated form of literature. It makes extensive and powerful use of figurative language and imagery. It need not be rhymed or rhythmic. Above all, it is artistic creation. Like other literature, it deals with the human condition: the writer attempts to communicate his experiences to the reader.

Why do people write poetry? Perhaps it is because they want to describe for others how they perceive life and their relation to it. At the same time they are making a significant statement in an artistic form. Certainly the biblical poets wanted to share with others their conclusions and ongoing experiences in their relation to God. And it also appears that there is a degree of satisfaction derived from crystallizing a portion of one's experience in a work of art. René Wellek and Austin Warren have captured this well:

> It is probable that all art is 'sweet' *and* 'useful' to its own appropriate users: that what it articulates is superior to their own self-induced reverie or reflection; that it gives them pleasure by the skill with which it articulates what they take to be something like their own reverie or reflection and by the release they experience through this articulation.[19]

This suggests that there is an effect on the writer as he pursues his craft. In a sense, it is a statement about the writer and reflects his interaction with his subject. Very often there is a perceptible change that can be seen within the poem itself.

Now this way of seeing poetry can be extremely helpful in aiding our understanding of biblical poetry, especially the Psalms. For even though they are part of an inspired text, they are no less a product of all that goes into being human—joy, hope, peace, despair, sin, guilt, fear, faith, failure, praise, and dedication. There can be no question that God led individuals to write the Psalms in order that we might have somewhere in Scripture the record of people like us, who go through experiences like ours and who tell us their perceptions in artistic and creative ways. No wonder this body of poetry has through the centuries held a special place for believers as they reflect on life.

If we look closely we can often see what happens to the poet in the course of a psalm. We are not saying that he dashes off his words in a charged emotional state. All good poetry is carefully crafted, and biblical poetry is no exception. Its writers were clearly aware of different forms of literature and of how to use poetic elements. Doubtless many psalms, if not all, are the result of much careful work. Certainly the acrostic psalms are (these are psalms where lines or sections begin with successive letters of the Heb. alphabet). This does not mean they are any less the product of the inspiring Holy Spirit. But the writer may reveal what occurs in his experience, as if the poem were an account of his progress. This is really no different from Paul's very human cries in Rom. 9:1–3.

There are several important psalms in the O.T. that demonstrate this quite clearly.

One of these of Ps. 2. The following is an analysis of this psalm in which we attempt to bring out its literary features, showing how they are integrated with and enhance its spiritual information. We will also suggest ways in which other psalms can be similarly viewed. The reader should first consult the notes at 2:1, 6 and 12.

Psalm 2: an Extended Treatment

Any approach to this psalm must first be based on a recognition of its messianic nature (see note at 2:1). Different portions of it are quoted, some several times, in the N.T. Clearly the N.T. writers viewed it as predictive of the Person and work of the Messiah. However, one of the questions that must be answered concerns the precise way in which this psalm or parts of it look forward to Christ. In part the answer is tied up with the experience of the poet.

The Scofield note at 2:6 explains that this psalm can be divided into six sections. Actually there are more, and their identification is made easier when we recognize that this poem portrays a drama, with players, dialogue, an observer's commentary, suspense, imagery, conflict, climax, resolution, and personal or moral application.

In this interactive drama there are four speakers or groups. The writer, acting as a commentator/observer/poet, begins with a query (v. 1) and parallel comment (v. 2) concerning the nations, then quotes their cry of independence (v. 3). Thus these first three verses feature the poet and the direct speech of the nations. (The NIV and NASB helpfully mark off vv. 1–3 as a unit.) The second main section (vv. 4–6) provides the Father's response, although we do not discover a distinction among the persons until v. 7. The commentator first describes God's reaction, then quotes Him, after the pattern of vv. 1–3. We are thus introduced, in parallel, to the two conflicting parties: the nations and God. Also, the Scofield note points out that vv. 4–5 contain those topics— God's derision and rebuking, and the establishment of the King upon Zion.

Now it is crucial that we see that in vv. 7–9 a fourth speaker/figure appears in this dramatization. He is addressed by the LORD (also Father) as Son. So the psalmist is quoting the Son, who is in turn quoting the Father. The Son's words continue through v. 9.

The final section is quite different from the preceding. It is a long homily by the poet himself and mentions the other three characters/groups appearing in the psalm. But, as we will see, it is an important part of the structure of the poem. It is the outcome of the poet's interaction with the problem and the other figures.

Although the psalm is clearly predictive of the Person and work of our Lord Jesus Christ, we need to dwell on this last point of structure. As the psalm unfolds, something clearly happens to the writer. In a sense the framework of the psalm is established by the poet's asking a question, one which is, as the poem states, very real and pressing to him: Why do the nations rage, plot, take this stand, and gather together against the LORD and His Anointed One (whose identity we do not yet know)? No one gives a direct reply to his initial interrogation. From where does the solution come? Certainly, at one level, it comes from divine revelation, and this psalm is a poetic revelation/prediction of the kingship and dominion of Christ. But in the realm of the psalmist's experience, he receives the answer as he puts spiritual truths together and understands what he did not understand before—the certainty of the coming rule of Messiah, who is, interestingly enough, also a Son. In other words, the psalmist learns and grows during the progress of the psalm. And one of the very important lessons we are to take from this psalm is that *his* spiritual experience is to be *ours* also.

Through the vivid presentation of this literary drama, we are drawn into the poet's world so that our growth becomes like his, our new understanding a result of his. His question is genuine, and *we* should stop to ask it with him: Why *do* the nations and peoples and kings and rulers (note the string of terms) behave so belligerently? And if we "play the game" with the psalmist, we, like he, do not know the answer until v. 10. But by then we have learned truths about God and His King, as well as (and this is crucial) how to go about answering spiritual dilemmas. When we are able to grasp more of the plan and purposes of God, especially as they are centered on Christ, our spiritual difficulties are eased. This principle is found everywhere in the Scriptures. The poet's literary experience, then, is a spiritual one as well. Literary form carries spiritual lessons.

Now within this twelve-verse drama, with its questions, quotes, and commentary, there is a host of other literary features that flesh out the skeleton just described. The poet interacts with the machinations of some human beings, the general human condition, and truths concerning God and His Son. As he does so, he skillfully employs devices to enhance the poetic experience he has that we are to enter into. We are presented with intense imagery from the very start, with the fuming hosts described in double parallelism, as (1) raging/plotting and (2) taking their stand/gathering together. Here is hyperbole (exaggerated description) and metonymy (the substitution of the term for one entity for a closely associated entity) of a sort, since nations don't rage, only individuals do, and peoples don't plot, their leaders do. The effect is clear: sinful humanity is thoroughly, hopelessly, and collectively at odds with God. Their case is against both Yahweh (the Lord) and his Anointed One.

The distinctive feature of Heb. poetry mentioned above, its parallelism, is utilized here to express a key doctrinal truth: the Lord and his Anointed One are one and the same. This does not mean, of course, that the distinctions between the Persons of the Trinity are erased, but that the Persons are somehow a unity. The Anointed One, who with the flow of the psalm must be the Son and the speaker of v. 7, is anointed precisely because he is king (v. 6), since kings, prophets, and priests in Israel went through ritual anointing. Thus this psalm asserts the deity of the Anointed One, the King, the Son. It is interesting also that being anointed itself is a metaphor—in action—for becoming a king.

The poet continues his highly figurative description in v. 3 with another use of metonymy. There are no real bonds—the word *chains* is used for the sovereignty of God. This is expressive of the people's true condition because, since God restricts their freedom and sin, they actually view God's control as a chain. It may be that all of v. 3 has in the background the figure of animals under a yoke. Perhaps somehow they realize they are created to serve and cannot abide in that condition. Yet, certainly, a dumb beast would not think of revolting. In their chafing and plotting, they are more stupid than oxen.

As the poet shifts to the sovereign serenity of heaven in v. 3, the language portrays an atmosphere appropriate to the unquestionable grip of God. In contrast to the milling, haranguing nations, God is at ease and enthroned (an anthropomorphism—a description of God in human terms). The first part of v. 4 at once expresses peace, control, and omniscience. None of the turmoil of vv. 1–3 goes unnoticed, yet none of it disturbs

God. In a second anthropomorphism, God is described as laughing. Of course God doesn't laugh, but when we find out what He is like, as the psalmist does, then it is reasonable to describe His undisturbed reaction as laughter.

But things become more serious in v. 5, where the description of God in human terms turns to anger and wrath. Without actually doing anything, He can cause terror by exposing His face of judgment. We should not miss the progression here: God laughs . . . scoffs . . . rebukes . . . terrifies (with the last two terms of the quartet introduced by "then"). The tables will turn; the mad career of organized rebellion of humanity against God will not go unchecked. As each step of God toward the visible rule of the King (v. 6) occurs, the clamps are tightened, and the principal described effect is upon the rebels. Their braggadocio of vv. 1–3 turns to terror at the disclosure of the King. Here then is God's perfect and long-awaited solution to the problem of collective rebellion against Him—a revolt that was earlier anticipated in Gen. 11 with the tower, and mushroomed in the Babylonianism of Dan. 2 and 7 and Rev. 13–19. The answer is a real King ruling on the earth over humanity. Does v. 6 have a particular human king in mind? Commentators on the psalm have difficulty pointing to one particular enthronement occasion. Yet the anointing of kings to reign in Jerusalem was a clear type of the recognition of the great King. All that they were to be—and so often failed to reach— in God's theocracy *will* be achieved under the reign of Christ in the kingdom.

An important element is still missing: no human king could ever subdue the nations. And those nations here include Israel, since Peter, in his interpretation of this psalm in Acts 4:27, tells us that the people of Israel stood with the Romans against Christ. We learn from this that the crucifixion was a manifestation of the spirit of rebellion of Ps. 2:1–2. But from the poet's perspective, no Israelite king could last long enough to have the power to subdue the nations. Furthermore, since their argument is against God Himself, He would have to defeat them. It is this problem that the decree of v. 7 actually answers.The inheritance of v. 8 is possible because of the declaration of sonship that the Son quotes as from the Father. Certainly this is no casual statement, and we would be missing the psalmist's whole point if we failed to see that whatever God does to the nations He does through the Son.

But what is it about the sonship decree that makes it the key to dominion over the nations by a king appointed by God? From the O.T. alone this problem would be hard to answer. But the N.T. explains how v. 7 can effect the cure that the psalmist seeks, and which, in the development of the psalm, is the catalyst to bring about his new confidence in vv. 10–12. Rom. 1:3–4 tells us that the resurrection "marked out" (NIV— "declared") Christ with power as the Son of God. This new sovereign position of Christ based on the resurrection is taught in many places in the N.T. (Rev. 5; Eph. 1, etc.). Furthermore, Acts 13:32–34 links Ps. 2:7 with Isa. 55:3 through the topic of the resurrection. In fact, Paul makes Ps. 2:7 a prediction of resurrection by the way he introduces the quote in Acts 13:33. The sonship declaration was a promise that awaited fulfillment. And the logical outcome of such a new power-position is given by the words of Isa. 55:3 quoted in Acts 13:34. The *sure mercies* are traceable to 2 Sam. 7:12–16 and the statement of the Davidic covenant, the promise of a ruler on David's throne forever. Now this is the promise that the psalmist needs (but apparently never gets) in order to solve his dilemma. In the N.T. Paul teaches us that the resurrection, which yields an unconquerable and undying king, provides the solution to the rebellion of mankind. Psalm 2:7, then, is a prediction of the resurrection. The "day" referred to must be the day of resurrection.

How much of this did the poet comprehend? We have no way of knowing. But what we do know is that in the purpose of the psalm the resolution of his spiritual query comes after the sonship declaration, with its expansion in the imagery of vv. 8–9. That declaration, which comes as the poet suddenly finds himself listening to a conversation between members of the Godhead, establishes the right, power, and endless life that the anointed One needed to rule. And this He will do, in contrast to vv. 1–3. In a bold anthropomorphic figure the poet places an iron scepter (*He* needs no weapon) in the hand of the messiah. In the N.T. John reveals that the scepter does its work at the second advent (Rev. 2:27; 19:15).

As a result of what he has learned from the divine conversation, the psalmist now sets forth his conclusion (vv. 10–12, introduced by "therefore"), extending what he has learned to all who will hear. The rebellious need wisdom and warning: the sonship declaration provides that information. Their true response should be to serve and rejoice, contrasted with their taking their stand and plotting. There is a great doctrinal fact behind this change between vv. 1–3 and vv. 10–12: God's grace may allow even the hardened to turn to Him. The poem displays a striking literary contrast; the Bible's teaching elsewhere on God's longsuffering explains it.

Metonymy is once more employed as the poet exhorts the rebellious to "kiss the Son," a plea that must stand for "trust the Son." Such an act will make one "blessed," says the psalmist, in what must be taken as an emotional outburst, conditioned by the great recognition that the grace of God operates even when judgment is predicted. (See Pss. 1:1; 32:1, 2; 33:12; 34:8; 40:4; 65:4; 84:4, 5, 12; 89:15, etc., for similar expressions of emotion.)

Thus this psalm, in which poetry and prophecy are woven together, begins with a question and concludes with an appeal and the poet's own exclamation of confident joy: to trust the appointed Son brings not only safety, but also happiness. By figure and structure, this poem takes the reader through a literary process, one which is also a life and soul process. We may wonder where history is going and why God is mocked en masse, but when we learn that a resurrected Son will have the last word, then our response, along with the psalmist, must be to tell others of the grace that has been provided.

Prophetic Literature

Many of the Bible's most fascinating and perplexing literary features are found in its prophetic sections. By concentrating on one particular book—Revelation—we can see many of these literary qualities and how they interact.

The Importance of Literary Features in the Book of Revelation

Nowhere in the Bible are literary features more prominent and important than in the book of Revelation, the climax of God's disclosure of Himself to humanity. It is the most extensively prophetic book, is saturated with the rest of the Bible, and draws all of its major themes together. We ought not be surprised to see to what extent literary features are used to assist in carrying this complex, largely prophetic divine disclosure. Literary qualities make the information more vivid and interesting, and enable the writer to communicate large amounts of it in few words. The important doctrinal features of the book are mainly carried by its structural and symbolic features. As a matter of fact, the first verse tells us that God intends to use symbols extensively and that the book is a communication by symbols.

There is no question that this book is difficult to interpret. It has baffled many through the centuries. In large measure this has been due to the strange symbolism in this apocalyptic literature. Yet it is the very presence of certain literary features that gives us clues to enable us to decode the book successfully. One must always operate in Bible study with the assumption that God intends the Book to be understood. Somewhere within it must be material to help with the difficult parts, since it is self-interpreting. So, when we approach the book of Revelation we must ask the same questions as elsewhere: "What is there here that will assist me in understanding this book? Must it remain closed?" Actually, the book itself helps us. The American N.T. scholar Merrill Tenney points out that the figures in Rev. can be put into three classes with regard to interpretation: those that are interpreted in whole or in part elsewhere in the book; those that are interpreted elsewhere in the Bible (especially in the O.T.); and those that are not interpreted in the Bible but which have connections with extrabiblical literature.[20]

Although there have been myriads of significantly different interpretations of Rev., there are divinely given keys to understanding it, most of which are literary in nature. The book's internal literary features and connections with the rest of the Bible are determinative in providing a framework of interpretation. In fact, without such a framework the student of Rev. is left hanging.

Sketch of Revelation's Literary Features

In this section we will attempt to alert the reader to some of the many literary properties of the book of Revelation. Then we will provide a study guide to enable the reader to undertake his own analysis of a similar prophetic work, the book of Daniel. (See "Questions for Further Study: Prophetic Literature.")

In order to simplify the presentation of complex material, we will break down the literary features of the book into three main types: (1) those that have more evident connections with structure (divisions and arrangements), (2) those that involve symbolism, and (3) those that are part of the narrative presentation (characterization, plot, theme, development, etc.). Such a division is arbitrary and should not obscure the fact that many of the literary aspects of the book are interwoven. Symbol and structure may occur together.

Structural features. All of the books of the Bible possess definable structure. It aids in the communication of the written message. The book of Revelation, however, has a complex set of structural features; and it seems almost as if the more one studies the book, the more features come to light.

Perhaps the most important structural feature is the division of the book into three time periods relative to the author John himself. In ch. 1 the Lord Jesus Christ presents Himself to John, and in turn to the seven churches, as a priest and judge who has the churches completely under His control. In chs. 2–3 He sends messages to those churches. Then in chs. 4–22 we are given the apocalyptic portion of the book. We are helped to see this threefold division of the book by the divinely placed outline in 1:19 (see NSRB marginal references at 1:19). The things John saw are contained in vv. 9–18. The things present are the details of the seven churches, which were contemporaneous with John.

The things that would be "hereafter" (AV) must begin in 4:1, where the same phrase occurs. These are future with respect to John. Thus the book itself provides a basic structural pattern for the reader. This is the place to start in understanding it.

Within each of these sections are structural features, some more evident than others. Their presence, however, is designed to contribute to the overall meaning of the book. Some of these are: the use of themes or key concepts, often repeated with or without variation; the use of preview, review and repetition; the presence of movement toward a climax; divisions and connections with other parts of the book by restatement or allusion. We will discuss only some of the most notable of these.

The composite O.T. quotation in 1:7 can be viewed as the book's theme.[21] Drawn from Zech. 12:10 and Dan. 7:13, it brings to the introduction to the book (1:1–8) the concepts of the second advent, the death of Christ, Jewish guilt in the crucifixion, and salvation of Gentiles. The reader learns in a few words that this book is a continuation and fulfillment of those O.T. teachings. Furthermore, the verse alerts the reader to expect these topics. In a sense this is a summary of the book.

It is worth noting at this point that the position of the book of Revelation in the canon and its use of the rest of the Bible is a structural feature of the Bible as a whole. The use of O.T. themes in 1:7 is only one example of the way in which Rev. culminates previous revelation and history. This last book of the sixty-six can be viewed as a lens that brings into focus themes that have run parallel to each other throughout large portions of the Bible, even from Gen. Some of these are (1) the problem of our access to God and its solution, (2) the extent of human depravity, (3) the Edenic ideal, (4) angelic, and especially Satanic, activity, (5) the holiness and justice of God, (6) the provision of a redeemer, (7) the selection of Israel, (8) the nature of true worship, and (9) the relation of the Church to Israel.

Revelation sets these and other important features of God's activity with humanity in proper perspective. As the final element of progressive revelation, it shows how God's purposes will culminate in the resolution of long-standing problems, and especially in the universal dominion of the Lord Jesus Christ. Just as a glass lens can deflect parallel light rays, so the book of Revelation acts upon parallel themes from the whole Bible, causing them to converge in a real, short period of time in which the sovereign hand of God brings about the glorification of the Lord Jesus Christ. This is summarized in 19:10, where we are told that testimony about Jesus is the core of prophecy (see note). All of biblical and human history is designed to highlight Him. In another sense we are being told that if we do not see Him at the heart of this book, we will not understand it. Thus the position of Rev. in the canon, along with its use of the rest of the Bible from that final position, is itself a carrier of spiritual information.

One of the most prominent features of the structure of the book of Revelation is the network of patterns found in the letters to the seven churches (chs. 2–3). The numbers involved are part of the symbolism, which will be discussed below. But since they form such a prominent feature of the structure, they are worth noting here. Tenney has shown that beyond the basic sevenfold destination of the letters, there is also the basic pattern of seven parts to each letter.[22] With only a few exceptions, each little epistle contains (1) a charge to the angel of each church, (2) a description of Christ in His relation to the needs of each church, (3) a commendation, (4) a condemnation, (5) a warning, (6) a remedy, and (7) an encouragement/promise. It is significant that out of the expected forty-nine parts, only four are absent. In the presence of such a pervasive pattern, we might suspect that breaks would be meaningful—and they are. Two churches,

Smyrna and Philadelphia, receive no condemnation. But two (Sardis and Laodicea) receive no commendation. In both instances the alteration of a repeated form carries meaning. It is important, the writer is telling us, that we notice the particular states of those four churches.

A similar violation of pervasive pattern occurs in 16:17–21, where the seventh bowl is poured out almost immediately after the sixth. In the earlier series, the seals and trumpets, there is a break between the sixth and seventh. In fact, the seventh seal and seventh trumpet have no content other than the next series. The seventh seal *is* the seven trumpets, and the seventh trumpet *is* the seven bowls. (We conclude this in part from the fact that we expect the last of each series, yet have no specific mention of a conclusion; there are other reasons for this interpretation.) Why this alteration? Because at this point in the book, events are moving rapidly toward the climax, the judgment of Babylon and the second advent of Christ. There will be no delay in the pouring out of the bowl judgments. By the change of pattern we are told of inevitability and rapid-fire movements in the plan of God.

Another pattern of repetition is seen in the description at key points of the hardness of human hearts during the outpouring of judgments on the earth. After the first six seals are opened, we are told in 6:15–16 that the inhabitants of the earth are in a state of terror, but will certainly not turn to God. They would rather be buried under mountains that they might be hidden from God than come to Him. It is significant that the very next verse begins a description of the two groups who will enjoy God's presence. This extends through the end of ch. 7 (see note). The hardness of hearts is again described in 9:20–27. Even after the trumpet judgments, more terrifying than the seals, people turn their backs on God. In fact, after the description of the afflicting demonic hordes in 9:1–12, we should be startled to learn that people still worship demons, preferring them to God. So, 9:20–21 is stressing human depravity. Sin is so corrupting that those affected by it prefer its ugly associations to knowing the true God. Some do enjoy Him (11:1–2, 13, 17) but the structure of the book reveals further that outright blasphemy is the next stage for the hardened (16:9, 11). The book is presenting a progression: as time advances in the tribulation period, the real nature of the human heart will become clear. Of course, 13:4 tells us that for such a hardened heart the preferred alternative is to worship the beast, and, in turn, Satan himself (the dragon). The structure carries teaching.

Pure repetition can also be considered an element of structure. The significant use of *thousand years* six times in 20:2–7 should not be overlooked. God really needs to tell us something only once, and we stand responsible for it. But here there is a clear repetition of a number. We would do well to take this at face value, since it is clearly stressed by its appearance in a series of six occurrences (see discussion of this in ch. 5, Interpreting the Bible).

Another recurring structural feature of Rev. is the grouping and/or contrasting of chapters and other units. In chs. 1–3 the scenes and letters are revealed from the vantage point of the earth. In 4–5 John sees events in heaven, perhaps *from* heaven (4:1–2; see note at 4:1). These two chapters appear where they do to underscore the fact that God is in control before the horrors and disarray of the tribulation begin. They are an expansion of Ps. 2:4–9, where God's absolute, unruffled rule is presented in poetic form, and where the Son-Heir is promised rule. Revelation 4–5 also presents the initiation of that rule as the Son takes the scroll, appearing under the figure of a sealed last will and testament, and opens it to unleash the great time of testing. God is not worried or caught off guard, nor is heaven in turmoil, as the earth is spiritually and physically turned upside down. Saints reading this book are to be calmed by chs. 4–5. This is the chapters' main purpose (see Scofield paragraph headings in chs. 4–5).

This chapter-to-chapter structure recurs throughout the book. Chapter 7 is a parenthesis (see Scofield chapter heading) to give encouragement to the reader (yes, some will be able to stand; cf. 6:17), and includes a scene in heaven (7:9–17). The scene shifts to earth again in 8:7–11:14, and back to heaven in 11:15–19. A major break then occurs between 11:19 and 12:1, where the book turns to describe, not so much particular judgments as major figures and movements, even breaks, in Israel's history. John is told in 10:11 that he will have to tell the prophetic story again (see note), and so chs. 12–19 take the reader over the same ground as 6:1–11:14 from a different perspective. In fact, as 11:15–19 is reached it is clear that the kingdom is at hand (see note). The ark is revealed as heaven stands open—symbolizing the presence of God with humanity, and the possibility of access to Him (cf. Ezek. 1:1; Jn. 1:51 and Gen. 28:12; Acts 7:56; Rev. 4:1, and discussion of this theme of access in ch. 7, Relations Between the Testaments). The seals and trumpets have moved events to the establishment of the kingdom (see note at 11:5), and the narrative turns to view the action from another vantage point. We could say that the end-zone camera is now replaced by one high in the stands.

Symbols. The very first verse of Rev. discloses that the book will be a communication of information by symbols. The word translated "made it known" (NIV), "signified" (AV), "communicated" (NASB), suggests the impartation of information by signs or symbols.[23] Now the nature of sign systems is that they involve stand-ins for entities. A stop sign is not the actual stopping of a vehicle, but by its shape and color (even without the word) it can convey the message, "The law requires that vehicles cease motion at this intersection." As mentioned in ch. 6, The Language of the Bible, language itself is a sign system, where one thing stands for another: sound units have no meaning in themselves, but are arranged in the language and in speech to form complexes that people use for communication.

Similarly, symbolism in language involves the substitution of one description or term for another. As such, this lies at the heart of metaphor. Symbolic language can provide insights that can be gained in no other way. One biblical scholar has described metaphor this way:

> During the past generation there has been a new perception of metaphor as more than elegant decoration of information that could otherwise be communicated in a straightforward manner. It is now generally understood that far from being merely decorative, metaphors have real cognitive content. If one tries to paraphrase a metaphor, what is lost is more than just a certain effect. What is lost is part of the meaning itself, the insight which the metaphor alone can give.[24]

But symbolic language can have a negative function. It often veils. One writer has articulated, "The insight which metaphor gives into truth is properly tentative and hypothetical. It has . . . an is-and-is-not character."[25] Now clearly much of biblical revelation is designed to disclose some information while hiding other. God is very economical and very jealous of His holiness. He does not cast pearls before swine. For example, He tells us very little about the interrelationships among the Persons of the Trinity. He tells us almost nothing about the joy of being in His presence in the heavenly city (Rev. 22). He often guards His revelation from those who are speculative, careless, and sensationalistic. And, especially, He keeps truth from the hardened. Types, parables, and figurative language have as one of their purposes the hiding of truth. They reveal but they don't reveal. Note what our Lord says in Mt. 13:10–17 as He quotes Isa. 6.

Furthermore, symbolic language causes us to realize that at any point we have not said all that we could say about passages where it is used. This does not mean that we cannot reach firm conclusions, or that we can lapse into subjectivism. But within the strictures placed on interpretation by the need to compare Scripture with Scripture, we can view figurative passages as shading off into details difficult to unravel. Probably every serious interpreter of Rev. has come to this conclusion.

Symbolic language is clearly at the heart of this part of God's operations among human beings. It makes the message more interesting, but it also hides it. No doubt this is one of the reasons Rev. is a fascinating but cryptic book. We are told something of God's overall intentions in Dan. 12:4, where the prophet is instructed to close up the message that would be opened to understanding in the days of its fulfillment (cf. Hab. 2:3). In contrast, John is told in Rev. to publish the contents of that book.

Symbolic biblical language, then, encourages interaction and serious spiritual purpose, inviting the reader by its unexpected analogies to discover biblical meaning. American theologian John Walvoord also points out that undoubtedly one of the reasons for the extensive use of cryptic language was to hide from Roman authorities the spiritual and prophetic references to them in the book.[26]

Only a few of the symbols of Rev. can be discussed here. And this writer makes no claim to being able to understand them all. One of the initial tasks of the student of Rev. is to identify the symbols and to note which parts of the text are apparently intended to be symbolic. In a sense, the book as a whole, as noted above, is a communication by symbols. Yet clearly some parts, for example the names of the churches in chs. 2–3, are not symbolic. It might be better to speak of the book as communicated to John in something like a scenic panorama, wherein John saw figures and events that were real to him, but which stood for spiritual truths and acts and physical entities. Hence in ch. 12 he probably saw a real dragon, but we are to take the dragon as symbolically standing for Satan, as explained in 12:9. This is, however, a difficult area, for we do not know how much John understood or exactly what he saw. (Did he understand that the dragon represented Satan?) It is possible that in many instances he only gave from his human experience the closest approximation of what he saw. For instance, in 4:7 he says that "the first living creature was like a lion" (NIV). Did he see something that we might agree was lionlike, or was that simply the closest approximation of an other-worldly being?

Yet, seeing the book this way still does not make the sorting out and assigning of meaning to the symbols an easy task. Some types or groups are quite clear: numbers, colors, animals and their parts (horns, beasts, the Lamb, the dragon), implements (bowls, censers, lampstands), clothing (robes, garments, etc.). But here the grouping is still easier than the identification with the reality. In ch. 9 the animals are composite: they are somehow like locusts, scorpions, horses, and lions, but also like chariots and women. Certainly a compound metaphor! It is fairly clear that the horses in ch. 6 describe the role of a conquerer (6:2), bloodshed resulting from war (6:4), famine, (6:5) and death (6:8), where the horse is pale green, suggestive of decay. Notice that animals and colors are combined here! Similar to this is the 3×7 combination in the series of seven judgments (chs. 6–18). Whether or not the tribulation has started by ch. 6, the last days before the second advent will see all of these terrors. But the identity of animal associations in the figures in ch. 9 is more difficult to determine.

Tenney correctly points out that we are given help in interpreting the symbols, since there are some symbols that are explained in Rev., some that are paralleled by O.T. features, and some that may be explained by current history or culture.[27] Hence, we are told that the lampstands stand for the churches (1:20), and that the dragon is Satan (12:9). Yet sometimes even the explanations leave us wondering, as when the features of the beast out of the sea (13:1) are elucidated in 17:7–13. His horns represent kings (17:12, note), but how are they related to him and where do they come from? The explanation takes us only so far.

The reader should gain the impression that the symbols of the book are in some cases quite transparent but in others thoroughly enigmatic. As a whole they are certainly the most difficult literary aspect to grasp.

Narrative presentation. We are on firmer ground here, since we can often identify ways in which the writer uses literary features to display the ongoing narration of the events of the book, and can often explain them without great difficulty. Perhaps the reason for this is that it is the symbols that are designed in part to hide information that would be valuable, even crucial, to know, while the features of narrative presentation, such as suspense, dialogue, and contrast, are less tied to the identification of specific entities, such as the identity of the beast, etc. It should also be remembered that those characteristics that can be viewed as structural in nature (repetition, climax, contrast) can also be discussed in association with those that show the narrator's craft in portraying characters and in moving them and events across the stage of the book, etc.

We should be careful to note at this point that when we speak of a narrator we are describing an individual who is functioning with human consciousness and, in the case of Rev., with no small literary skill. The book is, quite simply, a manual of literary construction. This does not mean, however, that God is not behind the book. Theologians speak of ''concursive operation,'' meaning that it is possible to see in inspiration both God's hand and that of the human participant. It is entirely legitimate to speak of the human author's narrative presentation, while fully recognizing that God is the ultimate Author. The book of Revelation is not fiction, but it partakes of some of the same features as the very best fictional narrative ever produced by human beings.

As good literature skillfully employs such things as drama, irony, dialogue, commentary, anticipation, suspense, reticence of description, personification, etc., it draws the reader into the world of the narration and moves him and the narrative along toward a climax. All of these features and many others are used in Rev. A few can be described here.

The scene in chs. 4–5 is actually a drama involving several individual figures and participating groups (the whole book can be described in this way). The stage is set in 4:2, after the time indicator in 4:1 that shows that this is yet future with respect to John. We are then ushered into a great throne room, which is heaven itself. It should not be overlooked that here we are once again presented in symbolic form with the truth that heaven is accessible, and God can be approached (v. 1; see above in this ch.). Here, however, the purpose of chs. 4–5 is to show more than this—namely, that God is completely sovereign over the affairs of men. Of course, there is no literal throne of God that is a physical entity. John is ''seeing'' and consequently describing an element of the vision that has spiritual significance. The throne stands for God's rule. Interestingly, though, we are never told exactly who the occupant is. He is described three times simply as the one who sits on the throne. Here is an example of reticence on the part of John the narrator. Why doesn't he say it is God? It does not take much to conclude that it is. And we know it is not the Son, because He, in the figure of the Lamb, takes the scroll from the separate being on the throne (5:7). Perhaps John veils the identity slightly for a few verses in order to heighten the suspense. However, He is identified in 4:8 as the Lord God Almighty. And it seems that John is more concerned with describing Him symbolically, as he ascribes to Him in 4:3 the qualities of precious stones.

The mention of the rainbow should immediately alert us to the fact that we are on covenant ground. In His acts toward human beings, God is first of all a covenant-maker (see ch. 2, The Nature of the Bible, concerning covenants). The rainbow recalls the promise of grace to Noah and all humanity. It is noteworthy that in Ezek. 1, a chapter very similar to Rev. 4–5, the Lord Jesus Christ appears (in a theophany) in His sovereignty over Israel's affairs, sitting on a throne-chariot surrounded by a rainbow (Ezek. 1:28). There we are being told that God is present to fulfill His covenants (cf. Ex. 4). Indeed, Rev. 6–19 forms the last stage in the fulfilling of those covenants by the completion of the seventy weeks of Dan. 9:24 (see note).

This first, lone player in this drama is now seen to be surrounded by two groups, the twenty-four elders and the four living creatures. Clearly these players are being introduced one by one, or group by group, with definite stage placements. The elders are around the throne; the four living creatures are in the midst of it *and* around it. If, as they seem to be, the creatures are angelic beings, we are being told that they are somehow very close to God; they are in the midst of the throne, right where He is.

The creatures of vv. 6–8 are perhaps the more striking of the two groups, both of which seem to function like choruses in a Gr. drama. They not only comment on the action and advance it, but by their description help the reader understand the whole drama. That is, we are being told that angels are in the presence of God, understand events on earth, and have certain relations to God, to man, and to the events that follow in chs. 6–19. Tenney points out that elsewhere in this book angels act as, among other things, guides for John.[28] A careful reading of 4:7–8 will yield a puzzling picture. These beings are like both the cherubs of Ezek. 1:10, etc., in that they have four faces (exact correspondence to Ezek. 1:10), and the seraphs of Isa. 6, in that they have six wings and continually ascribe holiness to God. Yet there are not two kinds of being here, but one. Are these a third type of angelic order (assuming that seraphs and cherubs are angels), or are we being told by the symbolism that these creatures act like the cherubs and like the seraphs? (See note at Ezek. 1:5.) It is not inconsequential that the description in 4:7 (cf. Ezek. 1:10) appears to reflect attributes of God as seen in the incarnate Son: the majesty of a lion; the meekness of the ox/calf; the humanity of the God-man; the sovereignty—above all turmoil—of the eagle. All of these attributes of the Son are seen in the subsequent narrative as the Son of God/Son of Man assumes control of the earth at His second advent. Furthermore, we are to gather that these angelic beings are closely associated with and reflect His Person and work.

The situation in heaven here is far from static. The living creatures continually, even day and night (although there is no day and night in heaven!), proclaim the merits of the only Holy God, while the first group, the elders, *respond* with their own worship (vv. 9–11). One group leads, one responds; both worship. Some of the chapter is narration; some is dialogue, as in vv. 8 and 11. It is valuable in narrative to give direct speech where that will reveal more about the condition or acts of the participants. And it may be that John wishes to highlight here the holiness of God and His being worshipped as the sovereign Creator (v. 11). In fact, the main contrast between chs. 4 and 5 lies in the *reason* for worship. In ch. 4 God is viewed as the one who made mankind so He can dispose of human history as He wishes. In ch. 5 He is highlighted in the Person of the Son as Redeemer. It is interesting that these two worthy qualities of God are elsewhere brought together in Scripture: God is both our Creator and our Redeemer. The direct speech in chs. 4–5 highlights this.

After the description of the activity of the two groups, the focus returns to the figure on the throne. Now, however, a new entity is introduced—the scroll, whose identification is never given explicitly. We are told what is *in* the scroll (the judgments, 6:1ff), but its symbolism needs to be explored. Apparently the reader is to understand this as a spiritual inheritance document. The possessor of the scroll is the heir. Now if the inheritance figures were absolutely parallel, we would expect the Lamb to be mentioned in it, but He is not. Instead He seizes it, almost by force—or should we say, by absolute right?—after He is revealed in v. 5 as the Redeemer.

The dialogue now becomes rapid-fire, to heighten the intensity of the drama. An angel poses a question touching only on the issue of opening the scroll. He himself is strong, but is not eligible (v. 2). John's comment in v. 3 repeats the angel's dilemma but adds a short but significant fact: no one can even look at it, much less open it. Further, he adds the threefold spatial reference ("in heaven or on earth or under the earth" NIV), to stress the absolute inability of any being to possess and open it. His conclusion, in the midst of the drama (v. 4) is that the absence of a possessor/heir is tragic, and he weeps, adding the further stipulation that no worthy reader exists. Will he ever find out what is in it and what will happen? It appears from his interaction that he knows it must be opened, yet we are not told how he knows. But we should notice that he begins to empathize with the heavenly beings: their dilemma becomes his.

An elder (v. 5) steps in with the answer, as the dramatic dialogue continues. And what an answer it is! Verses 5 and 6 are two of the most symbolically charged verses in the Bible, and contain far-reaching interrelated spiritual teachings. There are several symbols: the Lion, the Root of David, the scroll/seals, the Lamb, the horns, eyes and spirits, and the act of taking the scroll. The Lion/Root of David figure speaks of the credentials and source of the Lord Jesus Christ (see note on 5:5). He is of the lines of Judah and David, and so can rule in the kingdom. He is lionlike in regard to His second advent, contrasted with His lamblike quality in the first. Further, in regard to His power He is like a lion; but in regard to His incarnational appearance, He is like a lamb and a small seedling shoot (cf. Isa. 11:1).

So we are reminded of His credentials, His two advents (especially as the Lamb), and of His death. But what is so significant here is that He is both dead and alive. John does not explicitly say He is alive. That would be too obvious. So he indirectly asserts it by saying he is standing. Dead beings do not stand; therefore, He must be alive. But the contrast is heightened by the fact that He is said to be in a slain condition (see "A Pervasive Literary Figure" above in this ch.). He is therefore seen by John symbolically as both dead and alive, and very much alert. He is dead and alive, came once and will come again, and possesses the credentials to rule in the coming kingdom—His own.

It is no accident that the unholy, counterfeit trinity attempts to duplicate this death and resurrection. This takes place when the one who speaks like a lamb, but is actually vicious, tries to trick the world into believing the first beast has been resurrected (13:11; see note).

Moreover, one does not expect a Lamb to have any power. But He does, and only because of His death (cf. Heb. 2:10ff). This is the central point of the figure. The genius of this metaphor lies, then, in its ability to tell us compactly yet graphically that the Father is pleased with the Son's cross-work; furthermore, that the Father establishes that work before heavenly witnesses as the key to the Son's inheriting the earth after its tribulation-throes, which the Son also controls.

Thus the initial questions (v. 2) are answered. Of course, they are not answered directly, but by the outworking of the drama and the bold, multi-part metaphor centered on the Lamb. The last half of ch. 5 forms an interlude before the next event concerning the scroll, the opening of the seals in ch. 6. But the interlude is important, because it expresses the correct response of the heavenly "chorus" to the newly confirmed rights of the Lamb to rule by reason of death. The chorus explains part of what was so compactly presented in vv. 5–7, and adds information on the extent of the effect of the Lamb's death (in the second half of v. 9: "You purchased men for God from every tribe and language and people and nation" [NIV]). This forms the needed counterpart to the praise of ch. 4. Thus our great God creates us and also rescues us *by Himself*. The Lamb alone deserves our praise, as will be true in the eternal state (ch. 22).

Questions for Further Study

Figurative Language

1. What is the theme of Hos.? Where does it appear, and how is it presented? Does the book have elements of allegory? (Of course, the events really occurred.)

2. List all the figures of speech you can find in 1 Pet. 1:22–2:10. How many varieties can you find?

3. The parable of the vineyard in Mt. 21:33–46 teaches a number of lessons. What is its setting (where and when)? What ministry has immediately preceded it? What is the reaction of the hearers, who react on the basis of what they understand, and apparently know exactly what Jesus means? How are Isa. 5:1–7, Ps. 118:22–23, and Dan. 2:34–35 connected with the parable? What are the elements of the figure in Isa. 5? In Mt. 21? What does each, in context, appear to point to? What parts of the parable are obvious or explained? Exactly how is the vineyard figure varied between Isa. 5 and Mt. 21? What is the prophetic teaching? What is taught about the kingdom? What do we learn about God's love? About human beings' ignoring it? How do Gentiles figure in the parable? Is the Church a vineyard in any sense? Attempt to state the main lesson of the parable in a single sentence.

Psalms

1. Read Ps. 22 through several times, along with the NSRB notes. The note at v. 22 points out that there is a clear break yielding two contrasting sections in the psalm. David must have had some kind of experience that is reflected in this psalm. Yet, what he went through is only a foreshadowing of the experience of Christ on the cross. David, like the poet, displays a change in his outlook, apparently in the middle of v. 21. His genuine cries of confusion in v. 1 are resolved at that point. Although we do not know what David went through, it is important to ask what Jesus went through. In

context, Mt. 27:46 helps us to see that the Son was in some way separated from the Father for our sins (see center-column reference in Ps. 22:1). He had always spoken of and to His "Father," yet now it is only "God." Why? Under the judicial hand of the Father the God-man was made sin for us (2 Cor. 5:21) and was alienated from a holy God. Separation from the Father accomplished payment for sin. In light of the fact that in the sixth utterance from the cross (Lk. 23:46) Jesus once again addresses His Father, and the fact that Jn. 19:30 records His cry of "It is finished" (which must be a reference to His substitutionary work) before He died physically, describe as carefully as you can the experience of Christ as reflected in the structure of the psalm.

2. List and identify as many figures of speech as you can in Ps. 22 (see note on 22:7). What is their effect in the verses where they appear? What might have been figurative for the psalmist but nonfigurative for the Son?

3. Compare the beginning of the psalm with the end. What has happened in between to cause the change?

4. Read Ps. 139 through several times. If you look carefully, you can see that the writer is describing his own outlook as He interacts with the attributes of God. What stages does he go through? How and where does He change? What does he learn? Why does he conclude as he does in vv. 23–24?

Prophetic Literature

For many reasons the book of Daniel furnishes good ground for application of what has been presented concerning the literary features of Rev. To begin with, it is a kind of twin book to Rev., dealing also with the destiny of Israel in the plan of God. Moreover, they are two of the few primarily apocalyptic books in the canon. Most important, Dan. presents a number of interesting and valuable literary features, many of which are easy to identify and explain. We will suggest some applications of what was said in regard to Rev., along with some projects for the Bible student to undertake independently.

1. Several key structural features overlap in Dan. and deal with significant information. To begin with, there is a clear distinction between sections of the book, based on the languages they are written in. Chapter 2, v. 4. to ch. 7, v. 28 is in Aram., the rest is in Heb. (see note, 2:4). In addition, the book appears to break between chs. 6 and 7 in regard to main emphases. In chs. 1–6 the stress is on the history of Gentile powers. The last half of the book presents events from Israel's perspective. For example, in chs. 1–6 the visions are all received by a Gentile, while they are given to Daniel in chs. 7–12 (see note at 7:3) Given that Aram. was an international trade language and that Israel was in captivity in Babylon (see introduction to Dan. in the NSRB), what significance do these two divisions seem to have?

2. The mention of the temple vessels along with the giving of them *by God* in 1:2 is important. They appear again in ch. 5. Certainly 1:2 is presenting a preview of a feature to be expanded later. Further, Nebuchadnezzar and his kingdom are described as a head of gold that would eventually be removed. Nebuchadnezzar also learned to appreciate God, according to ch. 4, a passage that, interestingly enough, is written in the first person, giving Nebuchadnezzar's account in his own words. Certainly Belshazzar was not like Nebuchadnezzar. How do these temple vessels and the downfall of Babylon (ch. 5, 539 B.C.) figure in the portrayal of Belshazzar in ch. 5?

3. There are clear correspondences between the symbolic features of the statue and the beast visions in chs. 2 and 7 respectively. Using the Scofield notes, try to list all

the features of each vision, and then compare the two lists. Can you expand on the note at 7:3? What is clearly repeated from the statements about the statue to those about the beasts? What is not repeated and why? What is added? What is significant about 7:7–8?

4. The vision of ch. 7 actually consists of three parts. Note the repeated *I saw* (or *beheld*). Yet the vision is a unity (7:1). Given that the third vision describes the second advent and kingdom, what does ch. 7 teach about the time and nature of the kingdom and Christ's second advent?

5. At first sight, 9:1–23 appears to be an unnecessary appendage to the vision of the seventy sevens in 9:24–27. However, careful study reveals that it is a prelude in which Daniel's personal involvement with the crucial four-verse revelation is described. After studying the notes to Dan. 9, describe how vv. 1–3 are connected with vv. 24–27.

7

Relations Between the Testaments

In Lk. 24:13–27 we find a stirring account of the self-revelation of the Person and work of our Lord Jesus Christ to two disciples by means of the O.T. Scriptures. After exploring their spiritual understanding, He graciously opens their eyes in what must rank as one of the greatest teaching sessions of all time. He proceeds to take them from one end of the O.T. to the other, all the while showing how He Himself was the center of that body of revelation: "And beginning with Moses and all the Prophets, he explained to them what was said in all the Scriptures concerning himself" (Lk. 24:27, NIV). Our Lord, then, described Himself by appealing to the O.T. This kind of use of the O.T. is foundational to the text of the N.T.

It is not necessary for us to read very far in the N.T. before we discover that there is some kind of extensive relationship between that portion of the Bible and the O.T. In fact, the more we study, the more we are faced with different kinds of connections between the testaments. The extent and the variety of intertestamental links proves to be one of the most important and rewarding areas of Bible study. On the basis of the pervasiveness of this relationship, one writer has been led to describe the use of the O.T. by writers of the N.T. as "the substructure of Christian theology." [1] The thrust of this perceptive assessment, that the O.T. is the foundation of the N.T., should be adopted as a guideline by all Bible students. It would alert the reader to areas for ongoing study, and also serve to correct many lingering errors. One such fallacy is that of thinking that there is a basic dichotomy between the testaments, to the effect that the O.T. is primarily an expression of law, while the N.T. is primarily an expression of grace.

In some ways the area of the relations between the testaments has been neglected in the history of Bible study. In other respects it has been the scene of heated debate, as in the case of the controversy over the relation of the law to the life of the believer. But in any case it is a feature of the biblical revelation that cannot be ignored.

Although this area of study is in many ways open-ended, we will suggest four avenues of approach to relations between the testaments: (1) structural, (2) theological, (3) analogical, and (4) quotational. It should be emphasized that these are not mutually exclusive. For instance, many theological relations between the testaments are carried by quotations of the O.T. in the N.T., and many structural features are expressed in the development of theological themes between the testaments. The very fact that the N.T. quotes the O.T. extensively is in itself a structural feature. That is, the Bible builds upon itself.

Some Features of Structural Relations Between the Testaments

Progressive Revelation

Hebrews 1:1–2 presents a principle that is crucial for the understanding of the Bible as a whole: "In the past God spoke to our forefathers through the prophets at many times and in various ways, but in these last days he has spoken to us by his Son" (NIV). God has maintained a continuity of revelation to human beings through the centuries. And His speaking in the past certainly refers here to disclosure of information before the incarnation of Christ. He communicated on various occasions to different individuals and groups, and did so through diverse means. For example, He spoke to Moses from a burning bush (Ex. 4), to Daniel directly in a dream (Dan. 7) and in a vision (Dan. 8), indirectly through an angel (Dan. 9) and through a Gentile ruler (Dan. 2). Nevertheless, the clear intent of these verses in Heb. is to teach that the former messages were somehow incomplete, and that they awaited further revelation at a more crucial point in human history, "in these last days."

Certainly, then, God spoke in segments. His earlier words were entirely reliable, but were partial compared to what He would disclose over the total course of revelatory history. Not all topics in the O.T. receive later expansion, since some are mentioned once or a few times and then never again. But many are expanded on, and it is these that the Bible student must pay attention to as features of progressive revelation. This constitutes part of the framework of the Bible, which is arranged in such a way that later Scripture illumines earlier. Often what is introduced in a matter-of-fact manner is later, by means of new revelation, found to have far-reaching significance. Or, what is mysterious is subsequently uncovered. For example, the beings in Ezek. 1 are identified in ch. 10 as cherubs, and we ought then to compare them to other appearances of cherubs in the Bible (see ch. 3, How to Study the Bible, on Ezek. 1).

Progressive revelation bridges the testaments when, for example, Zechariah's poetic prophecy of the animated sword (Zech. 13:7) is applied by our Lord Himself to His passion in Mk. 14:27: "I will smite the shepherd, and the sheep shall be scattered" (AV). It is here that we learn that ultimately Christ is the shepherd and the "man who is close to me" (NIV) of Zech. 13:7. And we discover that the verse also contains teaching concerning the relation of the Persons of the Godhead, for the LORD Almighty speaks of a "man" who is close to Himself as only an equal can be. The human Jesus is thus also on the same level as the LORD Almighty.

Furthermore, the divine speaker of Zech. calls up the sword of justice, the instrument that will satisfy the wrath of God against sinners. In a veiled way we are being told that the Father smites the Son, and as He does so He strikes down One who stands in a relationship enjoyed by no other. Of course, it is unlikely that the prophet or his audience understood any of this. Nor should we expect a modern reader to see it on his own in reading Zech. only. Both audiences—then and now—would envision some event associated with the final restoration of Israel, but not much beyond that. Our justification in seeing reference to the Father and Son in Zech. 13:7 comes from Jesus' application to the verse to Himself.[2] In addition, some would question whether it is legitimate to see all of this in the verse, and if so much information is actually present. But the quotation in the N.T. invites us to make the connection, and the theological particulars of the verse in Zech. are then unmistakable.

Another example of a cross-testamental expansion of an apparently insignificant statement is the inclusion of the words of Jacob from Gen. 49:9 in the dramatic description of the two advents of Christ in Rev. 5. The first coming is in lowliness and suffering, the second in power and majesty. He appeared initially as the Root of David, seemingly unimportant, yet qualified to reign (Isa. 11:10). He will subsequently return lionlike as *the* descendant of Jacob to possess the earth (see note, Rev. 5:5).

Contrastive and Completive Relations

There are several ways in which the testaments stand in binary contrastive relationships. These all stem from the presence of progressive revelation and the nature of the N.T. as the recorder of the anticipated completion of what was begun in the O.T. Many of these relationships are complex and overlap in their characteristics.

Preparation and fulfillment. An example of this pervasive feature is the whole sequence of historical events surrounding Israel's being given into the hands of the Gentiles (Dan. 1:1–2), the Babylonian captivity, and the return to the land, no longer having the privilege of self-governance under God. Domination by the Babylonians, Medo-Persians, Greeks, and Romans brought Israel to the time of the presentation of her true King, who was subsequently rejected. The anticipated dominion of a ruler who would crush all Gentile powers (Dan. 2:34–35) has not been completely achieved. The O.T. prepared for Him in prophecy and history, but, although the N.T. records His presentation as a King in fulfillment of the predictions, Israel's enjoyment of her King has been delayed.

In another sense, the prediction in Mal. 3:1 of the coming of a messenger before the Lord is a kind of preparation, subsequently fulfilled when John the Baptist appeared to carry out his ministry. That this interpretation is valid is confirmed in Mt. 11:10, where our Lord specifically states that Malachi's prophecy prepared Israel for John's appearance. In fact, the implication seems to be that Israel should have understood better what that preparatory revelation meant.

Introduction and conclusion. We could view the presentation of the Servant in Isa. 42–55 as an introduction of a figure and associated themes that are concluded in part at the first advent of Christ, the true Servant of God. As with many of these binary relations, the second element has been fulfilled only in part, since the ruling aspect of the Servant's ministry is yet to be manifested (see the second half of Isa. 42:1). This Servant figure, introduced to Israel by Isaiah, finds its explanation and conclusion in the Person and work of Christ.

Anticipation and climax. The vivid description of the regeneration of the remnant of

Israel at the second advent of her Messiah as presented in Zech. 12:10–13:1 and its fulfillment in Rev. 19 certainly gathers in itself many of the longings of the righteous in Israel for national cleansing. Although Rev. 19 itself does not allude to Zech. 12–13, the second half of Rev. 1:7 does, and the event predicted in the latter verse is itself an anticipation early in the book of the victorious advent of the pierced One, described at the climactic point of the book, the appearance of the King of Kings in Rev. 19. Even the book of Revelation serves to heighten the intensity of the longing for the climax anticipated in Zech. 12–13.

Shadow and reality. The writer to the Hebrews, more than any other writer in the N.T., underscores the opaque, anticipatory nature of the Tabernacle, with its numerous features, rituals, and seemingly pointless detail. In Heb. 8:5 the writer points out that the physical tabernacle sanctuary with its priestly functions was actually a "copy and shadow" (NIV) of corresponding heavenly realities. Of course we are moving here in the realm of types, to be discussed more fully below under "Types." But this type and its anticipated fulfillment have been intentionally designed by God to be both partial and unclear.

Much of the biblical disclosure partakes of this hiding quality, for God does not reveal everything at once, He does not reveal to everyone, and He does not reveal in such a way as to allow mockers to toy with His truths. Thus parables are employed in the Bible with the dual purpose of revealing and hiding—revealing to the spiritual, and hiding from the careless. This must be true of the Tabernacle also, especially as it portrays the precious Person and work of our Lord Jesus Christ in obtaining access to the presence of a holy God. But the shadow aspect—which includes both incompleteness and opacity—must have existed also, because the Tabernacle and associated rituals were all physical realities picturing a spiritual reality.

In a sense we see the same phenomenon in the book of Revelation, especially in ch. 9, where physical properties of locusts (like horses, but with human faces, women's hair, lions' teeth, iron breastplates, rushing wings that sound like hooves pounding the ground, tails and stings like scorpions) are all employed by John to describe the spiritual reality of demonic influence and activity. Physical features can only be shadows of the more significant and enduring spiritual realities with which they may be associated. The bread and cup of the Lord's Table are in this sense shadows—although now understood—of the cross-work of Christ. God uses physical things to accommodate our limited participation and experience in the spiritual realm. The Tabernacle is unique, however, in that it is so complex and lies at the very heart of the work of God in bringing people to Himself. We should also note that the Tabernacle is said to be a shadow of "what is in heaven" (Heb. 8:5, NIV). There has been debate over whether there is a "real" Tabernacle in heaven itself. To hold to this, however, is to miss the point. Heaven does not contain physical entities. The work of Christ touched space and time in order to effect the spiritual release of human beings locked in those realms. But God is a spirit-being who dwells in a spiritual realm, and the transaction between the Son, who paid our ransom, and the Father, who accepted it, needed no structure in heaven. The reality *is* the acceptance by the Father of the work of a perfect sacrifice in a manner corresponding exactly to the features of the Tabernacle with its ritual. Notice the words of the second part of Heb. 8:5: "everything according to the pattern" (NIV). We do not need to look for any kind of Tabernacle in heaven.

Thus the extensive revelation centered on the Tabernacle is intended to be anticipatory and preparatory, yet shadowy. Its "meaning" for the spiritual realm could only be dimly understood. This portion of the O.T. awaited the events recorded in the N.T., along with further commentary, to disclose its reality.

We might think here also of a passage such as Eph. 3:3–6. The Scofield note underscores that the union of Jew and Gentile in one Body was not revealed in the O.T. As we look back at the O.T., however, we are able to see that it made allowance for this.[3] Not all the details were given in the O.T., and certainly the essence of the nature of the Body of Christ was not. But many predictions, both direct and in the form of type, laid the groundwork for the revelation of the mystery. For instance, the sweeping prediction of Gen. 12:3 includes blessing for Gentiles, and is not in contradiction to the mystery of Eph. 3. We must be very careful to note, however, that it is very unlikely that any O.T. saint was able to put together the scattered pieces and guess ahead of time what was revealed to Paul. And if we take Eph. 3:3–6 at face value, as we ought to, then we must conclude that Paul was given something new.

Ineffective vs. effective or final. Hebrews 9:9 illustrates another of these binary relations between the testaments as it reveals that sacrifices under the law were unable to bring about the necessary spiritual change, that of a person's being cleansed from sin and being confident of access to God. The ceremonies were thus ineffective, and pointed forward to other kinds of events that would do what they could not. And in Heb. 9:10 the appearance of the effective is linked to "the time of the new order" (NIV). God allowed many centuries to pass with the ineffective but instructive ceremonies in place. In part, the long presence of what was weak highlights the appearance of what is powerful. This contrast forms a key part of the argument of the book of Hebrews, and contributes in an important way to our understanding of the work of Christ. His sacrifice accomplished what long-standing ritual could not. It was and is final, with no chance of being superseded. (See note, Heb. 8:8, and introduction to the book; see notes, Gal. 3:19, 24, and 25.)[4]

Expansion and Focusing of Themes

One of the most complex structural qualities of the relations between the testaments lies in the sequence in which themes or concepts are introduced in the O.T., broadened with added information, connected with other themes as progressive revelation unfolds, and then brought into focus in the N.T. This can be clearly seen as the book of Revelation, in its picture of the events of the millennium and eternal state, gathers together themes from all over the Bible, especially from the O.T. It displays them together and brings them into a state of clarity that did not previously exist. In chs. 21 and 22, especially, many O.T. groups, entities, and doctrines are juxtaposed in relationships that were at best only hinted at before. The throne of God, the river of life, the tree of life, the nations, the Lamb, the presence of God among men, all find their proper place in the New Jerusalem. Granted, we still find this description difficult to understand, but we now learn much more than before by this new focusing.

Certain events that occur earlier in the book bring into focus previous biblical references to Babylon, which appears as a city, a culture, and a spirit of rebellion against God. For the first time it is clearly connected with key spiritual issues. Thus we learn in Rev. 18:13 that it is the spirit of Babylonianism, organized defiance of God, that is the power and machinery behind the spiritual captivity of human beings ("bodies and souls of men" [NIV]). The merchants of the earth, who are far more than innocent traders, have been linked with Babylonian enslavement of their fellows. This must be primarily spiritual enslavement, since it is souls, along with bodies, that are affected. In fact then, Babylonianism has ensnared all, for merchants and victims alike are part of its cargo.

Continuity of Purpose

Pervasiveness of faith. A superficial popular notion concerning the Bible is that before the cross people were to approach God through the law, and after the cross, by faith. In Rom. 4 Paul takes pains to refute this idea, showing that even *before* the law Abraham was declared righteous by faith (see notes to that chapter). If God accepted individuals only on the basis of their faith before the Mosaic law was instituted, then faith must be the constant and uniquely effective way. Paul teaches the same truth in Rom. 1:17, where he quotes Hab. 2:4, showing that the words of God to Habakkuk concerning the centrality of faith fit perfectly with God's disclosure of the way of approach today.

Unified witness to Christ. One of the most fascinating parts of the relations between the testaments is the way Christ is presented uniformly over a long period of time. This is part of the message of Heb. 1:1–2. Not only was more information added through the centuries, but none of it led to contradiction. Such a uniform presentation is due in part to the uniform presence of Christ, as highlighted by statements such as that found in 1 Cor. 10:4, where we are told that Christ was the rock that followed Israel in the wilderness. Similar to this is Jude's statement that "Jesus saved a people out of the land of Egypt" (Jude 5), according to some early manuscripts of the book of Jude (see NIV Scofield note).[5]

Unchanging covenants. In a real sense all of God's dealings with human beings are based on covenants, formal promises He has made to individuals or groups (see note on Covenants, Heb. 8:8, and subject chain on the Covenants; see also in ch. 2, The Nature of the Bible, on covenants, and the following section in this chapter). Walter Kaiser points out how the New Covenant, as part of a larger set of covenants, conditions blessings over a long period of time for different groups:

> The "new" began with the "old" promise made to Abraham and David. Its renewal perpetuated all of those promises previously offered by the Lord and now more. Therefore Christians presently participate in the new covenant now validated by the death of Christ. They participate by a grafting process into the Jewish olive tree and thus continue God's single plan. However, in the midst of this unity of the "people of God" and "household of faith" there is an expectation of a future inheritance. The "hope of our calling" and the "inheritance" of the promise (in contradistinction to our present reception of the promise itself) awaits God's climactic work in history with a revived national Israel, Christ's second advent, his kingdom, and the [new] heavens and the new earth. In that sense, the new covenant is still future and everlasting; but in the former sense, we are already enjoying some of the benefits of the age to come. With the death and resurrection of Christ the last days have already begun (Heb. 1:1 [and 1:2]), and God's grand plan as announced in the Abrahamic-Davidic-New Covenant continues to shape history, culture and theology.[6]

God's rule. The term "kingdom" has different meanings in the Bible. One of these is its use to describe God's constant control of the affairs of humanity. This is expressed in such passages as Ex. 15:8, 18:

And at the blast of Thy nostrils the waters were piled up,
The flowing waters stood up like a heap;
The deeps were congealed in the heart of the sea. . . .
The Lord shall reign forever and ever. (NASB)

Similarly, we read in Ps. 2 of the "kings of the earth" who wag their fingers at God, yet will eventually be crushed by Jehovah's King (vv. 6–9; cf. Rev. 19:4–5, where it is quoted). We must be careful to distinguish between the millennial kingdom of Christ and the eternal kingdom of God. The thousand-year reign of the Messiah is a subdivision of the overall rule of God over humanity. The difference is seen in 1 Cor. 15:24–28:

> Then the end will come, when he hands over the kingdom to God the Father after he has destroyed all dominion, authority and power. For he must reign until he has put all his enemies under his feet. . . . Now when it says that "everything" has been put under him, it is clear that this does not include God himself, who put everything under Christ. When he has done this, then the Son himself will be made subject to him who put everything under him, so that God may be all in all. (NIV)

See note, 1 Cor. 15:24; see also ch. 19, Future Things, concerning the kingdom.

Some Features of Theological Relations Between the Testaments

The Character of God

Because of a superficial reading of the Bible, some conclude that the God of the O.T. differs from the God of the N.T. God seems to be vengeful and legalistically demanding in the O.T., and benign, love-motivated, and quick to forgive in the N.T. If we take the scriptural record as divine revelation we will find ourselves far from this interpretation, and will be guided by such teachings as that found in the words of God recorded in Mal. 3:6: "I the Lord do not change" (NIV). He does not alter, and, although we do not know everything about Him, we do know that He will never present any aspect of Himself which is at variance with what has already been revealed. We may learn more, and certainly will want to sharpen our understanding of what the Bible teaches, but we will not find that He changes in His Person or nature.

Another way to remedy this concept of what Scripture presents is to distinguish God's Person from the variety of His purposes. Various parts of His program appear in Scripture and may possess contrasting features, but *He* does not change.

The Bible emphasizes also that He does not vary in His existence as a trinitarian Being. The Persons of the Trinity are discernible in the O.T., although more is revealed in the N.T. The third Person was present at the creation (Gen. 1:2), etc., and the second Person appeared in preincarnate form on numerous occasions (Gen. 18:1ff, etc.).

There is an important consequence of the fact of the unchangeable nature of God between the testaments. Because God does not change, the way He acts and deals with people does not change either. His words in the O.T. are as true as those in the N.T. In fact, this is one of the keys to understanding the analogical relations between the testaments to be discussed below. God works in the same way throughout history (aside from His varying programs) because He *is* the same through history. Thus, speaking of the unity of God's redemptive activity, F. F. Bruce points out:

> Because it is one continuous history of salvation and the same God who is active throughout its course, words of warning spoken through the prophet Habakkuk at an earlier stage of the history are still applicable: Behold, you scoffers, and wonder, and perish; for I do a deed in your days, a deed you will never believe, if one declares it to you. [Acts 13:40 ff, quoting Hab. 1:5][7]

The words in the O.T. concerning how God saves are consonant with those in the N.T. That is why the N.T. can express its message in terms of the O.T. (see further on in this chapter on quotations). The constant character and nature of God, then, and its revelation in the two testaments is a guarantee of our being able to perceive unity in the Scriptures.

The Enduring Promises of God

The unchanging character of God comes to the fore in the relationships He secures with humanity by means of promises. These promises appear in Scripture as covenants, sovereign pronouncements of God "by which He establishes a relationship of responsibility" between Himself and individuals or groups.[8] In one sense they are the glue that holds God's plan for humanity together, for they connect His redemptive acts with the recipients of the results of those acts. And everywhere in the Bible God's covenants are connected with His nature. In fact, the verse from Mal. quoted above with reference to His constancy is, in context, an explanation of His covenant relations. He has promised to bless Israel. Yet Israel has rebelled and, from a human standpoint and from the perspective of God's anger against sin, deserves to be disinherited and destroyed. Yet it is precisely the promise of God by covenant, based on His character, that guarantees that God will abide by His earlier agreements and not act capriciously.

It is, in fact, a key feature of the biblical covenants that they are supported by the unchangeable God. If they were to depend upon human beings for fulfillment, they would surely fail. This can be seen very clearly in the unilateral nature of the Abrahamic Covenant as confirmed in Gen. 15, where God in a sense sealed the covenant to Abraham without the latter's participation: he was asleep! The covenant can thus be said to be unconditional.

In order to understand the presentation in the N.T. of the incarnation of the second Person of the Trinity and His redemptive work, we must see God's acts against the background of His covenants in the O.T. All He is doing in Christ occurs in fulfillment of covenants. For instance, Luke is quite careful to present the birth of Christ as a significant step toward the realization of the Davidic Covenant given in 2 Sam. 7:16: "And your house and your kingdom shall endure before Me forever; your throne shall be established forever" (NASB). To a people discouraged under Roman dominion, God announces that He has not forgotten His promises to provide Israel with a king to rule on David's throne. Along with other covenant-fulfillment indications (1:17, etc.), Luke records the angel's assertion that "he shall reign over the house of Jacob forever; and of his kingdom there shall be no end" (Lk. 1:32–33a, AV).

In Acts 13 Paul describes the covenant promises to David as a prediction and guarantee of bodily resurrection. Here the introductions to the quotations from the O.T. (see below in this chapter under "The Introductory Formulas") are crucial, for they point out that Paul is associating in a cause/effect relationship the existence of the O.T. statements with the fact of the bodily resurrection of Christ:

> The fact that God raised him from the dead, never to decay, is stated in these words:
> "I will give you the holy and sure blessings promised to David."
> So it is stated elsewhere:
> "You will not let your Holy One see decay." (Acts 13:34–35, NIV)

This double quotation (from Isa. 55:3 and Ps. 16:10) is introduced by Paul in a way that underscores the truth that the O.T. statement concerning the promises to David *had to* issue in the resurrection of David's greater son: "The fact that . . . is stated." It is left, then, to the writing of the N.T. to reveal that Isa. 55:3, the poetic statement of the Davidic Covenant, was actually prophecy. (For a discussion of the nature of the role of the prophet, see below under "Analogical Relations Between the Testaments.")

From the preceding verses in Acts 13 (32–33), we learn that Ps. 2:7 is also a prediction of resurrection:

> We tell you the good news: What God promised our fathers he has fulfilled for us, their children, by raising up Jesus. As it is written in the second Psalm:
> "You are my Son; today I have become your Father." (NIV)

The manner in which this quotation is introduced, along with its juxtaposition with the resurrection topic of vv. 34–35, argues for the fact that it contains an anticipation of the resurrection of one who is called *Son*. Romans 1:3 explains this aspect of Ps. 2 (by the way, a psalm of the messianic King!) by showing that Christ was declared by His resurrection from the dead to be the Son of God. That He was the Son during His earlier ministry is clear. But the resurrection itself was a powerful pronouncement of His new dominion, the same state predicted in Ps. 2. The Davidic descendant is, by resurrection, qualified to assume David's kingship. History now awaits that coronation. And it is Ps. 2 that provides the poetic account of the steps which must take place before the King reigns (see ch. 6, Literary Aspects of the Bible).

Isaiah 55:1–5, quoted in part in Acts 13:34 and one of several expansions of the Davidic Covenant in the O.T., refers to God's "faithful love promised to David" (NIV).[9] God's promises are thus associated with His attribute of faithfulness. They are certain. It is this continuity of the promises of God that the N.T. unfolds from the O.T. (for more on covenants, see ch. 2, The Nature of the Bible).

Examples of Doctrines Developed by the New Testament from the Old Testament

There are many teachings that are expanded and explained in significant ways across the testaments, topics such as grace (see note, Jn. 1:17), the kingdom (see note, 1 Cor. 15:24), etc.[10] One that is often neglected is that of the matter of obtaining access to God, a doctrine that also touches on worship and priesthood. Since the fall, humanity's greatest problem lies in its alienation from its Creator. If we remain alienated, we suffer spiritual death. If we are somehow able to obtain access, we can have life. God has established definite channels for obtaining and retaining access to Himself. These are inextricably bound up with worship and priesthood.

The earliest record of God's activity in this area is found in Gen. 3:21, where, after the fall, God Himself provides coverings for the guilt of Adam and Eve, reflected in part in physical embarrassment. Of course, the first and most telling indicator of their post-fall state was their hiding from the God with whom they had earlier had perfect fellowship (3:8). It is significant that they first tried to cover themselves (3:7). But God showed His demand for a superior covering. This duality between the attempt to face God while dressed in sin-covered apparel, and God's demand for and provision of a unique approach on His own terms, is continued throughout the Bible. It is one of the most pervasive unifying features between the testaments, since it is at the heart of God's work of grace toward humanity.

Shortly afterward, in Gen. 4:1–15, sacrifices appear in the account, associated with approaching God. We should not be surprised to see animals associated with the one who pleases God, and plant life with the displeasing brother. Interestingly, we are never told whether or not Abel knew that he was to bring animal sacrifices. It appears, though, that he was doing what he was supposed to do. Cain must have thought that he was bringing God quite a treat. Were his vegetable and perhaps fruit offerings arranged on trays in much the same way we might lay out decorated appetizers today, with sliced carrots, and radishes sculpted to resemble roses? In any case, the precise point is that even though Cain brought what he must have felt would be acceptable because *he* had toiled over it, his offering was rejected. We may conjecture that Abel brought what he had been told to bring and was accepted for his obedience (see notes, 4:4 and 4:7).

There are at least three important pairs of contrasting elements here. First, there is the polarity between God's appointed way of approach and man's self-designed way. This continues through all of human history, and is, of course, the same duality as expressed in such passages as Eph. 2:1–8 ("dead in trespasses and sins, in which you used to live when you followed the ways of this world . . . By grace you have been saved . . . the gift of God—not by works . . ." [NIV]). The second pair consists of the opposing stances of the righteous and the unrighteous toward each other, reflected, for example, in Ps. 2, where *the* Man of God, His anointed, is plotted against by the nations and their leaders. A third pair consists of human beings in rebellion against God. Hence Cain's murder of Abel (John actually calls it slaughter in 1 Jn. 3:11, where the context is an exhortation to love the brethren in a way the world cannot), his hostility toward his kin, was but a reflection of the deeper hatred he had toward God. This was intrinsic because of the fall, and was brought to the surface, in the biblical account at least, by God's rejection of his offering. He insisted on attempting to come to God by his own devices, a reflection of Satan's own assertion of Isa. 14:14: "I will be like the Most High" (AV).

This attitude is pervasive throughout humanity, and stands in sharp contrast to the biblical presentation of the approach delineated and provided by God. God solves the problems associated with all three pairs of conditions as He establishes a successful way of approach (Heb. 9:22—"without the shedding of blood there is no forgiveness" [NIV]), removes the enmity between human beings and Himself (2 Cor. 5:18—"All this is from God, who reconciled us to himself through Christ" [NIV]), and makes it possible for human beings to love each other as they are loved by God (Eph. 2:14— "made the two one and has destroyed the barrier, the dividing wall of hostility . . ." [NIV]; 1 Jn.

3:11–12a—''For this is the message which you have heard from the beginning, that we should love one another; not as Cain *who* was of the evil one, and slew his brother'' [NASB]).

The continual biblical emphasis, then, is that God Himself, by His grace, provides a means for human beings to approach Him. This is reflected in the establishment of sacrificial systems through the O.T. Actually, until the law, we are told very little about what sacrifices do and how they are to be carried out. In Gen. 8:20 Noah sacrifices animals after the flood subsides, apparently in thanksgiving for deliverance. But we learn (vv. 21–22) that God viewed it also as a request-sacrifice, since in response to it He gave the Noahic Covenant. Apparently here Noah is acting in the role that we later see as that of a priest, bringing sacrifices.

The next important scene in the sequence is in Gen. 14, where one who is specifically called a priest, the startling figure of Melchizedek, appears with Abraham (see note, Gen. 14:18). He acts in a role of spiritual superiority to Abraham, not that Abraham could not know God by himself, but that Melchizedek in some way possessed greater privilege in the matter of official access to God. He was the mediator of God's blessing to Abraham (Gen. 14:19 and Heb. 7:1) and is said to be superior to Abraham (Heb. 7:7). Although this may seem opaque in Gen. 14, a comparison with the priesthood under the law shows that Melchizedek is parallel in function to the Levitical priests, in that they both in some way mediate access to God and spiritual blessing. In other words, with Melchizedek we begin to see that God works through intermediaries.

Did Melchizedek offer sacrifices? It appears that he did, but in a fascinating way. Bypassing the animal sacrifices of the Mosaic Covenant, he brings to Abraham in a victory celebration the same two elements as were ordained for the Lord's Table. It seems that in this way he prefigures the work of our Lord Jesus Christ on the cross, reflected in the bread and wine. It is this, along with other tantalizing correspondences, that makes Melchizedek such a suitable, and important, figure in the unfolding of the Epistle to the Hebrews. The writer saw that in significant ways Melchizedek lay at the heart of the access-work of Christ. So the Son, the perfect Priest, like Melchizedek, finally obtains the perfect access no one else could, as described in Heb. 7:25: ''Therefore he is able to save completely those who come to God through him, because he always lives to intercede for them'' (NIV; Melchizedek is treated at greater length below in this ch. under ''An Example of Analogical Relationships Between the Testaments Centered in a Type'').

Up to the time of Melchizedek there is clearly a restriction on the function and office of priest. We are told nothing about how individuals became priests or what they were to do. How Melchizedek knew what his functions were, and how and when he was appointed by God, are details which God has not chosen to reveal. The same can be said of Noah. With the Mosaic law we get for the first time a clear picture of how God appoints priests, at least in one priestly scheme. It is noteworthy that under the law there is still a limited priesthood. Only a few can approach God in ceremonies. In the case of the Levites, it is a group working together.

It is with the priesthood of Christ that the picture shifts radically. The number of priests changes in an interesting way. Christ is the only priest who can do, and has done finally, what is necessary to bring human beings to God. He accomplished it with a perfect sacrifice (Heb. 7:27). But now there is also a large company of priests, as extensive as the number of the children of God in this age (1 Pet. 2:5), offering sacrifices spiritually, instead of physically, as the Levitical priests did in the Tabernacle and

Temple. As stones they form a new Temple, a spiritual one. And this is possible because, as they come through the perfect Priest, they have perfect access to God. The
sacrifice to end all physical sacrifices, superior to all those going back as far as Noah,
has made possible what they could not and what they only prefigured by their acts—
entrance into fellowship with a holy God. It is clear that God allowed access to Himself
before that perfect sacrifice was made. But all the O.T. sacrifices were in some way
instructive concerning the nature of the only effective one. And so the writer to the
Hebrews exhorts his readers to offer spiritual sacrifices (Heb. 13:15–16). All are now a
company of priests destined for rule with Christ (Rev. 5:10). The many sacrifices of the
Levitical priests are replaced by many sacrifices of believers looking back at the work
of the Son.

With this we see another important aspect of sacrifices in relation to the matter of
access to God. The acts of believer-priests today are retrospective in nature. Sacrifices
are offered in response to access which has been provided. Apparently Noah's sacrifice
was also a thanks-response. And Melchizedek prefigured this celebration aspect, also.
In effect their sacrifices were based on confidence in the provision of God. The Levitical
system involved both request- and thank-offerings. And, of course, the great high-priestly
act occurring once a year was a request for access done according to the ritual prescribed
by God. The believer-priest today looks back and says, in effect, "The matter of access
is settled. I can rest and, because of grace, need make no attempt to get to God, on my
own or through anyone else. He has provided a way. I do now, however, have the
responsibility of thanking Him." The believer's sacrifices take four forms today: (1) the
offering of the body (Rom. 1:12–13); (2) the offering of praise/thanks (Heb. 13:15); (3)
the offering of time and effort in doing good (Heb. 13:16); and (4) the offering to God
of our physical goods by sharing with others (Heb. 13:16). It is significant, in connection with this last sacrifice, that the giving of money by a believer in this age is clearly
described as a priestly act, as it is in Phil. 4:14–19.

We should ask how worship fits with all of this. Before revelation of the assurance
of access provided by the cross, those approaching God came with requests for access
and with thanks, if they understood His acceptance of them by grace. They were wor-
shipping. Now the believer worships with thanks only, for the issue of access is no
longer in doubt. Final access has been obtained (Heb. 10:19–20).

In several places in the O.T. and N.T. there is a beautiful figure associated with
this theological theme of access. Our need is for fellowship with God in this life, and
for future fellowship which is unhindered by sin. For some individuals in the Bible
these goals appear at times to be too distant. Can we have fellowship with God, and
will we ever dwell with Him apart from the confusion of this world? Will God's program bring about a time in which the righteous do enjoy Him, the unrighteous are
excluded, and sin is punished (see above on Cain and Abel)? In Gen. 28:10–22 Jacob
experiences the heavenly stairway dream. If we had only this passage we would have
some difficulty in understanding its significance. However, in Jn. 1:51 our Lord tells us
that He Himself is the ladder. Jacob must have seen what amounted to a picture of the
spiritual reality of the provision by God of access to heaven. Interestingly enough, his
conclusion is that he has seen "the gate of heaven" (Gen. 28:17, NIV). The work of
the Lord Jesus Christ, then, is described by these two passages from the O.T. and N.T.
as involving the provision of a bridge between earth and heaven, at one end of which
is the gate to heaven. Jacob correctly assesses the importance of the experience by
observing that God is present and the location is "awesome" (NIV). It is also interest-

ing that the specific content of God's words has to do with the Abrahamic Covenant, whose fulfillment demands participation by individuals in the eternal life provided by God. In other words, to enjoy the Abrahamic Covenant and the land (Gen. 28:15)— actually guaranteed by the Palestinian Covenant—an Israelite, including Jacob, would first have to experience fellowship with God through His provision of access.

We find a further development of the open heaven motif in the first vision given to Ezekiel. The specific statement of Ezek. 1:1 is that "the heavens were opened and I saw visions of God" (AV). The essence of the vision is that God is present with Israel in fulfillment of His covenants, and is very much involved with the affairs of the earth. He is not distant, but rather appears sitting on a throne-chariot surrounded by angels who are doing His bidding. This revelation of the nearness of God was designed to show Israel that they could count on His intimate interest in and direction of their affairs as they were in captivity in Babylon. They could, as the unfolding message of Ezek. explains, enjoy Him through obedience, national repentance and humility. We ought to be alert to this figure of the open heaven as being a way of describing fellowship with and enjoyment of God. It should also be a startling teaching, for the truth is that God does not have to come to human beings, much less have fellowship with them. He is under no obligation to give access to heaven. However, the pattern of His dealing with sin—begun with the skins in the garden—unfolds through the Scriptures with striking presentations of the gracious provision of God: He does allow human beings into His presence, He will permit them to enter heaven, and does interact intimately with affairs on earth.

It is not surprising that at the beginning of the ministry of the incarnate second Person there are two important openings of heaven, the ladder teaching of Jn. 1:51, and the description of the presence of God at the baptism of Christ, where Matthew records: "As soon as Jesus was baptized, he went up out of the water. At that moment heaven was opened, and he saw the Spirit of god descending like a dove and lighting on him" (Mt. 3:16 NIV). The ministry of Jesus, then, is announced at this point as being associated with an accessible heaven. In a subsequent N.T. book it is an individual who walked with God who is granted a glimpse into heaven at the most crucial point in his life. Stephen sees his Savior as he declares, moments before his martyrdom, " 'Behold, I see the heavens opened up and the Son of Man standing at the right hand of God' " (Acts 7:56, NASB). His access to God was such that He revealed to him a glimpse of his new home to assure him of the fact that he pleased Him by his message in the face of intense hostility. We should remember also the sudden departures of Enoch (Gen. 5:24) and Elijah (2 Ki. 2:11–12). Heaven was quite open to those godly individuals.

But it remains for the book of Revelation to tie together elements appearing earlier in Scripture, as in 4:1 the throne room of God is disclosed through "a door standing open in heaven." At this crucial point in the Apocalypse, the appearance of this access motif reveals that God is about to actualize a longed-for promise of the ages—that God would dwell with humanity. This is access to God with a plus: people can enjoy fellowship with Him over a period of time. Later we learn that this will occur in a kingdom presided over by the God-man, ruling on the throne of David. Further, the creation of the New Heavens and the New Earth will result in a sinless state where there will be perfect fellowship and perfect service—enjoyment of the presence of God and the opportunity to return to Him in love some of the grace shown to the redeemed. So John tells us, "The throne of God and of the Lamb will be in the city, and his servants will serve him. They will see his face, and his name will be on their foreheads" (Rev.

22:3–4, NIV). Those with access will be His possession! This is all attributable to the work of the perfect Sacrifice, the Lamb/Priest, Who gave Himself to obtain access for those who know Him. The curtain in the Temple, torn from top to bottom—because the solution to the access problem came from a heavenly source, not an earthly—showed the final provision of God for alienated humanity (see note, Mt. 27:51).

Thus we can see that a key biblical theme is unfolded step by step through the testaments as progressive revelation gradually expands the teaching and our understanding. The testaments depend on each other for the complete picture. And they complement each other in a beautiful presentation. God's acts from Gen. to Rev. are unified but multifaceted. We miss too much if we do not take the time to compare and search through both testaments in regard to this or any other area of revealed truth.

Analogical Relations Between the Testaments

The Nature of Analogy

In myriads of situations in life, we make use of our ability to associate like things. In particular, it is useful to be able to describe one entity in terms of another, especially where one is better known than the other. The process of reasoning in which we associate any two (or more) entities by means of like features is called analogy.[11]

In human existence almost anything can be viewed as standing in an analogical relation to something else. Two males who are six feet tall have such a relationship. If they are both blond, have two children and work as letter carriers, then the analogical relationship is compound. Now of course no one would attempt to say there could be perfect correspondence between them, that is, every possible feature that could be listed for each is exactly duplicated in the other. Life does not work that way. In the case of this pair, we can say that no two human beings are ever completely alike, even in the case of twins, where analogical relations would be quite extensive, although the relation between twins, especially identical ones, would be an excellent example of naturally occurring analogy.

The Bible is filled with analogical relationships extending in many directions. There is an analogical relationship between God and His creatures who are made in His image (see note, Gen. 1:26). We have been fashioned so that we are individual persons, having the ability for thought and possessing moral capacity. As the note points out, the analogy is not perfect, that is, it breaks down when we come to the categories of duration and magnitude (God is infinite and we are finite) and the realm of existence (He is a spirit-being and we are physical beings with a spiritual capacity).

There is such a relation between Christ and those united to Him in this age—the Body of Christ—and a human body (see notes, 1 Cor. 12:1; Eph. 5:32). The human body has diverse, interconnected parts which must all function according to their assigned task for the whole to prosper. All are directed by the brain, with its unique function of commanding and integrating. It is the same with the Body of Christ. Paul points out in 1 Cor. 12 that it is foolish for physical body parts to attempt to act in isolation out of feelings of uniqueness. And so also it is out of place and even harmful for members of the Body of Christ to exalt themselves over other parts of the body and try to live in isolation. The effectiveness of Paul's instruction in 1 Cor. 12–14 depends in great part on the existence and clarity of this Body/body analogy.

Certainly, then, Paul uses this anology, a structural and literary feature, in order to enhance his message. There are many other such comparisons found throughout Scripture. Many of these spring from ordinary relations and features in life: meals, occupations (shepherd, potter), animals (sheep, goats, birds), trees (branches, leaves, roots, grafting), etc. All help us to move from the familiar to the unfamiliar. We understand more quickly and remember better when such analogies are used, since we are accustomed to seeing them everywhere in life, and, more importantly, they help us to visualize in terms of our own existence spiritual concepts which by their very nature involve features that we cannot see or handle.

Categories of Analogy Found in Relations Between the Testaments

In the relations between the testaments there exist a large number of analogous situations and entities. They were put there by God to aid our understanding of Him and His purposes, and to tie together and illumine the two main parts of His revelation, given as it was over such a long period of time.

There are two main categories of analogical features that occur across the testaments—types and prophecy. Similar to them in many respects are two other features of the biblical text, allegory and parables. All four involve both literary and theological elements. Although the latter two do not figure prominently in intertestamental relations, we will discuss them here in order to illumine the use of types and prophecy.

One of the reasons all four must be discussed at the same time is that it is often difficult to define one apart from reference to the other, as K. J. Woollcombe indicates:

> It is not easy to give a precise definition of the nature and scope of typology. As an exegetical method, it bears some resemblance to allegorism; in so far as it deals with the linkages between the Old and New Testaments, it is akin to the study of the fulfillment of prophecy. Hence the word 'typology' has often been used in a broad sense to cover the study of *all* the linkages between the two Testaments.[12]

Types. It is in the realm of typological relationships that the fullest range of analogical elements can be seen. And it is the phenomenon of types that, of the four categories discussed in this section, contributes the most to our understanding of the relations between the testaments.

A type is usually defined as a divinely ordained prefiguration in the O.T. of some N.T. reality. Further, the O.T. entity must be historically real, and so must that in the N.T. The correspondence relates in some way to the redemptive work of God, and must show evidence of being established by God. This serves to rule out many fanciful correspondences. There is little debate among Bible scholars concerning the existence of at least some typology in the N.T.

It may be that simply calling an O.T./N.T. correspondence a type may be too restrictive. Types are only one part of a range of relationships that exists in Scripture because of such things as the unity of the divine program, the constancy of God, and the phenomenon of partial statement followed by fulfillment. The key to the whole matter may be to see the existence of the principle of correspondence in the divine ordering of events.

It is also helpful to distinguish between typology as a feature of the biblical text, and typology as a method of looking at the text. Woollcombe points out that:

Typology, considered as a method of exegesis, may be defined as the establishment
of historical connexions between certain events, persons or things in the Old Testament and similar events, persons or things in the new Testament.[13]

Allegory. The word *allegory* is also used in two ways. First, it can refer to allegory
contained in the Bible and manifestly placed there by the writers. The key elements in
allegory as a feature of the text are the existence of narrative (i.e., a story), continuity
of analogy (not just one or a few comparisons), and simultaneity of the events or ideas
on the two levels (see ch. 6, Literary Aspects of the Bible, for more on allegory).

On the other hand, *allegorical interpretation* is an approach to the Bible that looks
for certain kinds of relationships, attempting to find hidden meanings underneath surface
or obvious meanings. Utilized extensively by some Church fathers and rejected decisively by reformers such as Luther and Calvin, it is generally not accepted today by
orthodox interpreters as a valid method (see ch. 5, Interpreting the Bible).[14] As practiced in the early Church, it was based on a view of the Bible as "a single vast volume
of oracles and riddles, a huge book of secret puzzles to which the reader has to find
clues."[15] The ancient allegorists used the literal sense as a starting point, but viewed
the O.T. as applicable to Christ or Christians without much regard for its original significance.[16] There is only one passage in Scriptures that in some translations is described
as allegory, and that is in Gal. 4:21–31, where in the AV, for instance, v. 24 reads
"Which things are an allegory . . ." The NIV, however, places the account of Sarah
and Hagar in the realm of types, saying that the two women have a figurative significance and are part of a correspondence (vv. 24–25). Since Paul does not at all deny the
significance of the two women in their primary historical setting, this cannot be taken
as an allegory. Actually then, the NIV translation gives valid insight into the nature of
types, taking Paul to be saying that a representative relationship exists between the two
women and some features of God's redemptive plan.

Woollcombe suggests a distinction between typological interpretation (exegesis)
and allegorical interpretation:

> Typological exegesis is the search for linkages between events, persons or things
> *within the historical framework of revelation,* whereas allegorism is the search for a
> secondary and hidden meaning underlying the primary and obvious meaning of a
> narrative. This secondary sense of a narrative, discovered by allegorism, does not
> necessarily have any connexion at all with the historical framework of revelation.[17]

Parables. Parables are illustrative accounts in which the historicity of figures and events
is not necessary. The main point is the existence of a comparison between the elements
of the story and spiritual truths to which they correspond. Like types and all figurative
language, parables have the function of revealing and hiding at the same time. And they
may be prophetic in nature, as in the case of the kingdom parables (see note, Mt.
13:11ff). They can point beyond their time to future fulfillment by the appearance of
the greater reality corresponding to the elements of their particular account. Thus the
parable of the mustard seed (Mt. 13:31–32; Mk. 4:30–32) is predictive in that it describes conditions which will exist during the course of this age as it leads to the kingdom. Among the types of analogical reasoning in the Bible, parables especially make
use of the ordinary events of life: lost sheep, agriculture, etc. (see ch. 6, Literary Aspects of the Bible, for more on parables.)
Prophecy. The word *prophecy,* in biblical studies, and in the Bible itself, has varied

meanings. The words of a biblical prophet (one holding the office or one functioning as a prophet) may either foretell events to come, or refer only to contemporary events. At times, a prophet's utterances do both. Either type may be designed to comfort, exhort, or denounce. *Nabhi*, the term translated "prophet" in the O.T., means literally "forth-teller." The prophet is thus a spokesman for God, publicly designated or not. In the wider sense, all the revelatory words of a biblical prophet can be called prophecy. In what follows we will be speaking of prophecy as predictive utterance.

General Principles Associated with Analogy Across the Testaments

All of the analogical relations across the testaments depend for their existence and efficacy on several general principles connected with God's dealings with humanity.

1. There is a God who orders events in history and is completely sovereign over the affairs of human beings. We should not be surprised to see correspondences of events in one period of biblical history with those in another. God directs historical occurrences so that they achieve His purposes, which may at times involve illustration of other truths. It is likely that these correspondences are much more complex than is usually thought. We will undoubtedly continue to find more of them in the biblical text. In this connection it has been noted that history itself is prophetic.[18]

2. Progressive revelation is intrinsic to analogical relationships, because patterns of correspondence emerge as God adds new information to old. For instance, in the case of Jacob's stairway, it is only when our Lord declares in John's Gospel that He is the stairway (1:51) that we see how far-reaching that dream is. The addition of the N.T. then, establishes the O.T. as containing half of the analogy.

3. God deals progressively with humanity. Not only does He not reveal all at once, but He also takes people—both individuals and groups—through different steps. In the case of Israel, He establishes them as a people beginning with Abraham, guides the race through experiences in and out of the land, reveals the Law, brings a Savior-Messiah on the scene, provides for sin, revokes the Law, and places the nation under a judicial sentence due to its hardening. Different stages in Israel's history are occasions for the establishment of various analogical relationships, as in the case of Jacob.

4. The Bible everywhere testifies to the existence of an unchanging God. Relations of analogy draw much of their force from the fact that God always carries out what He purposes to do, and exactly as He predicts. He controls history, is never thwarted in doing so, and, based on His own immutable character, brings continuity to the human scene. The Tabernacle can thus be somehow like the Person and work of Christ, because God establishes unvarying relationships in life, history, and the unfolding plan of salvation—all connected with His constancy.[19]

5. One of the major features of God's revelation is that there is a progression in significance from the O.T. to the N.T. We must explain this carefully, however. It is not the case that the O.T. is less important than the N.T. Nor is it an inferior record. And its testimony to the character of God is no less accurate. But it is true that the announcements of the New in relation to the Old come as quantum leaps forward in the progression of the plan of God. It is this feature that lies behind the statement of Gal. 4:4–5, that "when the time had fully come, God sent his Son, born of a woman, born under law, to redeem those under law, that we might receive the full rights of sons" (NIV). The law has been superseded by a better way, but the law was no less from God because

of this. The revelations to the fathers through the prophets were all true, but the superior revelation has come in the Son (Heb. 1:1–2). This could be described also as an intensification or escalation.[20] It is based on the conviction that in the future God will do things similar to those He did in the past, but on a greater scale.[21] Thus we are to look forward with anticipation from the O.T. portions of the comparisons to those found in the N.T.—anticipation of greater insight into the wonderful things of God.

6. The inability of human beings to work confidently within the spiritual realm (see Rom 8:26) occasions God's grace to give us abundant pictorial portrayals of spiritual truths. The presence of analogies is an accomodation to our weakness as well as an indication of the wonderful complexity of the elements of the written Word of God. This is especially so in the case of those spiritual issues that have not touched space and time as much as others. We can understand the analogy between the death of Christ for helpless sinners and the love of a husband for his wife, because His death occurred in space and time, where we live. And we are familiar with human death, even though we cannot fully understand His kind of sacrifice. But when the Tabernacle is said to picture elements of the relationship between the Father and Son and the transaction that removed our sins (Heb. 9:21–25)—a purely spiritual reality—then we are indebted much more to the presence of this analogy/explanation in Scripture.[22]

7. Underlying analogical relations between the testaments is the unity of divine revelation, without which we could only see chance correspondences. Some recent theologians who have not held that the Scriptures are an inspired record have suggested that typology is the approach to Scripture that sees analogous relations between the testaments that exist because there are recurring patterns discernible in God's dealings with people and because the writers of the two testaments shared a common cultural and religious heritage.[23] In fact, for them these are the primary unifying factors of Scripture. Hence, in regard to prophecy, those representing this kind of position would say that the prophets did not foresee events as pure prediction, but rather that they were involved in cyclical patterns of God's activities.[24] They do not believe that Scripture is a single harmonious body of revealed truth, and so cannot see patterns established intentionally by God in the O.T. in anticipation of parallel events in the N.T.[25] It does not take much to see that this empties the Bible of the miraculous element of transcendence of time by means of precognition. Biblical typology, to be more than guesswork, must be viewed against the background of the divinely established unity of the testaments.

8. Part of the use of symbolism in the Bible occurs in the realm of analogical relations. Symbolic relations involve one entity standing in for another, and it is easy to see that this is involved in the analogical relations between the Testaments, where a N.T. entity is represented in some way by an entity in the O.T. As a kind of shorthand, symbols take the place, in particular contexts, of the entities they refer to, yet are never as necessary as what they represent. Once we know from the book of Hebrews that Melchizedek pictures Christ, the appearance of Melchizedek in Gen. 14 says to today's reader, in effect, "At this point skip in your thinking to the greater Melchizedek." This is not to say that Melchizedek is less historical or real than Christ, only that Melchizedek serves to point to Christ. And this is the nature of symbols. They are pointers that have secondary value within a structured system (in our case, the progress of revelation) in relation to what they point to. This is not to say that all symbols are types, or that the symbolic element is all there is to types.[26]

9. As implied by much that has already been said, the analogical relations between the testaments involve the issue of promise and fulfillment. Old Testament portions of

the analogies must have been given by God in part in order to encourage inquiry into what was to come. Those people described in 1 Pet. 1:10–11 were probably spurred to investigate the appearance of the Messiah by elements presented in types as well as prophecy, since many of the "sufferings of Christ" were presented in channels other than purely predictive utterances. So Peter comments on their intense interest in the fulfillment portion of the two-part work of God, preparation and realization:

> Concerning this salvation, the prophets, who spoke of the grace that was to come to you, searched intently and with the greatest care, trying to find out the time and circumstances to which the Spirit of Christ in them was pointing when he predicted the sufferings of Christ and the glories that would follow. (1 Pet. 1:10–11, NIV)

They had understood clearly that there was a promise. And they were correctly attempting to uncover its details. Interestingly enough, the statement of Peter in its context suggests that they would always be moving in the realm of incomplete and shadowy things, since it remained for those living in the new age to be able to see the whole picture. In fact, Peter tells his readers that the message was intended primarily for them, and not for the prophets (v. 12). And so Paul says in a similar vein, "Now these things happened to them as an example, and they were written for our instruction, upon whom the ends of the ages have come" (1 Cor. 10:11, AV). The "things" are part of a typological relationship involving disobedience in the wilderness and the spiritual life of the Corinthians. The O.T., by virtue of the promise and fulfillment element, has lessons that it is crucial for us to apply in the present age.

Relations Between Types and Prophecy

The relationship between types and prophecy is complex, but an investigation is very instructive. There are several descriptive categories which apply to both, so we will treat types and prophecy together.

In regard to time. It is usual to see types as extending from the O.T. to corresponding features in the N.T., fulfilled in the incarnation and the events surrounding the redemptive work of Christ. However, some types clearly possess application to the ongoing church age, as in the case of the rock in the wilderness, which, in 1 Cor. 10, has the Lord's Supper as its counterpart. In terms of the relation between the time of prediction and the time of fulfillment, we can say the following:

> 1. Prophecy may appear in the O.T. and be fulfilled there (e.g., Hab. 1:6; see note).
> 2. Prophecy may extend from the O.T. to the N.T. and be fulfilled in whole or in part there (e.g., Mic. 5:2).
> 3. Prophecy may extend from the O.T. beyond the N.T., without fulfillment having occurred yet (e.g., Ps. 110:1b; see note on Ps. 110).
> 4. Prophecy may be found in the N.T. and fulfilled in the N.T., as in the case of Christ's own predictions concerning His death.
> 5. Prophecy may be found in the N.T. with extension into what is still future (e.g., 2 Th. 2:8; see note at 2:3).

An example of the last correspondence would be the picture in Eph. 5:25–32 of the Church as the Bride of Christ. Strictly speaking, only v. 27 is predictive, and the other verses teach how husbands should love their wives on the basis of the ongoing and future love of Christ for the Church, His Bride.

Interestingly, this kind of nonpredictive N.T. correspondence to a yet future entity is not usually viewed as a type. It should be noted, however, that in a sense a type is no less predictive than a prophetic utterance that concerns a future event. Both are part of God's process of announcing ahead of time what He is going to do. Furthermore, a type gives information only in part, just as a prophetic utterance does.

In regard to events and utterances. One could say that prophecies are correspondences and predictions in words and verbal description, and types are correspondences and predictions in actions, characters and institutions. Necessarily, types have the quality of the real existence of those actions, characters, and institutions in the O.T., while prophecy need only have the real existence of the utterance. Both are miraculous because they transcend time.

It is usually said that David in Ps. 22 is a predictive type, but that Melchizedek (Gen. 14:18–20) is not. In part this is because all of what is described of Melchizedek was true of him, while probably not all that is described by David in Ps. 22 (aside from the fact that it was written by him) was true of him. At times the details of the psalm appear to pass beyond what he could have ever experienced, as with v. 18, for example.[27] Although the precise application to David may be debated, it seems true that at some points the psalm moves from being true of David in a literal sense to being true only of Christ. Then, of course, it is purely predictive and does not differ from prophecy, although it is still couched in terms of the poet's own experience. And, as mentioned above under relations to time, if a correspondence is God-intended, the type is necessarily predictive. Since a type, by definition, points to something future, it is a prediction, at least in some sense.

However, the other side of the coin is that some prophecies may have fulfillment in some way at the time of utterance, yet await a greater fulfillment in the N.T. In Isa. 7 the prediction of the virgin birth of Christ is at the same time a short-range prophecy of doom to come on Ahaz. The sign of v. 14 is designed to be an encouragement to those who trust God and a sign of judgment on the faithless king and his court (v. 13; see note at 7:14). Both type and prophecy, then, can be interwoven with the time and life of the individual associated with them. (For more on prophecy, see ch. 5, Interpreting the Bible.)

Extent of Occurrence of Types

The question of how many types exist in Scriptures has been much debated in recent centuries. (In one sense, along with explicit types (e.g., 1 Cor. 10:11), there are many implicit correspondences at different levels, some merging with prophecy.) Some have believed that only those N.T. features specifically labeled in the text as types should be viewed as such. Others have gone too far in the other direction, seeing specific correspondences to Christ and His work, for example, in every minute detail of the tabernacle. The problem that many sense with this is that there is no check on the fancy of the interpreter. The Scofield Bible is conservative in its approach to types (see note, Gen. 2:23). It recognizes only explicit types, but notes that the principle of analogy is inherent in many more relationships. Since the present chapter is not designed as an exhaustive treatment of types, nor as a justification for typological interpretation of Scripture, but simply as an overview of important issues with suggestions as to how to approach the Scriptures, we cannot deal at length with different occurrences of types.[28] But in one sense it could be said that since prophecy and typology are all part of one extensive, complex system of analogical relations, the question of *how many* types there are in the Bible or what specific entities are types is irrelevant. What is important is that the student of Scripture see the hand of God present in ordering events between the testaments.

One recent writer has said, "Almost every area of typological interpretation is unsettled."[29] Types have suffered from abuse as well as neglect. Well-meaning individuals have spent inordinate amounts of time looking for details of types, while systematic study of how to approach them as been scant.[30] They are too important, as part of what has been called the "divinely planned mosaic pattern of Holy Scripture,"[31] to be neglected. The following suggestions may be helpful in the study of types.

1. Identify those N.T. entities that are specifically labeled as having an analogical relation with something in the O.T. Sometimes the presence of analogical and perhaps typical relations can be indicated by words such as *tupikōs* ("typologically," 1 Cor. 10:10), *tupos* ("type," "example," "pattern," Heb. 8:5), *skia* ("shadow," "foreshadowing," Heb. 8:5; Col. 2:17).

2. Look for the presence of manifest connection between O.T. and N.T. entities. Does the correspondence show the hand of God in guiding history?

3. The O.T. portion must be real and present in history, as must the corresponding N.T. entity, the antitype.

4. Ask if the correspondence between type and antitype is valuable in illuminating teachings of the Bible elsewhere. In other words, is it useful, or simply entertaining?

5. Do not build essential doctrinal understanding on types. Since they are really a secondary element in revelation and are by their very nature veiled, it is easy to miss parts of correspondence or see what is not there. Use them to shed light on what is taught clearly elsewhere.

6. Be careful not to see types everywhere. Some have spent so much time on types that they have missed the main messages of the Bible.

7. Follow N.T. guidelines in seeing types. The N.T. shows that the Tabernacle and the wilderness wanderings are the two major areas of typical relations.[32]

8. Do not try to force every point of the two entities into a correspondence. This often leads to nonsense. Types are prediction woven into history. Try to separate what is intended as prophetic from what is simply natural in life. Analogical language, including types, metaphor, etc., is notorious for being ragged at the edges of the comparison.

The reader may consult standard works on interpreting the Bible, especially Mickelsen and Ramm (listed under "Biblical Interpretation" in ch. 23, Annotated Bibliography), for other guidelines for the study of types and prophecy. See ch. 5, Interpreting the Bible, for general approaches to prophecy. The detailed example of an analogical relationship given in the next section should serve to demonstrate interpretive methodology.

An Example of Analogical Relationships Between the Testaments Centered in a Type

One of the most interesting and complex types in the N.T. is found in the book of Hebrews, where Melchizedek is presented as standing in an analogical relationship to

Christ and His priestly work. It is rich in parallelism that contributes to the important theological points the writer is making as he presents the finality of Christ's sacrifice as the basis for the annulment of the law. A systematic approach to this typologically oriented passage will illustrate many of the points made in the previous sections.

The analogical elements are explicitly placed in the realm of types by the words of 7:3, where it is said that Melchizedek has been made like or has become like the Son of God (NIV—"like the Son of God," AV—"made like unto the Son of God"). When this relationship is seen as part of the general pattern of divinely ordered correspondences between the testaments, the words can be taken as a statement of divine intent. It was God who shaped Melchizedek's existence, ministry, and appearance with Abraham so that they formed a multifaceted parallel to the Person and work of the Son of God. Furthermore, in light of the sheer number of correspondences that are set forth by the writer (many of which are commented on), we would be negligent if we were to fail to see the typological significance of this presentation. The elements of the relationship are actually spread over several chapters in the book of Hebrews, in part because the theological issues are so complex, and in part because of the writer's habit of introducing a topic and not developing it until later.[33]

Some have argued that Melchizedek was simply an appearance of Christ in the O.T. The account in Gen. 14 would thus be only one of many so-called theophanies (appearances of God) before the incarnation. (It should be noted that all theophanies are Christophanies, appearances of Christ, the second Person of the Trinity, before the incarnation, since we are told in John 1:18 that no one has ever seen God, that is, God the Father. Likewise, all Christophanies are theophanies, since Christ is God.) But the existence of the illustrative parallels between Melchizedek and Christ, along with the theological foundation that is found in Melchizedek, would, if Gen. 14 were viewed as containing a theophany, make Christ a picture of Himself. In order for the account to have theological significance in relation to the cross-work of Christ, the priesthood of Melchizedek must be an independent one, held by a real human being living during O.T. times.

The analogical elements touching on the presentation of Melchizedek include prophecy as well as type, since the writer to the Hebrews takes the oath verse of Ps. 110:4 as a prediction of the new priesthood of Christ. As is true of the whole book, the writer to the Hebrews makes extensive use of the O.T. by way of direct quotation. In fact, it is safe to say that he could not have written the book that he wrote without the O.T., since the former is saturated with the latter in quotation, allusion, and theology. An O.T. prophecy serves as the first direct introduction of the topic of Melchizedek, since the quotation from Ps. 110 in 5:6 contains the book's first mention of the priest's name. Altogether this determinative O.T. verse is utilized in one form or another three times (5:6; 7:17, 21), and perhaps a fourth, if 6:20 is counted. Interwoven with these specific supportive quotes is the concept of approved sonship as a basis for priesthood, supported by quotations from Ps. 2:7, found in 5:5 and developed in 5:7–10 and 7:28. Sonship is introduced as early as 1:2, however, and supported by an explicit quotation from Ps. 2:7 in 1:5. It is interesting also that the concept of a solemn asseveration by God, as exemplified in the oath of Ps. 110:4, is introduced earlier in the book in a different but related connection (3:11). Thus prophecy and type are woven together in a complex presentation. The author sees both as contributing interactively to the development of his N.T. material.

The author uses the concept of Melchizedek to draw together a number of theological elements. The individual is first mentioned in 5:6 and 10 in connection with the appointment of priests. Then, after the issue of access to God by priesthood (a key issue throughout the book) is introduced (5:9ff), he appears again in 6:20, and full development follows in ch. 7. Yet the matter of priesthood is actually presented earlier in chs. 1 and 2 where the deity and perfect humanity of Christ are found as the prerequisites for His being a perfect Priest. The actual description of Melchizedek in ch. 7 is connected most closely with the issue of superiority of one priesthood over another in terms of providing and maintaining access to God. Since access, priesthood, Melchizedek, and Christ have already been introduced before ch. 7, the author can proceed to bring in, through a description of the correspondences, the issue of superiority. He will later add to this sequence topics such as the relation of Christ's priestly work to the New Covenant and the need for appropriation of the priestly truths by the readers. These and many other complicated relationships are the product of an author who "knows at each moment precisely what his next sentence will be, and . . . follows meticulously an elaborate outline."[34] At the heart of this exposition is the analogically based figure of Melchizedek. This type, then, is crucial to the argument of the whole book.

It is possible to list and compare the ways in which Melchizedek and Christ are alike. And, as we would expect, the ways in which they are dissimilar are not mentioned at all. In fact, although the argument's crucial point is that Melchizedek appeared on the scene and disappeared without any antecedent or subsequent personal history, the obvious fact that Melchizedek died is not given, since it would take attention from (but not weaken) the analogy. Every reader can reason that he must have died, but that feature of his life is not really relevant to the point being made. Rather, Melchizedek is like Christ because *within the text itself* he has no beginning or ending. So we find that the writer is very careful to use what supports his point. It is true, however, that he has been criticized at this point for using fanciful exegesis of the O.T., arguing from points that are not really there. He has essentially combined the information given in Ps. 110:4 and in Gen. 14 and set forth the analogical relationships. It is his argument that the *silence* of Scripture concerning Melchizedek's life is parallel to Christ's eternality that has proven to be a stumblingblock to some interpreters. Nevertheless, it must be that Ps. 110:4 gives the missing piece to the correspondence, since the *eternal* priesthood is predicted there for one like Melchizedek. And plainly the author took Ps. 110:4 as the divinely provided clue. It is simply a case of interpreting Scripture by Scripture.

The following are some of the key correspondences:

Melchizedek	*Christ*
King *(melchi)*	King
King of Salem (perhaps = *shalom*, "peace")	King bringing peace
King of righteousness *(zedek)*	Righteous
No (recorded) beginning or ending	No beginning or ending
Spiritually superior	Spiritually superior
Connected with Abraham (versus Moses)	Connected with Abraham (versus Moses)

Melchizedek	*Christ*
Non-Levite	Non-Levite
Priest by divine appointment	Priest by divine appointment
Celebrates a victory	Celebrates a victory
Involved with sacrifices	Involved with sacrifices

Melchizedek is unique among human beings in the Bible in that he is a priest-king. David, for example, was a prophet-king, and Ezekiel was a prophet-priest. But it falls to Melchizedek to prefigure these two offices of the three that our Lord possesses. In this two-part role Melchizedek is associated first with access to God and then with leadership of people. His access role is taught indirectly by the blessing of Abraham, which, according to the writer to the Hebrews, makes him "greater" in some sense (7:7). It is also suggested by the interesting celebration elements, bread and wine, which he shares with Abraham. The role as king finds him associated with Salem, a name whose meaning has been debated. If, as some have suggested, it is to be taken as the Hebrew word for peace *(shalom),* then Melchizedek is parallel to Christ in that both are involved with peacemaking roles. If it means Jerusalem, then Melchizedek's domain was Jerusalem, and the prefigurement is connected with Christ's future rule in Jerusalem on the Davidic throne. Melchizedek is also described as a king associated with righteousness *(zedek),* a role true of Christ, also. Thus both have two offices (priest and king) and are associated with two kingship characteristics (peace/Jerusalem and righteousness). Of course, Christ is also a prophet, a role not assigned to Melchizedek.

The Scofield note at Gen. 14:18 points out that Melchizedek is a priestly type of Christ in regard to His resurrection, since the elements of the celebration are bread and wine. It may be making too much of these two entities if we associate them directly with the bread and wine that are used in the celebration of the Lord's Supper. But if this is a valid association, it would confirm the predictive nature of Melchizedek's presentation in Gen. In any case, the essence of Melchizedek's work involves giving of thanks in celebration of a victory, and the writer to the Hebrews is concerned with showing that the response of his readers should be to react appropriately to a victory instead of *trying* to get to God. In other words, the opening of access through the work of Christ is over, so anyone who attempts to add to it is foolish. Furthermore, the priestly work of Christ *endures* because He Himself is not subject to death, a truth paralleled by Melchizedek's sudden appearance and disappearance.

The key issue in the parallelism is the lack of mention of Melchizedek's exit from the scene. Since nothing is *said* about the rest of his life, it is, reasons the writer to the Hebrews, as if he had no beginning or ending (7:3). It is the enduring nature of Christ's priesthood, and therefore of His sacrificial work, which is at the heart of the argument. If a priest who is not subject to death arises, and if his sacrifice is acceptable to God (which the writer also shows), then access is secured. The way to God is open and stays that way (see above in this chapter under "Examples of Doctrines Developed by the New Testament from the Old Testament" on the door to heaven). For Christ to be a priest in the order of Melchizedek means that He is eternal. Eternal priests live to give their subjects eternal privileges before God. The writer develops this in 7:11–25, concluding with the powerful statement of 7:25: "Therefore he is able to save completely those who come to God through Him, because he always lives to intercede for them" (NIV).

It is also important for the writer to show that this work of Christ is superior to that of the priests under the law. The Melchizedek parallel enables him to do that because it shows that an ancestor of the Levites was spiritually inferior to Melchizedek (in the matter of access to God). Implicit in the argument of 7:4–10 is the assumption that one can rise no higher in the spiritual order than one's ancestors. So if Abraham offered tithes to Melchizedek and in turn was given a blessing by him, then his descendents, even though they may be priests under the law of Moses, are inferior to Melchizedek. Thus, if Christ is a Melchizedekian type of priest, He is automatically superior to the priests under the law, and His sacrificial work is superior to theirs, too. So Melchizedek's, and therefore Christ's (as a Melchizedekian priest), connection with Abraham rather than Moses establishes Christ's sacrifice as better than those under the law.

One of the most interesting aspects of the Gen. 14 account is the *absence* of information. We have already mentioned the lack of revelation concerning the rest of Melchizedek's life in terms of birth and death. But we should also notice that the biblical record says nothing about how Melchizedek became a priest. Not only is he clearly a Gentile, since he is a contemporary of Abraham, the father of all Jews, but he appears as a priest without any indication of how he got his information or authority. The writer to the Hebrews does not make any points from this, but it is possible to say that it is Melchizedek's being *unlike* the Levitical priests in terms of appointment that makes him like Christ. Of course, the writer to the Hebrews underscores the fact that Christ became a priest by direct divine appointment, by oath (5:5–6, 10; 7:17, 20–22, 28). And presumably, Melchizedek received his priesthood the same way, although that information is not crucial for the correspondence to Christ, and we go beyond the account in Gen. 14 and Hebrews if we speculate.

That the writer to the Hebrews saw himself as working in the realm of divine analogies is clear from the fact that he takes pains to explain elements of the correspondence. He carefully translates the names of the figure in Gen. 14, although he does not develop them in relation to his argument. And he expounds on the superiority and eternality correspondences in such detail that his points cannot be missed. In effect, he is teaching at length on the basis of analogical relations between the testaments.

Prediction by Analogy

Logicians, concerned with describing how people ought to reason if they are to reason well, have analyzed the components used in analogical thinking. They have noted that much of human reasoning can be viewed as analogical in nature, as we constantly compare new things with old, looking for degrees of similarity and, by implication, degrees of difference. Some students of cognitive processes feel that all learning, formal or informal, takes place as we use our analogical facility, working from the known to the unknown.[35]

If we consider again the mail carrier example from the beginning of this section on analogical relationships, we will recall we noted that the two men are similar in certain ways, and, if we were to examine such a pair further, we would probably begin to observe that at certain places the resemblances were not as strong as in others, or that there were clear differences between the two. Such features are called negative analogies, as opposed to positive or reinforcing analogies.

Argumentation and conclusions are often based on analogical reasoning. This is true inductive thinking. For instance, I note that student A is a sophomore, studies less than is expected, is homesick, and lives 500 miles away, and that student B is a sophomore, studies less than is expected, is homesick, lives 500 miles away, and just left school to take a week off at home. I might reason that student A would be likely to do the same thing soon. Logicians have noted that the strength of such a conclusion—that student A may leave—can be increased by adding to the number of compared items. If, for example, I added five details in which the two individuals were alike (they are both males, do not play sports, have large, closely knit families, have poor grades, and have cars), in addition to those listed above, clearly my conclusion would be stronger. Further, if I were to note other individuals who are like student A and also left for home, the strength of my conclusion would be increased. Conversely, the presence of dissimilarities decreases the strength of the conclusion. Thus, if I noted that student B has no relatives in the area but A does and stays with them often, my conclusion would be weakened.

It should also be noted that arguments of this kind sometimes take the form of predictions. Reasoning from what has happened in the past and correspondences to existing entities, I make an induction, a prediction concerning a future occurrence. Such reasoning can never be classified as good or bad. But it can be said that it has degrees of strength.[36]

All of this has relevance to biblical analogies. In the case of Melchizedek, we find that the author is, in a sense, reasoning from the known to the unknown. Many things are "known" about Melchizedek, and the writer simply accepts them from the Genesis record. Christ's spiritual work is not so well understood. Melchizedek and Christ are alike in several ways. Therefore, he reasons, they must be alike in others. Perhaps we could say that the predictive element is found in the anticipation that the access-work of Christ will be eternally effective.

Quotational Relations Between the Testaments

It should be immediately evident to any student of the Bible that a large part of the N.T. is made up of words from the O.T. These may be obviously complete quotations, or simply allusions (the use of a word or two, seemingly done in passing, or of phrases reminiscent of a particular passage). Unfortunately, we seem to be so accustomed to seeing these words that we do not usually stop to notice their significance. Yet it is evident from the frequent usage of O.T. material by the N.T. that the events that transpired from the hand of God were vitally and intimately connected with the dealings of God with people, as recorded in the O.T. And when we learn that as much as four percent of the N.T. (or one out of every twenty-two verses) is made up of material clearly recognizable as a quotation from the O.T., we ought to alert ourselves that here is a significant factor in interpreting the Bible. And this does not include allusions, which may number in the thousands.[37]

The person who pays attention to these quotations is, first of all, ensuring that a larger part of the Bible will come into view. But just as important, the manner in which the N.T. makes use of the O.T. leads to many valuable insights that could not be gained in any other way. In other words, the Bible's own use of itself provides spiritual information about its overall message. In addition, this takes us to the heart of the nature of the Bible itself, showing us much about how it was put together, how God guided its authors, and how we ought to view its inspiration and inerrancy.

There are several other reasons for studying the quotations of the O.T. in the N.T.:

1. Since such a large part of the N.T. is drawn from the O.T., it is evident that the authors of the N.T. preferred at many points to use words that were originally penned by someone else. They felt that the O.T. said it better than they could!

2. Such a study provides insight into the interpretive practices of the N.T. writers. Knowledge of such practices may assist us today in formulating approaches to Scripture.

3. Important theological points often rest on certain features in quotes. In fact, many theological arguments can be illuminated or even resolved by careful attention to quoted material.

4. Our Lord Jesus Christ made dependence on and quotation from the O.T. an important part of His life and ministry.

5. Such study has been largely neglected over the centuries.

6. The issue of the quotational relations between the testaments is connected with key hermeneutical issues such as typology and prophecy.

The purpose of this section is to acquaint you with some of the basic features of the use of the O.T. in the N.T., to suggest ways to analyze such material, and to encourage you to develop the habit of continually examining these correspondences when they arise. The possibilities for gaining insight into the Scriptures through this approach are virtually limitless. As a Bible student you should add this to your repertoire of study tools.

Many notorious Bible difficulties are connected with quotation. An example is Mt. 2:15 (see note). Recently some who have espoused a view of the biblical text that allows for errors in the original writings have suggested that some quotations are points in the text where N.T. writers not only were careless with the O.T., but also utilized it erroneously, perhaps by unjustifiably changing the wording. Thus, significant contemporary issues in biblical interpretation and theology interface with this matter of the Bible's quotation of itself.

We cannot deal with every quotation/allusion found in the N.T. In fact, the exact number and identity of such references is debated. Our purpose here is to present principles and representative usages. But in order to assist you in ongoing study, this book also contains a guide to passages corresponding across the testaments. And at the end of this chapter we provide questions for further exploration of this often fascinating topic.[38]

The Material Used in Quotations

The most basic features of the use of O.T. material in the N.T. are the sources of quotations and the methods used to introduce them. A careful examination of these furnishes great insight into the attitude of the N.T. writer or speaker toward the O.T., and some of the basic principles of interpretation that the N.T. employs.

Sources of quotations. The various titles used in reference to parts of the O.T. show that N.T. writers viewed it as a unity. In Lk. 11:50–51 our Lord states that "the blood of all the prophets" is encompassed by "the blood of Abel to the blood of Zechariah." Although Abel is here called a prophet, in Gen. he is depicted simply as a historical figure without prophetic character. Zechariah is found in 2 Chr. 24:21. Thus our Lord views the whole O.T., canonically arranged in the Heb. Bible from Gen. to 2 Chr. (a different order from that of Eng. versions), as a unified document possessing prophetic significance. Other terms used in reference to the O.T. show this same view of its unity. In Rom. 3:19 Paul calls a composite quotation from Ps., Isa. and Prov. "the law." And we ought to be surprised to hear Asaph, the writer of Ps. 78, called a "prophet" (Mt. 13:35), and Isaiah's writings referred to as "the law" (1 Cor. 14:21). Roger Nicole summarizes this practice when he states, "New Testament writers viewed the whole Old Testament Scripture as having legal authority and prophetic character."[39]

Something of the writer's view of the unity of purpose contained in the Bible can be seen in Mt. 21:4–5, where Isa. 62:11 and Zech. 9:9 are linked under the introductory phrase "to fulfill what was spoken through the prophet." We gather from this that Matthew regarded both prophets as speaking accurately to the same point and picturing the same event in prophetic discourse. It should be noted also that the surroundings of both Isa. 62:11 and Zech. 9:9 are of significance for our understanding of Matthew's presentation at this point. Clearly Matthew also recognized the correspondence between what he was writing about and the wider portions of Isa. 62 and Zech. 9. Not only did he know the O.T. passages well, but he was able to relate them to the incident in our Lord's life about which he was writing. Similarly, in 1 Pet. 2:6–8 Peter unites Isa. 28:16, Ps. 118:22 and Isa. 8:14 under the introductory formula "for in Scripture it says." He views the three prophetic references as speaking authoritatively to the same subject and as saying more than he could in his own words. Peter's practice seems to support and illustrate the observation made long ago by Benjamin B. Warfield that *scripture* as used in the N. T. conceives of the O.T. as a unitary whole.[40]

A slightly different practice that we encounter is that of the linking of a prophet's words and historical material, viewing both as contributing prophetically to the N.T. situation. Acts 3:22–33 unites the prophetic statement of Dt. 18:15 and the historical statement of Lev. 23:29 regarding correct observation of the Day of Atonement. Both record the words of Moses, but with different contexts and intents. Peter views both as bearing prophetically upon the appearance of *the* prophet.[41]

We also find the quotation of originally historical passages in a prophetic sense. We would be inclined to view these passages as typical statements, i.e., presentations of types, in the O.T., were it not for the fact that the N.T. clearly regards them as prophetic in nature. For example, Mt. 2:15 quotes the words of Hos. 11:1 under the introductory words "and so was fulfilled what the Lord had said through the prophet." Hosea originally spoke the words in an attempt to move Israel to repentance. Matthew does not say that they have an antitype, but rather that they have a fulfillment. This illustrates what we said earlier in this chapter concerning analogical relations between the testaments. Apparently Matthew sees God's hand at work in the ordering of the historical events in Hos., performing a shaping that can be viewed as prophetic in that God's directing of human affairs in one age is often designed to illustrate later events, with varying degrees of correspondence. So certain is this relationship between prior and subsequent event that the first can be described as prophetic of the second.

Another interesting practice is that of joining quotations from several prophets and viewing them as contributing to the prophetic picture. Matthew 24:15–31 contains references to Dan. 12:11,1; Dt. 13:1–3; Isa. 13:10; Joel 2:10; Isa. 34:4; Dan. 7:13; Zech. 12:10; and Isa. 27:13. Some of these may be considered allusions, but the presence of the reference to Daniel in 24:15 suggests that for this quotation, and perhaps for several of the others, our Lord had the specific texts directly in mind, especially in regard to Mt. 24:29 and 30. This teaches us that varied parts of the O.T. were designed by God to speak to single situations in the unfolding N.T. accounts. And we can see from many of these examples that the N.T. views as prophetic a wide variety of material that in its original context would probably not have been so understood. We should learn from this to look for more of the hand of God in history, especially as revelation unfolds.

Introductory Formulas. Careful examination of the various methods employed to introduce O.T. material pays rich dividends. The methods used reveal a great deal about how the N.T. writers viewed the O.T. These introductory statements have been called by some *introductory formulas* (abbreviated *IF*) or *citation formulas.* Some of the key words that we encounter frequently are:

1. *anaginoskō* (''read'')—In Mt. 21:42 our Lord asks the leaders of Israel if they have ''never read in the Scriptures'' the words of Ps. 118:22–23 concerning His rejection. The point is not simply that they should have heard of the verses in some way, but that they should have been acquainted with their *meaning* and *purpose* because it was plainly accessible to them.

2. *gegraptai* and *gegrammenon estin* (''it stands written'')—These terms are found frequently in the N.T. in reference to prophetic material. Warfield has pointed out that the use of this kind of formula ''carries with it the implication that the appeal is made to the indefectible authority of the Scriptures of God, which in all their parts and in every one of their declarations are clothed with the authority of God Himself.''[42] Jesus used the first term three times in His temptation as recorded in Mt. 4:1–11, quoting three times from Dt. (8:3; 6:16 and 6:13).

3. *teleō* and related words (''fulfill,'' ''finish,'' ''complete'')—In Lk. 18:31 Jesus says, ''Everything that is written by the prophets about the Son of Man will be fulfilled.'' It is interesting that He points out that *everything* that appears in the prophets (the whole O.T.?) about Him will be brought to completion. His comment in Jn. 19:28 (''so that the Scripture would be fulfilled'') points to the ongoing purpose of Scripture and the precise, necessary, and intimate connection of events with the express biblical design for His life. In short, He was living out the O.T.

Although they usually consist of only a few words, introductory formulas contribute significantly to our understanding of the Bible. In a sense, they are the Bible's own commentary on itself. (Interestingly enough, even the absence of a formula can be instructive!) Here are some examples:

1. Origin of quotation assigned to God—Often the N.T. says that the words of O.T. individuals were spoken by God. We find this in Acts 4:25, where David's words in Ps. 2 are ascribed to God. Acts 13:34–35 and Heb. 1:5–8 and 7:21 are similar. To quote Warfield again:

> They could be attributed to God only through such habitual identification, in the
> minds of the writers, of the text of Scripture with the utterances of God that it had

become natural to use the term "God says" when what was really intended was "Scripture, the Word of God, says."[43]

2. Personification of Scripture—Several prophetically related passages refer to Scripture as speaking or acting. Thus in Jn. 7:38, 42; 19:37; Rom. 9:17 and 10:11, Scripture is specifically labelled as the speaker. In Gal. 3:8 Scripture both foresees and announces. Warfield's conclusion above under (2) applies similarly here.

3. The human role in the creation of Scripture—At times an introductory formula contributes to our understanding of the inspiration of the Bible in a different way from that just mentioned. Mt. 3:3 provides an example of a passage where it is clear that the N.T. regards human beings as having a necessary function in the recording of prophetic material: "This is he who was spoken of through the prophet Isaiah." Acts 1:16 shows that there was an ever-present divine guidance to ensure accuracy: "Brothers, the Scripture had to be fulfilled that the Holy Spirit spoke long ago through the mouth of David concerning Judas . . ."

4. Authority of Scripture—Many formulas serve to demonstrate that the N.T. writers regarded the O.T. as speaking with great authority to first-century situations. In Acts 13:47 Paul states that Isa. 49:6, originally addressed to the Servant, contained a divine imperative to the apostles: "For this is what the Lord has commanded us . . ." A reading of the O.T. verse by itself would probably not have led anyone to conclude that such a statement was actually prophetic and imperatival in nature. In another vein, the two formulas in Rom. 10:19–20 indicate that Paul is supporting his argument with quotations from two Jewish authorities, Moses and Isaiah. But he carefully arranges his material and formulas so that there is an unmistakable heightening of the authority he is bringing to bear upon the situation of Israel's unbelief, for he states, "First, Moses says, . . . And Isaiah boldly says . . ." See Rom 15:10 for a similar example.

5. Accuracy—The accuracy with which Scripture speaks to the N.T. situation is reflected in Mt. 15:8–9, where the introductory words are "Isaiah was right when he prophesied about you . . ." (v.7). Compare also Mk. 7:6–7.

6. Divine agency—N.T. writers use formulas to highlight the active hand of God behind prophecies, and, as an extension of the prophecies, their fulfillment. In Jn. 12:38–41 Jesus clearly attributes to God the blinding and unbelief of Israel, although in a similar passage, Mt. 13:14, the name of Isaiah alone is mentioned in relation to the blinding. John says, "As Isaiah says elsewhere: He [God] has blinded their eyes . . ." Jesus' words, as recorded by John, view Isaiah as the instrument not only to announce but to carry out the decree of God, for in v. 39 we read, "For this reason they could not believe, because, as Isaiah says elsewhere . . ." The next verse goes on to show that it was clearly God who did the blinding.

7. Close association of O.T. and N.T.—On several occasions the N.T. identifies a first-century situation as closely as possible with prophetic material by saying, "This is that" or "This is he." Matthew 3:3, 11:10, and Jn. 1:23 speak this way about John the Baptist. There is no statement of fulfillment; instead there is a close connection between John's appearance and what was foretold by the prophetic word. In Jn. 1:23 the writer simply links the first person singular nominative pronoun with the words of Isa. 40:3. "John replied in the words of Isaiah the prophet, 'I am the voice . . .' " The importance of this is that we learn that the N.T. writers firmly believed that what they were witnessing was exactly what the O.T. spoke about.

8. Absence of formulas—The appearance of a clear quotation without any formula

points in many cases to the intimate acquaintance of the speaker with prophetic material. Paul's quotation of Ps. 19:4 in Rom. 10:18 without a formula, but with predictive reference to Israel, indicates that he felt it more natural and proper to continue his sentence in the exact words of Scripture than in his own. Apparently he felt that Scripture could say it better than he could!

We can see, then, that various formulas are employed with often significant intent, and that the O.T. is regarded as authoritative and as having a living relation to N.T. situations.

Correspondence of Meaning

There are many instances where the correspondence of wording or meaning between the N.T. and the O.T. is not exact. Such apparent discrepancies are often a target of criticism, on the grounds that N.T. writers erred in their translation or understanding of the O.T., or engaged in unwarranted and fanciful interpretation. But C. H. Dodd, one who would be more inclined than many to criticize such usage, reaches the conclusion that "in general . . . the writers of the N.T., in making use of passages from the O.T., remain true to the main intention of their writers."[44]

Some quotations involve alteration of a basic or peripheral element in the O.T. material. Others show primarily an alteration of wording, although some change of meaning may also be involved. We will consider both types.

Quotations with modified meaning. We should point out initially that, in regard to understanding O.T. purposes, the case must be weighted in favor of the N.T. writers, because of their exposure to O.T. teaching, and, more important, to the interpretive principles of Christ. Roger Nicole states, "Few Christians, it is hoped, will have the presumption of setting forth their own interpretation as normative, when it runs directly counter to that of the Lord Jesus or of his apostles."[45]

At times we find that N.T. writers have seized upon a portion of the original sense that would not be immediately apparent to the reader and have made it a major feature of N.T. usage. In Mt. 13:35, which quotes Ps. 78:2, Asaph, the author of the psalm, is recorded as opening his mouth in parables. Matthew 13:35 has no meaning if what was fulfilled was "I will open my mouth," because that was simply Asaph's description of his own action. Nor was hiding of truth (which is present in the N.T. context) fulfilled, for that was not present in the O.T. context. The fulfillment consists of more than this. The fulfillment is rather a culmination of the purpose for speaking. The psalmist spoke didactically to bring understanding and a reaction. The context concerns Israel's disobedience and God's faithfulness. Our Lord speaks in a didactic manner to bring understanding and a reaction, and His material concerns Israel's disobedience and God's faithfulness, plus new truth. Note that the psalm ends with the Davidic glory, God's kingdom administered through a divinely appointed king. Our Lord seeks fulfillment of this. The psalmist seeks preservation of the institution as he knows it. The fulfillment is therefore a culmination of the teaching process toward humanity and of the content of the process. Matthew has in mind the revelatory nature of the fulfillment, the completion of the process of didactic exposition by means of the giving of final information. Thus Matthew has correctly seized upon the O.T. sense, although he has stressed a portion that might not be readily apparent.

In some instances the N.T. modifies O.T. statements that are viewed as having definite prediction/fulfillment significance. Thus, in Mt. 2:15 a historical statement from Hos. 11:1 is said to be "fulfilled." There are two problems here: first, what is actually fulfilled? and second, how is the staying in Egypt a fulfillment of leaving? We will deal here only with the first issue.

The experiences of Israel were prophetic in type of those of the Messiah (see note, Hos. 11:1). Note Ex. 4:22 where Israel is called "my son." In Hos. 11:1 God's care for Israel is stressed; in Mt. 2:15 His care for the Messiah is similarly emphasized. How then is this a fulfillment? The fulfillment comes from the fact that God's purpose of bringing His people Israel to union with Himself is being accomplished in the life and death of the Messiah (see note, Mt. 2:15). The incident of the Egyptian sojourn is part of this program. The historical events concerning Israel in and after Egypt under God's care are fulfilled in the perfect Son Who does please the Father and who will do His will perfectly where Israel failed. Matthew 2 shows God's care to raise the perfect Son, obedient unto death. The fulfillment is therefore not only that of historical type correspondence. Fulfillment here is the continued step-by-step movement toward completion of the plan of God to have an obedient people for Himself; that is, He desires perfect, obedient sonship. God is fulfilling His purposes, not just the type.[46]

At times we are initially surprised to find that the subject of the original O.T. statement is altered, or the background or frame of reference is in some way modified in the N.T. usage. In Mt. 21:33–46 Jesus interprets the parable of Isa. 5:1–2, which, in the O.T. context, identifies the vineyard as Israel (cf. Isa. 5:7). In the N.T., the vineyard is the kingdom, because it can be taken from Israel. What then is the correspondence between the two statements of the parable? In the O.T., unfruitfulness inside the nation leads to judgment. In the N.T., unfruitfulness inside and outside the nation in administration of the kingdom leads to judgment. So judgment on unfruitfulness is the common ground. Our Lord uses this theme and expands on the significance of the parable. In the O.T., judgment falls on the vineyard; in the N.T., on the administrators (vv. 40–41).

Paul shows a similar interpretive procedure in 1 Cor. 14:21 in quoting Isa. 28:11–12. In Isa. the tongues are the speech of foreign invaders. The sign was a judicial one upon Israelites who had disregarded Isaiah's message. Here is the application of a principle that held true in Isaiah's time and was still true for some disbelieving Jews in the first century.[47] But the judicial sign is now that of Christian tongues. We cannot grasp this controversial chapter unless we understand the judicial nature of tongues, as shown by this quotation. (Note also similar interpretations in Acts 13:41, 47, and Gal. 4:7.)

There are several citations in which an O.T. reference to Israel is interpreted as applying to believers in this age. It should be noted, however, that no promises made to Israel concerning the integrity of the nation or its future blessing are abrogated by this. Rather, the spiritual principles that characterized God's dealing with Israel are interpreted as applicable to His present dealings with believers in this age.

In Jn. 6:45 Jesus quotes Isa. 54:13, which contains a prediction concerning Israel, "They will all be taught by God." He does not limit the prophecy, but widens its scope, changing "sons" to "all." The range of the discipleship of those drawn by God is extended beyond Israel. It is a principle for all whom He chooses to draw to Himself.

Similarly, in 2 Cor. 6:16–18 Paul applies descriptions of Israel in the land (Lev. 26:11–12) and in millennial restoration (Ezek. 37:27; Isa. 52:11–12; Jer. 31:9) to the body of the believer as the temple of the living God. The millennial temple of Ezek.

37:27 is descriptive of the temple that is the believer's body. Note further that in 7:1 Paul goes on to state an inference from the preceding verses, which he regards as "promises." Prophecy for Israel is regarded as a truth partially applicable to believers in this age. Paul is not stating that these are fulfilled, but that they contain principles that apply to all believers. He does not say that Israel has lost her promises or that the Church has inherited them. We should notice the "as" in the introductory formula in this regard: Paul is giving a comparison. A similar formula and interpretation are found in Rom. 9:25–26 (Hos. 2:23; 1:10).[48]

Thus it can be seen that, although N.T. writers often alter the original sense of the O.T. prophetic passage, they remain true to a portion of the original meaning.[49]

Quotations with modified wording. REASONS FOR CHANGE. A second category of modified quotations concerns those references in which a significant change of wording either denotes interpretive intent or suggests error in translating or understanding the O.T. text. Roger Nicole gives several reasons to account for many of the N.T. practices of quotation.[50] Some of these are: (1) The N.T. writers had to translate their quotations from Heb. texts that may or may not have been accurate or the same as those we have today; (2) The Septuagint may have been used, with purposeful retention of variants in deference to the popular form of the text; (3) The writers of the N.T. did not follow the same quoting conventions we do today, especially in our scientific works; (4) Paraphrases were sometimes employed; (5) Some texts may contain textual corruptions; (6) The Spirit of God was free to modify the expressions that He inspired in the O.T.

Quotations with change in wording fall into two main categories, those with deletions and those that contain changes or supposed errors.

EXAMPLES. In Mt. 4:15–16 only a portion of Isa. 9:1 is quoted, and the phrase "In the past he humbled" is left out. Robert Gundry states:

> Mt leaves out this whole phrase as irrelevant to his purpose. He wishes to string together all the geographical terms in unbroken succession to emphasize the specifically geographical fulfillment, as further shown by the complete lack of grammatical relationship between the list and the rest of the quotation.[51]

Matthew thus takes only the geographical names, leaving out the affliction. But the affliction is still implied in Mt. 4:16. There are many other examples of this type of change, such as Mt. 21:5 (Zech. 9:9); 21:12–13 (Isa. 56:7 and Jer. 7:11); Mk. 1:2 (Mal. 3:1b); Lk. 4:18 (Isa. 61:1–2); Ps. 41:9 (Jn. 13:18); Rom. 1:17 (Hab. 2:4).

Changes in wording will often reveal a part of the writer's interpretive aim. Matthew does this in 1:23, where he changes "[she] will call" to "they will call." Matthew demonstrates that God has not forsaken His people, that the judgment incurred in part by Ahaz in Isa. 7 will eventually be abated. In the birth of the Messiah, God's faithfulness and provision of a sign (scorned by Ahaz) are proven. The whole nation would, in a sense, join in giving the name, although the existence of a national entity regarding Messiah with joy is still future. For other examples see Mt. 26:31 (Zech. 13:7); Mt. 21:5 (Zech. 9:9), Eph. 4:8 (Ps. 68:18).

In summary, it can be said that N.T. writers remain true to the intent of the O.T. passage they are quoting, although wording may vary in many instances. This practice does not in any way demonstrate a low regard for the integrity of O.T. Scripture. In regard to both sense and wording, the N.T. shows a confidence in its ability accurately to apply O.T. truths and predictions to N.T. times.[52]

Reasons for New Testament Quotation of the Old Testament

Why does the N.T. use O.T. material? How does it fit into the histories and teachings of the N.T. writers? What is the attitude toward O.T. truths in their appearance, fulfillment, and explanation in the N.T.?

There are two main purposes for the quotation of O.T. texts in the N.T.: literary and apologetic. This division is not entirely clear cut, since purposes often overlap (as do many other features of the whole area of usage of the O.T. by the N.T.). Yet it helps us to see many of the objectives of the N.T. in its employment of the O.T.

Literary Usage. Here we find that N.T. writers often used the O.T. as an integral part of the literary structure of a passage.

CLOTHING OF THOUGHTS. —In several instances O.T. material is used to clothe the writer's own thoughts or words. There is such a regard for the O.T. that its phrases are felt to be more fitting to express ideas than original composition. In Rom 15:3, where Paul has a sustained argument of twenty-five verses, he turns to Ps. 49:10 for words that describe a type to complete his presentation: "For even Christ did not please himself but, as it is written: 'The insults of those who insult you have fallen on me.' " Similarly, in Mt. 10:35 Jesus indirectly quotes words of the prophet Micah (7:6) to describe his own mission: "For I have come to turn 'a man against his father, a daughter against her mother . . .' "

EXPLANATION. A second literary use is where the evident contextual significance of an O.T. reference seems to be brought into play in order to give added depth and understanding to the N.T. reference and context. This is admittedly a subjective evaluation for the N.T. interpreter. However, in some instances there exists evidence of the sort that would lead us to the conclusion that a N.T. writer does have much of the O.T. context in mind, and views it as contributing to the N.T. situation he is describing. A natural extension of this, although one that would be difficult to prove, is that the N.T. writers, in all or the majority of instances, viewed the O.T. context as blending with the N.T. situation in which a quotation was employed.

An interesting example of such usage is found in Mt. 1:23 where Isa. 7:14 is quoted as a prophecy fulfilled in the virgin birth of Christ. The context of Isa. 7 presents the disobedience of the king, Ahaz, who is found in the genealogy in Mt. 1:9. Note that the Babylonian captivity is mentioned in 1:11. But the sign and deliverance that were once rejected are now being given. The statement of 1:23 includes more than a fulfillment of prophecy. It is the sign of God's program of intervention in visiting a rebellious people. Immanuel will save His people from their sins—transgressions that brought desolation and judgment. The birth of Immanuel overcame the failures of the line of David, and here particularly those of Ahaz, who denied God's faithfulness to His promise of 2 Sam. 7:14 (see notes at Isa. 7:14 and Mt. 1:23).

A similar use is found in Mt. 4:15–16, which quotes Isa. 9:1. In Isa. 9:7 the establishment of Davidic reign is foretold, accompanied by relief for a particular geographical area. In Mt. 4 our Lord begins to preach concerning the kingdom. Surely a Jew reading the account would have thought of the Davidic promises of Isa. 9:7. It is appropriate, therefore, that Matthew uses this quotation here, both to explain the significance of our Lord's dwelling place and to show God's hand in His movements. Matthew thus uses prophecy to elaborate upon his theme (rather than explain it himself) and to point out that His ministry fulfills Davidic promises, in spite of sin.

ANALOGY. —A third literary use of the O.T. is that of comparing items in the N.T. and the O.T. by means of similar features, attributes or characteristics (see above in this ch. under "The Nature of Analogy"). Thus in Rom. 1:17 Paul uses Hab. 2:4 not as a proof or a fulfillment, but rather as an O.T. truth that possesses certain qualities in common with the N.T. teaching he is setting forth. The contexts of Rom. 1 and Hab. 2 are remarkably similar. In Hab. the prophet anticipates a Messianic deliverance in the immediate future. Meanwhile, the faith principle is to guide the prophet and the remnant. Paul has received a message concerning the finished work of Christ. The common idea is that approach to God and blessing from God are based on trusting obedience—or, faith (see note, Hab. 2:3). Similar uses of the O.T. are found in Rom 2:24 (Isa. 52:5) and Acts 7:48–50 (Isa. 66:1–2).

Apologetic Usage. Among the examples of apologetic usage there seem to be four types: (1) proofs, (2) answers, (3) explanations, and (4) the special use of the O.T. by Christ in regard to the outworking of the events of His life and ministry. All of these have the underlying motive of convincing or of presenting authority.

PROOF OR SUPPORT. —A simple illustration of this is found in 1 Cor. 1:19, where Paul quotes Isa. 29:14. Isaiah's statement, introduced by "for it is written," is a fully authoritative proof of Paul's assertion in v. 18: "For the message of the cross is foolishness . . ." The prophet's words are a warning of impending judgment on Judah and Jerusalem for unbelief. Paul says this has ultimate reference to disbelief at the preaching of the cross. The supreme manifestation of this comes at the revelation of the Messiah. Thus Paul is not simply seizing and applying a principle that he found in the statement of Isaiah, but is using the prophet's words to highlight the continuity of unbelief. See also Rom. 3:10–18 (several sources), and Acts 2:34–35 (Ps. 110:1).

ANSWER. —A more evident type of use is where O.T. material is given as an answer to a question. This is, of course, similar to the practice of clothing one's words in O.T. language, but it goes a step further in that it has definite apologetic and argumentative intent. Thus, in Mt. 2:6 the answer to the question of the place of the Messiah's birth is given directly from Scripture, and in Jn. 1:23 John the Baptist quotes Isa. 40:3, adding "I" as the subject of the fulfilled prophecy: "John replied in the words of the prophet, 'I am the voice of one calling in the desert, "make straight the way for the Lord.' "

EXPLANATION. —A third type of apologetic usage is that in which an authoritative explanation is given from O.T. material. The purpose is not simply to give greater understanding, but to demonstrate that a correspondence exists between the O.T. and N.T. in regard to contexts or inherent details, and that the O.T. anticipated with precision and insight the N.T. reference to which it corresponds.

Matthew gives such an explanation in 2:23, asserting the reason for our Lord's dwelling in Nazareth: "And he went and lived in a town called Nazareth. So was fulfilled what was said through the prophets: 'He will be called a Nazarene' " (see note, Mt. 3:2). See also Mt. 3:3 (Isa. 40:3) and Lk. 22:37 (Isa. 53:12).

FULFILLMENT IN LIFE. —A unique category of usage consists of our Lord's application to Himself of O.T. prophecy, apparently acted out or lived out by Him in His circumstances in the N.T. Matthew 21:1–11 is a prime illustration of this. Our Lord intentionally fulfills the prophecy of Zech. 9:9 because it applies to Him as Messiah.[53] His act constitutes a giant object lesson, and is similar to the parables that were acted out by the prophets in order to make the importance of the message clear to the onlookers.[54]

Jesus' words on the cross show a similar intent. In Jn. 19:28 He recognizes the need for the fulfillment of the last prophetic detail concerning His passion: "Later, knowing that all was now completed, and so that the Scripture would be fulfilled, Jesus said, 'I am thirsty.' " It should be noted, however, that His speaking the words "I am thirsty" did not complete prophecy. He spoke in order that vinegar might be given to Him in fulfillment of the typical prophecy of Ps. 69:21. British writer R. V. G. Tasker points out concerning this type of usage:

> In the closing stages of the great drama of redemption, as our Lord drew nearer to His appointed cross, it was the Old Testament which interpreted for Him incidents that might otherwise have been bewildering. Sometimes He was able to anticipate events in the light of prophecy and so was unsurprised when they occurred; at other times any shock that events might at first cause Him was at once removed as He recollected how inevitable it was that all should happen in accordance with the Scriptures.[55]

There are many reasons other than those indicated above for the use of O.T. material in the N.T., and these reasons often overlap each other. But it is clear that the authority of the O.T. is always in the background, and that the O.T. is often regarded as more fitting than a writer's own words to describe a N.T. situation.

Doctrinal Uses of Quotations

The substance of O.T. thought and discourse is assimilated very naturally into N.T. books, because quotations are at the heart of the exposition of history and doctrine by N.T. writers. Thus, the sovereignty of God in all the events of the life of Christ and the early church is explained, reinforced, and in many places predicted, by O.T. statements. The details of the life and Person of Christ are not only foretold, but also given spiritual depth and significance by being part of the continued outworking of God's purposes in revelation. Not only is there advancement of specific subjects or themes, but there is also an application of O.T. truths along certain lines, such as (1) fulfillment, (2) the culmination of O.T. institutions, actions, or words in N.T. events, and (3) the relating of O.T. spiritual principles to people's lives and to the formulation of doctrine. Here are a few of the subjects with which quotations are associated.

The Sovereignty of God. Underlying all the usage of the O.T. by the N.T. is the continued outworking of the sovereign purposes of God. There are several passages in which N.T. writers show the specific intention of highlighting God's control over events.

It is clear that in Jn. 12:38–40 there is an emphasis on God's sovereignty in the life of the nation of Israel. There are several features that John uses to this. First, he states that Israel's not believing (v. 37), occurred in order "to fulfill the word of Isaiah the prophet." Divine hardening is implicit in this statement. Second, in v. 39 John makes the unequivocal statement that they could not believe. Third, he adds the authority of Isaiah's second statement, saying, "as Isaiah says elsewhere." Fourth, Isaiah's having spoken (the act itself in combination with the thrust of the words) is viewed as effecting unbelief. It almost appears that, in Christ's view, God and the prophet are merged in Isa. 6. Isaiah appears to be assigned the role of decreeing what will happen: he is God's instrument for effecting His decree, not just for prophesying. John thus goes a step further than Matthew, who says that the statement of Isaiah is fulfilled (13:14). John says that the condition described by the prophecy exists because it was stated by Isaiah. Fifth, the account in John shows word changes from the O.T. that highlight the sovereignty of God. Clearly, Jesus regarded the words of Isaiah as intrinsically connected with the outworking of the sovereignty of God over the nation.

Descriptions of Christ. Material from the O.T. is frequently used to reinforce the N.T. presentation of the various facets of the Person and work of Christ. Thus, according to such references as Mt. 1:23; 2:6, 15; Acts 2:25–36 and 3:18, He is the Messiah of Israel. And He fulfills what Isaiah predicted about the Servant in such places as Mt. 3:17; 8:17; Lk. 4:18, and 1 Pet. 2:24–25. In general, the picture of our Lord in the N.T. with reference to the O.T. is that He culminates God's purposes of salvation and revelation.

Types. Often an O.T. quotation is used in such a way that a relation of type and antitype is established or explained (see above under "Types" in this chapter). Psalm 69:4, quoted in Jn. 15:25, is an example: "But this is to fulfill what is written in their law: 'They hated me without reason.' " An experience of David finds its ultimate meaning in the life of Christ. Interestingly, Ps. 69:22 is interpreted by Paul in Rom. 11:9 as being prophetic in type of the unbelieving Jews of Paul's day. Apparently, evil elements touching the experience of the psalmist can have meaning as a type in anticipating N.T. situations. For similar examples, see Rom 8:36 (Ps. 44:22); Acts 2:25–28 (Ps. 16:8–11); Acts 13:33 (Ps. 2:7).

Truths gathered from the O.T. The wide scope of the Scriptures in predicting N.T. events is indicated in Lk. 24:44–46, where Christ states that the whole O.T. spoke concerning the Messiah. Sometimes gatherings of truth from the general words of the O.T. are specific, sometimes they are general. (The above statement is a general reference.) For both types, instances can be cited for which one or more O.T. locations could be the source of the N.T. statement. And both types have those statements for which only tentative suggestions can be made as to the source.

Specific statements with obvious O.T. references are found in Mt. 9:12; 26:54; Jn. 7:42; 17:12; 20:9; Acts 1:16; 3:18; 17:3, and 1 Cor. 15:3–4. The last of these reads "For what I received I passed on to you as of first importance: that Christ died for our sins according to the Scriptures, that he was buried, that he was raised on the third day, according to the Scriptures . . ." His resurrection was predicted, for example, in Ps. 16:10. Apparently Paul feels that the strength and extent of O.T. references to this event make it unnecessary that he quote any particular verse or verses (see note and marginal references at 15:3).

General statements with fairly evident O.T. sources are exemplified by Mt. 26:24 ("The Son of Man will go just as it is written about him."), which perhaps has Isa. 53 in mind, and by Mk. 14:21, 49; Lk. 18:31; 21:22; 24:27, 44–46, and John 1:45.

Among those places gathering quotations or allusions difficult to assign sources to are Mt. 2:23 (" 'He will be called a Nazarene.' " See note, Mt. 2:23); 26:56; Mk 9:13; Lk. 11:49; and Jn. 5:39, 44.

The significance of these is first that the writers of the N.T. viewed the O.T. as possessing authority even when no specific quotation was made, or was made but not identified, with only the word *Scripture* being present. Second, the O.T. is viewed as voicing unanimous opinions concerning N.T. events and persons, particularly regarding the Messiah.

Sources of the Interpretation of the Old Testament by the New Testament

Why did the N.T. writers use the O.T. the way they did? C. H. Dodd concludes his examination of a number of quotations by saying, "Our study has surely created a certain presumption that N.T. writers were guided in their use of the O.T. by certain agreed principles or conventions."[56]

Dodd believes that it was Jesus Christ himself who "directed the minds of His followers to certain parts of the Scriptures as those in which they might find illumination upon the meaning of His mission and destiny."[57] Certainly a basis for assigning the origin to Christ is found in Lk. 24:25–27. Note that in v. 27 He is said to have covered the entire O.T. in His teaching. R. H. Gundry states concerning the various interpretive procedures of the N.T., "That every principle of interpretation is exhibited in quotation occurring on the lips of Jesus suggests he himself was the author of this new and coherent method of OT exegesis."[58]

This suggestion should be taken one step further. Surely our Lord instructed the disciples concerning basic principles by example and explicit direction. But the final detailed application in each situation of composition by the N.T. writers was under the guidance of the Holy Spirit. This is not meant to be an assertion of the abrogation of the personal qualities of the N.T. writer during composition. Rather, they used their own personalities in accord with the principle laid down by our Lord in Jn. 16:13–15:

> But when he, the Spirit of truth, comes, he will guide you into all truth. He will not speak on his own; he will speak only what he hears, and he will tell you what is yet to come. He will bring glory to me by taking from what is mine and making it known to you. All that belongs to the Father is mine. That is why I said the Spirit will take from what is mine and make it known to you. (NIV)

We should note that there are many unanswered questions concerning methods of interpretation. The field offers many opportunities for careful interpretation.[59]

Conclusion

One of the most striking features of N.T. use of the O.T. is the great familiarity that writers have with earlier revelation. Not only is the O.T. authoritative, but it also has something to say to every type of situation. Tasker concludes concerning Christ's intimate acquaintance with Scripture:

> At every point in our Lord's earthly ministry the Old Testament was there, in His heart if not in His hands, in His thoughts if not in His words, determining the course that ministry should take, and providing the only possible language for its interpretation.[60]

Further, the O.T. is used to prove that the Person of Christ was predicted in detail. In its statements of history and principle and in its prophetic utterances, it is viewed as anticipating the events of the N.T. age. This is, of course, within the limitations of the undisclosed mystery of the Church. But it should be noted that the continued purpose of God is always in view; His will deserves primary consideration in expression of the message.

It is this sense of God's explicit direction of human affairs that shapes the N.T.

writers' view of the O.T. The Scriptures they work with are a living book. But more significantly, examination of N.T. usage reveals that careful reading and study by the writers led them to apply scriptural texts and principles to situations in which they found themselves. A forceful example of this is Peter's reasoning from Scripture in Acts 1:16. Thus, N.T. use of O.T. material discloses careful attention to the details of Scripture by individuals. Tasker cogently summarizes our Lord's relation to the Scriptures:

> How naturally and how readily does our Lord turn from the stories of the patriarchs to the utterances of the prophets and vice versa in the sayings that fall on various occasions from His lips. The language of the Bible is His native language. It is also His natural, or perhaps we should say His supernatural, channel of expression, because it is with His Father's business that He is concerned, and the Old Testament is His Father's living and abiding word. That word had gone forth to His servants in ancient days to find a permanent record in the Old Testament; and that word had now descended into human flesh in the person of His incarnate Son.[61]

As with all other facets of Christ's Person, this is an example to be emulated by believers today.

Summary of the Chapter

This chapter has shown some of the links between the Old and New Testaments. Perhaps you have concluded that there are far more than you had ever suspected. Due to the complexity of the Bible and the wisdom of God, it is safe to say that there are many more! At least we can see that comparisons, predictions, doctrines, themes, quotations, and other elements glue the Old and New together. You should acquire the habit of looking for such relations. The Guide to Old Testament Quotations in the New Testament (ch. 22) in this book, which provides a list of O.T. quotations in the N.T., is one tool that will assist you in this.

Questions for Further Study

1. In Acts 1:12–26 Peter and the disciples are led by Scripture to choose an individual to replace Judas. Where are the quotations in v. 20 from? Read the notes associated with their sources in the O.T. Are there any verses in the context of the O.T. passages that are quoted in the N.T.? Would you have connected these two verses as Peter did? What is the logical connection between the two verses? What does v. 16 tell us about Peter's thinking? What do vv. 21–22 tell us about his view of the O.T.? How are these O.T. quotations used here?

2. We mentioned above that Hab. 2:4 is used in Rom. 1:17. Where else is it used? Read the note at Hab. 2:3. How is the O.T. wording changed in each occurrence, if at all? What is the connection in meaning between Hab. and the N.T. uses? Do the N.T. passages use the verse in different ways? Are any differences associated with variations in authorship? Why do the authors use the verse? How does each use contribute to the N.T. passage in which it is found?

8

Essentials of Biblical Geography

Significance for the Bible Student

Step into the realm of biblical geography and you immediately find yourself amid the swirling currents of interactions among nations, some powerful and some not so powerful; the mighty and lowly individuals of biblical and secular history; the forces of topography, climate, and distance; and a God who designed a particular land to enhance His lessons for His people. Far from being a field in which you can rise no higher than the memorization of key place names and a few dates and people associated with them, biblical geography can actually be looked upon as something that links a number of important approaches to the Bible. Why is this so?

First, biblical events occur in real physical settings and involve people who walked in places that are known and accessible today. The sites where they lived, journeyed, fought, preached, faltered, and triumphed for God are significant, for the Bible often teaches us as much by the location of an event as by the details of the event itself. It is not fanciful to view the Bible as revealing spiritual details by means of the relations of people to topography, geography, and climate. It is certainly true that the God of the Bible is not a physical God who is limited to activity in the physical realm. John 4 teaches us this quite clearly, as does Acts 17. He is supraspatial because He is an omnipresent spiritual Being. Nevertheless, He has chosen to use His created physical realm, including rocks, wadis, rivers, deserts, and rain, to enhance encounters between Himself and those He speaks to and walks with, and future times of glory are described in terms of approved and reshaped physical features, as in Zech. 14. Seen in this light, geographical details are neither accidental nor incidental. Biblical geography is truly providential.

Second, biblical geography is intimately connected with history, societies and cultures, archaeology, and language. If you study any one of these fields you are forced to foray into one or more of the others. None can be understood without some comprehension of those related to it. But, looked at from a different perspective, it can be said that each realm is enriched and embellished by the others. When you study geography you learn about cultures automatically. Further, history comes alive when it is seen as occurring in real places, many of which have been opened to contemporary understanding by the tools of the archaeologist. Biblical geography is fascinating!

Third, the Bible student who neglects biblical geography simply omits a vast portion of the Scriptures from his purview, since so much of both the O.T. and N.T. is given to the description of geographical and related details. Their study makes for a more well-rounded Bible interpreter. Biblical geography provides balance.

Fourth, the solution of many issues of interpretation depends on knowledge of biblical geography. The susceptibility of the Sea of Galilee to sudden storms (Mk. 4:35–41), the extent of the influence of Solomon, whose public works for Israel extended to the Persian Gulf (1 Ki. 9), the sequence of the letters in Rev. 2–3, and the events of ch. 19 of that same book, where the nations opposed to Israel and to God gather in a battlefield that is now one of the most fertile areas in modern Israel—all of these points and myriads more are tied intimately with biblical topography and geography, often as these fields of study have been colored with exciting hues by the findings of modern research. Biblical geography unlocks doors to interpretation.

Confluence of Continents

Although most of biblical history is centered on the tiny land of Palestine, the geographical references found in the Bible touch on three continents. Eastern and western boundaries for the range of biblical geography are given by Paul's reference to Spain (Rom. 15:28) and references to the Persian nation (Ezek. 27:10; 38:5). References to the Scythians (north of the Black Sea; e.g., Col. 3:11) and Ethiopia (e.g., Ezek. 38:5) show the north-south range. What is important here is that Europe, Africa, and Asia are all significant in the events of the Bible. A large number of nations occupying these continents over many millennia figure in the affairs of the patriarchs, Israel, and the Church.

But there should be no doubt that the dealings of God with humanity are centered on the land given to His chosen people, Israel. In a number of ways that land possesses a strategic location among the nations of the ancient world. First, it was close to areas such as Sumer, Babylon, Egypt, Greece, and Rome, where advances in civilization were made that would prove to have great significance—the invention of writing systems, the development of great forms of art and literature, and experimentation with various forms of government. All of these would ultimately influence Israel, and in turn the early Church.

Second, Palestine was uniquely situated along trade routes that were pounded firm with the hooves of thousands of caravans passing in early centuries between Asia and Africa, and then later to Europe also. Those trade routes served to give Israel contact with the outside world, but also from a human point of view seemed at times to be detrimental, as God brought invading nations along those same routes to clash against each other or to pressure Israel.

Third, the key location of Palestine at the confluence of three land masses is significant, because it provided an opportunity to show God to others. Israel was not commanded to reach out beyond her borders, except in the case of Jonah as he was sent to Nineveh, but there were many nations that were exposed to Jehovah's work in Israel as they came in contact with the people in the land. And by the apostolic age, the ease of travel from Palestine in all directions facilitated rapid publication of the Gospel, especially to centers such as Rome. The Great Commission as restated in Acts 1:8 based its directions on the location of Palestine in the midst of nations easily reached by land and sea travel. In fact, the book of Acts shows movement toward the Mediterranean seacoast, as the Gospel spreads from Jerusalem to Lydda (Acts 9:32), Joppa (9:42), and Caesarea (10:1). In addition, the first missionary home base, Antioch in Syria, was contiguous with both Jerusalem (the "mother church") and the Roman Empire.

Influence of Secondary Nations

Early Biblical History

Although many have speculated concerning the location of the garden in Gen. 2–3 (where it is associated with the Tigris and Euphrates rivers), the exact place remains unknown. We do not have to proceed much further in the biblical narrative before we encounter more familiar geographical references. Today we know a great deal about the geographical and cultural world of the patriarchs.

The Sumerians were a non-Semitic people who inhabited the southeastern part of what has been described as the Fertile Crescent, which extends from the Persian Gulf to the Sinai (NSRB map 5). Sumer was the ancient name of southern Mesopotamia. The Sumerian civilization was at its height between 2800 and 2370 B.C.[1] Cities belonging to this culture, such as Erech, Kish, Lagash, Nippur, and Ur, have yielded instructive archaeological finds. To the north, but still within the plain formed by the Tigris and Euphrates Rivers, lived the Akkadians, whose civilization flourished after 2000 B.C. The mention in Gen. 11:2 of the "plain of Shinar" is apparently a reference to Sumer, i.e., southern Mesopotamia (a Gr. term meaning "the land between the rivers"). Mesopotamia is usually taken to refer to the whole area between the lower Tigris and Euphrates Rivers, roughly modern Iraq. The geographical region of Babylon encompassed the territory of both the Akkadians and the Sumerians.

Abraham migrated from Ur at the end of the third or beginning of the second millennium B.C. (i.e., just before or after 2000 B.C.), at a time when the Mesopotamian region was under the domination of the Amorites. (See notes at Gen. 11:27 and 28.) He journeyed by way of Haran, a city on the upper Euphrates. From there he entered a land (Gen. 11:31; 12:4–5) inhabited in part by the Canaanite peoples (cf. Gen 10:15–20), whose name apparently meant "red-purple," in keeping with an important product of the area, dye and cloth of that color. His migration took him into the Negev (see note, Gen. 12:9) and into Egypt.

Egypt and the Sinai

This region figures most prominently in the Bible in connection with the sojourn in Egypt and the Exodus. The people who entered the land of Goshen in Gen. 46 eventually served as slaves to Pharaoh and built the cities of Pithom and Rameses for him (Ex. 1:11). It was to the latter city that Moses was brought, where he was raised by Pharaoh's daughter (NSRB map 2). He subsequently fled to Midian (Ex. 2:15), perhaps east of the Sinai. There God appeared to him in a burning bush to commission him to lead Israel out of Egypt. The actual departure from Egypt proceeded from Rameses to Succoth and into the Sinai. The body of water they crossed is referred to in Ex. 13:18 as the "Red Sea," a rendering of the Hebrew name *Yam Suph,* apparently meaning "Sea of Reeds." The exact location has been the subject of much debate. Map 2 in the NSRB shows two routes that have been suggested for the continued journey, labeling them "The Way to the Land of the Philistines" and "The Way to Shur."

Assyria

Assyria first ascended to world power status in the twelfth c. B.C. The fortunes of the Assyrian Empire, which was centered at Nineveh in the heart of Mesopotamia, rose and fell under numerous kings over a period of several centuries. Most significant for biblical studies was the Assyrian invasion of Judah and Ephraim (Samaria) in the eighth century B.C., with the subsequent defeat of the latter in 721 B.C. Over 27,000 people from the northern kingdom were deported to Assyria (2 Ki. 17–18). By the early decades of the seventh c. B.C., the Assyrian Empire covered most of the Fertile Crescent, from Babylon to the Sinai (NSRB map 5).

Babylon and Medo-Persia

The role of dominant nation in the Middle East shifted from Assyria to Babylon after victories at Babylon (626 B.C.) and Nineveh (612 B.C.) and over Egypt (allied with Assyria) in 607. Shortly after assuming the Babylonian throne in 605, Nebuchadnezzar (or Nebuchadrezzar) initiated a series of attacks on Judah, and Jerusalem in particular. In 597 he overthrew Jerusalem, sending into exile Jehoiachin and many Judeans. The destruction of the Temple followed in 586, along with further deportations. Apparently, there was another shipment of captives to Babylon in 582 or 581.

Although extensive geographical details of this period are not chronicled in the O.T. in connection with the exile, the significant point is that Judeans found themselves in bondage once again at a great distance from their land and center of worship. But the O.T. highlights this time as one of great national change. In spite of the idolatry and neglect of the Temple and regulations of the law (Jer. 34:12–22; Ezek. 8:15–18) that occasioned the Babylonian captivity, God used that period of approximately seventy years to turn a large number to dependence on Him. And it is not insignificant that the O.T. clearly tells us that Babylon itself was raised up by God to accomplish His purposes for Israel, and was then removed from a place of influence as soon as the work was finished (Jer. 25:12; 1:5; Dan. 5:30). The ascendancy of the Medo-Persian Empire, which defeated Babylon in 539 B.C., is clearly connected with God's plan to bring the majority of Judeans back into the land. King Cyrus is portrayed as a beneficent instrument in the hand of God to enable Judah to return home after God's spiritual purposes had been accomplished (Isa. even refers to Cyrus as God's "messiah" or "anointed one" [45:1]). But in the meantime the distress over absence from the land (as in Ps. 137) had served as part of the chastising instrument of God to bring repentance and remove idolatry. In this case then, being under an idolatrous oppressor away from the previously neglected land and Temple had caused a rethinking of the value of God's love and concern for Judah. This simple fact of geographical distance is of great significance in the history of Israel (see NSRB map 5).

Greece

Greek influence in the Middle East rose abruptly with the conquests of Alexander the Great of Macedon. Subduing the Medo-Persian Empire within a matter of a few years, he extended his domain into Africa and as far as the borders of what is now India (NSRB map 8). The death of Alexander in Babylon in 323 B.C. resulted in the division of his empire into four parts, each under the administration of one of four prominent generals. The relations between two of the resulting regions are especially important for the history of the intertestamental period (see NSRB note on the intertestamental period, "From Malachi to Matthew," and map 7). The spiritual significance of this period for Israel is given in prophetic form in the book of Daniel (see notes at Dan. 8:1–23; 11:1–36.) In fact, the most detailed extended prophecy in the Bible (Dan. 11–12) has this period mainly in view. The position of Israel between Egypt and Syria, and the intense desire of Antiochus Epiphanes (175–164) to impress Greek culture upon the Jews resulted in the revolt of the second c. B.C. against Greek rule, chronicled in 1 and 2 Maccabees. As in the case of the Babylonian captivity, the presence of idolatry and foreign culture, along with zeal for the land and independence, led to significant events in Israel's history. It is noteworthy that the details of Hellenistic abuse, leading to the events of the Maccabean revolt, are described in Dan. 8 as prefiguring the acts of the great persecutor of Israel, the world-ruler of the tribulation period.

Rome

The intertestamental period drew to a close with Palestine under Roman domination. In 63 B.C. the Roman general Pompey extended Roman rule to Palestine, placing the Idumean Antipater over Judea along with his sons Herod and Phasael (NSRB map 7). It was into a land ruled by the Herodians by permission of Rome that the God-man entered by humble birth at Bethlehem. The extent of Roman influence on Israel's cities, ports and military activity is quite visible today, and provides fascinating illumination of the days in which N.T. events occurred. Furthermore, Roman control of the Mediterranean area is significant for understanding the events of the apostolic age, as the Gospel was taken beyond the borders of Palestine (NSRB map 8). For example, Paul's journeys, and especially his trip to Rome as a captive, come alive to the Bible student who makes use of knowledge of Roman history in the Mediterranean.

The Centrality of Palestine

Although surrounding nations and societies figured significantly in Israel's history, it is the land of Palestine itself that is most intimately connected with the experiences of the children of Abraham. There is, of course, clear biblical reason for this, for in Gen. 12 God promised that territory (and more) to Abraham and his descendants. The fortunes of Israel have been and will continue to be tied to that small area between Egypt and Syria, the Mediterranean and the Arabian Desert. In beautiful ways God has taught Israel in and through that land and its features, and will reshape that land as part of His ultimate blessing of that distinct and covenanted people (see Zech. 14). Ongoing lessons and provisions from God (beginning with Abraham, who was called out of Ur to Palestine) are intimately tied with geographical, topological, and climatic features.

The Nature of the Land

The report by the spies who searched out the land (Num. 13:29) broke the land down into four sections: the Negev, the mountains, the seacoast, and the Jordan. This is a valid and helpful outline of the topographical variation within the land of Israel as it exists today.

Negev is actually a transliteration of a Heb. word meaning ''arid'' (see note, Gen. 12:4), and came to be used to describe the arid region in the land, the southern sector between the mountains of Judea and the Sinai desert (NSRB map 2). Its condition can be directly attributed to an average annual rainfall of less than ten inches. Although such a region was and is physically uninviting, a number of significant biblical events occurred there. Beyond the constant feature of the use of the Way of Shur (NSRB map 2) as a trade route to Egypt, with its bringing of traffic through the land, we find in the Negev the experience of Hagar in flight from Sarah (Gen. 21), and the flight of Elijah from Jezebel under the protecting hand of God (1 Ki. 19). Especially in the latter account, we see that topographical hostility can be used to highlight the power and provision of God.

The mountains or highlands of central Palestine are actually a continuation of the Lebanon mountain range that extends far to the north. A parallel range is found on the eastern side of the Jordan River valley (shown on NSRB map 6, extending through the region of Gilead). The highest point in the central range is Mt. Merom (biblical Jebel Jermaq?) in upper Galilee, with a height of 3,962 feet. The elevation at Jerusalem, by comparison, is about 2,500 feet above sea level. An important break in this range of hills is the plain of Megiddo (also known as Jezreel and Esdraelon), a fertile strip running from north of Carmel to Bethshan, from northwest to southeast. It is here that significant future military movements will occur (Rev. 19) as they have in the past. The intermediate region between the coastal plain and the central mountains is known as the Shephelah. Numerous east-west travel passages cross it, providing access between the hills to the east and the coast itself. David's encounter with Goliath occurred in one of these valleys (Elah, 1 Sam. 17:2), as did some of the recorded exploits of Joshua, Samson, and Assyrian kings (2 Chr. 32:9–19).

To the west of the highlands lies the coastal plain. It is topographically interesting in that it lacks suitable natural deep-water port facilities and is abruptly terminated by the cliffs just south of Tyre (the Ladder of Tyre), where the hills of Galilee reach the seacoast. The whole plain is normally divided into four regions. Between Mt. Carmel and Tyre the plain of Acco expands at the northwest end of the plain of Megiddo. South of Mt. Carmel, between what is now Haifa and the Roman city of Caesarea, lies the

Plain of Dor, which opens into the Plain of Sharon. South of Joppa is the broad Plain of Philistia, which was already well populated when Joshua entered the land, and figured significantly in the history of Israel under Joshua.

Since major trade routes between the Fertile Crescent and Egypt/Africa passed through the coastal plain, the region had continued significance for Israel's contact with other nations. In particular, the mountain passes at Megiddo, Taanach, and Jokneam (NSRB map 4) offered strategic control of the passage of armies and caravans. Such a location made Megiddo (which gave its name to the plain) one of the most significant biblical cities. Solomon recognized its crucial role and made it, along with Hazor, Jerusalem, and Gezer, one of his principal fortified cities.

Although the topography of Palestine is varied and often striking in many places, the most unusual feature of the region is the Jordan River valley. Part of a long geological formation extending from Syria into central Africa, this natural border between the western and eastern mountain ranges contains the lowest land point on earth, that at the surface of the Dead Sea, 1,285 ft. below sea level. The bottom of the Dead Sea is approximately 1,300 ft. below that (NSRB map 6). In contrast, Mt. Hermon rises above the northern reaches of the depression to a height of 9,232 ft. As the Jordan flows southward from its source tributaries south of Mt. Hermon, it lives up to its name, which means "that which goes down,"[2] flowing into and out of the Sea of Galilee, already 695 ft. below sea level, and traveling three times the air mileage between that body of water and the Dead Sea. It is significant that there is no outlet from the Dead Sea (called Salt Sea [Gen. 14:3], Eastern Sea [Ezek. 47:18], and Sea of the Arabah [Dt. 4:49]), a fact which contributes to its rich mineral deposits. The whole depression from the Sea of Galilee to the Gulf of Aqabah is known today as the Arabah (Heb. "wasteland"; NSRB map 6) or Ghor (Arabic for "rift").

Several locations around the Dead Sea figure in biblical history. Moses was permitted to view the land from Mt. Nebo (Dt. 32:49). David encountered Saul at En Gedi (1 Sam. 24, NSRB map 3). The Essene community at Qumran yielded perhaps the most startling modern archaeological find when the so-called Dead Sea Scrolls were discovered in 1947 in caves near the community's living center along the western shore. Postbiblical events associated with Israel's subsequent history under Rome are illuminated by the features of Herod's massive palace-fortress, Masada, farther south along the western shore.

Questions for Further Study

1. What sites are possible for Mt. Sinai?

2. How far would the Israelites have traveled from Egypt to Canaan if they had gone in a straight line, assuming they reached Beersheba?

3. What area did the Edomites settle?

4. Where was the city of Hazor that Joshua took as recorded in Josh. 11:10?

5. Where were the first three cities that Joshua took?

6. In Josh. 11:16 Joshua's route of conquest is described. Trace it on a map. What is significant about this particular description?

7. In Isa. 7 Ephraim is said to be in league with Assyria against Syria (see note at

7:20). What are the relative positions of these three nations? Which was the most powerful at the time?

8. In Zech. 14:4 we are told that at the second coming of Christ the Mount of Olives will be altered. What can you tell about the topography of the area that enables you to picture what will occur?

9. Where are the two Caesareas that are mentioned in the N.T.? The two Antiochs?

10. Where did each of Paul's journeys start? Trace them using the text of Acts.

11. What continent is Thessalonica on?

12. Trace the locations of the events of Acts 16:6–9. In what direction was the Spirit moving Paul and his company? How far is Troas from Philippi?

13. Why might the N.T. speak of going "up to Jerusalem"? (Mt. 28:18, etc.)

14. Locate the cities of Rev. 2–3. Are there other cities nearby that are known to have had local churches? Suggest a reason why these particular seven cities were chosen. What kind of geographical pattern do they form?

15. Where will the events of Rev. 19 take place?

II

Summary of Bible Doctrine

9

Introduction
to Bible Doctrine

Any field of study demands summaries, comprehensive statements and practical over-views. For example, a physicist works with little pieces of information to begin with, attempting to understand what he has observed, but eventually at some point has to make organized conclusions about all his findings. A summary of all the areas of phys-ics would include all that is believed to be true in the realm of physics. It should be up to date, orderly, and should cover every area touched on by physics.

Biblical studies also needs such summary statements. They serve to give global understanding, reveal weak points as areas of study are compared and systematized, and furnish a picture of the view of interpreters of the Bible at a point in history.

Elsewhere in this book we deal at length with theology and its relation to interpre-tation (see ch. 5, Interpreting the Bible). Theology, a frightening word to some, is simply the attempt to draw together in our own words all that we understand about the Bible and its relation to humanity. One of the most obvious reasons this is needed is that the Bible, although organized for certain purposes, does not lay out its complete content in a systematic way. For example, we learn certain things about God in Gen., other things in Phil. and still more in Rev.

The word *doctrine* is used by some to describe systematized statements about the Bible. This word can actually be used with regard to any subject. It simply denotes any portion of a system of ideas, belief, or study. There is doctrine in the field of sociology, in particle physics, in microbiology, and in literary criticism.

In a sense, doctrine (when it refers to biblical studies) and theology amount to the same thing. Both are concerned with making organized summary statements about what we believe the Bible is saying. There are, to be sure, different uses of the word *theol-ogy*.

Systematic theology, as defined by a conservative Protestant, attempts to organize data from all sources concerning God and His activities. As such, it may draw on history, philosophy and other fields. It is important to note that in the last hundred years many nonconservatives have attempted to write about God without significant reference to the Bible. The name *theology* may be used for this, but its connection with the Bible varies, and sometimes it is not biblical at all, dealing almost exclusively with philosophical, linguistic, or sociological matters. Anyone can label as theology anything he wishes. But for our purposes it is important to realize that theology, as the field that ought to make comprehensive statements about God and His activities, is most fruitful if it centers on the revelation He has given of Himself in Scripture.

In this sense, some have spoken of *exegetical theology,* as an endeavor that in its summarizing and explanatory work consciously keeps the careful examination of minute parts of Scripture in the center of its attention.[1]

The term *biblical theology* has been used by some to describe an approach to summarizing that consciously avoids data from outside the Bible. We would be practicing biblical theology if we studied only what *the Bible* says about the Church, for example. Some have used *Bible doctrine* in roughly the same sense. However, we should admit that it is actually quite difficult to study any part of the Bible without touching on other areas, such as philosophy, history, the history of doctrine, and archaeology. In the final analysis, we cannot do complete Bible study without such outside helps.

Historical theology is the field that traces beliefs, particularly in the Christian Church, through the centuries. It attempts to form a history of conclusions about the Bible. Interestingly enough, such history of theology is indispensable for doing theological work in any age, for the errors and insights of the past should always form the background of current thinking. The history of any field of study is always relevant to new formulations.

On hearing the term *practical theology,* some might conclude that it is simply the useful application of otherwise dry studies. But this term denotes the employment in life of what is concluded from the Bible, and is used especially of ministry in the Body of Christ. It is, in the highest sense, the fruitful outcome of what the mind has concluded about the Bible.

There is at least one other term using the word theology that we should note— *theology proper.* This refers to a narrow portion of theological study, that centered on the nature of God as a trinitarian Being. In a real sense it is the place to begin in our thinking as we summarize the Bible, since God Himself is the reference point for all things. Theological studies that in the twentieth century have turned theology into expositions of humanity and have put man at the center of the universe, often asserting that we cannot know much about God anyway, have missed the all-important truth that we are beings who owe our existence to a personal God to whom we are responsible for all that we do. When we make doctrinal summaries, then, we are organizing in our own words what we believe the message of the Bible is. This is a great aid to our understanding, because we have difficulty grasping or considering many things at once. Further, we can compare points more easily and find out where we are inconsistent.

Unfortunately, some people believe that there is something unbiblical about doctrine or theology. They say something like, "Just give me the Bible. Don't give me human opinions." The problem with this is that as soon as anyone speaks about the Bible (unless he simply reads verses, in which case he is reflecting the decisions of translators, which in turn involve opinions about the Bible), he is rendering an opinion. When a person says "Don't give me doctrine" he is really saying "Don't give me your doctrine, for I prefer mine (although I won't call it that)."

Doctrinal/theological statements (when they are centered on the Bible) are invaluable to anyone who wants to learn more about the things of God. The following chapters, then, have the modest goal of offering a simple summary of doctrine of the type found in the Scofield Bible, which itself has many valuable doctrinal observations. In fact, the nature and extent of these observations make the Scofield unique among study Bibles.

10

The Bible

The Need for Authority

Although God Himself should be the center of our thinking as we deal with doctrinal matters, it is appropriate that we first consider how He has communicated with us. What is the nature of that permanent written record we call the Bible? The answer to this question belongs to the province of *bibliology*.

When we come to the study of the nature of the Bible, we are involved with systems of belief—Why do I believe one thing as opposed to another? And why, on the basis of what I believe, do I do one thing and not something else? This is a question of authority, i.e., what belief-action system do I place myself under, using it as the reference-point or basis for what I think, and how I act? This is significant for every human being, because it obviously determines much of what we think and do.

Since the fall, human beings have always, in regard to moral and spiritual issues, tried to avoid the authority system that comes from God. In its place they have erected many alternatives, all of which are counterfeits, some more blatant than others. In essence, the substitutes all put the individual at the center, investing him with the capability to make his own decisions without an outside reference point. To be sure, when this obviously damages society, enough people get together and alter or abolish particular variations of authority systems. But in the final analysis, according to these systems, a human being is his own authority.

It is significant that in spiritual matters there have been within the last hundred years blatant attempts to make individual-centered systems the official position of Christianity. The extreme liberal of the nineteenth and early twentieth centuries was very much influenced by philosophical trends that suggested that human beings could not know God as He was, and so people might as well talk only about their thoughts concerning God. Friedrich Schleiermacher (1768–1834) was influential in popularizing this view. It is only one step from this to the position that human beings, individually or collectively, are the standard for knowing, grasping, and recognizing truth, if any such thing is left! In the nineteenth c. this was funneled through seminaries, and led to the theological position that the Bible is only a human book, since people couldn't know anything about God apart from their own thoughts. In the classic liberal view the Bible is only a record of human beings' experiences of God.

Fortunately, there has been a swing away from that position in nonconservative theological thinking. But that position—which amounts to subjectivism—is always at odds with the Bible and God's system, no matter how vigorously it is espoused. Many nonconservatives today believe that the Bible is not a message from God in and of itself, but becomes the word of God to an individual when he finds something in it that touches his experience. If we look at this from the standpoint of authority, then we realize right away that the individual has managed to come to a place where he believes he is responsible to no one but himself, that he is his own authority.

God's Provision of a Source of Authority

It does not take much thinking to realize that the Bible makes claims about itself that are totally contrary to this kind of position. For example, integral to the outlook of the O.T. especially is the idea that God has been present in history, that He has communicated with us. In Isa. 7:14 we are taught by the concept of "God with us" that His purposes in history are focused on the incarnation. Our Lord Jesus Christ is called the Word of God, God's ultimate revelation to humanity (Jn. 1:1, note).

According to Rom 3:23 we are, because of sin, unable to reach in any way the perfections of a holy God. This includes communication with Him. In addition to sin, there is also a separation between God and the created being. Eternal is contrasted with temporal, infinite with finite, uncreated with created. Thus, we are separated from God in two basic ways: creatureliness and sinfulness.

Thankfully, God has intervened. Left to ourselves we would bring our entire race to destruction. But God has revealed to us both Himself and His will for us. He has not left Himself without witness in nature. We have only to realize that there is a clear revelation in nature of the general character of God, His power, and His wisdom. We see also that humanity has denied this revelation and gone its own way, creating its own objects of worship. Rom. 1:19–32 portrays this graphically (Rom. 1:18, note).

In addition, God has revealed Himself in special, direct ways. There is much to think upon in the hymn verse that reads:

> How firm a foundation, ye saints of the Lord,
> Is laid for your faith in His excellent Word.
> What more can He say than to you He hath said,
> To you who for refuge to Jesus have fled?

We see here the concept of a basis of faith, trust and salvation, and a foundation for life, not only in this world but also in that to come. The Word of God meets us in our need and directs us to Jesus Christ, who provided refuge from the penalty of our sin. The words of this hymn serve to point out to us many of the issues involved in this matter of revelation, and the authority of God's disclosure to us of a message that we needed to hear.

Perhaps it would be helpful at this point to summarize what we have just said as an introduction to the doctrine of bibliology:

> 1. The orthodox doctrine of the Church until the eighteenth century was that the Bible is a supernatural revelation from God.
>
> 2. Much of so-called Christendom has fallen prey to a reversal in the basis of theology, namely that since we can't know God as He is, we cannot know if He has spoken, and the Bible is certainly not revealed truth from God.
>
> 3. The basis for a good part of Christian theology has become the individual, rather than a God who has revealed Himself.
>
> 4. The whole matter is an issue of having a basis for what we believe.
>
> 5. We asserted that we are separated from God, and in His grace He has intervened to reveal to us how we can reach and please Him. This is the clear teaching of Scripture about itself. If it were not for philosophical assertions to the contrary, and our bent toward turning from God to ourselves, we would read Scripture this way.

The question of an authoritative revelation of a self-disclosing God is crucial for any work in spiritual matters. In many instances it provides the key to discerning errors in doctrine among those who study the Bible.

Revelation

General Revelation

It will be helpful if we take the word *revelation* as equivalent to "disclosure" or "communication." There are several avenues through which God has carried out revelatory activity. To begin with, there is information that is available to every human being without exception, and since it is so widespread it is called *general revelation*. Because it is available to all, and yet all do not come to God through it, it is limited in content and effectiveness.

As an example of this kind of revelation, He has communicated with us through all that we see around us in nature. Taught in such passages as Rom 1:18–21 (see v. 18, note); Ps. 19:1–2; Isa. 40:12–14, 26, this revelation provides us with information about God as powerful, purposeful and creative. This is stressed in Isa. 40:26, where we are told that we can perceive His "great power and mighty strength" from the "starry host" (NIV).

In another vein, Mt. 5:45 reminds us that God exercises continual care over humanity, and indeed the whole universe—that He allows and even supports life for those who are in rebellion against Him, as well as those who love Him—and tells us that He is long-suffering and loves His creation. Colossians 1:17 adds another detail, that the Lord Jesus Christ is holding the universe together. Of course, we cannot discern this from looking at nature. But we should be able to sense that there is someone behind life who does good things for us (although, admittedly, we are still faced with the problem of evil and catastrophes in nature).

We do not even need to go beyond ourselves to gain some information about God, for He has given us all a certain measure of ability to discern right from wrong, a conscience. We might not be able to identify this capacity specifically on our own, but Rom. 2:14–16 points out that our consciences, implanted by God, give us some ability to differentiate among moral and spiritual alternatives.

It is important to realize that these disclosures available to everyone have their limitations. They can only tell of God's existence (perhaps), personality (in limited ways), power, and purposefulness. They do not disclose His righteousness or moral attributes. However, they can give us impetus to look further for more about God. And they certainly put us in a position where we are responsible to God. Romans 1:19–20 is quite clear about this, teaching that even the knowledge gained from creation concerning God's power and deity are enough to obligate us to Him as a superior to us.

Special Revelation

But that same chapter in Rom. shows that humanity has for the most part rejected God's disclosures through these channels. It can only be the grace of God that has led Him to communicate patiently with us in other ways. To meet our need of knowing how to get to our Creator, He has told us much more in more direct ways, through the medium of language itself. This kind of disclosure has been called *special revelation*. It is special, or limited, in that it has taken place on specific occasions with certain people. It partakes of evident supernatural qualities, since it occurs as a kind of intervention into the natural course of things in human existence. It differs from general revelation in that it gives information that we need to help our situation as sinners, while disclosure in nature, conscience, and providence is addressed more to all of us as human beings.

Some might criticize this division of revelation and its purpose into two segments. It is certainly true that the words *general* and *special* do not appear in the Bible in connection with God's disclosure of Himself. But they are helpful in describing the areas or channels through which God has chosen to reveal Himself. There is no break in the unity of God's revelation—whatever the source, the same God is behind it all—but the twofold division speaks of God's desire to communicate to us in diverse ways, an activity of God that should lead us to appreciate Him more, since due to our sinful condition He is under no obligation at all to tell us anything.

In comparison with general revelation, God's activity in special revelation has been more diverse. This is described in Heb. 1:1: "In the past God spoke to our forefathers through the prophets at many times and in various ways . . ." (NIV). But there were even channels beyond those of the prophets. At times God communicated directly (Gen. 17:1) in some kind of appearance (Jn. 1:18, note), but at other times only a voice could be perceived (Ex. 3:2ff, where apparently only the burning bush was seen). Although every communication from God by the vehicle of language can be called a miracle, we would be inclined to view incidents such as the burning bush as more miraculous than God's speaking through Moses to Pharaoh, as described in Ex. 4:12.

The greatest revelation connected with a person is centered on the Lord Jesus Christ. Quite apart from anything He ever said, He Himself was a disclosure by God (Heb. 1:2). The very fact that God, in the Person of the divine-human Being, walked among us, constitutes a giving of information about Him. In fact, Jn. 1:18 (see note) tells us that this revelation, the incarnation itself, is unique, since it somehow tells us more about God, and takes us closer into the divine presence than any other communication from God. The reason for this is given in Mt. 11:27: "No one knows the Son, except the Father; nor does anyone know the Father, except the Son, and anyone to whom the Son wills to reveal Him" (NASB). Thus, although God Himself spoke to people previously, the constant presence of a divine Being, who could be observed rigorously, was the greatest of all disclosures of God. Paul describes this in 1 Tim. 3:16 as "God manifest in the flesh" (AV). Certainly Jesus disclosed God's nature as a perfect Being, since He Himself never sinned. The existence of God was clearly established. And the very obedience of our Lord Jesus Christ, apart from His words, constituted a lesson concerning the existence of a divine will for human beings.

Although the revelation taking us closest to God Himself occurred in the Person of Christ, the most valuable for later generations is the revelation which is Scripture. For, although God spoke and appeared to many, we would have no record of any of it—no trustworthy record, that is—if it were not fixed in a lasting medium. We couldn't know anything of the previous types of special revelation that we have mentioned if they hadn't been preserved.

We should remember that all of the Bible is really a revelation, even though some of the content was known previously (see discussion of sources in ch. 2, The Nature of the Bible, under "Types of Material"). Historical and geographical records may have been generally accessible, and may even be mentioned outside the Bible in other literature. But their arrangement and inclusion with material that no human being had access to—data concerning God and His will—amounts to a revelation.

There are some obvious advantages of Scripture over the other forms of special revelation. To begin with, the written text preserves messages originally given orally or in writing. They could easily have been lost over the years during transmission. Of course, the Holy Spirit preserved some information over long periods of time before it was written down. Moses wasn't present at the Creation, and wrote somewhat after the fact!

Written revelation also has the advantage of being transportable. In fact, God has made taking Scripture with us anywhere quite easy due to ready access to writing materials and the ability to translate, advancements that were both in place during and before Abraham's time.

Because the Bible can be brought to people who are in diverse locations and removed in time from those who experienced God directly as recorded in the Bible, individuals in every generation around the world become responsible to it. If we only heard about some message that God had given to people many years ago in a distant place, we might not feel it was worth investigating, and might not even be able to go and check on it even if we wanted to. But the grace of God has made the Bible accessible to many different language groups, societies, and generations. The fact that in any generation, including the present one, there are many around the world who do not have the Bible in their own language should spur us to be more involved in translating and publishing this precious revelation.

The Bible is quite clear in teaching that the Holy Spirit of God is the Agent of revelation, as described in Acts 1:16: "This scripture must needs have been fulfilled, which the Holy Spirit spoke before concerning Judas, who was guide to them that took Jesus" (AV). David, who is listed as the human author of Pss. 69 and 109, could not have spoken about Judas ahead of time, since he could not have known about his life and existence at all. But God knew it perfectly, and revealed to David what he could not know himself. (Whether or not David understood what the Spirit was leading him to write is another matter. See ch. 7, Relations Between the Testaments). In 2 Pet. 1:21 this work of the Spirit is described as "carrying along" the prophets of the O.T. (see note, 2 Pet. 1:19). That the human authors participated intelligently is clear from the many biblical indications of their emotions, desires, etc., indicated in their writings. But it is also quite clear that the Spirit of God used them as channels for the message exactly as He intended it to be given through them.

To be sure, there are limits to special revelation (whether it is a dream or vision, or Scripture itself) as there are to general revelation. Deuteronomy 29:29 reminds us that God has not told us everything that can be known about Himself: "The secret things belong to the Lord our God, but the things revealed belong to us and to our children . . ." (NIV). There are many things we would like to know, and probably many things we would not understand, that God in His wisdom has kept closed to us. But we are responsible for what we do have, for it is what we need for pleasing God: "All Scripture is Godbreathed and useful . . . so that the man of God may be thoroughly equipped for every good work" (2 Tim. 3:16–17, NIV). Although special revelation has been given in stages, so that each new disclosure adds more to the picture, we are obligated to attempt to get the most from the whole written message and obey what we find.

Inspiration

Description of the Doctrine

In describing the process of revelation we have already mentioned that God took steps to ensure that the written record of His communication corresponded with His character. If He spoke to us and yet we became confused in carefully following what He said, then He would be leading us into error. Not only would such a revelation be worthless, it would give us the wrong concept of God. He would be inconsistent with Himself.

The means God used to insure accuracy is presented in many places in the Bible. We read descriptions such as "The Spirit of the Lord spoke by me" (2 Sam. 23:2–3, NASB) and "David himself said by the Holy Spirit" (Mk. 12:36, AV). Clearly God was intimately involved in communication of the message through and to human beings. This superintending *inspiration* was an act of God that guaranteed an error-free product from the hand of the original writers. And, although the Bible never tells us exactly how inspiration took place, we can understand certain aspects of what God did.

Both of the previous examples, and many other portions of Scripture, indicate that in very natural ways human beings were a part of the process. Scripture is thus the product of a significant two-sided activity involving God and individuals. God supervised and saw to it that the message was recorded as He wanted it to be. And human beings, not always knowing that they were part of a momentous spiritual activity, recorded the revelation. The outcome is an error-free, multi-part document.

There are several qualifications that we should note, since some people have ridiculed this doctrine without having a proper concept of it to start with. First, the Bible indicates that usually God worked behind the scene, so to speak, leading in the writing, but not turning the people who wrote into robots. Only at times do we read that He directly dictated information to be inscribed (Jer. 30:2; Hab. 2:2), and then the writers were alert to what was going on.

It is also quite evident that God used people with normal human qualities that often surfaced in the inscripturation process, as in Rom. 9:1–3, where all of the longing for his kinsmen and the intense personal will of the Apostle Paul come to the fore:

> I am telling the truth in Christ, I am not lying, my conscience bearing me witness in the Holy Spirit, that I have great sorrow and unceasing grief in my heart. For I could wish that I myself were accursed, separated, from Christ for the sake of my brethren, my kinsmen according to the flesh . . . (NASB)

Also there is no indication in the Bible that we are to assign to any copies of the Bible the same qualities as those of the original writings. Admittedly, this is a difficult area. Some might ask how we could have a Bible that could help us if the translations or copies we read are not just as accurate as the originals. Or, what good does it do to talk about inspiration and accuracy of the originals if we don't have them? We need to talk about the Bibles we have and what qualities they possess today. These are legitimate questions, but they ignore several important other facts.

First, since we have copies that disagree, we would be faced, if we looked for inspiration of the copies, with the problem of deciding which one is inspired. To be sure, when we do textual criticism, we are asking which text represents and corresponds to the original, but that is a different matter. It is generally assumed that we are one step away from an original text that possessed perfection of content. And to get anywhere, we assume in doing textual criticism that one of the variant readings at any point represents the original, although it is hypothetically possible that we do not have what represents the original at particular points. (See ch. 2, The Nature of the Bible, on textual criticism.)[1]

Further, all evidence points to the fact that although we talk about error-free originals and flawed copies, the Bible still possesses God-given authority over our lives. It never gives human beings justification for passing judgment on it. Instead, it stands as a standard for us, a measure that we must always brings ourselves into line with.

It is also quite evident that if we could point to certain copies and say, "These preserve the original exactly," we would tend to pay more attention to them than to God. He has evidently given us the message in such a form that we are obligated to search continually to try to recover its original condition. Yet at the same time we are to approach the matter by faith, trusting Him to have watched over the process of transmission of the text so that we still have essentially what we need and can through textual criticism gradually weed out errors introduced along the way. If we recognize that we are led to greater trust through this transmission process and the resultant condition of the text, then we have taken the right approach.

Circular Reasoning?

Sometimes people wonder if the Bible's statements about itself should be the source for our understanding of its characteristics. Is this arguing in a circle? The Scriptures tell us truths we cannot discover in any other way. If we turn to the Bible for testimony to the otherwise unknown, we certainly can accept its testimony concerning itself. Furthermore, we look to it for information on other doctrines. Why can't we ask it about itself? It really boils down to whether we trust the Bible as a guide to itself or choose to erect some outside standard. We are in unique territory here, since the Bible is unlike any other book or document. Usually the reluctance to allow the Bible to speak about itself in regard to inspiration is a result of a predisposition to find errors in it. We are in the best position if we give the Bible every benefit of the doubt, allowing time for apparent errors to be resolved while taking the Bible's claims for itself at face value. To do otherwise is to set ourselves up as judges of the Scriptures. We should always assume that we do not know enough, as opposed to thinking that we have finally proven an error in the Bible. The biblical revelation is so much greater than human beings that we dare not do otherwise.

The Scriptural Picture of Inspiration

As God worked in and through individuals to achieve the written record He desired, He led writers to use different kinds of materials. Some were known before, some were not. Some were written, some oral. The whole process, however, involved His creative and directive hand. Two key passages provide extensive teaching on this.

The first is 2 Tim. 3:16–17: "All Scripture is God-breathed and is useful for teaching, rebuking, correcting and training in righteousness, so that the man of God may be thoroughly equipped for every good work" (NIV). When we come to this passage we realize that in some ways the term *inspiration* is misleading. The one Gr. word that is variously translated "given by inspiration" (AV) and "inspired by God" (NASB) really does not refer to in-spiring, that is, of breathing into something. Instead, v. 16 tells us that Scripture comes from God. What we should avoid thinking is that God took existing writings and put His stamp of approval on them. The initiative and the material were clearly from Him.

The word inspiration has led some to think of the process of giving Scripture as similar to our concept of a thinker or writer getting a sudden flash of intuition. We speak of a poet or a musician rising above himself and accomplishing something extraordinary. The use of the word inspiration in some translations and as the name of a doctrine should be understood quite differently, however. 2 Tim. 3:16 actually says that the Scriptures are "breathed out." Exactly what happened to the individual writers is not stated here. But we do know that the writings are "breathed out" from God. Simply stated, Scripture came from God. As Benjamin Warfield said many years ago, "The Scriptures owe their origin to an activity of God the Spirit and are in the highest and truest sense His creation."[2]

We need to understand Paul's statement from his first-century perspective. Although Paul could have already (at this point, after sixty A.D.) possessed N.T. writings that he regarded as Scripture, the only "Scriptures" that Timothy could have known and used "from infancy" (v. 15) were the O.T. These were the "holy Scriptures" to any Jewish person. It is significant that for Paul the whole body of O.T. revelation was God-breathed, for v. 16 specifies that no part is excepted from the process ("all").

Our discussion of this passage would not be complete if we failed to observe the practical outcome of inspiration. Precisely because it comes from God, Scripture is useful in generating and guiding spiritual growth and service. It teaches, convicts of error, leads to the proper realm of behavior, and generally brings about righteousness, ultimately leading to fruitful service for God (v. 17). The Bible student should also observe that 2 Tim. 4:1ff contains an exhortation to *use* Scripture for those very ends, especially in ministry to others. This is essential because correct teaching—which the Bible always provides because of its source—is ignored in every age and will be increasingly shunned in the future (vv. 3–4). Because it is God-breathed, the Bible always offers us the truth of God and always withstands error (see note, 2 Tim. 3:16).

Although 2 Tim. 3:16–17 does not take us very far into the interaction between God and the writers of Scripture, 2 Pet. 1:19–21 does provide some insight into that cooperative activity. In this passage Peter is concerned with showing the same value of Scripture in counteracting error. In the face of ever-present moral murkiness (v. 19), the Bible appears as a light—the only light—giving us hope that the things of God will prove to be lasting and worthwhile. (One of the main purposes of the epistle is to encourage the readers to maintain a pure life in the face of many spiritual dangers around them.)

This passage speaks of the process of revelation specifically from the point of prophecy. But there is no reason that we could not legitimately apply its teaching to the rest of Scripture. For Peter, prophecy was not given to arouse curiosity (there were some who were mocking prophecy itself, as indicated in 3:3ff). Instead, it had its source in God. Peter underscores its superhuman origin in two ways. To begin with, it did not arise through discoveries by the prophets who spoke in the O.T. (v. 20). It was not as if they had searched and searched on their own and were finally able to put together something later regarded as Scripture. No, neither their minds nor their wills (v. 21) produced Scripture. They could not, because a higher source was needed. Instead, the prophets (and others, we assume) were "carried along" (NIV) by the Spirit of God. As a ship is empowered by and at the mercy of the wind, so also the writers of Scripture were totally dominated by God, here, in bringing the prophetic writings to others. Nothing that the Holy Spirit did not want to be inscribed ever was. And everything that He did want to appear, was written.

Once again, we should not overlook the connection between inspiration and the life and service of the child of God. The Bible is the only light in moral darkness, because it is from God. Anything less would make it part of the confusion. Scripture can only help us see through and rise above ever-present distortion of spiritual realities if it is from God. This is one reason we can never presume to pass judgment on the Bible. We are to study it, yes. But when we do not understand it we are to let it have the final say. Otherwise we contaminate it with the error that surrounds us and which we are trying to avoid (see note, 2 Pet. 1:19).

The Extent of Inspiration

We have not yet addressed the question of how much of the Bible is the product of this kind of supervisory activity. We might think that parts of the Bible were written under it, but others somehow were left out. There are, however, many indications that we should view every part of the Bible as coming from God, down to the words themselves. In Jer. 30:1 God told Jeremiah to write specific words in a book. In addition to statements of this kind, we should stop to consider the fact that as human beings we cannot send or receive significant messages without reference to words. Even Morse code, although it does not utilize words at its lowest level, reflects words. While some have suggested that God simply gave individuals general suggestions concerning what He wanted them to write and they filled the rest in on their own, that kind of view flies in the face of the implicit and explicit statements of Scripture and leads to serious problems. For the Bible to be breathed-out and thoroughly trustworthy it would have to be exactly what God intended. Human elaboration of God-given ideas would not achieve this.

This quality of possessing God-given detail at the level of the individual words of the Bible is called verbal inspiration. We should not search to try to figure out which parts of the Bible are breathed out and which are not. For the message to be from God all the parts have to be from Him.

This brings us to a concept that many have overlooked in recent discussions of inspiration and the error-free nature of the Bible. It is perfectly all right to say that the Bible teaches implicitly and explicitly that the words themselves are what God intended the original readers to receive. But we should not overlook the fact that messages using human language carry meaning not by stringing together the meanings of successive words. Instead, meaning, that is, the content of information that a message moves from one person to another, is carried at many points and in many ways in texts. Individual words have meaning only in connection with other linguistic items, some of them words, some of them parts of words or relative placement of words. For example, a particular word in Gr. or Heb., by virtue of its position in a sentence, may carry the message ''view this word and therefore what it stands for in this text as emphasized.'' It does this not because it is a particular word as opposed to another, but because it appears in the text in a different place from what might normally be expected. In other words, meaning can be indicated by *relations* within texts. Many more examples could be given (see ch. 4, The Language of the Bible, under ''Language as Code.'')[3]

One of the implications of this for inspiration is that it is not accurate to make the formulation, as many have made over the years, to the effect that we should be concerned with the very words of the Bible because the words are the place where the exact intended message of God is carried. The exact words are certainly necessary. And inspiration does not involve the concepts only. But the information God has given us is carried in complex, interlocking ways in the text. This kind of view of inspiration, linguistically based as it is, actually enhances our view of the activity of God in giving the Bible, since it brings to the fore the intricate nature of the Bible and reminds us that it had its origin totally in the perfect purposes of a God who is able to design beyond our capacities to do so.

Someone might also say that they can believe some of the details of the Bible are a product of the creative and supervisory activity of God, but that there might be some question as to whether every single section or book of the Bible is included in that activity. In other words, the statement in 2 Tim. 3:16 certainly includes all of the O.T., since we have every reason to believe that Paul saw the O.T. Scriptures as a canonical unit even in his own time, but it doesn't necessarily say that any of the N.T. is ''breathed out.''

We have help in this in Jn. 14:26, where Jesus, in predicting the coming ministry of the Holy Spirit, said, ''He will teach you all things, and bring all things to your remembrance, whatsoever I have said unto you'' (AV). Now that is just the kind of ministry that would give the Gospels, especially, the same qualities as the O.T. Scriptures, which were given through the ministry of the Spirit. Also to the point is Jn. 16:12–15:

> I have much more to say to you, more than you can now bear. But, when he, the
> Spirit of truth, comes, he will guide you into all truth. He will not speak on his own;
> he will speak only what he hears, and he will tell you what is yet to come. He will
> bring glory to me by taking from what is mine and making it known to you. All that
> belongs to the Father is mine. That is why I said the Spirit will take from what is
> mine and make it known to you. (NIV)

This broadens Jn. 14:26 to include material not already spoken by Jesus, and especially
mentions prophetic truth. Together these two passages describe all the material of the
N.T. written after Jesus' death as being under His authority and from Him (see note,
Jn. 16:12).

There are other lines of evidence that we are to regard the N.T. as just as much a
product of the creative breath of God as the O.T. In 1 Cor. 14:37 Paul indicates that,
at that point at least, he was aware that what he was writing was "the Lord's command" (NIV). Similar to this is 2 Pet. 3:2, where Peter places his writings on a par
with the O.T.: ". . . the words spoken before by the holy prophets, and . . . the
commandment of us the apostles of the Lord and Savior" (AV). For a first-century Jew
to elevate his writings to the same level as those of the revered prophets was quite a
claim! A few verses later Peter specifically places Paul's writings in the category of
"Scripture," which for Peter must have been, as for Paul in 2 Tim. 3:16, the O.T.
writings: ". . . as also in all *his* letters, speaking in them of these things, in which are
some things hard to understand, which the untaught and unstable distort, as *they do* also
the rest of the Scriptures, to their own destruction" (2 Pet. 3:16, NASB).

Although not all of the writings of the N.T. are specifically assigned to the category
of "Scripture," the process of canonization, the acknowledging that books had their
source in God, argues for the inspiration of all twenty-seven. Even in the last book of
the N.T. there was a consciousness of writing God's words (Rev. 1:1–3; see also the
note at 1 Cor. 2:13).

Jesus and Inspiration

It is interesting that some Bible students suggest that what is important is not a "rigid"
doctrine of inspiration, but simply paying attention to the words of Jesus. Not only does
this immediately imply that He could be in conflict with Scripture (which is not borne
out by the N.T.), but also that His words might be somehow superior. However, examination of His views of the O.T. is quite revealing, and actually adds a great deal to
our understanding of inspiration.

On many occasions He quoted the O.T. and described the cited material with the
phrase "it stands written," as in Mt. 4:4, 6, 10. As He used the O.T. in those verses
to ward off Satan's temptations, He showed that He believed it had permanent authority
and was capable—on its own—of defeating the tempter. In one writer's view, "Jesus
backed up [spiritual principles] with Scripture, which for Him as for all Jews, would
endow it with indisputable authority."[4] It is very significant that the God-man put Himself behind the shield of Scripture. We might think that as God He could ignore the
O.T., since He had created it. But just the opposite is true. We never find Him contradicting Scripture, and in fact find Him depending on it for everything. He gives every
indication of consciously living out the prophecies that concerned Him (see for example,
Jn. 19:28, where He seems to quote an O.T. verse in order to fulfill prophecy). He

would not have acted this way if He did not believe that the Bible had absolute authority over Him—authority that comes from its complete accuracy.

We see this exemplified in a significant passage, Mt. 5:17–20. Here Jesus declares that His purpose is to fulfill the O.T. Scriptures, i.e. to act in such a way that He furthers their prophecies and other prefigurements. He must do this because every portion is binding (vv. 18–19), and also will find fulfillment. In other words, no one can thwart the ongoing purpose of God as carried in Scripture. As we read Mt. 5:18, we might at first think it is a promise that the original writings of the O.T. will not perish: ''For verily I say unto you, Till heaven and earth pass, one jot or one tittle shall in no way pass from the law, till all be fulfilled'' (AV). A jot is the smallest letter of handwritten script in the Heb. text, equivalent to our *i* in some respects. A tittle is any small portion of a written letter that serves to distinguish it from other similar letters. A moment's reflection will lead us to conclude that every portion of the autographs had by that time indeed disappeared, yet the law, which included predictive elements, had not yet seen complete fulfillment. Either Jesus was wrong, or there must be something else involved.

Jesus must have meant that the smallest details of *meaning* would eventually find fulfillment, even though the physical letters might disappear. No part of the message would fail to find its place in the outworking of history. But for this to happen, the small parts must be from God as much as the larger parts. In fact, everything forms a web of meaning. Nothing is dispensable. Now if this is so, what Jesus is really saying is that all of the law, in this case, has its origin in God. Otherwise the little parts could not be so important. Every part is significant to God, and so He insured that every part was exactly the way He wanted it. This is then an implicit argument for the inspiration of the O.T.

Jesus' view of the O.T. is very instructive to the Bible student, forming a whole area of investigation. Among other things, it shows that He always put Himself under the authority of Scripture, viewing it as having all the answers for His life. This is nowhere more evident than at the crucial points of His life and ministry, e.g., the temptation in the wilderness and His passion (see note, Mt. 4:1). He knew the O.T. well, quoting relevant portions from memory at just the right time, with perfect application. As in all things, He provides an example for us in this. Believers in every age should likewise put themselves completely under the Word of God. This is both possible and rewarding because of the inspiration of Scripture.

Those who appeal to the authority of Jesus as opposed to that of Scripture have entirely missed the point. Jesus continually supported the highest view of the O.T. Those who choose to reject His outlook on the O.T., or to pit Him against the O.T., have misread the Bible.

Help for Our Understanding—Illumination

Up to this point in this ch., we have not spoken about how we can interact with the Bible. Through the centuries many have wondered if there are special keys for approaching and understanding it. 1 Cor. 2:10–14 provides an answer. The context deals with taking in revealed truth from God. To begin with, v. 14 shows that there is a basic requirement for receiving information from God: possessing the Spirit of God. This is true because a person in his natural unregenerate state considers the things of God to be nonsense. He cannot understand them and does not accept them (v. 14, NIV). Spiritual discernment is necessary. This ministry of the Holy Spirit is called *illumination* (see note, 1 Cor. 2:13).

Some distinctions must be drawn here. Revelation concerns the material, the information, the content that God has communicated in the form of the Bible. Inspiration is a term that describes the process of writing down that disclosure. Illumination is the Spirit's work in providing understanding of that written message.

In Jn. 14:16 and 26 our Lord predicted the coming ministry of the Holy Spirit to teach His followers. But Jesus first carried out this ministry Himself. This is recorded in a beautiful account in Lk. 24:13–45, where in a postresurrection appearance He thrilled the hearts of two discouraged disciples on the way to Emmaus. According to vv. 44–45 they could not make a connection between His death and the teachings of the O.T. So He first expounded the Scriptures (v. 27), explaining how they pointed to Him. As a result, they possessed a desire to know more, recognizing the importance of what He said (v. 32). Finally, He opened their understanding for a very specific purpose—to understand the Scriptures, particularly concerning His death, burial, and resurrection (vv. 44–46). So, His ministry was a forerunner of that of the Spirit in this age to individuals concerning Scripture. The Spirit continued His work because He was no longer present in the flesh.

This activity of the Spirit is described in 1 Jn. 2:20 and 27 as an "anointing." In looking at this passage some have quickly concluded that there is some special work of the Spirit that is to be sought and brings some special blessing. But v. 27 shows clearly that the anointing is a ministry of teaching. The context tells us that this task of the Spirit is needed to keep us from falling for error (vv. 20, 26–27). And what is most important is that every believer has this ministry (v. 20). No limitations of time or frequency are placed on it. We conclude, then, that it is always available.

Some cautions are needed at this point. First, we cannot expect the Spirit of God to teach us what the Bible means if we do not work and study. It would make learning the Bible easy if God put us into a trance and poured into us all He wanted us to know from the Bible. He could do that. But all the biblical evidence points to the fact that He expects us to put forth effort. The simple fact that we are commanded to study is proof enough of that (2 Tim. 2:15).

A second guideline: be aware that every time you look at the Bible you need illumination. That constant ministry of the Spirit must exist to meet constant need. It is not presumptuous to ask God to teach you whenever you study. Such dependence reminds us how much we need God's help and that we are venturing into spiritual territory, where we cannot operate directly.

A third caveat: be careful not to confuse inspiration and illumination, as some do, supposing that God gives us the same supernatural help that the authors of the Bible possessed. Those groups that put their authority on a par with Scripture in effect do that, supposing that God will show them today information equal or superior to what is in the Bible. The biblical writings were *inspired*, breathed out by God; readers of the Bible are *illumined*, taught to understand what has already been written and takes precedence over their insights.

Finally, we should be careful to avoid the common error that suggests that a light within the individual is more accurate than the writers of the text of Scripture were and than the original text itself was. This is a form of subjectivism and allows the individual to set himself up over the Bible.

Authority

C. H. Spurgeon once said, "There is no need for you to defend a lion when he is being attacked. All you need to do is to open the gate and let him out!" The Bible in action is like that. As a result of their inspiration, the Scriptures possess a quality that has been described as *authority* and that assures that they are the complete expression of God's sovereign will for human beings.

We already saw above in the discussion of Jesus' view of the O.T. that He believed that He had to depend on it entirely, and that it had permanent spiritual validity. This is suggested, for example, by the little phrase "it stands written," as found in Mt. 4:4, 7, and 10, and elsewhere. There are other passages where Jesus' outlook on the Scriptures comes through clearly.

In Mk. 12:18–23 Jesus is queried by the Pharisees, who pose a hypothetical riddle in an attempt to trap Him. His reply amounts to a rebuke: "Are you not in error because you do not know the Scriptures or the power of God?" (NIV). The Sadducees should have known Ex. 3:6, which He goes on to cite. Consequently, Jesus chides them for not knowing from Scripture what God said, and not applying it to give them the answer and to correct their error. Scripture would have told them the correct and spiritually valid answer because of its authority.

Here, then, is an important sequence. The Bible possesses authority over life; it brings correct doctrine (teaching) into a life; the result, all other things being equal, is correct practice.

Similarly, in Jn. 10:34 Jesus refutes a false doctrinal view resulting in a false practice by referring to the authority of Scripture. Certain Jews had accused Him of blasphemy. In making this charge and attempting to stone Him, they were acting incorrectly. Jesus' quotation of Ps. 82:6 provides the needed corrective to their behavior. They had an improper estimate of Him. They would have understood Him and acted properly on the basis of spiritual understanding, if they had known the Scriptures ("Is it not written in your Law . . . ?"[NIV]).

Perhaps they might have thought or said, "We are not bound by the words of Ps. 82:6." Jesus' words indicate that (1) Scripture carried full weight over them, (2) they were responsible to it, (3) it stands alone as an unchangeable reference point, and (4) they came under its jurisdiction. This provides us with a succinct and powerful statement of the authority of Scripture.

Earlier in this chapter we indicated that the issue of authority is of immediate relevance for every person's life. We automatically assume some source of authority, some reference point for our lives, whether ourselves, or something or someone external to us. The Bible provides that authority because, due to revelation and inspiration, it is authoritative in itself. It is a unique and sufficient guide for life, and claims to be the very best one.

We encounter some very foundational matters here. As the British theologian J. I. Packer points out in his very fine book on this topic, there are only three possible answers to the question of authority.[5] We are either traditionalists, subjectivists, or biblicists. The traditionalist (in regard to "Christian" issues) holds that the Bible isn't a safe guide. Instead, he claims, we can look to tradition to supply what is lacking in Scripture, which isn't a sufficient authority because it isn't self-contained (outside information must be added to it) or self-interpreting (outside institutional sources must interpret it for the average person).

The subjectivist holds that human reason is the standard for authority. This position is decentralized (as opposed to the institutional/traditional) and has as many submanifestations as there are individuals. But wherever it is found it has the same simple pattern: human beings believe they are qualified to pass final judgment on the trustworthiness of the Bible and, if it is deemed unreliable in whole or in part, to substitute for it anything else they wish.

The biblicist holds that the Bible is the final authority for everything in life. Even if we don't understand it (and no one understands all of it), we are answerable to it. As a matter of fact, even if we never hear it we are still answerable to it. If a person never hears a word from the Bible, and hence never hears the Gospel, he will be lost just as surely as if he had heard the Gospel over and over for years and rejected it. The Bible possesses its authority over us independently of us.

There are several very practical implications of this. To begin with, every word of the Bible is binding on our lives. Just as our Lord Jesus Christ was in subjection to its authority, even in its finest points, so we should be, too. This means we have to study it and soak in it, then ask God how to apply it. No area of our lives is exempt from its scrutiny. We are in trouble before God if we don't say in everything, "I will start with Scripture. What does Scripture say? I will look to it first and construct my ways of behavior from it." Remember, because of the authority of Scripture, service in an organization, in a church, in a Christian school—anywhere—is of no value to God unless it is done in accord with Scripture.

This applies positively as well as negatively. We are obligated to find out what the Bible says. But we are also obligated to discern when what we are doing and what it says do not match. We are always under a divine injunction to search for and discard error, whether in what we believe or what we do. Packer summarizes this forcefully:

> Inevitably, we grow up children of our own age, reflecting in our outlook the mental environment in which we were reared. The process is as natural as breathing in the air around us, and as unconscious. It is easy to be unaware that it has happened; it is hard even to begin to realize how profoundly tradition in this sense has moulded us. But we are forbidden to become enslaved to human tradition, whether secular or Christian, whether it be 'catholic' tradition, or 'critical' tradition, or 'ecumenical' tradition, or even 'evangelical' tradition. We may never assume the complete rightness of our own established ways of thought and practice and excuse ourselves the duty of testing and reforming them by Scripture.[6]

Trustworthiness—Inerrancy and Infallibility

The historic position of the Christian Church has been that the Scriptures are free from error and correspond at every point to what is true, with God as the reference point. Of course, this is a quality claimed only for the originals, not for copies or translations. (See above in this ch. under "Inspiration," concerning the quality of the kinds of manuscripts and translations that we do have.) This doctrine is called *inerrancy*.

If we think more in terms of actual use of the Bible, the term *infallibility* has been used to describe the trustworthiness of Scripture, indicating that it can in no way lead us astray from true doctrine or practice.

These two doctrines are actually two sides of the same coin, since we cannot have one without the other. Because of this, some have suggested that they are essentially synonyms for the purposes of discussion of biblical matters,[7] especially since some evangelicals in recent years have attempted to say that the Bible may be infallible in certain areas that it speaks to, but may not be inerrant.

Both of these doctrines are intimately connected with inspiration.[8] Since inspiration is the process in which God by His superintendance assured that the original writings were exactly what He desired as His word to us, then as a result they are inerrant, and are therefore infallible. If we have God's word, and it is without error, then because it is from God and not from us it must be totally trustworthy for doctrine and practice, that is, infallible. So inspiration leads to inerrancy, which in turn leads to infallibility. Each link is vital. In what follows we will assume that inerrancy and infallibility cannot be separated.

How can we demonstrate inerrancy? Perhaps one of the primary sources for establishing the doctrine lies in the character of God and His relation to the Scriptures. If, as is presented in places such as Jn. 3:33 ("He who has received His witness has set his seal to *this,* that God is true" [NASB]), then God is absolutely truthful; He is incapable of communicating error or deception. Any product of His creative activity—especially in the light of 2 Tim. 3:16—must also be inerrant and trustworthy. The universe was in a perfect condition originally. Both it and the copies of Scripture were subsequently corrupted by human beings. God's initial product was perfect.

Some clarifications are needed here. Some people are all too eager to see "errors" in the Bible, but have overlooked some rather obvious features of Scripture. First, inerrancy does not mean that there will be total verbal correspondence between parallel accounts appearing in different places in the Bible. The fact that Mt., Mk., and Lk. do not agree on a particular incident in the life of Christ does not warrant immediately jumping to the conclusion that one or more is wrong. Often a plausible explanation— one of many possible ones—is that the writers are all reporting true details, but are highlighting or picking and choosing according to their specific purposes in writing. An assumption of this kind gives the Bible the benefit of the doubt until apparent errors can be clarified.

The Bible is a genuine book with normal literary features. To opt for error in response to figurative language is an invalid approach. The Bible is not presenting error when Jesus claims He is a door. It should be expected to make effective use of symbols and pictures.

Similarly, we should not expect the Bible to employ a technical and scientific vocabulary, matching the standards of rigorous description of any particular age. And the Bible can hardly be faulted for saying "the sun rises and sets" when we do the same—and know that the sun does no such thing.[9]

Furthermore, inerrancy does not usually depend on the matter of establishing the Heb. or Gr. text. Those who claim the Bible has errors do not usually point to variant readings as examples of errors.[10]

Recent Objections

There is an important movement among a minority of evangelicals in the last half of the twentieth c. that is attempting to refine doctrinal statements about the nature of inspiration, inerrancy, and infallibility. Some have claimed such things as the following: (1) inerrancy should be ascribed only to revelational matters that have to do with salvation or explicit teaching; (2) the express teaching of the Bible concerning its own inerrancy (and inspiration) may not be sufficient to establish the real nature or extent of inerrancy, or conversely, although the Bible may state explicitly that it is inerrant, the actual embedded details may show errors.

Although some have come to these and similar conclusions, they are often reluctant to say there are clearly errors in the Bible. But often this position seems to involve a willingness to allow for error.

Both positions, however, have been strongly criticized by the majority of evangelicals, and rightly so. Either one amounts to setting oneself up as a judge of Scripture, assuming that one has the insight and sufficient information to determine conclusively exactly where there are errors. But who decides what is to be called error? Where do we draw the line? How do we keep this from affecting other doctrines? Questions such as this have been raised by Harold Lindsell, among others.[11] Furthermore, isn't God quite able to preserve the Scriptures from error in the process of inspiration? Apparent errors can very well be just that—apparent. We do not have to assume that so-called errors are valid, since we do not possess enough evidence to label them as such.[12] Although it is entirely possible that what the Bible teaches about its own inspiration— and most are agreed that it *teaches* inerrancy—could be contradicted by embedded details elsewhere (a geographical or chronological item or the like), the best course, according to most, is to hold judgments in abeyance and give the Bible time to be proven correct, through new discoveries, etc. This amounts to a faith position, of course, and involves suspending our judgments even though there may appear to be problems. Many recent studies by those concerned with upholding inerrancy have shown that features of the Bible that seemed to be erroneous can be easily explained, if there is enough careful study.[13]

This is an important area of discussion, for many reasons. It is vitally linked with the issue of inspiration. What we believe about inspiration determines what we believe about inerrancy, and vice versa. Secondly, those who are quite willing to allow for errors in the Bible assert that we can still hold to the full authority of the Bible over us even without inerrancy. However, given a toehold, the depravity of human beings will always lead them to discard the demands of Scripture. None of us by nature looks for an authority from God. Rom. 1 is quite clear on that.

Questions for Further Study

1. Using passages such as 2 Tim. 3:16–17; Tit. 1:9, and Eph. 4:11–16, suggest some ways in which doctrine and practice are related.

2. Try to make a comparative and contrastive chart of the various kinds of reve-

lation (general and special) that will give you a helpful visual picture. What kinds of revelation are found in the following passages:

Acts 9:4–6	1 Tim. 3:16
Num. 12:6–8	Ex. 33:11
Rev. 1:10–11	Jn. 1:18
Acts 17:24–28	Jn. 14:9
Ps. 94:9–10	Mt. 11:27

3. Examine carefully 1 Tim. 5:17–20. Verse 18 consists of two quotations from the O.T. Using references in the margin or at the bottom of the page (or from ch. 22, Guide to Old Testament Quotations in the New Testament), determine (1) the sources of the quotations; (2) the reason these two are put together; (3) why both are called Scripture. What does this tell us about Paul's view of the books he quotes from?

4. Read carefully Gal. 3:8 and Gen. 12:1–3. Who spoke in Gen. 12:1–3? What does Gal. 3:8 do with Gen. 12? What is unusual or striking about Paul's wording? What qualities are ascribed to Scripture? How could Paul be justified in doing this?

5. Read Rom. 9:17 and Ex. 9:13–16. What quality is ascribed to Scripture in Rom 9:17? Who actually spoke to Pharaoh? Paul would not say that Scripture is the same thing as God. What kind of connection is he making, then, between God and Scripture?

6. Using scriptures given above and found in the Scofield notes, attempt to assess which passages, if any, best describe or characterize the different types of special revelation. See notes at 1 Cor. 2:14; 2 Tim. 3:16; 2 Pet. 1:19.

11

God

His Characteristics or Attributes

It should come as no surprise that it is very hard to describe what God is like. We are created beings attempting to talk about the One who made us. Since He gave us our existence, He is in every way greater than we are. We are derived. He is not derived at all. The best we can do is to say as much as the Bible says, noting points where we correspond to Him in some way, making helpful categorizations, and giving illustrations. Often in order to describe Him we must resort to saying what He is not, for instance, in regard to His holiness, since we have never experienced such a quality, and since we can know what the absence or opposite of holiness is—that we *have* experienced!

Over the centuries Bible students and scholars have suggested various ways of dividing the discussion of God's attributes and the qualities of His essence. But it will be helpful if we notice that there are some qualities that describe what His basic nature is, some that describe the qualities He has by Himself, and some that describe qualities of which we are allowed to partake.

The Bible speaks of characteristics or qualities of God that involve not doing but being or existing. He is a spiritual Being, without physical properties (here is a negative definition already!) and invisible to human beings (Jn. 1:18). Yet He is alive and personal (we have trouble thinking of something that can't be seen as alive and able to interact with living beings).

Because we are created and live in a cause and effect environment, we have difficulty conceiving of anything that exists without reference to anything else. Yet God is like that because He is totally independent of all other things and beings for His existence and all He does. He reveals Himself in Ex. 3:14 as the God who will not fail to keep His promises because nothing can change Him, since everything depends on Him. He does not need anything from anyone or anything in order to be everything He can and wants to be.

We must describe negatively when we come to what theologians have called His immensity. He is not limited in regard to space. He can be everywhere in His creation—physical and spiritual—and yet not be part of it. The pantheist says God is part of the universe and the universe is part of Him; he cannot thus have a personal God. The God of the Bible is both personal and immense.

God's infinite quality with regard to time is described as His eternality. Again, we have great difficulty thinking about living without succession of events. And yet God, as the cause of time—He has created it for His purposes—is not bound by it in the least. All things and events, in any and all of what we know as time periods, are equally present to Him (Isa. 57:15; Gen. 21:33, note).

The great *Shema* of Dt. 6:4 (note) expresses a crucial attribute of God: He is uniquely God; there is no other God but Him; He is not a plurality, and cannot be looked at as divisible into parts (1 Cor. 8:6). One very common error outside the Judeo-Christian tradition is polytheism, holding to the existence of many Gods. This biblical teaching concerning His unity counters this fallacy as well as the error of seeing the Persons of the Trinity as separate gods (see "The Trinity" below).

The Bible reveals several qualities of God that are not so much descriptive of what He is in Himself but of how He is related to His creation. But again, it is difficult to place satisfactory titles on these divisions. Ps. 139:7–12 teaches that God is personally present everywhere in regard to His creation and all living beings. He can function this way because of His immensity, his teaching is a great encouragement to believers, and should serve as a deterrent to sin, since there is no act anywhere in the universe that escapes His notice. This attribute is often called God's omnipresence.

Not only can God be present everywhere, He also knows everything there is to know: He is omniscient. This includes not only what actually occurs—the kind of things we can know, up to a point—but also what could possibly occur, all the potential combinations of events out to an infinite number. Both His omnipresence and His omniscience are taught in Jer. 23:23–25.

A third characteristic of God that is seen especially in His activities is that of His omnipotence, His ability to do whatever He wants to. This is subject, of course, to His other attributes. He could not will to sin in any way, or to be other than what He is. Jer. 32:17 emphasizes the power side of this attribute; other passages remind us that it can never get Him into trouble. He cannot be inconsistent with Himself.

An attribute repeatedly brought to the fore in God's dealings with His own is His immutability. As described, for instance, in Mal. 3:6, this means that He does not vary from what He is and always has been and always will be. Furthermore, nothing could possibly influence Him in such a way as to bring about change in Him. Appealing to His immutability, God speaks through Malachi to confirm that His promises to Israel are still in effect, in spite of the nation's sins. In other words, circumstances do not disturb God or cause Him to change His plans.

There are qualities of God that are associated with behavior, and are especially connected with human existence, as He interacts with us. They are also attributes that we can share in to a degree. One of the most difficult to describe is His holiness. This is found so often in the Bible that we might think it would be easy to nail down. Perhaps we might initially say that it means He does not sin. But if we were to stop and think about that, we would realize that sin is defined only with respect to God Himself. So we would be going in a circle. It certainly involves His being separate from sin, but we should also add that it is His moral perfection, although this is again perhaps circular. We end up essentially defining God's holiness negatively. This may not be such a bad way to approach this attribute, since we know what sin and error are, and can understand at least a little about what living apart from sin might be like. In fact, the process of sanctification for a believer should involve our sinning less and less, and thus being more and more like God in regard to His holiness. Isa. 57:15 paints a beautiful picture of the God who is so much different from all of us in morality: "For this is what the high and lofty One says—he who lives forever, whose name is holy: I live in a high and holy place, but also with him who is contrite and lowly in spirit, to revive the spirit of the lowly and to revive the heart of the contrite" (NIV). Even God's name—biblical names are so often reflections of character—is pure.

Often confused with God's holiness is the attribute of righteousness. Although at times in the Bible they seem to be used interchangeably, righteousness, especially in Rom. 3:21–26, speaks of meeting a standard, in this case, holiness. Paul's argument is that God could have been called into question for forgiving sins before the cross. Now that the proper payment for sin has been made, however, the whole world can see that God had a plan in mind to take care of previous sins. He never "cheated" on people's accounts with Him, cancelling debts without warrant. This vindication is described as righteousness. He can be declared righteous as a result of the cross, and can turn around and pronounce human beings righteous, that is, completely in accord with His demands for holiness.

God reveals Himself to us as beneficent in many ways, all of which theologians have described with the cover term *goodness*. One of the ways He shows this is by loving those He has created. He always extends Himself toward human beings, wanting them to experience Him, even when that does not involve an election relationship. Certainly there is a special degree of love exercised toward the elect, but He is so much characterized in general by love that John says simply, "God is love" (1 Jn. 4:8). This does not mean that love and God are interchangeable, that when a person loves someone else then that is somehow part of God. Nor does it mean that love is an attribute of God to be viewed as dominant over others. It does mean that love is such an evident and pervasive quality of God that He can be equated with it.

The contrast between God's nature and ours is highlighted throughout the Bible through His attribute of mercy. When Paul describes God as "rich in mercy" in Eph. 2:4, he is indicating that God extends Himself to us especially to overcome our human frailty. When we cannot help ourselves, even if we wanted to, His mercy brings His goodness to us. Our greater need, however, is to have God reach out to us to overcome our sinfulness. This act is described as His grace. In fact, it comes toward the elect so abundantly that it seems like an overflowing treasure (Eph. 1:7–8). It is amazing that God would show grace and mercy and love toward sinners. But He extends Himself through these characteristics continually, often over long periods of time (as in the case of Israel, especially) in spite of repeated rejection. He is thus a long-suffering God, as described in 2 Pet. 3:9.

Finally, there is abundant indication everywhere in the Bible that God never deceives us, never leads us into error, never tricks us. He has the pervasive attribute of truth, taught in such a pithy manner by John in his first epistle: ". . . we are in him who is true—even in his Son Jesus Christ. He is the true God and eternal life" (5:20b, NIV). We can always count on Him to be totally straightforward and to act in complete accord with actuality, whether in His written revelation or in His leading day by day.

A moment's reflection on these attributes will lead us to realize that we can share in some of the latter ones: holiness, righteousness, love, mercy, grace, truth, long-suffering. However, God is always the standard, and our enjoyment or practice of them is based on their extension from Him to us and to the work of the Holy Spirit in us. In another vein, we are spirit beings as He is, but have great difficulty operating in the spiritual realm, unlike angels, for instance. This quality of spirituality that we partake of, along with others such as the capacity to know, understand, think, and have personality, are all part of our resemblance to God as made in His image and likeness (Gen. 1:26, note).

The Names of God

Throughout the Bible there is a constant emphasis on relations between an individual's name, on the one hand, and his character, on the other. This is especially true in regard to God, who lives up perfectly to descriptions through His appellations. Although there are many names for God in Scripture, we will consider only three here. Explanations of many others can be found in ch. 20, Guide to Bible Study Terms, and in the Scofield notes, especially at Mal. 3:18.

Jehovah

Strictly speaking, this is the only name of God in the Bible. The other terms point to aspects of His character or of His relations with people. *Jehovah* is actually a word that was created in the Middle Ages by the rabbis. Reverent Jews traditionally did not pronounce the proper name of God when they encountered it in the Hebrew text. That word was apparently to be pronounced as *Yahweh*. Instead they substituted the word *Adonai*, "Master," "Lord." Several centuries after Christ Jewish scholars inserted the vowels of *Adonai* between the semivowels and consonants (*h* and *h*) of *Yahweh*, thus creating *Jehovah*.

Although the term Jehovah is found before Ex. 3, in that chapter God speaks of Himself as the self-existent One who is able to keep promises all by Himself. Many scholars make a connection between the name and the phrase *I am,* from the verb *to be.* If this association is correct, *Yahweh/Jehovah* has to do with independent existence. It would thus point to the God of the Bible as the only entity in the universe that does not depend on anything else. This is, of course, a perfectly appropriate name for Him, since He is the Creator of all things, and everything depends on Him. *Yahweh/Jehovah* teaches us through His personal name that He is unique, powerful, different from every other being, the sustainer of everything, and the One who alone can keep His promises perfectly. It is the name especially of the covenant-keeping God of Israel.

El/Elohim

El is well known as the generic name for deity, and has counterparts in Semitic languages other than Heb. It is thus equivalent to Gr. *theos,* and is employed similarly. *El* in the O.T. and *theos* in the N.T. are both used for the unique deity of the Bible, Jehovah, as well as for any claimed deity (e.g., the god of this world). *Elohim* is a plural, and can mean gods, but is applied also to the God of the Bible (see note, Gen. 1:1). Many have suggested that this grammatically plural form is designed to reflect the plurality of the Trinity. It also appears that *El,* which appears often in compound forms (*El Shaddai,* etc.), suggests strength and power, although we should be careful not to read earlier meanings into later occurrences of words. (We may be justified in doing this with *Jehovah/Yahweh,* however, since Ex. 3:14 may be a deliberate word play.)

Adonai

This term, mentioned above in connection with *Jehovah,* is the Heb. word for "Lord" or "Master." When the God of the Bible is thus addressed or identified, we are to view Him as the One who demands and expects obedience and controls the affairs of individuals as well as the universe (Gen. 15:2, notes).

For explanations of the other terms associated with the God of the Bible, see the note at Mal. 3:18 and the passages and notes it refers to. The student of Scripture should conduct independent studies of the names and descriptions of God, for they are a rich mine of devotional and doctrinal help.

The Trinity

One of the hardest doctrines of the Bible to grasp is the teaching that God is three Persons and yet one God—the Trinity. But this does not mean that it cannot be one of the most precious areas of understanding or the believer. Statements such as "There is in the Divine Being but one indivisible essence" are certainly likely to turn most people off. And they do not seem to have much everyday relevance. We will attempt to be practical in the following discussion.

One reason the Trinity is difficult to understand is that it is not something we have any analogy for in our existence. It is found only in the Bible. Partly because of this, some have shown great skepticism. Thomas Jefferson said it was "incomprehensible jargon." Some have called it a fairy tale. If we look in the heavens, we see a revelation of God, but not of the Trinity. It cannot be proven. It cannot be illustrated. It is unique in the universe. Yet this uniqueness has a significant implication. Because of the existence of such a Being, I am obligated to acknowledge that I am created, I am derived, I am dependent, and I must worship Him. In fact, any attempt to put away the biblical teaching on the Trinity must be viewed as an effort to make God like me.

There are several basic elements to the biblical picture of the Trinity. To begin with, God is both a unity and a plurality. His unity is stressed in the Bible in order that we might not fall into the very common error of polytheism, even when talking about the God of the Bible. That pronouncement of Dt. 6:4 (note), so precious to the Jew, is evidence enough of God's singularity: "Hear, O Israel! The LORD is our God, the LORD is one!" (NASB). As soon as we speak of separate Persons, it is easy to think of separate gods, but the Bible warns us against that.

Further, the God of the Bible is not one Person who shows Himself to human beings in three ways or forms (an error called Sabellianism). There are three separate Persons comprising one God. This is suggested or taught in such passages as Gen. 1:26; 11:7; Ps. 2:7 (see ch. 6, "Literary Aspects of the Bible"); Isa. 6:8; Mal. 3:1; Mt. 3:16–17 (see note, v. 16); Jn. 14:16–17. Mt. 28:19 (see note) and Jn. 10:30 underscore the equality of and agreement between the Persons. The many passages that teach the deity of Christ and of the Spirit demonstrate that each Person is just as much God as the others.

But what about passages such as Phil. 2:5–8, where it appears that one of the Persons can be dominant over the other or have more power? The Bible indicates that in God's program of dealing with humanity and the universe, especially in regard to providing salvation, the Persons of the Trinity are distinguished by certain things they do. In Phil. 2 the incarnate second Person is said to change something in relation to deity. Reading carefully we notice that He subordinated Himself—as the God-man—to the will of the Father in order to go to the cross for human beings. This was part of the outworking of the distinct roles of the Persons. The Holy Spirit did not become joined to humanity, nor did the Father; the Father never appeared to individuals, nor did the Spirit; neither the second Person nor the Father is said to have directed the writers of Scripture: the Spirit did. And so it was the second Person who voluntarily submitted Himself to the Father for the sake of sinners.

We have already used several terms for the Persons of the Trinity. Actually the Bible never speaks of the first Person, second Person, and third Person of the Trinity. As a matter of fact, it never uses the word *Trinity*. But all are convenient in helping us to understand this difficult doctrine. The Bible does speak of the Father, the Son, and the Spirit. The word *God* can refer to the Trinity in general or to each of the Persons. *Lord* is used often of both the Father and the Son.

It is important that we understand that the second Person of the Trinity and the Jesus that we encounter beginning at Bethlehem are different in some important respects, and this also complicates the picture when we are talking about the second Person. But, in general, the same features hold concerning the second Person before and after being joined to humanity. We will discuss this further in ch. 12, The Person of Christ.

It might be helpful at this point for us to provide a definition of the Trinity, keeping in mind that the Bible does not give such a succinct statement and does not use the term *Trinity:* There is only one true God, existing as a single Being comprised of three Persons who are equal in every way, yet distinct in their tasks and relations to humanity.

Especially with the doctrine of the Trinity, we should stress the practical connections with our lives, lest we see this teaching as dry and of little importance for us. In addition, applications will help us to understand the Trinity better.

To begin with, each of the Persons is equally worthy of worship, equally powerful and equally glorious. We often tend to forget to be thankful for each Person, perhaps thinking only of the work of the incarnate second Person. But all deserve our praise. And if we think of the Father as dwelling in glory, we should conceive of the Son and the Spirit the same way, especially in light of such passages as Heb. 4:14 and 9:24, where the Son is described as being in the presence of the Father, certainly sharing His glory.

While what we have just said stresses the equality of the Persons, their special functions have practical aspects, too. Each has a complex and extensive role, especially toward believers. We ought to cultivate, for example, the special presence of the Holy Spirit to teach and encourage us (Jn. 14:25), and the distinctive and crucial work of the Son in providing high priestly victory over temptation (Heb. 4:14).

At times we are careless with these special roles, however. One of the key features of the Son's work was to provide access to the presence of the Father (Heb. 10:19–22). The Son is now occupied with keeping that way open, lest sin somehow close it (Heb. 7:25). He is the permanent bridge to the Father. As such we go to the Father through Him, and of course all our approaching is done through prayer. That is the reason our prayer is to be directed to the Father on the basis of the work of the Son (Heb. 7:25; 10:19–22). Certainly all three Persons are aware of our praying, but approaching the Father through the Son indicates that we understand the roles of the Persons concerning our salvation, and that pattern is also the one presented in the N.T. in the prayers that we have recorded after the cross.

Another often neglected teaching associated with the Trinity is that the believer actually has all three Persons within him. We think most often of the Spirit's presence (Eph. 1:13, note; Jn 14:17), but Col. 1:27 and Jn. 14:20 (see note) and 23 teach the indwelling of the Son and Father. This alone—the spiritual presence of all three Persons of the Godhead—provides every believer with all the comfort, teaching, and encouragement that he will ever need. None of us ever needs more of God, although we do need to submit ourselves more. And all three are active in keeping the believer secure (Eph. 1:13, note; Heb. 7:25; Jn. 10:29). We are thus triply guarded. There is enough here for endless contemplation—and thanks!

Certainly the O.T. revelation touching the Trinity is scant compared to that in the N.T. In the wisdom of God He told us little of what He is like as a Trinity until that Trinity acted on behalf of sinners to provide salvation. We find out what the Trinity is like when we see in full operation the Godhead's work for us. It takes the Trinity to save us—that's how sinful we are!

Errors Concerning God and the Trinity

Erroneous views of the Trinity and of the nature of God are highly instructive to us. We may take it as a biblical principle that the importance of a doctrine can be evaluated by the extent of satanic efforts to distort it. In this sense, the doctrine of the Trinity ranks at the top.

Atheism, outright denial of the existence of God, is a position that many hold. If you are an atheist, you believe that man is alone and life is meaningless. This is the Soviet cosmonaut's view of the universe ("I can't see God, so He must not exist."). It is contradicted by evidence in nature, the conscience, and the spiritual makeup of the individual, as well as by biblical teaching. At heart, it is a rejection of the self-revelation of the personal God of the Bible, who has on innumerable occasions communicated with human beings for their benefit. Many people are practical atheists because they have not bothered to inquire about the existence and character of God.

Agnosticism, the belief that one cannot know if God exists or not, amounts to a suspension of knowledge. As with atheism, it rejects the many self-disclosures of God. It is an affront to the God who has spoken, is based on pride, and offers no hope for life now or after death. Both positions are contrary to the basic makeup of human beings, who desperately need contact with their Creator and have the spiritual capacity to interact with Him.

Pantheism is an often sophisticated but actually illogical view of God. It denies the existence of a personal God who interacts intelligently with human beings. Instead, God is the same thing as the universe, and, in turn, the universe is God. Of course, in this view we are part of God and He is part of us. If you are a pantheist, then you have to conclude that at any given moment you are sitting or standing on God! It actually sacrifices God's personhood for His infinity, and, in some forms of the view, makes God physical, although in some variations everything is supposedly nonmaterial and spiritual, including the universe. Pantheism is an attempt to reduce God to identity with His creation.

Polytheism, the belief in a plurality of gods (equal or differing in rank) is prevalent throughout the world, as is pantheism. This view clearly contradicts the biblical teaching that there is only one deity and that He is unique in power and position. In polytheism in general, the adherent can never know if he has pleased the right god. We might call this the Alka-Seltzer view of God. Like a medicine that covers all the bases, polytheism, by encouraging placating all the gods to obtain favor, assuages the conscience—at least it attempts to!

Deism is the view that God exists and can interact with human beings, but has withdrawn from contact with them. In some forms it involves denial of a Trinity, the incarnation, miracles, and other orthodox doctrines.[1]

Many organized groups, and individuals also, deny the equality of the Persons of the Trinity or the existence of the Trinity itself. This may be due to a denial of the deity of the Son or Spirit (for many the Spirit is just an "influence"), or to a rejection of the concept of the Trinity as mathematically incomprehensible. Jehovah's Witnesses are an example of a popularly presented denial of the deity of the Son and Spirit. They are strongly anti-Trinitarian: there is only one God, whose name is Jehovah. According to them, Satan himself originated the doctrine of the Trinity. In their literature the Trinity is sometimes represented as three gods in one person. The Son is not God, and the Spirit is not God and not a Person.

In Christian Science, actually religious pantheism, God is not personal, but is the whole universe, rather, the universe is God. In this system, angels are pure thoughts from God, the Holy Spirit is Christian Science, and Jesus Christ was not deity.

Mormonism is a sophisticated version of polytheism. Latter-Day Saints say they believe in the Father, Son, and Spirit, but these are for them only three of many gods. Among their gods are human beings who have, through works and time, become divine. The heart of the Mormon system involves the doing of good works leading to a physical existence after death, with the prospect of becoming a god. Such gods have physical bodies (another serious error of biblical understanding), have mates, and engage in procreation.

Granted, the Trinity is not completely explainable in human language, and probably could not be understood while we are under the limitations of our present existence. Still, such positions, if they are conscious, evidence an unwillingness to accept the data of Scripture. There can be no question that the downplaying of the deity of Christ, for instance, and His equality with the Father, is connected with erroneous views of salvation, since the Bible is quite clear that it took a perfect sacrifice—that could be provided only by deity—to take away sin. Denial of the deity of Christ always leads to autosoteriology, the attempt at self-salvation.

Many of these errors that can be seen at the present time correspond to views held through the Church Age. For example, Arianism, propagated initially in the fourth century, held that the second and third Persons were created, and thus not eternal, or deity. Many hold essentially the same position today. This and other errors concerning the Trinity tend to deny three key features of the Trinity taught in the Bible: the deity of the Son and the Spirit; the equality of all three Persons; and the distinctiveness of the three Persons.

No area of doctrine is more important, and none more rewarding to careful study— and devotional consideration—than that of the Trinity. Errors concerning the Person of God lead easily to errors concerning His work and relations to human beings. Many of the most significant movements away from orthodox positions have had errors concerning the Trinity at their core. On the other hand, the spiritual health of the believer is always helped by careful consideration of the nature of the God who both creates and saves.

Questions for Further Study

1. Where is the Scofield note on *El Olam* located? How do different translations render it? Is it more a title or a description? What does it reveal about God? How is it connected with people and events in contexts where it appears?

2. Where is *Jehovah-Nissi* found? What does it suggest about God?

3. What does *Jehovah-Tsidqenu* signify?

4. What does Mt. 3:16 teach about the Persons of the Trinity and their relations?

5. From Jn. 14–16 list as many relationships as you can between the Father, Son, and Holy Spirit.

12

The Person of Christ

He is described, among other ways, as the Son of God, the Son of Man, the Messiah, the Lord, the I AM, Immanuel, the Lamb, the Child (Isa. 9:6), Our Great High Priest, the Vine, the Word of God, the Savior, the Rock, the Stone, the Servant, the Branch, and King. He is the dominant theme of the Bible—the Lord Jesus Christ. Most Christians know of His Person and work only in fragments. They need a comprehensive study of both areas in order to get a grasp of the overall teaching of the Bible and to put together and relate to each other His Person in its various aspects and His works for human beings. This section will deal mainly with His Person, but will necessarily touch on His activities, which are covered more fully in a subsequent chapter (The Doctrine of Salvation, ch. 17).

Just as with our study of the Bible's teaching on the Trinity, our study of the Person of the Lord Jesus Christ should be a lifelong endeavor. We can never know too much about the One who took on human flesh that He might die in the place of sinners. The Bible student should use this section as a springboard to long-term investigation of that One to whom all the Scriptures point.

His Titles

Sometimes when we name our children we select words—if we know their meanings—that suggest concepts we want to associate with our offspring. And these concepts may involve things we project or wish on them as extensions of us. Of course, in many instances, the original sense of names has been lost, especially when they are imported from one language to another. Parents naming a son Daniel, for instance, might bestow that name on him partly because they like its sound, perhaps partly because they know individuals with the name whom they like, and partly because they know that it means "God is my judge." Human beings may or may not appreciate their names, and may or may not live up to their meanings, but in the case of the Lord Jesus Christ, His names are clearly designed to reflect what He actually is.

Son of God

In Heb. the term *son of* followed by a noun meant that the people or concepts so linked grammatically were to be taken as having a special connection. A son of thunder was a person who was characterized by thunder, was thunderlike, or, simply, had a thunderous personality. *Son of* did not imply physical descent. In the case of Jesus, the title Son of God describes His deity. He has a relation to deity that is similar to but far deeper than a human being could have.

Aside from the use of this specific phrase, the concept of Jesus' divine sonship is implied when He refers to God as His Father. Although the term is used of angels (Job. 1:6) and ordinary human beings (2 Sam. 7:14; 1 Jn. 3:1), it has special significance when applied to Jesus.

It may be helpful to point out what Son of God does not mean before showing what it does. It does not indicate that Jesus is derived from God, as some groups say. If He were He could not be as fully deity as the Father. Since His deity is fully affirmed in the Bible, He must be eternal, as are the Father and Spirit. This also rules out the view that He was created. When Col. 1:15 describes Jesus as the firstborn, it is speaking of rights of inheritance, not generation. He did not begin at a point in time. Nor does the term mean that Jesus was or is in any way inferior to God.

What does the term mean, then? One passage that helps us understand the meaning of this title is Jn. 5:17–23. Here Jesus describes how He and the Father are in perfect harmony (v. 17). What one does the other also does. The Son is completely dependent on the Father (v. 19). As such He perfectly reflects the Father's will. In v. 18 Jesus clearly asserts His deity, indicating that God is His Father in a special sense: ". . . he was even calling God his own Father, making himself equal with God" (NIV). The following verses (19–23) are an elaboration of the unity and equality of the Father and Son as shown in their activities and the honor people ascribe to both equally. This relationship is eloquently affirmed by the centurion in response to the miracles after the death of Christ: "Surely he was the Son of God!" (NIV).

It is important to inquire how long Jesus is the Son of God. Did His sonship start at the incarnation? Matthew 3:17 emphasizes the sonship at His baptism, and Rom. 1:4 does the same in connection with His resurrection. But Jn. 10:30 may tell us that the Father/Son relation has been eternal, since certainly He was always one with the Father. It is certainly true that it is not until the incarnation that the relation becomes noticeable, and we have little revelation in the O.T. concerning it (Ps. 2:7; Isa. 9:6; and, in a more veiled sense, 2 Sam. 7:14).

What significance does this term that underscores Jesus' deity have for believers? First, as Son of God He reveals God to us. In Jn. 1:18 we have God revealing God: "No one has ever seen God, but God the One and Only, who is at the Father's side, has made him known" (NIV). What is disclosed must be given perfectly. Second, as

Son of God He is sinless and can die for us, as described in Mt. 27:54 (above): God dies for human beings. Third, as Son of God He will judge the world after resurrecting the righteous (Jn. 5:25ff). It will be God in the Person of the Son who will judge. And finally, as the resurrected Son of God now invested with power (Ps. 2), He will rule the nations and believers with Him. God will rule in the Person of the Son of God (see ch. 6, Literary Aspects of the Bible, for an exposition of Ps. 2).

Son of Man

We do not have to look very far to realize that our planet with its societies is in poor condition. The earth has been mismanaged in many ways, economies are never stable, there is persistent starvation. We may conclude that the earth is a mess. Closer to home, we are quite aware that jobs take perspiration, it is hard to make ends meet, and sometimes there are no jobs at all. We may conclude that in many ways life on this planet can be very nasty. Further, without a biblical viewpoint, most people believe that human beings are not worth very much and are the victims of fate: what good is life, anyway? There are several passages in the Bible that address these things. Romans 8:18–22 acknowledges that the earth is out of kilter, and humanity along with it. This sense that we are overwhelmed by life and cannot overcome our weakness, particularly in regard to the sin that besets us, is underscored in Heb. 4:15–16. And the whole book of Ecclesiastes addresses the question of the value of life in general (concluding that apart from God nothing counts).

It is against this background that God's provision comes, the encouragement of a name for the incarnate Lord Jesus Christ—Son of Man. Above all it stresses that God knows just what it is like to be human. If the title Son of God describes Christ's deity, glory, and infinity, then Son of Man highlights His humanity, humility, and finiteness. If as Son of God Jesus is omnipotent and self-sufficient, as Son of Man He is pushed around and dependent. The Son of Man got wet when it rained. To bring it closer to home, if the Son of Man were here today, there would be times when His car wouldn't start! And we should be struck by the fact that this is the term that Jesus used for Himself more than any other—more than eighty times. He wanted us to know that this characterization would be especially helpful for us.

It is this title of Son of Man, then, that should be especially dear to us in our humanity. Its content is taught both by specific uses of the phrase and by passages where Jesus' humanity is highlighted. When we are tired, we are to look to the Son of Man who got tired, too (see note, Mt. 8:20). When rejected, we are to remember that it was the Son of Man who was rejected (Mk. 8:31). At those times when we feel as if heaven is far away, we are to recall that the Son of Man has opened the way into it (Jn. 1:51), since to take humans to the presence of God He has to be human, too. If we long to know God better, we are to look to the Son of Man, who reveals Him, remembering that God is just like the Son of Man. Should death touch our lives, our consolation is the Son of Man who suffered, hurt, cried over Lazarus, and died (Heb. 2:14ff). We are commanded to go to God at the time of temptation through the one who was also tempted, yet never conceded (Heb. 2:18; 4:15). Should we ever feel that life has no point, we must recall that with the Son of Man we have a glorious future (Dan. 7:13; Heb. 2:9–10).

Martin Luther effectively summed up the concept behind the Bible's use of this title in his "A Mighty Fortress Is Our God" (italics mine):

> Did we in our own strength confide,
> Our striving would be losing:
> Were not the right *Man* on our side,
> The *Man* of God's own choosing:
> Dost ask who that may be?
> Christ Jesus, it is He;
> Lord Sabaoth, His name,
> From age to age the same,
> And He must win the battle.

Messiah

One of the most frequently used terms applied to our Lord Jesus Christ is *Messiah*. Unfortunately it is the center of much confusion. For example, for an unbelieving Jew, has Messiah come? Is Messiah a person? Is a believing Jew today related to the Messiah? Is he "fulfilled" in the Messiah, as some teach? Is a Gentile today in the Messiah?

There are many ways that the concept of Messiah is presented in the Bible. One way is through the meaning of the term itself. The Heb. word *mashiach,* transliterated "Messiah," is an adjective made from a verb, and could be translated roughly "anointed one." The N.T. *christos,* made from the verb meaning "anoint," has an equivalent meaning. Thus Messiah and Christ represent the same concept. (It should be remembered that Christ is not a last name, with Jesus as the first name, as many seem to think).

The concept of ritual anointing lies behind these words. The anointing of any individual in connection with the offices of prophet, priest, and king signified two things: God's appointment, and identification of that person with a sphere of service to be performed for God and human beings. The term *Messiah* points, then, to one who is appointed by God and serves Him and humanity.

In addition, because of the significance of these offices in Israelite life, any one who fulfilled all three was an extraordinary person. Because he does just that, the Messiah is presented as the ideal Israelite. Thus Ps. 45:1 (see note) appears to point beyond a mere human king to the very best king that could be contemplated, who would be the Messiah. (Although the term *Messiah* is not used in the ps., the king is described as having received a spiritual anointing [vv. 2 and 7].) As to the offices of priest and prophet in relation to the ideal Israelite, all Israelites were originally to be priests (Ex. 19:6) and prophets (Num. 11:29), but the only perfect priest/prophet is the Messiah.

There are many other terms that suggest this same concept of God's perfect delegate. Seed of Abraham, Son of David, Son of Man, My Son, My Servant, My Elect, the Branch, Prince of Peace, Word, Counselor, Mighty God, Everlasting Father—all of these are Messianic terms in the sense that they point forward to or describe the work of God's ideal individual, although they also may suggest other features of Christ's character or work.

An important question related to how the N.T. presents Him is that of what kind of Messiah the Jews expected. More than 400 O.T. passages were taken by ancient Jewish teachers to speak of the Messiah (Gen. 3:15; Ps. 2:2; 22:7, etc.). But in spite of the extensive O.T. revelation, Jews did not expect the Messiah as He is found in the N.T. They correctly looked for a king, and saw the Messiah's existence before the world, superiority to Moses and the angels, sufferings and violent death, redemption of Israel, Gentile opposition to Him, and the universal blessings and kingdom that He would bring. Yet they failed to see His priesthood (as indicated in part by the extensive revelation of it in the book of Hebrews), providing access to God by dealing with sin. Further, in a sense they slighted his role as a prophet, not earnestly seeking a true revelation from God to meet their needs. In short, they looked for kingship and deliverance, not release from the guilt of sin. Today orthodox Jews have many of the same expectations as the Jews of the first century. Reformed and nominal Jews tend to look at the Messiah as perhaps a person, but possibly an age or the fact of Israel's being in the land.

New Testament writers clearly quote O.T. passages that Jews had regarded for centuries as messianic and apply them to Jesus. Acts 2:35–36 and 13:33 are two examples. In the latter reference, Paul explicitly states that the resurrection of Jesus was a fulfillment of Ps. 2:7.

The relation of individuals today to the Messiah is an important doctrinal issue. To begin with, all believers are the recipients of divine favor through the Messiah. The O.T. promises of a Messiah are unfolded as God deals with Israel, primarily from Gen. 12:1 onward. Through Israel all the elect from the nations are blessed secondarily through association with God's chosen ideal individual. This is the point of Rom. 11:12–24 and Paul's concept of grafting.

Second, Jesus is not the Messiah for the Church, since "Messiah" is an office exercised toward Israel as a nation. Anyone—Jew or Gentile—who comes to Christ during this age is part of the Church, the Body of Christ. Certainly Jesus and the Messiah are the same Person, but we should remember that *Messiah* is a title descriptive of His ministry toward the chosen nation. Since the Church and Israel are not the same entity, creating a group (as some say, "returning to the Messiah") that emphasizes Jesus as the Messiah, while slighting His role as the Head of the Body for Jews *and* Gentiles today, violates what is taught in the N.T. about erecting barriers between Jew and Gentile after those divisions have been torn down (Eph. 2:14; see note, 3:6).

Perhaps the dominant lesson for us that is taught in the concept of Messiah is that God's grace overcomes man's depravity. Throughout the whole O.T. there is the emphasis that God will reverse the effects of the fall through a redeemer who is prophet, priest, and king. This is grace and the theme of the O.T. Further, when we think of Jewish understanding then and now, we are reminded of the nation's spiritual hardening. They wanted a king-messiah for national hopes, but did not want a sin-bearer. The outlook is the same today: we don't think we need a redeemer. As with the hardness in the heart of any individual, God can overcome this through His grace. And this is pictured especially in the figure of the Messiah.

Other names of the God-man are described in ch. 20, Guide to Bible Study Terms.

The Work of Christ Before Bethlehem

Where was Jesus before Bethlehem? What was He doing? How is He described? Was He a priest? Was He a king? Who was He? In one sense, He was simply the second Person of the Trinity, and so it is not quite correct to speak of a "Jesus" before Bethlehem. But for the moment, we will use the term for the sake of simplicity. The important thing is to inquire whether that Person was active in ways that had continuity with the activities of Jesus after Bethlehem. It is likely that if any average Christian were asked what the second Person was doing before Bethlehem, he would not be able to say very much. And that is unfortunate, because we lose out when we don't see His work before the incarnation. Jesus did exist *in some way* before Bethlehem (something called His *preexistence,* and different from His *eternality,* which denotes that He has always existed), and was very active in human affairs.

To begin with, He was active in the creation of the universe (along with the Spirit [Gen. 1:2]; see also Jn. 1:3; Col. 1:15–17, etc.). The latter passage also reveals that one of His tasks has been to uphold the universe and enable it to function since the Creation (see note, Col. 1:15).

Several names provide insight into His activity. For example, when John quotes Zech. 12:10 in Rev. 1:7 he is making an equation between the "Jehovah" of the O.T. ("me" in Zech. 12:10) and the "Jesus" of the N.T. The same truth is taught when Ps. 110:1 is quoted in Heb. 1:13. The "Lord" of the ps. is the "Jesus" of the N.T.

Jesus' activity before Bethlehem is emphasized by His many appearances to groups or individuals in the O.T. All of these are describable as theophanies. A theophany is by definition an appearance of God. A Christophany is an appearance of Christ. In a strict sense, all theophanies are Christophanies, since no one has ever seen the Father (Jn. 1:18). And, since Jesus is God, all Christophanies are also theophanies.

Perhaps the most striking of these are the incidents involving the angel of the Lord. While not all angel of the Lord appearances involve the preincarnate Son (as in Zech. 1:12–13), most do. His appearances show a great breadth of work, mainly for Israel. For example, in Gen. 22:11–18 He appears to stay Abraham's hand in sacrificing his son, and to promise further blessings for the patriarch. In Jud. 2:1–4 (v. 1, note) it is the angel of the Lord that warns and judges Israel, reminding them of the covenant He made with them; clearly we are to take the angel and Jehovah as one and the same.

Other incidents, although they do not speak of the angel of the Lord, clearly involve the preincarnate Son. Certainly He was one of the three men who appeared to Abraham in Gen. 18:1–33, since v. 1 tells us that the Lord appeared to Abraham, and v. 10 records that He spoke as one of the men.

What can we conclude from this kind of O.T. evidence? First, when N.T. writers interpret O.T. divine names as applying to Jesus, we can learn that through progressive revelation God was preparing people to understand Jesus' work after the incarnation, and so we can comprehend better God's desire that we grasp the meaning of that event. Second, Jesus' appearances before Bethlehem help us to see the preincarnate Son of God as doing the same things in the O.T. for Israel as He does today for us: comforting, guiding, empowering, protecting, correcting, warning, chastising, promising, and testing faith. This is an example of Rom. 15:4: "For everything that was written in the past was written to teach us, so that through endurance and the encouragement of the Scriptures we might have hope" (NIV).

We should learn also by noticing what is missing from the O.T. descriptions. Jesus was not the Son of Man before Bethlehem, since He is that only after being joined to humanity. The various kinds of appearances, and the emphasis on the birth in Bethlehem, indicate that He did not have a body before then. Nor was He the Messiah before Bethlehem, since His roles as prophet, priest, and king toward Israel did not begin in the formal sense until after Bethlehem. He was not a king yet, and He is not really ruling publicly as a king even now although that is just a matter of time (Ps. 110:1; Heb. 10:13). Jesus' prophetic ministry did not begin until after the incarnation, a role described, for example, in Rev. 1:5 ("the faithful witness" [NIV]), and Jn. 1:18, where

He is characterized as the perfect revealer of God, the basic function of the prophet. And His role as priest could only be carried out after humanity was joined to deity, since His priesthood involved knowing both sides perfectly and bringing them together. The fact that all these roles began or had their basis in the events at Bethlehem should make us very alert to the significance of the incarnation.

The Incarnation

J. I. Packer has described the incarnation as the "supreme mystery" associated with the gospel.[1] It is more of a miracle than the resurrection, because somehow a holy God and sinful humanity are joined, yet without sin being present. In Jesus God enters the human realm. "Nothing in fiction is so fantastic as is this truth of the incarnation."[2]

The word *incarnation,* which means "coming to be in the flesh," is used to describe the event of Bethlehem and its continuation. It is the permanent joining of the nature of God with the nature of a human being. Although it began at a point in time, that union will continue through eternity, for the work of the God-man for His own never ceases.

If we grant that it was God's desire that the preexistent second Person of the Trinity enter into the human realm to deal with sin and become truly human, the question arises of how that end could be achieved. He couldn't just take up residence in an existing human body. He had to have a natural human origin and enter the human family as all others do. The result of the way that God chose was that He did possess a fully human and fully divine nature. On the one hand, He had to be fully human to be the heir of the promises to David to sit on his throne, to fulfill the earlier promises of blessing to Abraham, and to be able to help fallen humanity (Heb. 4:15). On the other hand, the testimony of Scripture (Col. 2:9) is that "in Him dwelleth all the fulness of the Godhead bodily" (AV). We could say that God's purpose of redemption was achieved through the incarnation, and the incarnation with its particular necessary details was achieved through the virgin birth.

The biblical description of how God brought God to humanity is a beautiful example of how miracle is woven into the fabric of the description of real life, with several important lessons for the student of the Scriptures. Although the coming of a redeemer is predicted as early as Gen. 3:15, it is in Isa. 7:14 (see note) that we first find predictions of an unusual birth. There a promise is given to faithless, doubting, rebellious Ahaz and his court that a virgin would conceive, bear a son and should name Him Immanuel. The terminology used in Isa. 7:14 clearly points to the mother as a moral, unmarried woman, hence, a virgin. Matthew tells us that this prediction found its fulfillment in the events of Bethlehem.[3] We should not miss the main point of the prophecy: it brings God to Israel, since *Immanuel* stresses the very presence of God with and among human beings. The child born in Bethlehem, the same one as described in Isa. 9:6, brought to humanity the longing of the ages to be fulfilled ultimately as portrayed in Rev. 22: God will actually live among us.

It is important to note that in the context of the prediction in Isa. 7 and the fulfillment in Mt. 1, the sin of Israel is stressed. The naming of the babe as Jesus (Mt. 1:21) would be connected with salvation from sins. Further, the sins of the nation are prominent in the genealogy in the earlier verses of Mt. 1, where the Babylonian captivity is used to mark out sections in the history of Israel from Abraham to Christ. And in Isa. the sign of the virgin birth came from God in the midst of rebellion against Him. As such, it highlights humanity's rebellion and God's grace. The virgin birth brings God to humanity to save us from our sins.

The only way God can save us is through one who is really human but also really God and thus sinless—''from the Holy Spirit'' (Mt. 1:20, NIV). The solution to the relation between God's justice and our sinfulness is provided through the incarnation, which in turn is carried out through the virgin birth. It brings into existence a Person who is fully human and fully God, yet without a sinful nature.

What is important to note in this is that the normal transmission of the sinful nature is overridden in the case of Christ. Heb. 4:15 tells us that He was without sin, and Lk. 1:35 speaks directly concerning the incarnation:

> The Holy Spirit shall come upon thee, and the power of the Highest shall over-shadow thee; therefore also that holy thing which shall be born of thee shall be called the Son of God. (AV)

The great theologian Benjamin Warfield said cogently, ''Born into our race he might be and was; but born of our race, never—whether really or only apparently.''[4]

If there had been no virgin birth, we would face the despair of the fall with no hope. It is the God-man who is the great Reverser. He can do this because He did not partake of Adam's sin. If he had our nature He would not be able to counter Adam's act.

If there had been no virgin birth, there would be no future for humanity on the earth. It is clear that we cannot live peaceably on the earth in societies. God will rule the earth with people on it through a man, the ideal man, the sinless man, so made by the virgin birth.

If there had been no virgin birth, we would not know what God is like. In the O.T. we get only a few glimpses of the nature and heart of God. Jn. 1:18 confirms this, but tells us how we have come to know what God is like. One who is God can reveal God. One who is human can show this to humans. There is considerable emphasis on this in the N.T. The God-man was God tangibly among human beings (1 Jn. 1:1–2) and a testifier of heavenly things (Rev. 1:5). Without the virgin birth and resulting incarnation it would be impossible to overcome the estrangement between us and God.

If there had been no virgin birth we would have no example to show us how to please God in life. He alone of all who ever walked on earth has lived the perfect life before God.

If there had been no virgin birth, we would have no one who really knows what it is like to be one of us, trying to resist sin. As a sinful One, with no sinful nature to lead Him to strike back, He could endure trials without sinning (1 Pet. 2:21–25). This, by the way, is the basis for the exhortation of Heb. 4:15–16 to use His tested priesthood when we need it, in order to overcome temptation ourselves.

Packer forcefully summarizes the incarnation:

> The really staggering Christian claim is that Jesus of Nazareth was God made man—that the second person of the Godhead became the 'second man' (1 Cor. 15:47), determining human destiny, the second representative head of the race, and that He took humanity without loss of deity, so that Jesus of Nazareth was as truly and fully

divine as He was human. Here are two mysteries for the price of one—the plurality of persons within the unity of God, and the union of Godhead and manhood in the person of Jesus.[5]

The Humbling of Christ

The therapists and positive thinkers encourage us to say, "I'm somebody." And the ad makers advise us that, "It may cost a little more, but you're worth it." The common feature in these is that the individual is important. Biblically, it is true that the individual is valuable. I am thinking in keeping with the Bible when I believe that I have significance before God and am important to Him as a person. On the other hand, we all have a perverted idea of our place in the universe, and it is this that the positive thinkers and ad makers are appealing to. I will always want to promote myself, believing that I am the most important person in the world, and feeling justified in making demands, expecting good treatment, and viewing others as less valuable than I am—unless God enables me and leads me to do otherwise.

In the incarnation we see the very antithesis of unredeemed individualism. Our Lord Jesus Christ put Himself last among human beings. He did this not only to go to the cross for others, but also to give us a way to live. According to Phil. 2:1–11 He became the scourge of humanity, a slave. What happened as He did this?

We must first of all think of the position of a slave, especially in the first c., since that is the culture from which this figure is drawn. A slave was lower than a servant, who had certain privileges. His time and abilities were at the disposal of others. He was obligated to let others be first in everything. He was trained and expected to notice the needs of others and ignore his own. He had to put his own safety and welfare last. He was not his own master, had essentially no rights and no respect. In short, he was, for all practical purposes, a nonperson.[6] When we read in Phil. 2:1–11 that our Lord Jesus Christ became a slave for us, we can see that several of these points have immediate application to His Person and work.

To begin with, He was God in every way, as indicated by v. 6 (see note), translated by the NIV as "being in very nature God." Moreover, He lived the way God lived. This is indicated in v. 6b, although it is not brought out by most translations. The Gr. text refers to a manner of existing, of carrying out one's affairs. There is a pattern to the existence of God. He demands instant obedience, is completely free to do what He desires, and cannot be changed by anyone or anything. It was this way of existing that Jesus did not try to keep in His grasp. Instead, He relinquished it in subjection to the Father in order to accomplish salvation. A point of contention throughout the history of the Church and especially within the last century is the statement at the beginning of v. 7, translated variously as "emptied himself" (NASB) and "made himself nothing" (NIV). Since the Gr. verb behind this is *kenoō*, one approach to this passage has been known as the kenosis theory. It asserts that Jesus surrendered some of His attributes in order to become humanity. Aside from the fact that such a change would entail His ceasing to be God, that is simply not taught here. Instead, 7b tells us that the emptying, which must be taken metaphorically, involved becoming a slave. It was a lowering, an emptying, to go from living as God lives to living as a slave lives. This is one of the changes that is described in this passage. The other change involves a feature that accompanies the first. Whereas before the incarnation the second Person existed as God only (v. 6), after Bethlehem He existed as the second Person joined to a human nature. This is clearly asserted in 7b and 8a. If He was genuine deity before, then He was genuine deity and genuine humanity afterward. He was just like any other human being and looked like it, too.

The key question is "What did the second Person give up?" If He gave up any of His attributes such as omniscience, omnipotence, infinity, eternity, or glory, then He could not have continued to be God. Some say He gave up all but love (as in Charles Wesley's hymn, "Emptied Himself of all but love," which some have changed, recognizing the error, to "Emptied Himself in matchless love"). What was lost in the "emptying"? The change was from living the way God lives to living the way a slave lives. To be a slave is totally unlike existing in the manner of deity. He forsook the privileges (but not the attributes) of God to be a slave, at the mercy of human beings. None of His attributes as God were ever affected. The second Person is God. God is unchangeable. Therefore the second Person could not change.

What is of immense doctrinal and practical significance in this is that the Son subordinated His will to that of the Father beginning at Bethlehem in order to go to the cross as the object of human hatred (Jn. 5:30). In fact, that willing subordination is the very reason the Father gave the God-man the highest place in the universe (vv. 9–11). In discussing the relations between the Persons of the Trinity (in ch. 11, Doctrine of God) we pointed out that the three carry out different tasks in the overall plan of God. One of those responsibilities on the part of the second Person was to be joined with humanity and be at the mercy of human beings—up to a point. For at times people could see his glory. There were occasions when He used His omniscience. And He definitely controlled His own march to the cross. His obedience to the Father and control of His life are seen in Jn. 10:17–18: "The reason my Father loves me is that I lay down my life—only to take it up again. No one takes it from me, but I lay it down of my own accord. I have authority to lay it down and authority to take it up again. This command I received from my Father" (NIV). His cross-death, reserved for criminals and slaves, involved shame and suffering, yet He willingly went through it to redeem sinners. As He experienced the manner of death cursed by the Mosaic law (Dt. 21:23) and considered the lowest form of punishment by Gentiles—a Roman citizen could not undergo it—He went as low as He could go. He died as a slave for sinners under the will of the Father.

What our reaction should be is evident. First, we should be led to thank God when we realize how far He went for us. Second, we cannot help but understand better how sinful we are, in that the second Person of the Trinity gave up so much and went through so much for sinners. Third, the main point of Phil. 2:1–11 is to lead us to emulate His attitude of self-denial in every way. Paul views Jesus' acts as driven by an "attitude" (v. 5, NIV): self last. Very simply, the believer is obligated to be a slave to others. Our time is to be at the disposal of others. They are to be first in reward, joy, and attention. There is no room for jealousy. The believer is to look for needs (the slave is trained to watch out for others) and put his own welfare last, not seeking his own comfort. And, according to v. 16, the result is the favor of God. Appropriate are the words of Thomas Kelly:

> Look, ye saints! The sight is glorious:
> See the Man of Sorrows now;
> From the fight returned victorious,

Ev'ry knee to Him shall bow:
Crown Him! Crown Him!
Crowns become the Victor's brow.

Results of the Incarnation

One of the most puzzling questions of biblical interpretation concerns the relation between the elements of God and humanity in the incarnate Lord Jesus Christ. We do not claim to be able to explain everything involved, since, as mentioned above, the incarnation is perhaps the greatest mystery of Christianity. But there are some doctrinal distinctions that can be made.

The Person of Christ possessed both a divine and a human nature. At times His humanity could be seen, when He was hungry, for example. At times His deity was seen, as when He showed He knew people's hearts. But we cannot peel one nature away from the other, as we could with a person who was demon-possessed, where the demon and the individual are two separate beings. And we should be careful not to mix the two natures together, thinking of Jesus as a super human being. Nor is the relation between the two natures like the indwelling of the believer by Christ, since that still involves two separate people.

But although there are many unfathomable aspects to the incarnate Person—keep in mind that we do not have anything to compare it with in all the universe—we can mention certain things that we are quite sure about. He had a genuine human nature, a fact that we gather not only from the express statements in passages such as Phil. 2, but also from implicit information concerning the genuineness of His body (such as being born of Mary and seen and touched by human beings). One of the most explicit expositions of His true humanity is found in Heb. 2:9–18, where the bedrock fact is that unless He had a true human nature He could not help us get out of sin. (See *Docetism* in ch. 20, Guide to Bible Study Terms). And there are many explicit and implicit points in the N.T. (and O.T.) that indicate He possessed genuine deity (such as in Phil. 2, explained above, under "The Humbling of Christ").

We would be going beyond the biblical revelation if we expected to know how Jesus' deity and humanity interacted on every occasion. The Bible simply does not tell us. But there are some things that we do know about what it meant for Jesus to be God but like you and me, too. To begin with, He was like us in every way except one. Rom. 8:3 explains that He had all the necessary human qualities, but the similarity stopped short of including participation in the condemnation resulting from the Fall. As a result, His life experiences could be just like ours except for acts of sin (Heb. 4:15). (In fact, there is every indication that He could not sin, not just that He somehow avoided it. See the discussion of the temptation in the next section.) What is significant about this? The effects of the fall touch every human being. Jesus in His incarnation had to be *unlike* us since we are under judgment in Adam. This highlights the point at which we are condemned. It is not that we don't manage to please God, but rather that we cannot. The sooner we recognize this, the better (see ch. 14, The Doctrine of Sin; see *Total depravity* in ch. 20, Guide to Bible Study Terms).

We also know that Jesus never used His attributes to benefit Himself. Although He was hungry in His wilderness isolation for forty days, He did not succumb to Satan's suggestion to turn stones into bread to satisfy His hunger (Mt. 4:2–4). Despite the taunting of those who hated Him while He hung on the cross, He refused to use His power to make Himself more comfortable (Mt. 27:39–44). This is a doctrinal point that has immediate relevance to the way the believer is to live (based especially on Phil. 2:1–11). We regularly seek to profit ourselves. He had every reason and right to do so but did not. He could have done more public miracles to gain a following, but avoided it. He never tried to make Himself popular—as we do.

Jesus apparently depended on the Spirit for empowerment for some of His miracles. This is disclosed in Mt. 12:28, where He asserts that He drove out demons by the Spirit of God. Certainly He was able to do this on His own. This tells something very important. If He, as part of His humbling (see above on Phil. 2 under "The Humbling of Christ") voluntarily depended on the Spirit, yet did not need to, why don't we, who really do need to? His pattern reveals our foolishness.

Many people have suggested that the second Person "laid aside His glory" in order to take on human nature. However, although He did not look like God, we have clear indications that His glory was very much present, although veiled. After all, no human being could live in the presence of the full glory of God, the magnificence of God that stems from His perfection in every way (see *Glory* in ch. 20, Guide to Bible Study Terms). The statement of Jn. 1:14, "We have seen his glory . . ." (NIV) is enough to prove that it was not laid aside (see also Jn. 2:11; 17:22; 18:6). It is significant that Jesus never sought false glory and fame to substitute for what was veiled. In the temptation one test was for Him to claim the homage of human beings (Mt. 4:8–9). He could take a shortcut and get instant honor, but that would violate God's plan and would be incompatible with Jesus' sinlessness. Contrast this with fallen humanity: we regularly seek glory for ourselves when we deserve none (Phil. 2:3–4).

One of the ways in which the incarnation should affect us most deeply is in the area of Jesus' ability to empathize with us. He can do this because His humanity was subject to temptation, distress, weakness, pain, and sorrow. This is nowhere exemplified better than in Mt. 26:36–38, where He wrestled with the prospect of bearing sin: "My soul is deeply grieved, to the point of death . . ." (NASB). Why are we told things like this? It shows God is concerned with our weakness. It is not sin to be tempted, to be distressed, to hurt, to grieve. Because Jesus endured these as a human being, we know God knows in Christ what life is like for us (Heb. 5:1–11).

God is very concerned about order in the universe. There is one way of salvation. There is to be order in the local assembly (see ch. 18, The Church), in marriage, in employer/employee relations, even among the angels. So we should not be surprised to find that there is order among the Persons of the Trinity (see ch. 11, Doctrine of God). To accomplish salvation for sinners, the self-imposed order is Father, Son, Spirit. Although all three Persons are fully God, there has clearly been voluntary self-limitation within the Godhead (as seen in Phil. 2:6–8). Why would the Son subject Himself entirely to the Father, with the Spirit supporting the Son? God regulated Himself in this way in order to bestow grace-based salvation on sinners. If we can begin to understand this, then we are seeing a lot of the heart of God. Think for a moment about the temptation. It tested exactly this point: would the Son step outside the order? Would He act on His own? It doesn't take much thinking to realize that just as the God-man trusted the Father for all things, so also we are to trust our saving God in everything. The temptation for us is always to act on our own, out of God's expected order of our dependence on Him. Faith is the opposite of acting on our own. A feature of this ordering is Jesus' perfect obedience, even to the point of death. Philippians 2:8 emphasizes how far He went as a slave, subject to mistreatment: ". . . and became obedient to death—even death on a cross!" (NIV). In some way the divine and human natures cooperated to lead Jesus to be completely obedient, even when He as God was being buffeted by the ones He Himself had created. 1 Pet. 2:21–25 presents His pattern of obedience as an example for us to obeying God in everything.

When in *Jesus Christ Superstar* Pilate asserts "He's a sad little man, not a king or God,"[7] we see a perfect example of how many have mistaken for weakness the perfect cooperation of the two natures present in Jesus, working together within the subjection of the Son to the Father to save sinners. If those around the cross made this error, it's not surprising that writers and others today would, also. We are correct in seeing Him as like us in almost every way. Let no one forget that that one exception—due to the presence of deity—makes the difference we desperately need, enabling the God-man to be a perfect sacrifice for sinners.

Some Roles of the Incarnate Lord Jesus Christ

During His earthly ministry and after His resurrection, Jesus was and continues to be occupied with many activities, some directed especially toward the elect. Some of these are presented in the N.T. under expressive poetic figures, such as the vine and the branches (Jn. 15:1–8; see notes, 15:1,2,4,8) the Shepherd and the sheep (Jn. 10:1–17; see note, 10:7) and the chief shepherd over the Church, which He desires to control (see ch. 17, The Doctrine of Salvation, concerning sanctification). At the very least we should realize that Jesus is not on some cosmic vacation, having left us to fend for ourselves. One particular ongoing work is that of His priesthood. It deserves special treatment here in connection with the Person of Christ, since it is interwoven with His makeup as the God-man and the work He accomplished on the cross.

The essence of priesthood is the work of taking human beings to God. There are, of course, many false "priests" in heathen religions, attempting to do just that. However, it is quite clear in the Bible that God has given specific stipulations concerning priesthood in relation to Him. A priest has to be appointed (Heb. 5:4), must know humanity and deity (Heb. 5:1–2), must, to be effective, open the channel to God (Heb. 5:3) and keep it open (Heb. 7:23). Jesus fulfilled all these requirements in that He was appointed (5:10), knows both sides (Heb. 1 presents His deity, Heb. 2, His humanity), opened the channel successfully (9:23–24), and is able to keep it open (Heb. 7:25).

Several crucial events in the earthly life of Jesus are intimately related to this feature of His work. Heb. 5:8 indicates that His life experiences were such that they enabled Him to learn how to function as a priest for us. This enabled Him to empathize with our weaknesses (Heb. 5:2), as One who was fully human. And, of course, as God He maintained separation from sin, and could thus be a perfect sacrifice for sinners (Heb. 9:26).

It is at this point that we must deal with the biblical picture of the temptations that occurred during His life. They reveal a great deal concerning His makeup as the God-man and the nature of His sacrifice and continuing work for us. Augustine understood this when he remarked that Adam turned a garden into a wilderness; in His temptation in the wilderness Jesus brought us back to the garden. How could this be so? And how is the cross involved?

As we read Mt. 26:36–38, one of the key temptation passages in the N.T., we may be led to feel that it is one of the strangest scenes in the whole Bible. In fact, some have felt that it was so unusual it must be fictitious. Actually, it is so degrading, no one would have dared to invent it.[8] Why is it odd? Because the God-man looks and feels the way we do. He's not supposed to, is He? As He wrestles with what He knows will come the next day—His being viewed as a sinner—He displays human reactions just like ours, only certainly much deeper and more agonizing. Actually we have here one of the greatest and most helpful gifts of God's love and grace for us. But to understand this we have to understand several things about His temptations and temptation in general.

What is a temptation? First, it is not the same as sin, as 1 Cor. 10:13 points out. It is neutral, and is the invitation to sin, not the sin itself. It can be viewed as a testing to see if sin will result.

When was Jesus tempted? We know of several prominent occasions: (1) in the wilderness; (2) on the eve before the cross; and (3) on the cross itself. But certainly He must have been tempted every day, for Heb. 4:15 indicates that His temptations correspond to every kind that we face—covetousness, lust, anger, disobedience to God, etc.

Can we assess the reality of His temptations? Some people have asserted that Jesus was not really tempted, since He couldn't sin anyway (the temptations must have come from outside Him in any case, because He did not have a sin nature as we do). But Heb. 4:15 couldn't be clearer in teaching that He was really tempted. And not only were the temptations real, they were more intense than what we face, and probably more in number. Every human being becomes callous to sin because of having given in so easily on so many occasions. We don't often struggle, agonize, and resist sin. After a brief contemplation, in the majority of instances we yield. Not so with the God-man. He was tempted by things we are hardened and wide open to. His agonizing resistance is suggested in Heb. 12:1–4.

Could Jesus have sinned, as some have suggested? Did He simply manage to depend on the Holy Spirit every time, or face the temptations in His own strength and somehow go through His whole earthly life without committing one act of sin? If that were the case, then our salvation would have been accidental, and He would have provided it by the skin of His teeth. Further, the view that He could have sinned misunderstands His Person, with the intertwined divine and human natures. A human being is weak in regard to temptation. God is not. God cannot sin (Jas. 1:13). Some have compared the temptation of the God-man to the attempt to break a glass rod that is wrapped with steel. Yes, the glass could be broken, but the steel prevents that. Admittedly this analogy is imperfect. But it does highlight the reinforcing character of the divine nature.

Perhaps the most significant question we could ask about Jesus' temptations is, Why was He tempted? In short, the temptations were provided by God in order to demonstrate that He could not sin. When we first think about this we are inclined to suspect that in order to be real the temptations all had to be carried out in all kinds of circumstances in order to see if there might be some situation in which He might sin. But, given the understanding of His Person that we have presented above, the temptations must be viewed as taking place not to see if He would sin, but sovereignly planned by the Father to show that He would not and could not yield.

This teaching has immense significance. It demonstrates why Jesus needed no savior Himself (Heb. 7:27) and so could be the perfect provider of redemption (Heb. 9:26). It proves his genuine humanity—being exposed to real temptations is at the heart of being human. It enabled Him to grow—as He resisted—as a priest (Heb. 2:10; 5:5–9). In short, it put Him in a position where He could help us when we are tempted. We are not to think that for Him to help us when we are tempted He had to commit the same sin. Instead, it was His steadfast resistance that put Him in a position to sympathize, no matter what temptation we are facing. That is the point of Heb. 4:14–16:

> "Therefore, since we have a great high priest who has gone through the heavens, Jesus the Son of God, let us hold firmly to the faith we profess. For we do not have a high priest who is unable to sympathize with our weaknesses, but we have one who has been tempted in every way, just as we are—yet was without sin. Let us then approach the throne of grace with confidence, so that we may receive mercy and find grace to help us in our time of need." (NIV)

This establishes the biblical doctrine of the correct behavior of the believer when tempted. We are to turn to the high priestly work of Christ to enable us to overcome temptation just when it appears to be overwhelming us (or sooner!). Heb. 4:14–16 does not refer to coming to God with various prayer requests and general needs. That is certainly taught elsewhere. The crucial practical truth the passage presents is that we do not have to sin because we have available One who never yielded and promises to get us out of the temptation. This passage tells us how God carries out 1 Cor. 10:13, where He promises an escape. Of course, we are foolish if we don't use this provision. Under the law the high priest could approach God in the Tabernacle only once a year. And no one else could. But sinners need no longer keep their distance. Once under the blood, they can draw near with confidence, especially coming to God pleading for the ever-available temptation-defeating work of the One who went through what we go through and never yielded.

Not only do those He died for as a priest have this particular ministry available, they also are the recipients of His continual ministry of intercession to keep them secure. Hebrews 7:25 presents one of the most significant ongoing works of our Lord Jesus Christ—keeping the believer secure in salvation. None of the redeemed can be lost, because the Sacrificer Himself never stops reminding the Father that they are under the blood: "Hence also He is able to save forever those who draw near to God through Him, since He always lives to make intercession for them" (NASB; see ch. 7, Relations Between the Testaments, regarding Melchizedek and Christ's eternal priesthood.)

It is in His perfect sacrifice as a priest and His continued work to protect His own from sin and loss of salvation that Jesus truly, as Augustine said, has brought us back to the garden.

Questions for Further Study

1. Does Gen. 32:24–20 contain a Christophany?
2. Make a chart of all the works of Christ before His incarnation, showing which were continued.

3. Read carefully Isa. 7:1–17. To whom is the prophecy of 7:14 addressed? The "sign" is one of judgment and hope. Why might this be so? According to Isa. 7:14, who was to name the child? Who was to do it, according to Mt. 1:23? What might be the significance of this?

4. Using Scofield notes concerning our Lord Jesus Christ, list as many reasons as you can why He needed to be fully human.

5. What does Jn. 5:25 teach about the relation between the first and second Persons of the Trinity?

6. What do you make of the future relations between the Father and Son as described in 1 Cor. 15:24–28?

7. Find examples in the Gospel of Mk. of Jesus' divine attributes, and list them. Do the same for His human qualities. Where do you see the two interacting?

13

The Holy Spirit

There are many ways to organize an approach to the biblical revelation concerning the Holy Spirit. In this section we will approach the material by discussing first His Person and deity (both of which are found throughout the Bible) and then His ministries, prior to, during, and after the N.T. age. All of this is described by theologians as pneumatology.

His Person and Nature

Because He cannot be seen, the Holy Spirit's actual existence and personal nature have often been doubted through the years. But the Bible declares in many places and in many ways that we are to regard the Holy Spirit as just as real as the Jesus who walked in Palestine, with the same ability to interact rationally with human beings, as well as with the universe with whose creation the Spirit Himself was involved. In fact, His role in creation (along with the Son; Gen. 1:2 and Col. 1:6) demonstrates His intelligence and purposefulness, qualities attested by His interaction with individuals (Acts 5:3; Eph. 4:30, etc.). This and other evidence disallows the position of some that the Holy Spirit is simply an influence or a feeling.

Closely connected with the preceding kind of error is the position that the Spirit is somehow less of a deity than the Father and Son, a view held by some cults. If we take the biblical record seriously, we have to acknowledge that creation is something only God can do, and the Holy Spirit did it. Further, He is intimately connected with God in other activities and abilities (e.g. 1 Cor. 2:11–12, where the Spirit of God knows and imparts to believers the things of God). The Scofield note at Zech. 12:10 offers many more evidences of the deity of the Holy Spirit, most drawn from the O.T.

Perhaps in interpretation of the Bible the Holy Spirit has been slighted because He is invisible and is the least prominent of the three Persons of the Godhead. Clearly, He is indispensably involved in God's design for the provision of salvation, but He has assumed a role supportive of the Lord Jesus Christ, who in turn acts in obedience to the Father. But we must not mistake such purposeful direction as indicating inferior status. If we did, we would, for example, slight the great works done in each believer during this age through the Holy Spirit. In fact, the most prominent presence of God with the believer is expressed by the teaching on the Spirit's activity in and through individuals. The Son is in us (Col. 1:28), as is the Father (Jn. 14:23, the only description of that indwelling), but the Spirit's presence is described the most. Keep in mind that it would be a logical strategy for Satan to minimize the deity of the Holy Spirit (as well as His personality and even His existence) in order to prevent the believer from entering into and enjoying to the fullest the wonderful works of God toward him during this age through the third Person of the Trinity.

A significant consequence of all this is that the Holy Spirit brings to the believer all of God He ever could dream of having. In a genuine sense, the Holy Spirit is our representative from God during this age (see note, Jn. 14:16). This is a biblical fact that is designed to lead us to dependence as well as boldness. In spite of the great things people have accomplished for God since Pentecost, it is safe to say that no human being has ever drawn on that indwelling presence as fully as he could. There is always more of God available to us through the presence of the third Person in us.

Ministries Before the New Testament Age

Because the Spirit is by comparison much more prominent in the N.T. records, many have assumed that He was essentially inactive before N.T. times. Just the opposite is true. As mentioned above, He was involved in the creation of the universe, including people (Job 33:4—an ongoing activity). He did not indwell individuals as He does during the present age, and was present with some only intermittently. But He did work in evident ways in and through some, empowering and even being in some (Gen. 41:38; Jud. 3:10; 14:6, 19; see note, Zech. 12:10). The biblical record concerning these ministries is significant for what it does *not* tell us, in comparison with His ministry during this age, which, as we will see below, is for crucial reasons far more extensive.

As the Person of the Trinity most involved with individuals in the recording of biblical revelation, the Holy Spirit had a nearly continuous ministry throughout the period in which the O.T. was written. Both the N.T. and the O.T. tell us that the Holy Spirit spoke through individuals (2 Pet. 1:21; Isa. 59:21). His work thus involved what is described as revelation (disclosure) as well as inspiration (guidance concerning the exact message to be preserved). We might expect that such a ministry concerning Scripture would continue through the apostolic age, and this is confirmed by our Lord's prediction in the Upper Room Discourse just before His death. There He anticipated the Spirit's ministry in bringing to the disciples' minds the exact details of what He had said (Jn. 14:26) and also giving understanding of that material (Jn. 16:14). Strictly speaking, the N.T. never says that the Holy Spirit guided the writers of the N.T. But the fact that N.T. writers considered their words to be on a par with and one piece with those of the O.T. writers indicates that they were conscious of God's guiding, and since it was the province of the Holy Spirit to guide in the giving of Scripture *before* the N.T. age, we are safe in assuming that He also did during apostolic times (Acts 1:16; 1 Tim. 5:18, etc.).

Ministries Distinctive to the New Testament Period and Afterward

On the face of it, the notion that God would support and help God seems superfluous and perhaps even nonsensical. Yet that is what the Holy Spirit did for the God-man, the Lord Jesus Christ. Of course, the second Person needed no such assistance. But as God joined with humanity, there were many occasions for the supportive strength and miraculous working of the Spirit. Thus we find that, for example, the Spirit effected the incarnation, causing Mary to be pregnant with the One who was deity joined to humanity (Lk. 1:35). The Spirit was subsequently present at His baptism (Mt. 3:16), and filled Him and led Him into the wilderness to be tempted (Lk. 4:1–2). At a crucial point in His ministry, Jesus declared that His miracles were performed by the Spirit of God (Mt. 12:28). The accusation by the Pharisees that He had been healing the demon-possessed by Satan (Beelzebub) led to Jesus' pronouncement of the so-called unforgiveable sin (Mt. 12:31; see ch. 20, Guide to Bible Study Terms). That sin was limited to those who were witnesses of Jesus' earthly ministry and cannot be committed in the same way today. At the end of Jesus' ministry, the Spirit was clearly involved in the very death of Christ, for Heb. 9:14 says: "How much more will the blood of Christ, who through the eternal Spirit offered Himself without blemish to God, cleanse your conscience from dead works to serve the living God?" (NASB).

The day of Pentecost marked the beginning of a radically new complex of ministries on the part of the Holy Spirit. It is important that the Bible student understand that what the Spirit is doing during the Church Age is distinctive to the present time period and is linked with unique purposes that God is carrying out in the era bounded by Pentecost and the rapture. What He is doing is part of a larger plan centered on the creation of the Body of Christ.

This caution should be broadened. There are three interlocking subfields of Bible doctrine or theology: pneumatology (the doctrine of the Holy Spirit), ecclesiology (the doctrine of the Church, local and universal), and eschatology (the doctrine of future things, or, roughly, unfulfilled prophecy). Only a premillennial interpretation of Scripture with an emphasis on the separation between what God is doing with Israel and what He is doing with the Church now can do full justice to the data in the Bible (see ch. 5, Interpreting the Bible). Our understanding of the Church is at issue, since the distinction between Israel on the one hand and the Church as the Body of Christ on the other defines the people God is dealing with during this age, and marks off a separate people who will inherit promises made to them in the O.T.

Where does the work of the Holy Spirit enter the picture? It is His ministry in starting the Church, the Body of Christ, at Pentecost that gives this age its uniqueness. Its formation takes place through the particular work of baptizing individuals, at the point of salvation, into the Body of Christ. That work is continued by ongoing ministries of the Spirit, tasks that were never seen before Pentecost. The Spirit's activity in the present age provides the key to the unique character of this Church period. He will eventually cease these ministries and allow conditions to revert very much to what they were (in terms of His relation to individuals) before Pentecost (described in 2 Th. 2:6–7). His role thus causes this age to have a parenthetical function. This coincides with the parenthesis in the seventy weeks of Daniel (Dan. 9:24–27; see note, 9:24) and the goal of the tribulation as part of the seventy weeks—to bring Israel to a place of blessing before God. The Spirit will certainly be active in the tribulation, as indicated, for example, by Joel 2:28–29, where as part of the unusual events taking place on the earth there will occur significant revelations from God initiated and empowered by the Spirit. Certainly it will be the Holy Spirit who will bring about the regathering of Israel and the regeneration of a remnant (Zech. 12:10; 10:1, note) to enter the millennium under the headship of Messiah. But the Bible student must see that particular ministries of the Spirit are tied to certain times and portions of God's program. If we do not do this, endless confusion results.

Since the present works of the Spirit are so unique to this Church Age and provide so many benefits to each believer, every child of God should be fully acquainted with biblical teaching about them. Neglecting what the Spirit can do and wants to do—even already has done—for the believer, is a way of telling God that what He has taken pains to provide doesn't make much difference to us.

It is the baptizing ministry of the Holy Spirit (discussed more fully in ch. 17, The Doctrine of Salvation) that initiates His relation to us and establishes our connection with Christ. The most far-reaching ministry after this is indwelling. This is the spiritual presence of the Holy Spirit in every individual who has placed personal trust in Christ as Savior. Described in Jn. 14:17, this is the basis of His other ministries to the believer. In relation to the disciples, the Spirit was formerly present "with" them; He would subsequently be "in" them.

The presence of the Spirit is itself a promise by God of future activity on behalf of the one who is indwelt. This sealing work of the Spirit, described in Eph. 1:13 (see note), is a guarantee that God will take the believer fully into His presence. Having a portion of God now will issue in full enjoyment of Him in the future. The Spirit is thus viewed as a pledge that God will take the believer out of his world and make his salvation (here "redemption") complete.

The Spirit's ministry of indwelling makes constant teaching available. Because we cannot understand the Bible and spiritual issues on our own, we must have divine assistance. God has given us the very best—the author of the Book Himself. This is what Paul described in 1 Cor. 2:12: "We have not received the spirit of the world but the Spirit who is from God, that we may understand what God has freely given us" (NIV). This ministry is also characterized as an anointing in 1 Jn. 2:27, and is especially valuable in showing the believer what is true in contrast to erroneous teaching. Although this anointing ministry is not specifically described in 1 Jn. 2 as emanating from the Spirit, Jesus' prediction in Jn. 14:26 that the Spirit would initiate a teaching ministry— continuous because of His unchanging presence—is sufficient to enable us to identify the Holy Spirit as the One who carries out the anointing ministry. While the indwelling and sealing are constant, this teaching ministry, while always available, obviously operates when it is needed, as the believer looks to God to teach him God's Book.

A fifth ministry of the Spirit is that of empowering believers for service. This is called *filling*. Especially prominent in the book of Acts, filling sometimes appears as a constant characteristic of life, as in the case of Stephen (Acts 6:5), and sometimes as an enablement to meet unusual needs (Acts 4:8). We should avoid thinking of filling as something that can be turned on and off as we would a faucet. Filling is a result of a consistent walk with God, and depends on a genuine and mature relationship with the Holy Spirit. Simply asking to be filled will not bring it.

Of all the ministries of the Spirit during this age, none is more visible than His provision and administration of spiritual gifts. These abilities, called in 1 Cor. 12:1 simply "things that have to do with the Spirit" *(ta pneumatika),* are the empowerments God has provided for service today. They are apparently grouped into oral and non-oral, or simply serving, patterns (1 Pet. 4:10), and are based on the triumph of the resurrection (Eph. 4:7–10; see notes, 4:11). Although the complement for each individual varies in its composition, every believer has at least one (Eph. 4:7; 1 Pet. 4:10). It is likely that we are to take the N.T. lists (Rom. 12:6–8; 1 Cor. 12:7–11; Eph. 4:11; 1 Pet. 4:11) as complete, making a distinction between natural abilities (musical, athletic, etc.) and enablements given by the Spirit at salvation.

Some gifts are associated with particular places of service. For example, 1 Pet. 5:2 indicates that elders in a local church are supposed to shepherd believers. In order to do that they must have the gift of shepherding or pastoring. Elders thus carry out pastoring through the channel of their spiritual gifts. It stands to reason that a man who does not have the gift of shepherding/pastoring should not be an elder. Elders are also required to be able to teach (1 Tim. 3:2). It is likely, then, that they are to have what Eph. 4:11 describes as a two-part gift, shepherding/teaching. Another gift that seems to be associated particularly with them is the gift of leadership or administration, seen in Rom 12:8. However, other individuals can have the gift of teaching (Rom. 12:7), even of shepherding/teaching. In fact, the exhortation by Paul in 1 Th. 5:14 addressed to believers in general to exercise pastoral care toward each other argues for the possession of the gift by many. But elders need a particular minimum set of gifts.

There can be little question that in the latter part of the twentieth c. there has been a significant increase in attention paid to the gifts of the Spirit. Many believers have realized that everyone in the Body should be about the task of ministry, and that demands understanding and use of gifts, (see notes, Eph. 4:11–12). The Spirit gives gifts so that everyone can build up the Body of Christ. All have a part; none are exempt. The job cannot be left to one or a few in a local church who are assumed to have the needed gifts. As a matter of biblical fact, the picture of the local church involves multiple input into the life of individual gatherings, with various individuals ministering through their gifts (1 Cor. 14:26). It is a critical error to assume that one individual in a local church has all the requisite gifts to minister to the needs of a group of believers. The N.T. teaches that on the basis of the gifts we have been given we are all to minister to one another (Eph. 4:11ff; 1 Th. 5:14; 1 Pet. 4:10, etc.). When we look at ministry this way, we see that God has provided a network (suggested by 1 Pet. 4:10: serve each other by means of gifts) of gifts so that many can help a particular individual grow to maturity in Christ (Eph. 4:11–16). For example, we find that during the apostolic period the church at Antioch had many teachers (Acts 13:1). While God is sovereign in how many He will give to a local church, we can expect from the patterns in churches in the first c. and from apostolic teaching concerning spiritual gifts that God will provide multiple teaching where we ask for it. This provides a check against error and a healthy diet of balanced ministry (all other things being equal). This is only one example of the many benefits to be had from paying attention to developing gifts in all the individuals in a local church. We cannot expect the Spirit to give gifts beyond those given at salvation, but certainly we are to cultivate what we have (see ch. 18, The Church).

Certainly the twentieth-century emphasis on the Holy Spirit has been due also to a movement introduced by the Spirit Himself aimed at removing sterility in life and worship. The Spirit of God wants us to depend on Him, not on patterns for behavior or service that we have developed in the past and then followed slavishly. This is no less true of our gatherings in local churches. An evaluation by James Denney (writing in the nineteenth c.) is especially appropriate here:

> I have hinted at ways in which the Spirit is quenched; it is sad to reflect that from one point of view the history of the Church is a long series of transgressions [by such quenching], checked by an equally long series of rebellions of the Spirit. . . . [It] came to pass at a very early period, and in the interests of good order, [that] the freedom of the Spirit was summarily suppressed in the Church. . . . In plain English, the Spirit was quenched when Christians met for worship. One great extinguisher was placed over the flame that burned in the hearts of the brethren; it was not allowed to show itself; it must not disturb, by its eruption in praise or prayer or fiery exhortation, the decency and order of divine service. I say that was the condition to which Christian worship was reduced at a very early period: and it is unhappily the condition in which, for the most part, it subsists at this moment.[1]

Perhaps we can learn from the lessons of history and give the Holy Spirit more freedom.

However, we must always be careful to maintain balance and pay attention to the Bible. Unfortunately, some appear to be preoccuppied with the Holy Spirit and His ministries through gifts. This has occurred especially where people have sought to make the gift of tongues and even the supposed utterance of prophecy standard experiences, even marks of spirituality, for believers during this age. While a full discussion of what is really a network of issues is beyond the scope of this chapter, we should note certain biblical facts. First, the N.T. associates the gift of tongues with God's special first-century work of alerting unsaved Jews to a new work of God in the midst of Israel, as well as to the danger of rejecting the Messiah. Both elements are found in Acts 2, the first in 2:5–12 and the second in vv. 15–21, where Joel's prophecy actually describes such outpourings of the Holy Spirit as a prelude to conversion for some, but destruction for many. Throughout the book of Acts, Luke strikes this same ominous note over and over, as he portrays Israel's progressive hardening that actually began not in the early chapters of Acts but during the earthly ministry of Jesus (see Mt. 12 and the comments on it above in this section on ministries of the Holy Spirit). This function of tongues as a warning is found even more clearly in 1 Cor. 14:21–2, where in quoting from Isa. 28:11–12 Paul says unequivocally that tongues were a sign for the Jews, intended to shake them up. In fact, the following verses (22–26) show that prophecy, not tongues, would bring a person to Christ. Tongues had a different function, that of alerting Jews to their plight. It is interesting that whenever tongues appear in the book of Acts the main impact is on the Jews who are present.

Paul's general outlook on tongues stands in marked contrast to the preoccupation of some today. In 1 Cor. 14 he indicates that prophecy was the gift that would lead a person to Christ, and that He was not concerned with speaking in tongues (v. 19). In fact, such interest was a sign of immaturity (v. 20). Further, tongues were not to be spoken unless interpreted. By the way, this indicates that the tongues that occurred in the first c. were genuine languages (not gibberish or "angelic" speech, whatever that may be), since only language can be interpreted. One must seriously ask if those who espouse the gift of tongues for today are concerned with having an interpreter.

It is clear that some people spoke in tongues during the apostolic age. Shouldn't that continue today? The Bible actually teaches that some gifts were foundational in nature. Eph. 2:20 indicated that the gifts of apostle and prophet (needed for the giving of new revelation and interpretation of the great, new events of the unfolding apostolic age) were for the early stage of the building of the Body of Christ. Once they had fulfilled their purpose they would no longer be needed. We have historical evidence that tongues faded out at the end of the apostolic age. This, along with the clear biblical purposes for tongues, argues for the fact that they are not part of God's purpose at this point in the Church Age. While God certainly can do anything He wishes, we expect Him to act in accord with His Word. In fact, He promises that He will never violate it and that it is always true; our Lord Jesus Christ put Himself in complete subjection to it. Whatever the phenomenon of tongues today is, it does not match the biblical revelation and must be explained on other grounds.

It should not be overlooked that in the twentieth c. preoccupation with tongues has often gone hand in hand with another error of biblical interpretation, namely, the assertion that one must undergo an experience of the "baptism" of the Spirit in order to arrive at a higher plane in the Christian life. This demonstrates confusion concerning baptism as the foundational work of the Spirit toward believers during this age. Baptism places a person in the Body of Christ, identifies him with the crosswork of Christ, is entirely unseen and unfelt, cannot and need not be sought, and happens only once. Even the worldly and divided Corinthian believers had been baptized by the Spirit (1 Cor. 12:13). They did not need a new "experience of the Spirit," but needed to practice simple obedience and adherence to Scripture. The Bible does not give warrant for looking for a second blessing, a baptism, a spiritual experience. And that kind of error is especially misleading when associated with unbiblical ideas concerning tongues and the believer today.[2]

Questions for Further Study

1. Using the marginal note at Jn. 14:17, locate the other references to the indwelling ministry of the Spirit.

2. Make a chart of all the spiritual gifts present today, along with places where they might be used, if such information is given.

3. Using the Scofield notes on the Holy Spirit and a concordance. lay out the role of the Spirit toward individuals in the O.T.

4. Trace the Spirit's ministry through the book of Acts.

5. Suggest five practical results of anointing/teaching.

6. Consult a Bible encyclopedia, dictionary, or compendium of Bible customs on the subject of ancient seals, and relate your findings to the work of the Spirit in Eph. 1:13.

14

Sin

Someone has suggested that two great doctrines of Scripture go hand in hand: sin and redemption. "It is sin that has drawn out redemption from the heart of God, and redemption is the only cure for sin."[1] As we study the doctrine of sin (called *hamartiology*) one of our purposes will be to show how offensive sin is to God, and how much it has damaged the human race. In ch. 17, The Doctrine of Salvation, we will describe how God has provided everything necessary to overcome sin—past, present, and future. We should always keep in mind that it is logical strategy for Satan to minimize the sinfulness of sin, and thereby slight the greatness of the cross-work of Christ.

Backgrounds

Although human sin began in Eden, to get the full picture of its career we must go back further to the offense of the first angel. It is there, at a time not delineated in Scripture, that sin entered the universe, and with it the great distortion of the goodness and purposes of God. Some have suggested that the time of the sin can be located between vv. 1 and 2 of Gen. 1 (see notes at Gen. 1:2 and Isa. 14:2). According to this view, Satan's first sin and consequent fall from his place of privilege before God occurred after the creation of the earth and the passing of a considerable period of time, during which extensive life forms existed on earth. His fall occasioned a judgment of the earth by God, resulting in the condition described in Gen. 1:2. Since there is a considerable period of time between vv. 1 and 2, this view has been described as the gap theory.

However, this writer prefers the alternative view indicated in the NSRB note at

Gen. 1:2, to the effect that Gen. 1:1 describes the original creation of the physical universe, with no gap between vv. 1 and 2. Under this view, v. 2 describes the condition of the earth immediately after the initial act of creation.[2]

The background to that first transgression is found in two passages: Ezek. 28:11–19 and Isa. 14:12–17. In the former passage, the reason for Satan's sin is not indicated. Instead, we are simply told (v. 15) that wickedness was discovered in him—quite an understatement! Although he had a favored position, including access to God as a "guardian cherub" (NIV), apparently he was carried away with his great beauty and power. Needless to say, this pattern of being taken up with self has spread to the human race, too, and is repeated over and over (see notes at Ezek. 28:12 and 19).

A direct biblical statement concerning the exact nature of Satin's sin is found, however, in Isa. 14:13. In power and importance he wanted to be a duplicate of God. This was clearly an act of his will—a will in opposition to God's. The result was the spiritual fall of v. 12 (see note).

These two passages delineate the pattern sin would follow as it spread through angelic ranks and entered humanity. Sin would manifest itself as an act of the will, a desire to function in the place of God and to be like Him through self-effort (note that the goal of the believer is to be like God as He produces that likeness in us!), overestimation of one's position and assets, and disregarding of the consequences of thus rebelling against God. We should learn a great deal from these short but pithy accounts of the fall of the one who introduced sin into the universe. As much as we dislike saying it, we act like him and, outside of Christ, face the same consequences (Rev. 20:10–15).

The Spread of Sin to Humanity

Although many modern theologians have viewed the account of the experience of Adam and Eve in the Garden of Eden as mythical and attempt to explain existing realities by resorting to a contrived account, there is every reason to take it as factually true. The account is presented as genuine history and was regarded as such by other biblical writers, as by Paul in 2 Cor. 11:3. It fits integrally with the rest of the Word of God and explains many facts that we cannot account for otherwise. We should take it as a description of real events, recorded by Moses under the guidance of the Holy Spirit as he wrote Genesis (see note at Gen. 2:16).

Genesis 3 records the presence of three individuals in the Garden—Satan, Adam, and Eve (actually she is simply "the woman," since she is not named until 3:20). How could a serpent as we know it today act in the manner given in this account? To begin with, we are not dealing with a snake or other reptile that we know now, since it is clearly described as being the most wily of all the animals that had been created (see note, v. 1). Furthermore, Satan must have been possessing the serpent, since the curse of 3:15 (as taken by most Bible interpreters) goes far beyond the serpent—although the curse is addressed to it—and focuses on Satan himself. Further, both Rev. 12:9 and 20:2 identify Satan as the serpent. Exactly how he possessed or utilized a real serpent for his purposes is never disclosed in the Bible, and we should not speculate beyond what the text tells us. At least we should notice that at the very beginning of Satan's dealings with humanity we see deviousness that channels his attacks through nonsuspect vehicles. He delights in approaching us in disguise.

Concerning the restriction of eating from the tree (v. 3), we are simply told that God prohibited it. In itself it may not have been wrong. And Eve must have reasoned that evident damage would not be done if she were to eat. That, of course, is the way sin always proceeds. We attempt to rationalize around God's prohibition. What makes an act sin is the fact that God has prohibited it. Whether it seems good to us, appears to do no damage, or may even feel good, is irrelevant. God's Word is sufficient to establish something as right or wrong.

At the very beginning of the experience in the Garden, then, we see part of the essence of sin. It is disobedience to the revealed will of God. There are other components, but it always starts there. This is confirmed in the account by the fact that Satan himself reversed the statement of God, saying that there would be no resulting death, when God had said there would. It is significant that though Satan and the woman both tried to dismiss God's Word, it turned out that God's Word had the final say. What it predicted was exactly what happened. Failure to believe what God says to us is always disastrous (see note, 3:6).

As she reasoned—really already in sin—concerning the restriction, Eve evidently thought it presented an unnecessary limitation on her freedom (see Isa. 14:12–17). In doing this she had already set herself up as entity operating against God, since up to this point there had been perfect fellowship with Him, as evidenced by the fact that shortly after the fall the previously pristine conditions of contact between God and the pair were suddenly altered (v. 8). Thus before she ate the fruit—which, by the way, is never said to be an apple!—she had already pulled herself away from God, and thus had sinned.

The Consequences of the First Human Sin

The most far-reaching of the immediate results of Eve's sin was loss of fellowship with God (3:8; see note on the second dispensation, 3:7). This separation from God is the essence of spiritual death. Along with it came the knowledge of what it means to sense guilt before God, and so Adam and Eve attempted to cover themselves, certainly in relation to each other and probably partly from the sight of God, too. The long-term consequence in the life of every human being since them is physical death, described in v. 19. Spiritual alienation from God leads to aging and dissolution of the body, a proof and demonstration that we are all affected by the fall and its resulting curse. Physical death is unavoidable and unalterable, because the fact of our spiritual death is unalterable, also. We should never try to minimize its terrible effects.

By the way, it is biblically significant that although the woman is the first of the human race to sin, Adam is blamed for her actions (Rom. 5:12–19). He was responsible for her and failed to direct and control her. Several principles that we see in life today are inherent here. First, the male of our species is responsible for the spiritual welfare of the female. That does not mean that she cannot approach God. But she was created as his helper, not as his head. Since the moment of the fall, she has attempted to reverse that God-given order. One of the judgments on her (Gen. 3:16) places her under his headship—however unwilling she may be to be there. That this will always be a problem is indicated in 1 Tim. 2:11–15, where the prohibition against a woman's teaching *or* usurping authority comes because, in Paul's words, the woman was thoroughly tricked by the serpent. (The Gr. of 1 Tim. 2:12 cannot be construed to mean "I do not permit a woman to teach if she usurps authority over a man," as some suggest. In such a view women would be allowed to teach if they didn't try to "lord it" over men in the church. Instead, Paul prohibits a woman's teaching biblical things to men *and* usurping authority over them—here, in the context of the local church and its functions.) In the light of this spiritual weakness—not that she cannot be as spiritual as a man, but that she is more easily tricked in doctrinal matters—she is to be under the sheltering control of her husband. It is important that we realize that this restriction is actually a blessing, since the balancing role of the husband is to be a help to enable her to fulfill herself. Paul's promise in 1 Tim. 2:15 "She shall be saved in childbearing" (AV, where "be saved" means "find fulfillment") is thus positive, giving a place of worth and value to the woman after the fall. Of course, the fact that Paul had to give the prohibition concerning teaching and usurping authority indicates that lack of subordination has continued since the fall. One of a woman's greatest problems, then, since the fall, is that she tends to act on her own apart from restrictions by her husband (or any other male spiritual head, for that matter). The fall obviously has highly practical consequences for life through every age. We should be very careful not to minimize God's analysis of our condition—whether male or female—before Him.

There are three parts to the specific judgment section of Gen. 3:14–19. There is to be a change in the condition of the serpent and an ultimate conquest of the one behind the serpent by the offspring of the woman (see notes, v. 15). This is clearly a predication of Satan's apparent victory over Christ from the cross to the resurrection, and then of the final triumph by the God-man. Interestingly enough, then, the outcome of the course of the ages is predicted right at the beginning, perhaps lest there be discouragement from then on that the results of sin might never be reversed.

The judgments upon the woman include the restriction in relation to the man and increased pain in childbearing. Since these are new pronouncements, we are led to believe that both areas would have been less difficult for the woman had the fall not occurred.

Falling upon the man is the curse of pain in making a living. Prior to the fall, work was present and expected, since Adam was to tend the Garden (2:15) and subdue the earth (1:28). Yet there was no sin involved. God exerted effort in creation, yet there was no sin or curse present. Work itself is not a curse, and is not to be associated with sin. The difficulty of work comes as a result of the fall. As a matter of fact, the ground itself is cursed.

Finally, Adam and Eve are expelled from the Garden, indicating that idyllic conditions could not be retained, and confirming the severity of God's reaction to their crime. Human beings have lost the privilege of special communion with God. Unless some way back were to be found, the cherubs and the flaming sword would exclude them permanently from the place of joyful fellowship with Him. This is not to say that they could not be and were not the recipients of grace, and even of salvation. Genesis 3:21 (see note) is clearly an act of grace on God's part. The fig leaves that Adam and Eve used to cover themselves were inadequate—for two reasons: (1) they themselves constructed the covering, and (2) vegetable material and not animal was used. God initiates the provision in v. 21: that is grace. The material is superior to fig leaves because it prefigures the animal sacrifices to come, first in the case of Cain and Abel

(4:3–4; see notes, 4:1 and 2), later under the law, and especially in the sacrifice of our Lord Jesus Christ. Adam and Eve were probably horrified as they witnessed the first slaying of animals to provide those skins. But they also could not help but be struck, as we should be, by the gracious act of the God whose commands they had so recently flouted.

The Nature of Sin

What is sin? We have already discussed its origins, and in so doing have uncovered many of its properties. Can we give a comprehensive description?

Some have simply dismissed the idea of sin as being any kind of problem for humanity. Many philosophers and psychologists have done this, as well as the Christian Scientists, who assert that sin is an illusion. Such an approach is enmeshed with the Christian Scientist's pantheistic (or monistic) view of the world, and we would have to say that it clearly does not match reality, if we are at all honest with our condition in life (see ch. 11, The Doctrine of God).

Those who have suggested that sin is disobedience to the law of Moses fail to provide a definition for sin outside the period of the law. Further, any description of sin as a violation of God's law in general, though correct as far as it goes, fails to deal with all the manifestations of sin, such as sin that is resident within us, and acts of sin that do not violate a specific prohibition from God.

Those who say that sin is acting in independence from God are also partly correct, as we saw above in our description of the fall. Every act of sin has this component to it. But we need a more encompassing definition.

In our discussion above of the nature of God, we stressed that God's holiness cannot be defined by comparison with anything that we know in this life. Since God is unique, in a sense He is the standard for Himself. This is the point where our definition of sin must begin. Anything that does not correspond to the nature of God is sin. Sin draws its essential character of sinfulness from the fact that it is unlike God. We will see that this enables us to view sin as having the same qualities whether we are thinking about acts of sin or the nature that every human being possesses that leads to those acts. In the latter case, there is a part of us that is confirmed in being unlike God, and that comes from the fall (as exemplified by the fact that Adam and Eve were no longer fit for God's presence and were thrust from the Garden). This kind of definition enables us to identify as sin those things that are not mentioned in specific biblical prohibitions, and helps us to see how there can be a part of each of us that wants to sin; since the fall we want to be unlike God—as exemplified by Satan's words in Isa. 14:13–14: "I will . . . I will . . . I will . . . I will . . . I will." We are the same. Isn't the comment of the seaman prior to the maiden and only voyage of the Titanic a perfect example: "God Himself could not sink this ship."[3]

We get a good idea how awful sin is—because it is offensive to God—from the details of His provisions for salvation. The error by many, especially in this century, that suggests that God could or would save out of generosity overlooks completely the biblical teaching that sin is antithetical to God. It is not just a minor deviation, an error, a false step. It is gross aberration from God's original purpose for all created rational beings, angelic and human alike. Lewis Sperry Chafer has cogently observed:

Too little, indeed, is it realized by many who attempt to preach the gospel, that the grace of God which saves the lost is not mere big-heartedness of generosity on God's part. He could have saved souls without the sacrifice of His Son had that been the case. The death of His Son as a sacrifice is required only because God cannot compromise His holy character by making light of sin. . . .[4]

Romans 3:23 describes how important it was for God to deal with sin in the right way, and this in turn shows how evil sin is. Paul's argument is that those before the cross could have called God into question for not remedying sin with an adequate penalty. The sacrifices under the law could not take away sin (see also Heb. 10:4), so how could God allow anyone into His presence? That He did so seemed to indicate that He wasn't a just God, since sin and a holy God were not compatible, and an effective removal had to be made. That the cross finally accomplished that is for Paul a point to be published abroad, announcing to the world that finally something strong enough to match sin had come on the scene.

Sin's Relations to the Human Race

There are at least three significant ways in which sin touches our lives or is connected with us. As we think about these we ought to keep in mind that sin, as that which is unlike God, is always sin no matter where we find it.

What We Do

The manifestation of sin that is easiest to understand and recognize is that which occurs when we do something that is unlike what God would do. This has been called by some personal sin (see notes, Mk. 7:21; Rom. 3:23) and is exemplified by 1 Jn. 1:10: "If we say that we have not sinned, we make Him a liar, and His word is not in us" (NASB). In this manifestation of sin, the inward bent toward being unlike God comes to the surface, and includes the kinds of things described in Gal. 5:19:

> The acts of the sinful nature are obvious: sexual immorality, impurity and debauchery; idolatry and witchcraft; hatred, discord, jealousy, fits of rage, selfish ambition, dissensions, factions and envy; drunkenness, orgies, and the like. (NIV)

The counteracting provision for sin of this kind is found in 1 Jn. 1:9: confession brings forgiveness.

What We Are

A relation that sin has to us that is more difficult to grasp is the inherited pollution we have from our first parents, that inward bent already mentioned above. This is sometimes called inherited sin, the sinful nature, or the sin nature. It is always present and evokes our acts of sin, personal sins, yet we try to minimize it, as described in 1 Jn. 1:18: "If we claim to be without sin, we deceive ourselves and the truth is not in us" (NIV).

There are three special questions associated with this manifestation of sin. The first is this: if it is there, where is it in me? What part of me is it? Of course the Bible views human beings as more than electrical impulses running through and between cells. As creatures made in the image and likeness of God, we have spiritual, rational, and emotional capacities. The Bible does not really tell us exactly which parts have been affected by the fall, but it is very explicit in declaring that there has been a permanent change in our constitution, centered in the spiritual part of us and affecting all the others. Eve's act altered her makeup, that of Adam, and that of every one of their offspring. We are permanently bent out of shape as far as godliness is concerned. To be sure, the Bible does not tell us how that one act introduced a permanent condition in Eve, nor how that state could be continued through subsequent generations. But the fact of it is indicated: "Surely I was sinful at birth, sinful from the time my mother conceived me" (Ps. 51:5, NIV). We are not being overly literal if we point out on the basis of that verse that such internal pollution begins its relation to an individual not at the first act of sin, not even at birth, but from the moment in time he or she begins to exist. In short, the nature of every human being has been damaged by what Eve and Adam did in Eden.

This aspect of sin has also been described as total depravity. This term sounds too harsh to some, seeming to suggest that we are all raving beasts of some kind. After all, we can be kind to children and do many "good" things. Yet, none of us can do anything that helps us get access to God, and that is what is at issue. If we could, it might be possible for someone to be good enough to be accepted on his or her own merits by God. Of course, that would take a sinless life. But we only have to take one look at Rom. 3:10–18 to realize that God's evaluation is that no one is able to do that. Not only is there no one who is sufficient in himself to match God's expectation (no one is righteous, v. 10; no one does good, v. 12), as a matter of fact, everyone is running from God (v. 11). The specific sins listed in vv. 13–18 are an outworking of this spiritual pollution and resulting hostility toward God. Total depravity, then, is our spiritual inability to please God. It is a condition participated in by every human being who ever lives. We cannot escape it, and it is one reason we are condemned before God.

Ephesians 2:1–3 (see note, v. 5) shows us that this condition fosters a complete style of living that enjoys participation in Satan's own world system. The result is universal condemnation—everyone is headed for judgment by God and eternal separation from Him (v. 3; see note, v. 5). It isn't the specific acts of sin that bring this, although they are enough to do it. It's the internal condition. It cannot be reformed, cleaned up, mollified, or covered over. It is in every way hostile to a righteous God. The only remedy is a new capacity to please God. And that is just what our gracious God provides at salvation. This was what Nicodemus needed to hear about, and in Jn. 3 our Lord showed him that he needed an infusion of spiritual life (v. 6). God's work of regeneration is what brings this new capacity into a life, although the old nature is still present (see notes, Rom. 6:6 and Jn. 3:3; see "Regeneration" in ch. 20, Guide to Bible Study Terms, and in ch. 17, Salvation).

What Someone Else Did

The preceding aspect of sin's effect on us is often confused with another one that is equally universal and invisible—imputed sin. It can be defined simply as this: Adam sinned for everyone else. The key passage describing this is Rom. 5:12–21. As Paul demonstrates the imputation of Christ's righteousness to those who are His, he also shows that Adam's act is imputed to every human being. Those in Christ do nothing to gain His merits. Similarly, those in Adam—everybody—have done nothing to be condemned; yet they are. Both sets of people are the recipients of imputation, first of sin, then of righteousness. The imputation of sin brings death (v. 14); the imputation of righteousness brings freedom from condemnation, release from a curse.

This is different from the sinful nature described in the previous section. There every human being has been altered spiritually, in terms of ability to do what pleases God, interest in spiritual things, and volition to obey Him. With imputed sin, nothing we have or do is involved. Instead, we have been evaluated as guilty on the basis of the act of one person, Adam.

It is at this point that many object to this doctrine. It could not be fair for God to condemn Adam's descendents on the basis of what he did. We weren't there. Give us a chance! Yet, the evidence from Rom. 5 is overwhelming. God chose Adam as a representative for all the race. He failed, and we were adjudged to fail with him.

There are several other points in Rom. 5 that support this conclusion. Verse 12 says that all die because all sinned, and also that all died because one sinned. This could only be true if one person's sin were being imputed to others. Further, it does not say that all become sinful. Thus the point of condemnation is not a sinful nature but some act of sin. Then in vv. 13–14 Paul indicates that in the period from Adam to Moses, before the law, sin was not charged. At first glance this seems to be a contradiction. People died because of sin, but sin was not charged to them. The only possible resolution would be that they were charged with someone else's sin. They weren't charged with their own personal sins because the law, containing an explicit catalogue of sins, had not yet come on the scene. Death was proof enough that some act or acts of sin (not a sin nature here) had triggered God's judgment. It must have been Adam's. Further, v. 19 clearly states that one man's disobedience made many (here, "many" means everyone who has ever lived after Adam) sinners (not "sinful"). And finally, the work of Christ occurs vicariously without our asking for it, and is here made parallel with the act of Adam, also done vicariously without our requesting it.

It should be evident from this that God Himself has provided a phenomenal reversal to the situation of Adam's imputed sin. The act of our Lord Jesus Christ not only erased Adam's condemnation, it provided more cancelling power than we could ever need (v. 19; 5:14, note).[5]

Forgiveness for acts of sin, a new nature to counteract the sin nature, more than enough merit to cancel our condemnation in Adam—all of these provisions portray for us what grace is. We ought always to stand amazed that sin, which has so pervaded our existence, has been met so completely by the grace of God toward sinners.

Questions for Further Study

1. What does Eph. 2 tell us about what God does to counteract our sinful nature? Does it say the sinful nature is removed? See also Col. 3:1–14.

2. According to Rom. 6:1–14, what kind of relationship does sin have to us before salvation? Afterward?

15

Humanity

Why Human Beings?

One of the fundamental questions of our existence is, "Why are we here?" Many thinking people through the ages have pondered this, and some have arrived at answers that others accept to various degrees. But the Bible—and particularly the first three chapters of Gen.—is the only source for satisfying answers to questions such as this. Human beings exist and are on this planet because God had certain specific purposes for them.

In fact, God, human beings, and the earth are tied together inseparably. God chose the earth as the arena for the creation of people and for the outworking of their responses to Him. The early chapters of Genesis record that the first human beings were formed from the earth, worked on and with it, and would return to it. Romans 8:19–22 teaches that when Adam and Eve fell, the earth was affected (see note, Rom. 8:22). Finally, when God brings about the full glory of the redeemed, the earth will be refashioned, too (Rev. 21:1–5).

As we scan human history, one of our conclusions has to be that the events found in worldwide records cluster around two focal points: our relating successfully to the planet, and our relating to each other on the planet. The provision of food, control of disease, development of transportation, as well as negative events such as loss of life in earthquakes, disasters at sea, and snakebite, are all examples of the former. Problems involving human interaction are evidenced in the rise and fall of kings and kingdoms, the events associated with legal enactments (the Magna Charta, the U.S. Constitution), as well as overcrowding of prisons, and crimes themselves. We might conjecture that the negative examples shed little light on our purpose for being on earth. However, when we are given enough information, they turn out to fit perfectly into a picture that has its roots in the first three chapters of the Bible. In fact, we cannot understand history itself without understanding why we are here and what has happened to us along the way in our relation to God. God's placing us on this planet with responsibility for it— and that includes the earth and all living matter—is the key to history. Perhaps saying more than he realized, Alexander von Humboldt concluded: "World history is incomprehensible apart from world government."[1]

A Key Source of Information

Any careful reading of the early chapters of Gen. leads to this conclusion, among others: we do not have all the information we would like to have about the beginnings of people and the earth. We wonder how much time elapses between Gen. 1:1 and events at or after the time of the flood, where names of people and places begin to match existing extrabiblical records. Where was the garden? Exactly what were weather conditions like and how did they differ from those of today? How much did Adam and Eve know about God? What did newly created living and inanimate objects look like? Not only are there many points where interpretation is difficult, there are apparently many intentional gaps in the flow of information.

But in a sense we are asking the wrong question. Yes, it is right to ask questions of the Bible. But in this case there is a missing observation: the purpose of the first two chapters of Gen. is not to give a detailed and scientific report (although we must assume that the Bible will not contradict science), but to provide a rationale for our existence on this planet.[2] Only enough historical detail is given to provide an adequate setting for the more important spiritual issues. Erich Sauer, a perceptive German writer, says:

> The chief and essential interest of the creation-narrative is a spiritual one. Its real concern is not to give a report about cosmogony but rather a manifestation of revealed truths, not to give a *history* of creation but to testify to its *meaning*.[3]

That meaning is in turn centered on human beings. Even a casual reading of Gen. 1–2 will yield the fact that the events of creation lead to the appearance of Adam. Yet he comes on the scene as frail, alone, and shaped from the huge earth he stands on. His first job is to name the animals as God parades them past him, and they obviously outnumber him. Almost as an afterthought God gives him help in the form of an alternate human being. From this we gather that Adam needs assistance: even before sin enters the picture he is set over against his environment.

In a literary sense it is the very fact that he is outnumbered that immediately sets up a conflict. Somehow this solitary individual has to pit his equipment against everything around him. If we read honestly and naively, we would ask, "Will he make it?" (It is significant that in the late twentieth c. we are asking if we will destroy the whole planet, including humanity). And yet we sense that he will, because, although he seems weak, he has not been neglected. God has made him like Himself in some ways, and has given him a special commission. God must think he can make it. In fact, God simply tells him to go ahead and live successfully. Survival doesn't seem to be an issue.

These and other factors lend support to the conclusion that the creation account is centered on human beings. They are the goal as well as the focus of God's mighty acts, the "head and crown of all visible, created beings."[4] We should not be surprised that even a Nietzsche would say, "Man is the reason for the world."[5]

The Commission

We should look carefully at God's initial interaction with Adam. After creating him, God gave him a specific two-part responsibility (Gen. 1:28): (1) produce more human beings, and (2) bring the earth under control. The second element has more spiritual significance than the first, and we might conclude that increasing in number would be a means toward achieving the subjugation of the earth. In any case, the main import of this commission is that Adam and Eve and their descendants are to be rulers of the earth—kings, in a sense. Contained within the mandate is permission to utilize innate abilities as well as external means to bring this to pass. All the seeds of culture, science, and technology, are here. God gave the earth to the human race to administer, and to do it in His place. This commission is part of the crowning point of creation (1:31) and concludes God's creative activity. Galileo's words concerning an instrument fashioned by human beings are to the point:

> O telescope, instrument of much knowledge, more precious than any sceptre! Is not
> he who holds thee in his hand made king and lord of the works of God?

Psalm 8 provides us with further insight into God's purpose in creating human beings, presenting God's activity poetically, but agreeing with the emphasis of Gen. In this psalm we are tiny and insignificant compared to the heavens. Even though the psalmist knows that God made us, he wonders how God could have any interest in us. Yet in the order of living beings we are positioned just below the angels, and, in fact, given glory and honor that they are never said to have (see note, v. 5). These endowments are explained in v. 6: the glory and honor consist of being established as ruler over the earth—over everything! We might ask why the psalm concludes in v. 9 by turning from our position to God's. It must be because the plan of our ruling on the earth is something that brings glory to God. Though we are kings on the earth, God is still greater. We should never forget He has commissioned us to act under Him. We are kings, yet weak without God's help.[6]

The Equipment to Carry Out the Commission

The result of God's creative activity on the sixth day was a being made in the image and likeness of God (see note on Gen. 1:5 concerning the days of Gen. 1–2). Like Him, we have intellectual ability, make moral/ethical decisions, operate in the spiritual realm (although He is a pure spirit being—we are not), and are social beings (for God this is seen in the love among the Persons of the Trinity and His love for sinners).

Although interpreters have debated the possible differences between the "image" and the "likeness," there does not seem to be a great distinction between the two.[7]

If these were the components of the image and likeness before the fall, we should ask what their condition is now. Clearly we still have these qualities, as suggested by 1 Cor. 11:7. But because of the fall we can never utilize these capacities to their fullest without distortion. We cannot, for example, operate well at all in the spiritual realm, whereas Adam could speak to God directly. Adam displayed intellectual ability during his first task, that of naming the animals. Many feel that the most brilliant individuals since Adam display minds that are only shadows of his.

However, Eph. 4:24 and Col. 3:10 suggest that parts of the image undergo renewal in the believer. If, as some believe on the basis of Eph. 4:24, righteousness and holiness were part of the original image of God, then certainly they were lost. But the believer regains them as he becomes more like Christ. It is part of the great and gracious plan of God that since the fall He has been in the process of making individuals like the perfect, unfallen human being, the Lord Jesus Christ. Thus Rom. 8:29 reveals God's new program since the original makeup of human beings was so terribly distorted by the fall. Colossians 3:10, which speaks of a person's "being renewed in knowledge in the image of [his] Creator" (NIV), apparently describes our ability to interact with God in the spiritual realm, gaining understanding of those things that outside of Christ are beyond our comprehension. Thus we can become more like Him because, in part, we can think like He does.

It is significant that the Bible nowhere records that anyone who faces eternal separation from God ceases to be a person with the attributes of the image (aside from holiness). People will still have spiritual, moral, intellectual, and social capacities in the state of endless punishment, and having them without fulfillment will make their condition even more miserable. For example, the Bible gives no indication that any individual will have contact with another after death. This lack of fulfillment of the social capacity will in itself be a source of torment. Perhaps we could even say that eternal punishment will consist in part of being denied the opportunity to fulfill in any way the elements of the image and likeness of God. Thus, the most basic human capacities will be unfulfilled, with resulting torment.

Obviously, understanding the basic makeup of human beings as created in the image and likeness of God has great significance for interpreting the behavior of people in any age. We should not be surprised when psychologists discover that a person who is denied adequate social interaction, especially human love, as a youth, will manifest patterns of distorted behavior in life. From another standpoint, we should realize that good health and the ability to live normally (as much as can be done since the fall) depend on an understanding of how God made us in His image and likeness. It is there in the Bible for us to see and understand.

There is another piece of equipment that we possess from creation: language, the ability to interact with other human beings and with God. Many animals have signaling systems: honeybees, dogs, chimpanzees, etc. But only people have an information system that utilizes a small set of signals that can be combined in an infinite number of ways to produce an infinite number of different messages (see ch. 4, The Language of the Bible). This capacity is so unique to human beings that we would not be far from the mark if we suggested that it was tied up in some way with the features that are part of the image and likeness of God. It may be that our language ability has been given to us to enable us to communicate primarily in the spiritual dimension. One writer has put it this way:

> The spiritual nature expresses itself chiefly in man's power of speech. Speech is the direct self-revelation of the human spirit. . . . Classical writers tell how the Greek philosopher Socrates met a young man who devoted himself to ideological and moral problems and who had been hoping to be further stimulated by meeting Socrates. But contact with this intellectual "giant" so overawed him that he scarcely dared to open his mouth to speak, or to ask a question. So they walked side by side for a while without conversation. Then Socrates suddenly broke the silence and said kindly but briefly to his young companion, "Speak, that I may 'see' you."[8]

This ability to communicate the most significant elements of our personal existence corresponds to our need to interact with the One responsible for that existence. The very fact that human language possesses the capacity to speak about things that are displaced from us and abstract, nonvisible entities, argues for its source in a God who designed us to have fellowship with Him.[9]

Although we may not initially think of it as such, the creation of human beings in the form of two sexes constitutes equipment for carrying out God's commission. We should note several significant doctrinal points:

> 1. Mankind consists of male and female (Gen. 1:26–27); the most immediate implication of this is that neither is complete without the other (see 1 Cor. 11:8–12). Many marriage problems would be avoided if people lived in the light of this simple biblical principle.
> 2. Woman was created as a helper (Gen. 2:18); this implies first that Adam would have to work, and second, that he would need assistance; God provided the perfect assistant.
> 3. She was made from the man (Gen. 2:21), and so enjoys the closest communion with him, and he with her.
> 4. God's intention is one man for one woman. Although God permitted polygamy in His own purposes during the O.T. period, it is clearly not His ideal. Further, the spiritual, emotional, social, and physical union between the two (Gen. 2:24) is such a fundamental part of their existence that we have to view divorce as a terrible disruption of the divine order.
> 5. Careful attention to the details of the creation of male and female should immediately lead us to rule out homosexuality as having any legitimate part in the purpose of God for the sexes. Romans 1:24–29 describes homosexuality as unnatural, a perversion, depravity, and a kind of idolatry. In short, it is at odds with God's created order.

Although the human body is not part of our resemblance to God, since God is a spirit Being, it is part of our God-given equipment to carry out our commission on earth. It is tied directly to the earth by its composition and destiny (Gen. 3:19). It is significant, then, that after death we receive a new body, one suited for eternal spiritual existence (see note, 1 Cor. 15:52).

One of our main perversions since the fall touches our acts of worship, which should be to give the Creator/Commissioner/King of the universe His due. Since the fall we have, out of keeping with our position under Him, directed our worship toward three other focal points—ourselves, nature, and Satan and other fallen angels (demonic worship). Part of our worship of ourselves involves undue attention to the human body, either our own (narcissism) or those of others (lust). Both are perversions of true worship of God (see Rom. 1:21–32). Along with worship of nature, they are simply examples of our bent toward giving homage to anything but the only deserving Object, our Creator. In contrast to some pagan philosophies, the Bible teaches that the body itself is not evil, as witnessed by the fact that our Lord Jesus Christ possessed one just like ours (Phil. 2:7–8) and yet never sinned and had no sin capacity. But the body can obviously be used to serve sin, and the Bible exhorts the believer to direct its actions toward serving God (Rom. 6:13). In this capacity the body is a channel for the outworking of the image and likeness on this earth.

There has been much discussion over the centuries concerning the relation between the human soul and spirit, as well as with other nonphysical aspects. Do the soul and spirit have mutually exclusive functions? Does the Bible indicate capacities for the heart and mind that overlap those of the soul or spirit? The dichotomist views man as consisting of two basic parts: soul and spirit on the one hand, and body on the other. The trichotomist holds that soul and spirit can be validly distinguished. In general it appears that Scripture most often speaks of the spirit as that part of a person that participates in life with God. The soul, on the other hand, seems more to connect us with the everyday aspects of life as human beings. But the facts that the same activities can be predicated of the soul and spirit, and that the heart (in 1 Pet. 3:15 it is used of the spiritual life) and mind can also be involved in some of these functions, argue against either of the above views. For example, in Lk. 1:46–47 Mary exclaims, "My soul glorifies the Lord and my spirit rejoices in God my Savior" (NIV). The best view is that we possess many capacities within our immaterial natures, a view that has features in common with both the dichotomous and trichotomous views.[10] This appears to do justice to the variety present in the biblical material.

Another oft-disputed area concerns the transmission of the nonphysical side of humanity. Does God create a new soul, spirit, etc., when each individual comes into existence (creationism), or has he simply set into motion, as part of human reproduction, those processes that bring new immaterial capacities into existence along with new bodies (traducianism)? What is clear from Scripture is that immaterial natures do not exist prior to union with human bodies, as some ancients held, and many hold today (Mormons, reincarnationists). In the final analysis, the distinction is not crucial for one's system of doctrine, but both views seem to have an element of truth. God is certainly responsible for the creation of each new life, yet the human race possesses certain nonphysical unifying features. The pollution inherited from Adam is passed from parent to child, and it is certainly to be associated with our nonmaterial side. Perhaps we could compare the issue to God's role in connection with weather on this planet. Does He directly control or create each thunderstorm, or are they the result of ongoing forces that He set in motion long ago? Both sides are true. And certainly He participates in some way in the creation of each new human being's immaterial properties, while the process is the result of His establishment of regulative forces during the creative week of Gen. 1 and 2.

Table 15.1 summarizes the relation of some of the components of the image and likeness to various points in biblical history and the history of individuals who obtain salvation. The body, not part of the image, is included for comparison. A + indicates the presence or restoration of a feature. A − indicates loss.

TABLE 15.1.   Human Components Through Time

	Pre-fall (Adam)	Post-fall	Salvation	Death	Final State
Righteousness/ holiness	+	−	+	+	+
Knowledge (of God)	+	−	+	+	+
Moral capacity	+	+	+	+	+
Rational capacity	+	+	+	+	+
Language/communi- nication capacity	+	+	+	+	+
Body	+	+	+	−	New kind

The Effects of the Fall

Although they occupy only a small portion of the totality of written revelation, the tumultuous events of Gen. 3:1–24 bear witness to a colossal perversion of God's initial plan for human beings. Every problem, every distress, every shortcoming in life can be traced to the transgression and subsequent judgments. We have all incurred altered relations to our own selves, to other human beings, to nature and the whole earth, and to God.

The existence of fragmented and ill-functioning personalities demonstrates that the fall damaged that object of creative activity who was designed to be a king on the earth. Instead of dominating his surroundings, he is a slave to his own fears, to an easily distorted conscience and to a sin-capacity that cannot be turned off (see note, Rom. 7:21). We cannot do what we ought, or even what we know we should.

We hardly need to give proof that our basic relation to each other is skewed. Adam and Eve once lived in perfect harmony without shame over their differences. But now our differences are such a point of contention that one of the major features of the reversal of the fall in Christ consists of God's introducing a new unity. We are made members of each other, with the result that all of us, male and female, are obligated to put each other first. In fact, we are to exercise the same self-denial toward every human being we come in contact with.

Our place as royalty over the earth has seen incomplete, even perverted fulfillment. Although we can make great strides in science or medicine, for example, we can use the very same discovery for great beneficence or for horrifying destruction, as in the case of harnessing the atom for use in radioactive diagnostic procedures or for the annihilation of masses of people made in the image and likeness of God. In Rom. 8:22 (see note) the physical earth seems almost to be weeping for restoration of the original created state of affairs, while showing the effects of one single momentous act. We cannot even reciprocate its personified concern, but instead turn to our globe and its parts as objects of our adoration. One of the grossest perversions of God's original intent occurs when we worship the realm we were to administer for God—including its trees, animals, and source of light—instead of the Creator who made them (Rom. 1:21–25; see note, 1:18). A classic biblical example is the creation and worship of the golden calf, as recorded in Ex. 32, an event that occurred in the midst of far-reaching revelations from God. Perhaps most amazing is the fact that Aaron, whose high-priestly office had just been explicitly described, led in that perverted worship. Of course, the Bible clearly shows that any such worship of nature is associated with demon-worship, since Satan so easily turns distorted allegiance toward himself. Thus we become slaves— spiritual slaves, the worst kind—of nature and everyday life. This is expressed in pantheism, where the world is God; in animism, where animals or inanimate objects are viewed as having consciousness, and by extension are viewed as gods; and in evolution, where development of life forms (the biblicist would say that random occurrence is the basis of this system) makes nature a glorious realm and makes human beings the pinnacle of an aeons-long process, an error that actually tends toward worship of mankind.

It is important to remember that evolutionary views, which deny God's direct creation of human beings in His image and likeness, lead to absolving individuals of their responsibility toward God. The human race is an accident, the product of nature's "wisdom" (not God's), not a royal race placed on earth to rule it as kings for God. Bruce Waltke gives penetrating commentary on this situation:

> Until about a century ago, most persons living within Western culture found their answer to the question of cosmogony in the first words of the Bible: "In the beginning God created the heavens and the earth." But today their descendants turn more and more to encyclopedias or other books on universal knowledge. There, both in text and in picture, an entirely different origin is presented. In place of God they find a cloud of gas, and in place of a well-organized universe they find a blob of mud. Instead of beginning with the Spirit of God, the new story begins with inanimate matter which, through some blind force inherent in the material substance, brought the world to its present state during the course of billions of years. This substitution of matter for spirit accounts for the death of Western civilization as known about a century ago.[11]

One contemporary view sees the universe as proceeding through a series of forms, from a small size with infinitely great mass, to stages where expansion proceeds until the energy responsible for such motion dissipates and the universe shrinks again. It is interesting that astronomers may appear to proceed with careful scientific investigation, reasoning from effect to cause, until they come to origin issues:

> An oscillating universe has the satisfying property that it does not single out any particular point in space-time as a "creation." In this picture, the universe does not need to be created, because it has always existed. It is infinitely old and will continue infinitely far into the future, periodically going through a fireball stage.[12]

It is not difficult to see that chance and matter (wherever it came from!) are substituted for a creating God. In fact, the above paragraph, from a recent college textbook, seems to be a polemic against creation views.

So we worship all the wrong objects, demonstrating little of the nobility we were originally endowed with. We casually take human life, whether in individual murders, wars, or abortion, demonstrating the lowest regard for what God brought into existence at the crowning-point of His creative work. We should not be surprised that the first murder occurs in the biblical record in Gen. 4, immediately after the fall; the stage was set for it before Cain and Abel were born. That we can save lives and take them by abortion in the same hospital is testimony to the gross perversion of relations between human beings.

The misuse of what was entrusted to us, and the abomination of worshiping it instead of God, are pointedly summarized by Sauer:

> Thus man's vocation to nobility, which was made known to him in Paradise, has also an earthly and moral aspect. Man should not be a *tyrant* over nature. He should not misuse it by senselessly destroying beautiful landscapes, by the predatory exploitation of field and forest, by harnessing the strength of animals so ruthlessly, that it becomes sheer cruelty. Equally he should not become a *slave* to nature—through pagan deification of nature, through the vague, modern enthusiasm for nature in pursuing gold and possessions as though true happiness were dependent on the possession of material goods. . . . Let us not forget that the whole creation waits for *our* perfecting.[13]

Of course, all of these sinful acts demonstrate that our most basic disruption since the fall has to do with our relation to God Himself. All He offered us—fellowship with Himself, developing dominion over a perfect earth, idyllic relations with others and a personal wholeness none of us can imagine—has been lost, and with it the initial opportunity to be all we could be before Him.

The Restoration

That the story does not stop there is but cause for amazement and thanksgiving. The cross-work of Christ not only reverses the fall, with its blight on humanity and its future, it more than makes up for it. Although not all will enjoy this reversal, those who do will be the recipients of a gusher![14]

The incarnation is at the heart of God's method for restoring our fortunes. Where the first human being failed, the perfect, ideal Person will not, indeed, cannot. As far as our position before God is concerned, He has determined in His wisdom to deal with the whole human race on the basis of the acts of two human representatives. The Lord Jesus Christ is described as (1) the last Adam, since there are no further significant individuals as far as determining our destiny by representation is concerned, and (2) the second man, stressing the fact that God only needs two to establish our basic relations with Him (1 Cor. 15:45–47).

There can be no question that this perfect human being bears an uncorrupted image and likeness, since there is no sin in Him. Thus, by looking at the Lord Jesus Christ as He lived on earth, we get a good idea of what Adam must have been like, although Adam did not possess the attributes of deity, with the ability to do miracles. In many places the N.T. holds Jesus up as our example (Heb. 12:1–4; 1 Pet. 2:21–24). He is all that we can and should be.

In what must be regarded as the most significant ironic turn in human history, God restores what Adam lost through a second, superior human being (joined with deity, of course; see ch. 12, The Person of Christ). The crucial difference in terms of performance is that whereas Adam was able not to sin, but chose to transgress, Jesus was not able to sin, and so could not fail any test that came to him. He thus demonstrated that

He was the perfect and ideal human being. This doctrine is particularly described in Heb. 2:5–18, where, interestingly enough, the original commission to control the earth is adduced in poetic form through quotation of Ps. 8. In short, the writer to the Hebrews explains that we will not see everything put under *our* feet (v. 8) until everything is put under *His* feet (1:13, quoting Ps. 110:1). But we should not dismiss the crucial fact that to accomplish this Jesus did one thing that Adam could not: He died as an acceptable substitute for those ruined through Adam (2:9). The result for Him is glory and honor (2:9), now simply awaiting their full manifestation. This same passage further recalls primeval events when it describes the crushing of the power of Satan (2:14–15). Finally, in what should be a precious teaching for every believer, the application of Christ's sacrifice and victory is portrayed as a union of siblings (vv. 11–14); we regain what was lost by our father through One who is our Brother, who knows what it is like to live under the curse, but has the riches to buy us out of slavery. Romans 6:1ff describes how God connects us with Christ, who is to God what we could not be. God views us, joined to Him, as if we had not failed to reach the original commission.

We should note one further step in this sequence of the restoration of our fortunes. The victory does not come easily, and although the cross sealed Satan's defeat, he will resist until permanently put out of the way (Rev. 20:10). As his end draws near, he will attempt to duplicate the work of the Lord Jesus Christ as the ideal human being by installing his own king over the earth, the false messiah of Rev. 13 (see note, v. 1). In a disgusting parody of the reign of the perfect human being, the "man of sin" (2 Thess. 2:3; see note) will present his false claims for control of the earth. But his career will be short-lived, and the true King of the earth and universe will appear personally to present His credentials and punish all pretenders (Rev. 19:20). That perfect human being has been described this way:

> He is, as the Son of Man, the unique one of our race. He is the true Man, the goal of all human history. He is the Representative of mankind itself, the embodied pattern of true humanity. In Him not merely isolated aspects of human nature but the whole of human nature in all its Divinely willed truth and purity receives its perfect expression.[15]

Questions for Further Study

1. Colossians 3:10 speaks of a restoration of knowledge through Christ. This must refer to the ability to understand the things of God, something very natural for Adam before the fall. Although this is not purely intellectual in nature, what does this restoration imply about the Christian's mind versus the mind of one outside of Christ, part of the world's system with its way of thinking?

2. Although the body is not part of our resemblance to God, it is part of our identity as individuals. Make a chart showing our relationship to the body throughout life, as well as after death. What is the purpose of resurrection? Consult works on cults and world religions and determine differences from the biblical teaching on the body. Does this seem to be an area of significant perversion?

16

Angels

If you were asked to list on paper five things you know from the Bible about who angels are and what they do, would you have trouble? Probably many Christians would, because the doctrine of angels may be one of the most neglected areas of biblical study. As a result, we tend to be oblivious to significant spiritual activity, and slight some of our best friends in the process.

Today we are all somewhat like the proverbial Missourian in one respect: we don't believe in what we can't see. So we don't bother with angels—at least we don't think we do. Really, today there may be more angelic activity than at any time since the ministry of our Lord, and more people involved in it, although they may not know they are at all.

We actually have no way of knowing angels exist apart from the Bible. But once we see who they are in Scripture, a lot of things around us become more understandable. Such diverse areas as the preservation of Israel, the life of the local church, astrology, fortune-telling, spiritism, and sometimes even discouragement or depression in the Christian life could involve angels. If you are a member of the human race, you should know about angels!

Unfortunately, since they can't usually be seen, they are hard to recognize. It's not like the western movies where the good guys and bad guys could be clearly distinguished by their white and black hats. In the case of angels, it's clear that the bad ones don't want to look bad. So they're hard to spot, for instance, when they are promoting false teaching in churches, or influencing important people, or causing illness or disease. But the fact remains that angels are a significant element in God's plan for the universe. They affect us, and what we do can affect them.

Created to Serve

A foundational portion of Scripture concerning angels is Heb. 1:14 (see note, Heb. 1:4). Perhaps we could take it as a summary of one of God's basic intentions for angels: they are to minister to the elect. The terms used in v. 14 indicate that they are involved with general service, and in particular spiritual service, the kind that has to do with things that priests in the O.T. might do in approaching God. That they do not have physical bodies is indicated by their description here as spirit beings (see also Eph. 6:12). (It is difficult to say whether the bodies they assumed on some occasions are real or only apparent, as in Gen. 18:2, where one of the men is apparently the preincarnate second Person of the Trinity).

We probably do not usually think of angels as having distinct personalities. But their intellectual capacity is clearly indicated by their rational interaction with human beings, as in Dan. 9:21ff. And they have interests and desires, as indicated by such verses as 1 Pet. 1:12, where they are described as wanting to know more about the progress of the Gospel. They can also rejoice and show excitement, as demonstrated by Job 38:7, which concerns their response to God's creation of the earth.

One common error among people who have not looked very carefully at the Bible is the belief that angels are a subsequent stage of people who have died. Nothing could be further from the truth. Angels are created by God for certain purposes (Heb. 1:7). They are below God and above human beings in power and privilege before God (Heb. 2:7). Interestingly enough, we have no indication in the Bible that specific angels ever cease to exist, so we have to assume they are eternal.

Used by God in Many Places

It is interesting that the words translated "angel" in Heb. and Gr. both denote a messenger. Perhaps their basic function is that of carrying out God's purposes as emissaries and couriers. This is certainly Gabriel's role, for every time he appears in the Bible he is functioning as a carrier of information (Dan. 8, 9; Lk. 1). Cherubs, which seem to be angelic beings, appear especially in Gen. 3:24 as guardians of Eden after the fall and in a similar role (represented by carvings, at least) over the Ark of the Covenant as protectors of the holiness of God. Similarly, the seraphs, named only in Isa. 6, constantly labor at proclaiming His holiness. The beings in Rev. 4:6–8 appear to have features of both the seraphs and cherubs (as found in Ezek. 1).

There are only three named individual angels in the Bible, Gabriel, Michael, and Satan. Michael, who always appears in connection with Israel, is the only named "archangel," or ruling angel. His function appears to be that of protecting God's chosen people in some special way. According to Rev. 12:7–9, he will be successful in defeating Satan during the tribulation period.

In addition to having assigned functions, angels have divisions, as suggested by Col. 1:16. Apparently these have to do with organization to carry out specific functions or assignments. These patterns extend also into the realm of angels that are now opposed to God (Eph. 6:12). These "fallen" angels deserve separate treatment here.

Some as Servants of Satan

To the modern mind Satan is only a joke. How much more foolish, then, to believe in an organized group of followers of Satan who do his bidding. And yet that is exactly what the Bible teaches. Revelation 12:4, although figurative, may describe the fall of a large segment of angels along with Satan. If so, this accounts for the existence of some angels, confirmed in evil, that are in complete opposition to God. Matthew 25:41, which speaks of "the devil and his angels" (AV), indicates that he has a role of leadership over such rebels (see also Mt. 12:24).

There is good warrant for taking evil angels and demons to be the same group, although some have seen them as two different groups. Satan is associated with both as a leader, indicating that they are synonymous (Mt. 12:24–26; 25–41).

The Bible nowhere indicates that an angel once fallen can return to service to God. Instead, it seems to be that every act of a fallen angel in Scripture is an occasion for venting hostility against God and those that belong to Him, as in Acts 16:24, where demonic opposition through a young girl led to the incarceration of Paul and Silas. Such free angels appear to be allowed by God to carry out Satan's bidding.

However, some angels are confined, as indicated by Jude 6 (see note) and 2 Pet. 2:4. The context of the latter passage has suggested to some interpreters that the sin of those imprisoned angels was connected with the great violation of Gen. 6:4 (see note). In any case, some angels are permanently out of the way. Why some are still allowed their freedom, as if they had not sinned as much as the others, is not revealed in the Bible. We only know that God permits them to be active in a kind of perverted service—now directed toward another angel, Satan—in the lives of individuals and nations, and ultimately He will receive glory in spite, or even because of, what they do.

We probably underestimate the degree of demonic activity in any age, including our own. For example, through its window on the angelic realm, Dan. 10 reveals that fallen angels (apparently the category to which the "prince of the kingdom of Persia" belonged) back some governments, and unfallen angels may be engaged against them.

Interference in the personal lives of human beings must be equally extensive. The presence of the Holy Spirit in each believer will not allow a demonic being to be present also, ruling out the possibility of a Christian being demon-possessed. But such control must be extensive among the unregenerate. In 1 Tim. 4:1 Paul teaches that demons have their own system of teaching and propagate it through false teachers. We should always be alert to and realistic about the possibility and presence of such deception.

Functions

We might wonder why an omnipotent and omnipresent God would create and use such things as angels. Can't He do what they do instead? Why should He share the credit? The answer is revealing. Angels (unfallen ones, at least) remind and teach us of the power and character of God. And as they function intelligently, doing exactly what He appoints, they are superb examples of how we ought to serve God. We have no indication that any unfallen angel ever deviated in the least from the task set by God. Take Michael and Gabriel, whose names even contribute to this. Michael means "Who is like God?'' and Gabriel means ''man of God'' or ''God has shown Himself strong.'' In function and appelation these two, especially, display the angel's role as reflecting characteristics of God Himself. This is nowhere more evident than in the complex apocalyptic passage of Ezek. 1:1–28, where living beings (identified in Ezek. 10:15 as cherubs) are described in physical terms as dashing to and fro to attend to the bidding of God, who is seated on a throne-chariot. These cherubs are portrayed in this extended figure as extensions of God. From this we are to learn that they act in perfect compliance to God and follow no will other than His (see ch. 3, How to Study the Bible, concerning Ezek. 1).

Biblical descriptions of some of the tasks of unfallen angels provide fascinating reading, and open for us new vistas into divine activity. Especially they teach us about God's concern for our welfare and growth in the faith. It's not likely that we will experience the direct visible intervention of an angel, as in Peter's miraculous escape from prison recorded in Acts 12:5–11. But angels are quite active behind the scenes during this age. Concerned with the progress of God's plan, they observe God's workers (1 Cor. 4:9), inquire into the progress of the Gospel as people handle it, and evaluate relations within local churches (1 Cor. 11:10, where they are interested in the balance between men and women and God-given authority structures). Matthew 18:10 seems to suggest that some angels carry out a representative function before God on behalf of children, at least. When we realize that there is a huge amount of unseen activity between fallen and unfallen angels in the spiritual realm, touching individuals as well as nations (as taught, for example, in Dan. 9–12), we should be led to conclude that we would be open to much more influence from evil angels if it were not for work of the unfallen ones on our behalf. They must be involved with restraining sin and furthering the Gospel. And the most exciting moment for any believer, the rapture of the Church, will be introduced by an angel—in fact, an archangel (Michael?)—as indicated by 1 Th. 4:16.

Figure 16.1 may help to clarify the relations between different groups of angels:

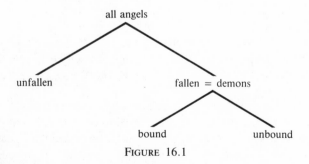

FIGURE 16.1

The basic teaching of the Bible is that there are three groups of angels: unfallen and free, fallen and free, and fallen and confined. All of the free ones are very active in things that touch the lives of believers and unbelievers alike. As opponents of God and perverted servants, the fallen angels attempt to thwart His purposes. As perfect servants, the unfallen angels actually form a company of friends of the elect. Although we cannot see them, we can be alert to ways in which they aid and protect us, both physically and spiritually, just as we might naturally want to know the identity of any anonymous benefactor.

It is also crucial to remember that Satan has many henchmen and can apparently assign several to each of us. This can result in demonic presence, but not possession. As an organized force (Eph. 6:12) and a part of Satan's schemes (Eph. 6:11) they amount to a formidable enemy. The Christian cannot afford to ignore them. The activities of evil angels are becoming more extensive as this age progresses, but certainly also more subtle. Both the boldness and the subtlety will increase to their culmination in the tribulation period, when demonic forces will be involved in the deception of the majority of inhabitants of the earth (Rev. 9:1–22; 12:9; 18:23). Ignorance of such increasing activity leaves the believer wide open to spiritual attack and defeat.

The Great Imposter

Our attention to angelic activity should be directed most toward discerning the purposes and activity of Satan. A local church once announced one Sunday that a prominent individual would be visiting the entire Sunday school the following week. As the congregation eagerly anticipated some sports or political figure the next Sunday morning, in strode one of the men of the church dressed as Satan. Well, he *was* well-known, wasn't he? The whole thing had been staged to demonstrate that Satan *wasn't* nearly as well-known as he should be. We should always be alert to his presence and work. It is likely that most believers go for long stretches of time without making a connection between something that happens in their lives and Satan's work and presence. 1 Pet. 5:8 is still true: "Be self-controlled and alert. Your enemy the devil prowls around like a roaring lion looking for someone to devour" (NIV). We can count on the fact that he is always opposed to the will of God in our lives—both for individuals and the local church and any kind of ministry. His name (Satan means "adversary") tells us that up front. He is an opponent of God and the elect. And he would like nothing more than for us to be oblivious to what he is up to. It is part of his plan.

But we have sufficient help in the Bible to discern and oppose what he does. The details of his fall tell us how he works. According to Ezek. 28:11–19 (see note, v. 12), Satan is a cherub expelled from heaven because of his pride. Although he had great privilege, walking in the presence of God, his original beauty entrapped him and he lost his first position. However, Job 1:6–12 tells us that he can still come before God when allowed.

Isaiah 14:12–17 (see note, v. 12) furnishes what no other passage does concerning the reason for and details of Satan's fall: he wanted to become like God. He is described in v. 12 as "morning star," "star of the morning" and "Lucifer," depending on the translation (NIV, NASB, and AV, respectively). "Lucifer" is a transliteration of a Latin term for the planet Venus and means literally "light-bearer." This was used by the translators of the AV to translate the first part of the Heb. phrase that is literally "shining one, son of dawn," since Venus possesses early-morning (as well, of course, as early-evening) brilliance. By the way, he must still possess this attractiveness to a great degree, since 2 Cor. 11:14 emphasizes his present magnetism. That title in Isa. 14:12, along with the information given in Ezek. 28, underscores the fact that His pride was centered on his concept of his own beauty and eminence. Such a perversion of God's original intention—that he should be a servant reflecting God's own glory—led him to think he could quite literally be just like God.

It is especially important for us to remember that our sin follows this pattern. Although Satan had been given great privileges by God—he was wise, beautiful, powerful and had a role in God's administration of the universe—he turned from God toward himself. In spite of blessings given to us by God, we tend to do the same thing, focusing on what we have been given and thinking it is ours by right, instead of acknowledging the Giver.

Satan's other names or titles are as revealing as the Bible's descriptive statements about him. In Rev. 12:3 he is called a "dragon," suggesting ferocity and perhaps, through reptilian similarities, a connection with the serpent in the garden, which he certainly empowered (see note, Gen. 3:1). This is made explicit in v. 9, where he is called "the serpent." The name *devil* in v. 9, derived as an Eng. word from Gr. *diabolos,* meaning "hurler," is descriptive of his role as a slanderer, a function that is elucidated in v. 10, where the heavenly chorus exults in Satan's defeat and rejoices that his accusing activity is over. Apparently this consists of attempting to get God to condemn those He has brought under the cross-work of Christ, in a manner similar to his attempted entrapment of Job.

Isaiah's description in particular shows us Satan's basic operational strategy: he offers counterfeits to God's will (see note, 1 Tim. 4:1). He may not offer something that is evil in itself, just something other than God's best. But, of course, knowingly pursuing something other than God's will is always sin. An example is found in the temptation of Christ, where the offer of the kingdoms of the world was not entirely misplaced: Jesus would get them eventually. But the timing and method were completely wrong. For us, Satan may lead us to spend time and energies on otherwise good pursuits that take us from God's revealed will for our lives. He can accomplish this through various channels.

Just as Satan was involved in the life and ministry of Christ, and affects unbelievers by blinding them to the Gospel (2 Cor. 4:4), he may bring different pressures to bear on believers—from family, health, or other circumstances, to bring about discouragement, confusion, or outright sin. We see an example of this in 1 Th. 2:18.

Satan is the master of an organized life system that is in complete rebellion against God. With its structuring, goals and staffing (demonic), it touches every aspect of life on earth. John's writings describe it as a *kosmos,* a complex world system with its own values, energized by a nefarious ruler (Jn. 14:30; see notes, Rev. 13:8 and Mk. 10:30). There is no question that Satan would like us to adopt and put primacy on the values of this system. It is totally evil. Following it leads to confusion, defeat, and sin. Matthew 13:22 describes how the world system can cut off the Gospel in the life of someone who has heard it.

Satan gives evidence of not believing what God has said, especially what He has written. When God has predicted Satan's end (Rev. 19:20, etc.), how can he continue to rebel? But this inveterate doubt of God's word is a basic part of his personality and strategy. He would dearly love to get us to fail to believe God. After all, he succeeded with Eve (Gen. 3:1) and attempted it with our Lord Jesus Christ (Mt. 4:6, where he was corrected in His misuse of Scripture by Jesus; see notes, Mt. 4:1 and Lk. 4:10), so why wouldn't he try it with us?

Part of Satan's strategy is to make his alternative offerings look good. 2 Cor. 11:13–15 unmasks this approach, labeling him as a masquerader (NIV). He utilizes disguises in order to get people to think he is something other than what he is. While God, who is benevolent, has revealed Himself over and over in various ways, Satan, malevolent, hides himself.[1] In the light of this, the believer's first line of defense is to know what Scripture says about him. Then, as described in Eph. 6:10ff, 1 Pet. 5:8, and Jas. 4:7, we are to resist or take a firm stand against him. Ephesians 6 in particular provides several additional weapons, from truth to prayer. (See note, Rev. 20:10, for a summary regarding Satan.)

Questions for Further Study

1. After studying the Scofield note on angels and the above text, describe as fully as possible the role of good angels in the present age.

2. Study Lk. 4:6; Jn. 12:31; 14:30; 16:11; 17:14; 18:36. List as many ways as you can where Satan's world system touches our lives, where we may follow it, and where Satan's standards are designed to become ours.

3. After studying the Scofield notes referred to in this ch., make a chart of the classes of angels and their activities since creation.

17

Salvation

The Background

Many have asked whether it was absolutely necessary for God to send His Son to die. Could His demands have been satisfied in any other way? Since God is omnipotent, couldn't He have just forgiven us? Couldn't He forgive by divine generosity? Why did God have to go so far as to put the only perfect human being on a cross?

Although we cannot attempt to fathom the purposes of God, we can at least note that God's justice is infinite in scope and demand, because of His infinite and perfect holiness. Any sin must result in a necessary penalty, which must in turn be infinite. However, God's infinite love matched the full demand of justice. Although He did not have to pay the penalty for us, He did, and in such a way as to satisfy the needs of the parties involved. The solution He chose, the death of a sinless sacrifice, must have been absolutely necessary. If God could have done it in any other way than by the sacrifice of His beloved Son, He would have.

The Value of Christ's Death

Down through the history of the Church there have been various statements as to who was affected by the death of Christ and in what way they were affected. Many of them have some scriptural support, but only one of them really takes into account the full biblical picture of the death of Christ and its results. Each view must be evaluated according to the following scriptural details concerning the death of Christ: (1) God's holiness; (2) our sinfulness; (3) God's demand for punishment of sin; (4) our inability to help ourselves; (5) the work of Christ described as redemption, reconciliation, and propitiation; (6) the sacrificial nature of the death of Christ.

Passages such as Heb. 2:14–15 appear to teach that the death of Christ was designed to affect Satan (see also 1 Jn. 3:8; Col. 2:15; Jn. 12:31; 16:11; Isa. 14:17; 61:1). As a result, some have held that the death of Christ was a ransom paid to Satan to cancel any claims he may have had on us. Although Satan's defeat is clearly taught in the Bible, and predicted as early as Gen. 3:15, this view does not take into account the full scriptural picture concerning God's holiness and our sinfulness.

Some, noting the biblical emphasis on the suffering of Christ, have suggested that God wanted to show His displeasure against sin. The Father commiserated with the Son in His suffering, and thus showed His compassion toward sinners. God forgives sinners when they are deterred from sin by contemplating the death of Christ. The emphasis is on God's compassion on Christ and humanity, rather than His judgment. The weakness in this is that there is a lack of emphasis on God's demand for the satisfaction of a violated holiness. One should also ask what basis there would be for forgiveness in O.T. times. This view, sometimes called the *governmental theory,* is essentially the Arminian view of the atonement.

Because the love of God appears to be connected with the death of Christ, some have made God's love a central feature of the explanation of the cross. In the "moral influence" view of the atonement, the death of Christ is viewed as a manifestation of the love of God as he suffered with His creatures. This love of God removes our opposition to Him, we forsake sin, and He forgives it. But again, this view does not deal with God's offended holiness, our sinfulness and inability (the biblical teaching is that only in Christ can we please God), salvation before Christ (see below in this ch. under "Faith"), and the actual sacrifice of Christ.

Jesus' death as a victim comes to the fore in the "martyr" view of the death of Christ. In this approach the cross portrays the way of dedication and obedience to God. As we follow it, God pardons us. It hardly needs to be said that this view has a very low view of sin, and really no connection with the bedrock issues of salvation. In fact, it confuses the life of sanctification with entrance into that life. It denies human depravity (as do many other views), assuming that we can please God on our own. One of the great errors inherent in most variations of this view is that Christ was only a man, perhaps deluded, confused, and misguided, at that. In a sense, it also puts the effects of Christ's life above those of His death. And, once again, it does not account for the possibility of salvation before the cross.

The "mystical" view of the death of Christ is similar to some of the previous ones in that it views the life and death of Christ as having a mystical influence on us, lifting us to a higher and perhaps divine plane of existence. As with the above views, it slights God's holiness, our guilt, and our sin, and does not touch the issue of pre-cross salvation. Nor does it do justice to the sacrificial nature of the death of Christ.

Since the Bible does represent sin as an affront to God, some have suggested that this is the key element in the cross-event. God's honor was offended by sin. Since He was sinless Christ didn't need to die. This earned him merit with God, which he passed on to us, thus compensating for our lack of merit. Once again, in this "satisfaction" or "commercial" view God's holiness is neglected, as well as our sinfulness.

To summarize, all of the above theories fail to do justice to the work of Christ as redeemer, sacrifice, and substitute. They fall short on the application of the work of Christ to individuals. In most of these, it is our task to change ourselves. None put great emphasis on the holiness of God. Most direct the results of the cross at human beings, or even Satan, rather than God. And some confuse the value of the cross with the act of salvation itself, and the act of salvation with ongoing life with God.

Perhaps all of the above inadequate views grow out of the idea that it would be unthinkable for God to transfer His wrath against sinners to an innocent victim. It seems that this is based in great part on the unwillingness of human beings ultimately to acknowledge their complete depravity before God. God's holiness is at issue, and we can in no way help ourselves. Thus a substitute is necessary.

Although we do not know all that went into the death of Christ, and probably will not be able to give anything near a complete explanation during this life, the full doctrine of the value of Christ's death must be based on the following scriptural points:

1. God is holy (Lev. 19:2; Isa. 57:15; 1 Pet. 1:15–16)
2. This holiness is offended by sin.
3. We are totally guilty and unable to help ourselves (Rom. 2:1–3:20; see note, 3:23).
4. The ideas of sacrifice and substitution are essential.

They run from the beginning of the Bible to the work of Christ and then to the book of Revelation, where the Lamb appears in Rev. 22:1. Hebrews 9:28 could not be clearer: "So Christ was once offered to bear the sins of many" (AV). We will now explore this emphasis further.

Substitution

The essence of substitution is that God provides what we cannot. If something is done in our place, then we are not a party to the transaction. This simple logical fact is combined with the numerous biblical evidences to give the picture of God Himself doing what His hand of justice required. This is expressed in such passages as Gen. 22:8— "God will provide for Himself the lamb for the burnt offering" (NASB) and Jon. 2:9— "Salvation is of the Lord" (AV). One writer has put it this way: "The Christian discovers that the grace by which he is saved is exercised toward him by the very tribunal which condemned him."[1] (See Zech. 13:7 for a prophetic and poetic description of this.)

In the Bible the concept of substitution is bound up with the work of priests. Starting with inconclusive references early in the Bible, the written revelation eventually presents a full-blown priestly system under the law, with minute details concerning activity, locations, timing, and qualifications. It is significant that many recent views of the death of Christ have dismissed that system as simply one among many found around the world, simply another attempt to placate God through "primitive," bloody means. However, the Bible extends that system into the N.T. in its description of the death of Christ, especially as found in the book of Hebrews.

What Christ performed was a vicarious act, a substitution that consisted of a sacrifice. This is the essence of the work of a priest, one who stands—in the biblical system—between us and God. How could we be reconciled? Only through the meeting of God's demands (we didn't have any!). Our Great High Priest stepped in through grace to meet those demands for us.

The Person and Death of Christ as a Priest

There are many scripture passages that speak of the death of Christ as a sacrifice, for example:

1 Cor. 5:7—"For even Christ, our passover, is sacrificed for us." (AV)

Eph. 5:2—"Christ . . . gave himself up for us as a fragrant offering and sacrifice to God." (NIV)

Jn. 1:29—"Behold, the Lamb of God who takes away the sin of the world!" (NASB)

The Bible views this sacrifice as intimately connected with one aspect of His person and work, namely, His priesthood. The function of a priest is to offer sacrifice. And Christ is qualified both to be a priest and to do the work of one.

Our Lord is specifically called a high priest in several places: Heb. 5:6, 10; 6:20; 7:11, 15, 17. In each place the writer to the Hebrews links Him with Melchizedek, the striking figure of Gen. 14:18–20. There are two purposes for the unusual passage of Heb. 7:1–28: (1) to show that Christ's priesthood is superior to that of Aaron, and (2) to show that it lasts forever: it cannot be quenched by death. The consequences of this are: (1) Aaron's priesthood was no longer needed; and (2) Christ's priesthood, since it lasts forever, is the *final* priesthood. Hence, if Christ can get us to God, He can keep us there forever.

In the Bible a priest is one who works as an intermediary, attempting to take us to Him (see ch. 18, The Church, where teaching and priestly activity are distinguished). The best kind of intermediary is one who understands both sides. The author of Heb. presents Christ as One who understands both sides because He has the nature of both sides:

1. Heb. 1:8—"Thy throne, O God, is forever and ever" (addressed to the Son; AV). Along with other verses, this demonstrates His deity.

2. Heb. 2:9–18 is a lengthy exposition of His humanity. It is necessary to recall something concerning the nature of the incarnate Son of God. He was (and is) fully God and fully human. He had two natures that were united in one Person forever. And because deity was present in this Person, He could not sin. A priest who is sinless can offer a perfect sacrifice. Christ offered Himself (Heb. 9:25–26): all other priests offered the blood of animals (9:25). Christ was thus both priest and victim. So, His service as a priest was acceptable before God (He was sinless, obedient, and eternal) and His sacrifice was acceptable before God (it was spotless and didn't have to be made for Himself [Heb. 9:7]).

Whereas the Levitical priests had to enter the tabernacle continually (9:6), Christ's sacrifice was given once. In five places (9:26, 28; 7:27; 9:12; 10:10) the author uses two different and very pointed Gr. adverbs to indicate the finality of the sacrifice. Furthermore, it lasted forever (10:14), was made not in an earthly sanctuary but in a heavenly one (9:11, 24), did what animal sacrifices could never do (9:12; 10:4), and was spotless (9:14). All this amounts to a perfect sacrifice in the sight of God.

The result of a perfect sacrifice is perfect access to God. We will examine below some of the other accomplishments of the death of Christ, such as redemption and propitiation. But there can be no greater achievement than that a lost sinner can obtain perfect access to God. All of the other benefits of the death of Christ are details of the achieving of this access. Access to a holy God is the goal and end of salvation.

Other Results of the Death of Christ

Redemption

Redemption, propitiation, and reconciliation are the three main concepts used in the N.T. to describe the effects of the death of Christ. Several passages of Scripture establish the need for the first:

1. Jn. 8:34—"Whosoever committeth sin is the servant of sin." (AV)
2. Rom. 7:14—"But I am of flesh, sold into bondage to sin." (NASB)
3. Rom. 6:17—the Romans "used to be slaves of sin." (NIV)

So the picture is of the sinner as a bondservant to sin, yielding to its power, and unable to escape by himself. God's reversal of this pitiful condition becomes the basis for His appeal to us to respond to Him with our lives. Redemption, we will see, is designed to lead to eager obedience to God.

The presence of the concept of redemption in the O.T. sheds light on the redemptive aspects of the death of Christ. In the book of Ruth, Boaz acts as a "kinsman-redeemer," operating under the law of levirate marriage and the regulations given in Lev. 25:25–27, 47–49 concerning buying land or individuals who are in poverty. Boaz is able to buy Ruth's land that had passed out of the family because he is related to her and has the funds to meet the price. This corresponds to features of the Person and work of Christ in redemption. He is related to sinners (Heb. 2) and can meet the price (an infinite payment).

In the N.T. the presentation of redemption focuses particularly on several individual words. One (*lutroō* and related forms) points to our release or ransom from sin's grasp, as in Mt. 20:28. Another (*agorazō* and related forms) emphasizes our being purchased by God (Rev. 5:9–10). A third (*peripoieō*) speaks of God's acquiring us for His possession (Acts. 20:28). The combined picture of these words is that those in bondage to and under sin (we were condemned and couldn't help ourselves) have been released, purchased, removed, and acquired for possession. In each case the transaction was made with the sufficient price, the blood of Christ.

We would be giving an incomplete picture of redemption in the N.T. if we left the believer at the point of his exit from slavery. For although he indeed steps from slavery to freedom in one sense, at the same time he enters into slavery again, but this time it is joyful service to the King of Kings. That freedom is underscored in Gal. 4:1–14. Paul points out that under the law a person could never keep God's decrees (ch. 3). The law showed a person's actions to be sin. No matter how hard he tried, he was proven over and over to fall short of keeping the law, and therefore to be sinful. In Gal. 4:3 Paul calls this bondage, or "slavery." But after the application of redemption an individual is no longer a servant to sin, but a child of God (4:7). The problem of bondage and work as a slave is taken care of. The believer is free from the law, which actually highlighted his service to sin. As a result he is no longer obligated to produce works of sin (which under the law everyone did at every point) but is now free to walk in the Spirit and able to produce righteous acts (Gal. 4:6; ch. 5; see notes at 5:22, 3:19, and 3:25).

Romans 6 takes us even further in our understanding of this freedom. Romans 7:5–6 shows how a Jew was held in the law, which worked in us to bring forth sin. We served sin (6:6) and the law (7:5–6). Romans 6:14–23 shows the new relationship to God, consisting of being servants to righteousness that leads to holiness. This is especially a great Pauline concept: four of Paul's epistles begin with the statement that he is a bondslave of Christ.

The doctrine of redemption is also the basis for the Bible's teaching on our physical surrender to God, as seen in 1 Cor. 6:19–20. Not only do our nonmaterial parts belong to God, but our bodies do also. For a believer overcome by some bodily sin, the most solid ground to proceed on is to trace what God has done in purchasing that person, body and all.

Finally, redemption has good works as its goal. Notice that we've come full circle here. Works under the law were of no avail. They only demonstrated our sinfulness. The sinner is redeemed from the law, from slavery to it and to sin, and is now a servant to God to perform a new kind of works!

Propitiation

The English word *propitiation* is only found a few times in the Bible (six times in the AV: 1 Jn. 2:2; 4:10; Rom. 3:25; Lk. 18:13; Heb. 2:17; 8:12). Although this is a small number of passages, the *concept* of propitiation is found throughout the O.T. (usually translated "atonement") and is central to the work of Christ.

In studying propitiation it is important that we fix in our minds the nature of the reaction of God toward sin. We will describe the results of His reaction with the word wrath. There are more than twenty words in the O.T. used to refer to the wrath of Jehovah, and altogether there are over 580 occurrences of these words referring to God's wrath. God's wrath is not a capricious passion that can be turned on and off or that subsides with time, but is the stern reaction of a holy God to our evil nature and our evil acts. After Israel fashioned the golden calf and worshipped it, God said, "Now leave me alone so that my anger may burn against them and that I may destroy them" (Ex. 32:10, NIV). In Ps. 60:1–3 the displeasure of God against Israel's sin results in His meting out "wine of staggering" (AV). When we turn to the N.T. we find the writers using the word *orgē,* denoting a settled emotion, "a strong opposition to all that is evil arising out of God's very nature." [2] The word *thumos,* pointing to passionate anger, is used much less in regard to God. While human beings experience both controlled and passionate anger, what we know of the nature of God prevents us from concluding that He could lose His temper and become enraged as we do. The controlled aspect of God's anger against sin is expressed clearly, for example, in Jn. 3:36, where the wrath of God is said to remain on the unregenerate individual.

This concept of the wrath of God, who expresses just indignation against sin, is far removed from many modern concepts of God that view Him as a God of love only. He must judge what is contrary to His holiness, and that's one reason we ought to define sin as anything that is contrary to His person (see ch. 14, The Doctrine of Sin).

So where there is sin there is wrath. But the grace of God operates, too. Because all are under God's wrath, only God can do something about it, and in fact He does. Leviticus 17:11 provides a clear expression of this in connection with the provisions of the law, as it speaks of the blood: "I have given it to you upon the altar to make atonement [propitiation] for your souls" (AV).

Although the usual view of interpreters concerning propitiation in the O.T. is that it consists simply of a covering for sin, there is a clear connection with the wrath of God. Once a year the high priest was allowed to enter the holy of holies and place blood on the mercy seat (the place of propitiation). This was the cover on the ark of the covenant (Ex. 25:10, 11, 17, 21), which contained the law tablets, Aaron's rod, and the pot of manna. The broken law led to wrath, judgment, and death. The cover is a picture of the stopping of God's wrath against the broken law, and is incomplete without the blood's being applied, after which God can commune with people there (Ex. 25:22). The mercy seat is thus a covering in a rough sense, but it is involved in something more complicated: blood is used to turn away wrath against sin.[3]

In Rom. 3:21–26 propitiation is linked with the doctrine of justification. This passage indicates that our justification is based on the removal of God's wrath. Our failure to meet God's demands for holiness led to God's wrath, which in turn led to death. The payment of the blood of a substitute removes that wrath. As a result the failure by sinning is of no consequence, and so legally God's demands are satisfied. The declaration of this legal verdict is justification (see below in this ch. under "Justification"). As the Scofield note on Rom. 3:28 says, "The justified believer has been declared by the Judge Himself (Rom. 3:31) to have nothing laid to his charge (Rom. 8:1, 31–34)." The hymnwriter William Cowper was brought to Christ through this passage, and later wrote:

> There is a fountain filled with blood,
> Drawn from Immanuel's veins;
> And sinners plunged beneath that flood
> Lose all their guilty stains!
> E'er since by faith I saw the stream
> Thy flowing wounds supply,
> Redeeming love has been my theme,
> and shall be till I die.

Reconciliation

While the doctrine of redemption teaches that the cross-work of Christ dealt with our condition of slavery to sin, and propitiation speaks of our escaping God's wrath, the doctrine of reconciliation indicates that our hostility toward God has been changed.

Romans 5:6–11 describes our alienation from God, speaking of our being God's enemies (v. 10). Reconciliation turns alienated parties back to each other. But who is the active enemy, God or the individual sinner? Which one is subsequently turned around? Earlier in Rom. Paul demonstrates by quoting from the O.T. that we are the ones who ran from God (3:7–18). Although His wrath is against us, He is the one who seeks us out. We could not say that He is our enemy. But outside of Christ a person is hostile toward God and actually hates Him. God does not hate His creatures. Thus, in 2 Cor.

5:20 the turning of reconciliation is predicated of sinners, not God. We need to be reconciled to God, not He to us. We are the ones who are changed in our orientation. However, it is also true that this occurs when God has certain requirements satisfied. In a sense we could say that redemption and propitiation make reconciliation possible. Redemption involves the payment of a price to release us from sin and to become God's possession (versus sin's). Propitiation describes a payment toward God to turn away His wrath against sin. In the first, God redeems us as He satisfies His requirements. In the second, He changes His outlook as He meets His standards. When both of these have taken place, the elimination of hostility is possible. Strictly speaking, God does not remove the enmity until a person accepts Christ as Savior. Thus Paul pleads in 2 Cor. 5:20: "Be reconciled to God" (NIV). In fact, the death of Christ only provisionally effected all three doctrines—redemption, propitiation, and reconciliation—and they become actual when saving faith is exercised.

We should add a word concerning the relation of these three doctrines to our lives before we come to Christ. Redemption stresses aspects of the cross-work of Christ that negate our misery in sin, our slavery to a master that can do no good for us, and our hopelessness. Similarly, propitiation teaches that outside of Christ we face certain judgment and destruction. There is no way we can effect our own salvation. There is nothing that we do that pleases God. All that we do morally and spiritually only adds to our punishment through His wrath. And reconciliation teaches that we are in a position of hostility toward God. We hate the things of God. If we are to be saved, it will come only through His breaking into our situation. It is not difficult to see that it is grace operating upon all three problems that alone can help us. The biblical exposition of these three doctrines is a parade-ground for the unmerited favor, the saving grace, of a loving God.

The Resurrection of Christ

Many people, especially at Easter time, describe the resurrection as the evidence that there is life after death. This is not true at all, of course, since many passages teach that no one ceases to exist. Does the resurrection provide life with God after death, then? No, not really, since spiritual death is our problem, and Christ's bearing of the penalty of sin satisfied God's demands and made it possible for Him to give life only to those in Christ.

A startling statement will help us see the importance of the resurrection: Jesus actually died twice. He was first forsaken by the Father during His time on the cross. This is described in Ps. 22:1–21, especially v. 1, the cry of dereliction He quoted on the cross: "My God, my God, why have you forsaken me?" (Mt. 27:46, NIV). This separation from the Father was spiritual death, experienced for others as He was "made" sin (2 Cor. 5:21). It is significant that Jesus addressed the plea not to His Father, but simply to God. The father/son relation had been broken for a few hours as sin was being dealt with. But Lk. 23:46 records that just before His death, in what must have been the seventh utterance from the cross, He once again addressed God as His Father: "Father, into your hands I commit my spirit" (Lk. 23:46, NIV). The union, which had existed until a few hours earlier, then had been broken, was restored. In fact, the first cry was "Father, forgive them." Yet before He expired, He revealed that the transaction had been completed, as He cried, "It is finished" (Jn. 19:30). We should note then, that utterances addressed to the Father surround one addressed only to God. Furthermore, the purpose of His dying was completed before He died physically. That period of forsaking, involving spiritual death, was what actually paid for sins.

What then was the purpose of His physical death and of His subsequent resurrection? For every human being physical death comes as a result of being under the curse of the fall. The decay and final failing of the body is a vivid demonstration of something that we cannot see but all possess—spiritual death. Only a few individuals in history have escaped the sequence—Enoch and Elijah—who both went directly to God, avoiding bodily death. Jesus' body died partly as a result of His spiritual death and partly as a demonstration of it. We know from His physical death that He was, even for a short time, made like us and subject to the curse of returning to dust, placed on everyone since the fall. Of course, the immediate cause was the physical mistreatment He received. But the ultimate cause was His coming under the judgment of God on sinners.

In speaking of the resurrection we should stress that Jesus' *body* was brought from the grave. Jesus as a person never ceased to exist. Where He was for three days, the Bible doesn't say. But His bodily resurrection reunited His nonmaterial nature with His body, thus setting the pattern for all who follow the same sequence, with Him as the firstborn (Col. 1:18). So we should stress, at Easter and all other times, that Jesus' resurrection made it possible for those who know God to enjoy meaningful life after the grave, with the whole person put back together—body, soul, spirit, heart, mind, and all. In God's sight, the individual is incomplete without his body. And even though the body that believers receive at their resurrection will be different (the issue that perplexed the Corinthians and that is addressed in 1 Cor. 15), it will somehow be like the body they had earlier, retaining personal identity. Jesus possessed this kind of body after His resurrection, so that His friends were able to recognize Him.

The bodily resurrection of Jesus was a demonstration that the Father approved the cross-work of the Son. Romans 4:25 indicates that He was "raised on account of our justification," i.e. because justification had been accomplished (not brought out in most translations). Without the bodily resurrection we would never know if the basic problem of sin and spiritual death had been solved. All that was needed for justification had already been accomplished, so the Father raised the Son as a visible proof that the sin question had been settled.

There are other significant spiritual issues connected with the resurrection. Among other things, it is a fulfillment of many O.T. prophecies, a demonstration of the power of God, and the prerequisite for Jesus' occupying the throne of David over Israel in the kingdom.

Events surrounding the resurrection are treated in books that deal with the life of Christ. The reader should consult such works in ch. 23, Annotated Bibliography, for details concerning the sequence of events and proofs for the resurrection.

The Application of the Death of Christ

Selection of Recipients

Mention election in any average gathering of evangelicals and you immediately have several diverse reactions. "It's too difficult!" "It's divisive!" "If theologians haven't solved it, I won't even touch it!" "It hinders my freedom!" "It makes God look arbitrary!" and so on. It is instructive for us to notice, however, that both Paul and Peter begin epistles with the doctrine (Rom. 1:6; Eph. 1:4; see note, 1 Pet. 1:1). In fact, without this important work of God, no one would have a share in the death of Christ.

Here are some questions that reflect problems that we often have concerning election:

1. What is the basis for election?
2. Is God fair in electing some and not others?
3. What does *foreknowledge* mean?
4. How does foreknowledge relate to other aspects of election?
5. Does election eliminate a genuine Gospel offer?
6. Does election discourage evangelism?

It may help to provide some guidelines for approaching the whole area of election. First, we must pay careful attention to Scripture. It anticipates confusion and problems of understanding that we may have. Too often we don't bother to go to it carefully in this or other doctrines. We have to be willing to believe what it says, not to come to it with preconceived notions. Second, it is always valuable to state the full counsel of Scripture (as much as there is room to do so!). Third, where there are problems, interpret the less clear Scripture by the more clear, or more explicit. Fourth, try to look at whole passages and not just isolated verses. Fifth, keep in mind what the Bible teaches about God's Person and character. The more we know about His Person, the more we appreciate His sovereignty. Sixth, remember the nature of Christ's work: (1) It is free for the one who believes; (2) We did nothing and deserve nothing. Our position outside of Christ is that of slaves to sin, under God's wrath and alienated from God. So, whatever election is, it must be viewed against the backdrop of our being under the wrath of God. And whatever God does in His sovereignty to apply the cross-work of Christ must be in keeping with the nature of that work. Seventh, we are limited by sin, and God has not told us all there is to know. Eighth, we may have our own ideas of how we would like God to act in saving people, but that may not be the way God does it. We must always bring our thoughts into subjection to what God actually tells us. Ninth, we have to recognize our limitations. We can explain as far as we can from Scripture, but cannot speculate in going beyond it. Finally, remember that if you pray and expect God to be the only One who can answer, then you already believe in the sovereignty of God.

Romans 8 and Foreknowledge

The five terms in Rom. 8:29–30—foreknew, predestined, called, justified, glorified—form a chain "connecting God's gracious purpose in the eternity past with its consummation in the eternity to come."[4] Verse 28 moves from the problems of this life to God's counsels and work in eternity past and future—from foreknowing to glorifying. In the midst is the wonderful v. 29, which has been for so many an encouragement to confident trust. But the reason for the promises of vv. 28 and 31–39 is God's sovereign purpose in election. God's providence depends on His elective work, that is, His choosing. When we have problems with election, we should keep in mind that this passage teaches that our blessings depend on it!

What does the term *foreknowledge* mean? This is an important question, because it is the most misunderstood of the five words and the key to the rest, since it starts the sequence. Whatever benefits there are in the following verses depend on it. The crucial question is, did God simply see ahead of time that some would believe and call them the "elect," or did He plan for their faith, too?

Several other biblical passages aid our understanding at this point. In Jer. 1:5 the same concept of "knowing" is present (see also Gen. 18:19). It cannot simply mean "to know about," but must describe a personal relationship. Certainly God "knew about" Israel before her founding (in Gen. 12); there must be more than that. In Amos 3:2 the Heb. word behind the "known" of the AV is appropriately rendered "chosen" by the NIV. In Rom. 11:2 the same base word as Amos 3:2 and Rom. 8:29 is used (the prefix differs). Once again the concept is the same, and we could legitimately translate the word as "plan for." The idea of simply knowing about the people of Israel ahead of time does not make sense here (i.e. knowing about them or knowing they would do something). Besides, the crucial question in Rom. 11:1ff is, if God planned for them, why aren't they blessed now? This is like the idea expressed in Amos 3:2: God "planned for" a people to have a special relationship with Him. In 1 Pet. 1:19–20 there is, first of all, a term found in the AV—foreordination—that does not correspond to the Gr. word *proginoskō,* usually translated elsewhere "foreknow." What, however, is the meaning of the foreknowing here? It would not make sense to say here that God knew about Christ ahead of time. That goes without saying. The translators of the NIV have rendered this as "chosen." This indicates more clearly that before the creation of the world God planned for Christ to have the role of the sacrificial lamb. A final passage is Acts 2:23, where God's foreknowledge is the instrument, along with His counsel (they are grammatically parallel in the verse), of handing Christ over to the cross. Foreknowledge could only be instrumental if it involved planning.

We must always be careful not to read meanings of words in various contexts into occurrences elsewhere. However, there is enough evidence concerning the word foreknowledge to warrant our taking it in Rom. 8:29 as equivalent to choosing. Especially conclusive is Paul's own use in Rom. 11:2, within the same epistle. Thus, in Rom. 8:29 the word does not indicate that God simply saw ahead of time that some would exercise faith. It is actually the initial, determining, selecting step in God's arranging for some to be His own. It leads to blessing for the elect, essentially because it does not leave their relationship to God to chance.

What are the results of God's planning foreknowledge? Four benefits come to us in the chain begun by choosing. First, it brings our greatest good. The promise of v. 28 is linked to vv. 29–30 with the word *for,* which gives the reason for God's working in such a way that good results from all the events in a life given over to God. Apparent evils or problems work for good because of His initial foreknowledge that chooses us to be objects of His love.

Second, God's planning foreknowledge is related to Christlikeness. Verse 29 literally says we will be inwardly and outwardly just like Him. This is really the greatest thing God could do for us. Predestination is what plans this out. The Gr. word translated "predestine," when found without the prefix equivalent to *pre,* can mean "to mark a boundary around something." So we are kept and guarded for God's purpose. Today and tomorrow are part of His plan to bring the believer to the place of being like Christ. This obviously establishes foreknowledge and predestination as eminently practical doctrines.

Third, foreknowledge makes it possible for us to believe. The word *called* in v. 30 does not simply mean "invite." There *is* a general call to elect and nonelect alike, as seen in Mt. 22:14. Here, though, this is the call to the elect, those foreknown, i.e., *chosen.* (Cf. 1 Cor. 1:24.) The same people are involved with all five acts of God. Calling is the work of the Holy Spirit that moves a person to believe in Christ as Savior. Paul tells us in Phil. 1:29 where our faith actually comes from: it is God's gift to us.

Fourth, foreknowledge guarantees our security (vv. 31–34). We will discuss the security of the believer further below. But the issue is this: Is it possible for some who have genuinely believed in Christ as Savior to lose their salvation through their own sin or the act of someone else (Satan, for example)? If God just saw ahead of time who would believe, then there would be no guarantee of the constancy of a person's faith— it would be essentially his own doing. But because foreknowledge (equivalent to planning for) starts the chain of vv. 29–30, then the blessings of vv. 31–39 are certain. In other words, our view of eternal security depends on our view of election. We should also notice the four questions in vv. 31–35. The answers result from the links in the chain, going back to foreknowledge. Furthermore, the works of Christ that guarantee our security are ours because of planning foreknowledge.

Romans 9 and Choosing

Starting in Rom. 9, Paul turns from his description of the provision of salvation to its application to Israel. This exposition, which continues through the end of ch. 11, provides crucial information concerning God's choosing process. It answers several basic questions that we often have about election.

To begin with, it answers the question of what election is. It appears that Israel has been forgotten by God (vv. 1–5). They have privileges (vv. 4–5), but now Gentiles are being favored. Why? The principal of *selection* (given exposition in vv. 8–13) accounts for the apparent disfavor. There are Jews within the totality of Judaism who are dealt with in a special way—an Israel within Israel. This does not mean they are all brought to God. The issue here is not that of salvation (as it is in 9:23–24). Paul simply wants to establish the principle of selection, of choosing from a mass. God chooses some individuals within Israel for blessing, and so the promise of national blessing comes only to some. (In ch. 10 he shows who the promise of salvation comes to: those of faith.) The demonstration is simple: not all of Abraham's offspring are heirs to the promises God made to him. Ishmael is excluded. God's selecting activity separates some from a mass to be the objects of blessing.

Does this passage shed any light on who the objects of choosing are? Yes, it does, in that it shows that some individuals are singled out. Isaac (v. 10) is blessed in regard to the promises on the basis of selection. The selecting principle then follows the line of a second individual, Jacob. Although salvation is not directly in view in 9:7–13, chs. 9–11 is a unit, and Paul's ultimate purpose is to show how some from Israel can and will be saved. So, the principle of selection applies to (1) the limitation of blessing to parts of Abraham's line and (2) the choice of some for salvation.

One of the most perplexing problems that some people wrestle with is, How does God choose? On what basis does He select? The basic answer, as given in this passage, is that He chooses in His sovereignty, as He desires. Esau was the older brother. God's selection went counter to the law of primogeniture regarding inheritance (here, again, the inheritance of the blessing promised to Abraham). So, selection does not operate on the basis of human claims, merits, or expectation (cf. 1 Cor. 1:26–27). We often hear it said, "He's so nice, he'd make a good Christian." God does not work that way. In the case of Jacob and Esau, selection operated before birth, so no human act at all conditioned it (not even an anticipated act that God would have known about ahead of time). Their destiny was settled before they were born and without reference to their character, abilities, or actions.

Is there a discernible goal in God's selecting? Why does He choose? The statement in v. 13, "Jacob I loved, but Esau I hated" (NIV), has seemed to be at variance with what we know from elsewhere concerning the character of God. Divine displeasure and disfavor is indicated here, but not malice or vindictiveness.[5] God's controlling "purpose in election" (v. 11, NIV) is that some might become the objects of God's favor. He wants some to enjoy His special love. Beyond that, the Bible does not tell us why He selects the ones He does.

The Question of Fairness

The issue of the equity of God arises often in Scripture. The Bible always vindicates God, and in doing so shows that we need to know more doctrine about Him (see Job; Heb. 12; Rom. 3:25–26; all of Hab.). The question of God's righteousness arises in Rom. 9 in regard to election. In vv. 7–13 we are told that God chooses individuals without reference to their merit or actions or desires. How can God do this? Is this a fair thing to do? There are two similar questions that Paul raises and answers (vv. 14 and 19): (1) Doesn't this method of choosing and rejecting really make God unrighteous? This calls God's character and nature into question. (2) If God works this way, how can He possibly blame anyone for not responding to invitations to obey Him? He hardens some and then, when they do not do His will, He holds them responsible. How can He do that?

The answers to both questions come from two O.T. passages.[6] It is significant that the Bible already contains answers to problems we imagine concerning election. The first question has two parts and is answered in vv. 14–18: Is God unrighteous in choosing as He does? Paul's first response is found in v. 14: "Not at all!" (NIV). This quick denial is followed by a more lengthy explanation. The quotation in v. 15 from Ex. 33:19 is a statement of the absolute sovereignty of God. Interestingly enough, it is given no explanation, apparently because in Paul's mind it needed none. Moses was favored simply because of God's sovereign mercy. Moses had no claim on it. Verse 15 stresses God's freedom in bestowing mercy. There is no issue of justice when God does His selecting. Mercy is never given on the basis of merit, anyway. It comes freely; human effort or desire can never lay hold of it. If it operated any other way, it wouldn't be mercy.

If we were to look at Ex. 3:19ff and the sequence regarding Pharaoh and his hardening, we would find that God first predicted that Pharaoh would not release Israel (3:19), and that He would harden Pharaoh's heart (4:21). Subsequent verses describe God as the agent of hardening nine times and Pharaoh himself two times, and twice hardening is mentioned without an agent's being indicated. Is it the case that God simply allowed Pharaoh to harden himself? Pharaoh did harden his heart. But even one reference is sufficient to show that it was not just Pharaoh's act. The context of Rom. 9:17 leaves no room for a conclusion other than that it was God who actively hardened Pharaoh's heart (cf. Jn. 12:39–40). The purpose of God in all this was to show His power and name. That is God's goal in all His works.

We must conclude, then, that there are two directions to sovereignty: having mercy, and hardening. They are the only two. Note that the two directions of sovereignty are not mercy and nonattention. Further, note that His will is mentioned as the cause. Now most people do not have trouble with vv. 15–16, especially if He shows *us* mercy. But we rebel at vv. 17–18, which are of a piece with vv. 15–16. If there is not a showing of mercy, there is hardening. There is no middle ground. But at the same time human beings are held accountable for any evil they do, and for unbelief. Pharaoh's own hardening is present, and he is guilty for it. This is exactly parallel to election as the call to faith and salvation (although the topic of coming to God doesn't enter until 9:23). Some are called and saved. Those not chosen, the hardened, are responsible for their actions. We should not forget that all deserve to be hardened. No one deserves God's mercy. The fact that it is mercy means that it is not deserved. Our depravity (we do not want to come to God) means that salvation will not work without election that is based on mercy alone. Finally, in Ex. 3–14 it is clear that God's offer of mercy to Pharaoh and His hardening activity stand side by side. There is no injustice in this (v. 18). His will is sovereign. That is the point of vv. 14–18.

The second question Paul asks and answers in this passage is found in v. 19: How can God condemn anyone if He works this way? He hardens a person, then when they do not do what He asks, holds them responsible. Is this fair? Isn't He inconsistent in what He does? It is almost humorous that Paul's initial response is that the question itself is improper: "But who are you, O man, to talk back to God?" (NIV). Paul immediately turns the imaginary questioner to contemplation of his own creaturehood. Since we are created by God, He can dispose of us as He wills, and we cannot legitimately call God into question for hardening or showing mercy. God can harden and still hold the one hardened responsible because He is the sovereign Potter (v. 21). Paul's exposition of the potter figure is drawn from four O.T. passages: Isa. 29:15–16; 45:9–13; 64:8–9; Jer. 18:1–6. Clearly he believed that such O.T. references would demonstrate his point. The sovereignty of the Potter is especially related to our status as sinners. As the potter is free to do as he wishes with clay (and not be questioned) so God is free to deal with people as He wishes and not be questioned—because of their sin and God's creatorship. We should note especially that, as in vv. 13 and 18, there are only two directions—honor and dishonor. There is no middle ground. Vessels/pots are destined for wrath and mercy.

Although the matter of salvation is not in view until 9:23 (as mentioned earlier, up to that point Paul is dealing with the question of selection for favoring by God), God's dealings with Pharaoh and the figure of the potter are instructive concerning the Gospel offer. When a person is told he or she can have salvation simply by exercising faith in Christ, that offer is absolutely genuine, even though the principle of selection determines who will actually believe. Every person who responds will obtain salvation. We are not to say that, since some cannot possibly believe, God is taunting people. On the other hand, those who do not respond are described in the Bible as responsible for not doing so, just as Pharaoh was responsible for his not letting Israel go.

In spite of the electing work of God, believers are always responsible for evangelizing.[7] They can never legitimately say that the elect will eventually come to God on their own and no human intermediaries are necessary. God has decreed that people hear the message through human spokesmen. Election does not obviate the responsibility to believe or the responsibility to publish the Gospel.

These verses in Rom. 9 reveal three purposes of election. God works in two directions (hardening and showing mercy) to show His wrath toward sin, to display His power, especially toward those hardened, and to display His glory by means of those who are shown mercy: He is glorified by choosing some! That God shows mercy to anyone is amazing. We ought to be satisfied that He does the rest as He wishes.

The Grace of God

In our discussion of the doctrine of salvation to this point we have already mentioned the grace of God several times. What is this feature of God's activity toward human beings? In the O.T. two different words are frequently involved in the presentation of God's gracious work, one indicating unmerited favor of a superior to an inferior (Ex. 33:19, translated "gracious" [AV, NASB] and "merciful" [NIV], and the other suggesting faithful lovingkindness, particularly in covenant relationships (2 Sam. 7:15, translated "mercy" [AV], "lovingkindness" [NASB], and "love" [NIV]). In the N.T. the word *charis* (often used in the Septuagint to translate the above-mentioned Heb. words) is used of general goodwill, loving-kindness, and favor (Acts 7:10, 46) as well as of the benefits of the death of Christ (1 Pet. 1:10: the appearance of Christ was the coming of grace; Jn. 1:17: grace and truth were brought through Jesus Christ; see note). In 1 Cor. 15:8–10 Paul underscores the undeserved nature of grace as he emphasizes his unworthiness ("the least of the apostles" [NIV]). We could examine more passages, but the essence of the biblical picture of grace is this: (1) It was undeserved favor on the part of God that sent the Son; (2) It is undeserved favor that applies His work to some individuals.

One particular passage that portrays the relation between our need and God's response in grace is Rom. 4, where grace is related to the provision of righteousness. Abraham was justified, declared righteous, by the grace principle (v. 16). He could not obtain right standing before God by his works, because (1) no one can gain any merit before God, since our works are evil, and (2) works simply gain us wrath (4:15). But righteousness comes through grace because (1) we can't earn it, and (2) we don't deserve it, since we're under wrath. The only responsibility we have in a grace transaction is faith. In the application of righteousness, works are not compatible with grace. But faith is (v. 16).

Grace, then, is God's undeserved and unsolicited favor toward those who cannot help themselves because of sin. God's provision of salvation in sending Christ to die on the cross is an act of grace, as is its application to each individual. Works on our part are totally excluded. Faith can be part of the process because it is not a work, indeed, it has its source in God (Phil. 1:29; see also notes at 1 Cor. 1:2; 2 Pet. 3:18).

The Requirements for Salvation

Faith. Since the grace method of salvation is incompatible with works, it must also be true even by logic alone that the application to individuals of the salvation provided in that grace principle must also be of such a nature as to exclude works. And we do indeed find that the biblical presentation confirms our logical supposition. In order to see this it is necessary to look at (1) the meaning of faith, (2) the object of faith, and (3) the source of faith. We should note that the words variously rendered in English as "faith," "faithful," "believe," "belief" and "trust" are translations of related words in Gr.

The first presentation of the faith principle in Scripture is found in Gen. 15:1–6. There Abraham, who was childless, simply trusted God when He said He would give him physical heirs even though he and Sarah were past the age of having children. The exposition of this is found in Rom. 4. The point is that God promised, and Abraham believed He would do what He had promised. Abraham acknowledged that he could not establish his own line of physical descent (vv. 17, 19) and that God could and would do it. Abraham's faith is not specifically exercised with regard to his own eternal welfare, but only with regard to God's provision of an heir. But this was the issue for him. Further, Abraham believed that God was able to bring life from where there was death (vv. 17, 19; cf. Heb. 11:19). So Abraham acknowledged his inability, relied on God's promises and ability, put confident trust in God despite outward circumstances (v. 17—God views the things that don't exist as though they did), and counted on the life-giving ability of God. Paul's discussion of Abraham's faith is designed to show what saving faith is for those in any age. In general, then, we can say that faith is firm reliance, trust, and confidence in a God who provides what we cannot, especially when it comes to providing life (see Rom. 1:16–17 and its quotation of Hab. 2:4).

From what we've already said, it is evident that the object of trust, saving faith, is the God who saves. It is not the faith that saves a person, but the object of faith. It's not the faith itself as a psychological phenomenon that saves, but the work of Christ applied by the Spirit. Faith is the human requirement used by the Spirit. It is important to notice that the Bible never says that a person is saved on account of his faith, but rather through it.

Why isn't faith really a kind of work on our part? Our previous illustrations clarify this:

    1. The grace principle excludes works.

    2. Faith acknowledges our inability to do what is required to correct our relationship with God.

    3. Faith is simply saying "I can't, but God can. I can't work, but God can and will."

    4. God has already provided salvation. It is spoken of as a "gift of grace." (AV)

J. Gresham Machen says:

> The reception of that gift is faith; faith means not doing something but receiving something; it means not the earning of a reward but the acceptance of a gift. A man can never be said to obtain a thing for himself if he obtains it by faith; indeed to say that he obtains it by faith is only another way of saying that he does not obtain it for himself but permits another to obtain it for him. Faith, in other words, is not active but passive; and to say that we are saved by faith is to say that we do not save ourselves but are saved only by the one in whom our faith is reposed. . . ."[8]

As to the origin of faith, it is God Himself. There are a number of direct statements that demonstrate this:

1. Heb. 12:2—Jesus is the "author and perfector of our faith." (NIV) Although the primary emphasis here may be on Jesus as an example for us to follow, it is also likely that the verse indicates that He is the source of our faith. One writer points out that our faith "is initiated and sustained by him because he has prayed the Father that we may come to faith." [9]

2. Phil. 1:29—Here our suffering and believing are linked; if we believe, then we can expect suffering, and both have their source in God. In fact the verb translated "given" (AV) and "granted" (NASB, NIV) suggests, more than the usual verb for "give," a free, unsolicited gift.

3. Acts 3:16—faith comes through the name of Jesus, apparently as individuals give Him His due.

4. Acts 13:48—those appointed to eternal life believed (exercised faith). Although it is not specifically stated that faith comes directly from God, it is implied that they could not have had faith without some work of God.

5. Acts 16:14—Lydia's response is made possible only by God.

We conclude, then, that faith has its source in God, is the only divinely appointed channel for receiving God's gracious provision in Christ, and is not a work (see also notes at Mt. 12:46; Lk. 7:44; Rom. 3:28; Heb. 11:39; Jas. 2:26).

Additions to Faith. Although the Bible is quite clear that faith is the only means for obtaining the salvation provided by the cross-work of Christ, many have intentionally or unintentionally substituted other requirements, or taken faith as a base and added stipulations to it.

Some have asserted that faith and confessing Christ publicly are both required for salvation. This view is based on a faulty understanding of Rom. 10:9. Confession there is best viewed as the conduct of life that follows true belief (cf. Jas. 2). The O.T. passage quoted in part in v. 8 (Dt. 30:10–20) speaks of doing something in obedience while making sure the primary act is that of loving the Lord. Works follow belief.

Noting that baptism is often closely connected with salvation, some hold that baptism is necessary in order to obtain it. In addition to the fact that this adds a requirement beyond faith, this misses the point that for N.T. writers salvation was naturally and immediately expressed in the act of baptism. It was the expected thing to do after trusting Christ. A verse often adduced in support of this erroneous view is Acts 2:38, which in context applies to the particular need of the generation of Israelites that crucified Christ to repent of what they had done, accept the Messiah they had crucified, be baptized, and thus receive forgiveness for their particular crime. Because of the particular situation in which this verse appears in Acts and the clear statements throughout the Bible to the effect that faith alone will bring salvation, it is erroneous to assert that baptism is a requirement for salvation.

There is another form of the error of adding to faith as the sole requirement for salvation. It actually has several variations, all of which amount to imposing a work requirement on the sinner in order for him to come to God. The most frequent form is something like: "You must receive Jesus as Savior and Lord in order to be saved." Variants are "believe and surrender" and "believe and give your life to God." Usually based on Rom. 10:9, this view confuses the requirements for salvation with those for sanctification (see "Life as Possessors of Salvation: Sanctification," below, in this ch.). In the context of Rom. 10:9, Paul is addressing the problem of Jewish unbelief. The crucial issue for his readers was that they acknowledge that the Jesus who walked among ordinary people and died on the cross was the Jehovah of the O.T., i.e., Lord. In fact,

v. 13 shows that calling on that "Lord" is the key to salvation. 1 Cor. 12:3 enunciates a similar principle: "No one can say, 'Jesus is Lord,' except by the Holy Spirit" (NASB). Knowing God and regarding Jesus as Jehovah go hand in hand. We should also note that the N.T. never speaks of "making Jesus Lord of one's life." Instead, it speaks of submitting, obeying, and imitating, all as elements of sanctification. To insist that a person "receive Jesus as Savior and Lord," in the sense of promising obedience, is to add to the requirement for salvation a promise that no unsaved person knows how to keep. He does not know what is involved in the Christian life, and is not expected to know. Promised obedience cannot be a condition of obtaining eternal life. It is a work, and is at odds with the grace principle of salvation.

In presenting the Gospel, many people probably add this condition inadvertently to the simple "You must receive Christ as Savior" (a correct condition based on Jn. 1:12 and equivalent to faith). And many individuals sincerely come to Christ through this kind of invitation. But it is important to stress what the Bible stresses, to make the distinctions the Bible makes, and to avoid any possibility of adding an unbiblical requirement to the terms of salvation.

Repentance. This important biblical doctrine is often a source of confusion in connection with exercising saving faith. What is its place? The word is used correctly (biblically) if it describes one of the parts of a person's act in coming to Christ that does not involve an outward emotional response. It is erroneous to teach that a person must experience emotional remorse before or while exercising faith.

The O.T. and N.T. presentations of this concept involve the ideas of turning (2 Ki. 17:13; Acts 3:19) and changing one's mind (Acts 20:21). In fact, the Gr. word often translated "repentance" can also mean "a change of mind." In Acts 11:21 the turning is inseparably linked with believing: "A great number of people believed and turned to the Lord" (NIV). Repentance is thus a real part of the salvation process (see also Acts 26:20; 2:38). It involves the mind (Acts 2:38) and the will (implied in commands to turn and rethink), and can involve the emotions, but is not necessarily accompanied by outward signs and does not necessarily include confession of sin. It is required for salvation in that no one can turn to Christ without a change of mind with regard to who He is, as exemplified by Acts 17:30: "In the past God overlooked such ignorance, but now he commands all people everywhere to repent." In many passages it is simply used as a synonym for believing, i.e., emotion is not necessarily involved; e.g., Lk. 24:47; Acts 2:38 compared with 2:41; 11:18, compared with 10:43; 17:30; Acts 20:21; Rom. 2:4, compared with 1:16–17; 2 Tim. 2:25; 2 Pet. 3:9.

The basic error connected with repentance is saying that it's necessary to experience anguish and remorse before one can be saved. That is a way of looking at ourselves, rather than at Christ, and conditioning salvation on feelings, not on faith. The meaning of the word as "changing one's mind," along with the many clear references to salvation's coming on the basis of faith alone argue for the fact that repentance is simply a valid part of faith. It is not a separate act. Therefore, when we come to a passage such as 2 Cor. 7:10 we are able to deal with it by comparison with the rest of Scripture. This refers to Christians who change their minds about their relation to Paul, and so a sin is taken care of. The result is glad salvation—entrance into the presence of God without regret for the way one lived. The command to repent in Acts 2:38 is a call to Israel (only) to change their minds about the Messiah they had crucified. Those who did repent were those who believed (vv. 41, 44). The problem is that this verse appears to teach that repentance and baptism are needed for salvation. It has special application to the generation that crucified the Messiah (see above on baptism).

Works of God at the Time of Salvation

It will be helpful if we distinguish between what God has accomplished provisionally through the cross and what He does for each individual at the time of salvation. The death of Christ secured redemption, reconciliation, and propitiation for sinners. These are applied to the elect as they exercise faith that that death will provide what they cannot. At that time a person experiences justification, regeneration, and the beginning of many continuous works of the Holy Spirit.

Justification

This doctrine is intimately linked with a quality of God—His holiness, His separation from moral evil or sin (Hab. 1:13), and ethical perfection (see ch. 11, The Doctrine of God). In reference to believers there are two sides to holiness: first, separation from the world and consecration to serving God, and second, as an extension of the first, sharing in God's purity. Sanctification is the process subsequent to salvation in which through the Spirit there is less yielding to the old nature and more production of fruit by the new (maturity and many other things are involved; see below in this ch. under "Life as Possessors of Salvation: Sanctification"). The new nature that a believer receives at salvation, and through which the Spirit works, is holy and unable to sin. The new birth thus produces a holy nature that makes fellowship with God possible (cf. Eph. 1:4; 5:27; Col. 1:22; 1 Pet. 1:16).

In the O.T. as well as the N.T., God is presented as One who has definite standards. In the O.T. particularly, God is often seen as a judge, making a pronouncement as to right or wrong (Ps. 50:6; 96:13). God acts in holy ways and demands that His people do the same. He punishes evildoing and rewards holiness. His own moral demands are the standard for what is right and wrong, that is, He is holy and expects everyone to be and act holy. If a person does not, then he is unrighteous, or not in accord with God's holiness. We can even define righteous as "being in accord with God's character, particularly, His holiness." Revelation 16:5 is helpful here in enabling us to see the difference between holiness and righteousness: "You are righteous, Who is and Who was, the Holy One, because You did so judge" (AV). The word *justify* is a translation of a Greek word *(dikaioō)* that means "to declare righteous." The words for "righteous," "righteousness," "justify," etc., are all from the same root in Gr. They describe the legal status of individuals (see note at Rom. 3:28).

Romans 3:21–28 illumines our understanding of justification. In vv. 25 and 26 Paul explains that one value of the cross was to demonstrate that God had the proper penalty in mind when He forgave sins before the death of Christ. A godly individual before that point could have called God's character into question, noting that God was holy and yet allowed sinners to approach Him without the proper effective payment to remove sins (of course, that person would have had to see that the sacrificial system that existed under the law was not able to remove sin). Although God could have been accused of not acting in accord with His own standards, now He has been "declared righteous," i.e. justified, and can thus declare individuals righteous (v. 26).

A closely related concept is that of imputation. The Gr. word used in the presentation of this teaching describes crediting something to someone's account, calculating, counting something for (or even against) someone (see note, Rom. 4:3; Jas. 2:23; Phile. 18). In the description of Abraham's status before God in Rom. 4, Paul shows that the patriarch's faith was counted to him (reckoned) for righteousness. This is another way of describing justification.

It is significant that in the unfolding of the message of Rom., Paul describes in 5:1 one of the immediate results of justification: peace with God and access to Him. Our guilt before God is no longer an issue, since He has given a declaration of acquittal. 2 Cor. 5:19 provides the other side of the coin as far as justification is concerned: sins are no longer charged against those in Christ. It is very important that we understand that this is a legal (in God's system) and positional matter. Clearly, believers do commit sins after exercising faith in Christ. But sins cannot altar one's basic position before God, i.e., they do not bring condemnation. They are a matter of practice, which will be discussed below under the topic of sanctification.

Regeneration

The second great work that God performs on behalf of the sinner the moment he believes is regeneration, the provision of spiritual life. It is clear from such references as Eph. 2:1, Rom. 8:8, 11, and Jn. 3:3 that in his natural state an individual is dead because of sin, and unable because of that condition to enter into the kind of life that belongs to God, that is, eternal life. He must somehow lay hold of a new life principle.

In general we can state that the Bible presents two sides of the fulfillment of this requirement. They seem to be very close in sense and application. This first is the fact that God provides a new birth, a birth from above (Jn. 3:3—be born again), and the second is that God infuses new life (Eph. 2:5—makes alive) and a new *kind* of life where there was formerly death. Both are described with some of the same terms.

In Jn. 3:1–17 Jesus confronts Nicodemus with his need for a radical transformation. There was no way for him (or any Jew) to enter the kingdom (v. 3) except by means of a drastic change, so far-reaching as to be described as a new birth. The word translated "again" can also be translated "from the top" or "from the beginning," and may very well be purposely ambiguous. But both sides can stand together. Any such birth from above is of course a radical and thus new one. The meaning of *kingdom* is important in this passage. Nicodemus must have understood the term to refer to the same sphere of rule that Israel expected (cf. Acts 1:6, note). When, after the second advent, an Israelite (or anyone) enters the kingdom, he will be born again. But it is also true that there is no entrance into the present "kingdom" of the Son (Col. 1:13) without the same new birth.[10]

This new and from-above birth is also described in v. 5 as being "of water and the Spirit." It is thus the Spirit of God who effects this transformation, through the cleansing power of Scripture (Eph. 5:26; cf. also Jas. 1:18; 1 Pet. 1:23). This great work of the Spirit stands in contrast with what human physical birth produces (v. 6). It can only bring about the existence of another human being. This work of the Spirit that produces a kind of birth takes people into the presence of God.

1 Peter 1:3, 23–24 indicates that this spiritual birth stands in strong contrast with

the natural means of birth, which produces individuals destined to die. The Word of God is the channel of God's regenerative activity. Since it is eternal, what it begets is eternal. From this we conclude that the Word of God must be present in some way for a person to be born again.

There are several passages that point to the results in our lives of being begotten of God:

1. 1 Jn. 2:29—We are capable of doing righteous things.
2. 1 Jn. 4:7—Being born of God is the basis of true Christian love, since we have a new capacity to love others.
3. 1 Jn. 5:4—We are able to overcome the world because of the radical change of life that has taken place.
4. Eph. 2:5—Formerly dead in sins, we are made alive together with Christ. Here this transformation is described with the word *zōopoieō*, "make alive." This union brings us into permanent contact with His unending life.

Thus regeneration gives the sinner a new capacity to please God, a "nature" that is eternal and is actually part of the life that is in the resurrected Lord Jesus Christ. This capacity is brought in alongside our old nature that is unable to please God or enter His presence. God achieves this transformation through a new birth, a birth from above, using the Spirit of God and the written Word of God. The results are the ability to love as God loves and to do righteous acts, which we could not formerly do.

The Certainty of Ultimate Salvation: Eternal Security

Can a person who has genuinely believed be lost? Will God ever let that person go? The biblical answer is a flat "NO!"

We must state the issue very carefully. It is not a question of those who outwardly appear to be believers and genuinely saved, but are not, and later turn from any interest in the faith. That is, it is not a problem of apostates.

If there are passages that clearly teach security, then the passages that those who favor nonsecurity cite as support for their view must be carefully interpreted. In other words, Scripture does not contradict itself. If it is clear in teaching security, then passages that seem to present nonsecurity must refer to something else.

The best understanding of security comes through seeing what God has done in providing for salvation and how He applies it. The believer is secure because of the way God saves, what He does when He saves, and what He does for believers after they are saved.

To begin with, the provision and application of salvation are completely free. Right standing with God is provided by a substitute. Through grace, God imputes righteousness and even provides faith (Phil. 1:29). Second, God makes each individual a "new creation" (1 Cor. 5:18), and provides a new life principle—actually the life of Christ by regeneration (see the preceding section in this ch.). If a person were to lose his salvation, then both of those monumental works would have to be undone. The very presence of a new life principle through regeneration disallows by definition the possibility of spiritual death. Further, some view salvation as a repeatable experience. One can be saved, then lost, then saved again, etc. It does not take much thinking to realize that if that were true, then the creation of a new person in Christ, and regeneration with its infusion of the life of Christ, would have to be undone, then redone, theoretically many times. Taking the works of God in salvation seriously shows how contradictory the nonsecurity position is.

The present work of God for believers is an area of revealed truth that could support security all by itself. In Eph. 1:13–14 the very presence of the Holy Spirit is described as a seal signifying that our destination is heaven and the presence of God. If loss of salvation were possible, then the Holy Spirit could be defeated (He would have failed as a seal), which of course is impossible. The intercessory work of Christ is described in both Heb. 7:25 and Rom. 8:34. It is especially clear in the first passage that He is presently active to bring before the Father His perfect completed work and its application to the elect. His intercession would be meaningless if it didn't keep its objects with God; it could be said that Christ failed. Three especially important passages that teach security from different viewpoints are Rom. 5:1–11, where Paul underscores the fact that trials cannot separate us from God; Rom. 8:28–39, where God's planning foreknowledge and the following elements in the chain (see above in this ch. on election) guarantee that we cannot be separated from Christ (v. 39); Jn. 10:28–29, where the Father will not allow the sheep, for whom Christ died (v. 15), to be lost. The reader should notice that in this paragraph we have included all three Persons of the Trinity as active in keeping the believer secure. Once again, if a believer were to be lost, then the Father, Son, and Spirit would have failed to make good on what the Bible promises they will do.

Space does not permit a detailed discussion of all the passages that are adduced in support of "insecurity." However, in the light of the overwhelming evidence that God will not fail to bring the elect into His presence, the Bible student is obligated to search for alternative explanations of such scriptures. For example, in context, 1 Cor. 9:27 refers not to loss of salvation, but to failing to gain reward for service (see note). John 15:1–8, often used by those who do not hold to security, is addressing the issue of fruit-bearing and fellowship, not salvation. Finally, Heb. 6:4–6 can be seen, in the context of the whole book of Hebrews, to refer to apparent believers who give up any pretense of belonging to God and turn away to their own ungodliness. It is "impossible" to bring these apostates back even to the place where they were previously (having some interest in spiritual things), since they have hardened themselves to the things of God (see note, 6:4). This admittedly difficult passage cannot be understood apart from a careful study of the doctrine of apostasy in the book of Hebrews. See also notes on security at Ezek. 18:24 and Jude 1.

Life as Possessors of Salvation: Sanctification

God's goal for believers is to bring each one to the point of being like Christ. While this cannot be completed in this life (sin is always present), He expects us always to move in that direction (Phil. 2:10–16; 1 Jn. 3:2–3). This process (and it is a process, not an instantaneous event) is called sanctification. We must be careful to distinguish two uses of this word in the Bible. The Eng. word translates biblical words that portray our being set apart to God and separated from sin. In one sense, the death of Christ applied to the believer sets that person apart for God, as described in 1 Cor. 6:11: "But you were washed, you were sanctified, you were justified in the name of the Lord Jesus Christ and by the Spirit of our God" (NIV). This describes a position determined by God's outlook toward us as associated with the work of Christ. On the other hand, God expects believers to grow continually toward the point of matching the standards of Christ (1 Th. 4:3–4; 5:23; see notes, Zech. 8:3 and Rev. 22:11). It is crucial that the Bible student distinguish what God does for us in associating us with Christ (our "standing") and what we do in service and growth toward everyday likeness to Christ that is visible in our lives (our "state").

One of the key elements in sanctification is achieving spirituality. Unbiblical ideas of spirituality include: (1) getting more of the Holy Spirit (we have all of Him we will ever need); (2) attempting to eradicate the sin nature (1 Jn. 1:8 proves that false); (3) gradual sinless perfection (1 Jn. 1:8 again); (4) experiencing certain gifts, such as tongues; (5) following some formula, such as asking Jesus to be Lord of one's life. As described in 1 Cor. 2:15, spirituality is simply maturity in regard to spiritual things, for in 2:6 Paul holds up the ideal recipient and doer of his message as the "mature" person. It is noteworthy that when Paul wrote to the Corinthians this first time they had been saved only a few years. So, it is normal in God's plan to move to maturity in Christ within that time. The spiritual person is able to penetrate into spiritual issues and come up with the right answers (2:15). He can identify sin and righteousness when it shows up in life, while others (the nonmature) are puzzled at his insight. He has the spiritual sense to do this because He has so grown to be like Christ that He has started to think like Him.

Of course, this includes many other spiritual components. A person cannot simply say, "I want to be spiritual," and expect it to happen. There are no shortcuts to spirituality, although God promises it if we are earnest and get right at the task. A proper relation to the Holy Spirit, obedience to Scripture and the revealed will of God, dedication, separation from sin, and becoming more and more like Jesus Christ Himself, are all involved. Certainly the believer must pay close attention to sin in his life, which breaks fellowship with God, confessing it as it occurs and obtaining forgiveness (1 Jn. 1:9). He will exercise his spiritual gifts in service, will be careful with his stewardship of what God has entrusted to him (time, body, gifts, money). He will make prayer a significant component of his life, taking advantage of the privilege of taking his needs and concerns to God through the access Christ has provided. He will do everything to shape his life so that bountiful rewards will await him in the presence of his Savior (see note, 1 Cor. 9:27; see 1 Pet. 5:4 regarding elders). Colossians 3:1ff describes the process of rejecting acts of the old nature and performing those suitable to the new. This brings the believer more and more under the dominion of Christ, serving Him as Master (Eph. 6:6). We noted above in the section on the terms of salvation that it is unbiblical to insist that an individual "accept Jesus as Savior and Lord." The N.T. does not speak of "making Jesus Lord" either at salvation or during sanctification. After salvation the emphasis is on obedience, doing the will of God and rejecting impulses of the flesh.

Several roles of the Lord Jesus Christ provide enablement and direction to the believer in this process. John 15:1–14 portrays Him as the Vine from which we are to derive strength and power for fruitbearing (see notes, vv. 1, 2, 4, 8, 15). Elders in local churches especially have the encouragement of His presence with them, in the role of the Chief Shepherd, for guidance and wisdom. This is a biblical guarantee that they as undershepherds can count on the interest and direction of the Lord Jesus Christ in the assembly of Christians (1 Pet. 5:1–5). This is but one facet of His ongoing provision as the "great Shepherd of the sheep" (Heb. 13:20).

An important first step in sanctification is given in Rom. 12:1–2. Here Paul exhorts us to give our bodies over entirely to God. It is easy, of course, to say that we are *spiritually* yielded, for no one can disprove that. But it is a greater step to yield the body, because that involves what people see and so is a proof of our sincerity. Besides, since the body can be a source and channel of sin, yielding it brings an important part of our existence under God's control. Some people claim that this act of dedication can be performed over and over. To counter that view, which seems to trifle with a very serious command by making it possible to do it insincerely, many have appealed to the particular tense (aorist) of the Gr. verb meaning "present" (AV, NASB), "offer" (NIV). The assertion commonly made is that an aorist verb denotes an unrepeatable event. However, there are so many examples to the contrary in the N.T. that the interpreter should avoid such a conclusion. Aorists often describe events that are repeated. However, in Rom. 12:1–2 the act of presentation (v. 1) is contrasted with the ongoing process of transformation of the mind, carried by a "present" tense in Gr. It is the *contrast* between these two acts in vv. 1–2 that strongly suggests that dedication, the surrender of the body, is to occur decisively.[11]

Although this act of dedication may come at a point of crisis—emotional or not—in a person's life, spirituality still does not come all of a sudden. In fact, the road to Christlikeness is fraught with danger. Romans 6:1–14, a passage that expands on Rom. 12:1–2, describes our task as cutting off obedience to the old nature and yielding only to the new (as in Col. 3:1ff, mentioned above in this section). This is possible because at the cross sin's control over Christ, and therefore over those associated with Him, was broken.

A similar exhortation passage is Eph. 6:10–20, where Paul warns us of the spiritual perils that await us that have their source in Satan himself. The believer is to stand his ground after making the proper spiritual preparation. Though final success is guaranteed, ease is not.

The danger of not heeding such warning passages, in fact, of not growing to maturity and Christlikeness, is not growing at all or so yielding to the pressures of the world that they become the dominant influence in the life of the believer. 1 Cor. 3:1–4 describes this condition. Some of the Corinthians (remember, they should have gone on to maturity) remained babyish (v. 1) so long that they left themselves wide open to extensive influence from Satan's world system. They were then "carnal" or "worldly." Although two different Gr. words are used in 3:1 and 3, unfortunately most translations fail to distinguish between them. Babyhood at the beginning stage of the faith is normal. Staying that way has either of two results: conformity not to Christ (spirituality) but the world (worldliness or carnality). Sad to say, many Christians live long stretches of their lives in carnal conditions. It is instructive to notice that Paul goes on in 1 Cor. 3 to say that one of the marks of carnality is divisiveness. Those who divide groups of believers on the basis of such things as adherence to personalities (how often do we see that!) should be labeled for what they are—Christians who are not right with God.

While for some people the road to spirituality is paved with negative bricks, the N.T. emphasis is on positive surrender and doing the will of God. Certainly this involves commands not to do certain things. But some people enjoy majoring in what should not be done, instead of what should be done in positive, joyous obedience to

Christ. Legalism is one such negative route. Legalism is the attempt to please God by erecting hard and fast rules where the Bible does not give them, and then making them binding on oneself and others. It is not a matter of following those things that are commanded, or that have clear biblical principles associated with them. It is a matter of raising decisions on so-called doubtful things to the level of commands. Doubtful things are those that have no N.T. commands associated with them, and which the consciences of various believers lead them to decide on in different ways. Such things include kinds of activities allowed on the Lord's day, dress practices, and, in N.T. times, abstaining from food that has been associated with heathen practices (the issue in Rome; see note, Rom. 14:3). The issue is not that of obeying biblical commands. The N.T. has many laws or commands that we are to follow, such as those in Eph. 4–5 ("speak truthfully," 4:25). God does not give us a choice on these. We are expected to obey. But there are issues with which no express biblical command can be associated. Several principles must be followed in order to avoid legalistic reactions:

1. In every instance of doubtful things, we are to decide what to do on the basis of love for each other and a desire to be like Christ (Rom. 14:13–15:3).

2. We are not entirely free to do what we want. Although we are not bound by the law, we do not have freedom to act in excess or in such a way as to hurt another (Gal. 5:13).

3. In all doubtful things, we are to accept and not judge each other (Rom. 14:1–12). The "strong" believer is one who on a particular issue believes he can do certain doubtful things. The "weak" believer is one who believes, for the sake of his conscience, that he cannot. The tendency of the strong believer is to look down disdainfully on the weak believer. The weak, conversely, looks at the strong and condemns him, or, following the example of the strong, goes ahead and does the same thing. In doing so he violates his conscience, and ends up feeling guilty. In fact, he has actually sinned, because the doubtful thing really is sin for him (Rom. 14:14).

The Bible gives no warrant for thinking that the strong believer is more spiritual than the weak. It is better to be a strong believer, but every believer is probably a mixture of both strong and weak.

The overriding guideline in all of this is that the believer is under the grace principle of life. Aside from specific biblical commands, he is to live toward God and others in conscious knowledge that he owes everything to God, and in conformity to the life of the Lord Jesus Christ (see Rev. 22:11 for a summary note on sanctification; see also note at Rom. 1:16).

Questions for Further Study

1. Hebrews 2:14–15 has been used by some to support the view that Christ's death consisted of a payment to Satan. What does the passage teach about the relation to Satan of Christ's Person and death?

2. Compare Rom. 1:17 and Hab. 2:4 concerning the nature of faith. Who is the trusting person in Hab. 2? How is that concept parallel to that in Rom. 1? Where else

is Hab. 2:4 quoted in the N.T.? How is the verse varied in the quotations? The Scofield note at Hab. 2:3 should prove helpful.

3. Some have held that if God alone leads a person to faith, then evangelism is unnecessary. What is the relation between the two sides in Acts 16, where Lydia is converted?

4. Skim through 1 Cor. and note some of the characteristics that qualified the Corinthians as carnal believers. What is the biblical remedy for each?

5. Make a list of "doubtful things" you are able to notice that fit the description of Rom. 14–15. Which seem to be most difficult for Christians to see as doubtful things? See note at 14:3.

18

The Church

The Universal Church

A Key Doctrine

Let's say it up front: what you believe about the Church is highly determinative for your understanding of the Bible as a whole. Some might say, yes, that must be true, because the main purpose of the Bible is to show how God worked over centuries, through the O.T. era and into the N.T. age to bring the Church into existence. Others might suggest that since the Church is at the heart of Christianity, and the Bible, with the O.T. and N.T., is a Christian book, the Bible must have the Church as its central concern. Or it might be noted that since Jesus is the most prominent figure of the Bible and He founded the Church, the focus of the Bible, now and into the future, since He is gone, is the Church.

What we believe about the Church is crucial, not for reasons such as these, but because of the way the Church fits into the overall plan of God. There is no question that it is highly distinctive and prominent in the Bible. But that does not mean that it is the goal of God's plan. To be sure, the Church is at the heart of Christianity, but we must not forget that there are others in different ages who share the same faith as those in the Church (see notes, Heb. 11:35 and 39). And although Jesus did found the Church, He also sustained in the past, and continues to sustain, relations with other individuals and groups, particularly Israel. No, the doctrine of the Church is significant for one's overall understanding of the Bible, not so much because of any properties it might have in itself, but because of the way it fits into what God is doing with humanity. And as a matter of biblical fact, building the Church is not the goal of God's overall plan. The

Church is important, but we must see it in perspective and not allow it to dominate or distort other doctrines.

It would be helpful at this point to give a definition of the Church. It is the totality of all individuals saved from Pentecost to the rapture, an event described especially in 1 Th. 4:12–18, and is formed by the distinctive work of the Holy Spirit who at the point of their salvation through Christ joins individuals to the living Head, and to each other as sharers in Him (1 Cor. 12:13). An individual automatically becomes a member of the Church, the Body of Christ, at the point of exercising faith.

Although many individuals and groups call themselves Christian and profess to be part of the Church, the Bible is clear that there is a core element that is genuine, a true Church within a professing Church (2 Tim. 3:1–9; see note, 3:1). That false segment eventually shows itself as untrue and unbelieving, falling away in apostasy or simply being left behind when the Church leaves the earth at the rapture.

There are two key elements in that definition: the time span for the Church, and the manner in which it is formed. Both set the Church off from all other groups that God has dealt with in the past and will in the future. It is contrary to the Scriptures to see the Church as being in existence on earth before Pentecost or after the rapture and second advent. Furthermore, the acts of the Holy Spirit in forming the Church were not seen before the present age. The Church is thus bound by time and created by ministries of the Spirit unique to that time span.

Is it possible to demonstrate conclusively when the Church began? Yes, it is, and those ministries of the Spirit figure prominently in our understanding of its beginnings. In Eph. 4:22–23 the Church is described as the Body of Christ. It does not take much thinking to realize that this is a spiritually based concept. The Body of Christ consists of individuals with physical bodies, but the connections those people have are spiritual. It is this group, unified spiritually, that forms the Church. 1 Cor. 12:13 teaches us that Spirit baptism places individuals into the Body of Christ. If we knew, then, when Spirit baptism began, we would know when the Church began.

As a matter of fact, the Bible provides us with just such information. In Acts 1:5 Jesus predicted that the Holy Spirit would baptize the disciples within a few days. If we take vv. 4 and 8 at face value, then a new and special ministry of the Spirit would start at the same time (v. 4—a promised gift; v. 8—power received when the Spirit came upon them). This different kind of ministry, which would include baptism, would be experienced in a short time. There is no question that Acts 2 describes such a new kind of ministry, although it does not mention baptism, only tongues and filling. However, in recounting what happened at the conversion of Cornelius, Peter (Acts 11:15–17) compares the coming of the Spirit in Cornelius' house with the coming "at the begin-ning," describing both as baptisms. The only event recorded for us in the book of Acts that could qualify as a beginning and a giving of the Spirit ("God gave them the same gift as he gave us," v. 17, NIV) would be Pentecost in ch. 2. We conclude, then, that the Church, the Body of Christ, began at Pentecost, just fifty days after the death of Christ (see note, Acts 2:1).

If we are honest with the Bible, we must conclude that this new work of the Spirit is not found before the book of Acts. If the Body of Christ did not exist before Pente-cost, then the Church did not either. This doesn't mean people were not able to come to God before Pentecost, or that the way they came was different from the faith channel evident since the cross. But it does mean that the group of believers that form the Church is a different entity from previous groups, especially Israel. Ephesians 3:6 clearly indicates that the Body as the point of union of Jew and Gentile is a new thing, a mystery in the sense of something previously unknown (see note, 3:6). Israel as a group that God dealt with was well known. The Body/Church was not. Israel and the Church cannot be the same entity. It is absolutely essential that the Bible student recognize that the Bible teaches that the Church is not a continuation of Israel. Endless confusion in biblical interpretation results if the two are not kept distinct. Since its first edition the Scofield Bible has stressed this doctrine, and because of this and related emphases has proven to be of great help to Bible students in keeping God's overall plan in perspective. Many other passages support this understanding of the Church. We will deal with some of them in connection with eschatology in ch. 19, Future Things (see also ch. 2, The Nature of the Bible, concerning dispensationalism).

A New Unity

One of the most salient features of the Church as the Body of Christ is its unity. When we stop to think about how the Body is formed, the reason for this unity becomes evident. In Rom. 6:1–11 Paul discusses the same work of the Spirit as in 1 Cor. 12:13, showing that Spirit baptism connects the believer with the death, burial, and resurrection of Christ. Before a person comes to Christ he has no intrinsic connection with any other human being other than coparticipation in the human race, and such essentially social unions as family relations (of course, marriage involves physical union, too). But when an individual is joined with Christ through becoming—in the sight of God—a participant in the work of Christ, he becomes at that time a coparticipant with every other person who has exercised faith, and all become part of the invisible, spiritual Body that is the extension of the Lord Jesus Christ through them. Our union, then, results from having died, having been buried, and having been raised to a new kind of life. This is such a momentous and far-reaching experience that it transcends normal social and familial relations, creating a family of brothers and sisters related through Christ, the living Head. Interestingly enough, these new family relations are so significant that they bring individuals closer than any physical siblings could be. Being "in Christ" can and does take the place of what the unbeliever takes to be the closest relations on earth.

In fact, this unity is so complete that it can bring together on the same ground parties that previously lived in absolute hostility. This is exemplified in Eph. 2:14–15 and 3:6, where Jews and Gentiles are brought together, with former barriers removed. Thus Paul can speak of "one body" in Eph. 4:4—a spiritual unit that is to be kept intact by believers (v. 3). We ought to notice that individuals do not create the unity of the Body; they are simply called on to avoid acting in ways that disturb it.

It is significant that the ministry of the Spirit toward the Body of Christ, first evident at Pentecost, involves a network of tasks affecting individual believers, and, in turn, the Body as a whole. The Spirit's baptism, an associative work, is accompanied by four other permanent ministries that run throughout this age: indwelling, sealing, anointing, and filling. Three of the four are distinctive to the Body of Christ, that is, they are not found in the O.T. in relation to Israel under the law or before (see ch. 13, The Holy Spirit; see also notes at Jn. 14:20; Eph. 5:25; 1 Tim. 3:15; Heb. 12:23).

The Local Church

Definition

While the Body of Christ consists of all individuals who know Christ as Savior during the present age, no one can actually see them all. Not all are alive at any one time, and even at a point in time they are scattered around the world and cannot reasonably be brought together. God has made it possible for believers to interact successfully, even apart from the marvels of modern electronic communication, by providing the groundwork for local units—individual churches.

Something of the importance of the local church can be seen from the fact that it is the only institution that our Lord Jesus Christ ever established. He did not found any educational entity, any mission organization or any other kind of instrument for outreach or edification. We give tacit assent to this when we speak of such groups or institutions as "parachurch" in nature. Although such groups may accomplish great things for God, the fact remains that in the Bible we see only one instrument for carrying out His work on earth—the local church.

Before we go any farther, we need to provide a definition of local church. It is a group of believers meeting together in a given location for several purposes, all described in Scripture, namely, to edify each other, to worship, to observe the two ordinances of baptism and the Lord's Supper, and, in general, to seek the will of God together. A local church is composed of individuals who are all in turn members of the Body of Christ. According to the N.T. there is no qualification other than saving faith for membership in a local church. But it is clear that in the apostolic age it was known who was affiliated with a local church, that is, people did not simply wander in and out at will.

It is very important to remember that a local church is not the visible building that people meet in. It is the group of believers meeting at a particular location. Some translations speak of the local gathering of believers as the "church," others as the "assembly." Today the latter term may have the advantage in English-speaking areas of reminding us that the local church is the people, not the wood, brick, or stone edifice.

Three Spheres

In this treatment of the doctrine of the local church we will attempt to describe what the N.T. presents as the picture during the apostolic age. Although there is no question that there is an almost innumerable variety of groups meeting in local churches today around the world, it does not take much thinking to reach the conclusion that at least some are on the wrong track. The very fact that so many are at odds with each other over the way they should meet should lead us to suspect that God has a more coherent plan, especially in the light of such an exhortation as Eph. 4:3–4, mentioned above, where God expects unity in the Body of Christ. If we are honest we have to admit that the Body of Christ is not presently displaying that attribute as well as it could! So we would like, instead of listing the group distinctives as practiced today, to look at the biblical teaching on the local church. It is this author's view that there is a coherent and noncontradictory presentation of the local church in the N.T.

One way to approach this is by thinking of the information given in the N.T. on the local church as involving three related spheres of activity, each one shaped by

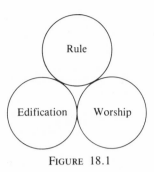

FIGURE 18.1

biblical information and instruction: rule, edification, and worship. The relationship of these three spheres is shown in figure 18.1.

The sphere of rule involves leadership activity carried out *under God*. It is best seen for example, in the teaching Peter gives to elders in 1 Pet. 5:1–5. There the pervading element is that the elders are to carry out their task of shepherding (a spiritual gift) under the Chief Shepherd, the Lord Jesus Christ. As undershepherds, they are only mediators of His will.

Within the sphere of edification the most evident activity is that of the use of spiritual gifts, that is, God-given abilities for service (see ch. 13, The Holy Spirit). This activity is carried out in order to build up the Body, and in the N.T. we see it done among believers gathered at a particular location, the local church. The passage that speaks most fully on this is Eph. 4:11–16. There we are told that unless the Body edifies itself it cannot bring its parts (individual people) to the point of being like Christ, and it remains weak and susceptible to the intrusion of error. The key to achieving edification is the use of gifts, some of which are listed in Eph. 4:11 (see notes). This sphere could be described as involving activity coming *from God,* as exemplified particularly by the function of teaching, which brings truth from God (in accord with His revelation in Scripture, of course). The exhorter, using his gift, also speaks from God (1 Pet. 4:11). Worship, in contrast, involves activity, especially speaking, directed *toward* God. The Bible distinguishes between teaching and worship.

These three spheres intersect with three principles of activity: diversity, freedom, and restriction. The issue of diversity concerns contribution to the life of the Body of Christ by believers, each of whom possesses a gift-complement, a personality, and a set of natural talents and abilities that differ from those of every other believer. How can a local church best utilize this range? The issues of freedom and restriction have to do with the extent of the imposition of regularity and order on the participants in a local church. How much can they do on their own, and what are the boundaries of individual activity? And how can there be diversity, freedom and restriction in a working balance? (In a sense, every human institution must face this same question.) When we examine the spheres of rule, edification, and worship we can see how diversity, freedom, and restriction are handled by the N.T.

Rule. Not everyone has the right to rule in the local church: God does not allow for anarchy. Hebrews 13:17 instructs believers to obey their overseers. Only some can rule, those that have the moral qualifications (1 Tim. 3:1–7), the doctrinal abilities (Tit. 1:9), and the gifts (e.g., ruling, in Rom. 12:8). Further, as the Scofield note at Tit. 1:5 points out, the N.T. pattern in the apostolic churches was to have a plurality of elders (that note also provides a comprehensive description of elders' tasks). Most biblical scholars take the terms "overseer" and "elder" to be descriptive of the same individual, the first word describing function (superintending the affairs of the local church) and the second pointing to the need for a degree of maturity or even physical age (since the term is also used for "an older man" elsewhere in Gr.). According to Heb. 13:17 these elders/overseers have final authority in the local church, yet also bear final responsibility before God for its success. It is not an overstatement to say that the most important feature of the local church is the presence of qualified and functioning elders.

In addition to gift, spiritual health, and doctrinal sharpness and ability, there is a further restriction on the eldership: it is for males. 1 Timothy 3:11–13 clearly prohibits women from exercising authority over men in spiritual things (see ch. 14, The Doctrine of Sin, concerning the fall). So here there is *freedom*—a man can develop to the point of being qualified as an elder, if God has so equipped him (notice 1 Tim. 3:1, where it is a good thing to want be an elder). And there is *diversity*—the presence of many elders serves to prevent error by providing wisdom from many sides. This provides *restriction* on the usurpation of power by individuals, a frequent problem in the local church.

The term *deacon* describes an individual ministering under the elders in a local church. The Gr. word behind the term simply means "servant," and so expresses the function of serving other people, rather than a fixed office or even a place of leadership (1 Tim. 3:8–13, especially v. 10). Since elders have control over all of the affairs of a local church, the corps of deacons is answerable to them.

Edification. Here we find that every believer is to be involved. Peter tells us that every single individual in the Body of Christ is to use the gift(s) given by God, and the goal is helping each other (1 Pet. 4:10). This is certainly diversity!

There are many fine studies available in print today that outline the N.T. picture of spiritual gifts. What is not usually noted, however, is that there are both ministry gifts and utterance gifts (1 Pet. 4:10–11). The latter profit the whole assembly of believers. Thus, there must be opportunity for their exercise. Interestingly enough, the meeting of the N.T. church was such that there was *freedom* and occasion for edification of the body by gifted individuals. The N.T. presents a picture of many gifted men teaching and preaching in a given assembly (Acts 13:1–2; 1 Cor. 14:26). The Spirit may provide one or many for ministry of the Word and for shepherding of the local church, but it is ultimately His choice, and the pattern in the N.T. is for multiplicity of edification and oral gifts. So here is, once again, *diversity* along with *restriction*. Many may teach the assembly, but only if they are gifted in teaching. Clearly those in the local church must look for and encourage gifts (1 Th. 5:19–21).

In Eph. 4:11–16 Paul presents details concerning gifted individuals and their function in the Body of Christ: apostles, prophets, evangelists, and pastor-teachers (the last is a single gift, as indicated by the grammar, although this is not brought out clearly in many translations). Elsewhere apostle, prophet, and teacher are given as gifts, so there is every reason to take pastor-teacher and evangelist as gifts also. Now if pastor-teacher, or more clearly, shepherd-teacher, is a spiritual gift, then it is not a ruling or overseeing function, but a channel for edification. In addition we are told in Acts 20:28 that the Ephesian elders were instructed by Paul to do the work of shepherding the flock of God over which the Spirit made them overseers. What is crucial here is that the *gift* of shepherd-teacher may reside in many men—or even women—in the local church. It is not necessarily restricted to elders, but at least the elders should have it (1 Tim. 5:14; 1

Pet. 5:1–4). Thus shepherding and teaching are done by many people, especially elders, and here again is *diversity*.

Worship. Here we find that *all* believers are priests (Rev. 5:10, NIV; 1 Pet. 2:5–9; see note, v. 9). So all can respond to God with sacrifices—praise, doing good, giving (all three are found in Heb. 13:15–16) and yielding the body (Rom. 12:2). Here, then is *diversity*. The acts of priests are both corporate and individual. Obviously the yielding of the body is an individual act. But the worship of the local church when it comes together is corporate (1 Cor. 14:26). How much *freedom* is there here? *All* are to worship, but only some are to do it orally; there is a *restriction* on the oral participation of the women (1 Cor. 14:34; 1 Tim. 2:11). This may seem harsh, but in 1 Tim. 2:14 Paul relates this particular restriction to the fall. Perhaps what is most difficult for us to understand today is that in the apostolic age all were expected to be prepared to worship: in 1 Cor. 14:26 all brought something to the meeting of the saints. They were eager. Although the believers at Corinth had many problems, and Paul takes time to correct them, he appears to be perfectly satisfied with their participation as described in that verse. Worship and participation in the meeting that gave opportunity for that flowed from grateful hearts.

We find in the N.T., then, that there is much *diversity* and *freedom*—more than in most churches today. But there are also careful *restrictions,* especially on participation and qualification. God always restricts for our good, although we chafe under it. For instance, elders are to rule, even though believers may not always like what they do. Of course, such leaders must be sensitive and Spirit-led. And these features of diversity, freedom, and restriction are clearly seen in three important functions in the local church: rule, edification, and worship. Together these six elements give us a picture of the basic N.T. philosophy of life and activity in the local church.

Giving and the Local Church

Confusion. Giving money and possessions is one of the most practical, yet frustrating and abused, areas in the Christian life. Every believer must make decisions as to how, when, why, and to whom to give. Yet many find that they do not have helpful guidelines in the form of teaching. And further, many assume things about giving—and getting—that are not in the N.T. Should I tithe? How often should I give? How much is enough? What if I just can't give? Is it all right to pledge or make a faith-promise? Who or what should I give to? These are all legitimate questions that all believers must answer. Perhaps the best way to summarize this area of doctrine concerning the local church is this: every believer is obligated to give—but only in accordance with the teaching of the N.T. The following discussion necessarily deals with practical aspects of giving, since this is not a doctrine (there is a N.T. doctrine of giving!) that can be treated in the abstract.

Principles and Guidelines. In Phil. 4:18–19 and Heb. 13:15–16 giving money is described as a priestly act, a form of worship, a response to the grace of God. Just as my public worship is to be directed by the Spirit, so also is my giving. Such giving is pleasing to God, as an O.T. sacrifice might have been (Phil. 4:18–19). Because of the priestly nature of giving—a response to grace shown to individuals—no one can tell a believer how much to give, or where to direct his giving. Further, this rules out appeals to those outside the Body of Christ, since they are not priests and cannot give as such to the Lord's work; they have never experienced the grace of God.

One area of giving involves those who minister the Word of God in teaching: "Anyone who receives instruction in the Word must share all good things with his instructor" (Gal. 6:6, NIV). Providing for teachers is an obligation for every believer, for essentially everyone is taught by someone. Unfortunately this kind of giving is often neglected. 1 Cor. 9:11–15 describes this from another perspective. The one who ministers has a right to be supported, but that right can be forfeited, as in the case of Paul. It is important to remember that he never asked for money for himself, thus living in the Gospel ministry entirely by faith. Another aspect of giving to those who minister is found in 1 Tim. 5:17–18, where some elders may spend more time in ministry and do better at leading than others, and should be compensated proportionately.

Two important passages dealing with giving that also form a unit are 1 Cor. 16:1–2 and 2 Cor. 8:1–9:15. In 1 Cor. 16 Paul mentions the collections for the believers, and then resumes the same topic in 2 Cor. 8:1, written a short time later. In 1 Cor. 16 we learn:

1. Paul taught the same principles in Asia and Europe. His teaching was universal (see also 1 Cor. 4:17 for the same principle). Therefore these principles of giving must have universal application.
2. The collection was part of ministry to the poor.
3. This is part of apostolic command.
4. Giving is to be done by individuals ("each one of you" [NIV]).
5. Money is to be put aside, as in a fund.
6. There are to be no public collections.
7. Giving is to be done out of what is earned already (v. 2), not out of what is anticipated.

In 2 Cor. 8:1–9:15 we learn:

1. Giving is a part of grace (v. 7), as opposed to the O.T. tithe. Tithing (one tenth plus) was for those under the law. We are not under the principle of tithing today, since we are not under the law.
2. Giving comes after seeking God's will (v. 5). It is to be a matter settled personally between the individual and God after dedication to His direction.
3. The Corinthians had on their own asked if they could give. The amount and time were not specified. Paul, a third party, urges them to finish this commitment. The money is not for him. It is not a fixed, promised amount—that would violate 8:12. When the Macedonians had heard about the need in Jerusalem they had begged to participate on their own (8:4). Paul exhorts them to give, but not to him. The N.T. does not condone the requesting of money for one's own ministry or other needs. It is not found here and would violate 1 Cor. 16:1–2 and the free leading of the Spirit. God is quite able to supply the needs of those who minister in His name, by leading other individuals to give to those ministries He wants supported. Many have found that this works and brings great honor to God.

Giving is a privilege under grace, a responsibility under priesthood, and can be a blessing to believers and glorifying to God, if done in conscious obedience to the N.T. As in all things, God prospers us as we follow His word. He does not promise to bless what is not done in accordance with His word. It is thus a biblical principle that the will of God can be discerned by the way God provides for lives and ministry through others. Dependence on the Spirit of God to supply financial needs is thus a key ingredient in determining how and where God wants us to serve Him. Forcing people to give eliminates this important part of God's leading.

The Ordinances

"A picture is worth a thousand words" because we understand and remember better what we see portrayed visually. God understands this, of course, and uses this principle throughout the Bible. Types, for instance, are pictures in the O.T. of events or persons yet to come in the N.T. (see ch. 7, Relations Between the Testaments, on typology). In the book of Ezekiel, God commands the prophet to act out certain spiritual truths. These visual lessons would help the Israelites in captivity to understand better their spiritual predicament. We especially need pictures and illustrations, because we do not operate well in the spiritual realm (unlike angels, for instance). So God often illustrates and explains spiritual realities by means of physical acts that we can directly relate to. Baptism and the Lord's Supper are two of these. They are the two ordinances of the Church.

The Nature of Ordinances. The term *ordinance* is often confused with the word *sacrament*. Neither term occurs in the Bible in reference to baptism and the Lord's Supper, although *ordinance* probably comes into our usage from its occurrence in 1 Cor. 11:2. There, however, Paul is speaking of those truths to be put into practice—all the teachings he had presented to them. The NIV translates the word as "teachings," and the NASB renders it "traditions."

These two acts are symbolic rites that set forth essential truths of the Christian faith and must be practiced by all Christians. Sadly, both are frequently neglected and misunderstood. 1 Cor. 11:2 tells us we are to hold on to the elements of apostolic teaching (here Paul's), that is, to see them as important, to teach them, and to do them. These two ordinances represent in physical, pictorial form two aspects of our experience with Christ: (1) Baptism pictures our identification with Christ and His work, and (2) The Lord's Supper pictures our ongoing union with Him and His work. As such they are mnemonic in nature; they are designed to help our weakness in comprehending great spiritual realities. Their practice does not gain us merit before God, and especially not salvation. The term *sacrament* usually carries with it the implication that, as under the Roman Catholic system, certain acts bring merit from God. An ordinance does not have such properties. If we understand the word sacrament to refer to practices that do not bring merit, then its use is biblical; otherwise, we should avoid it.

Baptism. There are actually several baptisms in the N.T. (we do not see baptism in the O.T., although we do see ceremonial cleansings, e.g., Lev. 8:6). All of them have to do with association or identification. John's baptism was part of his preparation of people for the coming of the Messiah, and when individuals were baptized they identified themselves with John's message of a coming One. John's baptism of Jesus shows His identification with the needs of Israel, to be met through His roles as Prophet, Priest, and King (Mt. 3:15, note). Our Lord also spoke of the baptism of the cup (Mk. 10:38–39). This refers to His undergoing death as a sinner. He would be associated with death and all its terrors. The fourth baptism in the N.T. is the work of the Spirit that associates us with Christ (1 Cor. 12:13). It is this that is pictured by water baptism for the believer. As such it portrays our entrance into life with Christ. Baptism is not the equivalent of circumcision in the O.T. The erroneous view that equates the two is based on the assumption that the Church is found in the O.T. and that a person identified then with the covenant people by circumcision and identifies now with the new covenant people by baptism.

As taught in the N.T., baptism is for believers only, is for all believers (no exceptions), and pictures our being identified with Christ spiritually. The reality behind this is delineated in Rom. 6, where Paul teaches that every believer has been identified with/baptized into Christ's death, burial, and resurrection. Going under and coming out of the water graphically portrays this spiritual reality as an aid to our understanding. It is a public demonstration that the inner act has been accomplished. It is for this reason that we do not, as some say, "follow our Lord in baptism," since we are not identifying ourselves with the needs of the nation of Israel! Furthermore, Jesus was not baptized as a public confession of his salvation, as we do (1 Pet. 3:21).

Since the whole tenor of the N.T. points to baptism as expected after salvation, those in places of leadership in local churches should stress the need for baptism for every believer as soon after salvation as is reasonable. By the way, because water baptism is so closely associated with salvation in the N.T. (as the expected outward step reflecting the inner spiritual reality), some people have interpreted some passages as teaching the need for baptism in order to gain salvation. One such passage is 1 Pet. 3:18–22, where in v. 21 it appears at first sight to say that baptism saves a person. If this verse were teaching that, it would contradict the rest of the N.T., where faith is regularly presented as the sole channel of salvation. But the fact that in the apostolic age baptism was an expected thing—not optional, as it is for some today—led some, such as Peter in this passage, to speak of baptism and salvation in one breath.

The mode which best pictures the truth of Rom. 6 is immersion. This is supported by the meaning of the Gr. words for baptism that mean "immerse" or "dip," as one would dye cloth in a vat of liquid dye. The earliest mention of sprinkling comes in the late second century. If this were the biblical method, baptism would picture cleansing. But the symbolism of baptism is identification with Christ's death, burial, and resurrection. The normal Gr. word for "sprinkle" is never used in the N.T. of the baptism of believers. Furthermore, since baptism pictures the experience of a sinner coming to Christ and being identified with His work, it cannot be done legitimately to infants, since it would have no meaning (see Acts 8:12 for summary note on baptism).

The Lord's Supper. This ordinance is, like baptism, a physical act picturing a spiritual truth. In this case the invisible reality is our ongoing life with Christ, derived from His death and resurrection. This is summarized in 1 Cor. 11:23–26, where the Lord's Supper is described as a proclamation to be repeated throughout this age, picturing Christ's death. It actually looks forward as well as backward, anticipating the enjoyment of His presence. Clearly one of its functions is to remind us of what Christ has done, is doing, and will do for us. As such it is an aid to our memory and a stimulus to our spiritual senses. We get a good idea of its importance when we see that it was the focal point of the meetings of the church in the apostolic age. According to Acts 20:7 the purpose of meeting together on the Lord's Day was to "break bread," Luke's phrase equivalent to Paul's "the Lord's Supper." The fact that it is commanded in 1 Cor. 11:25 indicates that the believer cannot view it as optional. As the focus of worship—the function of believer-priests—we can hardly regard it as in any way secondary to other things we may do in meeting together as a local church.

It is noteworthy that during the apostolic age the pattern was to have the Lord's Supper weekly. That did not mean that every believer was obligated to participate that often, but the opportunity was given. When we remember that worship is a response to grace, then we should approach this activity that is at the core of our response to grace with a grateful heart. That kind of outlook evidently led believers during the apostolic age to want to meet weekly for an event they invested with great significance.

The personal requirements for participation in the Lord's Supper are given implicitly and explicitly in the N.T. Since the ordinance portrays our ongoing life with Christ, it makes no sense for a person who does not possess that life to partake. The Lord's Supper is thus for believers only. Paul adds a further explicit qualification in 1 Cor. 11:27–28: the person partaking should have first searched himself for sin. Coming to the Lord's Table with unconfessed sin is an offense to God, since it indicates that the individual does not take the ordinance seriously.

If we investigate what procedure the N.T. displays for the Lord's Supper, we find that there is very little information. At the heart of it is gratefulness, especially evidenced in the expressions of thanks associated with the bread and the cup. Beyond that, there are no explicit directives. In 1 Cor. 14:26 and 31, Paul enjoins orderliness and the goal of edification on the meetings of the local church, and that must apply to the Lord's Table. Otherwise, the N.T. portrays it as a simple act. It's safe to say that over the centuries human beings have complicated what God originally instituted as a straightforward picture to remind believers of some of the great acts of God toward them.

Discipline

Believers in the last half of the twentieth century have become increasingly concerned with the lack of order in the home and society. There is biblical warrant for viewing such things as the increase in crime in society as the outcome of the lack of parental guidance, including discipline, in the home. Yet we fail to realize that discipline is just as important among groups of believers—in the local church. We rarely hear teaching on it, and it is a neglected practice. Too often we are afraid to do it. As in a family, we don't want to be too harsh. The same results occur in the local church as in the home if discipline is neglected: anarchy, increasing disrespect for authority, breaking up of churches just as with homes, and lack of joy. Indulgence does not make a happy or useful child in a family; discipline is essential. The same is true in general for the life of the believer: we must know our position in the order of the Body of Christ and its local manifestation. Without discipline the local church in any age or culture is impoverished. Even when it is done, often individuals under discipline simply go to another church, taking their problems with them, and are accepted. Several passages—more than we might expect—speak to the issue of discipline in the local church.

Matthew 18:15ff stresses the steps to take when sin is suspected in another person. The concerned individual is to approach the other alone, then, if there is no positive response, take one or two witnesses and approach him again. If he still denies there is a problem, the local church is to be informed. (Strictly speaking, the "assembly" in Mt. 18:17 is simply a group to be informed; at this point the disciples could not know what a local church was: none existed yet. We should not read later revelation into earlier.) Finally, if all of those steps fail, the believer in question is to be shunned. There is an important safety factor in this kind of sequence: the "accusing" individual has had his case verified by two witnesses.

Much confusion has resulted from not connecting Mt. 18:18–29 with the preceding verses concerning discipline. Verse 18 indicates that the decision whether or not to carry out discipline has already been made in heaven. For that reason, Jesus is in the midst in order to guide (v. 20) in the painful process of discipline. In context, v. 20 is not a blanket promise of the presence of the Lord Jesus Christ with believers.

The shunning described in Mt. 18:17 is treated more fully in 2 Th. 3:14–15. We can view Mt. 18 as a first stage in the discipline process. If the three steps described there do not result in a turnaround in the sinning individual, then more severe action must be taken, equivalent to treating the individual as "a pagan or a tax collector" (Mt. 18:17, NIV). In 2 Th. 3:14 Paul prescribes a three-part second stage: (1) mark the sinning brother out in some way, apparently by public announcement; (2) stop regular socializing in order to induce shame and repentance; and (3) continue to admonish him, since he is still a brother in Christ. Believers are not to break off all contact, since some opportunity for continued work with the individual is needed. It is significant that disobedience to apostolic doctrine is grounds for taking these discipline steps.

No believer is exempt from discipline, as indicated by 1 Tim. 5:19–20, where the rules for disciplining a sinning elder are laid out. As in Mt. 18, there is the safeguard of the requisite two or three witnesses. But here especially, if guilt is established— apparently by the other elders and the local church as a whole—public (in the local church) rebuke is to be given, with the goal of warning others of the danger of sin, which is especially dangerous for the local church when it occurs in the life of the leaders.

Scripture records the results of not carrying out discipline or the failure of the sinning individual to acknowledge guilt. The extreme situation in 1 Tim. 1:19–20, where two sinning individuals are "handed over to Satan," must represent a third stage in the discipline process. It is possible that the three steps of Mt. 18 had already been done, along with the shunning of 2 Th. 3:14, although we cannot be certain. Verse 19 appears to say that these men were believers. If they were, then they were far from the path of obedience. A Hymenaeus is mentioned in 2 Tim. 2:17–18, and described as having wandered away from the truth. And in 2 Tim. 4:14–15 Paul speaks of an Alexander who opposed his message. If these are the same men and they are believers, they are indeed hardened to the things of God. We should not be surprised, then, at Paul's extreme step of giving them over in some way, by apostolic decree, to be exposed to satanic pressure. Apparently this pressure would be the result, in part, of excluding them from fellowship with other believers.

Although 1 Tim. 1:19–20 offers some problems in interpretation, the severe steps of 1 Cor. 11:30 and 1 Jn. 5:16 are more transparent. Both describe situations where sin is so advanced that from God's standpoint the only solution is to remove the individuals from this life. 1 Cor. 11:30 also indicates that some believers were physically ill because of their abuse of the Lord's Table, a condition undoubtedly coming from the chastising hand of God. In both the illness and death, God intervenes either because believers have not disciplined their own, or because they have and it has not been accepted by the sinning party. In 1 Cor. 11 it is clear that this drastic discipline by God is designed in part to uphold His honor and that of the Gospel (see 1 Pet. 4:18).

No Christian enjoys thinking about having to apply discipline. However, when we see what it is designed for and the conditions to which it is to be applied, we should be led to avoid the sin that can bring discipline. That preventative effect is at the heart of the N.T. teaching on discipline in the Body of Christ.

Questions for Further Study

1. Compare and contrast the qualifications of elders and deacons. What gifts are associated with each?

2. After looking at N.T. passages on spiritual gifts, try to determine what spiritual gifts people have used that have benefited you the most in your spiritual growth.

19

Future Things

Introduction

The subject of frequent abuse and widespread disagreement, sadly neglected throughout most of the history of the Church, always fascinating—biblical prophecy is at the core of God's written revelation. Far from being icing on the cake and a topic of marginal value (some evangelical seminaries essentially avoid the subject), the Bible's description of things to come has its roots in the plan of God for the ages. Understanding the purpose of God in human history and unraveling prophecy not yet fulfilled are complementary tasks. This section will touch on both areas.

Needless to say, prophecy that has not yet come to fruition is only a portion of the totality of biblical predictive material. Fulfillments have occurred at different times and at varying distances from the time of utterance. For example, some of the prophecies of Dan. were fulfilled within the time covered by the events of the book itself (e.g., the fall of Babylon), some within the intertestamental period (the rise of the Greek and Roman Empires), some during N.T. times (the Roman destruction of Jerusalem), and some are unfulfilled at the present time. A discussion of all prophecies and their fulfillment would demand a very large volume. The purpose of this section is to outline biblical teaching on events that have not yet taken place at this point in the present age. This is eschatology, or the doctrine of last things. Most students of the Bible agree that the details yet to take place will bring human history as we know it to a close. In this sense, unfulfilled prophecy describes final or last events. As with all of the doctrines in this section, our treatment can only be summary in nature, and we cannot present all the arguments for and against particular positions. The reader should look in the Scofield notes and at works on prophecy in ch. 23, Annotated Bibliography, for more discussion of particular points that may be under current debate in this area of perennial interest.

The Kingdom

For several reasons, the kingdom promised to Israel is a key issue in biblical prophecy. It is portrayed as a goal of God's activity among human beings, the culmination of the agonizing progress of the ages. Further, as far as interpretation is concerned, it is the watershed of two currently competing and major systems of approaching the Bible espoused by theological conservatives—amillennialism and premillennialism. We are fully justified, then, in saying that the issue of the kingdom is important not only for the interpretation of prophecy, but also for our understanding of the Scriptures as a whole. Put another way, if you were to ask a person what he believed about the kingdom, the answer would enable you to anticipate many of his views on the rest of the Bible. For these reasons, we will treat the kingdom first in this section.

Some preliminary definitions are in order:

1. Millennium—a thousand-year period (can refer to anything, biblical or otherwise).
2. Millennial—having to do with a period of a thousand years.
3. Chiliasm—belief in a thousand-year kingdom, on earth or otherwise (but usually a chiliast believes in a thousand-year earthly kingdom); same as millennialism.
4. Kingdom—a sphere of God's rule; may describe the whole universe, a spiritual rule, or an earthly rule.

In what follows we will approach biblical teaching on the kingdom by examining three competing views. These have been touched on in connection with other issues in ch. 2, The Nature of the Bible, and ch. 5, Interpreting the Bible. A few particulars will be repeated here to clarify kingdom issues.

Postmillennialism

Although this is not a widely held view today, we will describe it for purposes of distinguishing it from amillennialism and premillennialism. The essence of this view is that there will be a period of special blessing from God, a millennium, on the earth during the present age. The length of the time of blessing varies within this position, and a definite thousand-year period is not essential to it. The Church will be responsible for bringing in an age of unprecedented prosperity and spiritual health. At the end of that time, Christ will return. His coming is thus *post* or after the millennium. Interestingly enough, Christ is not visibly present on the earth during this time. If the period is considered in any sense a kingdom, then the King misses the whole thing! Postmillennialism is actually a fairly recent system, having been formulated after the Protestant Reformation. As a system of interpretation, postmillennialism does not allow literal fulfillment of O.T. prophecies of a kingdom for Israel on earth. Instead, such predictions are given meanings other than those that would be assigned if they were taken at face value. This enables postmillennialists to apply them to the Church Age. Postmillennialism is very similar to amillennialism in its approach to O.T. kingdom promises.

Because it does not fit the facts of history—we are obviously not in and have never been in such a golden age—postmillennialism has declined from the position of favor it enjoyed at the beginning of this century.

Amillennialism

Held by many fine evangelicals, including Reformed churches in general, it is the position of the Roman Catholic Church, as well as many Lutherans, Presbyterians, and Southern Baptists. Our discussion will center on the Protestant versions of it.

As implied by the name, it is essentially negative. There will be no kingdom on earth with Christ reigning over it (the a-prefix indicates the denial of a millennium.) Strictly speaking, the name is not quite accurate, since a kingdom (if it does not have to be a literal thousand years in length) is allowed for. But what is denied is a visible, physical kingdom with Christ present. We are in the kingdom in some way right now. Christ will return after the Church Age has run its course, and subsequently the "eternal state" will begin. Many amillennialists see a tribulation period at the end of the present age, but in any case the creation of the new heavens and new earth (Rev. 21:1) could not be far away from any time during this present age. The imminent return of Christ is His coming to resurrect the dead of all ages, to judge the unsaved dead, and to usher in the joy of the redeemed in the presence of God.

The history of amillennialism is significant. It can be traced to the Church Fathers, and particularly the approaches to Scripture of Origen and Clement of Alexandria, who believed that the Bible was to be interpreted allegorically, with the true meaning discovered beneath the surface. Augustine applied this especially to prophecy.[1] In allegorical interpretation it is quite easy to impose any preconceptions on Scripture, since the most evident meaning is tossed aside in favor of one that is actually arrived at subjectively. The clear prophecies in the O.T. of an earthly kingdom for ethnic Israel could thus easily be applied to the Church. As a result of this methodology of Augustine, the Roman Catholic Church was amillennial. Although the Reformers did reassert the truth of several great biblical doctrines, they did not really deal with eschatology. Thus Reformed theology as a whole has been amillennial.[2]

Covenant theology, systematized only within the last 350 years, is a theologically conservative approach to the Bible that sees all of God's dealings with humanity as based on two or three covenants, particularly a "covenant of works" and a "covenant of grace." (As promises made by God, covenants are found in the Bible. But these are not.)[3] In covenant theology there is one central purpose of God in history, to create through election and the application of the work of Christ one redeemed people, saved through the covenant of grace. This underlying feature of covenant theology, actually a presupposition concerning God's purpose in and beyond history, has plausible elements. God is certainly saving people from all ages, and He does it always through the cross. However, for such a presupposition to be workable it must fit the facts, and this one is too often contradicted by the facts. Its adherents must bend biblical data in order to keep the position alive (see ch. 5, Interpreting the Bible).

Although amillennialism as a system existed before covenant theology was formulated, the union of the two in some schools of Protestant interpretation has tended to lend continued support to amillennialism. Since God's purpose, according to covenant theology, is singular, there can be no room for separate tracks or sidings. Thus Israel and the Church are part of the same stream, two manifestations of the "covenant" people. The covenant theologian often speaks of believers before the cross as "the Church," and believers after the cross as the true Israel.

It is especially in the area of the purpose of God during this and coming ages that the covenant theologian runs into difficulty. He cannot account for the very distinctive present-day works of the Holy Spirit, for much teaching concerning the nature of the universal Church and the local church, and for much of the biblical revelation concerning unfulfilled prophecy. It is no accident that these three areas are affected, for they are connected, and in order to lay them out fully one must note distinctions that the Bible makes. For example, the very practice (noted in the previous paragraph) of seeing the Church in the O.T. and confusing Israel and the Church in the N.T. clearly flies in the face of biblical evidence. Yet, unfortunately, presupposition is allowed to take precedence over biblical data.

To cite another example, Rev. 20:2 describes the binding of Satan during a predicted thousand-year period (even leaving aside for now the question of exactly how long that period is; see ch. 5, Interpreting the Bible). Since the amillennialist assumes that whatever form the kingdom/millennium will have already exists now, i.e., we are in the kingdom, he posits that Satan is bound now. It does not take much biblical investigation, however, to conclude that such an assumption—a central one to the amillennialist's position—stands in absolute contradiction to 1 Pet. 5:8–9: "Be self-controlled and alert. Your enemy the devil prowls around like a roaring lion looking for someone to devour" (v. 8, NIV).

There are thus two main assumptions that the amillennialist makes that determine his position. The first is that O.T. prophecies concerning a physical kingdom for ethnic Israel have been absorbed by the Church. In this approach such predictions need not be taken at face value, since kingdom prophecy need not be interpreted literally. It is of great significance that some amillennialists have admitted that if they took prophetic Scripture at face value they would have to be premillennialists.[4] It is also of no small moment that such an interpretation of prophecy—part of a dual treatment of the biblical text—contains another two-part approach: prophecies concerning the first advent of Christ are always taken at face value, but kingdom-associated prophecies are treated differently, i.e., in a metaphorical sense. (However, predictions of the second advent of Christ *are* taken at face value.) We could diagram this as shown in figure 19.1

The second basic assumption—one that is historically more recent—is that there is a single company of the redeemed, and no room for distinctive groups. Redeemed ethnic Israel has no separate future involving an earthly kingdom with Christ reigning over it.

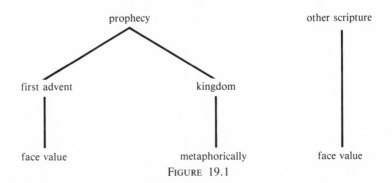

FIGURE 19.1

No student of the Bible can avoid making assumptions. Such presuppositions are part of our limitation as non-omniscient beings, and are a needed part of the investigative process. But they must always be checked and reformulated, if necessary, according to data that is available. In the case of the assumptions of covenant amillennial theology, the facts of Scripture have not been given priority (see ch. 2, The Nature of the Bible; ch. 5, Interpreting the Bible; ch. 18, The Church).

Premillennialism

The essence of this position, espoused without apology in all editions of the Scofield Bible, is that the second advent of Christ will occur at the end of the present age, after which He will establish a physical kingdom on earth. This thousand-year reign will be followed by the re-creation of the universe and the unhindered fellowship of the redeemed of all ages with God.

The belief in a physical return of Christ is, of course, shared with amillennialism and postmillennialism. However, connected with that return will be another appearance, one having the specific purpose of removing the Church from the earth. There are four main views on that lesser coming, or *rapture,* and they will be discussed below. There is little question among historians that premillennialism was the view of the early Church, which believed that Christ could come at any moment to establish His kingdom.[5] Even if it were new (as some assert) there would not be a problem, since many doctrines have been unsettled in the Church for long periods of time. The goal of all Bible interpreters should be to find out what the Bible actually says.

Dispensationalism is premillennial in its view of the kingdom, but there are other premillennialists. In other words, all dispensationalists are premillennialists, but not all premillennialists are dispensationalists. Thus, there are some premillennialists who hold that there will be a future millennium preceded by the second advent, but the kingdom will not have a strong Jewish character.

Table 19.1 and figure 19.2 will serve to clarify the relation of millennial views. They approach the views from two different angles: (1) a general overview and (2) a timeline perspective. Some of the points represented will be discussed further below.

TABLE 19.1. Overview of Dispensational, Amillennial, and Nondispensational Premillennial Views of the Present and Future Ages

	Beginning of Church	Nature of Church	Rapture Timing	Second Advent Timing	Kingdom	Promises to Israel
Dispensational	Pentecost	Those baptized into Body of Christ in this age	Before tribulation	After tribulation	1000 yrs. on earth for Israel	Literally fulfilled
Amillennial	In the O.T.	Saved of all ages	= 2nd advent	After this age	In heaven during this age	Given to Church
Nondispensational Premillennial	Varies	Varies	Varies	After tribulation	1000 yrs.	Varies—often slighted

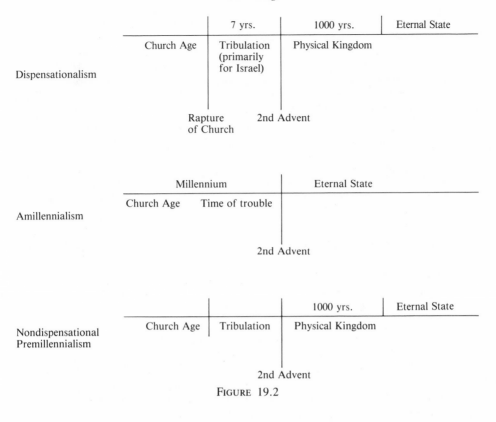

FIGURE 19.2

The Tribulation

Most students of the Bible acknowledge that it teaches there will be a time of great upheaval on the earth during the end times. For example, in Mt. 24:21 Jesus speaks of a "great tribulation" (AV, NASB), and the major part of the book of Revelation appears to chronicle that time. What is that strange period, and when and why will it occur?

As with all interpretation of prophecy, we cannot make sense of the biblical data about it unless we take Scripture at face value. The Bible actually tells us why the tribulation period will take place (Dan. 9:24–27; see below under "Overview of the End Times"). Unless we come with preconceptions about the time, we can follow this major clue and other biblical information to lead us to fit the tribulation with other prophetic information.

Among premillennialists there are several different positions on the nature and purpose of the tribulation. However, they can be conveniently distinguished on the basis of their view of the relation of the Church to that period. It should be remembered that for the postmillennialist and amillennialist the rapture is not a significant issue.

1. Pretribulationism—the Church will be taken from the earth by means of the rapture (1 Th. 4:13–18) before the events of the tribulation begin. Usually in this view the events to follow are designed to accomplish the purpose of bringing a large

portion of ethnic Israel to Christ (see previous section, "Premillennialism"). Dispensationalists are almost always pretribulationists.

2. Posttribulationism—the Church will remain on earth through the events of the tribulation, and the rapture will occur along with the second advent of Christ. The wrath of God during that time will be experienced by the Church as well as Israel and the world.[6]

3. Partial rapturism—only those believers who possess sufficient spirituality and are watching for the coming of Christ will be raptured at the beginning of the tribulation. The rest will go through it as a kind of purgation. This view is not held by many and is beset by a number of obvious contradictions.

4. Midtribulationism—stressing the biblical distinction between the two halves of the tribulation (three and a half years each), this view sees the Church as raptured at the midpoint of the period. However, this is also a minority view containing evident contradictions.

Table 19.3 displays millennial positions as they are connected with the kingdom and tribulation.

In recent years there have been several lengthy apologetics for posttribulationism that have appeared in print. While it is not possible to deal with them at length in this book, a few points should be noted:

1. Any view of the tribulation that views the Church as passing through it fails to take seriously several pieces of biblical data. As mentioned above, Dan. 9:24–27 gives as the purpose of the tribulation the purification of Israel. While that alone does not prove that the Church cannot be present, certainly the emphasis will be upon God's dealing with Israel. Further, the wrath involved, while compatible with the hardness of Israel's heart and the rebellion of the nations during the last days, is totally incompatible with the idea of the Church as the Bride of Christ. In fact, 1 Th. 1:10, in the context of the coming wrath of God in the Day of the Lord, specifically states that believers of this Church Age are to be rescued from the wrath to come by the Lord Jesus Christ. That very point is expanded in 1 Th. 4 and 5, where the rapture of the Church is described. In addition, it is a simple biblical fact that the Church is never mentioned as part of the tribulation in the passages where the tribulation is described, such as Rev. 6–18. In fact, the Church is clearly present in Rev. 2 and 3, but all mention of it suddenly ceases when the wrath of God begins to be poured out. It does not appear again until ch. 19, after the second advent, where the marriage supper of the Lamb is celebrated (although the word *church* is not mentioned; see note, Rev. 19:7). Revelation 3:10 is a prophecy of the safety of

TABLE 19.3. Millennial Positions Concerning the Kingdom and the Tribulation

	Physical 2nd Advent	Earthly Kingdom	Rapture			
			Pretrib.	Midtrib.	Posttrib.	Partial
Dispensational	yes	yes	yes	no	no	no
Amillennial	yes	no	n/a	n/a	n/a	n/a
Postmillennial	yes	yes (before 2nd advent)	n/a	n/a	n/a	n/a
Premillennial Nondispensational	yes	yes	——————— varies ———————			

the Church from the horrors of the tribulation. If its phrase "kept from the hour" is taken at face value, then we must conclude that the Church will not be present at all during that time. One of the purposes of 1 Th. 5:4–8 is to show that the believers who are addressed—Church-Age people—are not part of the darkness characterizing the Day of the Lord, which begins at the rapture.[7]

2. The Bible presents the rapture as imminent (1 Th. 4 and 5), meaning that Christ could return for the Church at any moment. Posttribulationism and midtribulationism cannot maintain this view, since if Christ has not come and people know they are in the tribulation, they can predict the time that must elapse before the appearing of Christ.[8]

Overview of the End Times

It is not difficult to place the major events at the end of this age in relation to each other. Most premillennialists hold not only that the rapture of the Church is imminent, but that events of the twentieth c., especially in regard to the Middle East, have prepared the world for the fulfillment of the great prophecies connected with the regathering of Israel and the second coming of Christ. Certainly the stage is set in terms of moral, political, and economic climates.

In relation to the present age in which we are living, the next great event in the prophetic scheme will be the removal of the Church from the earth (by the rapture) and the beginning of the seventieth week of Dan. 9:24–27 (see note, 9:24). It is this crucial passage that lays out God's plan for human history from the fifth c. B.C. to the kingdom. Daniel 9:24 clearly states that the prophecy is intended to bring in righteousness for Daniel's people. To take this as other than Israel (as the Church, for example) is to impose on the text what is not there (see notes, 1 Th. 4:17; 2 Th. 2:3; Mt. 24:16). While we are not specifically told anywhere that the seven-year period will begin immediately after the rapture, it is reasonable to assume that the removal of the evil-restraining effect of the Holy Spirit through the Church will allow satanic influence to spread rapidly. The first three and a half years of the seventieth week are a period of outward calm, but of behind-the-scenes fomenting of anti-Semitism, especially on the part of the world leader of that time (see note, Rev. 13:1). At the middle of the seven years he breaks a peace treaty made with Israel (Dan. 9:27) and proceeds to promulgate intense persecution of Jews. As this terror mounts, a judgment that is actually part of the wrath of God (Rev. 6:16–17; 7:14, note), He continues to regather Israel in the land and to work in individual hearts to turn a remnant to the Messiah.

Spiritual deception will reach an all-time high as Satan promotes a false trinity imitating God, with himself corresponding to the Father, and the two beasts of Rev. 13 as the Son and Spirit. Yet at the same time God will be saving many from among Jews and Gentiles (Rev. 7; see note, 7:14). The tribulation is a time of pressure to bring Israel to God, and others incidentally along the way. As the political, social, economic, and deceptive spiritual movements of Daniel's seventieth week reach a peak, God will conclude that rescuing work, drawing probably one third of ethnic Israel to Himself (Zech. 13:9).

The second advent of Christ will bring the period to a conclusion, as the King Himself returns to the Mount of Olives, bringing physical safety to a large number of believers, while defeating military forces arrayed against Jerusalem itself (Zech. 14:1–5). Probably between the rapture and the second advent the marriage supper of the Lamb occurs (Rev. 19:7–9), along with the judgment seat of Christ, where the works of believers during the Church Age are judged, the outcome to be bestowal of rewards, not loss of salvation (see note, 2 Cor. 5:10; 1 Cor. 3:11–15). After the second advent individual Gentiles will be judged, as the Lord Jesus Christ separates the "sheep and goats" (true and false Gentile believers who are alive at the time of His coming; Mt. 25:31–46; see note, 25:32). Following a time of cleanup (Ezek. 39:12–15; see note, Dan. 12:12; Zech. 8:23) and publication of His return, the Lord Jesus Christ will reign as the Davidic King in Jerusalem for a thousand years, fulfilling the kingdom promises of the O.T. and those surrounding His birth (Lk. 1:32; see note, 1 Cor. 15:24).

This messianic kingdom—the final dispensation—will demonstrate, however, human beings' inveterate sinfulness, for even in the presence of the King, they will rebel and attempt to overthrow Him (Rev. 20:7–8). We should note that this will happen while Satan is bound. People will show that their sin natures alone (with no outside help from Satan) are confirmed in rebellion against God. These events at the end of the final dispensation, just prior to the judgment of the unsaved of all ages (Rev. 20:11–15; see notes, vv. 12, 14) will serve to highlight God's grace and our failure, even under near-ideal conditions.

The final judgment of human beings occurs in conjunction with the beginning of Satan's eternal confinement. All of the unregenerate of all ages are brought to life to face God (see note, Rev. 20:12). They will be evaluated on the basis of their works and the presence of their names in the book of life, and will fail on both counts. Along with Satan, they will be cast into the lake of fire (see note, Rev. 20:10).

After this the so-called eternal state will be instituted, inaugurated by the creation of the new heaven and new earth (Rev. 21:1; see note, 21:2). Actually the Bible tells us very little about it, devoting only the last two chapters of the book of Revelation to it. Many of the things we see there are even more difficult to understand than details of the earlier chapters of the book, due in part to the fact that we are being given insight into new creations of God that are far removed from anything we know around us in life during this age (1 Cor. 15:24–28).

Questions for Further Study

1. Dan. 9:1–23 forms a significant prelude to the revelation by Gabriel of the seventy weeks/sevens prophecy. Using the Scofield notes, carefully study the text of the chapter, listing the elements of the prayer that correspond to features of the prediction.

2. Rev. 6:15–17 describes one of the reactions of enemies of God to the pressures of the tribulation period. As terrible as life will be during that time, most will still not turn to Him. Look through chs. 6–18, noting similar reactions. What is God's response? Where can you see grace? What can you say about God's patience?

III

Reference

20

Quick-Reference Guide to Bible Study Terms

This glossary presents terms that are frequently encountered in Bible study. The following types of entry are omitted:

    1. most geographical terms
    2. most names of ethnic groups
    3. most plants and animals, except when they are associated with a problem of interpretation or play a significant doctrinal role, e.g., wormwood.
    4. most minerals
    5. names of Bible books
    6. proper names of people
    7. weights and measures (see notes at 2 Chr. 2:10 and Acts 27:28)
    8. coins (see notes at Ex. 30:13 and Mt. 5:26)
    9. terms in common use today, such as those referring to pottery, except where the terms are used in a special sense or are invested with special significance, such as *rainbow*
    10. most terms relating to theological movements after N.T. times

Definitions cannot be exhaustive. The most frequent uses, or those most relevant for study throughout the Bible, are given; for example, *bread* is found throughout the Bible but is especially important as a figure of Christ.

    The abbreviation *S.* instructs the reader to see another entry or section in this book; esp. = especially; n = note; Scr. = Scripture. The abbreviation (q.v.) following a term means to see the entry for that term.

A

Abaddon. Heb., "destruction"; name given to angel of the abyss in Rev. 9:1ff; probably Satan.

Abba. Aram., "father"; used in N.T. to address God; Rom. 8:15.

Abiding. The privilege and imperative for the believer, involving confession of sin, dependence on God, and resulting spiritual sustenance; Jn. 15:4n.

Ablution. S. Washings.

Abomination of desolation. (AV, NASB) A particular profane act or person of the last days; Dan. 8:13n; Mt. 24:15; NIV = *rebellion that causes desolation.*

Abrahamic Covenant. Promise made to Abraham in Gen. 12; establishes blessings for racial Israel (and for others through them) and is the basis for all other convenants with that people; Gen. 12:2n. *S. Covenant; S.* ch. 2, The Nature of the Bible.

Abraham's bosom. From oriental dining language, denoting proximity to someone; used of Lazarus' state after death (Lk. 16:22–23); in the *Talmud* (q.v.), being in Abraham's bosom was equivalent to being in paradise; Lk. 16:23n.

Abyss. (NIV) Residence of imprisoned demons, as in Rev. 9:1ff; AV, NASB = *bottomless pit.*

Access. Crucial issue for human beings in relation to God; it is the privilege of being able to enter God's presence; made possible by the substitutionary sacrifice of Christ; Eph. 2:16; Heb. 10:19–22; *S.* ch. 7, Relations Between the Testaments.

Acts (of righteousness). (NIV) Outward religious behavior; Mt. 6:1n; AV = *alms;* NASB = *righteousness.*

Adam, the last. S. Last Adam.

Adamic Convenant. Covenant made with Adam determining life after the fall;

Gen. 3:15n; *S.* ch. 2, The Nature of the Bible.

Adonai. Heb., "master," "sovereign," "lord"; used of human beings and God; Gen. 15:2n.

Adonai Jehovah. Compound name of God; translated in the AV and NASB as "Lord God" and in the NIV as "Sovereign Lord"; Gen. 15:2n.

Adoption. Spiritually, the act of God at salvation that transfers a sinner into His family by grace, bestowing the rights and privileges of a naturally born offspring; complement to new birth, which involves bestowal of a new nature; Eph. 1:5n.

Adultery. A married person's having sexual relations with someone other than his or her spouse; condemned by Scr.; Lev. 20:10; used also figuratively of appearing to belong to God and turning to other objects of worship; Jer. 3:8; *S. Fornication.*

Advent. First or second appearance of the second Person of the Trinity joined with humanity; Acts 1:11n.

Advocate. One who assists in time of hardship; used of Christ and the Holy Spirit; the Gr. word behind it is also translated "comforter"; 1 Jn. 2:1n; Jn. 14:16n.

Affliction. Difficulty in life, used of believers and unbelievers alike; only the child of God can see purposes in it, but sometimes not until he is in the presence of God; Job 42:6n.

Agape. Transliteration of a Gr. word for love; used esp. of the unselfish love of God; *S.* also *Love feast.*

Age. A period of time, with length specified or unspecified; may have spiritual characteristics or purposes of God associated with it; Mt. 24:3n; Mk. 10:30n.

Agrapha. Sayings of Christ not recorded in the Gospels.

Akeldama. (AV = *Aceldama*) Aram., "field of blood," (Mt. 27:8; Acts 1:19); earlier called Potter's Field; traditionally in the Hinnom Valley south of Jerusalem; purchased by chief priests with Judas' betrayal money.

Alexander the Great. King of Macedonia who conquered the Mediterranean world between 336 and 323 B.C.; Dan 8:9n.

Allegory. (1) The literary device of portraying one thing (the "deeper" meaning) in terms of a second (the "shallower") and less important thing; (2) the interpretive practice of seeking or observing such figures; the word is used only once in Scr., Gal. 4:24 (AV, NASB); *S.* ch. 5, Interpreting the Bible, and ch. 6, Literary Aspects of the Bible.

Alleluia. S. Hallelujah.

Almighty. Name of God translating Heb. *shaddai* ("mighty"?) and Gr. *pantokrator,* "all-powerful"; also used in combination with *el* and translated "God Almighty" or "Almighty God"; Gen. 17:1n.

Almond tree. Early-blooming tree used to signify impending fulfillment of God's plan; Jer. 1:11n.

Alms. Act of giving; the term was applied by Jesus negatively to ostentatious religious behavior; Mt. 6:1n.; *S. Acts.*

Almug. Possibly the sandalwood tree; 1 Ki. 10:11n.

Alpha and omega. First and last letters of the Gr. alphabet; used to describe the eternality of Christ; Rev. 1:8n.

Altar of burnt offering. Large piece of "furniture" for sacrifice, with particular dimensions, used in the Tabernacle and Temple, and a type of Christ as a sacrifice; Ex. 27:1n.

Altar of incense. Sacrificial instrument with particular dimensions, used in the Tabernacle and Temple, and a type of Christ as Intercessor; positioned next to the veil containing the ark of the covenant; Ex. 30:1n.

Amen. Heb. word denoting agreement, confirmation, certainty; used of Christ, as the channel of fulfillment for the sure promises of God, Rev. 3:14.

Amillennialism. The view of the plan of God that holds there is no physical/spiritual kingdom on the earth over which Christ reigns visibly and personally; contrasted with *premillennialism* and *postmillennialism* (q.v.); *S.* ch. 5, Interpreting the Bible, and ch. 19, Future Things.

Amulets. Decorative jewelry or inscriptions worn to protect from evil spirits; condemned by Scr., as in Isa. 3:20.

Anathema. Gr. term; (1) an offering set up in a temple (Lk. 21:5); (2) LXX translation of Heb. term, denoting a person or thing devoted and separated to the Lord, sometimes with need for its total destruction; also translated as "devoted thing."

Ancient of Days. Descriptive term and name for God, esp. the Father, as in Dan. 7:19, denoting eternality.

Angel. One belonging to an order of powerful and intelligent beings, created to serve God; some are fallen (e.g., Satan), others are confirmed in holiness (Heb. 1:14); the Gr. word from which it is transliterated, and the Heb. word used parallel to it, simply mean "messenger"; Dan. 10:13n; Heb. 1:4n; Jude 6n; Rev. 1:20n; *S.* ch. 16, Angels.

Angel of the Lord. (1) An appearance of an angel as a special emissary of God, or (2) a preincarnate appearance of the second Person of the Trinity; Jud. 2:1n; *S.* ch. 12, The Person of Christ.

Anger. In relation to God, His controlled displeasure against sin.

Annihilationism. The unscriptural view that at death an individual ceases to exist; Mal. 4:1n.

Annunciation. The revelation to Mary in Lk. 1:26–38 that she would give birth to the Messiah; important, esp. in the context of Lk. 1, as confirmation of Davidic promises (vv. 32–33).

Anointing. (1) A ritual act performed for persons or objects (e.g., the Tabernacle) in the O.T., signifying separation or consecration to God, where it was viewed as a picture of a previous spiritual anointing by God, to which nothing could be added by human beings; 1 Sam. 10:1; esp. of God's chosen representatives (prophets, priests, and kings), and the supreme embodiment of these, the Messiah Himself; Messiah is a transliteration of a Heb. word meaning "anointed one"; Gr. *christos* has the same meaning; (2) a medical procedure, as at Jas. 5:14 (a different Gr. word is used).

Anthropology. The study of the biblical teaching concerning the nature and makeup of human beings as created in the image and likeness of God; *S.* ch. 15, Humanity.

Anthropomorphism. A figure of speech in which an act or attribute of God is described in terms of human activity or qualities, e.g., the "hand" of God (Ps. 119:73); cp. *Anthropopathism.*

Anthropopathism. A figure of speech in which an act or attribute of God is described in terms of human emotion or sensitivity, e.g., "God hates sin"; cp. *Anthropomorphism.*

Antichrist. (1) The manifestation of any satanically induced counterfeit of the work or presence of the true Messiah, as in 1 Jn. 2:18, 22; 4:3; 2 Jn. 7; (2) used generally in biblical studies (though not found in Scr. this way) of the world-ruler of the tribulation period; Rev. 13:11n.

Antilegomena. A term used by the Church historian Eusebius to describe biblical books whose canonicity was a point of debate; cp. *Homologoumena.*

Antinomianism. (1) Any position based on the view that rejects God's laws as binding; (2) more specifically, rejection of the moral law of the O.T. as binding on individuals.

Antitype. As used of correspondences between the testaments, the N.T. event, person, or entity paralleled and pictured by an O.T. feature; *S. Type,* and ch. 7, Relations Between the Testaments.

Apocalypse. (1) Generally a type of literature (usually prophetic) that opens vistas into the spiritual realm by means of visions and striking and unusual descriptions (adj.: *apocalyptic*); (2) specifically, the last book of the N.T., the unveiling par excellence, as described in Rev. 1:1, the "revelation of Jesus Christ"; the Gr. word means "an uncovering" or "an unveiling."

Apocalypticism. The belief that the future will include startling, unusual, and previously unseen events as part of the climax of the ages.

Apocrypha. Transliteration of the Gr. word for "hidden"; a set of noncanonical works descriptive of events, some historical and some not, occurring in O.T. and N.T. times.

Apocryphal Gospels. Group of noncanonical writings in various languages from the early Christian era, ostensibly giving information on the life and ministry of Christ.

Apologetics. Argumentation supportive of the veracity of the Christian faith.

Apostasy. The deliberate act of departing from a position of profession of faith in Christ; outward appearance of genuineness that eventually gives place to complete rejection of the things of God; 2 Tim. 3:1n.

Apostle. A human emissary of God, commissioned with delegated authority; used of Christ, the disciples, Paul, and others; Mt. 10:2n.

Apostolic Fathers. Writers, such as Ignatius and Polycarp, from the early part of the postapostolic era (ca. 90–150 A.D.), who may have known some of the apostles.

Arabah. Heb., "dry," "waste"; used of

(1) the valley extending from the Sea of Galilee to the Gulf of Aqabah; (2) certain areas within that region; Dt. 1:1n.

Aramaic. Language of the Aramaeans, a Semitic people; related to Heb.; one of the two languages in which the O.T. was written; Dan. 2:4n; *S.* ch. 4, The Language of the Bible.

Archaeology. The study of cultures, sites, and artifacts of past human life; of great significance as an aid in interpretation and confirmation of biblical history and the written record.

Archangel. (1) A particular named angel (Michael; Jude 9) or (2) a leading angel in the service of God, e.g., 1 Th. 4:16, perhaps also Michael.

Areopagus. S. Mars Hill.

Arianism. A view found in the fourth-century Church, asserting that Christ was created by God, and hence not deity; named for Arius, a priest in North Africa; the view was condemned at the Council of Nicaea in 325.

Ark. (1) The vessel made and used by Noah at God's direction; Gen. 6:14n, 15n; (2) the vessel used to save Moses by water (Ex. 2:3–6).

Ark of the Covenant. The sacred container located behind the veil in the Tabernacle and Temple, holding the broken tables of the Law, Aaron's rod that budded, and the pot of manna; Ex. 25:10n.

Armageddon. Gr. equivalent of Heb. *harmegiddo* ("Mount Megiddo"); site of O.T. events and the great conflagration of the latter part of the tribulation period, according to Rev. 16:16; apparently near Mt. Megiddo at the edge of the Jezreel Valley; *S. Jezreel.*

Arminianism. Theological position stressing the freedom of human beings to cooperate with God in securing their salvation; named for James Arminius, sixteenth/seventeenth-century theolo-gian; in general, holds to (1) election on the basis of God's awareness of who would believe, (2) resistable grace, (3) possible loss of salvation, (4) unlimited atonement, (5) the death of Christ as a suffering for human beings, not the payment of a penalty.

Ascension. The change in ministry of the resurrected Lord Jesus Christ from visible presence with the disciples to presence with God; an event viewed by the N.T. as a continuation of the sequence begun by the resurrection and as placing Him in the position of offering continual intercession and preparing for His return in power and glory; Acts 1:9–11.

Ashtaroth. S. Ashtoreth.

Ashtoreth. Canaanite mother goddess, equivalent to the Phoenician Astarte, goddess of fertility; AV = *Ashtaroth,* NASB = *Astartes;* Jud. 2:13n.

Assurance. (1) Used generally of confidence in spiritual things; (2) a person's inner knowledge, given by the Holy Spirit in conjunction with the Scriptures, that he is a child of God; involves understanding the "terms of salvation," namely that, if a person has taken a step of exercising genuine faith in Christ, he is accepted by God and becomes the recipient of all the blessings of salvation; cp. the related but distinct doctrine of *security* (q.v.); Jude 1n.

Assyria. Major Middle Eastern power of the ninth to seventh c. B.C.

Astartes. S. Ashtoreth.

Atheism. Position that no deity exists, whether the God of Scripture or otherwise.

Atonement. A general term for the cross-work of Christ, a translation of O.T. and N.T. words more accurately rendered by Eng. "propitiation" (q.v.); Lev. 16:6n; Rom. 3:25n.

Atonement, Day of. S. Day of Atonement.

Attributes of God. Features of the nature

and character of God; He is a spirit being, alive, present everywhere, perfect in every way, etc.

Authority. (1) Quality inherent in Scr. by virtue of which human beings are completely answerable to its content; (2) in regard to the Church, the governing structure established by God for local bodies of believers, representing His will and expectation of allegiance from Christians.

Authorized Version (AV). The King James translation of the Bible, published in 1611.

Autographs. The original documents produced by the writers of Scripture; none are in existence today.

Avenger of blood. Provision in the O.T. for an individual to make restitution for the murder of a relative, based on existing Eastern custom of family revenge for personal damage; limited by specific stipulations and the provision of *cities of refuge* (q.v.); Gen. 9:6; Num 35:6.

B

Baal. Heb., "master," originally a plural deity of Canaan, then the name for the god of fertility; observed throughout the Middle East, Baal worship was a great stumbling block for Israel; often connected with worship of *Ashtoreth* (q.v.); found in place names, since for the Canaanites property was owned by various Baals.

Baal-zebub. Heb., "lord of flies," god of Ekron, a Philistine city (2 Ki. 1:2–16); in the N.T. it is used of Satan in Mk. 3:22 and parallels; also found as Beelzebub, Beelzebul, Beezebul.

Babel. Name for early Babylon, a city established by Nimrod (Gen. 10:10;

NIV = Babylon); site of attempt to build tower to reach heaven, clearest early manifestation of the Babylonian spirit of organized rebellion against God.

Babel, Tower of. S. Tower of Babel.

Babylon. Ancient culture and city located on the Euphrates River in what is now Iraq; one of the significant civilizations of the ancient world, also known as Shinar (Gen. 11:1); its spirit of independence is continued and reaches its ultimate expression in the organized system of the tribulation period, described in Rev. 13–19; Isa. 13:1n, 19n; Rev. 18:2n.

Babylonia. The area in what is now Iraq deriving its name from its capital city, Babylon; called Shinar in Gen. 11:1; *S. Babel, Babylon.*

Backsliding. (1) Used of Israel in the O.T. to refer to continued failure to obey and trust God (Jer. 5:6); (2) although the term is not found in the N.T., it is used generally to describe the spiritual change in a believer who lapses into continued sin; does not involve loss of salvation; may result in severe chastisement or being taken home by God (1 Jn. 5:16); treated especially by 1 Jn.; the remedy is confession and obedience (1 Jn. 1:9).

Badgers' skins. Valuable skins used especially as covering for the Tabernacle; perhaps actually from marine animals such as the seal, dolphin, porpoise, or dugong.

Balm. A medicinal product exported from the region of Gilead; exact content unclear.

Baptism. (1) A ritual act expressing indentification and association; a public acknowledgement that spiritual new birth has taken place; cannot bring life *(S. Baptismal regeneration):* not a continuation in this age of *circumcision* (q.v.); (2) the work of the Holy Spirit performed for each individual at salvation (*S. Baptism of the Spirit);* (3) for our Lord Jesus Christ, the ritual that signified His association as Messiah with the needs of Israel (Mt. 3:16); (4) for our Lord, also, a figure for His undergoing death (Mk. 10:38); Mt. 3:15n; Acts 8:12n.

Baptismal regeneration. The view that water baptism is necessary for, and brings, the new birth; contradicted by the many biblical references to faith alone as the condition of salvation.

Baptism for the dead. A concept found in 1 Cor. 15:29 (see note); probably descriptive of the practice of replacing believers who have died with new ones who fill their ranks; to claim, as some cults do, that this refers to baptizing living people as stand-ins, in order to effect the salvation of dead people, is a contradiction of Scr.— baptism cannot save, and there is no indication in the Bible that after death a person has a second chance to come to God.

Baptism of the Spirit. The nonphysical act of the Spirit of God that places a believer in the Body of Christ and makes him a partaker, along with all other believers, of the work and merits of Christ; should be distinguished from filling, sealing, and indwelling; cannot be felt or noticed, and hence must be appropriated by faith; there is no warrant in Scripture for assuming a second act of God for power, a "baptism," after salvation; 1 Cor. 12:13; *S.* ch. 13, The Holy Spirit.

Barbarian. From the Gr. word *barbaros,* meaning "foreigner," "non-Greek"; in Rom 1:14 it is used with "Greeks" to encompass the whole world; borrowed into Eng., where it has a different meaning, "uncivilized person."

Beast, the. The world-ruler of the tribulation period who comes to be worshiped as a counterfeit Messiah; Rev. 19:20n.

Beatitude. Term not found in the Bible; used generally to refer to spiritual benefits or blessings, especially as found in Mt. 5:3–11 and Lk. 6:20–22.

Beelzebub, Beelzebul. S. Baal-zebub

Beezebul. S. Baal-zebub.

Behemoth. Plural of Heb. word for "beast"; used throughout the O.T. of cattle, but of a larger animal in Job. 40:15ff, perhaps the hippopotamus, although other animals have been suggested.

Bel. The principal god of Babylon; Jer. 50:2.

Belial. A Heb. word of uncertain meaning, apparently denoting evil or wickedness; not a proper name; used of human beings or Satan (2 Cor. 6:15).

Belief. Confident trust, esp. in the assertions of God; more than simple mental assent; the sole condition of salvation; synonymous with faith in the Bible; Jn. 3:16n.

Believer-priest. Used to describe one of the functions of the believer during this age; not a biblical term per se; based on priesthood passages such as 1 Pet. 2:9 (see note); Rev. 1:16; *S.* ch. 18, The Church.

Bible. From the Gr. *biblos,* "book"; the sixty-six canonical books comprising the written revelation from God.

Bibliology. The doctrinal study of the nature of the Bible; *S.* ch. 10, The Bible.

Binding and loosing. Words used in Mt. 16:19 (see note) and 18:18, based on a rabbinic phrase describing decisions connected with the law involving forbidding or allowing certain practices; in the N.T. they refer to authority given to the apostles or believers in the local church to carry out (in the context of Mt. 16:19 and 18:18) decisions already made in heaven.

Birthright. S. Firstborn.

Bishop. S. Overseer.

Bitter herbs. Vegetables used as part of the sequence of the celebration of the Passover; Ex. 12:8.

Blasphemy. Ascription of an evil character or act to God (or a king, in the O.T.), willful or otherwise.

Blasphemy against the Holy Spirit. S. Unpardonable sin.

Blessing. (1) Expression of favor from God to human beings (Eph. 1:3b) or from human beings to each other (Gen. 49:1ff); (2) thankfully acknowledging the true characteristics of God (Eph. 1:3a).

Blindness. Aside from physical reference, it is used of a spiritual condition involving absence of spiritual understanding; Mt. 15:14.

Blood. Since the death of a substitute is required for atonement, blood is regarded as the key to securing forgiveness; Lev. 16:5n; 17:11, two notes.

Blood, Field of. S. Akeldama.

Blood sacrifice. A substitutionary act in which the death of an animal victim is accepted as the death of another.

Bodily resurrection. Physical resuscitation after death; the claim of some that resurrection involves only the spirit, which is more suited to life after death, is foreign to the Bible; the N.T. emphasizes that the resurrection of Christ involved the same body that was put in the tomb. although naturally altered to be suitable for a new sphere of life; 1 Cor. 15:52n; *S. Resurrection.*

Body. A feature of the original composition of human beings as creations of God; not part of the image and likeness of God per se (Gen. 1:26), since God is a spirit being; assigned great worth in the Bible (1 Cor. 6:19), it is, as the vehicle for the soul and spirit, a channel for glorifying God; *S.* ch. 15, The Doctrine of Humanity.

Body of Christ. S. Church, universal.

Book of Life. (1) In the O.T., those alive and under the care of God (Ps. 69:28);

to be "blotted out of the book of life" was to die and be outside any possible blessing; based on practice of keeping civil records; (2) in the N.T. it speaks of those who alone will inherit eternal life; Phil. 4:3; Rev. 3:5, etc.

Book of the covenant. (1) A term used in Ex. 24:7, where Moses read apparently from the Decalogue of Ex. 20:1–17; (2) also applied to Ex. 20:22–23:33, the fuller statement of Jewish law.

Booths, Feast of. S. Tabernacles, Feast of.

Bottomless pit. S. Abyss.

Branch. (1) In addition to other symbolic uses, a figure of Christ as an heir to royal privilege, the King of David's line; Jer. 23:5; 33:15; Isa. 4:2n; Zech. 3:1n, 8; (2) a figure of the believer as joined to Christ the vine, drawing sustenance from Him; Jn. 15:1ff.

Brazen serpent. S. Bronze serpent.

Bread. A symbol of Christ as an offering, undergoing the fires of the wrath of God for sinners, and as the source of spiritual nourishment for all who are in Him.

Bread of the Presence. S. Showbread.

Breaking of bread. Luke's term for the *Lord's Supper* (q.v.).

Breastplate of the high priest. An intricately fashioned portion of the garments of the high priest, carrying, among other things, twelve stones in each of which were carved the name of a tribe of Israel, signifying the priest's function of bearing the people to God.

Bride of Christ. A figure of the Church as those chosen by and cared for by Christ, the Bridegroom, to be fully united with Him in the future; Rev. 19:7n; different from Israel as the "wife" of Jehovah (Hos. 2:2).

Brimstone. A flammable substance, esp. sulfur; one of the instruments of the destruction of Sodom and Gomorrah (Gen. 19:24).

Bronze. In addition to denoting metals, used figuratively of Christ undergoing judgment; Ex. 27:17n; Num. 21:9n.

Bronze (brass, brazen) altar. A type of the cross as the offering-place of Christ; Ex. 27:1n.

Bronze (brazen) serpent. A type of Christ undergoing substitutionary judgment for sinners; Num 21:9n.

Burning bush. Locus of the miraculous appearance of God to Moses in Ex. 3:2ff; the bush symbolized both the suffering of Israel in the "fires" of Egypt and the presence of God in the midst of that trial.

Burnt offering. Animal offering under the law that symbolized Christ's complete, free, offering of Himself as a spotless victim; offered on various occasions; Lev. 1:3n; Ex. 27:1n.

C

Call, calling. Invitation by God to enjoy His favor; may be general (Mt. 11:14), without divinely induced effect, or specific ("special" or "efficacious" grace), not resistable, and sovereignly effective, as in Rom 8:28.

Calvary. Lat., "skull"; not found in N.T.; the place of the crucifixion of our Lord Jesus Christ; exact site unknown; *S. Golgotha,* which is the term found in the N.T. in Mt., Mk., Jn.; Lk. has *kranion,* Gr. "skull," and the AV transliterates its Lat. equivalent, *calvaria.*

Calvinism. A term used to describe (sometimes loosely) the theological system of John Calvin (1509–1564), emphasizing the sovereignty of God, human corruption, and free grace.

Camp. Used of the elaborately regulated ordering of the stopping places of Israel in the wilderness, and a type of legalistic Judaism as a whole; "outside the camp" therefore points to something beyond Judaism, and is where Christ suffered and where we are to walk (Heb. 13:12–14); Lev. 4:12n.

Canon. Transliterated from a Gr. Word meaning "standard"; as used of the Bible, it refers to books authenticated as possessing divine origin and therefore authoritative; the Jewish canon consists of thirty-nine books, the Protestant of sixty-six and the Catholic of eighty (including apocryphal books); *S.* ch. 2, The Nature of the Bible.

Canticles. A name for the Song of Songs or Song of Solomon; used in the Vulgate, the Lat. translation of the Bible.

Captivity. Used esp. of the exile of first Israel and then Judah at the hand of the Assyrians and Babylonians, respectively; Jer 25:11n.

Carnality. A spiritual condition in which a believer is dominated by the old, sinful nature; in 1 Cor. 3:1–3 there are actually two conditions, as indicated by two different words: (1) spiritually weak and immature, like a baby (3:1); (2) controlled by the old nature, exhibiting strife, etc., and for the Corinthians a result of remaining too long in the first condition. The AV translates both as "carnal," the NIV translates both as "worldy," but the NASB uses "men of flesh" and "fleshly"; Rom. 7:14n.

Catholic Epistles. S. General Epistles.

Celibacy. Remaining unmarried for spiritual purposes.

Censer. Instrument for burning incense under the law.

Centurion. Transliteration of a Gr. word borrowed from Lat., denoting a Roman military position, involving leadership of a group of soldiers; the Lat. word *centuria* means "a division of 100" or "a company of soldiers."

Chaff. Waste portion of grain blown away

during winnowing; a figure of worth-less teaching or behavior.

Chaldean. (1) Descriptive of a small region in southern Babylon; (2) later used to refer to Babylon in its entirety.

Chariot. Used figuratively of God's judgment; Zech. 6:1n.

Charismata. A transliteration of the Gr. for "gifts"; used by Paul in 1 Cor. 12:4 of the enablements of the Spirit given for service in the Body of Christ; 1 Cor. 12:1n.

Charismatic. Used today generally to refer to concentration on experiences of certain miraculous spiritual gifts, esp. tongues; not a term found in the Bible.

Charity. AV term = *love* (q.v.).

Chastisement. The loving, gracious work of God that disciplines His people, whether Israel or the Church today, in order to remove sin; its goal is always to produce godliness; Heb. 12:4–15.

Cherub. A heavenly being, apparently an angel, concerned with upholding the holiness and glory of God; plural is cherubim (a transliteration of the Heb. word) or cherubs (Eng. plural added to the Heb. *cherub*); Ezek. 1:5n.

Children of God. A N.T. term denoting those who have placed saving faith in Christ; as such they are recipients of all the benefits of the work of Christ and are members of the family of God; *S. Regeneration;* Jn. 1:12–13.

Chiliasm. Theological position involving belief in a millennium; from the Gr. word for one thousand, based on the description of the 1000-year kingdom in Rev. 20:2ff; one who holds to the return of Christ and subsequent kingdom on earth is a chiliast (and pre-millennialist); Rev. 20:2n; *S. Millennium.*

Christ. A transliteration of Gr. *christos,* meaning "one who has been anointed" (ritually); not a proper name, as many assume, but a title equivalent to Heb. *mashiach,* "anointed one," the title

for the promised Deliverer; *S. Anointing;* Mt. 1:16n.

Christian. In the biblical sense, a person who has placed saving faith in Christ; first used in Acts 11:26; Gal 5:22n.

Christology. That branch of theology that deals with the makeup of the Person of Christ, and sometimes His work (which is also considered under the area of *soteriology* [q.v.]); *S.* ch. 12, The Person of Christ.

Christophany. An appearance before the incarnation of the second Person of the Trinity.

Chronology. The study of sequences and datings of events, esp. important for biblical studies in relation to individuals, groups, kings, and the Exodus in the O.T., and the life of Christ, identity and sequence of rulers, events of the book of Acts and other elements of the apostolic age; *S.* the Introduction in the NSRB and NIV Scofield; Gen. 1:1n; 5:3n; 11:10n.

Church, local. The manifestation of living Christians in a particular geographical area during this age, meeting regularly for the purpose of giving and receiving teaching, sustaining Christian fellowship, celebrating the Lord's Supper and praying (Acts 2:42); has visible leadership, shepherding ministry and the authority to carry out discipline; association with a local church is obligatory for believers (Heb. 10:25) and is the prime source of strength and nurture; a subset of the Body of Christ, the universal Church *(S. Church, universal);* Phil. 1:1n.

Church, universal. The Body of Christ, all believers from Pentecost to the rapture who have placed faith in Christ; although *church* is a translation of a Gr. word whose component parts add up to "a called-out entity," and indeed those in the Body of Christ have been called by God, one should be careful not to take "called out" as the meaning, since it is inaccurate to assume meanings on the basis of etymology as opposed to usage; the most general meaning of the word is to refer to an assembly, i.e., a group gathered for a particular purpose; Heb. 12:23n.

Church Age. That period of time from Pentecost (Acts 2) to the rapture (1 Th. 4); involves a people of God distinct from Israel in the O.T.; one of the dispensations; Acts 2:1n; *S.* ch. 2, The Nature of the Bible.

Church Fathers. The leaders and writers of the postapostolic Church to the sixth c.

Church government. The patterns of authority in the local church; Tit. 1:5, two notes; *S.* ch. 18, The Church.

Circumcision. A ritual predating the law, signifying membership in the community of Israel; not replaced by baptism today; Gen. 17:10n; Josh. 5:2n; *S.* ch. 18, The Church.

Cities of refuge. Locations provided after entry into the land, in order that those committing manslaughter might have a place of safety; Num. 35:6n.

Cleansing. Freedom from physical, and esp. spiritual, contamination; for the believer the latter is obtained positionally at salvation and practically through confession (1 Jn. 1:9); Lev. 14:3n; Ps. 51:7n; Jn. 13:10n.

Codex. Ancient form of book, as opposed to a scroll, the older form; codices (plural) came into widespread use in the Western world just after the apostolic era.

Colony. City or region with special Roman status and privilege, enjoyed, for instance, by Philippi.

Comforter. S. Advocate.

Commandments. S. Ten Commandments.

Communion. (1) Spiritual unity, a concept expressed especially by the Gr. word *koinonia,* denoting things held in common; hence (a) spiritual oneness with God, unimpeded by sin (Song

2:14n; Ps. 51:1n); (b) the content of all in the spiritual realm that is shared by Christians because they are sharers in the work of Christ; (2) from 1 Cor. 10:16, the *Lord's Supper* (q.v.) or *Breaking of Bread* (q.v.), the focal point of the meetings of the early Church (Acts 20:7).

Concision. A term meaning "mutilation," and used by Paul (Phil. 3:2) in condemning the practice of making Gentiles subject to circumcision; such legalism amounted to spiritual mutilation.

Concubine. A woman held as a secondary or lesser wife; although practiced in the Middle east, Greece, and to some extent in Rome, and allowed by God in Israel, it violates God's ideal for marriage and was clearly condemned by our Lord Jesus Christ.

Concursive operation. God's working through human beings in the composition of Scr.; God used human personalities, yet achieved exactly what He intended as inerrant revelation.

Confession. The act of acknowledging one's sin (1 Jn. 1:9, 7n) or faith (Mt. 16:16).

Conscience. (1) A God-given internal guide that leads us to discern right and wrong; however, it can be damaged by sin (1 Tim. 4:2; Tit. 1:15), and hence is not entirely reliable; in this age the child of God is to rely on the infallible Holy Spirit; (2) the second dispensation; Gen. 3:7n; *S.* ch. 2, The Nature of the Bible.

Conversion. (1) A general term for the new birth; (2) more specifically, a translation of Heb. and Gr. words descriptive of turning from sin to God (Acts 3:19); Rev. 7:14n (regarding conversion during the tribulation).

Conviction. The inner witness of the conscience or Holy Spirit concerning some aspect of the will or truth of God; Acts. 3:27.

Corban. From a Gr. word for "offering" in the sense of a presentation gift; the

Pharisees allowed an individual to label his goods as "corban," thus avoiding using them for another person, i.e., they were "dedicated" to God; condemned by Jesus in Mk. 7:11–13 (7:11n).

Cornerstone. A figure of our Lord Jesus Christ, descriptive of His role in regard to the saving purposes of God; as such He is the foundation and beginning point, and provides perfect spiritual alignment, i.e., the work of God in saving human beings is perfectly accomplished through Him; this is an element of the larger figure of Christ as the *Stone* (q.v.); Isa. 28:16–17; 1 Pet. 2:6.

Cosmos (Kosmos). Transliteration of a Gr. word translated "world"; (1) some segment of humanity in general, the extent determined by the context, e.g., in Rom. 1:8 the word is used of the Mediterranean "world"; Mt. 4:8n; (2) as used esp. by John it refers to Satan's organized world system, in rebellion against God; Rev. 13:8n; Mk. 10:30n; cp. Lk. 2:1 (see note) where *world* represents a different Gr. word.

Council, Jerusalem. The meeting convened in Jerusalem as described in Acts 15:1–29; as a result of the conversation of many Gentiles, the question was raised as to whether they needed to observe the law after salvation; certain practices were enjoined upon them to keep from offending Jews; a crucial meeting, historically and theologically, since it shows that believers are not under the law; Acts 15:13n, 16n, 19n.

Covenant. (1) Generally, an agreement between two parties; (2) used esp. of the compacts between God and human beings, initiated and upheld by God; as such, these form the framework of the outworking of the purposes of God with humanity; Gen. 2:16n; Heb. 8:8n; *S.* ch. 2, The Nature of the Bible.

Covetousness. A sin, condemned under the law, consisting of a person's illegitimately desiring what does not belong to him; can be used in a positive sense, as in 1 Cor. 12:31.

Creation. The act of the eternal God of bringing both the physical and spiritual worlds into existence; Heb. 11:3 underscores the need to approach this doctrine from the standpoint of faith; Gen. 1:1n; 2:4n.

Creationism. (1) The view that the nonmaterial parts of the individual are fashioned by God for each new person; (2) the modern evangelical movement stressing the direct and nonevolutionary work of God in bringing the universe into existence.

Cross. As the immediate instrument for the death of Christ, this came to signify the work of God in providing salvation, as in 1 Cor. 1:18; Lk. 23:35n.

Crown. Used esp. of certain rewards promised to believers, e.g., the elder's crown in 1 Pet. 5:4.

Crucifixion. The form of punishment used to bring death to our Lord Jesus Christ; employed by the Phoenicians, Persians, Egyptians, Carthaginians, Indians, Assyrians, and others; considered by Jews to be the worst kind of death; Mt. 27:33n; Ps. 22:7n.

Cult. Used in biblical studies of any nonorthodox offshoot of biblical Christianity.

Cuneiform. Ancient writing system utilizing wedge-shaped elements; employed by various linguistic groups.

Cup. In addition to general use of physical items, this is used figuratively, e.g., "the cup of salvation" (Ps. 116:13), or the cup that contained the wrath of God, which Jesus in a sense had to "drink"; Mt. 26:39n.

Cupbearer. Wine taster and court official of ancient times, known in Egypt, Sumer, and Israel; Gen. 40:1ff; 1 Ki. 10:5.

D

Dagon. A Middle Eastern deity worshipped in several cultures, esp. by the Philistines; Jud. 16:21–23.

Damnation. Eternal separation from God.

Darkness/light. In addition to use in regard to physical conditions, darkness is a symbol of death, spiritual blindness, and the satanic realm (Eph. 5:11); light is associated with the Person and activities of God (1 Jn. 5:5).

Davidic Covenant. The promise made to David, guaranteeing eternal kingship over Israel through his offspring; 2 Sam. 7:16n; *S.* ch. 2, The Nature of the Bible.

Day of Atonement. One of the festivals of Israel; set aside as the single day on which the high priest entered the holy of holies; points to Israel's national cleansing, provided for in the cross but still to be effected; Lev. 16:30n, 23:27n; Zech. 13:1.

Day of Christ. Period of time associated with the fulfillment of promises of blessing for the Church, as it is removed from the earth at the rapture to enjoy the presence of Christ; not the same as the *Day of the Lord* (q.v.); 1 Cor. 1:8n.

Day of Destruction. That aspect of the Day of the Lord in which judgment falls upon those outside of Christ; occurs after the second advent; a concept described differently by various passages; Rev. 20:11n.

Day of the Lord. The important period of time beginning after the rapture of the Church, including the messianic kingdom of our Lord Jesus Christ, and culminating in the creation of the new heavens and the new earth; involves the fulfillment of promises—for judgment and blessing—for Israel; Rev. 19:19n; Ps. 2:9n; 1 Th. 5:2; Isa. 10:20n; Joel 1:15n; Zeph. 1:7n.

Daysman. A mediator or adjudicator; used in the AV in Job 9:33 (see note) to refer to the need for someone who could bridge the gap between human beings and God (NIV = *arbitrator;* NASB = *umpire*).

Dayspring. A term found in the AV of Job 38:12, where NIV and NASB have *dawn;* used figuratively in Lk. 1:78 in the AV (where NIV has *rising sun* and NASB has *sunrise*) to describe the coming of the Messiah (whether universally or personally is not clear).

Deacon. A translation of the Gr. word for "servant"; used generally for a servant (Rom. 13:4) and even of Christ (Rom. 15:8); one of two places of service in the local church; perhaps first established in Acts 6; qualifications are given in 1 Tim. 3:8–13; in a sense, being a deacon is being a servant; cp. *Overseer* (q.v.) and *Elder* (q.v.).

Dead Sea. Body of water in southern Palestine around which many biblical events occurred; lowest point of land surface in the world, almost 1300 ft. below sea level; contains unusual rich mineral deposits because of lack of outflow of water; also called Salt Sea.

Dead Sea Scrolls. A collection of documents dating from the second c. B.C. to the latter part of the first c. A.D.; discovered in caves near the residence of a Jewish sect *(S. Essenes),* at the northwest end of the Dead Sea; significant for studies of the O.T. text and N.T. backgrounds.

Death. (1) Spiritual death is a state of separation from God, caused by sin (Jas. 1:15); it is the condition of every human being born since the fall; reversed by the sacrifice of Christ; Eph. 2:5n; (2) physical death is a separation of the immaterial part of a person from the body; resurrection leads to a body suited for eternal existence; Heb. 9:27n.

Decalogue. The *Ten Commandments* (q.v.).

Decrees of God. God's overall plan for the universe, established in eternity past and worked out in time and eternity; Eph. 1:11.

Dedication, Feast of. An extrabiblical festival, instituted in the second c. B.C. during the Maccabean period; occasion for one of Jesus' discourses (Jn. 10:22ff).

Deism. The belief that God is not personally involved with the universe, although He may have created it; Eccl. 3:16n; cp. *Theism* (q.v.).

Deliverance. Used of physical escape, or change of situation (Rom. 4:25), it is also a general word for the sinner's escape from difficulty, esp. divine punishment; Dan. 12:1; Rom. 11:26.

Deluge. The flood of Gen. 7ff; *S. Flood.*

Demon. Evil spiritual being, apparently to be equated with the fallen angels, since Satan is called the prince of demons (Mt. 9:34); AV "devils," should be translated as "demons"; Mt. 7:22n.

Demonology. The area of theology devoted to the study of demons, their attributes and work; *S.* ch. 16, Angels.

Demoniac. A person possessed by a demon, as in Mt. 4:24.

Descent into Hades. The view that between His death and resurrection Christ visited those in Hades, the N.T. equivalent of the O.T. Sheol, the place of the dead, in this case, the unsaved dead, for the purpose of proclaiming salvation as a result of His recently accomplished cross-work; appeal for the view is made on the basis of such passages as Eph. 4:9–10; 1 Pet. 3:19–20; but see 1 Pet. 3:19n.

Devil. From a Gr. word meaning "hurler," "slanderer"; a fallen angel, apparently the highest of all created beings; Isa. 14:12–17; Ezek. 28:11–19.

Devoted thing. S. Anathema.

Diana of the Ephesians. Lat. name for a goddess worshipped in the Mediter-

ranean world (= Gr. Artemis, as in AV and NASB); Acts 19:28n.

Diaspora. S. Dispersion.

Dichotomy. Descriptive of the view of the makeup of the individual that sees him as made up of two parts, material/physical on the one hand and soul/spirit, etc., on the other; cp. *Trichotomy; S.* ch. 15, Doctrine of Humanity.

Dictation theory. The view that God impressed the revelation of Scr. on the human authors in such a way that their own personalities and conscious participation were suppressed; not consonant with the biblical evidence.

Disciple. Although a translation of a Gr. word meaning "learner" (and in the O.T., where it occurs once, Isa. 8:16, a translation of a Heb. word with a similar meaning), the term is used in a wider sense for any follower of Christ; Acts 11:26.

Discipline. Chastisement from man or God that has the purpose of improving behavior; for local churches, strict regulations are given regarding treatment of individuals; 2 Th. 3:14, etc.

Dispensation/Dispensationalism. A dispensation is a period of time during which God is dealing with human beings according to certain divine goals and human responsibilities; dispensationalism is the view that the Bible sets forth such distinctions, although there are different opinions on the exact number, from four to eight; Gen. 1:28n; *S.* ch. 2, The Nature of the Bible.

Dispersion. A translation of a Gr. word meaning "scattering"; used of forced or voluntary migration of Jews from the land, with subsequent resettling outside Palestine.

Dives. S. Lazarus and Dives.

Divination. The heathen practice of attempting to predict the future by any one of various means; condemned in Scripture and associated with demonic activity; Dt. 18:10.

Docetism. The view that our Lord Jesus Christ only appeared to possess humanity, but that He could not have because a union of deity with humanity would be unlikely or impossible; held by some in the early Church.

Doctrine. What is taught or held as true; in relation to the Bible, it is the Bible's teaching on a particular topic; *S.* ch. 9, Introduction to Bible Doctrine.

Documentary theory. The view that the Pentateuch was written in stages by (apparently) four authors/editors ("redactors"), each with a particular doctrinal and historical perspective associated especially with differing uses of the divine names; also known as the Graf-Wellhausen theory, after those who developed it; it is not compatible with the biblical text; Ex. 6:3n; Gen. 2:3n.

Dominion. Used esp. of God's entrustment of the earth to humanity, with responsibilities to fill and master it; Gen. 1:26n.

Doubtful things. Those practices for which there are no specific N.T. commands, and concerning which different believers may be led to view as either allowed or not allowed; *S. Legalism* and ch. 17, The Doctrine of Salvation.

Dragon. In addition to other uses, a figure of Satan, used in Rev. 12:3ff; stresses his power and ferocity.

Dream. In addition to ordinary usage, often a means of revelation from God; Gen. 12:6.

Drink offering. One of the sacrifices prescribed under the law, consisting of wine, pointing to the complete yielding of Christ as he poured out his life to death (Ps. 22:14).

Dualism. The view that the universe (or parts of it) operates under the influence of opposing and often contradictory principles or powers, such as spiritual versus material substance.

E

Earnest. As used in Eph. 1:14, the presence of the Spirit in the believer, guaranteeing the completion of the purchase transaction by God; Eph. 1:13n.

Ecclesiology. The study of the nature of the Church, esp. local; *S.* ch. 18, The Church.

Eden, Garden of. The location of the first home of humanity and the sin of the first pair; apparently in Mesopotamia, although exact site is unknown.

Edenic Covenant. Compact made by God with Adam; involved responsibilities on the earth and in the garden, having dominion over animals and nature, abstaining from eating of the tree of knowledge of good and evil; Gen. 2:16n; *S.* ch. 2, The Nature of the Bible.

Edification. Building up in the faith through teaching and fellowship; Eph. 4:12.

Edomites. A group descended from Esau that settled in southern Palestine on both sides of the *Arabah* (q.v.) or great depression; source of difficulty for Israel; Gen. 36:1; Obad. 9–18.

Efficacious grace. The working of God in an individual to lead that person to faith in Christ; it does not fail to reach its goal of eventually bringing the person into His presence; Rom. 8:29–30; Phil. 1:19; Jn. 1:17n; *S.* ch. 17, The Doctrine of Salvation.

El. Heb. generic word for deity, apparently denoting strength; used esp. of the God of Israel; Mal. 3:18n.

El Elohe Israel. A name for God appearing in Gen. 32:30; can mean "God, the God of Israel" or "the God of Israel is Mighty"; Gen. 33:20n.

El Elyon. Name for God translated "Most High" or "God Most High"; Gen. 14:18n; Mal. 3:18n.

El Gibbor. Name for God translated "Mighty God"; Isa. 9:6; Mal. 3:18n.

El Roi. Name for God appearing in Gen. 16:13 and translated "the God who sees me"; Mal. 3:18n.

El Olam. Name for God translated "Eternal God" or "Everlasting God"; Gen. 21:33n; Mal. 3:18n; *S. Eternality.*

El Shaddai. Name for God translated "God Almighty" or "Almighty God"; Gen. 17:1n; Mal. 3:18n.

Elder. Used generally of mature men who carried authority and were repositories of tradition; one of the two offices or places of service in the local church according to the N.T.; suggests age and maturity; *S. Overseer;* cp. *Pastor* (q.v.), a spiritual gift; Tit. 1:5n; *S.* ch. 18, The Church.

Election. Choosing, esp. of God's selecting individuals to be recipients of the blessing of salvation; 1 Pet. 5:13n; 1:20n; *S.* ch. 17, The Doctrine of Salvation.

Elohim. A plural noun, based on *El* (q.v.); generically, used of plurality of gods; esp. used of the God of the O.T.; Mal. 3:18n; Gen. 1:1n.

Eloi, Eloi. Aram. words used on the cross by our Lord Jesus Christ as He experienced separation from the Father; the name for God with suffix added indicating direct address: "My God, My God"; Mt. 28:46.

Emerods. As described in 1 Sam. 5:6, an incurable disease resulting from disobedience, involving tumors or swelling of some kind; some think it may be bubonic plague.

Emmanuel. S. Immanuel.

Encampment by the Sea. The temporary stopping place of Israel during the escape from Egypt, just before the miraculous deliverance through the Red Sea; Ex. 14:2.

Enoch, Book of. One of the O.T. pseudepigraphical books; *S. Pseudepigrapha.*

Ephraim. A son of Joseph; tribe, and land region allotted to it; name (along with "Israel") for the northern of the two Hebrew kingdoms; cp. *Judah* (q.v.).

Ephod. (1) An ordinary garment; (2) part of the prescribed dress of the high priest; Ex. 29:5n.

Epicureans. Followers of the philosopher Epicurus (341–271 B.C.); held that the goal of life was to seek happiness; encountered by Paul in Athens; Acts 17:18n.

Epistle. A letter, esp. those books of the N.T., such as Rom. or Gal., that were originally penned as correspondence to individuals or groups.

Eschatology. The study of future, and esp. final or last events in the divine program; ch. 19, Future Things.

Esdraelon. S. Jezreel.

Essenes. A Jewish sect that flourished between the second c. B.C. and the first c. A.D.; emphasized strict ceremonial life; *S. Qumran* and *Dead Sea Scrolls.*

Eternal God. S. El Olam.

Eternal life. Endless enjoyment of the fellowship of God; not simply endless life, since all, regenerate and unregenerate alike, possess that; the result of the new birth; Cp. *Eternal punishment;* Rev. 22:19; Jn. 3:36.

Eternal punishment. The antithesis of eternal life; endless separation from God under torment; Rev. 20:11–15.

Eternal security. The biblical teaching that God will not fail to bring into his presence for unending enjoyment of spiritual blessings those who have placed their faith in Christ; a corollary of election and efficacious grace, since what God purposes for those He chooses is certain to be accomplished; Jude 1n; Ezek. 18:24n; *S.* ch. 17, The Doctrine of Salvation.

Eternality. An attribute of God (also *eter-*

nity); He is above time, there was never a time when He did not exist, and He will never cease to exist; insofar as eternity involves human beings, it is not to be taken as endless time, since time as we know it is temporary; the concept, though impossible for us to fathom, can only be defined with reference to the Person of God; Gen. 21:33n; *S. El Olam.*

Eucharist. A term for the Lord's Supper, not specifically found in the Bible, but taken from the Gr. for "give thanks," after the words of our Lord as He took the bread and cup and gave thanks (Mt. 26:26–27); *S. Lord's Supper;* Mt. 26:20n; 1 Cor. 11:23n.

Euroclydon. A term used in Acts 27:14 for a Mediterranean storm, reflecting one of several variant readings *(S. Variant)* (Euroquilo, Eurakulon, and Eurokoidon are also found, for example); apparently, as suggested by modern meteorology, a storm with violent winds from the East-Northeast; transliterated from one Gr. reading in the AV; the NASB has Euroquilo; the NIV has "northeaster" (in quotes).

Evangelist. A person who does the work of evangelism, esp. a person with the spiritual gift of evangelizing; but note 2 Tim. 4:5, where Timothy is exhorted to do the work of an evangelist—apparently all are to be doing it, even though some may possess a special enablement from God to carry it out with greater fruit (as with the gift of giving); See Acts 21:8, where this is applied as a title to Philip, apparently for his possession and eminent use of the gift; the term also came to be used later for any one of the writers of the four Gospels; Eph. 4:11, two notes.

Evangelize. To proclaim the good news of free salvation in Christ.

Evangelism. The act of proclaiming the good news of salvation in Christ.

Evil. Physical or moral alteration of the divine harmony of the universe resulting in hurt and pain; ultimately due to sin, which has disrupted the earth and its systems as well as the internal character of human beings.

Evil speaking. As found in the N.T. and the O.T., defaming or slandering another person, as in Ps. 15:3 (AV); condemned in Ps. 34:13 and 1 Tim. 3:8, etc.

Evil spirits. Term for demons, esp. as they affect human beings; sometimes described as involved with or promoting sinful practices; probably the same as "unclean spirits" (translated, e.g., in Rev. 16:13, as "evil spirits").

Evolution. Although the term can be used validly of various processes in life, it is used to denote the specific teaching that all life forms as we now know them, and that ever existed, developed from simpler forms of life over a long period of time, with or without divine direction; it should be firmly stated that such a view is antithetical to the biblical teaching of the origination of life forms by God in the original creative week.

Exegesis. The actual practice of interpreting a document or other message, of studying it to determine its meaning; differs from exposition, which is a setting forth for an audience of conclusions already arrived at by an interpreter; differs from hermeneutics, which is the set of rules or principles that is used to carry out exegesis; differs from theology, which in one sense is the summary of findings from exegesis, although theology and exegesis must go hand in hand.

Exhortation. An appeal made to assume a course of action or change one already in progress, esp. in regard to spiritual decisions, as in Rom. 12:1 (AV), Heb. 13:22 (NASB, NIV); also, a spiritual gift, enabling an individual to minister with fruit to others in the Body of Christ by bringing about change in their lives; Rom. 12:8 (AV, NASB; NIV = *encourage*).

Exile. In addition to general uses, the specific removal of major segments of Israel from the land of Palestine, as to Assyria in 721 B.C. and Babylon in 604 B.C.

Exodus. Israel's miraculously provided escape from Egypt and the control of Pharaoh, especially chronicled in the book of the same name; Ex. 1:8n; 25:1n; Num. 3:43n.

Exorcism. Attempts to alleviate demonic possession by use of magical formulas; exposed by Jesus in Mt. 12:25–28, as He showed He had true ability to control demonic forces and therefore the kingdom of Satan; Mt. 7:22n; *S. Demon*.

Expiation. A general term denoting the removal of the punishment due for sin; found in some translations, esp. where the concept of propitiation is present, although expiation usually has a wider reference.

F

Faith. Confident trust in the promises of God, centered in His provision of spiritual life through a sacrifice; it is the sole condition of salvation and is not a work, but, in fact, a gift of God (Phil. 1:29; Eph. 2:8); synonymous with *belief* (q.v.); Heb. 11:39n; Mt. 12:46n; Lk. 7:44n; Rom. 1:16n; 3:28n; Heb. 11; Jas. 2:26n.

Fall of man. The reversal of the original spiritual condition of humanity as a result of the sin of Eve and Adam, which was disobedience to God's express command; it resulted in a polluted nature, the inability to please God for spiritual benefit, and spiritual

and physical death; not a term found specifically in the Bible; Gen. 3:6n, 15n.

False prophet. Anyone who claims to speak from God but does not actually represent Him; condemned throughout the Bible; a key characteristic of the second beast of Rev. 13, who promotes deceptive teaching.

Familiar spirit. In occult practice, the presence of a demon with a conjurer, assisting in interaction with demons; condemned in Lev. 20:27.

Famine. In addition to expected use denoting absence of food, a sign, and instrument, of God's withholding of blessing, as in Amos 4:7.

Fasting. Abstinence from ingestion of food for a period of time; seen throughout the O.T. but specified under the law only for the *Day of Atonement* (q.v.); Lev. 16:29–30n; in the N.T. the legalistic fasts of the Jewish leaders were condemned by Jesus (Mt. 6:16), who fasted in the wilderness, although perhaps out of necessity; seen in the book of Acts, for example, at crucial times of decision making, e.g., 13:2–3; not specifically enjoined for believers today; Zech. 7:2n.

Fatalism. The view that events are impersonally determined and will come to pass regardless of our actions or intervention; a fallacious variant of the biblical teaching that events rest in the hands of a controlling, but benevolent, self-revealing, omnipotent, omniscient, personal, gracious God, who responds to prayer concerning the future and always seeks the best for His children; Eccl. 3:1n; 16n.

Father. In addition to the expected uses denoting human family relations (either in an immediate or more distant paternal relation, i.e., grandfather), the concept of father, with its corollary, offspring, is invoked in Scripture to describe the relation God sustains to

(1) the incarnate second Person of the Godhead (Jn. 8:38ff), (2) those who enter His family by the new birth and adoption (Rom. 8:15), (3) the nation of Israel (Isa. 63:16n; Mal. 1:6), (4) humanity in general (Isa. 9:6; Jas. 1:17).

Fatherhood of God. S. Father.

Fear of the Lord. Respect for God due to reverence and awe; not cowering or terror; although the unsaved may fear God for consequences due for their actions (Rev. 6:15–17), they are focused on themselves and what they will lose; reverential fear of God springs from knowledge of Him as a strict but loving heavenly Father, who never deviates from His promises for his own, both for blessing and (loving) chastisement; Ps. 19:9n.

Feasts. The seven yearly festivals of Israel; Lev. 23:2n; *S. Passover, Pentecost, Tabernacles.*

Federal theology. A view of the sin of Adam and the work of Christ that takes crucial acts of each as standing for those of others, that is, in a relation under a covenant (assumed to be invoked by God), with a representative acting for the benefit of others; the term *federal* in this sense is from the Lat. word *foedus,* "covenant"; this is supported by the biblical figure of the two Adams (1 Cor. 15:45) and the two "men" (1 Cor. 15:47), and especially by the crucial comparison in Rom. 5:12–21, where the sin of Adam becomes the sin of all by direct charge or imputation, and union with Christ (without our being present) effects salvation, just as union with Adam brought guilt (without our being present); Jas. 2:23n.

Fellowship. Based on the concept of sharing or holding something in common, fellowship can be (1) enjoyment of the presence of God by the believer, with sin confessed, obedience the prime goal, and fruit the result (1 Jn. 1:7n; Jn. 15:15n); (2) the possession of common spiritual assets by human beings (1 Jn. 1:7—"with one another"); (3) in some translations, giving financially to the needs of fellow believers (Phil. 1:5; 2 Cor. 8:4, both AV).

Fellowship offering. An NIV term rendered "peace offering" in the AV and NASB, this part of the sacrificial system pointed to the obtaining of communion with God; Lev. 3:1n; 7:1n.

Festivals. S. Feasts.

Field of Blood. S. Akeldama.

Figurative language. Any one of several linguistic features in which something other than the "expected," "usual," "frequent," or "normal" meaning is employed; involves a transfer of qualities from one object to another; includes metaphor, allegory, simile; *S.* ch. 6, Literary Aspects of the Bible, and ch. 5, Interpreting the Bible.

Fig tree. A tree native to the Middle East, with fruit that is an important feature of the diet; appears throughout Scr.; Adam and Eve made coverings from it (Gen. 3:7); its failure to produce was associated with difficulties of the nation (Jer. 5:17, etc.); in Mt. 11:18–21 and Mk. 11:12–14 Jesus curses a fig tree that had produced leaves but no fruit. This has been variously interpreted, but apparently has to do with the number of crops a tree produces during a year and the relation of leaves to fruit. In this case the tree should have had fruit as well as leaves, and is a figure of appearing to be useful but in reality producing no fruit; Mk. 11:13n.

Firmament. An AV term (NASB and NIV have "expanse") for the first element brought into existence on the second creating day; according to the NIV this refers to the sky, the physical "heavens."

First resurrection. As used in Rev. 20:5, this is the physical resurrection of believers before the millennium, and occurs after the second advent of Christ; it is not the new birth, as some amillennialists claim, since the context involves two instances of the Gr. word equivalent to "came to life," which must be parallel; since the second (v. 5a) is clearly physical, the first must be also; the event serves to populate the earth for the kingdom with saints who died during the tribulation period and probably O.T. saints; *S.* ch. 5, Interpreting the Bible, and ch. 19, Future Things.

Firstborn. An important genealogical and cultural feature; the firstborn in Israel enjoyed many privileges, in authority, inheritance, etc.; Mic. 6:7n; thus as applied to the work of our Lord Jesus Christ, it denotes His place of privilege as (1) the heir to power and glory (Heb. 1:6), (2) the first of many brought physically from the grave (Col. 1:18), (3) the Creator (Col. 1:16); in connection with the last passage, it should be emphatically stated that *firstborn* does not imply that He was created, since that is not the thrust of the passage and would also contradict other biblical passages.

Firstfruits. In the agrarian society of Israel, the sequence and production of crops played a major role in determining patterns of life; the first fruits of a crop were a reason for thanksgiving, which was to be directed to God (Ex. 23:18) along with the expectation that He would provide more; among other figurative uses (Rom. 8:23, etc.), *firstfruits,* when applied to the relation between the believer and Christ, points to His resurrection as the first of many more to follow (1 Cor. 15:20).

Flesh. A word found frequently in the AV as the translation of several different concepts, among which are: humanity in general (1 Pet. 1:4; Isa. 40:6); human tissue (Job 33:21); edible meat (Ex. 16:12); and the sinful human nature (Rom. 8:3; Jude 23n); the Heb. and Gr. words in such occurrences are rendered variously in other translations.

Fleshhook. Apparently forklike instrument used in manipulating meat sacrifices under the ceremonies of the law.

Fleshpots. Large containers, apparently made of bronze, used for washing or cooking; used figuratively in Ezek. 11:3 and elsewhere.

Flood. Usually used of the unique, world-encompassing catastrophe of Gen. 6–9; it occurred because of the sinfulness and rebellion of the race; was universal in scope; saw the deliverance of a righteous group; resulted in altered meteorological patterns; Gen. 7:10n; 8:14n.

Foot washing. An eastern practice quite reasonable in light of the conditions for travel; held up by our Lord Jesus Christ as an example of humility and a reminder of the need for inner cleansing (Jn. 13:4–17); mentioned in 1 Tim. 5:10 as an appropriate practice for widows.

Foreknowledge. More than simple prior awareness, foreknowledge involves God's active involvement in events and is causative, as in Acts 2:23; it is thus synonymous with planning or choosing (as translated by the NIV at 1 Pet. 1:20); 1 Pet. 1:20n; *S.* ch. 17, Salvation.

Foreordination. A word used in the AV at 1 Pet. 1:20; best translated "foreknowledge" or "choosing" on the basis of the Gr. word; *S. Foreknowledge.*

Forerunner. As found in some translations in Heb. 6:20 (AV, NASB), it denotes one who leads the way for others who will follow; a key element of the argument of the book of Hebrews, which conceives of life and the access to God as a journey: Jesus has completed the journey and will bring believers to the place where He is—the very presence of God.

Forgiveness. The condition of not being under condemnation for sin; this can be (1) positional in nature, as when God comes to view all who exercise faith as free from condemnation (Col. 2:13) or (2) practical, where the believer, who cannot come under judgment as a sinner, must nevertheless deal with those sins that cause disruption of the enjoyment of fellowship with God (1 Jn. 1:7n); Mt. 26:28n; 6:12n.

Former prophets. The books of Josh., Jud., (1 and 2) Sam. and (1 and 2) Ki. in the Heb. Bible.

Fornication. (1) In the narrowest sense, sexual infidelity while married (Mt. 5:32; 19:9); in wider senses, (2) any sexual relations outside of marriage or immorality in general (1 Cor. 5:1 = *incest*); universally condemned in Scr. and a figure of spiritual unfaithfulness to God (Hos. 6:10); *S. Adultery.*

Foundation. In addition to physical reference, the concept is used esp. of (1) the effects of the labor of the N.T. apostles and prophets in establishing the Church (Eph. 2:20) and (2) the work of Christ in establishing salvation (1 Cor. 3:11), suggesting its permanent effects and the ongoing constructive work of God in completing the Body of the redeemed; *S. Cornerstone.*

Fountain. Since water was a precious commodity in the usually arid regions of Palestine, the concept of plentiful supply provided an apt figure to describe the gracious provisions of God to satisfy spiritual thirst; Ps. 36:9 (of God Himself); Zech. 13:1 (of national cleansing for Israel); Jn. 7:37–38 (of the ample provisions of the Holy Spirit).

Frankincense. A prized incense and spice derived from certain trees, it was used in holy oil, burned with other materials for its fragrance, and even employed in the making of the showbread that appeared in the tabernacle; offered to Christ (Mt. 2:11) because of its value and perhaps because of its connections with priestly activity; Ex. 30:34n; *S. Incense.*

Free will. The extent of the actual freedom of human beings has long been debated by theologians and philosophers; the question centers on how much God determines human actions and how much He allows us to do on our own, and even how much our environment conditions us; relevant to how salvation is entered into, how we cooperate with God in sanctification, and the problem of the existence and source of sin.

Freedom. In addition to uses related to society, this is used of (1) an attribute of God stressing the unconditioned nature of God's activity: He does what He does in complete freedom; (2) the ability of human beings to make their own choices *(S. Free will);* (3) release from the control of sin, as in Heb. 2:14–15.

Free woman. As used esp. in Gal. 4:22ff, this helps establish the figure (v. 24) of the enslaving nature of the law and the gracious character of the provisions of God in the cross.

Friend of the bridegroom. As found esp. in Jn. 3:29, the use of the concept of the oriental equivalent of the contemporary best man to describe the joy of one who lives to serve another.

Fringes. The decorative hem of a Jewish garment, designed to remind of God's commands; Num. 15:38–39.

Fruit. A figure of spiritual productivity, stemming from the concept that the recipient of God's grace should return his time and energy to God in appropriate service; the conditions for bearing fruit are confession of sin, obedience, and dependence; Jn. 15:2n, 4n, 8n.

Fullness of the Gentiles. A term used in Rom. 11:25 (see note) in the AV and NASB to refer to the completion of the salvation of elect Gentiles during this age, with consequent national blessings for Israel; NIV = *full number of the Gentiles;* cp. *Times of the Gentiles.*

Fullness of time. As used in Gal. 4:4 and Eph. 1:10 (AV and NASB), this denotes the existence of the perfect time in the plan of God for certain events to occur; in the first instance it is the appropriate time for the incarnation, with international events, language features, the condition of Israel, etc., all in place; in the second instance, it points to the eschatological point where the events of human history are brought to a climax in Christ, namely the millennium and the New Heavens and New Earth *(S. Eschatology); S. Fullness of the Gentiles.*

Furnace. Figuratively, this is suggestive of trial, as in Isa. 48:10.

G

Gabriel. One of only two named angels in the Bible, the other being Michael (the only archangel?); always appears in an announcing role, so apparently he is God's messenger par excellence; the name means "man of God" or "strong one of God"; Lk. 1:26ff.

Gadara, Gadarenes. Gadara was a town several miles southeast of the Sea of Galilee, and the capital of a Roman province; the Gadarenes were its inhabitants; the site of the healing of the two demon-possessed men and the self-

destruction of the pigs, as found in Mt. 8:28ff and parallels; the term is one of several variant readings, among which are Gergesenes and Gerasenes, putting the exact intended location in doubt.

Galilee. Region of northern Palestine, significant esp. for the ministry of our Lord Jesus Christ there (site of the majority of His miracles and of His transfiguration) and the positive response of the people to Him.

Gall. (1) One of several bitter substances; (2) the product of a particular plant whose exact nature is difficult to identify; (3) a description for the bitter character of the drink offered to Jesus on the cross; (4) a metaphorical term for difficulty or trial (Acts 8:23).

Gap theory. The view that original creation is described in Gen. 1:1, but between vv. 1 and 2 there was a "gap" of an indeterminate length of time; during that period Satan fell, resulting in a condemned earth (which was his domain); that judged state is reflected in v. 2 by the description of the earth as "waste and void"; appeal is made to Isa. 45:18 in the AV to support the view; it attempts to allow for long geologic periods in the early verses of Genesis; however, the NIV of Isa. 45:18 will not allow that verse to be used to support the view; further the Heb. grammar of 1:1–2 stands against it; the role of Satan in regard to the earth required by the view does not fit with the rest of Scr.; the view's resulting interpretation of v. 3 as a re-creation forces us to view v. 1 as the only account of original creation; although the view was espoused in *The Scofield Reference Bible* of 1909, and is allowed for in subsequent editions, there are many exegetical points that militate against it; Gen. 1:2n; Isa. 45:18n.

Gehenna. The term "hell" in the N.T. is

the translation of the Gr. *geenna,* based on the Heb. *ge-hinnom,* "Valley of Hinnom"; this was the area directly to the south of Jerusalem, in earlier times the place of child sacrifice (2 Chr. 28:3), and in later times the site of a refuse dump with accompanying continual fires, thus engendering an image of everlasting punishment; whereas Sheol in the O.T. and Hades in the N.T. denote the place where dead people go, Gehenna has the aspect of torment, and is apparently identical with the lake of fire (Rev. 19:20); Mt. 5:22n.

Genealogy. Far from being lifeless records of obscure generations, the biblical genealogies are important elements of revelation; although many historical and chronological difficulties are associated with them, occasioning much scholarly research, they are useful in showing (1) God's concern with the contributions of individuals to His dealings with humanity (e.g. faithfulness), (2) the line of descent of the Messiah (Mt. 1:1n; Lk. 3:23n); Gen. 11:10n; Dan. 5:2n.

General Epistles. The books of James, 1 and 2 Peter, 1, 2, and 3 John, and Jude (some include Heb.); called "general" or "catholic" (= "universal") because of their audience and topics; also called Catholic Epistles; *S.* Scofield Bible, Introduction to the General Epistles.

General revelation. God's disclosure of Himself, available directly to all, given through means other than dreams, visions, direct words, and Christ Himself; seen in (1) nature (Ps. 19:1–6; cp. 8–14); (2) the composition of human beings as intelligent, rational, and spiritual (Acts 17:24–28); (3) the conscience (Rom. 2:15), (4) the events of history as they manifest a divine controlling hand (Acts 17:26); while falling short of showing attributes of God

such as holiness, omnipresence, etc., it is apparently designed by God to lead people to inquire further into spiritual realities, and, in fact, can itself be a point of condemnation, if rejected (Rom. 1:18–20).

Gennesaret, Lake of. S. Sea of Galilee.

Gentiles. The nations other than Israel; to the Jew, all non-Jews were Gentiles; they were established as "other" than Israel by the selection of the nation of Israel by God for blessing; Acts 15:19n; Ezek. 25:8n; Gen. 11:10n; Acts 10:11; Eph. 3:6.

Gergesenes, Gerasenes. S. Gadarenes.

Gethsemane. A translation of the Aram. term for "oil press"; a garden on the Mount of Olives east of Jerusalem and across the Kidron Valley; a frequent resting place for Jesus, and the scene of His agony on the eve before His crucifixion.

Gift, spiritual. S. Spiritual gift.

Giving. All believers are to give of their material possessions in response to God's grace (2 Cor. 8:9) and as *believer-priests* (q.v.) (Heb. 13:16); some are specially equipped by God to see needs and to give unselfishly, as a result of possessing the gift of giving (Rom. 12:8); 2 Cor. 8:1; 1 Cor. 16:2; *S.* ch. 18, The Church.

Ghost, Holy. S. Holy Spirit.

Glory. An attribute of God, describable as the sum total of His perfections; it cannot be defined with reference to anything we know.

Glossolalia. Speaking in tongues, as in Acts 2:4; *S. Tongues.*

Gnosticism. A religious philosophy prevalent in the ancient Middle East; it assumed many forms and was affected by other religious movements with which it came in contact (syncretism); it involved primarily an emphasis on dualistic principles (e.g., light versus darkness) and the acquisition of knowledge; posed problems for early

Christianity in that its ideas infiltrated Christian teaching; the exact extent of its influence on the churches, groups, and individuals for whom the N.T. documents were written continues to be a matter of debate; Col. 2:18n.

God. A personal, infinite, spiritual, rational, intelligent, holy, eternal, self-existent Being, the Creator of the universe and Sustainer of all things; He is three Persons in one, yet not divided or capable of division; *S.* also individual names of God; Rom. 1:18n; Nah. 1:2n; Ezek. 16:60n; Isa. 45:7n; Mt. 28:19n; Jn. 1:18n.

Godliness. The goal of true spiritual endeavor, correspondence to the characteristics of God Himself; 1 Tim. 4:8.

Gog and Magog. A phrase occurring in Rev. 20:8 and Ezek. 38–39; the former occurrence falls in a description of a rebellion that occurs after the kingdom, in which Satan, released from 1000 years of captivity, shows his inveterate sinfulness as he attempts once again to overthrow God; *Gog and Magog* is a phrase that apparently denotes representative rebellious nations or groups; the occurrence of the in Ezek. 38–39, where a defeat by the Lord Himself of an army invading Israel, has been associated with the middle and end of the tribulation period, and even the earliest stages of the kingdom, after the second advent; the last view has much to commend it; Ezek. 38:2n.

Golgotha. An Aram. word meaning "place of a skull"; the term used by Mt., Mk., and Jn. for the site of the crucifixion of Christ; Lk. has Gr. *kranion,* "skull," which in the AV is transliterated as "Calvary," from the Lat. word for "skull"; Mk. 15:22n; *S. Calvary.*

Good news. A translation of the Gr. word *euangelion;* another name for the message of the Gospel.

Gopher wood. Used in the building of the ark (Gen. 6:14); there is disagreement as to its exact source.

Gospel. (1) The message concerning the Person and work of Christ (the word is from Old Eng.); Rev. 14:6n; 1 Cor. 15:1n; Gal. 1:16n; (2) one of the four accounts (Mt., Mk., Lk., Jn.) of His life and ministry.

Gospels. The four accounts of the life and ministry of our Lord Jesus Christ; *S.* Scofield Bible, Introduction to the Four Gospels.

Government, human. A dispensation, instituted in Gen. 8 and establishing regulations for human social responsibility and rule; Gen. 8:15n; *S.* ch. 2, The Nature of the Bible.

Grace. The unmerited favor of God toward sinners, who are unable to please God; cp. *Mercy,* His goodness toward those who are helpless and weak; Jn. 1:17n; 2 Pet. 3:18n; 1 Cor. 1:2n.

Grafting. A term borrowed from horticulture, used by Paul in Rom. 11:17–24 to describe the relation between Israel and the Gentiles during this age and the coming period of national blessing for Israel.

Grammatico-historical interpretation. The approach to the Bible that seeks to take its words and setting at face value; allows the Bible to interpret itself in its linguistic, cultural, and historical matrices; *S.* ch. 5, Interpreting the Bible.

Graven image. A wooden or stone carved replica of a deity, Jehovah or otherwise; forbidden under the law (Ex. 20:4); also translated as "idol" or "carved idol."

Great commission. The multi-part command of our Lord Jesus Christ, incumbent on all Christians, to spread the Gospel; consists of making disciples, baptizing, and teaching obedience; Mt. 28:18–20.

Great tribulation. A term occurring in Rev.

2:22 and 7:14 and Mt. 24:21; in the latter passages it refers to that future period of time during which God will bring judgments upon the earth primarily to bring a remnant of Israel to repentance; part of the 70th week of Daniel (Dan. 9:24–28); some use the term for only the last half (3½ yrs.) of the 70th week; Rev. 7:14n; Dan. 9:24n; Rev. 11:15n; *S.* ch. 19, Future Things, and ch. 2, The Nature of the Bible.

Greek. The language of a major power in the Mediterranean world, esp. from the fourth to first centuries B.C.; the language in which the N.T. books were written; *S.* ch. 4, The Language of the Bible.

Grove. (1) A word used in the AV to translate (erroneously) the term for an image of a Canaanite goddess, Asherah (NIV, NASB), as at 1 Ki. 15:13; (2) actual trees associated with idolatrous worship.

Guilt. The condition of a human being or angel as a result of violating a moral code, esp. God's; in regard to God's standards, guilt is a result of sin (the violation) and leads to punishment; God allows removal only on the basis of a substitute who acts as a stand-in for the guilty party.

Guilt offering. One of the prescribed sacrifices under the law; used in the NASB and NIV where the AV has *trespass offering;* stresses the need to remove the damage done by sin; Lev. 5:6n; 7:11n.

H

Hades. Transliteration of the Gr. word *hadēs;* found in the NASB and NIV; term for the place where dead people go, equivalent to O.T. Sheol; is also translated as "the depths," "the grave," and "hell" (always that in the AV).

Haggadah. Portions of the *Talmud* (q.v.), the collection of Jewish law dating to the early Christian era; includes commentaries on the entire O.T.

Hagiographa. S. Kethubim.

Hallel. S. Hallelujah.

Hallelujah. Heb. for "praise Yah" (shortened form of Yahweh); an invitation to worship, found either at the beginning or end of certain psalms; translated "praise ye the Lord" in the AV, "praise the Lord" in the NASB and NIV; *allēlouia* is the Gr. word found in Rev. 19:1, 3, 4, 6 and rendered "Halleluia" in the AV and NIV, and "Alleluia" in the NASB; the "Hallel" is the group of psalms from 113 to 118, so called because they begin with "hallelujah"; Ps. 113:1n.

Hamartiology. The doctrine of sin, human and angelic; *S.* ch. 14, The Doctrine of Sin.

Hardening. Spiritual dullness, stubbornness, and rejection of the things of God; Ex. 4:21; Heb. 3:8.

Healing. In addition to references to normal and miraculous physical improvement, this is a spiritual gift in the early church; as with all miraculous activities by human beings, it is designed—as a sign-gift—to attest the message and those bringing it from God; neither our Lord nor the apostles healed everyone, although the former could have; hence, miraculous healings are designed to get attention and turn it to something else; for this reason they are found in periods when God is seizing our attention in drastic ways; of course, God can work miracles at any time; the issue, however, is one of determining what He has set forth as the trends, movements, and purposes in His plan; one should not look for the presence of this sign-gift today; 1 Cor. 14:1 Lk. 5:12n; 9:11n; Isa. 53:4n.

Heart. A term used esp. of the nonmaterial part of a person; it can refer to what might elsewhere be described as the mind, the emotions, the will, the spirit, etc.

Heave offering. An offering found in Lev. 7:28–34, involving particular animal portions lifted up ("heaved") toward God.

Heaven. (1) The physical canopy around the earth and space beyond it; (2) the spiritual realm, inhabited by God and angelic beings—not to be associated (except metaphorically) with a particular direction; the exact correlation of these two meanings with the tiers of heaven suggested by 2 Cor. 12:2 (see note) has been debated.

Heavenlies. A translation (AV) in Eph. 1:3; 2:6; 3:10 of a term found also in Jn. and Heb.; in Eph. Paul uses the Gr. word to point to the spiritual realm as the true source and center of our life after salvation, esp. as our assets are found in Christ (Eph. 1:3n).

Hebrew. A term used, beginning in Gen. 14:13, to refer to Abraham and his descendants; origin in dispute; the language of that people; Gen. 14:13n; *S.* ch. 4, The Language of the Bible.

Heifer. Denotes a young cow as used in various sacrificial ceremonies; used figuratively of Israel, as in Hos. 4:16.

Heir. Since eastern and Mediterranean societies had laws and customs much as we do today, the figures of heirship, inheritance (esp. as associated with death) and contracts for bequeathing were utilized in Scr.; Eph. 1:14; Heb. 8:6ff, 1 Pet. 1:4, etc.

Hell. Used as a translation of several biblical words: Heb. *sheol,* Gr. *hadēs, geenna* and *tartaroō* (= "confine to Tartarus," 2 Pet. 2:4 only); the first two words describe the place where dead people go, the third refers to a place of punishment; thus "hell," as used in various translations, encompasses a wide range of meanings; *S. Hades, Gehenna, Sheol, Tartarus.*

Hellenists. Jews who adopted the Gr. language and Gr. customs; Acts 6:1; 9:29.

Heresy. Departure (by an apparent believer) from doctrine considered to be normative or orthodox, as at 2 Pet. 2:1; the person can still be considered to be regenerate; heresy differs from apostasy in that the latter describes a person who appears to be genuine and at some point rejects association with the things of God, although it may be difficult to tell the difference in some instances; the term is used in the N.T. of a faction or splinter group (Acts 5:17, of the Sadducees; 1 Cor. 11:19, of sinful divisions at Corinth).

Hermeneutics. The science of interpreting documents; a hermeneutic (sing.) is a set of guidelines and procedures for deriving meaning from any document; used of the Bible student's system of approaching the Bible to understand it; *S. Interpretation* and ch. 5, Interpreting the Bible.

Herod. Family name of a number of part-Jewish, part-Idumean (Edomite) rulers appointed under the Romans to govern different parts of Palestine: Herod the Great (40–4 B.C.); Herod Archelaus (4 B.C.–6 A.D.); Herod Antipas (4 B.C.–39 A.D.); Herod Agrippa I (37–44 A.D.); Herod Agrippa II (53–70 A.D.); the history of the family is full of sordid intrigue; not to be confused with the *Herodians* (q.v.).

Herodians. A political party of the first century, opposed to Christ; favored Roman rule; Mt. 22:16.

High places. Raised locations used for worship, esp. heathen; encountered by Israel in entering the land; condemned throughout the O.T., they were nevertheless a stumbling block for Israel; the term can be used positively of any physical location; 1 Ki. 14:23b; some legitimate use in worship of Jehovah is observed, as in 1 Sam. 9:12; 1 Ki. 3:2n.

High priest. One of the order of priests under the law; Aaron was the first; had special duties, attire, marriage regulations, inauguration into office; as the leader in the task of bringing people to God, the high priest pointed to the work of Christ, the "great high priest" (Heb 4:14); Ex. 28:1n; Lev. 8:12n; Ex. 29:5n; Jn. 17:1n; Zech. 6:11n.

Higher criticism. (1) That portion of biblical studies that attempts to assess compositional features such as date of writing, authorship, destination, sources used in writing (oral, written, etc.), and general literary form (including comparison with contemporary nonbiblical literary features and styles); done constructively and with a high view of the integrity of Scr., this area of study can make important contributions; done without a high regard for Scripture it can be a destructive influence; hence, the term is sometimes used (2) for rationalistic approaches to the Bible over the last hundred years that tended to treat it solely as a human work, not as an integrated revelation from God; cp. *lower criticism* (= *textual criticism,* q.v.), which deals with establishing the best text of Scr. to work with.

Hinnom, Valley of. A steep depression located on the south and southwest sides of Jerusalem; named after a person; first mentioned in Josh. 15:8; site of idolatrous worship and human sacrifice by Israelites; later location of Jerusalem's refuse dump; *S. Gehenna.*

Hireling. A temporary laborer, often foreign, as opposed to a native worker with some share and interest in production of a crop or care of a flock: used in Jn. 10:12–13 as an illustration of one who does not exercise great care for those entrusted to him, as opposed to the concern of Christ for His own.

Historical books. That portion of the O.T. canon from Josh. through Est.; a modern, not ancient, distinction; *S.* Scofield Bible, Introduction to the Historical Books.

Hittites. A people inhabiting Asia minor beginning in the early second millennium B.C.; they were Indo-Europeans, coming originally from central Europe; hence, their language, as has been demonstrated in this c., is related to Gr. and Lat.; mentioned often in the O.T. in connection with frequent contacts with Israel after the latter entered the land; 1 Ki. 7:6.

Holiness, Holy. Holiness is an essential attribute of God; as such it involves separation from impurity and evil (although evil itself must be defined with reference to this quality of God Himself); positively stated, it is the quality of moral perfection; in human beings, it denotes separation from sin and evil and to God; Mt. 4:5n; the word *saint,* found in some versions, is a translation of a related form of the Gr. word behind *holiness* and *holy.*

Holy of holies. The inner section of the holy place, both together comprising the tabernacle; Heb. 9:6–7 refers to them as "the first tabernacle" and the "second tabernacle" or "the inner room" and "the outer room," and to the inner portion as "the most holy place"; the holy of holies was separated from the holy place by a veil; it contained the ark of the covenant and was the place where God dwelled in the midst of Israel; it pictures, as part of the ritual under the law, accessible as it was only by the high priest, the work of Christ as our High Priest, who alone can take us into the presence of God; Ex. 25:10n.

Holy One of Israel. A name for God, used particularly of Isaiah.

Holy place. The outer, larger, section of the tabernacle; it contained the golden candlestick, showbread, and altar of incense, and was accessible by priests other than the high priest.

Holy Spirit. The third Person of the Holy Trinity; translated as "Holy Ghost" in some versions; not a mode of manifestation of God or simply an influence, but a Person, as fully deity as the Father and Son; seen in the O.T. as active in creation, as speaking through the prophets (Isa. 10:10), as leading Israel in the wilderness and being rebelled against (Ps. 106:32–33); and more extensively in the N.T. as indwelling believers (2 Cor. 1:22), guaranteeing their salvation (Eph. 1:13), teaching (Jn. 16:12n, 13–14), guiding in the writing of Scripture (2 Pet. 1:21n), filling believers for control (Eph. 5:18), interceding (Rom. 8:26); giving assurance of salvation (Rom. 8:16), searching the heart (1 Cor. 2:10), giving spiritual gifts (1 Cor. 12:4n; Heb. 2:4), etc.; Zech. 12:10n; Acts 2:4n.

Homologoumena. Term used by Church Fathers for biblical books accepted as canonical.

Homosexuality. A sin condemned both in the O.T. and the N.T.; in that it involves sexual desire and activity directed toward a member of the same sex, it violates God's pattern given in creation for love and sexual activity in marriage between male and female; Lev. 18:22; Rom. 1:26–27.

Hope. The biblical picture of hope involves something quite different from everyday expectation of the future; it is conditioned by the promises of a God who controls history, has revealed His will to human beings, knows the end from the beginning, controls life and death, and delights in blessing his children; biblical hope has God Himself as its object and the center of its expectation of the future; intimately bound up with faith (Heb. 11:1).

Horn. In addition to references to physical objects, this is used figuratively to denote strength and ruling power; Dt. 33:17; Zech. 1:18.

Hosanna. A transliteration of the Heb. imperative (command) word for "save" combined with a word meaning something like "please," found in requests; used in the O.T. only in Ps. 118:25, and in the words of the crowd during the triumphal entry of our Lord Jesus Christ into Jerusalem.

Host (of heaven). Also *heavenly host;* (1) used of angelic beings (Lk. 2:13); (2) perhaps of Israel (Dan. 8:10); (3) heavenly bodies as associated with idolatrous worship (Dt. 4:19).

Hosts, Lord of. This name of God, also translated "The Lord Almighty" (NIV) and "Lord of Hosts" (NASB) stresses His power in commanding the hosts of heaven, i.e., angels; Mal. 3:18n; 1 Sam. 1:3n.

Human government. S. Government, human.

Humility. A necessary virtue for the child of God; exemplified in our Lord Jesus Christ, as described in Phil. 2:5–11.

Husbandman. This agricultural role serves in the N.T. as a picture of God's work in "cultivating" and nourishing His children; Jn. 15:1ff; 1 Cor. 3:9.

Hyssop. Translation of O.T. and N.T. terms for various plants used esp. in sacrificial rituals, as in Ex. 12:22; Ps. 51:7n.

I

"I am" sayings. A series of statements used in a kind of word-play in the Gospel of John (4:26; 8:58, etc.), probably drawing on the language of

Ex. 3:14, where God reveals Himself as the "I am," the self-existent One; in most of their occurrences they are assertions of the deity of Christ; Ex. 3:14n.

Identification with Christ. A N.T. concept descriptive of the position of the believer; the death, burial, and resurrection of Christ are transferred judicially to the believer, corresponding to the breaking of sin's control and the ability and obligation to lead a new kind of existence, one that pleases God; pictured in baptism by immersion; Rom. 6:1–14.

Idolatry. Worship of anything or anyone (visible or not) other than the true God; condemned throughout Scr.

Illumination. The teaching ministry of the Spirit of God that imparts understanding of the message of Scripture to the believer; not to be confused with inspiration, which in the Bible is used of the work of God in giving Scr. (2 Tim. 3:16); 1 Jn. 2:20; Jn. 16:13.

Image. Negatively, a man-made depiction of an object of worship; positively, the correspondence that human beings have to their Creator (Col. 3:10), and the correspondence in essence and attributes of the incarnate Lord Jesus Christ to God (Col. 1:15; Heb. 1:3).

Image of God. S. Image.

Immanence of God. The presence of God in the universe and with human beings; contrasted with *deism* (q.v.); the pantheist *(S. Pantheism)* erroneously views God as one with the universe, i.e., everything is God; biblically He is in the universe but not coextensive with it; not to be confused with *imminence* (q.v.); *S.* ch. 11, God.

Immanuel. Found only in Isa. 7, 8 and Mt. 1:23; a description, meaning "God with us"; as such it is the longing of the righteous and the great need of humanity since the fall; to be permanently actualized in the new heaven

and new earth, as described in Rev. 21:22ff; Mt. 1:23n.

Immersion. A mode of *baptism* (q.v.) reflecting the believer's death, burial, and resurrection with Christ; *S. Identification with Christ.*

Imminence. This word, used outside the Bible to denote that an event can occur at any time, is used of a quality of the rapture of the Church prior to the tribulation, an event that can occur momentarily (not necessarily "soon"); 1 Th. 4:13–5:11.

Immortality. Life beyond physical death; possessed by all human beings; the issue in human life is whether or not it will be in the presence of God; Rom. 2:7.

Immutability of God. The attribute of God that describes Him as unchanging and unable to change (or be changed); Rom. 1:18n; Mal. 3:6.

Impeccability of Christ. The quality in the incarnate Son of being unable to sin; Jn. 8:46; Heb. 4:15.

Imprecatory psalms. Psalms directed to God requesting that He bring wrath on the enemies of the writer or of Israel.

Imputation. A term suggesting judicial activity, referring to both sin and righteousness; Adam's sin becomes the sin of all human beings in the judicial processes of God, and Christ's sacrifice is credited to those who exercise faith in Him; Rom. 4:3n; Jas. 2:23n; Phile. 18n; present also in the concept of *justification* (q.v.); Rom. 3:28n; Gen. 15:6n; *S. Imputed sin.*

Imputed sin. The sin of Adam became the sin of all human beings by direct charge; *S. Federal theology; S.* ch. 14, The Doctrine of Sin.

Incarnation. The uniting, within time and history, of the preexistent second Person of the Trinity with a full human nature; this began at Bethlehem and continues forever; Phil. 2:6n; *S.* ch. 12, The Person of Christ.

Incense. Used in sacrificial ritual, the odor produced is a symbol of prayer (Ps. 141:2); Ex. 30:1.

Inerrancy. A term applied to the Bible, although not specifically found in it; it denotes that the Bible, as originally written, possessed no humanly induced deviations from the message God intended to be recorded, and that it is true in every respect; 2 Tim. 3:16; 1 Cor. 2:13n; 2 Pet. 2:19n; *S*. ch. 10, The Bible.

Infallibility. Although some assert that this term has a different meaning from *inerrancy* (q.v.), the two terms are, for purposes of biblical study, synonymous; the Bible is infallible because inerrant, and inerrant because infallible.

Infant salvation. The belief that those below an "age of accountability" can be (or are) recipients of the grace of God for salvation; a difficult doctrine, because little is said about it in the Bible.

Infinity. An attribute of God, difficult to define due to our limitations and the fact that it can be viewed ultimately only with reference to God; denotes that He is without limit in all His attributes.

Inheritance. Although employed of human relationships, this is used to denote both the treasure the child of God has in heaven (Eph. 1:14) and God's anticipation of completing the process of salvation by bringing believers into His presence (Eph. 1:18).

Inherited sin. The sin of Adam resulted in a polluted human nature, passed down from generation to generation; the source of our acts of sin *(S. Personal sin);* contrasted with *imputed sin* (q.v.); 1 Jn. 1:8; *S*. ch. 14, The Doctrine of Sin.

Iniquity. Translation of various Gr. and Heb. words for aspects of sin.

Inner man. Term used by Paul in Rom. 7:22; 2 Cor. 4:16; Eph. 3:16; found in the AV and NASB (NIV = *inner being, inwardly*); describes respectively (1) the new nature as it seeks to please God, (2) the whole portion of a person that cannot be seen by others, (3) the part of a person that interacts with God.

Innocence, dispensation of. The first dispensation, starting in the Garden with the creation of Adam and Eve and concluding with the fall; Gen. 1:28n; *S*. ch. 2, The Nature of the Bible.

Inspiration. A term applied to the Bible denoting that it is the product of God's creative activity, figuratively breathed out from Him (2 Tim. 3:16n); applies to the process of recording Scr., not specifically to the people involved; actually, *expiration* would be a better term to reflect the concept of 2 Tim. 3:16; the result is *inerrancy* (q.v.); 1 Cor. 2:13n; 2 Pet. 1:19n; *S*. ch. 10, The Bible.

Intercession. The concept of pleading on another's behalf is applied esp. (1) to the work of the Holy Spirit in praying for believers when they are too overwhelmed to pray (Rom. 8:26; (2) the constant activity of the Son in keeping believers secure (Heb. 7:25); (3) the prayer activity of believers as they take the needs of others to God (1 Tim. 2:1).

Intermediate state. Although not found in the Bible, this is used to refer to (1) the time between Christ's death and resurrection, and (2) the condition of human beings between death and the resurrection of the body; it should be emphasized that at death the unsaved have their spiritual destiny sealed, receive no second chance, and are conscious, awaiting the judgment of the wicked, and the believer has the joy of entering immediately into the presence of Christ.

Interpretation. The act of examining a document or listening to a message in order to determine the meaning (to take in all the information) intended by the author/speaker; *S. Hermeneutics* and ch. 5, Interpreting the Bible.

Interpretation of tongues. A spiritual gift present in the foundational stage of the Church that was necessary for the decoding of the real-language messages given by those exercising the gift of tongues; 1 Cor. 12:1n; 14:1n; 14:27n.

Intertestamental period. The time period between the writing of the last book of the O.T. (Mal.) and the beginning of revelatory activity by God through the ministries of John the Baptist and our Lord Jesus Christ, approx. 400 to 4 B.C. *S.* Scofield Bible, "From Malachi to Matthew."

Irresistible grace. Used theologically to denote that the work of God in saving an individual proceeds first from God and does not fail to bring that person under the saving benefits of the cross, since it cannot be thwarted by human beings; Acts 26:14; Rom. 8:28.

Israel. (1) The name given to Jacob in Gen. 32:28; (2) the whole of the descendants of Abraham through Isaac and Jacob; (3) the northern kingdom during the divided-kingdom period; (4) those from the line of Abraham who have entered into the saving work of Christ (Rom. 9:6n); Rom. 11:26n; Gen. 11:10n.

J

Jah. Shortened form of Yahweh/Jahweh; found in names such as Isaiah; *S. Yahweh.*

Jahweh. S. Yahweh.

Jannes and Jambres. According to 2 Tim. 3:8, two individuals who opposed Moses; extrabiblical sources describe them as two of Pharaoh's magicians; they are held up as a pattern of false teachers and those who resist the truth.

Jealousy. As used esp. of God, this *anthropopathism* (q.v.) denotes His righteous concern that He alone be honored, as opposed to worshiping false gods; Ex. 34:14; Jas. 4:5.

Jehoshaphat. In addition to use as the name of several O.T. individuals, this is applied to the valley between Jerusalem and the mount of Olives, i.e., the Kidron; since the term means "Jehovah has judged," it seems to be descriptive of a future event, the judgment of the nations, rather than a name that was actually used.

Jehovah. A word that actually comes from the early middle ages and the work of rabbinic scholars in editing the O.T. text; it consists approximately of the consonants of *Yahweh* (q.v.), the sacred name, and the vowels of *Adonai* (q.v.); Mal 3:18n; Ex. 34:6n.

Jehovah Elohim. A compound name of God, combining the personal (Yahweh/Jehovah) and the generic (Elohim) names for God; Mal. 3:18n; Ex. 34:6n.

Jehovah-Jireh. A compound name of God combining the personal name and a word suggesting God's knowledge of the human situation that leads to provision, e.g. "the LORD provides"; Gen. 22:14; Mal. 3:18n; Ex. 34:6n.

Jehovah-Nissi. A compound name of God combining the personal name and "my banner"; hence "the LORD my banner"; stresses that God is the object of trust and source of provision; Ex. 17:15; Mal. 3:18n; Ex. 34:6n.

Jehovah-Rapha. A compound name of God combining the personal name and a word referring to healing; hence "the LORD who heals"; Ex. 15:26; Mal. 3:18n; Ex. 34:6n.

Jehovah-Sabaoth. A compound name of God combining the personal name and a word meaning "hosts" (= armies); expresses God's power; translated "LORD of Hosts" or "the LORD Almighty"; 1 Sam. 1:3n; Mal 3:18n; Ex. 34:6n.

Jehovah-Shalom. A compound name of God combining the personal name and the word for peace; hence "the LORD is peace"; Judg. 6:24; Mal. 3:18n; Ex. 34:6n.

Jehovah-Shammah. A compound name of God combining the personal name and a word describing location; hence "the LORD is there"; emphasizes the presence of Jehovah in the midst of Israel during the kingdom; Ezek. 48:35n (*S. Immanuel* for a similar concept); Mal. 3:18n; Ex. 34:6n.

Jehovah-Tsidkenu. A compound name of God combining the personal name and a word meaning "our righteousness"; hence "the LORD our righteousness"; Jer. 23:6; Mal. 3:18n; Ex. 34:6n.

Jerusalem Council. S. Council, Jerusalem.

Jesus. The human or personal name given by divine order to the incarnate second Person of the Trinity (Mt. 1:21); related to Joshua and Jeshua, the name means "Jehovah saves" or "Jehovah is salvation"; emphasizes His humanity; Ex. 14:30n.

Jew. An English word reflecting the Heb. and Gr. words for a person living in Judah, a descendant of Judah, or simply descendants of Abraham in general.

Jezreel. Personal and place name, used esp. for the city and associated plain in Issachar; used also as equivalent to the plain of Esdraelon; *S. Armageddon.*

Jordan. River and associated valley, part of a long and significant geological feature extending into Africa; contains the lowest land point on earth; significant in Israel's history esp. as a boundary; Gen. 13:10n; Josh. 3:1n.

Jot and tittle. Jot is from Gr. *iota,* the name for the smallest letter in that alphabet, equivalent to Heb. *yod;* tittle is the term used to describe small marks distinguishing letters, esp. in the Heb. alphabet; the phrase thus is descriptive of small and minute detail, as of the revelation of God or the law.

Jubilee. A festival under the law celebrated in the year after every forty-nine years; involved release of Israelites sold into slavery, restoration of land sold due to poverty, and rest for the land; inaugurated by blowing of trumpets; Lev. 25:28.

Judah. Name of a son of Jacob (Gen. 29:35) and other individuals; name for the tribe descended from him and for the region settled by the tribe in the land (along with the area allotted to the tribe of Benjamin), the southern portion of the divided kingdom; 2 Ki. 18:7n; Jer. 29:1n.

Judaism. The culture and religion of the Jews; Rom. 1:29n; Gal. 1:14n.

Judaizer. A person who follows, or encourages others to follow, Jewish practices, esp. regarding keeping the law as a Christian; Gal. 2:14 (only N.T. occurrence); the statement in Est. 8:17 that "many people became Jews" (NIV) is a reference to the same concept.

Judea. The territory occupied by the tribes of Judah and Benjamin; the southern of the divided kingdoms (versus Ephraim/Israel).

Judges. In addition to being the name of a Bible book, this refers esp. to the period of time before the presence of kings during which Israel was ruled by a series of judges; Jud. 2:18n.

Judgment. As an extension of the familiar concept of accountability between human beings, this is used esp. of spiritual accountability, e.g., in the local church (1 Cor. 5:3), of the unsaved of all ages (see notes, Rev. 20:11–15), etc.; Rom. 2:2n.

Judgment of the nations. The event to occur at the second advent of Christ, involving the separation of the unrighteous from the righteous among those that are alive; Mt. 25:32n; Rev. 20:12n.

Judgment seat. From the Gr. term applied to the raised place where a judge listened to cases and rendered verdicts, this was applied to the work of Christ in evaluating the life of believers, as in 2 Cor. 5:10n; Rom. 14:10.

Just. A word used to denote equanimity and impartiality in decisions, this was used also as a positional term that describes a person's standing before God, viz., considered to be or viewed as righteous (Rom. 1:17; Hab. 2:3,4n); *S. Justification, Imputation.*

Justification. God's act whereby He declares that a person has met all His standards for holiness; the moral quality is God's holiness, the position is righteousness; God does not make a person holy, since moral perfection does not come until a person is in the presence of God; Rom. 3:28n; *S. Imputation.*

K

Kenosis. A term drawn from Phil. 2:7, where the Gr. word is *kenoō,* variously translated "emptied," "made [himself] nothing"; the question centers on what was "emptied" or in what sense there was a change in the second Person of the Trinity; unsatisfactory views have suggested, for instance, that in order to take on genuine humanity He laid aside His omniscience, omnipresence, glory, etc.; the biblical view must take into consideration that if He lost or even temporarily laid aside any of His attributes He would cease to be God; further, the text of Phil. 2:1–11 itself essentially defines the "emptying": it consists of taking on a human nature and being a servant; for God to live like a servant is truly an emptying, a degradation; Phil. 2:6n; *S.* ch. 12, The Person of Christ.

Kethubim. The Heb. word for the section of the Jewish canon known as the *writings;* also known as hagiographa (a transliteration of a Gr. word); consisted of Ruth, Chr., Ezra, Neh., Est., Job, Ps., Prov., Eccl., Song, Lam., Dan.

Keys of the kingdom. A phrase used in Mt. 16:19n, where in context Peter is given authority or power to carry out spiritual decisions *(S. Binding and loosing);* this is exemplified in the history of the book of Acts.

Kidneys. Kidneys were used in sacrifices and viewed as involved in what we would describe now as mental, emotional, or spiritual functions; in this latter use the word "reins" is found in some translations.

King. An important and pervasive biblical concept; human kings reign with the permission of God; Israelite kings were to reign in God's stead; all human kings are inferior to the greatest King, the Lord Jesus Christ (Zech. 9:9n).

Kingdom. As a portion of God's rule over human beings and the universe, the predicted kingdom for Israel is particularly prominent in the O.T., the gospels, and Acts; it is the time and configuration during which God is present with human beings in the Person of the God-man, who will rule visibly over humanity; the Kingdom Age is also one of the dispensations; *S. Millennium.;* Zech. 12:8n; 1 Cor. 15:24n; Rev. 20:4n; Ps. 72:1n; Ps. 2:6n; Isa. 65:17n; *S.* ch. 19, Future Things, ch. 5, Interpreting the Bible, and ch. 2, The Nature of the Bible.

Kingdom of God. In one sense, God's kingdom consists of all over which He holds sway, i.e., the whole universe

(Dan. 4:17n); although the kingdom of God and kingdom of heaven appear in some uses to refer to the same domain, each has distinctive references; the kingdom of God may refer to God's total rule over the universe or the sphere of the possession of life with God (Jn. 3:5–7); the kingdom of heaven (used only in Mt.) can refer to the sphere of profession, including true and false believers, etc.; Mt. 3:2n; 6:33n.

Kingdom of heaven. S. Kingdom of God.

King's highway. An important travel route from the Gulf of Aqabah to Syria, in use over two millennia by N.T. times; a contemporary north-south road through Jordan follows the same route; *S.* ch. 8, Essentials of Biblical Geography.

Kinsman. All cultures have what anthropologists today call kinship systems, known structures imposed upon certain human relations, blood and otherwise; Jewish society was no exception; the concept of kinsman, a male blood relative of specified distance from a given individual, figured in the practices of the avenging of blood (*S. Avenger of blood*) and slavery or debt redemption, a picture, esp. in the book of Ruth, of the redemptive work of Christ; *S.* the book of Ruth, Introduction, Ruth 3:9; 4:5; Isa. 59:20n; Lev. 25:49n; *S. Redeemer, Redemption.*

Knowledge. As an extension of normal use of the word in human activity (Gen. 1:28n), this is employed variously to describe the capability to take in spiritual truth, an ability given to the person who exercises faith in Christ (Eph. 2:8), and the particular spiritual gift of "knowledge," apparently special insight into divine activity and spiritual issues; the highest kind of human knowledge is that which has the Person of God as its object.

Koine. A transliteration of a Gr. word

meaning common, this was applied by the Greeks to languages that were in use across regional barriers and by significant numbers of people, as opposed to local dialects (the prevailing condition in the Gr. world until the time of *Alexander the Great* [336 B.C.], q.v.); *Koine* is used for the language of the N.T., a continuation of the form of Gr. of Alexander's time; Koine Gr. is the same as Hellenistic Gr.; *S.* ch. 4, The Language of the Bible.

Koinonia. A transliteration of a Gr. word, this denotes what is held in common or shared; often translated "fellowship"; spiritually, it describes (1) the portion that believers have of the life of God, (2) what believers hold in common with each other; *S. Fellowship* and references there.

L

Laity. Although this term is used by some to refer to believers in general who are not in ministerial service, it should be remembered that all believers in this age are priests before God and have equal access to Him; all stand on the same ground before Christ.

Lamb. This common animal is used esp. as part of the sacrificial ritual of the law, and as such, prefigures the Person and work of Christ, the Lamb of God; Jn. 1:35.

Lampstand. An article of furniture in the tabernacle; made of gold, with seven columns or branches, it portrayed God's attribute of light, esp. as seen in the incarnate Son; Ex. 25:31n; Zech. 4:2n.

Last Adam. As found in 1 Cor. 15:45, this portrays Christ as the one who reverses the effects of Adam's sin; in God's dealings with humanity, only two representative human beings are needed, a "first" and a "last" in the sequence of Adams, or a "first" and "second" man, again suggesting that only two human beings are needed to determine the destiny of the rest as far as condemnation and the possibility of life are concerned; Rom. 8:22n; 1 Cor. 15:22n.

Last days. This phrase, with variants *latter days, last day, last time,* points to the final stages of God's dealings with Israel and the Gentiles, esp. at the time of the second advent; Gen. 49:1n.

Last Supper. S. Lord's Supper.

Latin. The language of the Rom. people (actually a dialect spoken in and around Rome); since it was the language of those occupying Palestine during the N.T. period, a number of Lat. terms are found in the N.T., e.g., *centurion, colony.*

Latter prophets. Those O.T. books described as the major and minor prophets; the whole prophetic section of the Heb. canon consisted of the latter prophets plus the former prophets, Josh., Jud., Sam. and Ki.

Laver. The basin in which priests washed before ministering in the holy place or at the altar; a picture of the cleansing work of Christ; Ex. 30:17–21; 30:18n.

Law. Used in several senses in the Bible: (1) man-made rules governing relations between human beings; (2) the three-part code given through Moses at Sinai (Ex. 20:1n); (3) the general principle of God's governance of human beings through regulations (Rom. 3:21); (4) the first five books of the O.T. in the Jewish Canon; (5) the dispensation covering the period from Sinai to the cross; (6) the rule of life ("law of Christ") during the present age, freedom under the love of God (2 Jn. 5n; Gal. 3:24n); *S.* ch. 2, The Nature of the Bible.

Laying on of hands. Jewish practice symbolizing association (Lev. 1:4) and sometimes the impartation of ability or gift (Dt. 34:9; cp. 1 Tim. 4:14); in the N.T. in Acts in particular it is connected with the giving of the Spirit (Acts 8:17 and 19:6), although the associative aspect should not be lost sight of, since in both instances the apostles were bringing into the Body of Christ a separated group (the Samaritans and the unsaved followers of John) and we are not told that the apostles "gave" them the Spirit; the raising up of Saul and Barnabas in Acts 13:2 by the Holy Spirit is followed by laying on of hands by the sending believers, indicating their association with the ministry initiated by the clear direction of the Spirit of God; Acts 6:6n.

Lazarus and Dives. A name for the account found in Lk. 16:20–25; the name for the rich man, Dives, is mentioned only in the Vulgate translation; *S. Vulgate.*

Leaven. In biblical times this was usually a small piece of dough kept from a previous baking session and turned sour, although initially it was made by various processes; pictures the presence of sin and evil; Mt. 13:33n; Lev. 7:13n.

Lectionary. A document for use in religious services with Scr. readings arranged according to particular sequences of holy days or for other special purposes.

Legalism. The attempt to please God by erecting rules where the Bible does not give them, and then making them binding on oneself and others; is not a matter of following those things that are commanded, or that have clear biblical principles associated with them, but of raising decisions on so-called *doubtful things* (q.v.) to the level of commands; *S.* ch. 17, The Doctrine of Salvation.

Legion. (1) A division in the Roman army consisting of several thousand men; (2) a large number of angels (Mt. 26:53) or demons (Mk. 5:9).

Leprosy. Applied to what was probably a range of diseases of the skin, and not necessarily what is now called leprosy; applied also to other forms of ceremonial uncleanness, such as fungus and mildew; Ex. 4:6n; Lev. 4:6n; Lev. 14:3n.

Leviathan. As used, e.g., in Job 41:1, a term for a twisting, writhing animal, perhaps aquatic, such as a crocodile; other identifications have been suggested for other occurrences.

Levirate law. A regulation found in Israel and other cultures, according to which a brother or other relative of a deceased husband marries the widow in order to support her; subsequent children are viewed as from the first husband; the source of the term is the Lat. word *levir,* which means "husband's brother"; Ruth 4:5n.

Levites. The descendants of Levi, and the tribe assigned priestly duties; Num. 1:47.

Levitical cities. Because the Levites had no specific portion of the land of Canaan, they were given certain other privileges, one of which was special access to forty-eight cities (which may have been used by others) with surrounding land that was their possession; Num. 35:1ff.

Levitical priesthood. Composed of those of the tribe descended from Levi, they had responsibilities at the Tabernacle and Temple; the high priest was a Levite, drawn from the line of Aaron; other Levites had attendant sacrificial and housekeeping functions; Num. 1:47n; *S. Levites.*

Liberty. The position of the believer during this age according to which there is no obligation to obey the law (Gal. 5:1ff), believers are free from bondage to Satan (Acts 26:17–18), and are to exercise spiritual discernment concerning those practices for which there are no specific moral commands (Rom. 14:1ff).

Life, Book of. S. Book of Life.

Life, eternal. S. Eternal life.

Light. Physical light, expressly stated in Gen. 1:3 as having been created by God, serves as a figure of the perfection and esp. truthfulness of God; 1 Jn. 1:5; Jn. 1:4.

Limited atonement. The view that sees the value of the cross-work of Christ as intended only for the elect, although sufficient for all; cp. *Unlimited atonement* (q.v.).

Literal/literalism. Literal is used of (1) taking messages at face value, i.e., interpreting elements as figurative only if there is evident warrant (the term *normal* is sometimes used as equivalent to this use); (2) translating any document from one language to another in such a way as to preserve the "form" of the first language, i.e., keeping the order and arrangement of words, the same parts of speech, etc.; *literalism* is used (1) with a negative connotation concerning such translating practices, and (2) of understanding language in such a way that minute details are emphasized apart from the overall sense of texts, with resultant distortion of the meaning (the Pharisees often did this); *S.* ch. 5, Interpreting the Bible, and ch. 4, The Language of the Bible.

Little horn. A term used in Dan. to represent (1) the world ruler of the tribulation period (Dan. 7:8n) and (2) Antiochus Epiphanes (Dan. 8:9n).

Locusts. A scourge of agrarian societies, this insect is prominent in the Bible in the sequence of plagues on Egypt and as a portrayal of chastisement by God upon Israel through other nations; apparently the same as the palmerworm (at a different stage of development); Joel 1:4n.

Logos. A transliteration of a word used exclusively by John (although the Gr. word is found often in the N.T.) primarily to describe Jesus as Himself a communication from God; translation is difficult, since "word," "utterance," "statement," leave something to be desired; the same concept is found in Heb. 1:1–2; Jn. 1:18; Rev. 1:5; Jn. 1:1n.

Long-suffering. An attribute of God and a virtue to be displayed by the believer; restraining anger when provoked or wronged; Rom. 9:22; Gal. 5:22.

Lord. This is used to translate Heb. *adonai* and Gr. *kurios,* in the O.T. and N.T., respectively; when it is used in the O.T. to translate *Yahweh* (q.v.), the personal name of God, it is rendered in many translations with large and small capital letters (LORD); Gen. 15:2n; Mt. 8:2n.

Lord of Hosts. S. Jehovah-Sabaoth.

Lord's day. The first day of the week as a celebration of the resurrection of our Lord Jesus Christ; not in any sense a Sabbath.

Lord's Prayer. The name applied to the prayer of Jesus found in Mt. 6:8–15 and Lk. 11:1–4; a comprehensive prayer associated particularly with anticipation of the kingdom; perhaps in some sense a model prayer, but not to be slavishly repeated; Mt. 6:9n, 12n, 13n; Lk. 11:2n.

Lord's Supper. Paul's term for the ordinance involving partaking of the bread and cup (Luke's term in Acts is "breaking of bread"); a picture of our life with Christ made possible through His sacrifice; sometimes associated with a meal, as in 1 Cor. 11:17ff; also called *Lord's table* (1 Cor. 10:21), *communion, participation* (both, 1 Cor. 10:16), *eucharist,* and *Last Supper* (the latter two not in the Bible); oblig-

atory for believers during this age; Mt. 26:20n; 1 Cor. 11:23n.

Lower criticism. Textual criticism (q.v.).

Lots. A method of determining the divine will in various kinds of situations; last found in Acts 1:26 and no longer valid or useful due to the indwelling presence of the Holy Spirit in believers during this age; Prov. 16:33.

Love. (1) An attribute of God; He always desires to impart Himself to His creatures; (2) by extension a virtue to be displayed by believers; Jn. 21:15n; 21:17n; 1 Cor. 12:31n; Mal. 1:3n; Dt. 6:5n.

Love feast. A meal associated with the *Lord's Supper* (q.v.), as in 1 Cor. 11:17ff; apparently optional and not universally practiced in the early church.

Lucifer. A term found in the AV of Isa. 14:12, translating the first part of a Heb. phrase that is literally "shining one, son of dawn"; *lucifer* is the transliteration of a Lat. word meaning "light bearer," and was used in Lat. to refer to the planet Venus, because of its morning brightness; the NIV translates the Heb. "shining one" as "morning star," and the NASB renders it "star of the morning"; in context, the term is used of the king of Babylon, but points beyond him, as do the following verses, to Satan; it thus denotes the brilliance of the highest angel before his fall; Lk. 10:18; Rev. 9:1; Isa. 14:12n.

Lust. A particular sin, involving inordinate desire, sexual or otherwise.

LXX. S. Septuagint.

M

Maccabees. A name for the family, known also as the Hasmoneans, that first came to prominence in 167 B.C. during a revolt against the Hellenistic rulers of Palestine, described prophetically in Dan. 11:21–35; four apocryphal O.T. books speak of the revolt and the times; 1 Maccabees is considered the most reliable historically; some members of the Herodian family were descended from the Maccabees; *S.* Scofield Bible, "From Malachi to Matthew"; *S.* also *Herod.*

Magi. Plural of a common Gr. word for a religious functionary, this appears in the O.T. and the N.T., and is used esp. of the respected eastern (their exact homeland is unknown) visitors to the child Jesus in Mt. 2:1ff, where it is translated as "wise men" in the AV.

Magic. Associated in the Bible with idolatry and demonic activity, magic in the spiritual realm is consistently condemned; involves charms, spells, curses, witchcraft, etc.

Magnificat. The doxology of Mary given at the announcement to her of the birth of Christ, recorded in Lk. 1:46–55; it is prophetic in nature and speaks of the fulfillment of God's promises to Israel.

Magog. S. Gog and Magog.

Major prophets. The books of Isaiah, Jeremiah and Ezekiel.

Mammon. A transliteration of a Gr. word reflecting an Aramaic word meaning wealth; used negatively by Jesus.

Man of lawlessness. S. Man of sin.

Man of sin. Used of the world ruler of the tribulation period in 2 Th. 2:3; also translated "man of lawlessness" (NASB, NIV); 2 Th. 2:3n.

Manna. The Gr. form of a Heb. word meaning "what?" (i.e., "what is it?"); used of the food miraculously provided by God for Israel in the wilderness; Ex. 16:35n.

Manuscript. A handwritten portion of a document, may be a fragment or many books.

Maranatha. Transliteration of a Gr. word based on an Aram. word meaning something like "come, our Lord"; perhaps a slogan among Christians of the first c.; 1 Cor. 16:22n.

Mark of the Beast. The identifying symbol placed on followers of the world ruler of the tribulation period; Rev. 13:16.

Marriage. The institution involving one man and one woman, as established by God in the Garden; serves also as a picture of God's relation both to Israel (a wife) and the Church (a bride); Hos. 2:2n; Rev. 19:7n.

Marriage supper of the Lamb. AV and NASB term, appears as "wedding supper of the Lamb" in NIV; the celebration of the joy of the entire Church in the presence of Christ, occurring at the time of the second advent; Rev. 19:7–9, v. 7n.

Mars Hill. Mars was the Roman equivalent of the Gr. god of war, Aries; Areopagus ("Hill of Aries") is the name of a rocky hill in Athens; site of one of Paul's speeches (Acts 17:19, 22); may refer to the hill or to the council that met there.

Martyr. Anyone who gives his life for a cause; the Gr. word *martus* means "witness"; some died, as in the book of Acts, as a result of giving witness; strictly speaking, the word *witness* should not be taken to mean one who is ready to die for Christ, since that would be importing a later meaning; Rev. 2:13n.

Masoretes, Masorah. The Masoretes (or Massoretes), Jewish editors of the Heb. text of the O.T. from about 600 to 1000 A.D., devised vowel signs, punctuation, accent marks, and other textual helps; their comments on the textual problems are known as the *Masorah,* or "oral tradition"; their work forms the basis of Heb. texts used today; adj., *Masoretic.*

Meal offering. Also known as the grain

offering, this may refer to sacrifices in general or esp. to grain or cakes as offerings; Lev. 2:1n.

Measuring line. A cord or rope used in building; employed figuratively as a symbol of divine evaluation of spiritual conditions; Ezek. 40:3.

Meat offering. A translation in the AV of a term translated "meal offering" (q.v.) in others.

Mediator. Because of the inability of human beings to approach God due to their sinfulness, a go-between is necessary to bring them to Him; this concept is foundational to the work of Christ, the perfect and only Mediator, who opens the way to God and keeps it open; 1 Tim. 2:5; Heb. 2:1.

Meekness. A virtue enjoined upon believers; a fruit of the Spirit as found in Gal. 5:23; not timid acquiescence to all that occurs, but humility before God that trusts His purposes even in the face of personal insult and damage; rendered as "gentleness" in the NASB and NIV; Gal. 5:23.

Mene, mene, tekel, upharsin. As found in Dan. 5:25 and interpreted in 5:26–28, these words mean "numbered, numbered, weighed, and divided" in reference to the Babylonian kingdom of Belshazzar; Dan. 5:25n.

Mercy. The application of the goodness of God to those who are too weak to help themselves, and a trait expected of believers.

Mercy seat. The gold-covered lid on the ark of the covenant in the *holy of holies* (q.v.); it was the place where God dwelt among Israel; overarched by figures of two cherubim; Rom. 3:25n.

Messiah. A transliteration of a Heb. word meaning "anointed one"; used of the expected national deliverer of Israel; the linguistic equivalent of Gr. *christos,* "Christ" (q.v.).

Michael. One of only two named angels in the Bible (the other is Gabriel); also described as an archangel (ruling angel) in Jude 9; always appears in connection with Israel or an Israelite.

Midrash. A kind of commentary, esp. on the text of Scripture, compiled by rabbinic scholars.

Midtribulation rapture. The view that the Church will be taken to be with Christ before the second advent and at the middle of the tribulation period; *S. Pretribulation rapture* and ch. 19, Future Things.

Millennium. A word for the kingdom of Christ on earth; from Lat. words "thousand" and "year"; the reign of Christ is described as a 1000-year period in Rev. 20:2–7; Rev. 20:2n; *S.* ch. 5, Interpreting the Bible, ch. 19, Future Things, and ch. 2, The Nature of the Bible.

Ministry. In general, service, either public or religious; in the N.T. esp. it consists of service to those in need and to local groups of believers; all believers alike are called upon to be involved in ministry.

Minor prophets. The books of Hosea through Malachi in the O.T. canon.

Miracle. Any divinely introduced interruption of the "normal' order of life (of course life itself is sustained by God and is "miraculous"); in its use there may be an emphasis on God's power, on the signifying nature of the occurrence, or on the awe it engenders in the observers; Jon. 1:17n; Isa. 38:8n; Acts 28:8n.

Mitre. The headgear worn by the high priest, apparently a type of turban.

Mixed multitude. Those who were not of pure Jewish blood who accompanied Israel in the Exodus from Egypt.

Moabite stone. An archaeological artifact discovered in 1868 at Dibon in what is now Jordan; corroborates the biblical account of King Mesha in 2 Ki. 3:4–27.

Molech. An Ammonite deity, also found as "Moloch"; the cult devoted to this god practiced child sacrifice and was a condemned but continual bane to Israel in the O.T.

Molten sea. A large bronze basin in the Solomonic Temple, used by priests for washing (2 Chr. 4:6).

Moneychanger. Used in general of bankers who exchanged currency and performed other banking services (Mt. 25:27; NIV = *bankers*); also, the exchangers who conducted business in the Temple area to enable those making purchases and paying into the Temple treasury to convert their coinage to the required denomination; a malicious practice condemned by Christ (Jn. 2:13–17, etc.).

Monotheism. Belief in a single deity, whether the God of the Bible or otherwise (Islam is monotheistic).

Mosaic Covenant. Compact made by God with Israel detailing ordinances regulating Israel's life; Ex. 19:5n; *S.* ch. 2, The Nature of the Bible.

Most High. S. El Elyon.

Most holy place. S. Holy of holies.

Mount of Olives. The range of hills immediately to the east of Jerusalem and across the Kidron Valley from it; Zech. 14:4n.

Myrrh. A translation of words for two different kinds of resin used as an aromatic, in cosmetics and burial preparations, and as an analgesic.

Mystery. A truth hidden by God for a time and then revealed; not an "unfathomable truth," as some say; Eph. 3:6n; Mt. 13:3n, 11n; Col. 2:2n.

Mystery of iniquity. As found in the AV, the satanically energized plan that issues in the attempt during the tribulation to establish a human being, the Beast, as a counterfeit Messiah; the phrase is also translated as "mystery of lawlessness" (NASB) and "secret power of lawlessness" (NIV); 2 Th. 2:7.

Mysticism. The attempt at direct and unmediated knowledge and experience of God, as opposed to acting by faith based on written revelation from God.

N

Nabataeans. An Arab people who flourished from the third c. B.C. past the apostolic age; they occupied land in what is now southern Jordan, at times controlling territory into the Sinai peninsula and as far north as Damascus; their capital was the unusual rock-hewn, rose-red city of Petra (Isa. 16:1 = *Sela*).

Natural man. As used in 1 Cor. 2:14 (AV, NASB; NIV = *man without the Spirit*) it denotes the unsaved person; 1 Cor. 2:13n; Gen. 4:1n; 36:31n.

Natural revelation. Also called *general revelation* (q.v.).

Nazarene. A person from Nazareth; not to be confused with *Nazarite/Nazirite,* although the statement in Mt. 2:23 that Jesus would be "called a Nazarene" has been interpreted as possibly a reference to (1) Isa. 11:1, where a *netzer,* a "shoot," is predicted, or (2) the O.T. Nazarite; Mt. 2:23n; *S. Nazarite/Nazirite.*

Nazarite/Nazirite. A man or woman who voluntarily entered into a state of consecration to God marked by abstinence from wine and the fruit of the vine, allowing the hair to grow, and avoiding dead bodies; Num 6:2n.

Necromancy. Attempting to communicate with the dead; forbidden by the law; Dt. 18:10–11.

Negev/Negeb. The arid region south of Judea; the word means "south" or "dry"; Gen. 12:9n.

Neoorthodoxy. A twentieth-century theological movement, emphasizing Scr.

as a pointer to revelation that is centered in Christ, and holding that Scr. contains the Word of God but is not identical with it.

Nephilim. Heb. term found in Gen. 6:4 in the NIV (see note) and NASB; translated in the AV as "giants"; identification uncertain; some take them to be normal human beings, others view them as the offspring of fallen angels and human women.

Net, parable of the. A parable found in Mt. 13:47–50, picturing the mixture of true and false in the kingdom during this age; Mt. 13:47n.

Nethinim. Helpers to the priests in the sanctuary; the term is found only in Ezek. and Neh. and 1 Chron. 9:2; Neh. 3:26n.

New birth. The act of God that brings spiritual life to the sinner; *S. Regeneration.*

New Covenant. The last of the biblical covenants; provides for access to God on the basis of faith in Christ and His finished work; it promises the regeneration of a remnant of Israel; the Church is benefited by the application of the work of Christ and secondary participation in blessings to Israel; Heb. 8:8n; Jer. 31:31n; Isa. 61:8; Heb. 13:20; *S.* ch. 2, The Nature of the Bible.

New creation. The believer as remade spiritually, with a new hope, purpose, and outlook; 2 Cor. 5:17.

New Heaven and New Earth. The recreated form of the realm of human existence as we now know it, with sin removed and the glory of God evident; a result of the sweeping acts of God at the end of the millennium after sin and the curse on the earth have been removed; Isa. 65:17; Rev. 21:1.

New Jerusalem. The city described in Rev. 21:2ff; a dwelling place for Israel, the Church, and others after the millennium; some hold that it is the abode of the Church during the millennium; Rev. 21:2n.

New man. Regenerate human beings viewed in their capacity, given at salvation, to please God; an AV term; the Gr. words behind the phrase are also translated "new self" (NASB, NIV); Eph. 4:24n; *S. Self, new and old.*

New self. S. Self, new and old.

New Testament. Although used in biblical studies of the books from Mt. through Rev., the term is actually a translation of the phrase *New Covenant* (q.v.), as found in Heb. 8:8, the key feature of first-century revelation, the inauguration of provision of access to God through the cross-work of Christ.

Nicolaitans. A group mentioned specifically only in Rev. 2:6n, 15, although some believe that others condemned in the N.T. (as in 2 Pet. 2:5) are of the same party.

Noahic Covenant. Compact made by God with Noah promising that there will be no further universal floods and entrusting humanity with the responsibility to protect human life by rule involving capital punishment; Gen. 9:16n; *S.* ch. 2, The Nature of the Bible.

O

Obedience. Found throughout the Bible in regard to relations between human beings and between them and God; the disobedience of Eve and Adam was determinative for the race; conversely, the obedience of Christ makes salvation possible for those who believe; believers are to imitate His obedience; Rom. 5:19; 1 Pet. 2:21–23.

Oblation. A word used to refer to various types of offerings under the law; *S. Offering.*

Offering. As used of the ritual system under the law, something presented to God, concerning both obtaining access to God and thanking Him for access provided; this parallels the work of Christ as the final offering (Heb. 9:28) and our offerings as believer-priests (Rom. 12:1–2; Heb. 13:15–16) in thanksgiving to God; Lev. 7:11n.

Oil. Used in sacrifices, in food, medicinally, and as a symbol of the Holy Spirit; Ex. 27:20n; 30:31n.

Oil, anointing with. S. Anointing.

Old Covenant. As found in Heb. 8–9, the Mosaic law, viewed esp. as unable to bring people to God; Heb. 8:8n.

Old man. Unregenerate human beings viewed from the standpoint of being unable to please God and having no interest in the things of God; an AV term; the Gr. phrase behind this is also translated "old self" (NASB, NIV); Rom. 6:6n; *S. Self, New and Old.*

Old self. S. Self, New and Old.

Old Testament. Generally applied to the books from Gen. to Mal.; "testament" is taken from the rendering in some translations in Heb. 9 of the same word that is translated as "covenant"; strictly speaking, the "Old Testament" would include only those parts of the Bible that involved Mosaic law.

Olivet Discourse. The prophetic message delivered by Jesus on the Mount of Olives during His passion week, recorded in Mt. 24:1–25:46 and parallels; of great eschatological significance; Mt. 24:3n.

Omen. A supposed indication concerning divine will, made usually on the basis of condemned heathen rituals, such as examination of livers, attempts to contact the dead, etc.

Omnipotence. An attribute of God that describes His limitless power; it should be remembered that this is never to be viewed as putting Him in a place of contradiction, such as making something so large that He could not move it; Heb. 1:3; Eph. 1:19.

Omnipresence. An attribute of God according to which He is viewed as present everywhere in His creation at the same time, yet without being part of it *(S. Pantheism);* perhaps most eloquently described in Ps. 139:7–10.

Omniscience. An attribute of God according to which He is viewed as knowing all things, actual as well as possible; Ps. 139:1–6, 11–12.

Only Begotten. A term used exclusively of our Lord Jesus Christ; taken by some to refer to His eternal relation to the Father, by others to refer to His uniqueness, since the Gr. word behind the phrase can mean "unique" or "one-of-a-kind"; also translated as "One and Only" (NIV); Jn. 1:14.

Oracle. A disclosure from God, although in the O.T. heathen oracles are mentioned; also translated "burden" (AV, NASB); Zech. 12:1.

Ordain. In addition to general use regarding appointments, this is used of entrance into offices or positions involving spiritual service; in the N.T. it is a translation of words that simply mean "appoint," "set up"; *S. Laying on of hands.*

Ordinances. The Lord's Supper and baptism, ceremonies obligatory for believers in this age, outwardly portraying spiritual realities; they are not to be viewed as bestowing grace, as in the concept of *sacrament* (q.v.); *S.* ch. 18, The Church.

Original sin. The act of Eve and Adam (although Adam is charged with the guilt in Rom. 5:12ff) that determined the spiritual constitution of humanity, i.e., charged with sin and also polluted by sin.

Outward man. As found in 2 Cor. 4:16, Paul uses this to describe himself as others see him, esp. his physical attributes; also translated "outwardly" (NIV); *S. Inner Man.*

Overseer. One who occupies an office or place of leadership in a local church; the Gr. word behind it *(episkopos)*, which describes the function of oversight, is translated as "bishop" in the AV (NASB and NIV = "overseer"); generally accepted as descriptive of the same function as *elder* (Gr. *presbuteros*), although *presbuteros* suggests maturity of years; in the N.T., overseers are presented as existing in a plurality in each local church; 1 Tim. 3:1; Phil. 1:1n; Ti. 1:5n; *S. Elder* and ch. 18, The Church; cp. *Pastor* (q.v.), a spiritual gift, and *Deacon* (q.v.), one functioning under the overseers.

P

Palestine. Taken from the word translated "Philistine," this was used in the Bible and afterward to refer to the territory from the mountains of Lebanon to the Sinai Peninsula, and from the Mediterranean to the Arabian Desert on the east.

Palestinian Covenant. Divine commitment to provide a land for Israel under messianic blessing; Dt. 30:3n; *S.* ch. 2, The Nature of the Bible.

Pantheism. The view that God is coextensive with the universe, i.e., the universe is God; incompatible with a personal deity; the Stoics of Acts 17:18 held pantheistic views; *S.* ch. 11, Doctrine of God.

Papyrus. An ancient writing material made from the pith of reeds that grew esp. along the Nile; not to be confused with paper; was supplanted by *parchment* (q.v.) as the primary writing surface in the early centuries of the Christian era.

Parable. A method of communicating in which a story, often involving everyday events, is made the vehicle of spiritual truth; also used of short sayings (Lk. 4:23); important in the ministry of Jesus and esp. for understanding of prophecy; Zech. 11:7n; Mt. 13:3n; *S.* ch. 6, Literary Aspects of the Bible.

Paraclete. A Gr. word meaning "helper" or "advocate"; used of the Holy Spirit (Jn.) and Christ (1 Jn. 2:1) and translated "advocate," "comforter," "counselor"; Jn. 14:16n.

Parchment. An ancient writing material consisting of smoothed skins from sheep or goats; supplanted papyrus in the early centuries of the Christian era as the primary writing material; cp. *Vellum* (q.v.).

Paradise. A transliteration of a Gr. word meaning "park"; used of the place of bliss where the righteous go at death (Lk. 23:43), sometimes more specifically of the place where God is (2 Cor. 12:2–4; Rev. 2:7); Lk. 16:23n.

Parousia. A transliteration of a Gr. word meaning "coming" or "presence"; used generally with the meaning "arrival" and of the rapture (1 Th. 4:15) or the second advent (2 Th. 2:8) of Christ and translated "appearance," etc.

Passion. The suffering and death of Christ; Acts 1:3 (AV).

Passover. The ceremony instituted by God in Egypt and the most significant of Israel's three yearly festivals *(S. Pentecost* and *Tabernacles);* pictures protection from judgment by the application of blood; also called the feast of unleavened bread, since during the seven days of celebration no leavened bread was to be eaten. Ex. 12:11n; Lev. 23:5n, 6n; Mt. 26:20n.

Pastor. A spiritual gift (Eph. 4:11) in the Body of Christ that may be resident in any believer; in the one list of gifts that it appears in (Eph. 4:11), it is found connected with the gift of teaching, i.e., pastor-teacher is a two-part gift; is esp. to be possessed and used by those serving as elders (1 Pet. 5:1–4; Acts 20:28); the verb related to the Gr. noun behind *pastor* is translated "shepherd," "keep watch," "feed."

Pastoral Epistles. A recent term for the books of 1 and 2 Tim. and Ti.

Patriarch. Generally, any head of a tribe; applied esp. to Abraham, Isaac, Jacob, and even David; Gen. 26:3n.

Patristic literature. The noncanonical writings of the early Christian era; includes apocryphal literature and writings of the church fathers.

Pauline Epistles. The books written by the Apostle Paul, all epistles; *S.* Scofield Bible, Introduction to the Epistles of Paul.

Pauline Theology. The doctrinal system and distinctive features found in the writings of the apostle Paul.

Pavement, The. The location, probably outside Herod's Antonia Fortress, where Pilate sentenced Jesus; also called Stone Pavement and Gabbatha (Jn. 19:13).

Peace. In addition to use descriptive of relations between human beings, this concept is important in the relation of human beings to God; outside of Christ every person is alienated from God and is in a state of hostility and enmity; Eph. 2:14–18; Mt. 10:34n.

Peace offering. A sacrifice of cattle given on the basis of fellowship with God; pictures Christ as our peace with God; also translated as "fellowship offering"; Lev. 3:1n; *S. Fellowship offering.*

Pentateuch. A Gr. word applied to the first five books of the O.T. canon; the Torah or Law; Ex. 17:14n; *S.* Scofield Bible, Introduction to the Pentateuch.

Pentecost. One of the three most important

festivals in the Hebrew calendar under the law, fifty days after Passover; pictured the birth of the Church, hence the event described in Acts 2:1ff is the Pentecost for the Body of Christ, its birthday; also known as the Feast of Weeks and the Feast of Harvest; Acts 2:1n.

Perfection. (1) A feature coextensive with all the attributes of God: He is perfect in love, power, etc.; (2) a condition expected of all believers, better translated as "maturity," since the N.T. makes it clear that no one achieves sinlessness in this life; Phil. 3:12n.

Perish. As used in Jn. 3:16 (see note), this means to fail to obtain the life of God, not cessation of existence.

Perseverance. (1) Used of the quality enjoined upon believers, amounting to steadfastness in obedience and growth, esp. through trials; (2) used generally (theologically) to refer to the security of the believer: those who have truly believed will, by the grace of God, persevere in the state of salvation through this life, with entrance into the presence of God; *S. Security* and ch. 17, The Doctrine of Salvation.

Persia. A culture and nation that, in alliance with the Medes, overthrew the Babylonian Kingdom in 539 B.C.; the Persians were Indo-Europeans, and their language is related to Gr., Lat., Sanskrit and even Eng.; Ezra 4:3n; Dan. 5:28.

Personal sin. Acts of sin committed by an individual; remedied by confession; to be differentiated from *imputed sin* (q.v.) and *inherited sin* (q.v.); 1 Jn. 1:10; *S.* ch. 14, The Doctrine of Sin.

Pharaoh. The term for a king of Egypt; many are mentioned in the Bible.

Pharisees. A Jewish religious and political sect dating in origin perhaps to the time of Ezra; stressed adherance to the Torah, believed in the immortality of the soul, a kind of resurrection, the existence of spirit beings; Mt. 3:7n; *S. Literal/literalism.*

Philistia. The coastal territory occupied by the Philistines, a non-Semitic people whose civilization was centered in the cities of Ekron, Ashdod, Ashkelon, Gath, and Gaza; they were a constant threat to Israel over many centuries; Jdg. 13:1n; 1 Sam. 13:19n.

Phoenicia. Narrow coastal territory extending roughly from Arvad to just north of Carmel; occupied by a seafaring Semitic people, called Canaanites; main cities were Tyre and Sidon; their alphabet was adopted by the Hebrews and subsequently the Greeks.

Phylacteries. Small boxes attached to the left hand and forehead, containing certain Scr. passages, and worn by pious Jews while praying; not mentioned in the O.T.; a term found only in the N.T.; connected with a literalistic understanding of Ex. 13:9–16; Mt. 23:5n; *S. Literal/literalism.*

Pillar of cloud and fire. The visible evidence of the presence of God as He guided Israel in the wilderness, by a pillar of cloud during daylight and a pillar of fire at night; Ex. 13:21–22.

Pinnacle. A term used of a part of the Temple in Mt. 4:5; Lk. 4:9; of disputed meaning; also translated as "highest point" (NIV).

Plague. A term referring to diseases, natural calamities, and the judgments of God on Egypt prior to the Exodus; in some translations of the N.T., it is used to render a word meaning "smiting," "shock," or "blow" (e.g. at Rev. 9:20).

Pleasing aroma offerings. As found in Lev. 1:9 (see note), offerings that portray the perfection of Christ and His devotion to the Father; also translated as "sweet-savor offerings" (AV), "soothing aroma" (NAS).

Plenary inspiration. Used to describe a particular view of *inspiration* (q.v.), namely that the creative activity of the Holy Spirit extended to *all* the canonical Scriptures; i.e., all of the Bible is inspired; *S.* ch. 10, The Bible.

Pneumatology. The doctrine of the Holy Spirit; *S.* ch. 13, The Holy Spirit.

Poetical books. The books of Job, Psalms, Proverbs, and in some classifications, Ecclesiastes, Song of Solomon and Lamentations; *S.* Scofield Bible, Introduction to Poetic and Wisdom Books.

Polygamy. The practice of having more than one wife; allowed by God during part of the O.T. period; a violation of the divine purpose, as given in the Garden, of one man for one woman.

Polytheism. Belief in a plurality of deities.

Postmillennialism. Belief that Christ will return after a kingdom, the millennium, has run its course on earth; *S. Amillennialism* and *Premillennialism* and ch. 19, Future Things.

Posttribulation rapture. The belief that the Church will be taken to be with Christ after the tribulation has run its course and immediately before the second advent; *S.* ch. 19, Future Things.

Potter's Field. S. Akeldama.

Praetorium/Pretorium. Used of the residence of a governor or emperor (Mt. 27:27); in Phil. 1:13 it has been taken to refer to the emperor's residence in Rome or to the residence of the group comprising the emperor's bodyguard.

Praise. Expression of thankfulness to God; the privilege and responsibility of the believer-priest; Heb. 13:15.

Prayer. Communication with God that may involve *praise* (q.v.) or request (*S. Intercession*); believers are to engage in it continually (1 Th. 5:17); prayer is possible only through the access provided by our Lord Jesus Christ (Heb. 13:15); it is clear that God is moved by the prayer of the godly (Jas. 5:6); Hab. 3:1n; Lk. 11:2n.

Preaching. The proclamation of any portion of the message of the Gospel, and basic to its spread (1 Cor. 1:21); an activity, not an office or spiritual gift.

Predestination. A term found only in the N.T., although the concept is found throughout the Bible; generally, to order or arrange ahead of time (1 Cor. 2:7); esp. God's activity in arranging the aspects of a person's life so that he is certain to arrive at God's goal for him, given for believers as Christ-likeness (Rom. 8:29); Eph. 1:11n; *S.* ch. 17, The Doctrine of Salvation.

Preexistence of Christ. The doctrine that the God-man did not come into existence in Bethlehem, but that the second Person of the Trinity, who was joined with humanity, existed before that; the *eternality* (q.v.) of Christ describes the second Person's existence from before time and so says more than preexistence; *S.* ch. 12, The Person of Christ.

Premillennialism. The doctrine that Christ will return to establish a literal kingdom on the earth in fulfillment of O.T. promises; *S. Amillennialism, Postmillennialism*, and ch. 19, Future Things.

Presbyter. Transliteration of the Gr. word often translated as "elder"; suggests age or maturity; *S. Elder, Overseer*.

Pretribulation rapture. The view that Christ will take the Church to be with Himself before the seven-year tribulation period; 1 Th. 4:17n; *S.* ch. 19, Future Things.

Pride. A sin, characteristic of Satan and perhaps at the root of his and all other sins; as exemplified in Isa. 14:13–14, an explicit attempt to be like God, i.e., free of all restrictions as His creatures, whether angels or human beings; avoided esp. by following the example of our Lord Jesus Christ as seen esp. in Phil. 2:1–11.

Priest/priesthood. A priest is a human being who mediates between God and man; he must know what it is like to be both God and a human being, must be qualified before God, and must operate according to God's regulations; he attempts to open a channel of access to God—who is separated from human beings—and to keep it open, subsequently bringing additional needs to God's attention for His care; all priesthood in the O.T. points forward to Christ; all believers since the cross are priests and look back at His finished priestly work; Heb. 5:1–10; 1 Pet. 2:9n; Zech. 6:11n; *S.* ch. 18, The Church, and ch. 17, The Doctrine of Salvation.

Prince. A translation of several Heb. and Gr. terms suggest concepts such as "leader" and "ruler," and not always royalty.

Prison Epistles. The N.T. books written by the Apostle Paul during confinement in Rome: Eph., Phil., Col., and Phile.

Proconsul. A Roman title for a provincial governor, e.g., Sergius Paulus in Acts 13:7.

Procurator. Financial official in a Roman province or a governor, e.g., Pontius Pilate.

Promise, Dispensation of. The dispensation that began with the covenant with Abraham in Gen. 12:1–3 (see note) and ended with the giving of the law at Sinai; *S.* ch. 2, The Nature of the Bible.

Prophecy. A means of divine communication that may or may not involve prediction; Dt. 13:4n; Lk. 24:19n; 1 Cor. 12:10n; *S.* ch. 7, Relations Between the Testaments.

Prophecy, gift of. A spiritual gift for the foundational stage of this age (Eph. 2:20—"the foundation that consists of the apostles and prophets"), involving the ability to give new revelation from

God, not necessarily predictive; 1 Cor. 12:10n; 14:3.

Prophet. A person who spoke from God, predictive or otherwise (even Moses [Dt. 18:18] and David [Acts 2:30] are called prophets); *S. Prophecy.*

Prophetic Books. The books from Isa. through Mal., exclusive of Lam., in the modern order of the canon; *S.* Scofield Bible, Introduction to the Prophetic Books.

Propitiation. Although used of human relations, it is esp. important in the Bible denoting the payment of a price to turn away the wrath of God; also translated *atonement* (q.v.); Rom. 3:25n; *S.* ch. 17, The Doctrine of Salvation.

Proselyte. A person who was not an Israelite by blood but who voluntarily put himself under Jewish regulations (to greater or lesser degrees); in N.T. times these were not necessarily in Palestine (Acts 13:43).

Proverb. (1) An enigmatic saying or (2) a story cast in realistic terms used for the purpose of illustrating a spiritual truth.

Providence. God's continual care for and government of His created universe; Ps. 33:11–18; Acts 14:17.

Psalm. From the Gr. word *psalmos,* "song sung to a stringed instrument"; the Hebrew name for the book of Psalms was *Tehillim,* "songs of praise," since they are poems written for singing.

Psaltery. A stringed instrument probably like a modern harp.

Pseudepigrapha. A group of noncanonical Jewish writings, not classed with the *Apocrypha* (q.v.), mainly from the intertestamental period.

Publican. A translation of a word also rendered as "tax collector," i.e., for the Romans.

Purim. A name for the Jewish festival celebrated because of God's safekeeping of Israel under the Persians, as found in the book of Esther; not ordained by God.

Python. A demon involved in communicating through human beings whom it controlled, as in Acts 16:16; from the name for the serpent supposed to inhabit Pytho, under Mt. Parnassus, guarding the oracle at Delphi.

Q

Queen of Heaven. the Phoenician goddess Astarte, the Assyrian Ishtar; Jer. 7:18n; *S. Ashtaroth.*

Qumran. A living and work center of the *Essenes* (q.v.), a cult that flourished in N.T. times; site of discovery of the *Dead Sea Scrolls* (q.v.); located at northwest corner of the Dead Sea; apparently inhabited over many centuries.

R

Rabbi. A Heb. word meaning "my teacher"; used respectfully several times in the N.T. of our Lord Jesus Christ; *rabboni* (Mk 10:51; Jn. 20:16) is a similar term, showing even more respect.

Rabshakeh. An Assyrian title for a high-ranking military officer; 2 Ki. 18:17.

Rainbow. As a result of the flood and His promise never again to judge the earth in the same way, God changed atmospheric conditions and established the rainbow as a new meteorological phenomenon and as a covenantal sign; it appears elsewhere suggestive of God's covenant relations, e.g., Ezek. 1:28; Gen. 9:13n.

Ransom. The payment of a price to obtain release; as such it is part of biblical teaching concerning the work of Christ, particularly the concept of redemption; Rom. 3:24n; *S*. ch. 17, The Doctrine of Salvation.

Ras Shamra. Site on the Mediterranean coast, north of present-day Lebanon, of extensive and major archaeological finds beginning in 1929; discoveries consisted of documents, palaces, temples, and many other artifacts pertaining to Canaanite civilization there dating to the fourteenth c. B.C.; among the languages represented in the written materials is Ugaritic, a sister language to Heb.

Rapture. From a Lat. word meaning "snatch," this term is used of the removal of the Church from the earth prior to the tribulation period; 1 Th. 4:17n; *S*. ch. 19, Future Things.

Reconciliation. Changing a state of enmity to one of harmony; used of the work of Christ in turning human beings to God by His death; Col. 1:20n; *S*. ch. 17, The Doctrine of Salvation.

Red heifer. A sacrifice for removing ritual uncleanness (using fire and running water); a picture of the believer's cleansing from sin as he goes through life; Num. 19:2n.

Redeemer, Redemption. an important aspect of the cross-work of Christ; points to the enslaving power of sin and the payment of a price (the blood) to effect release; a redeemer is one who provides such release; the concept of redemption is elaborated especially by several biblical terms; *redemption* is also used as a cover term for all the aspects of the saving work of Christ; Rom. 3:24n; Ex. 6:6n; Isa. 59:20n; Gen. 3:15n; *S*. ch. 17, The Doctrine of Salvation.

Refreshing, times of. S. Times of refreshing.

Regeneration. Among other uses, this refers esp. to the work of God occurring at salvation that brings spiritual life and the capacity to please God; overcomes depravity; not seen or felt; ob-

tained by faith; the concept is taught, among other means, by words translated "born again," "born from above" and "regeneration"; Jn. 3:3n; Mt. 19:28n; *S*. ch. 17, The Doctrine of Salvation.

Reincarnation. The unbiblical idea that human beings proceed through more than one life form, e.g., a human being may return after death as another human being, or as an animal, etc.; part of the Buddhist and Hindu systems; Heb. 9:27 shows that human beings die once.

Remission of sins. Forgiveness of sins; remission means "putting away."

Remnant. A key biblical concept: (1) because of the faith principle of approaching God and the depravity of human beings, God works only with a portion of humanity to bless them (1 Cor. 1:26); (2) the remnant is that portion of national Israel that through the ages has placed or will place faith in the Messiah; Rom. 11:5n; Jer. 15:11n; Mic. 4:11n.

Repentance. The act of reversing one's outlook, opinion or position; with regard to salvation, it is changing one's mind about the Gospel, Christ, and God; may involve an emotional element, but that is not necessary; Zech. 8:14n; Acts 17:30n; *S*. ch. 17, The Doctrine of Salvation.

Reprobate. Can mean (1) not genuine regarding the faith (2 Cor. 13:5); (2) useless or unfit (Ti. 1:16); (3) depraved (Rom. 1:28).

Rest. In addition to usage describing normal human activity, rest is a concept that runs from the beginning to end of the Bible; God's resting on the seventh day of creation is a picture of (1) the rest of salvation, esp. in its eschatological manifestations (Heb. 4:4, 8); (2) Israel's entrance into the land (Heb. 3:11ff).

Restoration. As found, e.g., in Acts 3:21

(see note) and in the O.T., this involves the fulfillment of God's promises to Israel concerning the kingdom, esp. regathering in the land; that this would be mentioned in Acts indicates that the kingdom was being offered after Pentecost; Acts 15:16; *S. Times of refreshing* and Acts 3:20n; Jer. 23:3n; Ezek. 34:12n; 36:1n; 37:1n; Zech. 2:1n.

Restrainer. As described in 2 Th. 2:3ff (see note), the power that holds back the satanic plan until the rapture takes place; from the grammar involved in that passage and the concepts involved, this must be the Holy Spirit.

Resurrection. Although the N.T. revelation is fuller than that in the O.T., this refers to the restoration of the *body* after being in the grave, not the continued existence of the immaterial part of man after death—that is assumed; hence the resurrection of the believer and of Christ both involve a rejoining of the physical and nonphysical parts of a person; the spiritual rebirth of Israel is also spoken of in resurrection terms (Ezek. 37); 1 Cor. 15:52n; Rev. 20:5n; Mt. 28:1n (resurrection of Christ); *S.* ch. 17, The Doctrine of Salvation.

Return of Christ. The *second advent* (q.v.).

Revelation. The information about Himself given by God to human beings; may be *general* (such as the heavens, etc.) or *special* (such as Scripture, Jesus Himself, the prophets, etc.); 1 Cor. 2:13n; Cp. *Inspiration* (q.v.), which is a term describing how God controlled the process of giving information for writing; *S. General revelation, Special revelation,* ch. 10, The Bible.

Rewards. Spiritual "pay" springing from the grace of God (1 Cor. 3:14n) or from His retributive justice (Jude 11, AV).

Righteousness/righteous. (1) The standing before God in which the believer is viewed by God as meeting all His standards concerning holiness (Phil. 3:9); *righteous* is synonymous with *just,* and describes a person having such standing *(S. Justification);* (2) personal activity that is pleasing to God (1 Tim. 6:11); Gen. 15:6n; Lk. 2:25n; 1 Jn. 3:7n; Rom. 3:21n; 10:3n; 10:10n; 1 Jn. 3:7n; Rev. 19:8n.

Rock. This term for an everyday item is used in many places in the Bible as a figure of Christ, describing His solidity and suitability as a foundation for spiritual activity; Ex. 17:6n; 1 Pet. 2:8n.

S

Sabaeans. A nomadic merchant group of northern Arabia; their territory was known as Sheba (1 Ki. 10:1).

Sabaoth. S. Jehovah-Sabaoth.

Sabbath. The seventh day of the week in the Jewish calendar, set aside for rest and spiritual activity; patterned after the seventh day of creation; its observation has not been needed since the cross; Neh. 9:14n; Mt. 12:1n; cp. *Lord's Day* (q.v.).

Sabbath day's journey. The distance a person was allowed to travel on the Sabbath according to Jewish understanding of Ex. 16:29, i.e., a short distance, set by some Jewish leaders as about 3,000 ft.; often circumvented.

Sabbatical year. The year (every seventh) provided for under the law in which tilled land was to lie fallow; Lev. 25:1–7.

Sackcloth. Coarse dark cloth worn during mourning; Gen. 37:34.

Sacrament. Strictly speaking, this is to be differentiated from an ordinance; according to some, a "sacrament" is a channel of the grace that flows from God to human beings; in such a view, a sacrament can thus be a source of forgiveness, even a means of salvation, as when baptism of an infant brings salvation or predisposes that person to it; all such views are to be avoided; because of such confusion, the term "ordinance" is preferable; there are only two ordinances in the N.T., *baptism* (q.v.) and the *Lord's Supper* (q.v.); *S. Ordinance.*

Sacrifice. The presentation of a gift to another, esp. to God; behind the activity lie the concepts of priesthood, priestly work, and access to God; Heb. 10:18n; Ex. 29:33n; Lev. 16:5n; 17:11n; Heb. 13:15–16; *S. Priest/priesthood, Access.*

Sadducees. A Jewish religious and political party during the time of Christ; drawn from the wealthy, usually priests; dominated the *Sanhedrin* (q.v.); accepted only the Pentateuch; rejected doctrine of resurrection and the existence of angels.

Saint. A person who has placed saving faith in Christ; a Christian.

Salt Sea. S. Dead Sea.

Salutation. This word for human greeting is used in Bible study to describe the initial part of an epistle in the N.T., in which the writer greets His audience and introduces himself and his credentials; *S.* e.g., 1 Tim. 1:1–2.

Salvation. A general word for the activity of God that brings human beings into fellowship with Him; both the Heb. and Gr. words involved suggest safety and health; it is described in the Bible as having past (Tit. 3:5—"saved"), present (Phil. 2:12), and future (1 Pet. 1:5) aspects; Rom. 1:16n; 1 Cor. 3:14n; *S.* ch. 17, The Doctrine of Salvation.

Samaritans. A race that lived, and continues to live, in the region of Samaria, about thirty-five miles north of Jerusalem; Samaria was the capital of the northern kingdom during the period of the divided monarchy; during the Assyrian captivity colonists were brought in, who intermarried with the Jews; this half-Jewish group was continually at odds with those who considered themselves full Jews; this explains the importance of the encounter between Jesus and the woman at the well in Jn. 4 and the bringing of the Gospel to the region in Acts 8, accompanied by special signs to show that they were accepted into the Body of Christ; *S. Ephraim, Israel.*

Sanctification. The process, occurring between salvation and entrance into the presence of Christ, in which God is at work to make the believer like Christ (Rom. 8:29); it is continual (no one arrives at it all of a sudden); it is God's work (Phil. 2:13); it does not bring sinless perfection (1 Jn. 1:8, 10); it involves obedience and faith (1 Pet. 5:6); it is contrasted with the state of salvation and entrance into it (Eph. 2:8—"by means of grace you are in a saved condition"); Zech. 8:3n; Rev. 22:11n; *S.* ch. 17, The Doctrine of Salvation.

Sanhedrin. The Jewish civil and religious ruling body during N.T. times, comprised of Pharisees, Sadducees, and others, and presided over by the high priest; arose during the period of Gr. domination of Palestine; suffered various fortunes under the Romans; prominent in the Gospels and Acts; Acts 4:1; 5:17, 34, etc.

Satan. A name for the fallen angel also called the devil; a transliteration of a Heb. word meaning "adversary"; as such, he is the opponent of God and of those who belong to God; Rev. 20:10n; Gen. 3:1n; Isa. 14:12n; Ezek. 28:12n, 19n; *S.* ch. 16, Angels.

Satyr. An idolatrous figure, perhaps goat-like (as in Gr. and Rom. religions), or the demon associated with it; the object of sacrifices in heathen practices; Isa. 13:21 (AV).

Savior. As a term for anyone who brought deliverance and safety, this was applied esp. to the Lord Jesus Christ, the great spiritual Deliverer of His people; *S. Salvation.*

Scapegoat. The animal used in the ritual of the Day of Atonement; the high priest placed his hands on its head, confessed over it the nation's sins, and had someone lead it into the desert; this portrayed the removal and separation of sin from the sinner.

Schoolmaster. A term drawn from Roman culture and used in Gal. 3:24–25 for the law; it had a guiding and preparatory effect until the revelation of the annulling of the law at the cross; Gal. 3:25n.

Scribe. A teacher and interpreter of the law; the position apparently first appeared during the time of Ezra; the scribes were prominent as Jewish leaders during the ministry of Jesus; Mt. 2:4n.

Scripture. The Gr. word this is translated from denotes any written document; the term is applied esp., however, to the written documents viewed as revelation from God; Lk. 4:19; 2 Tim. 3:16n.

Scroll. A form of ancient written document, predating the codex, or book form; scrolls were used by rolling from one holder to the other.

Scythians. A nomadic people primarily inhabiting the area north of the Black and Caspian Seas; at times they ranged through the eastern portion of the Middle East; the occurrence of the term in Col. 3:11 may be a reference to one of this group or, as some hold, to someone enslaved by them.

Sea of Galilee. Body of water in northern Palestine, bearing four different names in the Bible: Sea of Chinnereth (Num. 34:11), Lake of Gennesaret (Lk. 5:1), Sea of Tiberias (Jn. 6:1), Sea of Galilee (Mt. 4:18); the first name includes the Heb. word for harp, descriptive of the shape; fed by three streams or rivers on the north, it empties into the Jordan at the southern end; surrounded by flourishing towns in N.T. times; subject, due in part to its location and elevation (almost 700 ft. below sea level), to sudden meteorological changes; site of many of Jesus' miracles.

Seal. This everyday item, found on documents, doors, etc., is used to represent the security of the believer in Eph. 1:13 (see note); *S.* ch. 13, The Holy Spirit.

Second advent, second coming. The appearance of the Lord Jesus Christ at the climax of the tribulation period to establish His millennial kingdom; this return fulfills, among others, the promise of Acts 1:11 (see note); *S.* ch. 19, Future Things.

Second death. The final judgment of the wicked of all ages, including their entrance into eternal punishment; Rev. 20:14n.

Security. A biblical doctrine with far-reaching significance; all those who have placed genuine faith in Christ will surely be brought by God into His presence; none will be or can be lost; to assert that a person can lose salvation, and perhaps gain it again, is to show misunderstanding of what God has done in placing that person into the cross-work of Christ; Jude 1n; Ezek. 18:24n; *S.* ch. 17, Salvation.

Selah. A term found in Pss. and Hab. whose meaning is uncertain, probably a kind of musical sign; Ps. 3:2n.

Self-judgment. Spiritual evaluation of a believer by that believer with the purpose of determining the existence of sin; 1 Cor. 11:31n.

Self, new and old. Terms found in the NIV and NASB at Eph. 4:22, 24 and Col.

3:9–10, where the AV has *old man* and *new man;* they refer to (1) the individual as possessor of life from God and the capacity and desire to please Him, as contrasted with (2) the individual in the natural, unsaved state, without life and desire for the things of God; Eph. 4:24n.

Semite. The Semites were a race descended from Shem; Gen. 9:16n, 26–27; 10:1n; the Hebrews are a Semitic people.

Separation. A constant topic throughout the Bible; the law taught separation by its regulations and sacrifices; the believer is commanded not to partake of the world system; this separation is *to* God and *from* evil; 2 Cor. 6:17n; Rev. 18:4.

Septuagint. A translation of the Heb. and Aram. O.T. into Gr.; done at Alexandria, Egypt, apparently in the third c. B.C., and purportedly by a group of seventy Jewish scholars, hence the abbreviated title LXX in modern use; important for O.T. and N.T. studies; *S.* ch. 4, The Language of the Bible.

Sepulchre. A carved-out or constructed burial place.

Seraph. A member of an order of spirit-beings, apparently angels, named specifically only in Isa. 6:2 (see note); similar beings appear in Rev. 4:6–8, although these also have characteristics of cherubs; the plural, as transliterated from Heb. is *seraphim;* but the anglicized form *seraphs* is also used; hence "seraphims," like "cherubims," would be redundant; *S.* ch. 16, Angels.

Sermon on the Mount. The discourse of our Lord Jesus Christ found in Mt. 5:1–7:29 and perhaps Lk. 6:20–49 and other parallels; delivered to the disciples and a gathered crowd; not a plan of salvation, but a picture of the one who has the righteousness necessary for entrance into the kingdom, a key feature of Matthew's gospel; its principles are timeless (those who mourn will be comforted by God) and as such can be applied to the Christian, but its primary thrust is to relate to the Jews of Jesus' day God's spiritual and moral requirements for the inauguration of the kingdom; Mt. 5:2n, 3n, 11n, etc.

Serpent. This everyday animal is used in many figurative senses; the serpent in the Garden was certainly an animal energized by Satan; *S. Bronze serpent;* Gen. 3:1n; Num. 21:9n.

Serpent, bronze. S. Bronze serpent.

Servant. This role, drawn from ordinary life, is used extensively in Scr. to describe one who has characteristics of humility and self-denial in relation to others, esp. the Lord Jesus Christ and the believer during this age in his role in the Body of Christ; a *deacon* is at heart a servant; Gen. 24:66n; Isa. 41:8n; 42:1n; 52:13n; *S. Deacon.*

Servant of the Lord. Used of various individuals who serve God in different capacities, and esp. the figure that appears in Isa. 421ff, the Messiah (Mt. 12:17–21).

Seventy weeks. A phrase used in Dan. 9:24 (AV and NASB) to describe the period of time needed in the plan of God to bring a remnant of Israel to the Messiah; in that verse the phrase is literally "seventy sevens" (the NIV represents this as "seventy 'sevens' "); in Heb. the word for *seven* was used (among other uses) for what we call a week, hence the AV and NASB translation; the actual duration of the period must be a multiple of time units longer than seven days, and is best taken to be seventy times seven years, or 490 years; Dan. 9:24n.

Shekinah. A name, not found in Scr., for the presence of God among human beings, esp. in the Tabernacle and Temple; Ex. 27:20n.

Sheol. In the O.T., the place where dead people go; it is dark and foreboding; it must be remembered that in the progress of revelation much less was known about life after death in O.T. times than after the N.T. revelation; apparently equivalent to the *Hades* of the N.T.; Hab. 2:5n; Lk. 16:23n.

Shepherd/shepherding. The figure of shepherd is used in Scr. to represent Christ as caring for, feeding, and protecting those who belong to Him (Jn. 10:7n); shepherding is the spiritual gift used to care for those in the Body of Christ; Eph. 4:11; 1 Pet. 5:1–4; *S. Pastor.*

Shiloh. A place name and apparently a Messianic title (Gen. 49:10n; Josh. 18:1n); the exact messianic significance is uncertain.

Shinar. Babylon (q.v.); Gen. 11:1.

Showbread. The specially made bread that lay on an ornate table in the Holy Place in the Tabernacle; pictures Christ as the one who sustains (spiritual) life; translated "Bread of the Presence" in the NASB and NIV; Ex. 25:30.

Sign. A pointer designed to draw attention to a revelation from God or to His messengers and the message they carried; signs can take several forms (Gen. 9:12, the rainbow; Jn. 2:11, the turning of water into wine); in the divine economy, they are not to be regarded as ends in themselves; Acts 28:8n; Heb. 2:4.

Sin. Anything that is contrary to the nature of God Himself; includes intentional and unintentional acts; includes more than what is covered by the regulations of the law; Mt. 12:31n; Mk. 7:21n; Jn. 13:10n; Rom. 3:23n; Rom. 5:12n; *S.* ch. 14, The Doctrine of Sin.

Sin nature. S. Sinful nature.

Sin offering. An animal or flour sacrifice prescribed under the law; pictures Christ bearing our sin; Lev. 4:3n.

Sin unto death. As found in 1 Jn. 5:16–17, this denotes a sin habitually practiced by a believer, leading to God's removing him from this life, but not taking away his salvation; those who are euphemistically described as "asleep" in 1 Cor. 11:30 have been taken to be with Christ "prematurely" because of their abuse of the Lord's Table.

Sinful nature. The NIV rendering of the AV and NASB "old man" (q.v.), the human being viewed as fallen, corrupt, and unable and unwilling to please God, always seeking his own ends; also found as *sin nature;* Jude 23n.

Skull, place of a. The translation of Aram. *Golgotha* (q.v.).

Slave. This unfortunate social institution is used esp. in the N.T. as a figure of service to God and to others; Rom. 1:1.

Sodom and Gomorrah. Two cities located at the southern end of the Dead Sea, associated with each other in sin and subsequent destruction; Gen. 19:28n; Mt. 10:15.

Son of God. In the singular this is used of our Lord Jesus Christ, denoting His deity; Mk. 1:1; from the beginning of the incarnation the God-man was the Son of God, but the resurrection marked Him out especially as the Son of God invested with supreme power; Rom. 1:4; *S.* ch. 12, The Person of Christ.

Son of man. Used to describe Jesus in His humanity; probably drawn by Him from Dan. 7:13; our Lord's favorite name for Himself; Mt. 8:20n; used also of any human being (Ezek. 2:1n); *S.* ch. 12, The Person of Christ.

Song of Degrees. A title for each of Psalms 120–134, given, according to some, because they were sung at particular levels while ascending Mt. Zion (there are other views); also called *Song of Ascents.*

Sonship. The figure used to describe the believer's relation to God by adoption;

involves privileges as well as responsibilities; Rom. 8:16n.

Sons of God. (1) The beings described in
Gen. 6:2–4, see note, v. 4, perhaps
angels; (2) angels (Job. 1:6); (3)
Christians, as members of the family
of God by adoption (Rom. 8:14; 16n);
S. *Children of God.*

Soothsayer. A person associated with demonic forces who purports to divine
the future; Josh. 13:22 (AV; NIV
= *[one] who practiced divination;*
NASB = *diviner*); condemned in the
O.T. (Lev. 19:26); Dt. 18:10n; 1 Sam.
28:7n.

Soteriology. The study of the work of God
in providing salvation; S. ch. 17, The
Doctrine of Salvation.

Soul. A segment of the nonmaterial part of
a person that is most often associated
with everyday life and being human,
although at times it can be synonymous with other features, such as the
spirit; 1 Th. 5:23n; cp. *Spirit* (q.v.);
S. ch. 15, The Doctrine of Humanity.

Sovereignty of God. God's control of all
that occurs in the universe; He causes
all things to work together for His
purposes; nothing is excluded; the degree of immediate control may not be
specified; ultimately, all will be seen
to bring glory to Him; Eph. 1:11n.

Special revelation. The disclosure of information from God that is not available
directly to all human beings *(S. General revelation);* it comes through the
channels of direct communication (as
through the prophets), dreams and visions, the very appearance of Christ
in the incarnation, the superintending
of those writing what would subsequently be viewed as canonical Scr.;
it tells what general revelation cannot,
the express will of God for human
beings as sinners who need to become
related to a holy God; 2 Tim. 3:16–
17n; Heb. 1:1–2n; S. ch. 10, The
Bible.

Spikenard. A plant-derived oil with aromatic properties, originally from India, where it is still used; imported in
sealed alabaster boxes; used by Mary
of Bethany to anoint Jesus' head;
translated in the NASB and NIV as
"nard."

Spirit. (1) An incorporeal being, with intelligence, desires, and feelings; God
and angels are spirit-beings; (2) the
immaterial part of a human being,
most often descriptive of the capacity
to interact with God in the spiritual
realm; 1 Th. 5:23n; cp. *Soul* (q.v.).

Spirit, Holy. S. *Holy Spirit.*

Spiritism. Involvement with demons for the
purpose of attempting to determine the
future, gain favor, etc.; condemned
throughout the Bible; 1 Sam. 28:7n.

Spirits in prison. A phrase used only in 1
Pet. 3:19 (see note); probably angels,
although some take them to be dead
people.

Spiritual body. The form of existence for
the believer after resurrection; a new
kind of body is necessary for enjoyment of the presence of God and continued service into eternity; it is an
important biblical teaching that a person is not complete after death until
the body is brought back together with
the nonmaterial part, but also the body
must have a new form; 1 Cor. 15:52n.

Spiritual gift. A bestowal of the Spirit of
God on every believer as the result of
the resurrection of Christ and the formation of His Body; provides ability
and empowerment to serve God during this age by bringing others into
the Body (by evangelism, Eph. 4:11n),
and by ministering to others in the
Body (1 Pet. 4:10); some gifts were
foundational to the apostolic period of
the Church (Eph. 2:20; Heb. 2:4); 1
Cor. 12:1n; 14:1n; S. ch. 18, The
Church.

Spirituality. One of the goals of the process
of sanctification; it consists of spiritual

maturity (1 Cor. 2:14n, 15) and Christlikeness (Gal. 5:22n–23) produced by the Holy Spirit; *S*. ch. 17, The Doctrine of Salvation.

Standing and state. An important distinction that must be made in order to understand much N.T. teaching; *standing* involves the following: God has placed the believer in a position that involves several unalterable features (he is justified, bound for heaven, there is no possibility that his sins can cause judgment and loss of salvation, etc.); on the other hand, the believer is to grow in Christ, increase in holiness, confess sins that break fellowship—all of these describe things contributing to his *state;* 1 Cor. 1:2n.

Stele. Erect block of stone with an inscription memorializing a person or event; also spelled *stela*.

Stewardship. As created by God, human beings are responsible to God in everything He has entrusted to them; this is especially true of those who are saved by grace and have been given the privilege of managing spiritual gifts, places of service, and material goods as entrustments from a wise heavenly Father; all such activity is to be done in such a way as to glorify the Bestower; Lk. 16:1–13 (money); 1 Pet. 4:10 (gifts); 1 Pet. 5:2–4 (use of gifts).

Stoicism. A Gr. philosophy prevalent in N.T. times in the Medit. world; held that God is one with the universe *(S. Pantheism)* and that life should be pursued with reasoned detachment and acceptance of fate; Acts 17:18n.

Stone. This common item is used as a figure of Christ in relation to Israel, the Church and the nations, stressing His role as a divider between those who are open to the things of God and those who are not, His role as a foundation, and His destruction of every power that would oppose Him; Mt. 21:44n; Dan. 2:31n.

Stoning. Method of capital punishment under the law.

Strong brother. The Christian who believes that he has liberty to practice so-called *doubtful things* (q.v.); Rom. 14:3n; *S. Weak brother; S*. ch. 17, The Doctrine of Salvation.

Stumbling block. A translation of a Gr. word that denotes something that causes tripping; in 1 Cor. 8:9 it refers specifically to actions of stronger believers that lead the weaker believer to sin in doing by imitation something that he is convinced is a sin; *S. Strong brother, Weak brother,* and ch. 17, The Doctrine of Salvation.

Substitution. Involved in God's provision of salvation is the fact that no human being can pay the debt owed to God; hence God has established the principle of substitution, by which He accepts a stand-in to pay the price to turn away His wrath and to release from sin's grasp, etc.; the sacrifices under the law pictured this vicarious activity, yet themselves could never take away sin; Heb. 10:1ff.

Symbol. As part of the literary nature of the Bible, some things are presented as representative of others, for the purpose of enhancing understanding, or hiding truth, etc.; *S*. ch. 6, Literary Aspects of the Bible.

Synagogue. A Jewish religious institution that arose during the period after the Babylonian captivity; its purpose was to offer instruction in Jewish tradition and understanding of Scr.

Synoptic Gospels. The books of Mt., Mk., and Lk.

Syriac. A language into which the O.T. and N.T. were translated; a sister language to Aram.

Systematic theology. The organizing, arranging and summarizing of the message of the Bible, and, indeed, all we know about God, using all relevant sources of help, e.g., philosophy, archaeology, language study, history; since the Bible does not present God's revelation in step-by-step fashion, our understanding is enhanced by laying out the message in an organized way.

T

Tabernacle. A portable center for observance of ritual, housing the presence of God in Israel; details for it were issued by God with the giving of the law; many of its features clearly portray the Person and work of the Lord Jesus Christ; the word itself is a translation of Heb. words referring to the top and walls; the term is used also of any temporary boothlike structure; Ex. 25:9n; 26:15n; 27:1n, 9n, 16n, 17n; 1 Chron. 16:37n; Jn. 12:24n.

Tabernacles, Feast of. One of the appointed festivals of Israel; it pictures the joy of Israel in the kingdom; also called the Festival of Booths, because celebrants were to live in booths; *S. Passover* and *Pentecost,* the two other main festivals of Israel; Lev. 23:34n.

Talmud. The collection of rabbinic oral law and comments on it.

Tammuz. A name that appears in Ezek. 8:14 for an Akkadian god who was the husband of Ishtar, and who, according to the lore, had died; had counterparts in other ancient religions.

Targum. A translation or paraphrase of the O.T. in Aram.; employed before and into N.T. times; those that exist are useful for biblical studies.

Tartarus. In 2 Pet. 2:4 the Gr. verb *tartaroō* ("confine to Tartarus"), usually translated "sent to hell," reflects Gr. mythology, in which Tartarus was a place of divine punishment below Hades.

Teaching, gift of. A spiritual gift involving the ability to teach spiritual things with fruitful results; need not coincide with an ability to teach nonbiblical subjects; listed alone in 1 Cor. 12:29 and Rom. 12:7, but linked as a two-part gift with shepherding in Eph. 4:11 (see note).

Temple. The religious center of Israel beginning with the construction in Jerusalem of the first Temple by Solomon; modeled after the Tabernacle, it had a number of changes, including increased size; the first Temple was destroyed by the Babylonians in 587 B.C.; a subsequent temple was erected by Zerubbabel and expanded by Herod; this was destroyed by the Romans in 70 A.D.; 1 Ki. 6:2n; 7:14n; Ezek. 40:5; Hag. 2:3.

Temptation/testing. These two associated terms overlap in their application to human life; a temptation is an invitation to sin; its source may be external or internal; a testing is a procedure designed to determine and demonstrate inner character; God tests, but does not tempt, although, as in the case of Job, He may test an individual by allowing Satanic temptation; Jas. 1:14n.

Ten Commandments. The ordinances written on stone and delivered to Moses on Mt. Sinai and recorded in Ex. 20:3–17; 19:1n; 20:1 (see notes); 20:13n.

Ten lost tribes. A feature of the fallacious belief of some, especially in certain cults, according to which ten tribes of Israel were removed into exile and never returned, showing up subsequently as Anglo-Saxons; 2 Ki. 17:23n.

Teraphim. Figures of heathen deities, used, among other things, as household gods (Gen. 31:34); condemned throughout the O.T.

Test. S. Temptation/testing.

Tetrarch. A Gr. and Rom. civil office, denoting varying spheres of authority;

Herod Antipas was tetrarch of Galilee and Peraea.

Textual criticism. The science and art of attempting to discover the original text of a literary work; especially important for biblical studies, and the foundational endeavor to all subsequent investigation of the Scriptures.

Textus Receptus. An edition (compilation made from manuscripts) of the Gr. N.T. made in 1633 by the Elzevir brothers, Dutch publishers; it was based on earlier editions; *S.* ch. 2, The Nature of the Bible.

Thank offering. An offering under the law that was a sub-offering (along with the vow offering and the freewill offering) of the peace offering; given on the basis of communion with God; Lev. 7:11n, 12.

Theism. Belief in the existence of God, as distinguished from *atheism* (q.v.); this can include *polytheism* (q.v.) and *deism* (q.v.); esp., the belief in a personal deity who communicates with human beings.

Theistic evolution. The view that God used evolutionary processes in bringing the physical universe, including life forms, into existence; does not take the Genesis account at face value.

Theology. In the narrower sense, the study of God; theology can be viewed as drawing its data from the Bible alone, in which case it is called biblical theology; *systematic theology* (q.v.) attempts to use all sources, with the Bible as primary, in order to arrive at comprehensive statements about God and His work; *S.* ch. 5, Interpreting the Bible.

Theophany. An appearance of God to human beings; Gen. 12:7n; *S. Christophany.*

Thorn in the flesh. A physical ailment afflicting the Apostle Paul, mentioned in 2 Cor. 12:7; exact nature not given.

Times of refreshing. A phrase found in Acts 3:19 (see note, 3:20), pointing to the possibility of the coming of the kingdom if there were national repentance.

Times of the Gentiles. That period of time of unspecified length lasting from the beginning of the Babylonian captivity (604 B.C.) to the end of the tribulation period; subject of much biblical prophecy; it is that time during which Israel is out of the place of direct national blessing, and which will culminate in the greatest persecution of Israel (under the Beast of Rev. 13) ever to occur; Dan. 7:8n; 7:26n; Mt. 25:32n; Lk. 21:24n; Rev. 16:19n.

Tirshatha. As found in certain translations, a title of civil rulers under the Assyrians, Babylonians, Medians, and Persians.

Tithing. The regulation under the law according to which an Israelite gave to God one tenth of his livestock and his gain from the land, and actually more if other sacrificial requirements are figured in; annulled with the law at the cross and replaced for this age with the principle of giving with joy as believer-priests (Heb. 13:16) and in proportion to God's financial provision (1 Cor. 16:1–3; 16:2n); *S. Giving; S.* ch. 18, The Church.

Tittle. S. Jot and tittle.

Tongues. The miraculous ability to speak in a language not previously learned; a spiritual gift for the foundation stage of the church (as the other sign-gifts) and a sign to Jews (1 Cor. 14:21; 14:27n); not gibberish (since it is to be interpreted, and one cannot interpret gibberish) and not the language of angels, since we can have no idea what language angels use, if they use any at all; *S.* ch. 13, The Holy Spirit.

Torah. The Heb. word for law; used of the first five books of the O.T. canon.

Total depravity. The inability of anyone to do anything that gains spiritual merit with God; does not mean that a person cannot contribute to society, commits every possible sin, or is as evil as he could be; the result of a sinful nature and the fall.

Tower of Babel. The edifice that rebellious nations attempted to build, as recorded in Gen. 11:1ff; an outworking of the Babylonian spirit, organized rebellion against God, to be fully manifested during the tribulation period and subsequently destroyed at the second advent of Christ, as recorded in Rev. 17–19.

Traducianism. The belief that the soul is received, along with the body, from parents; *S. Creationism* and ch. 15, The Doctrine of Humanity.

Transcendence of God. An attribute of God according to which He is greater than and distinct from His creation (cp. *Pantheism*) (q.v.), according to which He is part of the universe); Acts 17:24–25.

Transfiguration. The event recorded in Lk. 9:28–36 and parallels, in which our Lord Jesus Christ took two disciples and ascended a mountain; as He spoke with Moses and Elijah a portion of His glory became visible; it is a picture of His glory in the kingdom; Mt. 17:2n.

Transgression. Used as a general word for sin and also to teach that sin is a violation of what God has laid down as standards for human beings; Rom. 3:23n; 2:23; *S.* ch. 14, The Doctrine of Sin.

Tree of the knowledge of good and evil. Located in the Garden of Eden, it was a real tree that provided a test for Adam and Eve, which they failed; eating its fruit determined the relation of the human race to God, because humanity became partakers of evil; Gen. 2:17.

Tree of life. A real tree in the Garden of Eden; its purpose is unknown, except

that it appears again in Rev. 2:7 and 22:2ff, where a sinless environment is once again provided for humanity; Gen. 2:17n; Rev. 2:7n.

Trespass offering. A sacrifice, usually a ram, made to atone for particular sins (e.g., Lev. 5:15) and directed at the effects of the sin more than removal of guilt from the sinner, since penalties were also involved (Lev. 6:5); depending on the passage and translation, this is also found described as a guilt or penalty offering; Lev. 5:6n.

Tribes of Israel. S. Twelve tribes of Israel.

Tribulation. This general word for a trial or difficulty is used esp. to describe the period of time also known as the 70th week of Daniel (Dan. 9:24n); it appears alone in reference to that time in Mt. 24:29 and Mk. 13:24 (AV and NASB); in Mt. 24:21 (AV and NASB) and Rev. 7:14 it is modified by the word *great;* some take these latter occurrences to refer only to the last three and a half years of the seven-year period; Rev. 7:14n; 11:2n.

Trichotomy. The view that the individual is composed of body, soul, and spirit; cp. *Dichotomy* (q.v.); *S.* ch. 15, The Doctrine of Humanity.

Trinity. Although this word does not appear in the Bible, it is useful for describing the relations within the Godhead; God is a unity, one God, who cannot be split into parts; but within this unity the Bible reveals that there are also three separate Persons who are equal in every way, i.e., each fully God, but having different tasks, esp. in regard to human salvation; they are described as Father, Son, and Holy Spirit; some have suggested an alternative term, *triunity;* Mt. 3:16n; 28:19n; *S.* ch. 11, The Doctrine of God.

Trust. In regard to salvation, this expresses an aspect of faith, which is confident dependence on God to provide what we cannot; Ps. 2:12n; *S. Faith* and *Belief.*

Truth. An attribute of God that describes Him as never acting in a manner contradictory to Himself and what He has revealed; our Lord Jesus Christ is the embodiment of truth (Jn. 14:6).

Twelve tribes of Israel. The division of Israel into twelve sections based on descent from the twelve sons of Jacob; the basis of allotment of territory upon entrance into the land; Gen. 35:22n.

Type. From a Gr. word meaning pattern, this term is used theologically of events or institutions (or their parts) in the O.T. that have counterparts in the N.T.; the O.T. entity is thus a kind of prophecy in life, as when in Ps. 22:1 David's cry of dereliction is echoed in our Lord's words from the cross; Gen. 2:23n; *S.* ch. 5, Interpreting the Bible.

U

Ultradispensationalism. The position that views the Church as having begun after Acts 2, esp. in Acts 13 or 28.

Unction. A term found in the AV at 1 Jn. 2:20 that describes the ministry of the Holy Spirit in teaching believers; NASB and NIV = *anointing.*

Union with Christ. The spiritual relationship that exists between the believer and the Person and work of Christ; effected by God at salvation, it describes a position in which the merits and future of Christ are the possession of the believer; Rom. 6:3–10; Col. 3:1–4, 9–11.

Universal Church. *S. Church, universal.*

Universalism. The view that no human beings receive eternal punishment, all benefiting from the cross-work of Christ and being recipients of divine favor; a general tenet of modern liberal theology.

Unknown God. A term found in Acts 17:23, where Paul speaks of the Athenian practice of erecting altars to deities otherwise not named specifically, done to placate gods by not omitting them from worship.

Unknown tongue. A phrase used in 1 Cor. 14 in the AV; the Gr. text has simply *glōssa,* "tongue" or "language"; the emphasis of 1 Cor. 14 is that the gift involves genuine human language that is, however, unknown to the speaker.

Unleavened Bread, Feast of. *S. Passover.*

Unlimited atonement. The view that regards the death of Christ as made for all human beings but effective only for the elect; cp. *Limited Atonement* (q.v.).

Unpardonable sin. (1) A term applied loosely and unbiblically to any sin that God would not forgive; (2) applied specifically to the act of rejecting the work of the Holy Spirit in and through the Lord Jesus Christ during His public ministry, and ascribing to Satan (through blindness and hardness of heart) the works of the Spirit; called also blasphemy against the Holy Spirit; Mt. 12:31n; not to be confused with the *sin unto death* (q.v.) of 1 Jn. 5:16–17.

Upper Room. The place where Jesus spent His last evening with His disciples; apparently a large chamber on an upper story of a house in Jerusalem.

Urim and thummim. A phrase whose exact meaning has been debated, connected with the breastplate of the high priest; Ex. 28:30n.

V

Vanity. As used esp. in Ecclesiastes (AV and NASB; NIV = *meaningless*), this refers to approaching life without giving God His proper place, resulting in emptiness; Eccl. 1:2n.

Variant. A term used in *textual criticism* (q.v.); it is the point in a manuscript where it contains a word, phrase, sentence, etc., different from any other manuscript(s); wherever there is such variation, all of the alternatives from all the manuscripts containing the section of the text in question constitute the *variant readings; S.* ch. 2, The Nature of the Bible.

Veil. The fabric divider placed between the holy place and the most holy place in the Tabernacle and Temple; Ex. 26:31n; Mk. 15:38n.

Vicarious atonement. The view that the death of Christ occurred as an act of substitution for others, removing the penalty of sin for those who could not remove it themselves.

Vellum. Ancient writing material made usually from calfskin; the term is sometimes used interchangeably with *parchment* (q.v.).

Verbal inspiration. The view that the very words, not simply ideas, of the canonical Scriptures were the product of the process of inspiration; 2 Tim. 3:16n; 1 Cor. 2:13n; 2 Pet. 1:19n; *S.* ch. 10, The Bible.

Virgin birth. Refers to the incarnation of our Lord Jesus Christ; His birth was supernatural in that He had a real human mother but the Holy Spirit created in her the God-man; it should be remembered that the birth itself was entirely normal; only the conception was miraculous; Isa. 7:14n.

Vulgate. One of several Lat. translations of the Bible; made by Jerome (and perhaps others) in the late fourth c. A.D.; the official Bible of the Roman Catholic Church; the word vulgate means common.

W

Walking in the light. A phrase used in 1 Jn. to describe the obligation of the believer to conduct his life in correspondence with the attributes of God; 1 Jn. 1:7n.

Washings. Used of ceremonial cleansing under the law, involving people and objects.

Wave offering. Description of the way in which certain offerings were presented to God, involving specific movements of the priests' hands.

Weak brother. The Christian who believes that he cannot practice certain *doubtful things* (q.v.); *not* an immature believer, as some assert; *S. Strong brother* and ch. 17, The Doctrine of Salvation.

Weeks, Feast of. Another name for the Feast of Pentecost (q.v.).

Wheat and weeds. Found as "wheat and tares" in the AV and NASB, this phrase is used in one of Jesus' parables of the kingdom in Mt. 13 to describe the presence together of true and false Christians in the professing Church throughout the present age; Mt. 13:24n.

Will of God. The purposes of God for humanity and the universe (as in Rev. 4:11), expressed in various ways and with various components: there is a will of God for believers (1 Th. 4:3); the death of Christ was part of the will of God in providing salvation (Acts 2:23); 2 Pet. 3:9n.

Willful king. A term used to describe the end-time figure presented in Dan. 11:36–45, the one who "will do as he pleases" (NIV); Dan. 11:36n.

Wisdom. (1) An attribute of God, denoting His perfect coordination of events to accomplish His ends; (2) a virtue, particularly for God's children, consisting of the ability to apply knowledge (esp. spiritual) successfully to life; used in a narrower sense of a spiritual gift (1 Cor. 12:8); Prov. 8:22n.

Wisdom literature. The books of Job, Proverbs and Ecclesiastes; *S.* Scofield Bible, an "Introduction to the Poetic and Wisdom Books."

Wise men. S. Magi.

Witchcraft. A condemned, demonically associated practice, involving worship of and attempted contact with evil spirits, with the intention of affecting human lives; Ex. 22:18.

Witness. A concept prominent in the N.T., esp. the book of Acts; all believers are to publicize to other people what God has done for them and what they have seen of the grace of God; Acts 1:8n.

Word. S. Logos.

Works. As used of human activity in relation to God, this can refer to (1) attempts by an unsaved person to please God on his own merits (Rom. 4:2); (2) those things that believers do, either empowered by the Holy Spirit and therefore valuable in God's sight, or done from the sin nature and therefore worthless (1 Cor. 3:12–15).

World. Depending on the translation, this may refer to (1) the whole universe, (2) the entirety or some portion of humanity, (3) the organized spiritual activity of Satan, operating independently of God and seeking to counterfeit Him and His works; Mt. 4:8n; Mk. 10:30n; Lk. 2:1n; Rev. 13:8n.

Worldliness. S. Carnality.

Wormwood. A bitter desert plant, symbolic of adversity and grief.

Worship. The act of approaching God in thanks for His goodness and grace; involves acknowledging who He is (Rev. 4:11); is possible today because of the sacrifice and present work of Christ (Heb. 13:15); is to be distinguished from teaching, which in this age is a spiritual gift and involves communication from God to us,

whereas worship involves our going to God; is esp. associated throughout the Bible with priesthood; Heb. 13:15–16; 1 Pet. 2:9–10; Ex. 30:9n; *S.* ch. 18, The Church.

Wrath. God's intense, controlled hatred of sin, expressed in the condemnation of sin and the sinner; Rom. 1:18.

Y

Yahweh. Approximate pronunciation of the personal name of God; Heb. O.T. manuscripts have the consonant/semivowel sequence YHWH without interspersed vowels; also called in biblical studies the *nomen sacrum* and considered too sacred to pronounce; *S. Jehovah,* a late creation; Mal. 3:18n; Gen. 2:4n; Ex. 34:6n; Ex. 3:14–15.

Yeast. NIV translation equivalent to AV and NASB *leaven* (q.v.); Mt. 13:33n; Lev. 7:13n.

Z

Zealot. This term for an enthusiast for a cause is found as a translation for the name of a Jewish political party of the first c., best known for its stand against the Romans at Masada in 73 A.D.; perhaps the description of one of the apostles as "Simon the Zealot" in Lk. 6:15 and Acts 1:13 was used to identify him with this party.

Zion. Narrowly, the rock formation at the junction of the Kidron and Hinnom valleys; more broadly used of the southwest portion of Jerusalem and the whole city itself, including references occurring in prophetic contexts (Heb. 12:22–24); 1 Chr. 11:5n.

21

Outlines of Individual Books of the Bible

These outlines are based loosely on those of *The New Scofield Reference Bible*. Use them to gain an overview of a book and to see relations of parts to each other. Bible students frequently differ in their sectioning of books, so these outlines are meant to be suggestive and do not purport to provide the final word. You should endeavor to amplify them through your own study.

Genesis

I. Creation	1:1–2:25
A. Account of God's acts in creation	1:1–27
B. First dispensation instituted: Innocence	1:28–2:25
II. The fall and the promise of redemption	3:1–4:7
A. Account of the fall	3:1–6
B. Second dispensation instituted: Conscience	3:7–4:7
III. The diverse seeds of Cain and Seth to the flood	4:8–7:24
A. Murder of Abel	4:8–15
B. Origins of civilizations	4:16–5:32
C. The flood	6:1–7:24
IV. The flood to Babel	8:1–11:9
A. Subsiding of the flood	8:1–14
B. Third dispensation instituted: Human Government	8:15–11:9
V. From the call of Abram to the death of Joseph	11:10–50:26

A. Call of Abram	11:10–32
B. Fourth dispensation instituted: Promise	12:1–3
C. Abram's early experiences	12:4–20:18
D. Birth and life of Isaac	21:1–25:23
E. Birth and life of Esau and Jacob	25:24–37:1
F. Account of Joseph	37:2–50:26

Exodus

I. Israel in Egypt: oppression and conflict with Pharaoh	1:1–12:36
A. Bondage of Israel; birth and early life of Moses	1:1–2:25
B. Call of Moses	3:1–4:31
C. Contests with Pharaoh	5:1–11:10
D. Institution of Passover	12:1–36
II. The Exodus from Egypt and the journey to Sinai	12:37–18:27
A. First stage of the journey	12:37–13:22
B. Pursuit by Pharoah, and his defeat	14:1–15:21
C. Provisions in the wilderness	15:22–18:27
III. At Sinai: the giving of the law and the construction of the Tabernacle	19:1–40:38
A. Fifth dispensation instituted: Law	19:1–25
B. Details of the law	20:1–32:35
1. Commandments, judgments, and feasts	20:1–24:8
2. Moses on Sinai	24:9–25:2
3. Details of the Tabernacle	25:3–27:21
4. The priesthood	28:1–29:46
5. The Tabernacle's use	30:1–31:18
6. The broken law	32:1–35
C. Journey resumed	33:1–35:35
D. Construction of the Tabernacle	36:1–40:38

Leviticus

I. The offerings	1:1–7:37
A. Pleasing aroma ("sweet savor") offerings	1:1–3:17
1. The burnt offering	1:1–17
2. The grain (meal) offering	2:1–16
3. The fellowship (peace) offering	3:1–17
B. Other offerings	4:1–6:7
1. The sin offering	4:1–35
2. The trespass offering	5:1–19
3. The guilt offering	6:1–7
C. Law of the offerings	6:8–7:37
II. Consecration of Aaron and his sons	8:1–10:20

III. Laws of cleanliness and holiness: a holy God—a holy people   11:1–15:33
   A. Food   11:1–47
   B. Law of motherhood   12:1–8
   C. Infectious skin diseases   13:1–59
   D. Law of cleansing   14:1–57
   E. Necessity of cleansing   15:1–33
IV. The Day of Atonement: Christ as High Priest and sacrifice   16:1–17:16
V. Laws regulating the personal relationships of the redeemed
   people   18:1–20:27
   A. Unlawful sexual relations   18:1–29
   B. Idolatry   19:1–8
   C. Provisions for the unfortunate   19:9–14
   D. Righteous actions   19:15–37
   E. Various immoralities   20:1–27
VI. Laws regulating the priesthood and the seven great feasts of the
   Hebrew calendar   21:1–23:44
   A. Regulations concerning priests   21:1–22:33
   B. Feasts of the Lord   23:1–44
      1. Passover   23:1–5
      2. Unleavened Bread   23:6–8
      3. First Grain   23:9–14
      4. Wave Loaves (Pentecost)   23:15–22
      5. Trumpets   23:23–25
      6. Day of Atonement   23:26–32
      7. Tabernacles   23:33–44
VII. Additional laws, promises, and warnings   24:1–27:34

Numbers

I. Preparations for departure from Sinai: order of the host   1:1–10:10
   A. Moses' numbering of the able men of war   1:1–54
   B. Arrangement of the camp   2:1–34
   C. The priests   3:1–4
   D. The tribe of Levi   3:5–13
   E. The families of Levi   3:14–24
   F. The duties of the sons of Levi   3:25–39
   G. The redemption of the firstborn   3:40–51
   H. Service of the Kohathites   4:1–15
   I. The office of Eleazer   4:16–20
   J. Service of the Gershonites   4:21–28
   K. Service of the Merarites   4:29–49
   L. Necessity of purity; defilement banished   5:1–31
   M. The Nazarites (Nazirites)   6:1–27
   N. Gifts of the leaders   7:1–89
   O. The lamps and lampstand   8:1–4
   P. Cleansing of the Levites   8:5–26

Q. The Passover	9:1–14
R. The guiding cloud	9:15–23
S. The silver assembly trumpets	10:1–10
II. From Sinai to the plains of Moab	10:11–21:35
A. From Sinai to Kadesh Barnea	10:11–12:16
B. At Kadesh Barnea	13:1–14:45
C. The years of wandering	15:1–21:35
III. The prophecies of Balaam	22:1–25:18
IV. Instructions and preparations for entering the promised land	26:1–36:13

Deuteronomy

I. First discourse: review of Israel's history after the Exodus, and its lessons	1:1–4:49
A. Failure of Israel at Kadesh Barnea	1:1–46
B. Wanderings in the wilderness	2:1–37
C. Experience with Og	3:1–29
D. Greatness of the law	4:1–49
II. Second discourse: rehearsal of the Sinaitic laws, with warnings and exhortations	5:1–26:19
A. Teaching of fundamentals of the law to a new generation	5:1–6:25
B. Results of obedience and disobedience	7:1–26
C. Moses' look backward and forward	8:1–10:22
D. Importance of heeding God's word	11:1–32
E. Law of the central sanctuary	12:1–32
F. Forbidden practices	13:1–14:2
G. Dietary laws	14:3–29
H. Sabbatical year	15:1–23
I. The Passover and other feasts	16:1–17:1
J. Provisions and prohibitions	17:2–26:19
III. Third discourse: blessings and curses for obedience and disobedience	27:1–28:68
IV. Fourth discourse: the Palestinian Covenant—its warnings and promised blessings	29:1–30:20
V. Conclusion: final words and acts of Moses, and his death	31:1–34:12

Joshua

I. Preparation for entering Palestine	1:1–5:15
A. Moses succeeded by Joshua	1:1–18
B. Rahab's assistance	2:1–24
C. Crossing the Jordan	3:1–4:24
D. New generation circumcised	5:1–15
II. Conquest of the land	6:1–12:24

A. Conquest of Jericho   6:1–27
B. Achan's sin and Israel's experience at Ai   7:1–8:35
C. Experience at Gibeon   9:1–10:15
D. Victory at Makkedah and other southern cities   10:16–43
E. Northern Palestinian campaign   11:1–23
F. Roster of conquered kings   12:1–24
III. Allocation of territories to the tribes   13:1–22:34
IV. Joshua's final message and his death   23:1–24:33

Judges

I. Review of the past and institution of the office of judge   1:1–3:4
A. State of Israel at the death of Joshua   1:1–3
B. Judah's victories   1:4–20
C. Incomplete victories of Benjamin and Manasseh   1:21–36
D. Rebuke for disobedience   2:1–9
E. Wicked new generation   2:10–15
F. Raising up of deliverers by God   2:16–19
G. Leaving of Canaanites to test Israel   2:20–3:4
II. Five judges   3:5–5:31
III. Gideon   6:1–9:57
A. Gideon's appointment   6:1–24
B. Gideon's life   6:25–8:35
C. Career of Gideon's son, Abimelech   9:1–57
IV. Six judges   10:1–12:15
V. Samson   13:1–16:31
A. Samson's birth and early life   13:1–25
B. Slaying of the lion and Samson's riddle   14:1–20
C. Burning of the Philistine's crops   15:1–8
D. Slaying of a thousand Philistines   15:9–20
E. Samson's moral weakness   16:1–22
F. Samson's death   16:23–31
VI. Confusion in Israel   17:1–21:25
A. Religious confusion   17:1–13
B. Incidents involving the Danites   18:1–31
C. The Levite's concubine: moral degredation   19:1–20:17
D. Civil war   20:18–21:25

Ruth

I. Ruth deciding   1:1–22
A. Famine in Judah   1:1
B. Sojourn in Moab   1:2–5
C. Return to Judah   1:6–10

   D. Ruth's loyal decision   1:11–18

   E. Return to Bethlehem   1:19–22

  II. Ruth serving   2:1–23

   A. Boaz' compliment   2:1–18

   B. Ruth's disclosure to Naomi   2:19–23

 III. Ruth resting   3:1–18

   A. Naomi's instructions to Ruth   3:1–4

   B. Ruth's obedience   3:5–6

   C. Boaz' charge   3:7–13

   D. Ruth's return to Naomi   3:14–18

 IV. Ruth's reward   4:1–22

   A. Ruth requited with marriage   4:1–15

   B. Ruth as an ancestor of David   4:16–22

1 Samuel

  I. The youth and judgeship of Samuel   1:1–8:22

   A. Samuel's birth   1:1–2:11

   B. Eli's wicked sons   2:12–36

   C. Call of Samuel   3:1–4:1a

   D. Ark captured by the Philistines   4:1b–5:12

   E. Return of the ark to Israel   6:1–21

   F. Revival after twenty years   7:1–17

   G. Israel's demand for a king   8:1–22

 II. The anointing and rejection of Saul as king of Israel   9:1–15:35

   A. God's choice of Saul as king   9:1–27

   B. Saul's anointing as king   10:1–27

   C. Saul's victory over the Ammonites   11:1–15

   D. Kingship confirmed to Samuel   12:1–25

   E. Saul's self-seeking, cowardice, and intrusion into the priest's
       office   13:1–22

   F. Victory through Jonathan   13:23–14:23

   G. Saul's rash order overridden   14:24–46

   H. Historic and spiritual summaries of Saul's reign   14:47–15:11

   I. Samuel's rebuke of Saul   15:12–35

 III. The parallel lives of Saul and David, to the death of Saul   16:1–31:13

   A. Rejection of Saul and anointing of David   16:1–23

   B. David's victory over Goliath and the Philistines   17:1–58

   C. Jonathan's covenant with David   18:1–4

   D. Saul's attempt to slay David   18:5–16

   E. David's marriage to Saul's daughter   18:17–30

   F. David protected from Saul three times   19:1–24

   G. Renewal of Jonathan and David's covenant   20:1–23

   H. Saul's anger toward Jonathan   20:24–42

   I. Saul's pursuit of David   21:1–30:31

   J. Death of Saul and Jonathan   31:1–13

2 Samuel

I. The death of Saul to the beginning of David's reign	1:1–4:12
A. David's lament over Saul and Jonathan	1:1–27
B. David's reception as king	2:1–11
C. Civil war begins	2:12–32
D. David's strength increases	3:1–4:12
II. The anointing of David as king of Israel to the revolt of Absalom	5:1–14:33
A. David as king over Israel in Jerusalem	5:1–25
B. Ark brought to Jerusalem	6:1–23
C. The Davidic Covenant	7:1–29
D. Davidic campaigns	8:1–10:19
E. David's great sin	11:1–27
F. Nathan's rebuke and David's repentance	12:1–31
G. Consequences of David's sin	13:1–14:33
III. The revolt of Absalom to the numbering of the people	15:1–24:25
A. Absalom's rebellion and death	15:1–18:33
B. Restoration of David to his kingdom	19:1–40
C. Further revolt and dissension	19:41–20:26
D. Restitution to Gibeonites	21:1–14
E. Final campaign against the Philistines and the song of deliverance	21:15–23:7
F. David's mighty men	23:8–39
G. Aversion of plague	24:1–25

1 Kings

I. David's last days	1:1–2:11
II. The reign of Solomon	2:12–11:43
A. Beginning of Solomon's reign	2:12–4:34
B. Preparation for Temple construction	5:1–18
C. Construction of the Temple	6:1–7:51
D. Placing of the ark	8:1–11
E. Solomon's dedication of the Temple	8:12–66
F. Splendor of Solomon's reign	9:1–10:29
G. Solomon's forsaking God; his death	11:1–43
III. The division of the kingdom under Rehoboam and Jeroboam	12:1–14:31
IV. The kings of Judah and Israel to the accession of Ahab	15:1–16:27
V. The reign of Ahab	16:28–22:39
A. Elijah's ministry	16:28–19:18
B. Call of Elisha	19:19–21
C. Ahab's campaigns against the Arameans	20:1–22:28
D. Death of Ahab	22:29–39
VI. The reigns of Jehoshaphat and Ahaziah	22:40–53

2 Kings

I. The last ministry and translation of Elijah	1:1–2:12
II. The ministry of Elisha	2:13–8:15
A. Elisha succeeds Elijah	2:13–25
B. Elisha reproves Joram	3:1–27
C. Miracles of Elisha	4:1–8:15
III. The kings of Israel and Judah to the fall of Samaria	8:16–17:41
IV. The accession of Hezekiah to the captivity of Judah	18:1–25:30

1 Chronicles

I. Genealogies of the patriarchs and the twelve sons of Israel	1:1–9:44
II. The last days and death of King Saul	10:1–14
III. The reign of David	11:1–29:30
A. David in Jerusalem	11:1–9
B. Roll of David's men	11:10–12:40
C. Sin at the ark	13:1–14
D. Prosperous reign	14:1–17
E. Ark brought to Jerusalem	15:1–16:43
F. The Davidic Covenant	17:1–27
G. Fullness of David's kingdom	18:1–17
H. David at war	19:1–20:8
I. Plague resulting from sin of numbering the people	21:1–30
J. Temple begun	22:1–19
K. Organizing of Israel	23:1–28:8
L. Charge to Solomon	28:9–21
M. Solomon enthroned	29:1–25
N. Death of David	29:26–30

2 Chronicles

I. The reign of Solomon and the building of the Temple	1:1–9:31
A. Solomon blessed by God	1:1–17
B. Preparation for building the Temple	2:1–18
C. Building of the Temple	3:1–4:22
D. The Ark brought in	5:1–14
E. Dedication of the Temple by Solomon	6:1–42
F. Divine support	7:1–22
G. Solomon's accomplishments	8:1–9:28
H. Death of Solomon	9:29–31
II. The history of Judah from the reign of Rehoboam to the destruction of Jerusalem and the captivity	10:1–36:23

A. Reign of Rehoboam   10:1–12:16
B. Reign of Abijah   13:1–14:1
C. Reign of Asa   14:2–16:14
D. Reign of Jehoshaphat   17:1–21:1a
E. Reign of Jehoram   21:1b–20
F. Reign of Ahaziah   22:1–12
G. Reign of Joash; ministry of Jehoiada   23:1–24:27
H. Reign of Amaziah   25:1–28
 I. Reign of Uzziah   26:1–23
J. Reign of Jotham   27:1–9
K. Reign of Ahaz   28:1–27
L. Reign of Hezekiah   29:1–32:33
M. Reign of Manasseh   33:1–20
N. Reign of Amon   33:21–25
O. Reign of Josiah   34:1–35:27
P. Reign of Jehoahaz   36:1–3
Q. Reign of Jehoiakim   36:4–7
R. Reign of Jehoiachin: the Babylonian Captivity   36:8–23

Ezra

 I. The first return under Zerubbabel and the building of the second
    Temple   1:1–6:22
    A. Decree of Cyrus permitting Jews' return to Jerusalem to re-
        build Temple   1:1–4
    B. Contributions to those returning; Cyrus' restoration of the
        holy vessels   1:5–11
    C. Number of those returning   2:1–70
    D. Building of the altar and restoration of ancient sacrifice   3:1–7
    E. Laying of foundations of the Temple   3:8–13
    F. Attempts to hinder the work   4:1–24
    G. Completion of work on the Temple and restoration of Pass-
        over   5:1–6:22
II. The ministry of Ezra   7:1–10:44
    A. Ezra's return to Jerusalem   7:1–10
    B. Decree of Artaxerxes on Ezra's behalf   7:11–26
    C. Ezra's thanksgiving   7:27–28
    D. Ezra's companions   8:1–14
    E. Ezra's sending for the Levites and the Nethinim   8:15–20
    F. Ezra's proclamation of a fast seeking the Lord's protection   8:21–23
    G. Committing of the treasure to twelve priests   8:24–30
    H. Ezra's arrival in Jerusalem   8:31–34
     I. Governors given king's decree   8:35–36
    J. Failure of God's people to separate from surrounding nations   9:1–4
    K. Ezra's prayer of confession to the Lord   9:5–15
    L. Reconciliaton to God through confession and separation   10:1–44

Nehemiah

I. Artaxerxes' permission for Nehemiah to visit Jerusalem	1:1–2:8
A. Distress of the remnant in Jerusalem	1:1–3
B. Nehemiah's prayer	1:4–11
C. Answer to Nehemiah's prayer	2:1–8
II. The rebuilding of the walls of Jerusalem	2:9–7:73
A. Nehemiah's arrival in Jerusalem and encouragement of the people	2:9–20
B. The builders of the walls	3:1–32
C. Opposition and encouragement	4:1–6:14
D. Completion of the wall	6:15–19
E. Registration of the people	7:1–73
III. The great revival under Ezra	8:1–10:39
A. The law read and explained	8:1–12
B. Feast of Tabernacles and assembly of the people	8:13–10:39
IV. Conditions prevailing in Palestine	11:1–13:31
A. Inhabitants of Jerusalem and other cities	11:1–36
B. Identification of priests and Levites	12:1–26
C. Dedication of the wall	12:27–47
D. Reading of the Book of Moses	13:1–3
E. Repudiation of Tobiah and cleansing of the Temple	13:4–9
F. Proper provision for Levites and singers	13:10–14
G. Restoration of Sabbath rest	13:15–22
H. Enforcement of law against intermarriage with other peoples	13:23–31

Esther

I. Selection of Esther as queen	1:1–2:18
A. The feasts of King Ahasuerus in the citadel of Shushan	1:1–29
B. Deposing of Vashti	1:10–22
C. Search for Vashti's successor	2:1–14
D. Esther's accession as queen	2:15–18
II. Esther's deliverance of her people, the Jews	2:19–7:10
A. Mordecai's saving of the king's life	2:19–23
B. Haman's conspiracy against the Jews	3:1–15
C. Mourning among the Jews and Esther's discovery of the conspiracy	4:1–8
D. Mordecai's request to Esther to risk her life for her people	4:9–17
E. Esther's courageous request	5:1–14
F. The king's insomnia	6:1–3
G. Haman forced to honor Mordecai	6:4–14
H. Esther's plea for herself and her people	7:1–6
I. Haman's death	7:7–10

III. The Jews' revenge upon their enemies 8:1–10:3
   A. Defeat of Haman's conspiracy through the king's decree ... 8:1–14
   B. Exaltation of Mordecai 8:15–17
   C. Jew's destruction of enemies 9:1–19
   D. Institution of the Feast of Purim 9:20–32
   E. Mordecai's further advancement 10:1–3

Job

  I. Prologue 1:1–2:13
   A. Job's character, family, and piety 1:1–5
   B. Satan's assaults 1:6–2:13
 II. Job's dialogues with his counselors 3:1–31:40
   A. Job's lament 3:1–26
   B. Eliphaz' first charge and night vision 4:1–5:27
   C. Job's reply: a plea for pity 6:1–7:21
   D. Bildad's first speech 8:1–22
   E. Job's response 9:1–10:22
   F. Zophar's first charge 11:1–20
   G. Job's rebuttal 12:1–14:22
   H. Eliphaz' second speech 15:1–35
   I. Job's reply 16:1–17:16
   J. Bildad's second speech 18:1–21
   K. Job's reply 19:1–29
   L. Zophar's final speech 20:1–29
   M. Job's answer 21:1–34
   N. Eliphaz' final speech 22:1–30
   O. Job's reply 23:1–24:25
   P. Bildad's final speech 25:1–6
   Q. Job's reply 26:1–31:40
III. Elihu's monologue 32:1–37:24
 IV. The Lord's reply 38:1–41:34
   A. Interrogation of Job face to face 38:1–41
   B. Assertion of omnipotence 39:1–30
   C. Summary question 40:1–2
   D. Job's reply 40:3–5
   E. God's questioning of Job resumed 40:6–41:34
  V. Job's confession 42:1–6
 VI. Epilogue: renewed blessing and prosperity for Job 42:7–17

Psalms

The simple, ancient Jewish classification of the Psalms is as follows:
Book I   Psalms 1–41
Book II   Psalms 42–72

Book III   Psalms 73–89
Book IV   Psalms 90–106
Book V   Psalms 107–150

Proverbs

I. Fatherly exhortations addressed mainly to the young	1:1–9:18
A. The purpose of the book	1:1–6
B. Wisdom's foundation: the fear of the Lord	1:7–19
C. Wisdom's warning	1:20–33
D. Wisdom's ability to deliver from evil	2:1–22
E. The rewards of wisdom	3:1–35
F. Fatherly advice	4:1–27
G. Immorality rebuked	5:1–23
H. Parental warnings	6:1–35
I. The snare of unchastity	7:1–27
J. Praise of wisdom	8:1–9:18
II. Wisdom and the fear of God as contrasted with the folly of sin	10:1–24:34
III. Proverbs of Solomon selected by men of Hezekiah: warnings and instructions	25:1–29:27
IV. Supplemental proverbs by Agur and Lemuel	30:1–31:31
A. The words of Agur	30:1–33
B. The words of Lemuel	31:1–31
1. The curse of intemperance	31:1–9
2. Portrait of the virtuous woman	31:10–31

Ecclesiastes

I. The teacher's experience of the variety of earthly things	1:1–4:16
A. His theme: everything is meaningless	1:1–2
B. Proof of the theme	1:3–3:22
1. The ceaseless cycle of created things	1:3–11
2. Failure of wisdom to satisfy	1:12–18
3. Failure of pleasure and riches to satisfy	2:1–11
4. Failure of both wisdom and folly	2:12–26
5. The weary round of life	3:1–22
C. Life's oppressions and inequalities	4:1–16
II. Exhortations in the light of this experience	5:1–10:20
A. Failure of mere religious practices to satisfy	5:1–8
B. The futility of riches	5:9–20
C. The futility of life	6:1–12
D. Human wisdom's better findings	7:1–29
E. Importance of obeying rulers	8:1–17
F. Certainty of death despite wisdom	9:1–18
G. Danger of folly	10:1–20

III. The conclusion of the matter 11:1–12:14
 A. The best thing possible to the natural man 11:1–10
 B. Necessity of fearing God 12:1–14

Song of Songs

Canticle I: A Young Bride, a Shulammite Girl 1:1–6
Canticle II: The Perplexed Bride 1:7–8
Canticle III: Mutual Admiration 1:9–17
Canticle IV: The Shulammite Is Comforted 2:1–7
Canticle V: The Shulammite Describes a Happy Visit 2:8–17
Canticle VI: The Shulammite Tells of Her Troubled Dream 3:1–5
Canticle VII: Solomon Has His Bride Brought to Jerusalem 3:6–11
Canticle VIII: Solomon, the Bridegroom, Expresses His Message of
 Love 4:1–7
Canticle IX: Solomon's Proposal and the Shulammite's Acceptance 4:8–5:1
Canticle X: The Bride Tells of Another Distressing Dream 5:2–6:3
Canticle XI: The Bridegroom Praises His Bride 6:4–7:10
Canticle XII: The Bride Expresses Her Longing to Visit Her Home 7:11–8:4
Canticle XIII: The Past Is Recalled When Baal Hamon Is Revisited 8:5–14

Isaiah

 I. Prophetic messages concerning Judah 1:1–12:6
 II. Prophecies concerning the nations 13:1–27:13
 III. Prophetic warnings concerning Ephraim and Judah 28:1–35:10
 IV. Historical parenthesis: Sennacherib's invasions and Hezekiah's
  illness 36:1–39:8
 V. The greatness and transcendence of God 40:1–48:22
 VI. The suffering Servant of the Lord 49:1–57:21
 VII. Concluding exhortations and prophecies 58:1–66:24

Jeremiah

 I. Prophecies of judgment on Judah 1:1–45:5
  A. Jeremiah's call 1:1–19
  B. Jeremiah's first message 2:1–3:5
  C. Jeremiah's second message 3:6–6:30
  D. Message at the Temple gate 7:1–10:25
  E. Message on the broken covenant 11:1–12:17
  F. Sign of the marred belt 13:1–27
  G. Message concerning the drought 14:1–15:14
  H. Jeremiah's communion with God 15:15–21
  I. Sign of the unmarried prophet 16:1–17:18

	J. Sign of the potter's house	18:1–19:15
	K. Jeremiah's persecution by Pashhur	20:1–6
	L. Jeremiah's complaint to God	20:7–18
	M. Messages concerning Judah's last four kings	21:1–22:30
	N. God's true king: Messiah the righteous Branch	23:1–8
	O. False prophets denounced	23:9–40
	P. Sign of the figs	24:1–10
	Q. Prophecy of the seventy-year Babylonian captivity	25:1–38
	R. Message in the Temple court and its results	26:1–24
	S. Sign of the yokes	27:1–22
	T. Hananiah's false prophecy and death	28:1–17
	U. Message to Jews of the first captivity	29:1–32
	V. Message concerning the Day of the Lord	30:1–31:40
	W. Jeremiah imprisoned: the sign of Hanamel's field	32:1–15
	X. Jeremiah's prayer and the Lord's response	32:16–44
	Y. Prophecy of the Davidic kingdom	33:1–26
	Z. Message to Zedekiah concerning his coming captivity	34:1–7
	AA. Princes and people rebuked	34:8–22
	BB. The Rechabites' obedience contrasted with Judah's disobedience	35:1–19
	CC. Jehoiakim's burning of Jeremiah's scroll	36:1–32
	DD. Jeremiah's interview with Zedekiah	37:1–10
	EE. Jeremiah's imprisonment and release	37:11–38:28
	FF. Fall of Jerusalem	39:1–41:18
	GG. Jeremiah's warnings	42:1–45:5
II.	Prophecies concerning foreign nations	46:1–51:64
III.	Historical supplement: second account of overthrow of Judah	52:1–34

Lamentations

I.	The desolation of Jerusalem	1:1–22
II.	The day of the Lord's anger	2:1–22
III.	Jeremiah's sharing of his nation's affliction	3:1–66
	A. His distress	3:1–21
	B. Recounting of God's faithfulness	3:22–39
	C. A call to self-judgment and confession	3:40–51
	D. Jeremiah's prison experience	3:52–66
IV.	The horrors of the siege of Jerusalem	4:1–22
V.	A plaintive prayer to the Lord	5:1–22

Ezekiel

I.	The call of Ezekiel	1:1–3:27
	A. Ezekiel's first vision: the glory of the Lord	1:1–28
	B. Ezekiel commissioned	2:1–3:27

II. Warnings of judgment upon Jerusalem   4:1–24:27
   A. Signs of coming judgment on Jerusalem enacted by the
       prophet   4:1–5:17
   B. Predictions of judgment and departure of God's glory   6:1–24:27
III. Judgments upon the Gentile nations   25:1–32:32
IV. Ezekiel's responsibility as watchman   33:1–33
 V. Predictions of events at the end of the age   34:1–39:29
   A. Restoration of God's flock Israel   34:1–31
   B. Prophecy against Edom   35:1–15
   C. Restoration of Israel to the land   36:1–38
   D. Vision of valley of dry bones: Israel's restoration   37:1–28
   E. Prophecy against Gog: future invasion of Palestine by
       northern confederacy   38:1–39:29
VI. The millennial Temple and its worship   40:1–47:12
VII. The division of the land during the millennial age   47:13–48:35

Daniel

  I. Daniel's early life in the Babylonian court   1:1–21
   A. Nebuchadnezzar's siege of Jerusalem   1:1–2
   B. Daniel and his companions in the palace   1:3–21
 II. Nebuchadnezzar's vision of the statue   2:1–49
   A. Interpretation demanded   2:1–9
   B. Failure of soothsayers   2:10–13
   C. Daniel's desire to interpret the dream   2:14–18
   D. Revelation to Daniel   2:19–23
   E. Disclosure of the dream and its meaning to Nebuchadnez-
       zar through Daniel   2:24–45
   F. Promotion of Daniel   2:46–49
III. Deliverance of the three Hebrew youths from the fiery furnace   3:1–30
IV. Nebuchadnezzar's second vision and his humbling by God   4:1–37
 V. Daniel's experiences under Belshazzar and Darius   5:1–6:28
   A. The handwriting on the wall   5:1–9
   B. Daniel's interpretation   5:10–31
   C. Daniel under Darius   6:1–28
VI. Daniel's first vision   7:1–28
   A. The four beasts   7:1–8
   B. The Ancient of Days   7:9–12
   C. The Son of Man   7:13–14
   D. Interpretation of beast vision   7:15–28
VII. Prophecy of Greek and Persian history   8:1–27
VIII. The prophecy of the seventy sevens   9:1–27
   A. Spiritual preparation by Daniel   9:1–19
   B. The actual vision   9:20–27
IX. Daniel's final vision   10:1–12:13
   A. Divine and angelic strengthening   10:1–11:1

B. From Darius to the man of sin	11:2–45
C. The Great Tribulation	12:1
D. The two resurrections	12:2–3
E. Last message to Daniel	12:4–13

Hosea

I. The prophet's tragic experience	1:1–3:5
A. Introduction	1:1
B. The marriage: birth of Jezreel	1:2–5
C. Birth of Lo-ruhamah	1:6–7
D. Birth of Lo-ammi	1:8–9
E. Future restoration	1:10–2:1
F. Chastisement of Israel	2:2–13
G. Restoration of Israel, the adulterous wife	2:14–23
H. The future Davidic kingdom, when Israel will fear the Lord	3:1–5
II. An indictment of Israel	4:1–8:14
A. The Lord's charge against the sinful nation	4:1–5
B. Israel's willful ignorance	4:6–12a
C. Israel's inveterate idolatry	4:12b–19
D. The Lord's face withdrawn	5:1–14
E. A remnant in the last days	5:15–6:3
F. The Lord's lament of Ephraim's (Israel's) sin	6:4–11a
G. Ephraim's iniquity	6:11b–7:16
H. Reaping the whirlwind	8:1–14
III. Retribution upon Israel	9:1–10:15
A. Ephraim punished and cast away	9:1–17
B. Fallow ground to be broken up	10:1–15
IV. God's unceasing love for Israel	11:1–13:8
A. The Lord's past relationship with His people	11:1–11
B. Further reproof of Israel's sin	11:12–12:14
C. Ephraim's continuing wickedness	13:1–8
V. The ultimate restoration of Israel	13:9–14:9

Joel

I. The present chastisement and its removal	1:1–2:27
A. Introduction	1:1–3
B. Desolation by locusts	1:4–13
C. Desolation by starvation and drought	1:14–20
D. The victorious invading host from the north, Assyria	2:1–11
E. Repentance the only escape from invasion	2:12–17
F. Deliverance promised if Israel repents	2:18–27
II. The promise of the Spirit	2:28–29

III. The future deliverance in the coming Day of the Lord   2:30–3:21
    A. The signs preceding the Day of the Lord   2:30–32
    B. The restoration of Israel   3:1
    C. Judgment of Gentile nations   3:2–17
    D. Final restoration: full kingdom blessing   3:18–21

Amos

  I. The pronouncement of judgment   1:1–2:16
    A. Introduction   1:1–2
    B. Judgments on surrounding cities and nations   1:3–2:3
    C. Judgment on God's people: Judah and Israel   2:4–16
 II. Inevitable divine judgment because of sin   3:1–4:13
    A. Guilt of all twelve tribes   3:1–15
    B. The Lord's scorn of Bethel's sacrifices   4:1–5
    C. Unheeded chastening   4:6–13
III. God's pleading with Israel to return to Him   5:1–15
 IV. Some events connected with the coming of the Lord   5:16–9:10
    A. The Day of the Lord   5:16–20
    B. Worship without righteousness an abomination to the Lord   5:21–27
    C. Woes upon those complacent in a time of unrighteousness   6:1–14
    D. Warning through visions   7:1–9
    E. Amaziah's accusation against Amos sent to Jeroboam   7:10–13
    F. Amos' answer   7:14–17
    G. Basket of summer fruit: Israel's impending captivity   8:1–14
    H. The final prophecy of dispersion   9:1–10
  V. The final restoration   9:11–15
    A. The Lord's second advent and the reestablishment of the
       Davidic kingdom   9:11–12
    B. Israel's restoration in the kingdom   9:13–15

Obadiah

  I. The pronouncement of doom upon Edom: the deceitfulness of
     pride   1:1–9
 II. The cause of this doom   1:10–14
III. Edom in the Day of the Lord   1:15–21
    A. Judgment upon Edom   1:15–16
    B. Deliverance for the house of Jacob   1:17–21

Jonah

  I. The disobedience and flight of Jonah   1:1–11
    A. Introduction   1:1

B. Jonah flees from the Lord 1:2–11
    1. God's commission 1:2
    2. Jonah's disobedience 1:3
    3. The storm 1:4–11
II. Jonah and the great fish 1:12–2:10
  A. Jonah swallowed by the fish 1:12–17
  B. Jonah's prayer 2:1–9
  C. The Lord's answer 2:10
III. The greatest revival in history 3:1–10
  A. Jonah's obedience 3:1–3
  B. Nineveh's repentance 3:4–10
IV. The wideness of God's mercy 4:1–11
  A. Jonah's displeasure 4:1–3
  B. Jonah rebuked by the Lord 4:4–11

Micah

I. Condemnation and captivity 1:1–2:13
  A. Introduction 1:1
  B. Judgment upon Israel 1:2–5
  C. Prediction of Assyria's victory 1:6–16
  D. Reasons for judgment 2:1–11
  E. Deliverance promised 2:12–13
II. Reproof and restoration in the kingdom 3:1–5:15
  A. Faithless leaders rebuked 3:1–8
  B. Prediction of Jerusalem's destruction 3:9–12
  C. Vision of earth's golden age 4:1–5
  D. Israel to be regathered 4:6–8
  E. Intervening Babylonian captivity 4:9–10
  F. Armageddon predicted 4:11–13
  G. Birth and rejection of the King 5:1–2
  H. Interval between the rejection and the return of the King . 5:3–15
III. Pleading, and assurance of mercy 6:1–7:20
  A. The Lord's past and present controversy with Israel 6:1–5
  B. The Lord's requirements 6:6–16
  C. The prophet's confession of the truth of the Lord's indict-
    ment 7:1–6
  D. Submission to the Lord 7:7–9
  E. Ascription of praise 7:10–20

Nahum

I. The character of God 1:1–8
  A. Introduction 1:1

  B. The holiness of the Lord and judgment upon Nineveh   1:2–8
II. God's punishment of His enemies   1:9–15
  A. The certainty of God's judgment   1:9–14
  B. The joyful news   1:15
III. The destruction of Nineveh detailed   2:1–13
IV. The cause of the destruction   3:1–19

Habakkuk

 I. The perplexity of the prophet   1:1–2:1
  A. Introduction   1:1
  B. The problem of unjudged sin   1:2–4
  C. The Lord's answer   1:5–11
  D. Habakkuk's perplexity concerning God's use of wicked
     Babylon   1:12–2:1
 II. The answer of God   2:2–20
  A. The vision: the just shall live by faith   2:2–4
  B. The destiny of the proud   2:5–20
III. The triumphant faith of Habakkuk   3:1–19

Zephaniah

 I. The coming invasion of Nebuchadnezzar: a figure of the Day of
    the Lord   1:1–2:3
  A. Introduction   1:1
  B. The coming judgment of Judah   1:2–18
  C. Zephaniah's call to repentance   2:1–3
  II. Predictions of judgment on surrounding nations   2:4–15
III. The moral state of Israel   3:1–7
IV. Future judgment of the Gentiles, followed by kingdom blessing
    under the Messiah   3:8–20
  A. God's determination   3:8
  B. Israel's cleansing   3:9–13
  C. Israel's restoration and blessing; the King in the kingdom   3:14–20

Haggai

 I. The first message of rebuke   1:1–11
  A. Introduction   1:1–2
  B. The condition of the exiles: God's discipline because of dis-
     obedience   1:3–11
 II. The first message of encouragement: the work recommenced   1:12–15

III. The second message of encouragement: the future glory of the
Temple ... 2:1–9
IV. The second message of rebuke: cleansing and blessing ... 2:10–19
V. The third message of encouragement: the final overthrow of
Gentile world power ... 2:20–23

Zechariah

I. Call to repentance ... 1:1–6
  A. Introduction ... 1:1
  B. A solemn warning and call to repentance ... 1:2–6
II. A series of eight visions ... 1:7–6:15
  A. The rider on the red horse ... 1:7–17
  B. The four horns and four craftsmen ... 1:18–21
  C. The man with the measuring line in his hand ... 2:1–13
  D. Joshua the high priest; the Lord's servant, the Branch ... 3:1–10
  E. The golden lampstand and the two olive trees ... 4:1–14
  F. The flying scroll ... 5:1–4
  G. The basket and the women ... 5:5–11
  H. The four chariots ... 6:1–15
III. The delegation from Bethel concerning fasting ... 7:1–8:23
  A. The question ... 7:1–3
  B. The Lord's answer ... 7:4–7
  C. The reason for unanswered prayer ... 7:8–14
  D. The future restoration of Israel in the kingdom ... 8:1–8
  E. Exhortation to hear the prophets ... 8:9–19
  F. Jerusalem as the religious center of the earth ... 8:20–23
IV. Prophecies concerning the end of Israel's age and the return of
Christ ... 9:1–14:21
  A. Destruction of cities surrounding Israel ... 9:1–8
  B. Prophecy of the Messiah's triumphal entry at first advent ... 9:9
  C. Future deliverance of Judah and Ephraim (Israel) ... 9:10–17
  D. Future strengthening of Judah and Ephraim ... 10:1–8
  E. The dispersion and regathering of Israel ... 10:9–12
  F. Messiah the true Shepherd rejected at His first advent ... 11:1–14
  G. The foolish shepherd to be overthrown ... 11:15–17
  H. Jerusalem to be attacked but Judah to be delivered ... 12:1–9
  I. The Spirit poured out: the pierced One revealed to the re-
pentent and delivered remnant ... 12:10–14
  J. Cleansing of the remnant ... 13:1
  K. False prophets to be ashamed ... 13:2–6
  L. Prophecy of the true prophet, Messiah ... 13:7
  M. Israel to be refined and delivered ... 13:8–9
  N. The Lord's triumphant return to earth to bring deliverance ... 14:1–3
  O. The visible return in glory ... 14:4–7
  P. The establishment of the kingdom ... 14:8–21

Malachi

I. Israel's pretended unawareness of God's love	1:1–5
A. Introduction	1:1
B. The Lord's love for His chosen people, Israel	1:2–5
II. The priests' denial of their despising the name of the Lord	1:6–2:9
A. Sins of the restoration priests	1:6–14
B. God's discipline of the priests	2:1–9
III. Israel's sins against one another and against the family	2:10–17
A. Sins against brotherhood	2:10
B. Sins against God in the family	2:11–16
C. Sin of insincere religious profession	2:17
IV. The coming of the forerunner, John the Baptist	3:1–5
V. Two groups of Israel contrasted	3:6–18
A. The people's robbing of God	3:6–15
B. The faithful remnant: the Lord's book of remembrance	3:16–18
VI. The coming Day of the Lord and the return of Christ	4:1–6
A. The appearance of the Sun of righteousness	4:1–4
B. The appearance of Elijah	4:5–6

Matthew

I. Introduction of the King	1:1–4:25
A. Genealogy	1:1–17
B. Birth	1:18–25
C. Early life	2:1–23
D. Ministry of John the Baptist	3:1–12
E. Baptism of Jesus	3:13–17
F. Temptation of Jesus	4:1–11
G. Early ministry of Jesus	4:12–25
II. The principles of the King's rule: the Sermon on the Mount	5:1–7:29
III. The King's authority manifested and rejected	8:1–12:50
IV. The mysteries of the kingdom: the period between the two advents	13:1–58
V. The ministry of the rejected King	14:1–23:39
VI. The predicted return of the King: the Olivet Discourse	24:1–25:46
VII. The death and resurrection of the King	26:1–28:20

Mark

I. Introduction of the servant to His public ministry	1:1–13
A. Ministry of John the Baptist	1:1–8
B. Baptism of Jesus	1:9–11
C. Temptation of Jesus	1:12–13

II. The work accomplished by the Servant	1:14–13:37
A. Public ministry	1:14–9:1
B. The transfiguration	9:2–13
C. Further ministry	9:14–10:52
D. The triumphal entry	11:1–11
E. Ministry in Jerusalem	11:12–12:44
F. The Olivet Discourse	13:1–37
III. The Servant's obedience to the point of death	14:1–15:47
IV. The resurrection and ascension of the victorious Servant	16:1–20

Luke

I. Introduction	1:1–4
II. The early life of Christ	1:5–4:13
A. Announcement of the birth of John the Baptist	1:5–25
B. Announcement of birth of Jesus	1:26–33
C. Jesus' miraculous conception and Mary's reaction	1:34–56
D. Birth of John the Baptist	1:57–80
E. Birth of Jesus	2:1–38
F. Growth of Jesus	2:39–52
G. Ministry of John the Baptist	3:1–20
H. Baptism of Jesus	3:21–22
I. Genealogy of Mary	3:23–38
J. Temptation of Jesus	4:1–13
III. The public ministry of the Son of Man to the Triumphal Entry	4:14–19:27
IV. The rejection of Christ and His death	19:28–23:56
V. Christ's resurrection and ascension	24:1–53

John

I. Prologue: the eternal Word incarnate in the Son of God	1:1–14
II. The witness of John the Baptist to the Son of God	1:15–34
III. The Son of God manifesting His power in public ministry	1:35–12:50
A. First converts	1:35–51
B. The first miracle: at Cana	2:1–12
C. The first passover: first purification of the Temple	2:13–25
D. Encounter with Nicodemus: the new birth	3:1–21
E. Last testimony of John the Baptist	3:22–36
F. Encounter with the Samaritan woman	4:1–45
G. Healing of an official's son	4:46–54
H. Healing at pool of Bethesda	5:1–15
I. Assertions of deity	5:16–47
J. Feeding of the five thousand	6:1–15
K. Walking on the water	6:16–21

    L. The bread of life   6:22–71
    M. Feast of Tabernacles   7:1–8:1
    N. Woman taken in adultery   8:2–11
    O. The light of the world   8:12–59
    P. Healing of the man born blind   9:1–41
    Q. The good Shepherd   10:1–42
    R. Raising of Lazarus   11:1–44
    S. Conflict and conversion   11:45–57
    T. Anointing by Mary of Bethany   12:1–11
    U. Entrance into Jerusalem   12:12–50
  IV. The private ministry of the Son of God   13:1–17:26
   V. The sacrifice of the Son of God   18:1–19:42
  VI. The manifestation of the Son of God in resurrection   20:1–31
VII. Epilogue: the risen Son of God, the Master of life and service   21:1–25

Acts

   I. The waiting believers   1:1–26
    A. Introduction: Christ's 40-day ministry   1:1–7
    B. The commission to evangelize the world   1:8–9
    C. The promise of Christ's return to the earth   1:10–11
    D. Waiting for the Spirit   1:12–14
    E. Matthias chosen to take Judas' place   1:15–26
  II. From Pentecost to the conversion of Saul   2:1–8:40
    A. Sixth dispensation inaugurated: the Church; Pentecost: the
       Spirit sent from heaven   2:1–13
    B. Peter's sermon: theme—Jesus is Lord and Christ   2:14–47
    C. Miracles and persecution   3:1–5:42
    D. Martyrdom of Stephen   6:1–8:3
    E. Philip's ministry   8:4–40
 III. From the conversion of Saul to the first missionary journey   9:1–12:25
    A. Saul's conversion   9:1–31
    B. Ministry of Peter   9:32–12:25
  IV. The first missionary journey   13:1–14:28
   V. The council at Jerusalem   15:1–35
  VI. The second missionary journey   15:36–18:22
 VII. The third missionary journey   18:23–21:14
VIII. From Jerusalem to Rome   21:15–28:31
    A. Paul in Jerusalem   21:15–23:22
    B. Paul in Caesarea   23:23–26:32
    C. Paul sent to Rome   27:1–28:16
    D. Paul in Rome   28:17–31

Romans

Introduction and theme: the righteousness of God	1:1–17
I. The guilt of the whole world before God	1:18–3:20
A. The wrath of God revealed	1:18
B. The universe a revelation of the power and deity of God	1:19–20
C. Stages of Gentile world unbelief	1:21–23
D. Results of Gentile world unbelief	1:24–32
E. Gentile and Jew condemned	2:1–3:20
II. Justification by faith	3:21–5:21
A. Nature of justification	3:21–4:25
B. Results of justification	5:1–11
C. Justification versus condemnation	5:12–21
III. Sanctification through union with Christ in His death and resurrection	6:1–8:39
A. The principle of union with Christ	6:1–14
B. Life by the Spirit	6:15–8:11
C. Certainty of salvation	8:12–39
IV. The problem of Jewish unbelief	9:1–11:36
A. God's sovereign wisdom and grace	9:1–33
B. Unbelief and the explanation for apparent failure of the promises	10:1–21
C. Certainty of Israel's restoration	11:1–36
V. Christian life and service for the glory of God	12:1–15:13
A. Dedication and service	12:1–16
B. Relations with those outside of God's family	12:17–13:14
C. Debatable things	14:1–15:13
Conclusion: the outflow of Christian love	15:14–16:27

1 Corinthians

Introduction: the believer's standing in grace	1:1–9
I. Divisions in the Corinthian church	1:10–4:21
A. Division of the body by human wisdom	1:10–17
B. Human wisdom contrasted with God's wisdom	1:18–25
C. Corinthian believers not of the wise	1:26–31
D. Wisdom and spiritual truth	2:1–16
E. Worldliness and spiritual growth	3:1–8
F. Christian service and its reward	3:9–4:7
G. Apostolic example and authority	4:8–21
II. Immorality rebuked and discipline commanded	5:1–6:8
III. The sanctity of the body	6:9–20
IV. Regulations concerning marriage	7:1–40
V. Limitations of Christian liberty	8:1–13
VI. Discipline and ministry	9:1–27

VII. Biblical separation   10:1–11:1
VIII. Christian order and the Lord's Supper   11:2–34
  IX. Spiritual gifts   12:1–14:40
      A. Their distribution   12:1–31
      B. Their use in love   13:1–13
      C. Their regulation in the assembly   14:1–40
   X. The hope of resurrection   15:1–58
  XI. Conclusion: instructions and personal greetings   16:1–24

2 Corinthians

Introduction   1:1–11
  I. Principles of action in Paul's ministry   1:12–7:16
     A. Background to his appeal   1:12–2:13
     B. New Covenant ministry   2:14–6:10
        1. Triumphant   2:14–17
        2. Accredited   3:1–5
        3. Spiritual and glorious, not legal   3:6–18
        4. Honest, not deceitful   4:1–7
        5. Its suffering   4:8–18
        6. Its ambition   5:1–10
        7. Its moving motives   5:11–21
        8. Its supernatural character   6:1–10
     C. Appeal for separation and understanding of Paul   6:11–7:16
 II. The collection for the poor at Jerusalem   8:1–9:15
     A. Example of Macedonia   8:1–7
     B. Example of Christ   8:8–15
     C. Trusted representatives   8:16–24
     D. Encouragement based on God's generosity   9:1–15
III. Paul's defense of his apostolic authority   10:1–13:10
     A. Divine authentication   10:1–18
     B. Godly jealousy   11:1–2
     C. Warning against false teachers   11:3–15
     D. Paul's continual boasting   11:16–12:10
     E. Warning   12:11–21
     F. Exhortation to self-examination   13:1–10
Conclusion   13:11–14

Galatians

Introduction and salutation   1:1–5
  I. Occasion of the epistle: the Galatians' departure from the true
     Gospel   1:6–9
 II. Paul's defense of his apostolic ministry   1:10–2:21

A. His reception of the Gospel from God   1:10–24
B. The Jerusalem council   2:1–10
C. Withstanding Peter at Antioch   2:11–14
D. The Christian and the law   2:15–21
III. Justification by faith apart from the law   3:1–24
A. The gift of the Spirit by faith   3:1–5
B. The Abrahamic Covenant and faith   3:6–9
C. The curse of the law   3:10–12
D. Christ's bearing the curse of the law   3:13–16
E. The law preceded by faith   3:17–18
F. The intent of the law   3:19–24
IV. The rule of grace in the believer's life   3:25–5:1
A. The justified believer as a son   3:25–4:3
B. Redemption from the curse of the law   4:4–5
C. Sonship confirmed by the Spirit   4:6–7
D. Legality as an elementary religion   4:8–14
E. Loss of blessing in legality   4:15–18
F. Incompatibility of law and grace   4:19–5:1
V. Characteristics of the life of the justified individual   5:2–26
VI. The outworking of the new life in Christ   6:1–16
Conclusion: the new fellowship of suffering   6:17–18

Ephesians

Introduction   1:1–2
I. The believer's standing in grace   1:1–3:21
A. The believer in Christ in the heavenly realms   1:3–14
B. Prayer for knowledge and power   1:15–21
C. Christ exalted as the Head of His Body, the Church   1:22–23
D. Method of salvation   2:1–10
E. Position of Gentiles by nature   2:11–13
F. Jew and Gentile one Body in Christ   2:14–18
G. The Church a temple for the habitation of God through the
   Spirit   2:19–22
H. The Church a "mystery" hidden from past generations   3:1–12
I. Prayer for comprehension   3:13–21
II. The conduct and service of the believer   4:1–5:17
A. Conduct worthy of high position   4:1–3
B. Seven unities to be preserved   4:4–6
C. The gifts of the risen Christ and their purpose   4:7–16
D. The conduct of the believer as a new individual in Christ   4:17–29
E. The walk of the believer as indwelt by the Spirit   4:30–32
F. The conduct of the believer as God's dearly loved child   5:1–17
III. The conduct and warfare of the Spirit-filled believer   5:18–6:20
A. The inner life of the Spirit-filled believer   5:18–21
B. The married life of Spirit-filled believers   5:22–33

C. The domestic life of Spirit-filled believers   6:1–9
D. The warfare of Spirit-filled believers   6:10–20
Conclusion   6:21–24

Philippians

Introduction: greeting and thanksgiving   1:1–7
  I. Christ, the Christian's life: rejoicing in spite of suffering   1:8–30
     A. Joy triumphing over suffering   1:8–18
     B. Paul's expectation of deliverance   1:19–30
 II. Christ, the Christian's pattern: rejoicing in lowly service   2:1–30
     A. Exhortation to meekness and unity   2:1–4
     B. The self-humbling of Christ   2:5–8
     C. The exaltation of Christ   2:9–11
     D. The outworking of salvation   2:12–16
     E. The apostolic example   2:17–30
III. Christ, object of the Christian's faith, desire, and expectation   3:1–21
     A. Warning against legalizers   3:1–3
     B. Warning against legal righteousness   3:4–6
     C. Christ, object of the believer's faith for righteousness   3:7–9
     D. Christ, object of the believer's desire for fellowship in resur-
        rection power   3:10–14
     E. Appeal for unity among believers   3:15–16
     F. Impossibility of compromise for the sake of unity   3:17–19
     G. Christ, object of the believer's expectation   3:20–21
 IV. Christ, the Christian's strength: rejoicing without anxiety   4:1–19
     A. Exhortation to be in agreement   4:1–3
     B. The secret of the peace of God   4:4–7
     C. The presence of the God of peace   4:8–9
     D. The believer's sufficiency through Christ   4:10–19
Conclusion   4:20–23

Colossians

Introduction: greeting and thanksgiving   1:1–8
  I. The apostle's prayer for the Colossian Christians   1:9–14
 II. The preeminent glory of Christ   1:15–23
     A. The seven superiorities of Christ   1:15–19
     B. The reconciling work of Christ   1:20–23
III. The apostle's concern for the church at Colosse   1:24–2:23
 A. The Church a "mystery" hidden during past ages   1:24–29
 B. The Godhead incarnate in Christ   2:1–23
        1. Christ, the fount of wisdom   2:1–3

2. The danger of fine-sounding arguments   2:4–7
3. Twofold warning against false philosophy and legality   2:8
4. The believer complete in Christ   2:9–13
5. Law observances abolished in Christ   2:14–17
6. Warning against false mysticism   2:18–19
7. Warning against asceticism   2:20–23

IV. Some characteristics of the abundant life of the Christian based on union with Christ   3:1–4:6
  A. The extent of union   3:1–4
  B. Christian living   3:5–17
  C. Christian family relationships   3:18–21
  D. Servants and masters   3:22–4:1
  E. Earnest prayer; wise speech   4:2–6

Conclusion: personal exhortations   4:7–18

1 Thessalonians

Introduction   1:1–4
I. The model church and the three tenses of the Christian life   1:5–10
  A. The conversion of the Thessalonians   1:5–6
  B. The example of the Thessalonians   1:7–8
  C. The hope of the Thessalonians   1:9–10
II. The model servant and his reward   2:1–20
  A. Purity of motive   2:1–6
  B. Genuine love   2:7–12
  C. The result: genuine faith   2:13–16
  D. Joy in fruitbearing   2:17–20
III. The model brother and his sanctification   3:1–13
  A. The sending of Timothy   3:1–6
  B. Prayer for believers   3:7–13
IV. The model life and the believer's hope   4:1–18
  A. Abstaining from sexual immorality   4:1–8
  B. Love for the brethren   4:9–10
  C. Relations to others   4:11–12
  D. The revelation of the rapture   4:13–18
V. The model walk and the Day of the Lord   5:1–24
  A. The nature of the Day of the Lord   5:1–3
  B. The position of believers   5:4–5
  C. Exhortation to watchfulness   5:6–11
  D. Regulations concerning assembly life   5:12–28
    1. Relations to overseers   5:12–13
    2. Ministering to each other   5:14–15
    3. Corporate growth   5:16–22
    4. Prayer for sanctification   5:23–24
Conclusion   5:25–28

2 Thessalonians

Introduction and salutation   1:1–4
  I. Comfort in persecution   1:5–12
    A. God's recompense for suffering   1:5–10
    B. Prayer for a significant work of God   1:11–12
 II. The Day of the Lord and the Man of Lawlessness   2:1–12
    A. Exhortation to understanding   2:1–2
    B. The revealing of the Man of Lawlessness   2:3–12
      1. The rebellion   2:3
      2. Characteristics of the Man of Lawlessness   2:4
      3. The Restrainer   2:5–7
      4. Satanic activity   2:8–10
      5. God's judgment   2:11–12
III. Exhortations and instructions   2:13–3:15
    A. Plea for steadfastness   2:13–17
    B. Request for prayer   3:1–5
    C. Need for diligence in work   3:6–13
    D. Instructions for discipline   3:14–15
Conclusion: benediction and authentication   3:16–18

1 Timothy

Introduction and salutation   1:1–2
   I. Warning about heresy in doctrine and life   1:3–11
  II. Paul's personal witness and charge to Timothy   1:12–20
    A. The divine origin of Paul's ministry   1:12–17
    B. Commission to Timothy   1:18–20
 III. Instructions about prayer and the place of women in the church   2:1–15
 IV. Qualifications of elders and deacons   3:1–16
    A. Stipulations for elders   3:1–7
    B. Stipulations for deacons   3:8–13
    C. Importance of the local assembly   3:14–16
  V. The conduct of the good minister of Jesus Christ   4:1–16
    A. Prediction of apostasy   4:1–10
    B. Encouragement to exemplary behavior and character   4:11–16
 VI. The work of the good minister of Jesus Christ   5:1–25
    A. Relations to older believers   5:1–2
    B. Regulations concerning widows   5:3–16
    C. Guidelines on elders   5:17–25
VII. Warnings to the minister of Jesus Christ   6:1–19
Conclusion: another charge to Timothy   6:20–21

2 Timothy

Introduction and salutation	1:1–2
I. Paul's charge to Timothy	1:3–18
A. Personal remembrances	1:3–5
B. Reminder of need to be courageous	1:6–14
C. Paul's deserters	1:15–18
II. The path of an approved servant in a day of apostasy	2:1–26
A. Need to commit truth to faithful believers	2:1–2
B. The faithful servant	2:3–10
C. God's faithfulness	2:11–18
D. God's knowledge of His servants	2:19–26
III. The apostasy predicted: the Christian's resource—the Scriptures	3:1–17
A. Danger of the last days	3:1–9
B. Paul's steadfastness	3:10–13
C. Timothy's source of stability—the Scriptures	3:14–17
IV. A faithful servant and his faithful Lord	4:1–18
A. Charge to preach the Word	4:1–2
B. Need for sound teaching in the presence of spiritual error	4:3–4
C. Personal words of Paul	4:5–18
1. Prediction	4:5–8
2. Desire to see Timothy	4:9–11
3. His desertion by many	4:12–18
Conclusion	4:19–22

Titus

Introduction and salutation	1:1–4
I. The qualifications and duties of elders	1:5–16
A. Need for elders	1:5
B. Personal prerequisites	1:6–8
C. Doctrinal qualifications	1:9–16
1. Ability to refute opponents of sound teaching	1:9
2. Presence of deceivers	1:10–11
3. Character of Cretans	1:12–16
II. The pastoral work of a true minister	2:1–15
A. Ministry toward various groups	2:1–10
1. Older men	2:1–2
2. Older women	2:3
3. Younger women	2:4–5
4. Younger men	2:6–8
5. Servants	2:9–10
B. The appearance of life-changing grace	2:11–15
III. Exhortations to godly living	3:1–11
A. Subjection to others	3:1–3

B. Behavior to be based on mercy shown to sinners   3:4–7
C. Need for continual sound teaching leading to good works   3:8–11
Conclusion: personal remarks and benediction   3:12–15

Philemon

Introduction: Paul's greeting   vv. 1–3
 I. The character of Philemon   vv. 4–7
II. Intercession for Onesimus   vv. 8–21
Conclusion: personal remarks and benediction   vv. 22–25

Hebrews

Introduction   1:1–3
 I. Christ as a Person superior to all others   1:4–4:16
    A. The Son superior to angels   1:4–2:18
       1. Because of His superior name: Son   1:4–8
       2. Because of His deity   1:9–13
       3. Because angels are servants to believers   1:14
       4. Because of association with a superior revelation   2:1–4
       5. Because He is heir to the promises to humanity concerning
          the earth   2:5–9
       6. Because of His sacrificial death and victory over Satan   2:10–18
    B. The Son superior to Moses, the servant   3:1–4:16
       1. Because He is Creator   3:1–6
       2. Because of His provision of final rest   3:7–4:16
II. The preeminence and finality of the priesthood of Christ   5:1–10:18
    A. The importance of priesthood   5:1–6:20
       1. The office of high priest   5:1–4
       2. Christ, a high priest after the order of Melchizedek   5:5–10
       3. The danger of rejecting the priestly work of Christ   5:11–14
       4. Need for entrance into faith   6:1–12
       5. Access to God by the oath-based priesthood of Christ   6:13–20
    B. The Melchizedekian priesthood of the Son of God   7:1–28
       1. The historic Melchizedek a type of Christ   7:1–3
       2. Superiority of the Melchizedekian priesthood   7:4–28
    C. The superiority of the New Covenant   8:1–10:18
       1. The presence of our High Priest with God   8:1–5
       2. The temporary nature of the Old Covenant   8:6–9:10
       3. The reality of the sanctuary and sacrifice of the New Cov-
          enant   9:11–15
       4. The New Covenant as the last will and testament of Christ 9:16–22
       5. The cleansing of the heavenly sanctuary   9:23–28
       6. The superiority of the one New Covenant sacrifice   10:1–18

III. The life of faith	10:19–13:19
A. Encouragements and warnings to those wavering	10:19–39
B. The superiority of the way of faith	11:1–40
C. The worship and life of the believer	12:1–13:19
Conclusion: benediction and greeting	13:20–25

James

Introduction	1:1
I. Testing of faith	1:2–2:26
A. Purpose of testing	1:2–12
B. Invitation to evil not of God	1:13–21
C. Test of obedience	1:22–25
D. Test of true religion	1:26–27
E. Test of brotherly love	2:1–13
F. Test of good works	2:14–20
G. Abraham as an illustration	2:21–26
II. Reality of faith tested by control of the tongue	3:1–18
A. Principle of the power of the tongue	3:1–5
B. The sinfulness of the tongue	3:6–12
C. Exhortation to control the tongue	3:13–18
III. Rebuke of worldliness	4:1–17
A. The role of lust	4:1–5
B. Resisting Satan and drawing near to God	4:6–12
C. Folly of acting independently of God	4:13–17
IV. Warning to the rich	5:1–6
V. Exhortations in view of the coming of the Lord	5:7–18
A. Importance of patience in affliction	5:7–13
B. Directions concerning the sick	5:14–15
C. The power of righteous prayer	5:16–18
Conclusion	5:19–20

1 Peter

Introduction	1:1–2
I. Christian suffering and conduct in the light of complete salvation	1:3–2:8
A. The certainty of the salvation of the soul	1:3–9
B. Prophetic inquiry	1:10–12
C. Exhortation to sober living	1:13–21
D. Permanence of the new birth	1:22–25
E. Need for genuine worship as stones built on the Cornerstone	2:1–8
II. Christian life in view of the believer's position and the victorious suffering of Christ	2:9–4:19
A. The demand for proper behavior toward others	2:9–20

B. The vicarious suffering of Christ 2:21–25
C. Godly living in the home and in the church 3:1–12
D. Godly living before the world 3:13–17
E. The victory of Christ preached in Noah's time 3:18–22
F. Exhortation to cease from sin 4:1–6
G. Proper use of gifts 4:7–11
H. Necessity of distinctive Christian behavior 4:12–19
III. Christian service in the light of the coming of the Lord ... 5:1–9
Conclusion: benediction and personal greeting 5:10–14

2 Peter

Introduction 1:1–2
I. Great Christian virtues 1:3–14
   A. The sequence of spiritual assets 1:3–7
   B. The value of the assets 1:8–11
   C. Peter's personal appeal as he faces death 1:12–14
II. The Transfiguration recalled 1:15–18
III. Prophetic Scriptures exalted 1:19–21
IV. Warnings against false teachers 2:1–3:3
   A. The prediction about false teachers 2:1–3
   B. The fate of disobedient angels 2:4–5
   C. The fate of Sodom and Gomorrah 2:6–9
   D. Anti-authoritarian nature of false teachers 2:10–12
   E. Infiltration by false teachers 2:13–14
   F. Marks of false teachers 2:15–22
      1. Like Balaam 2:15–16
      2. Destitute of spiritual life 2:17
      3. Use learned and pretentious words 2:18
      4. Pervert Christian liberty 2:19–21
      5. Turn away from the faith 2:22
   G. The reason for the epistle 3:1–3
V. The second coming of Christ and the Day of the Lord 3:4–16
   A. The return of the Lord to be generally disbelieved 3:4–9
   B. The purging of the heavens and the earth 3:10–16
Conclusion: exhortation and benediction 3:17–18

1 John

Introduction: The incarnate Word 1:1–2
I. Little children and fellowship 1:3–2:11
   A. Fellowship with the Father and Son 1:3–4

B. The conditions of fellowship 1:5–2:11
  1. Position in the light 1:5–7
  2. Recognition of indwelling sin 1:8
  3. Sins confessed, forgiven and cleansed 1:9–10
  4. Maintaining of fellowship by Christ's advocacy ... 2:1–2
  5. Recognition of God's holiness 2:3–11
II. Little children and their enemies 2:12–27
  A. The family addressed 2:12–14
  B. Danger of loving the world 2:15–17
  C. Warning against apostates 2:18–27
III. Little children and the Lord's return 2:28–3:3
  A. Purity exhorted 2:28–29
  B. Future conformity to Christ 3:1–3
IV. Little children contrasted with children of Satan 3:4–24
  A. Distinguishing characteristics of the two groups . 3:4–12
  B. Primacy of love 3:13–24
V. Little children and false teachers 4:1–6
  A. Command to test spirits 4:1
  B. Marks of false teachers 4:2–6
VI. Little children assured and warned 4:7–5:19
  A. Basis of love: God's act 4:7–10
  B. God's indwelling love demonstrated 4:11–21
  C. Faith as the overcoming principle 5:1–8
  D. Assurance of salvation 5:9–15
  E. Sober warnings 5:16–19
Conclusion 5:20–21

2 John

Introduction and salutation .... vv. 1–3
I. The pathway of truth and love .... vv. 4–6
II. The mark of a deceiver and antichrist .... vv. 7–11
Conclusion .... vv. 12–13

3 John

Introduction: Gaius greeted and characterized .... vv. 1–4
I. Hospitality to traveling believers: God's work supported by His
  own people .... vv. 5–8
II. Domineering Diotrephes and his evil deeds .... vv. 9–11
III. Godly Demetrius .... v. 12
Conclusion .... vv. 13–14

Jude

Introduction	vv. 1–2
I. Occasion for the writing of the epistle: warning against apostasy	vv. 3–4
II. Historical examples of unbelief and rebellion	vv. 5–7
A. Israel in the wilderness	v. 5
B. Disobedient angels	v. 6
C. Sodom and Gomorrah	v. 7
III. False teachers described	vv. 8–19
A. Rebellious against authority	vv. 8–10
B. Greedy	v. 11
C. Hidden among true believers	v. 12a
D. Spiritually dead	vv. 12b–13
E. Facing judgment	vv. 14–15
F. Promoting personalities	v. 16
G. Devoid of the Spirit	vv. 17–19
IV. Exhortations to Christians	vv. 20–23
Conclusion	vv. 24–25

Revelation

Introduction	1:1–3
I. The messages of the ascended Lord to the seven churches	1:4–3:22
A. Things past: the vision of Christ	1:4–20
1. Divine source of the book announced	1:4–8
2. Appearance of Christ as divine Priest	1:9–18
3. Command to write	1:19–20
B. Things present: the seven letters	2:1–3:22
1. Ephesus: the Church at the end of the apostolic age	2:1–7
2. Smyrna: the Church under persecution	2:8–11
3. Pergamum: the Church settled in the world	2:12–17
4. Thyatira: the Church in idolatry	2:18–29
5. Sardis: the Church as dead, yet having a believing remnant	3:1–6
6. Philadelphia: the Church in revival	3:7–13
7. Laodicea: the Church in its final state of apostasy	3:14–22
II. Things yet to come: opening of the seven-sealed scroll	4:1–6:17
A. Scene in heaven before opening of the scroll	4:1–5:14
1. God worshipped as Creator	4:1–11
2. Lamb worshipped as Redeemer	5:1–14
B. The first six seals opened	6:1–17
III. Parenthetic section: Jews and Gentiles saved during the tribulation	7:1–17
IV. Seventh seal opened: the first six trumpet judgments	8:1–9:21
V. Parenthetic section	10:1–11:19

    A. Instructions to John — 10:1–11

    B. Ministry of the two witnesses — 11:1–14

    C. Seventh trumpet — 11:15–19

  VI. Prominent characters in Israel's history, past and future — 12:1–17

 VII. Rise and reign of the Beast and False Prophet — 13:1–18

VIII. Parenthetic section: summary of the tribulation period — 14:1–20

  IX. The seven plague judgments — 15:1–16:21

   X. The doom of Babylon — 17:1–18:24

  XI. The Battle of Armageddon and the millennium that follows — 19:1–20:6

 XII. The final judgment and the Holy City — 20:7–22:5

XIII. The last message of the Bible — 22:6–19

Conclusion — 22:20–21

22

Guide to Old Testament Quotations
in the New Testament

This chapter contains a two-part list giving the locations of many of the quotational uses of the O.T. in the N.T. Such correspondences of wording are called quotations or citations. Both terms are used to refer to both explicit quotations and allusions.

Explanation of the Choice of Quotations

This list is necessarily incomplete; the exact number of places in the N.T. where O.T. wording is used is difficult to determine. The choice of what to include is somewhat arbitrary. Some Bible students see correspondences that others reject. There are many places where it is simply very difficult to tell if there is quoting from the O.T. in the N.T.

A *quotation* is generally considered to be a lengthy correspondence, and when introduced with a phrase such as *Scripture says* or *as Isaiah says,* it is called an explicit quotation. An *allusion* is a fragment consisting of a word or two, and is not explicitly introduced. All explicitly introduced quotations are given in the lists. The key to inclusion of allusions in this list is evident correspondence of language. Choice of allusions is made easier when there is correspondence of contexts between the O.T. and the N.T.

Place names are omitted unless they are a central part of what on other grounds would be considered to be an explicit quotation or allusion. For example, Armageddon, found in Rev. 16:16, is also found in Jud. 5:19 as Megiddo, but is not included in the list. Most names of people are omitted for the same reason. An exception is the listing of Gog and Magog, found in Rev. 20:8, which quotes various places in Ezek. 38–39.

They are unusual figures that are central both accounts. Most historical references, as in Acts 7, are listed, even though they may not have direct quotation involved. Often the wording is heavily influenced by the O.T.

Multiple citations at a N.T. location are listed in biblical order, not necessarily in the order in which they may be quoted in the verse.

Where reference is made to a whole ch. (as at Gen. 3, found in Rev. 20:2), there are several words or topics that are being alluded to.

How to Use This Index

You should acquire the habit of regularly consulting the annotations on each page of the biblical text to determine where the O.T. is cited in the N.T. You can then use this index as a supplement to such identification.

You can easily find all the instances of an O.T. verse cited in the N.T. For example, you can determine that Gen. 2:24 is quoted at Mt. 19:5; Mk. 10:7–8; 1 Cor. 6:16, and Eph. 5:31. It is informative to *compare* uses to identify variations in the quotation made by the N.T. writers for certain purposes. Habakkuk 2:4 (or 2:3–4) is found in three places in the N.T.: Rom. 1:17, Gal. 3:11, and Heb. 10:37–38. The two uses by Paul are virtually identical in meaning. However, the use by the writer to the Hebrews is quite different, emphasizing the second advent of Christ. This fact may have a bearing on the question of the authorship of the book of Hebrews.

From both lists you can see at a glance patterns of usage. The book of Psalms is distributed throughout the N.T. The majority of citations from Jer., Ezek., and Dan. are found in the book of Revelation, which also draws heavily on Ex. Such patterns give clues as to the doctrinal interests of the N.T. writers. This helps us to see that N.T. books cannot be studied thoroughly without reference to these citations.

Marginal references for particular verses lead the reader to other places in the Bible where the same or similar words are used, or where there is correspondence of ideas. Quotations or allusions should be considered alongside these other verbal and nonverbal correspondences. For example, at Rom. 4:1ff the topic of imputation can be studied on the basis of (1) the uses of the word *impute, credit,* or *reckon,* (depending on the translation), indicated by the marginal references or the NSRB chain on *imputation;* (2) the general concept of imputation, as indicated by the marginal reference to the parallel passage Gal. 3:6 (which in this instance happens also to use the same word); or (3) the use of O.T. wording, in this case Ps. 32:1–2, quoted in Rom. 4:7–8. It is also helpful to notice how Paul introduces the quotation with a reference to David and an explanation of what he believes the portion of the psalm means in connection with his point in Rom. 4. Furthermore, we should notice that David is speaking not of the experience of salvation, but of the restoration to fellowship of one who is a child of God. For David, the "blessed" one is the believer who confesses his sins and finds complete forgiveness. Apparently Paul uses this portion of Ps. 32 because imputation works the same way for salvation as for restoration.

See. ch. 7, Relations Between the Testaments, for extended treatments of topics related to quotations.

The word *see* in the following lists directs the reader to other entries in the list itself.

Other Sources of Help on Quotations from the Old Testament in the New Testament

Aland, Kurt, Matthew Black, Carlo M. Martini, Bruce M. Metzger, and Allen Wikgren. *The Greek New Testament.* 3rd ed. New York: United Bible Societies, 1983.

Archer, Gleason L., and Gregory C. Chirichigno. *Old Testament Quotations in the New Testament: A Complete Survey.* Chicago: Moody Press, 1983.

France, R. T. *Jesus and the Old Testament.* London: InterVarsity Press, 1971.

Johnson, S. Lewis, Jr. *The Old Testament in the New: An Argument for Biblical Inspiration.* Grand Rapids: Zondervan, 1980.

Toy, Crawford H. *Quotations in the New Testament.* New York: Scribner's, 1884.

All of the above except Johnson contain lists of quotations.

Old Testament Verses Cited in the New Testament

Genesis

1:26–27	Jas. 3:9
1:27	Mt. 19:4; Mk. 10:6
2:2	Heb. 4:4
2:7	1 Cor. 15:45,47
2:9	Rev. 2:7; 22:2,14,19
2:24	Mt. 19:5; Mk. 10:7–8; 1 Cor. 6:16; Eph. 5:31
3	Rev. 20:2
3:17–18	Heb. 6:8
3:22	Rev. 2:7; 22:2,14,19
4:4	Heb. 11:4
5:2	Mt. 19:4; Mk. 10:6
5:24	Heb. 11:5
9:6	Rev. 13:10
12:1	Acts 7:3
12:3	Acts 3:25; Gal. 3:8
12:7	Acts 7:5; Gal. 3:16
13:15	Acts 7:5; Gal. 3:16
14:17–20	Heb. 7:1–3,10
14:19,22	Rev. 10:6
15:5	Rom. 4:18
15:5–6	Heb. 11:12
15:6	Rom. 4:3,9,22–23; Gal. 3:6; Jas. 2:23
15:13–14	Acts 7:6–7
15:16	1 Thess. 2:16
15:18	Acts 7:5
17:5	Rom. 4:17–18
17:7	Lk. 1:55; Gal. 3:16
17:8	Acts 7:5
18:10	Rom. 9:9
18:14	Mt. 19:26; Mk. 10:27; Lk. 1:37; Rom. 9:9
18:18	Acts 3:25; Rom. 4:13; Gal. 3:8
18:20–21	Rev. 18:5
19:24	Lk. 17:29; Rev. 14:10; 20:10
19:28	Rev. 9:2
21:10	Gal. 4:30
21:12	Rom. 9:7; Heb. 11:18
22:16–17	Heb. 6:13–14; 11:12
22:18	Acts 3:25; Gal. 3:8,16
23:4	Heb. 11:9,13; 1 Pet. 2:11
24:7	Acts 7:5; Gal. 3:16
25:23	Rom. 9:12
25:33–34	Heb. 12:16
26:4	Acts 3:25; Gal. 3:8,16
28:12	Jn. 1:51
28:14	Gal. 3:8
32:12	Heb. 11:12
37:9	Rev. 12:1
37:11,28	Acts 7:9
38:8	Mt. 22:24; Mk. 12:19; Lk. 20:28
39:2–3,21,23	Acts 7:9
41:37–41	Acts 7:10
41:54	Acts 7:11
42:1–2	Acts 7:12
42:5	Acts 7:11
45:1–16	Acts 7:13

46:27	Acts 7:14	19:18	Rev. 9:2
47:9	Heb. 11:13	20:11	Acts 4:24; 14:15;
47:31	Heb. 11:21		17:24; Rev. 10:6; 14:7
48:4	Acts 7:5	20:12	Mt. 15:4; Mk. 7:10;
49:9–10	Rev. 5:5		Eph. 6:2–3; Col. 3:20
50:13	Acts 7:16	20:12–16	Mt. 19:18–19; Mk.
			10:19; Lk. 18:20
		20:13	Mt. 5:21; Jas. 2:11
Exodus		20:13–15	Rom. 13:9
		20:14	Mt. 5:27; Jas. 2:11
1:7–17	Acts 7:17–19	20:17	Rom. 7:7; 13:9
2:2	Heb. 11:23	21:17	Mt. 15:4; Mk. 7:10
2:2–10	Acts 7:20–21	21:24	Mt. 5:38
2:11–15	Acts 7:23–29,35	22:28	Acts 23:5
2:14	Acts 7:35	23:20	Mt. 11:10; Mk. 1:2;
2:22	Acts 7:6		Lk. 7:27
3:2–3	Acts 7:30–31	24:8	Mt. 26:28; Mk. 14:24;
3:3–5,7–10	Acts 7:31,33–34		Lk. 22:20; 1 Cor.
3:6,15–16	Mt. 22:32; Mk. 12:26;		11:25; 2 Cor. 3:6; Heb.
	Lk. 20:37; Acts 3:13;		9:20; 10:29
	7:32	24:12	2 Cor. 3:3
3:12	Acts 7:7	25:9,40	Acts 7:44; Heb. 8:5
3:14	Rev. 1:4,8; 4:8; 11:17;	26:30	Acts 7:44; Heb. 8:5
	16:5	27:21	Acts 7:44
6:1,6	Acts 13:17	28:21	Rev. 21:12–13
7:17,19–20	Rev. 11:6	30:1–3	Rev. 9:13
7:17–21	Rev. 16:3–4	32:1,23	Acts 7:40
7:20–21	Rev. 8:8	32:6	1 Cor. 10:7
9:9–10	Rev. 16:2	32:13	Heb. 11:12
9:16	Rom. 9:17	32:32–33	Phil. 4:3; Rev. 3:5;
9:23–24	Rev. 11:19		13:8; 17:8; 20:12,15;
9:23–25	Rev. 8:7; 16:21		21:27
9:24	Rev. 11:19	33:19	Rom. 9:15
10:12–15	Rev. 9:2–9	34:6	Jas. 5:11
10:21–22	Rev. 16:10	34:29–35	2 Cor. 3:12–18
12:46	Jn. 19:36	37:23	Rev. 4:5
12:51	Acts 13:17	38:21	Rev. 15:5
13:2,12,15	Lk. 2:23	40:34	Rev. 15:8
15:1,11	Rev. 15:3		
15:18	Rev. 11:15; 19:6		
16:13ff	Jn. 6:31	*Leviticus*	
16:18	2 Cor. 8:15		
16:35	Acts 13:18	5:11	Lk. 2:24
19:5–6	1 Pet. 2:9	10:9	Lk. 1:15
19:6	Rev. 1:6; 5:10; 20:6	11:44–5	1 Pet. 1:16
19:12–13	Heb. 12:20	12:8	Lk. 2:24
19:16	Rev. 4:5; 11:19	14:4	Heb. 9:19
19:16–19	Rev. 8:5; 16:18	16:2,12	Heb. 6:19
19:16–22	Heb. 12:18–19	18:5	Rom. 10:5; Gal. 3:12

19:2	1 Pet. 1:16
19:12	Mt. 5:33; 19:18; Mk. 10:19; Lk. 18:20
19:18	Mt. 5:43; 19:19; 22:39; Mk. 12:31–33; Lk. 10:27; Rom. 13:9; Gal. 5:14; Jas. 2:8
20:9	Mt. 15:4; Mk. 7:10
21:9	Rev. 17:16
23:29	Acts 3:23
24:20	Mt. 5:38
26:11–12	2 Cor. 6:16; Rev. 21:3
26:21	Rev. 15:1,6

Numbers

6:3	Lk. 1:15
9:12	Jn. 19:36
12:7	Heb. 3:2,5
14:29	Heb. 3:17
16:5,26	2 Tim. 2:19
16:35	Rev. 11:5
19:6	Heb. 9:19
24:17	Rev. 22:16
27:17	Mt. 9:36; Mk. 6:34
30:2	Mt. 5:33

Deuteronomy

1:10	Heb. 11:12
1:31	Acts 13:18
2:5	Acts 7:5
4:2	Rev. 22:18–19
4:11–12	Heb. 12:18–19
4:20	Tit. 2:14; 1 Pet. 2:9
4:24	Heb. 12:29
4:35	Mk. 12:32
5:16	Mt. 15:4; Mk. 7:10; Eph. 6:2–3; Col. 3:20
5:16–20	Mt. 19:18–19; Mk. 10:19; Lk. 18:20
5:17	Mt. 5:21; Jas. 2:11
5:17–19	Rom. 13:9
5:18	Mt. 5:27; Jas. 2:11
5:21	Rom. 7:7; 13:9
6:4–5	Mk. 12:29–30,32–33

6:5	Mt. 22:37; Lk. 10:27
6:13	Mt. 4:10; Lk. 4:8
6:16	Mt. 4:7; Lk. 4:12
7:1	Acts 13:19
7:6	Tit. 2:14; 1 Pet. 2:9
7:19	Acts 13:17
8:3	Mt. 4:4; Lk. 4:4
9:3	Heb. 12:29
9:4	Rom. 10:6–8
9:19	Heb. 12:21
10:17	Acts 10:34; Rom. 2:11; Gal. 2:6; Eph. 6:9; Col. 3:25; 1 Tim. 6:15; Rev. 17:14; 19:16
10:22	Acts 7:14
11:14	Jas. 5:7
14:2	Tit. 2:14; 1 Pet. 2:9
17:6	Jn. 8:17; 1 Tim. 5:19; Heb. 10:28
17:7	1 Cor. 5:13
18:15,18	Acts 3:22; 7:37
18:19	Acts 3:23
19:15	Mt. 18:16; Jn. 8:17; 2 Cor. 13:1; 1 Tim. 5:19; Heb. 10:28
19:19	1 Cor. 5:13
19:21	Mt. 5:38
21:21	1 Cor. 5:13
21:23	Gal. 3:13
22:21,24	1 Cor. 5:13
23:21	Mt. 5:33
24:1,3	Mt. 5:31; 19:7; Mk. 10:4
24:7	1 Cor. 5:13
24:14	Mk. 10:19
25:4	1 Cor. 9:9; 1 Tim. 5:18
25:5,7	Mt. 22:24; Mk. 12:19; Lk. 20:28
27:26	Gal. 3:10
28:35	Rev. 16:2
29:4	Rom. 11:8
29:18	Heb. 12:15
30:12–14	Rom. 10:6–8
31:6,8	Heb. 13:5
32:4	Rev. 15:3–4; 16:5,7; 19:2

32:17	1 Cor. 10:20; Rev. 9:20
32:21	Rom. 10:19; 11:11; 1 Cor. 10:22
32:35	Rom. 12:19
32:35–36	Heb. 10:30
32:43	Rom. 15:10; Rev. 6:10; 16:6; Rev. 19:2

Joshua

7:13	1 Cor. 5:13
22:5	Mk 12:33; Lk. 10:27
24:32	Acts 7:15–16

1 Samuel

1:11	Lk. 1:48
2:1	Lk. 1:46–47
2:2	Lk. 1:49
2:4	Lk. 1:51
2:5	Lk. 1:53
2:7–8	Lk. 1:52
2:26	Lk. 2:52
4:8	Rev. 11:6
12:22	Rom. 11:1–2
13:14	Acts 13:22

2 Samuel

3:39	2 Tim. 4:14
5:2	Mt. 2:6
7:8	2 Cor. 6:18
7:12	Jn. 7:42
7:12–13	Acts 2:30
7:14	2 Cor. 6:18; Heb. 1:5; Rev. 21:7
22:3	Lk. 1:69; Heb. 2:13
22:4	Lk. 1:71
22:9	Rev. 11:5
22:50	Rom. 15:9

1 Kings

8:1,6	Rev. 11:19
8:10–11	Rev. 15:8
8:17–20	Acts 7:45–47

17:1	Rev. 11:6
18:24–39	Rev. 13:13
19:10,14	Rom. 11:3
19:18	Rom. 11:4
22:19	Rev. 4:2–3, 9–10; 5:1,7,13; 6:16; 7:9–10,15; 19:4; 21:5

2 Kings

1:10	Rev. 20:9
1:10–12	Lk. 9:54; Rev. 11:5
2:11	Rev. 11:12
9:7	Rev. 6:10; 19:2

1 Chronicles

17:13	2 Cor. 6:18; Heb. 1:5; Rev. 21:7

2 Chronicles

18:16	Mt. 9:36; Mk. 6:34
18:18	Rev. 4:2–3,9–10; 5:1,7,13; 6:16; 7:9–10, 15; 19:4; 21:5

Job

1:1,8; 2:3	1 Th. 5:22
3:21	Rev. 9:6
4:9	2 Th. 2:8
5:13	1 Cor. 3:19
12:19	Lk. 1:52
13:28	Jas. 5:2
26:6	Rev. 9:11
41:11	Rom. 11:35

Psalms

2:1	Rev. 11:18
2:1–2	Acts 4:25–26
2:2	Rev. 19:19
2:7	Acts 13:33; Heb. 1:5; 5:5
2:8–9	Rev. 2:26–27

2:9	Rev. 12:5; 19:15	34:14	Heb. 12:14
4:4	Eph. 4:26	34:20	Jn. 19:36
5:9	Rom. 3:13	35:8	Rom. 11:9–10
6:8	Mt. 7:23; Lk. 13:27	35:19	Jn. 15:25
7:9	Rev. 2:23	36:1	Rom. 3:18
8:2	Mt. 21:16	36:9	Rev. 21:6
8:4–6	Heb. 2:6–8	37:11	Mt. 5:5
8:6	1 Cor. 15:25,27: Eph. 1:22	39:12	Heb. 11:13; 1 Pet. 2:11
		40:3	Rev. 5:9; 14:3
9:8	Acts 17:31	40:6–8	Heb. 10:5–9
10:7	Rom 3:14	41:9	Mk. 14:18; Jn. 13:18
10:16	Rev. 11:15	41:13	Lk. 1:68
11:6	Rev. 14:10; 19:20; 20:10; 21:8	42:5,11	Mt. 26:38; Mk. 14:34; Jn. 12:27
14:1–3	Rom. 3:10–12	43:5	Mt. 26:38; Mk. 14:34
16:8–11	Acts 2:25–28,31	44:22	Rom. 8:36
16:10	Acts 13:35	45:6–7	Heb. 1:8–9
17:15	Rev. 22:4	45:13–14	Rev. 19:8
18:2	Lk. 1:69	46:2–3	Lk. 21:25–26
18:3	Lk. 1:71	46:6	Rev. 11:18
18:4	Rev. 12:15	47:8	Rev. 4:2–3, 9–10; 5:1,7,13; 6:16; 7:9–10,15; 19:4; 21:5
18:6	Jas. 5:4		
18:25	Mt. 5:7		
18:49	Rom. 15:9	51:4	Rom. 3:4
19:4	Rom. 10:18	53:1–3	Rom. 3:10–12
19:9	Rev. 16:7; 19:2	55:22	1 Pet. 5:7
22:1	Mt. 27:46; Mk. 15:34	62:12	Mt. 16:27; Rom. 2:6; 2 Tim. 4:14; Rev. 2:23; 20:12–13; 22:12
22:7	Mt. 27:39; Mk. 15:29		
22:7–8	Lk. 23:35–36		
22:8	Mt. 27:43	68:17	Rev. 5:11
22:15	Jn. 19:28	68:18	Eph. 4:8
22:18	Mt. 27:35; Mk. 15:24; Lk. 23:34; Jn. 19:24	69:4	Jn. 15:25
		69:9	Jn. 2:17; Rom. 15:3
22:22	Heb. 2:12	69:21	Mt. 27:34,48; Mk. 15:23,36; Lk. 23:36; Jn. 19:29
22:23	Rev. 19:5		
22:28	Rev. 11:15; 19:6		
23:1–2	Rev. 7:17	69:22–23	Rom. 11:9–10
24:1	1 Cor. 10:26	69:24	Rev. 16:1
24:4	Mt. 5:8	69:25	Acts 1:20
28:4	2 Tim. 4:14; Rev. 20:12–13	69:28	Phil. 4:3; Rev. 3:5; 13:8; 17:8; 20:12,15; 21:27
31:5	Lk. 23:46		
32:1–2	Rom. 4:7–8	72:10–11	Rev. 21:24,26
32:2	Rev. 14:5	72:18	Lk. 1:68
33:3	Rev. 5:9; 14:3	72:18–19	Rev. 4:11; 5:12
34:8	1 Pet. 2:3	75:8	Rev. 14:10; 15:7; 16:19
34:12–16	1 Pet. 3:10–12		

76:7	Rev. 6:17	109:8	Acts 1:20
78:2	Mt. 13:35	110:1	Mt. 22:44; 26:64; Mk.
78:24	Jn. 6:31		12:36; 14:62; Lk.
78:44	Rev. 16:3–4		20:42–43; 22:69; Acts
79:2	Rev. 11:9		2:34–35; 1 Cor.
79:3	Rev. 16:6		15:25,27; Heb. 1:13
79:6	2 Th. 1:8	110:4	Heb. 5:6,10; 6:20;
79:10	Rev. 6:10; 19:2		7:11,15,17,21
82:6	Jn. 10:34	111:2	Rev. 15:3
86:9	Rev. 15:4	111:4	Jas. 5:11
89:10	Lk. 1:51	111:9	Lk. 1:49,68
89:3–4	Jn. 7:42	112:9	2 Cor. 9:9
89:11	1 Cor. 10:26	113:7–8	Lk. 1:52
89:20	Acts 13:22	114:3–7	Rev. 20:11
89:27,37	Rev. 1:5	115:4–7	Rev. 9:20
89:37	Rev. 3:14	115:13	Rev. 19:5
90:4	2 Pet. 3:8	116:10	2 Cor. 4:13
91:11–12	Mt. 4:6; Lk. 4:10–11	117:1	Rom. 15:11
92:5	Rev. 15:3	118:6	Heb. 13:6
93:1	Rev. 19:6	118:22	Lk. 20:17; Acts 4:11;
94:11	1 Cor. 3:20		1 Pet. 2:7
94:14	Rom. 11:1–2	118:22–23	Mt. 21:42; Mk. 12:10–
95:7–11	Heb. 3:7–4:11		11
96:1	Rev. 5:9; 14:3	118:25–26	Mt. 21:9; Mk. 11:9–
96:11	Rev. 12:12; 18:20		10; Lk. 19:38; Jn.
96:13	Acts 17:31; Rev. 19:11		12:13
97:3	Rev. 11:5	118:26	Mt. 23:39; Lk. 13:35;
97:7	Heb. 1:6		19:38
98:1	Rev. 5:9; 14:3	119:137	Rev. 16:5,7; 19:2
98:3	Lk. 1:54	126:5–6	Lk. 6:21
98:9	Acts 17:31	132:11	Acts 2:30
102:4,11	Jas. 1:10–11	132:17	Lk. 1:69
102:25–27	Heb. 1:10–12	134:1	Rev. 19:5
103:8	Jas. 5:11	135:1	Rev. 19:5
103:13,17	Lk. 1:50	135:14	Heb. 10:30
104:2	Rev. 12:1	135:15–17	Rev. 9:20
104:4	Heb. 1:7	137:8	Rev. 18:6
104:12	Mt. 13:32; Mk. 4:32;	139:14	Rev. 15:3
	Lk. 13:19	140:3	Rom. 3:13
106:1	Rev. 19:1	141:2	Rev. 5:8; 8:3–4
106:10	Lk. 1:71	143:2	Rom. 3:20
106:36–37	Rev. 9:20	144:9	Rev. 5:9; 14:3
106:37	1 Cor. 10:20	145:17	Rev. 15:3; 16:5,7
106:45–46	Lk. 1:72	146:6	Acts 4:24; 14:15;
106:48	Lk. 1:68		17:24; Rev. 10:6; 14:7
107:9	Lk. 1:53	148:1	Mk. 11:10
107:26	Rom. 10:6–7	149:1	Rev. 5:9; 14:3

Proverbs

1:16	Rom. 3:15
2:3–4	Col. 2:3
3:3	2 Cor. 3:3
3:4	Lk. 2:52; Rom. 12:17; 2 Cor. 8:21
3:11	Eph. 6:4
3:11–12	Heb. 12:5–6
3:12	Rev. 3:19
3:25	1 Pet. 3:6
3:34	Jas. 4:6; 1 Pet. 5:5
4:26	Heb. 12:13
7:3	2 Cor. 3:3
10:12	Jas. 5:20; 1 Pet. 4:8
11:31	1 Pet. 4:18
12:15	Rom. 12:16
14:5	Rev. 1:5; 3:14
17:3	1 Pet. 1:7
18:4	Jn. 7:38
24:12	Mt. 16:27; Rom. 2:6; 2 Tim. 4:14; Rev. 2:23; 20:12–13
25:21–22	Rom. 12:20
26:11	2 Pet. 2:22
26:12	Rom. 12:16

Ecclesiastes

7:20	Rom. 3:10
12:2	Mt. 24:29; Mk. 13:24–25; Lk. 21:25–26

Song of Solomon

6:10	Rev. 12:1

Isaiah

1:9	Rom. 9:29
1:10	Rev. 11:8
2:10,19,21	2 Th. 1:9; Rev. 6:15
5:1–2	Mt. 21:33; Mk. 12:1; Lk. 20:9
5:9	Jas. 5:4
5:21	Rom. 12:16
6:1	Jn. 12:41; Rev. 4:2–3, 9–10; 5:1,7,13; 6:16; 7:9–10,15; 19:4; 21:5
6:2–3	Rev. 4:8
6:4	Rev. 15:8
6:9	Lk. 8:10
6:9–10	Mt. 13:14–15; Mk. 4:12; 8:18; Jn. 9:39; Acts 28:26–27
6:10	Jn. 12:40
7:14	Mt. 1:23; Rev. 12:5
8:8,10	Mt. 1:23
8:12–13	1 Pet. 3:14–15
8:14	Mt. 21:44; Lk. 20:18; Rom. 9:32–33; 1 Pet. 2:8
8:17–18	Heb. 2:13
8:22	Rev. 16:10
9:1–2	Mt. 4:15–16
9:2	Lk. 1:79
10:22–23	Rom. 9:27–28
11:1,10	Rev. 5:5; 22:16
11:4	2 Th. 2:8
11:5	Eph. 6:14
11:4–5	Rev. 19:11
11:10	Rom. 15:12
11:15	Rev. 16:12
12:2	Heb. 2:13
13:10	Mt. 24:29; Mk. 13:24–25; Lk. 21:25; Rev. 6:12; 8:12
13:21	Rev. 18:2
14:12	Lk. 10:18; Rev. 9:1; 12:9
14:13–15	Mt. 11:23; Lk. 10:15
21:9	Rev. 14:8; 18:2
22:13	1 Cor. 15:32
22:22	Rev. 3:7
23:8	Rev. 18:23
23:17	Rev. 17:2; 18:3
24:8	Rev. 18:22
25:8	1 Cor. 15:54; Rev. 7:17; 21:4
26:17	Rev. 12:2
26:19	Mt. 11:5; Lk. 7:22; Eph. 5:14
27:9	Rom. 11:26–27
28:11–12	1 Cor. 14:21
28:16	Rom. 9:33; 10:11; 1 Pet. 2:6
29:10	Rom. 11:8

29:13	Mt. 15:8–9; Mk. 7:6–7	47:9	Rev. 18:8,23
29:14	1 Cor. 1:19	48:12	Rev. 1:8,17; 2:8; 22:13
29:16	Rom. 9:20–22	48:20	Rev. 18:4
30:33	Rev. 19:20; 20:10,15	49:2	Eph. 6:17; Heb. 4:12;
34:4	Mt. 24:29; Mk. 13:24–		Rev. 1:6; 2:12,16;
	25; Lk. 21:25–26;		19:15
	2 Pet. 3:12; Rev.	49:3	2 Th. 1:10
	6:13–14; 8:10; 9:1	49:4	Phil. 2:16
34:10	Rev. 14:11; 19:3	49:6	Lk. 2:32; Jn. 8:12; 9:5;
35:3	Heb. 12:12		Acts 13:47; 26:23
35:4	Mt. 21:5; Jn. 12:15	49:8	2 Cor. 6:2
35:5	Acts 26:18	49:9–10	Rev. 7:17
35:5–6	Mt. 11:5; Mk. 7:37	49:10	Rev. 7:16
	Lk. 7:22	49:13	Rev. 12:12
35:10	Rev. 21:4	49:18	Rom. 14:11
40:2	Rev. 18:6	49:23	Rev. 3:9
40:3	Mt. 3:3; Mk. 1:3; Lk.	49:26	Rev. 16:6
	1:76; Jn. 1:23	50:8–9	Rom. 8:33–34
40:3–5	Lk. 3:4–6	51:8	Lk. 1:50
40:6–8	Jas. 1:10–11; 1 Pet.	51:17	Eph. 5:14
	1:24–25	51:17,22	Rev. 15:7; 16:19
40:10	Rev. 22:12	52:1	Eph. 5:14; Rev.
40:13	Rom. 11:34; 1 Cor.		21:2,27
	2:16	52:5	Rom. 2:24
41:8–9	Heb. 2:16	52:7	Rom. 10:15; Eph.
41:8–14	Lk. 1:54; Jas. 2:23		2:13,17; 6:15
42:1	Mt. 3:17; 17:5; Mk.	52:11	2 Cor. 6:17; Rev. 18:4
	1:11; Lk. 9:35; 2 Pet.	52:15	Rom. 15:21
	1:17	53:1	Jn. 12:38; Rom. 10:16
42:1–4	Mt. 12:18–21	53:4	Mt. 8:17
42:7	Acts 26:18	53:4–5,12	1 Pet. 2:24
42:10	Rev. 5:9; 14:3	53:6	1 Pet. 2:25
42:16	Acts 26:18	53:6,12	Rom. 4:25
42:18	Mt. 11:5; Lk. 7:22	53:7	Rev. 5:6,12; 13:8
43:6	2 Cor. 6:18	53:7–8	Acts 8:32–33
43:20–21	1 Pet. 2:9	53:9	1 Pet. 2:22; Rev. 14:5
44:6	Rev. 1:8,17; 2:8; 21:6;	53:12	Lk. 22:37
	22:13	54:1	Gal. 4:27
44:23	Rev. 18:20	54:5	Rev. 21:2
44:27	Rev. 16:12	54:11–12	Rev. 21:19
44:28	Acts 13:22	54:13	Jn. 6:45
45:3	Col. 2:2	55:1	Rev. 21:6; 22:17
45:9	Rom. 9:20–22	55:3	Acts 13:34; Heb. 13:20
45:14	1 Cor. 14:25; Rev. 3:9	55:10	2 Cor. 9:10
45:21	Mk. 12:32	56:7	Mt. 21:13; Mk. 11:17;
45:23	Rom. 14:11; Phil.		Lk. 19:46
	2:10–11	56:12	1 Cor. 15:32
47:7–9	Rev. 18:7	57:19	Eph. 2:13,17

58:6	Lk. 4:18–19	6:16	Mt. 11:29
59:7–8	Rom. 3:15–17	7:11	Mt. 21:13; Mk. 11:17;
59:17	Eph. 6:14,17; 1 Th.		Lk. 19:46
	5:8	7:34	Rev. 18:23
59:18	Rev. 20:12–13	8:3	Rev. 9:6
59:20–21	Rom. 11:26–27	9:23–24	1 Cor. 1:31; 2 Cor.
60:1	Eph. 5:14		10:17
60:1–2,19	Lk. 1:78–79; Rev.	10:6–7	Rev. 15:4
	21:11	10:25	2 Th. 1:8; Rev. 16:1
60:3,5,11	Rev. 21:24,26	12:3	Jas. 5:5
60:11,19–20	Rev. 21:25	14:12	Rev. 6:8
60:14	Rev. 3:9	15:2	Rev. 13:10
60:19–20	Rev. 21:23; 22:5	15:14	Rev. 14:10
61:1	Mt. 11:5; Lk. 7:22;	16:9	Rev. 18:23
	Acts 26:18	17:10	Rev. 2:23; 20:12;
61:1–2	Lk. 4:18–19		22:12
61:2–3	Mt. 5:4	18:2–4	Mt. 27:9–10
61:6	1 Pet. 2:5,9; Rev. 1:6;	18:3–6	Rom. 9:20–22
	5:10; 20:6	23:5–6	Jn. 7:42
61:10	Rev. 19:8; 21:2	23:6	Rev. 3:12
62:2	Rev. 2:17; 3:12	23:18	Rom. 11:34
62:11	Mt. 21:5; Jn. 12:15;	25:10	Rev. 18:22–23
	Rev. 22:12	25:15	Rev. 15:7; 16:19
63:1–3	Rev. 19:13	25:34	Jas. 5:5
63:3	Rev. 14:20; 19:15	31:9	2 Cor. 6:18; Heb. 1:5;
64:4	1 Cor. 2:9		Rev. 21:7
65:1–2	Rom. 10:20–21	31:15	Mt. 2:18
65:17	2 Pet. 3:13; Rev. 21:1	31:31–34	Heb. 8:8–12
65:19	Rev. 21:4	31:33–34	Heb. 10:16–17
65:23	Phil. 2:16	31:33	2 Cor. 3:3
66:1	Mt. 5:34–35	32:38	Rev. 21:3; 2 Cor
66:1–2	Acts 7:49–50		6:16
66:6	Rev. 16:1,17	33:15	Jn. 7:42
66:7	Rev. 12:2,5	43:11	Rev. 13:10
66:15	2 Th. 1:8	49:36	Rev. 7:1
66:22	2 Pet. 3:13; Rev.	50:8	Rev. 18:4
	21:1–2	50:15,29	Rev. 18:6
66:23	Rev. 15:4	50:38	Rev. 16:12
66:24	Mk. 9:48	50:39	Rev. 18:2
		51:3	Rev. 17:1
		51:6,9,45	Rev. 18:4
Jeremiah		51:7	Rev. 14:8; 17:2,4; 18:3
		51:8	Rev. 14:8; 18:2
2:13	Rev. 21:6	51:9	Rev. 18:4–5
5:14	Rev. 11:5	51:13	Rev. 17:1
5:21	Mk. 8:18	51:36	Rev. 16:12
5:24	Jas. 5:7	51:48	Rev. 18:20

51:49	Rev. 18:24
51:63–64	Rev. 18:21

Ezekiel

1:1	Rev. 19:11
1:5	Rev. 4:6
1:10	Rev. 4:7
1:13	Rev. 4:5; 11:19
1:18	Rev. 4:6,8
1:19	Rev. 4:7
1:22	Rev. 4:6
1:24	Rev. 1:15; 14:2; 19:6
1:26	Rev. 1:13; 4:2–3,9–10; 5:1,7,13; 6:16; 7:9–10,15,19; 19:4; 21:5
1:28	Rev. 4:3; 10:1
2:8–3:3	Rev. 10:9–10
2:9–10	Rev. 5:1
5:12,17	Rev. 6:8
9:2	Rev. 1:13
9:4	Rev. 7:3; 9:4; 14:1; 20:4
10:12	Rev. 4:8
10:14	Rev. 4:7
11:20	Rev. 21:7
12:2	Mk. 8:18
14:21	Rev. 6:8
17:23	Mt. 13:32; Mk. 4:32; Lk. 13:19
20:34,41	2 Cor. 6:17
20:35–36	Rev. 12:6,14
22:31	Rev. 16:1
24:7	Rev. 18:24
26:13	Rev. 18:22
26:16–17	Rev. 18:9–10
26:21	Rev. 18:21
27	Rev. 18:11–19
28:13	Rev. 17:4; 18:16
31:6	Mt. 13:32; Mk. 4:32; Lk. 13:19
32:7	Rev. 6:12
32:7–8	Mt. 24:29; Mk. 13:24–25; Lk. 21:25–26; Rev. 8:12
34:23	Rev. 7:17
36:20,22	Rom. 2:24

36:27	1 Th. 4:8
37:5,10	Rev. 11:11
37:9	Rev. 7:1
37:14	1 Th. 4:8
37:24–25	Jn. 7:42
37:27	2 Cor. 6:16
38	Rev. 20:8
38:22	Rev. 8:7; 14:10; 19:20; 20:9–10; 21:8
39	Rev. 16:14,16
39:6	Rev. 20:9
39:17–20	Rev. 19:17–18,21
40:2	Rev. 21:10
40:3	Rev. 11:1
43:2	Rev. 1:15; 14:2; 19:6
43:7	Rev. 7:15; Rev. 21:3
44:4	Rev. 15:8
44:17–18	Rev. 15:6
47:1	Rev. 22:1
47:12	Rev. 22:2
48:15–35	Rev. 21:10–21

Daniel

1:12,14	Rev. 2:10
2:20	Rev. 5:12
2:28–29	Rev. 22:6
2:34–35, 44–45	Mt. 21:44
2:44	Rev. 11:15
2:45	Rev. 22:6
2:47	Rev. 17:14; 19:16
3:5–6	Rev. 13:15
3:6	Mt. 13:42,50
4:12,21	Mt. 13:32; Mk. 4:32; Lk. 13:19
4:30	Rev. 18:10
5:23	Rev. 9:20
7:2,7	Rev. 13:1
7:3	Rev. 11:7
7:7	Rev. 12:3–4; 13:7; Rev. 17:3,12,16
7:8	Rev. 13:5–6
7:9	Rev. 1:14; 2:18; 4:2–3,9; 5:1,7,13; 7:9–10,15,19; 19:4; 21:5
7:9,14,22,27	Rev. 20:4

7:10	Rev. 5:11; 20:12,15; 21:27
7:13	Mt. 24:30; 26:64; Mk. 13:26; 14:62; Lk. 21:27; 22:69; Rev. 1:7,13; 10:1; 14:14
7:14	Rev. 11:15; 19:6
7:18	Rev. 22:5
7:20	Rev. 13:5–6; 17:3,12,16
7:21	Rev. 13:7
7:24	Rev. 17:3,12,16
7:25	Rev. 11:2; 13:5–6
7:27	Rev. 22:5
8:10	Mk. 13:24–25; Lk. 21:25–26; Rev. 12:3–4
8:26	Rev. 10:4
9:6,10	Rev. 10:7; 11:18
9:27	Mt. 24:15; Mk. 13:14
10:5	Rev. 1:13
10:6	Rev. 1:14–15; 2:18; 4:3; 19:12
11:31	Mt. 24:15; Mk. 13:14
11:36	2 Th. 2:4; Rev. 13:5–6
12:1	Mt. 24:21; Mk. 13:19; Lk. 21:22; Rev. 13:8; 16:18; 17:8; 20:12,15; 21:27
12:4	Rev. 10:4; 22:10
12:7	Rev. 10:2–6; 11:2; 13:5–6
12:9	Rev. 10:4
12:11	Mt. 24:15; Mk. 13:14

Hosea

1:10	Rom. 9:25–27
2:23	Rom. 9:25–26; 1 Pet. 2:10
6:2	Mk. 8:31
6:5	2 Th. 2:8
6:6	Mt. 9:13; 12:7
10:8	Lk. 23:30; Rev. 6:16; 9:6
10:12	2 Cor. 9:10
11:1	Mt. 2:15
13:14	1 Cor. 15:55

Joel

1:6	Rev. 9:8
2:2	Mt. 24:21; Rev. 9:2
2:4–5	Rev. 9:7
2:5	Rev. 9:9
2:10,30–31	Mt. 24:29; Lk. 21:25–26
2:10,31	Mk. 13:24; Rev. 8:12
2:11	Rev. 6:17
2:23	Jas. 5:7
2:28–32	Acts 7:17–21
2:31	Rev. 6:12; 8:12
2:32	Rom. 10:13
3:13	Mk. 4:29; Rev. 14:14–19; 19:15
3:15	Mt. 24:29; Mk. 13:24–25; Lk. 21:25–26; Rev. 6:12; 8:12
3:18	Rev. 22:1

Amos

3:7	Rev. 10:7
3:13	2 Cor. 6:18; Rev. 4:8; 15:3
4:11	Jude 23
4:13	2 Cor. 6:18; Rev. 4:8
5:25–27	Acts 7:42–43
9:11–12	Acts 15:16–17

Jonah

1:17	Mt. 12:40; Mk. 8:31

Micah

4:9–10	Rev. 12:2
5:2	Mt. 2:6; Jn. 7:42
7:6	Mt. 10:35–36; Mk. 13:12; Lk. 12:53
7:20	Lk. 1:55

Nahum

1:6	Rev. 6:17
1:15	Rom. 10:15; Eph. 6:15
3:4	Rev. 17:1

Habakkuk

1:5	Acts 13:41
2:3–4	Heb. 10:37–38
2:4	Rom. 1:17; Gal. 3:11

Zephaniah

1:14	Rev. 6:17
2:15	Rev. 18:7
3:8	Rev. 16:1
3:13	Rev. 14:5

Haggai

2:6,21	Mt. 24:29; Lk. 21:25–26; Heb. 12:26

Zechariah

1:1–2	Rev. 11:1
1:6	Rev. 10:7
1:8	Rev. 6:2,4–5,8; 19:11
1:12	Rev. 6:10
3:1	Rev. 12:10
3:2	Jude 9,23
4	Rev. 11:4
4:2	Rev. 1:12; 4:5

4:10	Rev. 5:6
6:2–3,6	Rev. 6:2,4–5,8
6:3	Rev. 19:11
8:16	Eph. 4:25
9:9	Mt. 21:5; Mk. 11:1ff; Jn. 12:15
9:10	Eph. 2:13,17
11:12	Mt. 26:15
11:12–13	Mt. 27:9–10
12:10	Mt. 24:30; Jn. 19:37
12:10–14	Rev. 1:7
13:7	Mt. 26:31; Mk. 14:27
14:7	Rev. 21:25; 22:5
14:8	Rev. 22:1
14:9	Rev. 11:15; 19:6
14:11	Rev. 22:3

Malachi

1:2–3	Rom. 9:13
3:1	Mt. 11:10; Mk. 1:2; Lk. 1:17,76; 7:27
3:2	Rev. 6:17
3:17	1 Pet. 2:9
4:2	Lk. 1:78
4:5–6	Mt. 17:10–11; Mk. 9:11–12; Lk. 1:17

New Testament Verses That Contain Citations from the Old Testament

Matthew

1:23	Isa. 7:14; 8:8,10
2:6	Mic. 5:2; 2 Sam. 5:2
2:15	Hos. 11:1
2:18	Jer. 31:15
3:3	Isa. 40:3
3:17	Isa. 42:1
4:4	Dt. 8:3
4:6	Ps. 91:11–12
4:7	Dt. 6:16
4:10	Dt. 6:13
4:15–16	Isa. 9:1–2

5:4	Isa. 61:2–3
5:5	Ps. 37:11
5:7	Ps. 18:25
5:8	Ps. 24:4
5:21	Ex. 20:13; Dt. 5:17
5:27	Ex. 20:14; Dt. 5:18
5:31	Dt. 24:1,3
5:33	Lev. 19:12; Num. 30:2; Dt. 23:21
5:34–35	Isa. 66:1
5:38	Ex. 21:24; Lev. 24:20; Dt. 19:21
5:43	Lev. 19:18

7:23	Ps. 6:8	24:15	Dan. 9:27; 11:31;
8:17	Isa. 53:4		12:11
9:13	2 Chr. 18:16; Hos. 6:6	24:21	Dan. 12:1; Joel 2:2
9:36	Num. 27:17	24:29	Eccl. 12:2; Isa. 13:10;
10:35–36	Mic. 7:6		34:4; Ezek. 32:7–8;
11:5	Isa. 26:29; 35:5–6;		Joel 2:10,31; 3:15;
	42:18; 61:1		Hag. 2:6,21
11:10	Ex. 23:20; Mal. 3:1	24:30	Dan. 7:13; Zech. 12:10
11:23	Isa. 14:13–15	26:15	Zech. 11:12
11:29	Jer. 6:16	26:28	Ex. 24:8
12:7	Hos. 6:6	26:31	Zech. 13:7
12:18–21	Isa. 42:1–4	26:38	Ps. 42:5,11; 43:5
12:40	Jon. 1:17	26:64	Ps. 110:1; Dan 7:13
13:14–15	Isa. 6:9–10	27:9–10	Isa. 18:2–4; Zech.
13:32	Ps. 104:12; Ezek.		11:12–13
	17:23; 31:6; Dan.	27:34	Isa. 69:21
	4:12,21	27:35	Ps. 22:18
13:42,50	Dan. 3:6	27:39	Ps. 22:7
15:4	Ex. 20:12; 21:17; Lev.	27:43	Ps. 22:8
	20:9; Dt. 5:16	27:46	Ps. 22:1
15:8–9	Isa. 29:13	27:48	Ps. 69:21
16:27	Ps. 62:12; Prov. 24:12		
17:5	Isa. 42:1	*Mark*	
17:10–11	Mal. 4:5–6		
18:16	Dt. 19:15	1:2	Ex. 23:20; Mal. 3:1
19:4	Gen. 1:27; 5:2	1:3	Isa. 40:3
19:5	Gen. 2:24	1:11	Isa. 42:1
19:7	Deut 24:1	4:12	Isa. 6:9–10
19:18	Lev. 19:12	4:29	Joel 3:13
19:18–19	Ex. 20:12–16; Dt.	4:32	Ps. 104:12; Ezek.
	5:16–20		17:23; 31:6; Dan.
19:19	Lev. 19:18		4:12,21
19:26	Gen. 18:14	6:34	Num. 27:17; 2 Chr.
21:5	Isa. 35:4; 62:11; Zech.		18:16
	9:9	7:6–7	Isa. 29:13
21:9	Ps. 118:25–26	7:10	Ex. 20:12; 21:17; Lev.
21:13	Isa. 56:7; Jer. 7:11		20:9; Dt. 5:16
21:16	Ps. 8:2	7:37	Isa. 35:5–6
21:33	Isa. 5:1–2	8:18	Isa. 6:9–10; Jer. 5:21;
21:42	Ps. 118:22–23		Ezek. 12:2
21:44	Isa. 8:14; Dan. 2:34–	8:31	Hos. 6:2; Jon. 1:17
	35,44–45	9:11–12	Mal. 4:5–6
22:24	Gen. 38:8; Dt. 25:5,7	9:48	Isa. 66:24
22:32	Ex. 3:6,15–16	10:4	Dt. 24:1,3
22:37	Dt. 6:5	10:6	Gen. 1:27; 5:2
22:39	Lev. 19:18	10:7–8	Gen. 2:24
22:44	Ps. 110:1	10:19	Ex. 20:12–16; Lev.
23:39	Ps. 118:26		19:12; Dt. 5:16–20;
			24:14

10:27	Gen. 18:14	1:53	1 Sam. 2:5; Ps. 107:9
11:1ff	Zech. 9:9	1:54	Ps. 98:3; Isa. 41:8–14
11:9–10	Ps. 118:25–26; 148:1	1:55	Gen. 17:7; Mic. 7:20
11:17	Isa. 56:7; Jer. 7:11	1:68	Ps. 41:13; 72:18;
12:1	Isa. 5:1–2		106:48; 111:9
12:10–11	Ps. 118:22–23	1:69	2 Sam. 22:3; Ps. 18:2;
12:19	Gen. 38:8; Dt. 25:5,7		132:17
12:26	Ex. 3:6,15–16	1:71	2 Sam. 22:4; Ps. 18:3;
12:29–30	Dt. 6:4–5		106:10
12:31	Lev. 19:18	1:72	Ps. 106:45–46
12:32	Dt. 4:35; 6:4; Isa.	1:76	Isa. 40:3; Mal. 3:1
	45:21	1:78	Mal. 4:2
12:33	Lev. 19:18; Dt. 6:5;	1:78–79	Isa. 60:1–2,19
	Josh. 22:5	2:23	Ex. 13:2,12,15
12:36	Ps. 110:1	2:24	Lev. 5:11; 12:8
13:12	Mic. 7:6	2:32	Isa. 49:6
13:14	Dan. 9:27; 11:31;	2:52	1 Sam. 2:26; Prov. 3:4
	12:11	3:4–6	Isa. 40:3–5
13:19	Dan. 12:1	4:4	Dt. 8:3
13:24–5	Eccl. 12:2; Isa. 13:10;	4:8	Dt. 6:13
	34:4; Ezek. 32:7–8;	4:10–11	Ps. 91:11–12
	Dan. 8:10; Joel	4:12	Dt. 6:16
	2:10,30–31; 3:15	4:18–19	Isa. 58:6; 61:1–2
13:26	Dan. 7:13	6:21	Ps. 126:5–6
14:18	Ps. 41:9	7:22	Isa. 26:19; 35:5–6;
14:24	Ex. 24:8		42:18; 61:1
14:27	Zech. 13:7	7:27	Ex. 23:20; Mal. 3:1
14:34	Ps. 42:5,11; 43:5	8:10	Isa. 6:9–10
14:62	Ps. 110:1; Dan. 7:13	9:35	Isa. 42:1
15:23	Ps. 69:21	9:54	2 Ki. 1:10,12
15:24	Ps. 22:18	10:15	Isa. 14:13,15
15:29	Ps. 22:7	10:18	Isa. 14:12
15:34	Ps. 22:1	10:27	Lev. 19:18; Dt. 6:5;
15:36	Ps. 69:21		Josh. 22:5
		12:53	Mic. 7:6
Luke		13:19	Ps. 104:12; Dan.
			4:12,21; Ezek. 17:23;
1:15	Lev. 10:9; Num. 6:3		31:6
1:17	Mal 3:1; 4:5–6	13:27	Ps. 6:8
1:37	Gen. 18:14	13:35	Ps. 118:26
1:46–47	1 Sam. 2:1	17:29	Gen. 19:24
1:48	1 Sam. 1:11	18:20	Ex. 20:12–16; Lev.
1:49	1 Sam. 2:2; Ps. 111:9		19:12; Dt. 5:16–20
1:50	Ps. 103:13,17; Isa.	19:38	Ps. 118:26
	51:8	19:46	Isa. 56:7; Jer. 7:11
1:51	Ps. 89:10	20:9	Isa. 5:1–2
1:52	1 Sam. 2:7–8; Job	20:17	Ps. 118:22
	5:11; 12:19; Ps. 113:7–	20:18	Isa. 8:14
	8		

20:28	Gen. 38:8; Dt. 25:5,7
20:37	Ex. 3:6,15–16
20:42–43	Ps. 110:1
21:22	Dan. 12:1
21:25	Isa. 13:10
21:25–26	Ps. 46:2–3; Eccl. 12:2; 34:4; Ezek. 32:7–8; Dan. 8:10; Joel 2:10,30–31; 3:15; Hag. 2:6,21
21:27	Dan. 7:13
22:30	Ex. 24:8
22:37	Isa. 53:12
22:69	Ps. 110:1; Dan. 7:13
23:30	Hos. 10:8
23:34	Ps. 22:18
23:35–36	Ps. 22:7–8
23:36	Ps. 69:21
23:46	Ps. 31:5

John

1:23	Isa. 40:3
1:51	Gen. 28:12
2:17	Ps. 69:9
6:31	Ex. 16:13ff; Ps. 78:24; 105:40
6:45	Isa. 54:13
7:38	Prov. 18:4
7:42	2 Sam. 7:12; Ps. 89:3–4; Jer. 23:5–6; 33:15; Ezek. 37:24–25; Mic. 5:2
8:12	Isa. 49:6
8:17	Dt. 17:6; 19:15
9:5	Isa. 49:6
9:39	Isa. 6:9–10
10:34	Ps. 82:6
12:13	Ps. 118:25–26
12:15	Isa. 35:4; 62:11; Zech. 9:9
12:27	Ps. 42:5,11
12:38	Isa. 53:1
12:40	Isa. 6:10
12:41	Isa. 6:1
13:18	Ps. 41:9
15:25	Ps. 35:19; 69:4
19:24	Ps. 22:18
19:28	Ps. 22:15
19:29	Ps. 69:21
19:36	Ex. 12:46; Num. 9:12; Ps. 34:20
19:37	Zech. 12:10

Acts

1:20	Ps. 69:25; 109:8
2:17–21	Joel 2:28–32
2:25–28,31	Ps. 16:8–11
2:30	2 Sam. 7:12–13; Ps. 132:11
2:34–35	Ps. 110:1
3:13	Ex. 3:6,15–16
3:22	Dt. 18:15,18
3:23	Lev. 23:29; Dt. 18:19
3:25	Gen. 12:3; 18:18; 22:18; 26:4
4:11	Ps. 118:22
4:24	Ex. 20:11; Ps. 146:6
4:25–26	Ps. 2:1–2
7:3	Gen. 12:1
7:5	Gen. 12:7; 13:15; 15:18; 17:8; 24:7; 48:4; Dt. 2:5
7:6	Ex. 2:22
7:6–7	Gen. 15:13–14; Ex. 3:12
7:9	Gen. 37:11,28; 39:2–3,21,23
7:10	Gen. 41:37–41
7:11	Gen. 41:54; 42:5
7:12	Gen. 42:1–2
7:13	Gen. 45:1–16
7:14	Gen. 46:27; Dt. 10:22
7:15–16	Gen. 50:13; Josh. 24:32
7:17–19	Ex. 1:7–17
7:20–21	Ex. 2:2–10
7:23–29,35	Ex. 2:11–15
7:30–31	Ex. 3:2–3
7:31,33–34	Ex. 3:3–5,7–10
7:32	Ex. 3:6,15–16
7:35	Ex. 2:14
7:37	Dt. 18:15,18
7:40	Ex. 32:1,23
7:42–43	Amos 5:25–27

7:44	Ex. 25:9,40; 26:30; 27:21	4:22–23	Gen. 15:6
7:45–47	1 Ki. 8:17–20	4:25	Isa. 53:6,12
7:49–50	Isa. 66:1–2	7:7	Ex. 20:17; Dt. 5:21
8:32–33	Isa. 53:7–8	8:33–34	Isa. 50:8–9
10:34	Dt. 10:17	8:36	Ps. 44:22
13:17	Ex. 6:1,6; 12:51; Dt. 7:19	9:7	Gen. 21:12
		9:9	Gen. 18:10,14
13:18	Ex. 16:35; Dt. 1:31	9:12	Gen. 25:23
13:19	Dt. 7:1	9:13	Mal. 1:2–3
13:22	1 Sam. 13:14; cf. 2 Sam. 7; Ps. 89:20; Isa. 44:2	9:15	Ex. 33:19
		9:17	Ex. 9:16
		9:20–22	Isa. 29:16; 45:9; Jer. 18:3–6
13:33	Ps. 2:7	9:25–26	Hos. 2:23
13:34	Isa. 55:3	9:25–27	Hos. 1:10
13:35	Ps. 16:10	9:27–28	Isa. 10:22–23
13:41	Hab. 1:5	9:29	Isa. 1:9
13:47	Isa. 49:6	9:32–33	Isa. 8:14
14:15	Ex. 20:11; Ps. 146:6	9:33	Isa. 28:16
15:16–17	Amos 9:11–12	10:5	Lev. 18:5
17:24	Ex. 20:11; Ps. 146:6	10:6–7	Ps. 107:26
17:31	Ps. 9:8; 96:13; 98:9	10:6–8	Dt. 9:4; 30:12–14
23:5	Ex. 22:28	10:11	Isa. 28:16
26:18	Isa. 35:5; 42:7,16; 61:1	10:13	Joel 2:32
26:23	Isa. 49:6	10:15	Isa. 52:7; Nah. 1:15
28:26–27	Isa. 6:9–10	10:16	Isa. 53:1
		10:18	Ps. 19:4
		10:19	Dt. 32:21
Romans		10:20–21	Isa. 65:1–2
		11:1–2	1 Sam. 12:22; Ps. 94:14
1:17	Hab. 2:4		
2:6	Ps. 62:12; Prov. 24:12	11:3	1 Ki. 19:10,14
2:11	Dt. 10:17	11:4	1 Ki. 19:18
2:24	Isa. 52:5; Ezek. 36:20,22	11:8	Dt. 29:4; Isa. 29:10
		11:9–10	Ps. 35:8; 69:22–23
3:4	Ps. 51:4	11:11	Dt. 32:21
3:10	Eccl. 7:20	11:26–27	Isa. 27:9; 59:20–21
3:10–12	Ps. 14:1–3; 53:1–3	11:34	Isa. 40:13; Jer. 23:18
3:13	Ps. 5:9; 140:3	11:35	Job 41:11
3:14	Ps. 10:7	12:16	Prov. 12:15; 26:12; Isa. 5:21
3:15	Prov. 1:16		
3:15–17	Isa. 59:7–8	12:17	Prov. 3:4
3:18	Ps. 36:1	12:19	Dt. 32:35
3:20	Ps. 143:2	12:20	Prov. 25:21–22
4:3,9	Gen. 15:6	13:9	Ex. 20:13–15,17; Lev. 19:18; Dt. 5:17–19,21
4:7–8	Ps. 32:1–2		
4:13	Gen. 18:18	14:11	Isa. 45:23; 49:18
4:17	Gen. 17:5	15:3	Ps. 69:9
4:18	Gen. 15:5; 17:5		

15:9	2 Sam. 22:50; Ps. 18:49
15:10	Dt. 32:43
15:11	Ps. 117:1
15:12	Isa. 11:10
15:21	Isa. 52:15

1 Corinthians

1:19	Isa. 29:14
1:31	Jer. 9:23–24
2:9	Isa. 64:4
2:16	Isa. 40:13
3:19	Job 5:13
3:20	Ps. 94:11
5:13	Dt. 17:7; 19:19; 21:21; 22:21,24; 24:7
6:16	Gen. 2:24
9:9	Dt. 25:4
10:7	Ex. 32:6
10:20	Dt. 32:17; Ps. 106:37
10:22	Dt. 32:21
10:26	Ps. 106:37
10:26	Ps. 24:1; 50:12; 89:11
11:25	Ex. 24:8
14:21	Isa. 28:11–12
14:25	Isa. 45:14
15:25,27	Ps. 110:1; 8:6
15:32	Isa. 22:13; 56:12
15:45,47	Gen. 2:7
15:54	Isa. 25:8
15:55	Hos. 13:14

2 Corinthians

3:3	Ex. 24:12; Prov. 3:3; 7:3; Jer. 31:33
3:6	Ex. 24:8
3:12–18	Ex. 34:29–35
4:13	Ps. 116:10
6:2	Isa. 49:8
6:16	Lev. 26:11–12; Jer. 32:38; Ezek. 37:27
6:17	Isa. 52:11; Ezek. 20:34,41
6:18	2 Sam. 7:8,14; 1 Chr. 17:13; Isa. 43:6; Jer. 31:9; Amos 3:13; 4:13

8:15	Ex. 16:18
8:21	Prov. 3:4
9:9	Ps. 112:9
9:10	Isa. 55:10; Hos. 10:12
10:17	Jer. 9:23–24
13:1	Dt. 19:15

Galatians

2:6	Dt. 10:17
3:6	Gen. 15:6
3:8	Gen. 12:3; 18:18; 22:18; 26:4; 28:14
3:10	Dt. 27:26
3:11	Hab. 2:4
3:12	Lev. 18:5
3:13	Dt. 21:23
3:16	Gen. 12:7; 13:15; 17:7; 22:18; 24:7; 26:4
4:27	Isa. 54:1
4:30	Gen. 21:10
5:14	Lev. 19:18

Ephesians

1:22	Ps. 8:6
2:13,17	Isa. 52:7; 57:19; Zech. 9:10
4:8	Ps. 68:18
4:25	Zech. 8:16
4:26	Ps. 4:4
5:14	Isa. 26:19; 51:17; 52:1; 60:1
5:31	Gen. 2:24
6:2–3	Ex. 20:12; Dt. 5:16
6:4	Prov. 3:11
6:9	Dt. 10:17
6:14	Isa. 11:5; 59:17
6:15	Isa. 52:7; Nah. 1:15
6:17	Isa. 49:2; 59:17

Philippians

2:10–11	Isa. 45:23
2:16	Isa. 49:4; 65:23
4:3	Ex. 32:32–33; Ps. 69:28

Colossians

2:3	Prov. 2:3–4; Isa. 45:3
3:20	Dt. 5:16; Ex. 20:12
3:25	Dt. 10:17

1 Thessalonians

2:16	Gen. 15:16
4:8	Ezek. 36:27; 37:14
5:8	Isa. 59:17
5:22	Job 1:1,8; 2:3

2 Thessalonians

1:8	Ps. 79:6; Isa. 66:15; Jer. 10:25
1:9	Isa. 2:19,21
1:10	Isa. 49:4
2:4	Ezek. 28:2; Dan. 11:36
2:8	Job 4:9; Isa. 11:4; Hos. 6:5

1 Timothy

5:18	Dt. 25:4
5:19	Dt. 17:6; 19:15
6:15	Dt. 10:17

2 Timothy

2:19	Num. 16:5,26
4:14	Prov. 24:12; 2 Sam. 3:39; Ps. 28:4; 62:12

Titus

2:14	Dt. 4:20; 7:6; 14:2

Hebrews

1:5	2 Sam. 7:14; 1 Chr. 17:13; Ps. 2:7
1:6	Ps. 97:7
1:7	Ps. 104:4
1:8–9	Ps. 45:6–7
1:10–12	Ps. 102:25–27
1:13	Ps. 110:1

2:6–8	Ps. 8:4–6
2:12	Ps. 22:22
2:13	1 Sam. 22:3; Isa. 8:17–18; 12:2
2:16	Isa. 41:8–9
3:2,5	Num. 12:7
3:7–4:11	Ps. 95:7–11
3:17	Num. 14:29
4:4	Gen. 2:2
4:12	Isa. 49:2
5:5	Ps. 2:7
5:6,10	Ps. 110:4; see Heb. 6:20; 7:11,15,17,21
6:8	Gen. 3:17–18
6:13–14	Gen. 22:16–17
6:19	Lev. 16:2,12
6:20	Ps. 110:4; see Heb. 5:6,10; 7:11,15,17,21
7:1–3,10	Gen. 14:17–20
7:11,15,17, 21	Ps. 110:4; see Heb. 5:6; 6:20
8:5	Ex. 25:9,40; 26:30
8:8–13	Jer 31:31–34
9:19	Num. 19:6
9:19	Lev. 14:4
9:20	Ex. 24:8
10:5–9	Ps. 40:6–8
10:12–13	Ps. 110:1
10:16–17	Jer. 31:33–34
10:28	Dt. 17:6; 19:15
10:29	Ex. 24:8
10:30	Dt. 32:35–36; Ps. 135:4
10:37–38	Hab. 2:3–4
11:4	Gen. 4:4
11:5	Gen. 5:24
11:9	Gen. 23:4
11:12	Gen. 15:5–6; 22:16–17; 32:12; Ex. 32:13; Dt. 1:10
11:13	Gen. 23:4; 47:9; 1 Chr. 29:15; Ps. 39:12
11:18	Gen. 21:12
11:21	Gen. 47:31
11:23	Ex. 2:2
12:5–6	Prov. 3:11–12
12:12	Isa. 35:3
12:13	Prov. 4:26

12:14	Ps. 34:14
12:15	Dt. 29:18
12:16	Gen. 25:33–34
12:18–19	Ex. 19:16–22; Dt. 4:11–12
12:20	Ex. 19:12–13
12:21	Dt. 9:19
12:26	Hag. 2:6
12:29	Dt. 4:24; 9:3
13:5	Dt. 31:6,8
13:6	Ps. 118:6
13:20	Isa. 55:3

James

1:10–11	Ps. 102:4,11; Isa. 40:6–8
2:8	Lev. 19:18
2:11	Ex. 20:13–14; Dt. 5:17–18
2:23	Gen. 15:6; Isa. 41:8–14
3:9	Gen. 1:26–27
4:6	Prov. 3:34
5:2	Job. 13:28
5:4	Ps. 18:6; Isa. 5:9
5:5	Jer. 12:3; 25:34
5:7	Dt. 11:14; Jer. 5:24; Joel 2:23
5:11	Ex. 34:6; Ps. 103:8; 111:4
5:20	Prov. 10:12

1 Peter

1:7	Prov. 17:3
1:16	Lev. 11:44–45; 19:2; 20:7
1:24–25	Isa. 40:6–8
2:3	Ps. 34:8
2:5	Isa. 61:6
2:6	Isa. 28:16
2:7	Ps. 118:22
2:8	Isa. 8:14
2:9	Ex. 19:5–6; Dt. 4:20; 7:6; 14:2; Isa. 43:20–21; 61:6; Mal. 3:17
2:10	Hos. 2:23
2:11	Gen. 23:4

2:22	Isa. 53:9
2:24	Isa. 53:4–5,12
2:25	Isa. 53:6
3:6	Prov. 3:25
3:10–12	Ps. 34:12–16
3:14–15	Isa. 8:12–13
4:8	Prov. 10:12
4:18	Prov. 11:31
5:5	Prov. 3:34
5:7	Ps. 55:22

2 Peter

1:17	Isa. 42:1
2:22	Prov. 26:11
3:8	Ps. 90:4
3:12	Isa. 34;4
3:13	Isa. 65:17; 66:22

Jude

9	Zech. 3:2
23	Amos 4:11; Zech. 3:2

Revelation

1:4	Ex. 3:14
1:5	Ps. 89:27,37
1:6	Ex. 19:6; Isa. 61:6
1:7	Dan. 7:13; Zech. 12:10–14
1:8	Ex. 3:14; Isa. 44:6; 48:12
1:13	Ezek. 1:26; 9:2; Dan. 7:13
1:14	Dan. 7:9; 10:6
1:15	Ezek. 1:24; 53:2; Dan. 10:6
1:16	Isa. 49:2
1:17	Isa. 44:6; 48:12
2:7	Gen. 2:9; 3:22
2:8	Isa. 44:6; 48:12
2:10	Dan. 1:12,14
2:12,16	Isa. 49:2
2:17	Isa. 62:2; Ps. 78:23–24
2:18	Dan. 7:9; 10:6
2:23	Ps. 7:9; 62:12; Prov. 24:12; Jer. 17:10
2:26–27	Ps. 2:8–9

3:5	Ex. 32:32–33; Ps. 69:28	6:16	Hos. 10:8; see Rev. 4:2–3
3:7	Isa. 22:22	6:17	Ps. 86:7; Joel 2:11;
3:9	Isa. 49:23; 45:14; 60:14		Nah. 1:6; Zeph. 1:14; Mal. 3:2
3:12	Isa. 62:2; Jer. 23:6	7:1	Dan. 7:2; Jer. 49:36;
3:14	Ps. 89:37		Ezek. 37:9
3:19	Prov. 3:12	7:3	Ezek. 9:4
4:2–3	1 Ki. 22:19; 2 Chr. 18:18; Ps. 47:8; Isa. 6:1; Ezek. 1:26; Dan. 7:9; similar are: Rev. 4:9; 5:1,7,13; 7:9–10,15,19; 19:4; 21:5	7:9–10	See Rev. 4:2–3
		7:15	Ezek. 43:7; see Rev. 4:2–3
		7:16	Isa. 49:10
		7:17	Ps. 23:1–2; Isa. 25:8; 49:9–10; Ezek. 34:23
4:3	Ezek. 1:28; Dan. 10:6	8:3–4	Ps. 141:2
4:5	Ex. 19:16; 37:23; Ezek. 1:13; Zech. 4:2	8:5	Ex. 19:16–19
		8:7	Ex. 9:23–25; Ezek. 38:22
4:6	Ezek. 1:5,18,22	8:8	Ex. 7:20–21
4:7	Ezek. 1:10; 10:14	8:10	Isa. 34:4
4:8	Ex. 3:14; Isa. 6:2–3; Ezek. 1:18; 10:12; Amos 3:13; 4:13	8:12	Isa. 13:10; Ezek. 32:7–8; Joel 2:10,31; 3:15
4:9–10	See Rev. 4:2–3	9:1	Isa. 14:12; 34:4
5:1	Ezek. 2:9–10; see Rev. 4:2–3	9:2–9	Ex. 10:12–15
		9:2	Gen. 19:28; Ex. 19:18; Joel 2:2
5:5	Gen. 49:9–10; Isa. 11:1,10	9:4	Ezek. 9:4
5:6	Isa. 53:7; Zech. 4:10	9:6	Job 3:21; Jer. 8:3; Hos. 10:8
5:7	See Rev. 4:2–3 above in this list	9:7	Joel 2:4–5
5:8	Ps. 141:2	9:8	Joel 1:6
5:9	Ps. 33:3; 40:3; 96:1; 98:1; 144:9; 149:1; Isa. 42:10; Rev. 14:3 is similar	9:9	Joel 2:5
		9:11	Job 26:6
		9:13	Ex. 30:1–3
		9:20	Dt. 32:17; Ps. 106:36–37; 115:4–7; 135:15–17; Dan. 5:23
5:10	Ex. 19:6; Isa. 61:6		
5:11	Ps. 68:17; Dan. 7:10		
5:12	Isa. 53:7; Dan. 5:12	10:1	Dan. 7:13; Ezek. 1:28
5:13	See Rev. 4:2–3	10:4	Dan. 8:26; 12:4,9
6:2,4–5,8	Zech. 1:8; 6:2–3,6	10:2–6	Dan. 12:7
6:8	Jer. 14:12; 15:3; Ezek. 5:12,17; 14:21	10:6	Gen. 14:19,22; Ex. 20:11; Ps. 146:6; Neh. 9:6
6:10	Dt. 32:43; 2 Ki. 9:7; Ps. 79:10; Zech. 1:12	10:7	Dan. 9:6,10; Amos 3:7; Zech. 1:6
6:12	Isa. 13:10; Ezek. 32:7; Joel 2:31; 3:15	10:9–10	Ezek. 2:8–3:3
6:13–14	Isa. 34:4	11:1	Ezek. 40:3; Zech. 1:1–2
6:15	Isa. 2:10,19,21		

11:2	Dan. 7:25; 8:13; 12:7	14:3	See Rev. 5:9
11:4	Zech. 4	14:5	Ps. 32:2; Isa. 53:9;
11:5	Num. 16:35; 2 Sam.		Zeph. 3:13
	22:9; 2 Ki. 1:10–12;	14:7	Ex. 20:11; Ps. 146:6
	Ps. 97:3; Jer. 5:14	14:8	Isa. 21:9; Jer. 51:7–8
11:6	Ex. 7:17,19–20;	14:10	Gen. 19:24; Ps. 11:6;
	1 Sam. 4:8; 1 Ki. 17:1		75:82; Jer. 15:14;
11:7	Dan. 7:3		Ezek. 38:22
11:8	Isa. 1:10	14:11	Isa. 34:10
11:9	Ps. 79:2	14:14	Ezek. 1:26; Dan. 7:13
11:11	Ezek. 37:5,10	14:14–19	Joel 3:13
11:12	2 Ki. 2:11	14:20	Isa. 63:3; Lam. 1:15
11:15	Ex. 15:18; Ps. 10:16;	15:1	Lev. 26:21
	22:28; Dan. 2:44; 7:14;	15:3	Ex. 15:1,11; Dt. 32:4;
	Obad. 21; Zech. 14:9		Ps. 92:5; 111:2;
11:17	Ex. 3:14		139:14; 145:17; Amos
11:18	Ps. 2:1; 46:6; 115:13;		3:13
	Dan. 9:6,10	15:4	Dt. 32:4; Ps. 86:9; Isa.
11:19	Ex. 9:23–24; 19:16; 1		66:23; Jer. 10:6–7
	Ki. 8:1,6; 2 Chr. 5:7;	15:5	Ex. 38:21
	Ezek. 1:13	15:6	Lev. 26:21; Ezek.
12:1	Gen. 37:9; Ps. 104:2;		44:17–18
	Song 6:10	15:7	Ps. 75:8; Isa. 51:17,22;
12:2	Isa. 26:17; 66:7; Mic.		Jer. 25:15
	4:9–10	15:8	Ex. 40:34; 1 Ki. 8:10–
12:3–4	Dan. 7:7; 8:10		11; 2 Chr. 5:13–14;
12:5	Ps. 2:9; Isa. 7:14;		Isa. 6:4; Ezek. 44:4
	66:7	16:1	Ps. 69:24; Isa. 66:6;
12:6,14	Ezek. 20:35–36; Dan		Jer. 10:25; Ezek.
	7:25; 12:7		22:31; Zeph. 3:8
12:9	Isa. 14:12	16:2	Ex. 9:9–10; Dt. 28:35
12:10	Zech. 3:1	16:3–4	Ex. 7:17–21; Ps. 78:44
12:12	Ps. 96:11; Isa. 49:13	16:5	Ex. 3:14
12:15	Ps. 18:4	16:5,7	Dt. 32:4; Ps. 119:137;
13:1	Dan. 7:2,7		145:17
13:5–6	Dan. 7:8,20,25; 11:36;	16:6	Dt. 32:43; Ps. 79:3;
	12:7		Isa. 49:26
13:7	Dan. 7:7,21	16:7	Ps. 19:9
13:8	Ex. 32:32–33; Ps.	16:10	Ex. 10:21–22; Isa.
	69:28; Isa. 53:7; Dan.		8:22
	12:1	16:12	Isa. 11:15; 44:27; Jer.
13:10	Gen. 9:6; Jer. 15:2;		50:38; 51:36
	43:11	16:17	Isa. 66:6
13:13	1 Ki. 18:24–39	16:18	Ex. 19:16–19; Dan.
13:15	Dan. 3:5–6		12:1
14:1	Ezek. 9:4	16:19	Ps. 75:8; Isa. 51:17,22;
14:2	Ezek. 1:24; 43:2		Jer. 25:15

16:21	Ex. 9:23–25	19:11	Ps. 96:13; Isa. 11:4–5;
17:1	Jer. 51:13; Nah. 3:4		Ezek. 1:1; Zech. 1:8;
17:2	Isa. 23:17; Jer. 51:7		6:3
17:3,12,16	Dan. 7:7,20,24	19:12	Dan. 10:6
17:4	Ezek. 28:13; Jer. 51:7	19:13	Isa. 63:1–3
17:8	Ex. 32:32–33; Ps.	19:15	Ps. 2:9; Isa. 49:2; 63:3;
	69:28; Dan. 12:1		Lam. 1:15; Joel 3:13
17:14	Dt. 10:17; Dan. 2:47	19:16	Dt. 10:17; Dan. 2:47
17:16	Lev. 21:9	19:17–18,21	Ezek. 39:17–20
18:2	Isa. 13:21; 21:9; 43:11;	19:19	Ps. 2:2
	Jer. 50:39; 51:8	19:20	Gen. 19:24; Ps. 11:6;
18:3	Isa. 23:17; Jer. 51:7		Isa. 30:33; Ezek.
18:4	Isa. 48:20; 52:11; Jer.		38:22; similar are: Rev.
	50:8; 51:6,9,45		20:10,15; 21:8
18:5	Gen. 18:20–21; Jer.	20:2	Gen. 3
	51:9	20:4	Ezek. 9:4; Dan.
18:6	Ps. 137:8; Isa. 40:2;		7:9,14,22,27
	Jer. 50:15,29	20:6	Ex. 19:6; Isa. 61:6
18:7	Isa. 47:7–9; Zeph.	20:8	Ezek. 38
	2:15	20:9	2 Ki. 1:10; Ezek.
18:8	Isa. 47:9		38:22; 39:6
18:9–10	Ezek. 26:16–17	20:10	See Rev. 19:20
18:10	Dan. 4:30	20:11	Ps. 114:3–7
18:11–19	Ezek. 27	20:12	Ex. 32:32–33; Ps.
18:16	Ezek. 28:13		69:28; Dan. 7:10; 12:1;
18:20	Ps. 96:11; Isa. 44:23;		Jer. 17:10
	Jer. 51:48	20:12–13	Ps. 28:4; 62:12; Prov.
18:21	Jer. 51:63–64; Ezek.		24:12; Isa. 59:18; Jer.
	26:21		17:10
18:22	Isa. 24:8; Ezek. 26:13	20:15	See Rev. 19:20 and
18:22–23	Jer. 25:10		20:12
18:23	Isa. 23:8; 47:9; Jer.	21:1	Isa. 65:17; 66:22
	7:34; 16:9	21:2	Isa. 52:1; 54:5; 66:22
18:24	Jer. 51:49; Ezek. 24:7	21:3	Lev. 26:11–12; 2 Chr.
19:1	Ps. 106:1		6:18; Ezek. 43:7; Jer.
19:2	Dt. 32:4,43; 2 Ki. 9:7;		32:38
	Ps. 19:9; 79:10;	21:4	Isa. 25:8; 35:10; 65:19
	119:137	21:5	See Rev. 4:2–3
19:3	Isa. 34:10	21:6	Ps. 36:9; Isa. 44:6;
19:4	See Rev. 4:2–3		48:12; 55:1; Jer.
19:5	Ps. 22:23; 115:13;		2:13
	134:1; 135:1	21:7	2 Sam. 7:14; 1 Chr.
19:6	Ex. 15:18; Ps. 22:28;		17:13; Jer. 31:9; Ezek.
	93:1; Ezek. 1:24; 43:2;		11:20
	Dan. 7:14; Zech. 14:9	21:8	See Rev. 19:20
19:8	Ps. 45:13–14; Isa.	21:10	Ezek. 40:2
	61:10	21:10–21	Ezek. 48:15–35

21:11	Isa. 60:1–2,19
21:12–13	Ex. 28:21
21:19	Isa. 54:11–12
21:23	Isa. 60:19–20
21:24,26	Ps. 72:10–11; Isa. 60:3,5,11
21:25	Isa. 60:11,19–20; Zech. 14:7
21:27	Ex. 32:22–23; Ps. 69:28; Isa. 52:1; Dan. 7:10; 12:1
22:1	Ezek. 47:1; Joel 3:18; Zech. 14:8
22:2	Gen. 2:9; 3:22; Ezek. 47:12
22:3	Zech. 14:11
22:4	Ps. 17:15
22:5	Isa. 60:19–20; Dan. 7:18,27; Zech. 14:7
22:6	Dan. 2:28–29,45
22:10	Dan. 12:4
22:12	Isa. 40:10; 62:12; Jer. 17:10
22:13	Isa. 44:6; 48:12
22:14,19	Gen. 2:9; 3:22; Ezek. 47:12
22:16	Num. 24:17; Isa. 11:1,10
22:17	Isa. 55:1
22:18–19	Dt. 4:2; 12:32

23

Annotated Bibliography of
Basic Books for Bible Study

Introduction

There is a wealth of books available to provide assistance in Bible study. Every student of the Scriptures should attempt to build up a library with a core that covers all the basic areas. This bibliography provides such a foundation. It is aimed at the needs of both the general reader and the beginning Bible student. Consequently, overly technical works are left out except where they make a unique contribution. Certain other categories of books are omitted also, e.g., commentaries and language-specific works such as Heb. and Gr. grammars. Many helpful studies are found in articles appearing in periodicals, and no effort has been made to include them. Not all of the books in the bibliography have been written by those who agree with the position of the Scofield Bible, or who are even dispensational, conservative, or Christian (e.g. Jewish geographical works are included). In some cases, alternatives are given where there are similar valuable books on the same topic, e.g., Young's and Strong's concordances. In a limited bibliography of this kind many good works must be omitted. The reader should consult the bibliographies listed below in the first category for further bibliographical information.

Bibliographies

Barber, Cyril J. *The Minister's Library*. Vol. 1, 1974; Vol. 2, 1983. Grand Rapids: Baker.
    A unique work; very comprehensive and well organized; in spite of its title, suitable for all Bible students.
Osborne, Grant, ed. *An Annotated Bibliography on the Bible and the Church*. Deerfield, IL: Open Door, 1982.

Compiled by the faculty of Trinity Evangelical Divinity School; covers O.T., N.T., missions and evangelism, philosophy of religion, systematic theology, church history, Christian education, pastoral counseling, and practical theology; very valuable annotations.

Concordances

Goodrick, Edward W., and John R. Kohlenberger. *The NIV Complete Concordance*. Grand Rapids: Zondervan, 1981.
> The only complete NIV concordance; contains a list of a relatively small number of words that are omitted from the list of total occurrences.

Strong, James. *Strong's Exhaustive Concordance of the Bible with the Exclusive Key-Word Comparison*. Rev. ed. Nashville: Abingdon, 1980.
> Contains comparisons of key words among AV, RSV, NEB, Jerusalem Bible, NASB, and NIV translations, and a unique cross-reference system that includes Gr. and Heb. words.

Thomas, Robert L. *New American Standard Exhaustive Concordance of the Bible*. Nashville: Holman, 1981.
> Indispensable for work with the NASB; like Strong and Young, has index to Heb. and Gr. words.

Young, Robert. *Analytical Concordance to the Bible*. Rev. ed. Nashville: Thomas Nelson, 1982.
> Contains reverse indexes of Gr. and Heb. words. Strong and Young are equally usable.

Dictionaries and Encyclopedias

Archer, Gleason L. *Encyclopedia of Bible Difficulties*. Grand Rapids: Zondervan, 1982.
> Approaches knotty problems book by book; strong on biblical inerrancy; has sections on how to deal with Bible difficulties and on relations between the testaments; done by a respected premillennial scholar.

Bromiley, Geoffrey, ed. *International Standard Bible Encylopedia*. Vol. 1, A–D, 1979; Vol. 2, E–J, 1981. Grand Rapids: Eerdmans.
> Fully revised edition of a classic work; not all volumes of the revision have appeared yet.

Douglas, J. D., ed. *The Illustrated Bible Dictionary*. 3 vols. Wheaton, IL: Tyndale, 1980.
> American publication of a British work; excellent graphics.

————*The New Bible Dictionary*. Wheaton, IL: Tyndale, 1982.
> A standard conservative one-volume dictionary by an international group of contributors (mostly British); not as theologically homogeneous as Unger; good scholarship.

Elwell, Walter A. *Evangelical Dictionary of Theology*. Grand Rapids: Baker Books, 1984.
> Compilation of articles contributed by an international group of conservative scholars who are usually sympathetic with the subject presented; touches on theological topics as well as biblical terms and even contemporary movements and individuals; a handy reference volume.

Tenney, Merrill C., ed. *Handy Dictionary of the Bible*. Grand Rapids: Zondervan, 1965.
> Easy-to-use alphabetic format; concise definitions.

———— *The New Zondervan Pictorial Encyclopedia of the Bible*. 5 vols. New ed. Grand Rapids: Zondervan, 1974.
> International contributors; conservative and complete.

Unger, Merrill F. *Unger's Bible Dictionary*. Chicago: Moody, 1961.
> Rich in archaeology and other background material; doctrinally homogeneous and dispensational.

Pfeiffer, Charles, et al., eds. *The Wycliffe Bible Encyclopedia*. 2 vols. Chicago: Moody, 1975.
    A recent, conservative American work; geared for the average reader, but backed by fine scholarship.

Handbooks and Almanacs

Packer, J. I., Merrill C. Tenney, and William White, Jr. *The Bible Almanac*. Nashville: Thomas Nelson, 1980.
    Lengthy treatments of forty-six topics related to Bible study, including archaeology, geography, agriculture, music, the apostles; excellent graphics with many charts.
Unger, Merrill F. *The New Unger's Bible Handbook*. Rev. by Gary N. Larson. Chicago: Moody, 1984.
    Book-by-book commentary plus many articles. Excellent color graphics; update of *Unger's Bible Handbook*
———*Unger's Bible Handbook*. Chicago: Moody, 1966.
    A mine of reference information plus chapter-by-chapter analysis of the whole Bible.

Geography

Aharoni, Yohanan. *The Land of the Bible: A Historical Geography*. Rev. and enlarged ed. Trans. A. F. Rainey. Philadelphia: Westminster, 1980.
    Thorough and detailed work by an Israeli scholar; treats Palestine both chronologically and topically.
——— and Michael Avi-Yonah. *MacMillan Bible Atlas*. Rev. ed. New York: Macmillan, 1977.
    More complete than many similar works; excellent graphics; done by Israeli scholars; contains maps for almost every biblical event or movement.
Baly, Denis. *The Geography of the Bible*. New York: Harper and Row, 1974.
    One of only a few full-length presentations of the geography of Palestine; thorough but readable; includes geological information.
Beitzel, Barry. *The Moody Bible Atlas*. Chicago: Moody, 1985.
    Interesting and unusual format; excellent graphics; theologically conservative dating of O.T. events.
May, Herbert G. *Oxford Bible Atlas*. 3rd ed. Rev. John Day. New York: Oxford University Press, 1984.
    One of the best available; excellent maps; contains articles on history, archaeology and geology.
Pfeiffer, Charles F., and Howard F. Vos. *The Wycliffe Historical Geography of Bible Lands*. Chicago: Moody, 1967.
    A thorough survey of geographical factors needed for understanding Bible history; includes Palestine, Egypt, Greece, Italy; many photographs; excellent maps.
Smith, George Adam. *The Historical Geography of the Holy Land*. Nashville: Abingdon, 1976.
    A classic; older, but still valuable; written by one who spent much time in Palestine.
Turner, George A. *A Geographical History of the Holy Land*. Chicago: Moody, 1984.
    Covers Palestine by sections (like Smith above) and details historical events in each area up to the present; extensive pictures and maps; readable by general audience although backed by thorough scholarship.

Biblical Background

Barrett, C. K. *The New Testament Background: Selected Documents.* New York: Harper and Row, 1961.
Collection of various background topics; older but valuable.

Blaiklock, E. M., and R. K. Harrison, eds. *New International Dictionary of Biblical Archaeology.* Grand Rapids: Zondervan, 1983.
Complete and up to date; international group of contributors.

Bruce, F. F. *New Testament History.* New York: Doubleday, 1972.
Conservative and thorough; backed by fine scholarship.

Chiera, Edward. *They Wrote on Clay.* Edited by George G. Cameron. Chicago: Phoenix Books-University of Chicago Press, 1955.
A classic, highly readable description of the bearing of Babylonian clay tablets on the understanding of ancient Near Eastern life.

De Vaux, Roland. *Ancient Israel: Its Life and Institutions.* 2 vols. New York: McGraw-Hill, 1965.
A comprehensive, scholarly work on Jewish life.

Finegan, J. *Light From the Ancient Past.* 2nd ed. 2 vols. Princeton: Princeton University Press, 1959.
An older classic by a respected archaeological scholar; thorough and interesting, although somewhat scholarly in tone.

Hoehner, Harold W. *Chronological Aspects of the Life of Christ.* Grand Rapids: Zondervan, 1981.
Written for the general reader; theologically sound; many charts, including Daniel's seventieth week; best chronological treatment of the time of Christ.

———*Herod Antipas.* Grand Rapids: Zondervan, 1980.
Scholarly, but current and theologically sound; many insights into first-century culture and history; treats a key biblical figure.

Jeremias, Joachim. *Jerusalem in the Time of Jesus.* Translated by F. H. Cave and C. H. Cave. Philadelphia: Fortress, 1975.
Provides very detailed description of the economic and social conditions in the first c.; scholarly but valuable for the average reader.

Josephus: Complete Works. Trans. William Whiston. Grand Rapids: Kregel, 1974.
A first-century work important for information on O.T. and N.T. history.

Packer, J. I., Merrill C. Tenney, and William White, Jr. *All the People and Places of the Bible.* Nashville: Thomas Nelson, 1982.
———*Daily Life in Bible Times.* Nashville: Thomas Nelson, 1982.
———*The World of the New Testament.* Nashville: Thomas Nelson, 1982.
———*The World of the Old Testament.* Nashville: Thomas Nelson, 1982.
The preceding four titles are popular-level works, but up to date and useful for reference.

Perowne, Stewart. *The Life and Times of Herod the Great.* London: Hodder and Stoughton, 1963.
Provides fascinating information on an important N.T. figure.

Pfeiffer, Charles F., ed. *The Biblical World: A Dictionary of Biblical Archaeology.* Grand Rapids: Baker, 1966.
Dictionary format covering whole field of biblical archaeology.

Pritchard, James B. *The Ancient Near East.* Princeton: Princeton University Press, 1958.
Collection of translations of documents and inscriptions relevant to O.T. studies; many photos of documents and archaeological finds.

Ramsey, William A. *The Cities of St. Paul.* Grand Rapids: Baker, 1965.
Older classic; detailed study of cities visited by Paul plus other essays on the apostle.

————*St. Paul the Traveller and the Roman Citizen*. Grand Rapids: Baker, 1966.
>Older but still valuable treatment of the ministry of Paul.

Tenney, Merrill C. *New Testament Times*. Grand Rapids: Eerdmans, 1965.
>Thorough treatment of N.T. backgrounds; theologically conservative; excellent scholarship but very readable for the general audience; many photographs and charts; essential for an understanding of N.T. customs and culture.

Thompson, J. A. *The Bible and Archaeology*. Rev. ed. Grand Rapids: Eerdmans, 1981.
>Compilation of earlier works; includes O.T. and N.T. studies; surveys whole field; fairly contemporary.

Unger, Merrill F. *Archaeology and the New Testament*. Grand Rapids: Zondervan, 1962.
>Although older, still a usable survey of archaeological findings significant in N.T. studies.

————*Archaeology and the Old Testament*. Grand Rapids: Zondervan, 1954.
>A classic; excellent scholarship but very readable; shows value of archaeology for biblical studies.

Vos, Howard. *Archaeology in Bible Lands*. Chicago: Moody, 1977.
>Covers all Bible lands in one volume (Greece, Italy, etc.); numerous bibliographies; extra material on the field of archaeology (purpose, methodology, etc.); an up-to-date treatment.

Wiseman, Donald J., ed. *Peoples of O.T. Times*. New York: Oxford University Press, 1973.
>Scholarly; various British and American contributors.

Yamauchi, E. M. *The Stones and the Scriptures*. Grand Rapids: Baker, 1981.
>Survey of archaeological findings relevant to biblical study; fine conservative scholarship.

Gospel Synopses

These arrange parallel sections of the gospels in columnar format, enabling the student to see treatments of the same incidents by different authors.

Aland, Kurt. *Synopsis of the Four Gospels*. New York: American Bible Society, 1983.
>Combines Greek text and the second edition of the Revised Standard Version translation of the Gospels.

Pentecost, J. Dwight. *A Harmony of the Words and Works of Jesus Christ*. Grand Rapids: Zondervan, 1981.
>Presented along a topical/theological outline of the kingdom, and based on the NIV text.

Robertson, A. T. *A Harmony of the Gospels for Students of the Life of Christ*. New York: Harper and Row, 1950.
>An older but standard English synopsis.

Thomas, Robert L., and Stan Gundry. *A Harmony of the Gospels with Explanation and Essays*. Chicago: Moody, 1981.
>Indispensable for gospel work with the NASB; includes several helpful essays on study of the gospels.

Biblical Interpretation

Fairbairn, Patrick. *The Typology of Scripture*. New York: Funk and Wagnalls, 1900.
>An important older work; extensive coverage of the field of types.

Habershon, Ada R. *A Study of the Types*. London: Morgan and Scott, 1915.
>An older classic; surveys categories of types.

Kaiser, Walter C., Jr. *Toward an Exegetical Theology*. Grand Rapids: Baker, 1981.
    Practical applications of hermeneutics with the goal of exposition of Scripture.
Marshall, I. Howard. *New Testament Interpretation: Essays on Principles and Methods*. Grand
    Rapids: Eerdmans, 1981.
    A collection of studies on key topics in N.T. interpretation, including the history of N.T.
    interpretation, presuppositions, semantics, critical methods, etc.; includes two lengthy ex-
    amples of interpretive methodology.
Mickelsen, A. Berkeley. *Interpreting the Bible*. Grand Rapids: Eerdmans, 1966.
    More recent than Ramm (see next entry); covers many topics Ramm does not treat.
Ramm, Bernard. *Protestant Biblical Interpretation*. 3rd ed. Grand Rapids: Baker, 1970.
    Long a standard in the field; surveys areas of interpretation; many useful examples; the
    1970 edition is inconsistent in the application of the general principles of interpretation to
    all areas of Scripture, but the 1956 revised edition is much more uniform.
Tenney, Merrill C. *Interpreting Revelation*. Grand Rapids: Eerdmans, 1965.
    Although this treats only the book of Revelation, it contains extensive exposition of her-
    meneutical principles and their application.
Unger, Merrill F. *Principles of Expository Preaching*. Grand Rapids: Zondervan, 1967.
    Covers many areas of interpretation in laying a foundation for exposition of Scripture;
    abundant practical discussion of particular passages and problems.

Bible Study

Danker, Frederick W. *Multipurpose Tools for Bible Study*. Rev. ed. St. Louis: Concordia, 1970.
    Surveys the history of many works; gives tips on using tools (concordances, Gr., Heb.,
    and LXX texts, grammars, lexicons, dictionaries, translations, background works, and
    commentaries.)
Traina, Robert A. *Methodical Bible Study*. Wilmore, KY: Robert A. Traina, 1980.
    A highly practical book that combines interpretive principles with careful Bible study
    methods.
Wald, Oletta. *The Joy of Discovery in Bible Study*. Rev. ed. Minneapolis: Augsburg, 1975.
    Encourages personal observation of Scripture; especially good for beginners; contains many
    illustrations of methodology.

Introductions

Archer, Gleason L. *A Survey of Old Testament Introduction*. Chicago: Moody, 1978.
    One of the best O.T. introductions; written by a premillennial author; strong on inerrancy.
Geisler, Norman L., and William E. Nix. *A General Introduction to the Bible*. Chicago: Moody,
    1970.
    A survey of introductory topics; conservative theology; not overly scholarly in tone.
Hiebert, D. Edmond. *An Introduction to the New Testament*. 3 vols. Vol. 1, *The Gospels and
    Acts,* 1975; vol. 2, *The Pauline Epistles,* 1977; vol. 3, *The Non-Pauline Epistles and
    Revelation,* 1977. Chicago: Moody.
    A thorough introduction to each N.T. book, as well as groups of books; conservative and
    appealing to a general audience.

Word Studies

Brown, Colin, ed. *The New International Dictionary of New Testament Theology.* 3 Vols. Vol. 1, 1976, vol. 2, 1977, vol. 3, 1978. Grand Rapids: Zondervan.
Treats Gr. terms by indexing them according to their English translations; thorough and scholarly, but usable by the average reader.

Vine, W. E., Merrill F. Unger, and William White, Jr. *An Expository Dictionary of Biblical Words.* Nashville: Thomas Nelson, 1985.
Combines Vine's *Expository Dictionary of New Testament Words* and *Nelson's Expository Dictionary of the Old Testament* by Unger and White; includes cross-index to Strong's Concordance; covers Heb. and Gr. words.

Theological Studies

Barnhouse, Donald G. *The Invisible War.* Grand Rapids: Zondervan, 1980.
Popular treatment of Satan, his ways, goals, and activities by a great Bible expositor; strong on the gap theory.

Berkhof, L. *Systematic Theology.* Grand Rapids: Eerdmans, 1978.
A standard one-volume work on reformed theology; weak on eschatology, ecclesiology, and pneumatology, but strong on organization and definitions.

Chafer, Lewis Sperry. *He That is Spiritual.* Grand Rapids: Dunham Publishing Co., 1965.
Practical presentation of the believer's relation to the Holy Spirit; full of Scripture.

————*Major Bible Themes.* Revised by John F. Walvoord. Grand Rapids: Zondervan, 1974.
A revision of a classic dispensational theology book; includes study questions.

————*Salvation.* Grand Rapids: Zondervan, 1972.
Especially good on the riches of grace in Christ for the redeemed, and on the terms of salvation.

————*Systematic Theology.* Grand Rapids: Zondervan, 1981.
Complete dispensational theology by the founder of Dallas Theological Seminary; older, but valuable, especially because of its openness to Scripture.

Feinberg, Charles L. *Millennialism: The Two Major Views.* Winona Lake, IN: BMH Books, 1981.
Older but valuable; presents differences between amillennial and premillennial positions; shows value of dispensationalism and premillennialism.

Henry, C. F. H. *Revelation and the Bible.* 4th ed. Grand Rapids: Baker, 1967.
A collection of authoritative articles by international writers; although somewhat scholarly, it contains many topics not usually treated elsewhere.

Inrig, Gary. *Life in His Body.* Wheaton, IL: Harold Shaw, 1975.
An attempt to allow the Scriptures to speak for themselves in the area of ecclesiology.

Lindsell, Harold. *Battle for the Bible.* Grand Rapids: Zondervan, 1978.
A key book in the current debate over inerrancy; a survey of the issues and movements; comes out strongly for an inerrant Bible.

MacClain, Alva J. *The Greatness of the Kingdom.* Winona Lake, IN: BMH Books; 1983.
A detailed study of the biblical concepts of the kingdom in its various manifestations; dispensational; written by a former president of Grace Theological Seminary.

Machen, J. Gresham. *The Virgin Birth of Christ.* New York: Harper, 1930.
A thorough work by an important orthodox theologian; scholarly but readable.

Morris, Leon. *The Apostolic Preaching of the Cross.* Grand Rapids: Eerdmans, 1965.

Unique treatment of key soteriological terms, including redemption, propitiation, and justification.

Nicole, Roger R., and Ramsey J. Michaels, eds. *Inerrancy and Common Sense*. Grand Rapids: Baker, 1980.

Readable survey of a key issue; excellent modern scholarship.

Packer, J. I. *Fundamentalism and the Word of God*. Grand Rapids: Eerdmans, 1967.

An important book that should be studied by all Christians; Packer shows the crucial difference between biblical and nonbiblical, and therefore spurious, forms of Christianity.

———*Knowing God*. Downers Grove, IL: InterVarsity, 1981.

As always, Packer's writing is clear and interesting; this work is practical especially because it is saturated with Scripture.

Pentecost, J. Dwight. *Things to Come*. Grand Rapids: Zondervan, 1962.

Detailed study of prophecy yet to be fulfilled; dispensational; surveys alternative views.

Ryrie, Charles C. *Biblical Theology of the New Testament*. Chicago: Moody, 1959.

A concise summary of N.T. doctrine that proceeds book by book.

———*Dispensationalism Today*. Chicago: Moody, 1973.

A significant full-length treatment of dispensationalism; covers its history and relations to covenant theology; necessary reading for all Bible students.

———*The Grace of God*. Rev. ed. Chicago: Moody, 1975.

Practical survey of the manifestations of grace in Scripture; important section on life under grace, including discussion of legalism.

———*The Holy Spirit*. Chicago: Moody, 1967.

Practical and insightful; doctrinally sound.

———*Understanding Bible Doctrine*. Chicago: Moody, 1983.

Sound treatment of nine areas of doctrine; includes study questions.

Sauer, Erich. *From Eternity to Eternity*. Grand Rapids: Eerdmans, 1966.

Individualistic but dispensational treatment by a German scholar of the overall plan of the Bible; emphasizes future for Israel; full of Scripture.

———*The King of the Earth*. Grand Rapids: Eerdmans, 1962.

Unusual approach to biblical anthropology; flawed to some degree by certain assumptions about the sequence and timing of creation events.

Strong, A. H. *Systematic Theology*. Westwood, NJ: Revell, 1962.

An older, standard, thorough one-volume work on theology.

Thiessen, Henry C. *Lectures in Systematic Theology*. Revised by Vernon D. Doerksen. Grand Rapids: Eerdmans, 1981.

Revision of a standard one-volume pretribulational, premillennial text; thorough and probably the best one-volume work for the general reader.

Unger, Merrill F. *The Baptism and Gifts of the Holy Spirit*. Chicago: Moody, 1974.

Dispensational treatment by a respected scholar; corrects doctrinal misunderstanding regarding gifts of the Spirit.

———*Biblical Demonology*. Wheaton, IL: Scripture Press, 1970.

Thorough treatment of a neglected area that is relevant in every age due to ceaseless demonic activity.

Walvoord, John F. *The Blessed Hope and the Tribulation*. Grand Rapids: Zondervan, 1976.

Discussion of late twentieth-century posttribulationism by a pretribulational theologian.

———*Jesus Christ Our Lord*. Chicago: Moody, 1974.

Complete exposition of the theology of the Person and work of Christ by a dispensational writer; not overly technical.

———*The Millennial Kingdom*. Grand Rapids: Zondervan, 1959.

Detailed survey of kingdom issues; emphasizes earthly future for Israel.

———*The Rapture Question*. Rev. ed. Grand Rapids: Zondervan, 1979.

Treats various views on the rapture; strong pretribulational emphasis.

Warfield, Benjamin Breckinridge. *The Inspiration and Authority of the Bible.* 2nd ed. Philadelphia: Presbyterian and Reformed, 1964.
> A collection of studies on bibliology; Warfield keenly anticipated many issues of today, although he wrote in the early part of this c.; saturated with scriptural understanding.

Whitcomb, John C., Jr. *The Early Earth.* Grand Rapids: Baker, 1976.
> Readable survey of the recent creation (non-gap) position on Gen. 1–2.

Translating and Translations

Bruce, F. F. *History of the Bible in English.* 3rd ed. New York: Oxford University Press, 1978.
> Surveys Eng. translations from Old Eng. versions in the early middle ages to modern ones in the 1970s; backed by comprehensive scholarship.

Carson, Donald A. *The King James Version Debate: A Plea for Realism.* Grand Rapids: Baker, 1979.
> Balanced discussion of issues related to the KJV-only debate; scholarly, but suitable for general audience.

Kubo, Sakae, and Walter F. Specht. *So Many Versions? Twentieth-century English Versions of the Bible.* Rev. ed. Grand Rapids: Zondervan, 1983.
> A survey of over twenty major twentieth-century Bible translations; describes key features and translational rationale; includes quidelines for choosing and using translations; revised to cover recent translations.

Nida, Eugene A., and Charles R. Taber. *The Theory and Practice of Translation.* Leiden: E. J. Brill, 1969.
> Excellent summary of modern translation methodology by a Bible societies consultant, linguist, and anthropological scholar.

The Old Testament in the New Testament

Bruce, F. F. *The New Testament Development of Old Testament Themes.* Grand Rapids: Eerdmans, 1968.
> Considers several theological themes (the rule of God, the people of God, etc.) as they extend across the testaments; sensitive use of Scripture.

Johnson, S. Lewis, Jr. *The Old Testament in the New: An Argument for Biblical Inspiration.* Grand Rapids: Zondervan, 1980.
> Careful exegesis of six quotations in the N.T. from the O.T.; demonstrates that apparent inconsistencies can be resolved and inerrancy upheld.

Tasker, R. V. G. *The Old Testament in the New Testament.* Philadelphia: Westminster, 1947.
> Very readable; surveys O.T. themes and quotes in all sections of the N.T.

Special Topics

Alter, Robert. *The Art of Biblical Narrative.* New York: Basic Books, 1981.
> A fascinating work by a Jewish author, providing insights into the O.T. that most interpreters have glossed over.

Baker's Handbook of Bible Lists, compiled by Andrew E. Hill. Grand Rapids: Baker, 1981.
>   A unique resource book; contains chronologies, lists of rulers, journeys, etc.

Ewert, David. *From Ancient Tablets to Modern Translations.* Grand Rapids: Zondervan, 1983.
>   Survey of the history of the texts of the O.T. and N.T.; very readable and backed by good scholarship; fills a need for Bible students.

Greenlee, J. Harold. *Introduction to New Testament Textual Criticism.* Grand Rapids: Eerdmans, 1964.
>   Perhaps the simplest of introductions to textual criticism of the N.T.; contains much the average reader can profit from; many good illustrations.

Guthrie, Donald. *Jesus the Messiah: An Illustrated Life of Christ.* Grand Rapids: Zondervan, 1972.
>   A thorough overview of the life of Christ by a respected conservative British scholar; interspersed with numerous pictures.

Habershon, Ada. *The Study of the Parables.* Grand Rapids: Kregel, 1967.
>   One of the few works dedicated to the parables; provides many fine insights.

Scroggie, W. Graham. *Know Your Bible.* Old Tappan, NJ: Fleming H. Revell, 1965.
>   Older, but still valuable for its insights into the plan of Scripture and evident great love for the Bible.

Ryken, Leland. *How to Read the Bible as Literature.* Grand Rapids: Zondervan, 1984.
>   Deals with several topics associated with the literary properties of the Bible; written with the average reader in mind; interesting and important.

———*The Literature of the Bible.* Grand Rapids: Zondervan, 1974.
>   One of the few modern conservative treatments of the Bible as literature; deals with types of literature in the Bible as well as special topics.

NOTES

1 Introduction

1. Frank E. Gaebelein, *The Story of The Scofield Reference Bible: 1909–1959* (New York: Oxford University Press, 1959), 14–15. For further history of Scofield and the Scofield Bible, see Charles G. Trumbull, *The Life Story of C. I. Scofield* (New York: Oxford University Press, 1920) and William A. Be Vier, "A Biographical Sketch of C. I. Scofield," thesis, Southern Methodist University, 1960.

2 The Nature of the Bible

1. Robert E. Longacre, *The Grammar of Discourse* (New York: Plenum, 1983), 355; Gordon H. Clark, "Special Divine Revelation as Rational," in *Revelation and the Bible: Contemporary Evangelical Thought,* ed. Carl F. H. Henry (Grand Rapids: Baker, 1958), 41.

2. See Bruce M. Metzger, "The Language of the New Testament," in *The Interpreter's Bible,* ed. George A. Buttrick, 12 vols. (New York: Abingdon, 1951) 7:43.

3. See, for example, Alan F. Johnson, "The Historical-Critical Method: Egyptian Gold or Pagan Precipice?" *Journal of the Evangelical Theological Society* 26 (1983):3–15.

4. Benjamin B. Warfield, *The Inspiration and Authority of the Bible* (Philadelphia: Presbyterian and Reformed, 1964), 31, 32, 33.

5. Gleason L. Archer, Jr., *A Survey of Old Testament Introduction,* (Chicago: Moody, 1974), 21.

6. For example, Archer, *Survey,* and David Ewert, *From Ancient Tablets to Modern Translations.*

7. See Eldon J. Epp, "The Eclectic Method in New Testament Textual Criticism: Solution or Symptom?" *Harvard Theological Review* 69 (1976):215.

8. Bruce Metzger, *A Textual Commentary on the Greek New Testament* (New York: United Bible Societies, 1971), 607.

9. Archer, 79.

10. Archer, 77; Edward J. Young, "The Canon of the Old Testament," in Henry, 156–164.

11. Archer, 69.

12. Archer, 68.

13. See works in the Annotated Bibliography such as Kubo and Specht, *So Many Versions?*; Bruce, *History of the Bible in English*; Greenlee, *Introduction to New Testament Textual Criticism*.

14. Archer, 21.

15. See Archer, 19–34.

16. The meaning of the term in Eph. 3:2 is debated; see Walter Bauer, *A Greek-English Lexicon of the New Testament and Other Early Christian Literature,* trans. and ed. William F. Arndt and F. Wilbur Gingrich; 2nd ed., rev. and augmented by F. Wilbur Gingrich and Frederick W. Danker (Chicago: University of Chicago Press, 1979), 559.

17. John S. Feinberg, "Salvation in the Old Testament," in *Tradition and Testament,* ed. John S. Feinberg and Paul D. Feinberg (Chicago: Moody, 1981), 52.

18. Feinberg treats this and other related issues in this important article.

19. See ch. 5, Interpreting the Bible, concerning George Ladd.

20. Oswald T. Allis, *Prophecy and the Church* (Philadelphia: Presbyterian and Reformed, 1945), 54.

21. See Charles C. Ryrie, *Dispensationalism Today* (Chicago: Moody, 1973), 65–85.

22. For example, Ryrie.

3 How to Study the Bible

1. Vance Havner, *The Best of Vance Havner* (Old Tappan, NJ: Fleming H. Revell, 1969), 17.

2. In *Calvin: Institutes of the Christian Religion,* ed. John T. McNeill, trans. Ford Lewis Battles, The Library of Christian Classics, vols. 20–21 (Philadelphia: Westminster, 1960) 20:246.

3. In the preface to his *Novum Testamentum Graecum* (Tübingen, 1734), quoted by F. F. Bruce in "The History of New Testament Study," in *New Testament Interpretation,* ed. I. Howard Marshall (Grand Rapids: Eerdmans, 1977), 56.

4. Graham Stanton, "Presuppositions in New Testament Criticism," in Marshall, *Interpretation,* 68.

5. See Eugene A. Nida and Charles R. Taber, *The Theory and Practice of Translation* (Leiden: E. J. Brill, 1969), 7.

6. Augustine, *Expositions on the Book of Psalms,* Nicene and Post-Nicene Fathers, vol. 8 (New York: The Christian Literature Company, 1888), 531.

4 The Language of the Bible

1. A. Berkeley Mickelsen, *Interpreting the Bible* (Grand Rapids: Eerdmans, 1963), 14.

2. Eugene A. Nida and Charles R. Taber, *The Theory and Practice of Translation* (Leiden: E. J. Brill, 1969), 7.

3. James Barr, *The Semantics of Biblical Language* (London: Oxford University Press, 1961), 296.

4. Eugene A. Nida, "Implications of Contemporary Linguistics for Biblical Scholarship," *Journal of Biblical Literature* 91 (1972):74.

5. For a concise discussion, see G. Douglas Young, "The Language of the Old Testament," in *The Expositor's Bible Commentary,* gen. ed. Frank E. Gaebelein, 7 vols. (Grand Rapids: Zondervan, 1979), 1:198.

6. Norman Geisler and William E. Nix, *From God to Us* (Chicago: Moody, 1974), 128.

7. Geisler and Nix, 129.

8. David Ewert, *From Ancient Tablets to Modern Translations* (Grand Rapids: Zondervan, 1983), 43.

9. Gleason L. Archer, Jr., *A Survey of Old Testament Introduction* (Chicago: Moody, 1974), 17.

10. Barr's *Semantics* forms an incisive critique of this view, known as the Sapir-Whorf hypothesis; see also Moisés Silva, *Biblical Words and Their Meaning* (Grand Rapids: Zondervan, 1983), 21.

11. For a summary, see Bruce K. Waltke, "The Textual Criticism of the Old Testament," in Gaebelein, 1:220.

12. For an interesting introduction to this area, see Paul Thieme, "The Indo-European Language," *Scientific American,* Oct. 1958, 63–74.

13. See, for example, C. D. Buck, *The Greek Dialects* (Chicago: University of Chicago Press, 1955).

14. See Buck, and also L. R. Palmer, *The Greek Language* (Atlantic Highlands, NJ: Humanities, 1980), 3–26, 57–82.

15. Walter Bauer, *A Greek-English Lexicon of the New Testament and Other Early Christian Literature,* trans. and ed. William F. Arndt and F. Wilbur Gingrich; 2nd ed., rev. and augmented F. Wilbur Gingrich and Frederick W. Danker (Chicago: University of Chicago Press, 1979), xix.

16. See Bauer, xx.

17. Many of these examples are from Bruce M. Metzger, "The Language of the New Testament," in *The Interpreter's Bible,* ed. George A. Buttrick, 12 vols. (New York: Abingdon, 1951) 7:46–53.

18. Metzger, 47.

19. Metzger, 47.

20. Metzger, 48.

21. Metzger, 50.

22. See Richard N. Longenecker, "Ancient Amanuenses," in *New Dimensions in New Testament Study,* ed. Richard N. Longenecker, and Merrill C. Tenney (Grand Rapids: Zondervan, 1974), 281–97.

23. See Longenecker, 293–96; Silva, 114–17.

24. E. M. Blaiklock, "Latin," in *The New Bible Dictionary,* ed. J. D. Douglas (Grand Rapids: Eerdmans, 1962), 718.

25. For a full discussion see Philip E. Hughes, "The Languages Spoken by Jesus," in Longenecker and Tenney, 127–43.

26. Robert H. Gundry, "The Language Milieu of First Century Palestine," *Journal of Biblical Literature* 83 (1964):408; Hughes, 142.

27. Silva, 56–57; Bauer, xviii.

28. Bauer, xxi.

29. Silva, 87.

30. Quoted in Sakae Kubo and Walter F. Specht, *So Many Versions?*, rev. ed. (Grand Rapids: Zondervan, 1983), 25–26.

31. Quoted in Kubo and Specht, 26.

32. But see F. F. Bruce, *The English Bible* (London: Lutterworth, 1961), 137, 228; Kubo and Specht, 342.

33. Nida and Taber, 4.

34. See Kubo and Specht, 259; John Beekman and John Callow, *Translating the Word of God* (Grand Rapids: Zondervan, 1974), 19–32.

35. Nida and Taber, 2.

36. Nida and Taber, 2.

37. See Charles H. Kraft, *Christianity in Culture* (Maryknoll, NY: Orbis Books, 1980.)

38. Nida and Taber, 2.

39. Nida and Taber, 13.

40. Quoted in Kubo and Specht, 334.

41. See Bruce 167–72; Kubo and Specht, 35–39.

42. Nida and Taber, 22.

43. Nida and Taber, 47.

44. See Kubo and Specht, 21; Bruce, 214.

45. Nida "Implications," 75.

46. See Bruce, 211, for an example of interpreting in translating.

47. See, for example, Bruce, and also Kubo and Specht.

48. See Bruce M. Metzger, *The Text of the New Testament* (New York: Oxford University Press, 1964), 102, 105–6.

49. See Donald A. Carson, *The King James Version Debate: A Plea for Realism* (Grand Rapids: Baker, 1979), 99; Marchant A. King, "Should Conservatives Abandon Textual Criticism?" *Bibliotheca Sacra* 130 (1973): 39; Douglas S. Chinn and Robert C. Newman, *Demystifying the Controversy Over the Textus Receptus and the King James Version of the Bible* (Hatfield, PA: Interdisciplinary Biblical Research Institute, 1979), 16–18.

50. Bruce, 101–3.

51. See Kubo and Specht, 19–20.

52. For further material on evaluating the AV, see Carson.

53. Kubo and Specht, 336–44.

54. See Kubo and Specht, 18; Barr, 288–96.

55. It should be noted that the Living Bible was not done originally as a translation from the original languages; see Kubo and Specht, 340.

56. Kubo and Specht, 337–38; 69.

57. Kubo and Specht, 207–9.

58. Kubo and Specht, 245; see also the section "Introduction" in the *Oxford NIV Scofield Study Bible*.

59. Graham N. Stanton, "Presuppositions in New Testament Criticism," in *New Testament Interpretation*, ed. I. Howard Marshall (Grand Rapids: Eerdmans, 1977), 60.

60. Stanton, 64.

61. Stanton, 65. This has been changed in *The New Jerusalem Bible* (Doubleday, 1985).

62. See Bruce, x.

63. See, for example, the description of Kenneth Taylor's background in Kubo and Specht, 232; the names of the translators of the NASB and the NIV are available from the Lockman Foundation and the New York International Bible Society, respectively.

64. An example is *About the New English Bible*, compiled by Geoffrey Hunt (Cambridge: Oxford and Cambridge University Presses, 1970).

65. C. H. Dodd, Introduction to the New Testament, *The New English Bible* (Oxford and Cambridge University Presses, 1970), vii.

66. Kubo and Specht, 200–2, 223, 269–70.

67. J. B. Phillips, in *The New Testament in Modern English* (New York: Macmillan, 1973); Arthur S. Way, *The Letters of Paul; Hebrews and Psalms* (Grand Rapids: Kregel, 1981).

5 Interpreting the Bible

1. Eugene A. Nida and Charles R. Taber, *The Theory and Practice of Translation* (Leiden: E. J. Brill, 1969), 7.

2. See Jeremy Campbell, *Grammatical Man* (New York: Simon and Schuster, 1982), 37, 48, 62–63 (communication of information as a way of bringing greater order into randomness); see also Robert de Beaugrande and Wolfgang Dressler, *Introduction to Text Linguistics* (London: Longman, 1981), 14, where the issue is stated in terms of "informativity," and 7, where they speak of "relevance for the receiver."

3. Bernard Ramm, *Protestant Biblical Interpretation,* rev. ed. (Boston: W. A. Wilde, 1956), 46.

4. A. Berkeley Mickelsen, *Interpreting the Bible* (Grand Rapids: Eerdmans, 1963), 24.

5. Ramm, 28.

6. F. F. Bruce, "The History of New Testament Study," in *New Testament Interpretation,* ed. I Howard Marshall (Grand Rapids: Eerdmans, 1977), 25.

7. Bruce, 31.

8. Bruce, 31.

9. Bruce, 32.

10. Alexander Souter, *The Earliest Latin Commentaries on the Epistles of St. Paul* (London: Oxford University Press, 1927), 7.

11. See, for example, de Beaugrande and Dressler, 15, 140.

12. See de Beaugrande and Dressler, 140.

13. See de Beaugrande and Dressler, 146.

14. de Beaugrande and Dressler, 208.

15. de Beaugrande and Dressler, 7.

16. de Beaugrande and Dressler, 88.

17. For a classic discussion showing the author was decades ahead in his thinking, see Benjamin Breckenridge Warfield, "The Real Problem of Inspiration," in *The Inspiration and Authority of the Bible,* ed. Samuel G. Craig (Philadelphia: Presbyterian and Reformed, 1964), 169–226; see also Gleason L. Archer, Jr., *A Survey of Old Testament Introduction* (Chicago: Moody, 1974), 32–34.

18. John Lyons, *Language and Linguistics* (Cambridge: Cambridge University Press, 1981), 290–92.

19. See also Donald Guthrie, "Questions of Introduction," in Marshall, 110–15.

20. Carol A. Newsome, "A Maker of Metaphors—Ezekiel's Oracles Against Tyre," *Interpretation* 38 (1984):153.

21. The problem of formalizing procedures to show how we decide when to take an element metaphorically, or, rather, of how we know (usually quite well in normal conversation) to make the jump, is for literary critics one of the central issues in the analysis of metaphor. See Monroe C. Beardsley, "Metaphor," in *The Encyclopedia of Philosophy,* ed. Paul Edwards, 8 vols. (New York: Macmillan and the Free Press, 1967) 5:285.

22. See de Beaugrande and Dressler, 8, 9, 40, 88, 139, and 144.

23. Eugene A. Nida, "Implications of Contemporary Linguistics for Biblical Scholarship," *Journal of Biblical Literature* 91 (1972):86.

24. Nelson Goodman, *Languages of Art* (Indianapolis: Bobbs-Merrill, 1968), 80.

25. See de Beaugrande and Dressler, 140, regarding expectation of information.

26. Graham N. Stanton, "Presuppositions in New Testament Criticism," in Marshall, 68; Robert Baum, *Logic* (New York: Holt, Rinehart and Winston, 1981), 465.

27. For a description of this process from a slightly different perspective, see Ralph P. Martin, "Approaches to New Testament Exegesis," in Marshall, 229.

28. J. I. Packer, *Fundamentalism and the Word of God* (Grand Rapids: Eerdmans, 1958), 106.

29. See, for example, S. Lewis Johnson, Jr., "Romans 5:12—An Exercise in Exegesis and Theology," in *New Directions in New Testament Study,* ed. Richard N. Longenecker and Merrill C. Tenney (Grand Rapids: Zondervan, 1974), 299:

> [The] divorce of theology from exegesis is frequently represented as primarily an impoverishment of theology, which, of course, it is. But it is sometimes forgotten that contemporary exegesis as well has lost its grip on systematics, with dire results for interpretation. We are quite willing to grant that theology cannot really be done well without exegesis, but we are not as willing, it seems to me, to grant that exegesis cannot be done well without systematic theology. Exegesis, armed with the original text and modern critical tools and methodology, too frequently sees itself as autonomously self-sufficient, pouring out its arid and superficial grammatical, syntactical, and critical comments, while the deeper meaning of the texts in the light of the broader problems at issue is lost to it. In the introduction to his commentary on 1 John, Principal Candlish spoke of his desire to "bring out the full mind of the apostle" upon the truths embodied in the letter, and then added, in words surely applicable to the study of all the biblical literature: "For I am deeply convinced after years of thought about it, that it can be studied aright exegetically, only if it is studied theologically." William Manson, late Professor of New Testament at the University of Edinburgh, Scotland, used to refer to this type of exegesis, the type that kept exegesis and theology in holy bonds of matrimony, as "depth exegesis." It might just as well be called "depth theology."

30. For a lucid discussion of prejudice as well as presupposition in biblical studies, see Stanton, 60–71.

31. Bruce, 40.

32. Bruce, 42, 43.

33. Stanton, 67.

34. For extended discussion, see Archer, 379–403.

35. Stanton, 68.

36. See John Feinberg, "Salvation in the Old Testament," in *Tradition and Testament,* ed. John S. Feinberg and Paul D. Feinberg (Chicago: Moody, 1981), 46.

37. Kenneth L. Barker, "False Dichotomies Between the Testaments," *Journal of the Evangelical Theological Society* 25 (1982):35.

38. Henry Alford, *The Greek Testament,* 4 vols. (London: Longmans, Green, 1894) 4:732–33.

39. Mickelsen, 304–5; Ramm, 206.

40. George Eldon Ladd, "Historic Premillennialism," in *The Meaning of the Millennium,* ed. Robert G. Clouse (Downers Grove, IL: InterVarsity Press, 1977), 28.

41. Ladd, 27; this article shows many of his inconsistencies.

42. Ladd, 28.

43. Feinberg, 46.

44. George Eldon Ladd, *The Blessed Hope* (Grand Rapids: Eerdmans, 1956), 126.

6   Literary Aspects of the Bible

1. See, for example, Robert Alter, *The Art of Biblical Narrative* (New York: Basic Books, 1981), 3–22.

2. See René Wellek and Austin Warren, *A Theory of Literature* (New York: Harcourt, Brace and World, 1970), 42, where they point out that there are hundreds of definitions of what literature is.

3. Robert Longacre, *The Grammar of Discourse* (New York: Plenum, 1983), 355; see also C. Hugh Holman, *A Handbook to Literature* (Indianapolis: Bobbs-Merrill, 1983), 436, concerning the symbolic character of all language.

4. Leland Ryken, *The Literature of the Bible* (Grand Rapids: Zondervan, 1974), 130; see also Carol A. Newsome, "A Maker of Metaphors—Ezekiel's Oracles Against Tyre," *Interpretation* 38 (1984):152.

5. Northrop Frye, *Anatomy of Criticism* (Princeton: Princeton University Press, 1957), 14.

6. See, for example, Monroe C. Beardsley, "Metaphor," *The Encyclopedia of Philosophy,* ed. Paul Edwards, 8 vols. (New York: Macmillan and the Free Press, 1967), 5:284–89.

7. Norman Freidman, "Allegory," *Encyclopedia of Poetry and Poetics,* ed. Alex Preminger (Princeton: Princeton University Press, 1965), 12.

8. A Berkeley Mickelsen, *Interpreting the Bible* (Grand Rapids: Eerdmans, 1963), 231.

9. Ryken, 301.

10. Ryken suggests (301–2) that the more explicitly the surface of a narrative forces the reader to the second level, the more we are justified in seeing allegory.

11. Mickelsen, 230.

12. Mickelsen, 213, 230.

13. Ada R. Habershon, *The Study of the Parables* (London: James Nisbet, 1904), 335–36.

14. Mickelsen has a helpful section (212–35) that presents guidelines for interpreting parables and allegory.

15. Ryken, 81.

16. Ryken, 58.

17. Ryken, 106.

18. Ryken, 122.

19. Wellek and Warren, 31.

20. Merrill C. Tenney, *Interpreting Revelation* (Grand Rapids: Eerdmans, 1957), 186–87; see illustrations, 187–89.

21. See Tenney, 68.

22. Pp. 50–69; his chart is especially interesting.

23. See Tenney, 186; "signify" implies a divine communication to human beings in symbolic terms.

24. Newsome, 152.

25. Paul Ricoeur, *The Rule of Metaphor* (Toronto: University of Toronto Press, 1977), 7.

26. John F. Walvoord, *The Revelation of Jesus Christ* (Chicago: Moody, 1966), 26.

27. Tenney, 186–93.

28. Tenney, 96.

7 Relations Between the Testaments

1. The subtitle of C. H. Dodd's *According to the Scriptures* (New York: Scribner's, 1953).

2. For one discussion of this fuller sense of Scripture, termed by some *sensus plenior,* and some of the necessary checks on it, see Ralph P. Martin, "Approaches to New Testament Exegesis," in *New Testament Interpretation,* ed. I. Howard Marshall (Grand Rapids: Eerdmans, 1977), 224–25.

3. See John S. Feinberg, "Salvation in the O.T.," in *Tradition and Testament* (Chicago: Moody, 1981), 52.

4. See Stanley D. Toussaint, "A Biblical Defense of Dispensationalism," in *Walvoord: a Tribute,* ed. Donald K. Campbell (Chicago: Moody, 1982), 85; Richard N. Longenecker, "The Pedagogical Nature of the Law in Galatians 3:19–4:7," *Journal of the Evangelical Theological Society* 25 (1982):53–61.

5. See F. F. Bruce, *The New Testament Development of Old Testament Themes* (Grand Rapids: Eerdmans, 1968), 35–36.

6. Walter C. Kaiser, Jr., "The Old Promise and the New Covenant: Jeremiah 31:31–34," in *The Bible in Its Literary Milieu,* ed. Vincent L. Tollers and John R. Maier (Grand Rapids: Eerdmans, 1979), 116.

7. Bruce, 37–38.

8. *Oxford NIV Scofield Study Bible,* ed. C. I. Scofield (New York: Oxford University Press, 1984), 4.

9. The discrepancy between Paul's form of Isa. 55:3 and the O.T. form is due to the fact that he used the Septuagint. See Bruce, 71.

10. See Bruce for detailed and informative expositions of a number of O.T. themes unfolded in the N.T.

11. "Analogy, in its broadest sense, comprehends any mode of reasoning that depends on the suggestion or recognition of a relationship of similarity between two objects or sets of objects. It includes not only four-term proportional relationships of the type A:B::C:D . . . but also both explicit and implicit comparisons, for example the use of models . . . and of images . . ." Armand Maurer, "Analogy in Early Greek Thought," in *Dictionary of the History of Ideas,* ed. Philip P. Wiener, 5 vols. (New York: Scribner's, 1973) 1:60.

12. K. J. Woollcombe, "The Biblical Origins and Patristic Development of Typology," in G. W. H. Lampe and K. J. Woollcombe, *Essays on Typology* (London: SCM, 1957), 39.

13. Woollcombe, 39.

14. See Richard N. Davidson, *Typology in Scripture,* Andrews University Diss. (Berrigan, MI: Andrews University Press, 1981), 21–31.

15. G. W. H. Lampe, "The Reasonableness of Typology," in Lampe and Woollcombe, 31.

16. Lampe, 15.

17. Woollcombe, 40.

18. Davidson, 43.

19. See Davidson, 82.

20. Davidson, 53.

21. See Davidson, 82.

22. Such a relationship between an earthly picture and a heavenly counterpart has been described as a vertical type, e.g., in Davidson, 336.

23. Lampe, 23.

24. Lampe, 23; Davidson, 74.

25. Lampe, 18.

26. See Davidson, 101–2.

27. See Franz Delitzsch, *Biblical Commentary on the Psalms,* trans. Francis Bolton, 2 vols. (Grand Rapids: Eerdmans, n.d.) 1:69.

28. For a lengthy treatment, see Bernard Ramm, *Protestant Biblical Interpretation* (Boston: W. A. Wilde, 1956), 196–219.

29. Davidson, 112.

30. Davidson, 45.

31. Lampe, 15.

32. Ramm, 211.

33. Bruce M. Metzger, "The Language of the New Testament," in *The Interpreter's Bible,* ed. George A. Buttrick, 12 vols. (New York: Abingdon, 1951) 7:47.

34. Metzger, 47.

35. Morse Peckham, *The Triumph of Romanticism* (Columbia: University of South Carolina Press, 1970), 415.

36. See Robert Baum, *Logic,* 2nd ed. (New York: Holt, Rinehart and Winston, 1981), 424.

37. See estimates in Roger Nicole, "New Testament Use of the Old Testament," in *Revelation and the Bible,* ed. Carl F. H. Henry (Grand Rapids: Baker, 1967), 137–38.

38. Much of the material in this section is adapted from my thesis "The Interpretation of Prophecy in the New Testament," Dallas Theological Seminary, 1969.

39. Nicole, 140.

40. Benjamin B. Warfield, *The Inspiration and Authority of the Bible* (Philadelphia: Presbyterian and Reformed, 1964), 234–35, 238.

41. See F. F. Bruce, *The Acts of the Apostles* (Grand Rapids: Eerdmans, 1968), 113.

42. Warfield, 240.

43. Warfield, 300.

44. Dodd, 130.

45. Nicole, 149.

46. See Gleason L. Archer and G. C. Chirichigno, *Old Testament Quotations in the New Testament: A Complete Survey* (Chicago: Moody, 1983), 147.

47. Rudolph Bultmann ("Prophecy and Fulfillment," in *Essays in Old Testament Hermeneutics,* trans. and ed. James Luther Mays [Richmond, VA: John Knox, 1964], p. 54) misses this and states that Paul is here perverting the meaning of Isa. to its opposite.

48. See discussion of this type of quotation in Feinberg, 46–47.

49. This is the thesis of S. Lewis Johnson, Jr., in *The Old Testament in the New* (Grand Rapids: Zondervan, 1980).

50. Nicole, 142–48.

51. Robert Horton Gundry, *The Use of the Old Testament in St. Matthew's Gospel* (Leiden: E. J. Brill, 1967), 105.

52. For alternate views, see Richard Longenecker, *Biblical Exegesis in the Apostolic Period* (Grand Rapids: Eerdmans, 1983).

53. See S. Lewis Johnson, Jr., "The Triumphal Entry of Christ," *Bibliotheca Sacra* 124 (1967):227.

54. Johnson, 222.

55. R. V. G. Tasker, *Our Lord's Use of the Old Testament* (Glasgow: Pickering and Inglis Ltd., n.d.), 8.

56. Dodd, 59.

57. Dodd, 110.

58. Gundry, xii.

59. See Johnson, *The Old Testament in the New Testament,* and also Longenecker, *Biblical Exegesis,* for examples of problems and approaches.

60. Tasker, 9.

61. Tasker, 13.

8   Essentials of Biblical Geography

1. Herbert G. May, ed., *Oxford Bible Atlas,* 3rd ed., rev. John Day (New York: Oxford University Press, 1984), 54.

2. May, 48; for a sensitive treatment of the relation of the land of Palestine to the nation of Israel, see Gordon G. Ceperley, *A Promised Land for a Chosen People* (Langhorne, PA: Philadelphia College of Bible, 1979).

9   Introduction to Bible Doctrine

1. See, e.g., S. Lewis Johnson, Jr., "Romans 5:12—An Exercise in Exegesis and Theology," in *New Dimensions in New Testament Study,* ed. Richard N. Longenecker and Merrill C. Tenney (Grand Rapids: Zondervan, 1974), 299.

10 The Bible

1. In *Grammatical Man* (New York: Simon and Schuster, 1982), 72, Jeremy Campbell discusses redundancy in messages, pointing out that redundancy increases reliability because it enhances the likelihood that a message will be understood. The biblical text possesses such redundancy at every level. This contributes to the trustworthiness of the text as the textual critic deals with it.

2. Benjamin B. Warfield, *Inspiration and Authority of the Bible* (Philadelphia: Presbyterian and Reformed, 1964), 296.

3. See Moisés Silva, *Biblical Words and Their Meanings* (Grand Rapids: Zondervan, 1983), 112.

4. Donald Guthrie, *Jesus the Messiah* (Grand Rapids: Zondervan, 1972), 45.

5. J. I. Packer, *Fundamentalism and the Word of God* (Grand Rapids: Eerdmans, 1958), 46.

6. Packer, 69–70.

7. Harold Lindsell, *The Battle for the Bible* (Grand Rapids: Zondervan, 1976), 27.

8. Lindsell, 31.

9. On such cautions see René Pache, *The Inspiration and Authority of Scripture* (Chicago: Moody, 1969), 123–24.

10. Lindsell, 37.

11. See *Battle for the Bible*.

12. See, e.g., Edward J. Young, *Thy Word Is Truth* (Grand Rapids: Eerdmans, 1957), 61.

13. One example is S. Lewis Johnson, Jr. *The Old Testament in the New* (Grand Rapids: Zondervan, 1980); see also ch. 5, Interpreting the Bible, concerning assumptions and interpreting messages.

11 God

1. M. H. Macdonald, "Deism," *Evangelical Dictionary of Theology,* ed. Walter A. Elwell (Grand Rapids: Baker, 1984), 304.

12 The Person of Christ

1. J. I. Packer, *Knowing God* (Downers Grove, IL: InterVarsity, 1973), 45.

2. Packer, 46.

3. While some have noted that there may be reasons to see in Isa. 8 a fulfillment of this prediction, the most significant correspondence of the prophecy is to what Matthew describes.

4. Benjamin B. Warfield, *Biblical and Theological Studies* (Philadelphia: Presbyterian and Reformed, 1952), 163.

5. Packer, 46.

6. Under Roman law, slaves were not viewed as people, but as property. See Francis Lyall, *Slaves, Citizens, Sons* (Grand Rapids: Zondervan, 1984), 35, 125.

7. Tim Rice and Andrew Lloyd Webber, *Jesus Christ Superstar: A Rock Opera* (New York: Leeds Music Corporation, 1973).

8. See S. Lewis Johnson, Jr. "The Agony of Christ," *Bibliotheca Sacra"* 124 (1967):305.

13 The Holy Spirit

1. James Denney, "The Epistles to the Thessalonians," in *The Expositor's Bible,* ed. W. Robertson Nicoll, 6 vols. (Grand Rapids: Eerdmans, 1956) 6:355.
2. Further help on this issue can be found in Merrill F. Unger's *The Baptism and Gifts of the Holy Spirit,* listed in ch. 23, Annotated Bibliography.

14 Sin

1. Lewis Sperry Chafer, *Systematic Theology,* 8 vols. (Grand Rapids: Zondervan, 1981) 3:224.
2. There is not sufficient space to discuss all the factors involved in the interpretation of this passage and the gap theory. For an easy-to-read introduction see John C. Whitcomb, Jr., *The Early Earth* (Grand Rapids: Baker, 1982); see also Bruce Waltke, "The Creation Account in Genesis 1:1–3," *Bibliotheca Sacra* 132 (1975):136–44.
3. Geoffrey Marcus, *The Maiden Voyage* (New York: Viking, 1969), 31.
4. Chafer, 2:257.
5. For a fuller treatment see S. Lewis Johnson, Jr., "Romans 5:12—An Exercise in Exegesis and Theology," in *New Dimensions in New Testament Study,* ed. Richard N. Longenecker and Merrill C. Tenney (Grand Rapids: Zondervan, 1974), 298–316.

15 Humanity

1. Quoted in Erich Sauer, *The King of the Earth* (Grand Rapids: Eerdmans, 1962), 16.
2. The issues connected with origins, as raised by creationism, evolution, etc., are important, but demand treatment too lengthy and detailed for a book of this kind. Suffice it to say that if we take the Bible at face value, the early chapters of Gen. present God's direct, immediate creation of the inanimate and animate universe. See John Whitcomb, *The Early Earth,* in ch. 23, Annotated Bibliography, for further study.
3. Sauer, 50.
4. Sauer, 49.
5. Sauer, 49.
6. See Sauer, 143, where he discusses our possession of kingship in spite of our impotence.
7. For a summary, see Charles L. Feinberg, "The Image of God," *Bibliotheca Sacra* 129 (1972):235–46.
8. Sauer, 141.
9. See Robert E. Longacre, *The Grammar of Discourse* (New York: Plenum, 1983), 353–56; Gordon H. Clark, "Special Divine Revelation as Rational," in *Revelation and the Bible,* ed. Carl F. H. Henry (Grand Rapids: Baker, 1958), 41.
10. Charles Caldwell Ryrie, *Balancing the Christian Life* (Chicago: Moody, 1969), 32; Henry C. Thiessen, *Lectures in Systematic Theology,* revised by Vernon D. Doerksen (Grand Rapids: Eerdmans, 1979), 161–62.
11. Bruce K. Waltke, "The Creation Account in Genesis 1:1–3," *Bibliotheca Sacra* 132 (1975):25.
12. William H. Jefferys and R. Robert Robbins, *Discovering Astronomy* (New York: Wiley, 1981), 414.
13. Sauer, 84.

14. See S. Lewis Johnson, Jr., "Romans 5:12—An Exercise in Exegesis and Theology," in *New Dimensions in New Testament Study,* ed. Richard N. Longenecker and Merrill C. Tenney (Grand Rapids: Zondervan, 1974), 316.

15. Sauer, 99.

16 Angels

1. See Erich Sauer, *The King of the Earth* (Grand Rapids: Eerdmans, 1962), 43.

17 Salvation

1. Lewis Sperry Chafer, *Systematic Theology,* 8 vols. (Grand Rapids: Zondervan, 1981) 3:59.

2. Leon Morris, *The Apostolic Preaching of the Cross* (Grand Rapids: Eerdmans, 1956), 163.

3. For a fuller discussion of these concepts, see Morris 125–85.

4. James M. Stifler, *The Epistle to the Romans* (Chicago: Moody, 1960), 149.

5. For further discussion, see John Murray, *The Epistle to the Romans,* 2 vols. (Grand Rapids: Eerdmans, 1965), 2:23.

6. I am indebted to S. Lewis Johnson, Jr., for many observations concerning Rom. 9.

7. For an excellent treatment of this issue, see J. I. Packer, *Evangelism and the Sovereignty of God* (Chicago: InterVarsity, 1961).

8. J. Gresham Machen, *What is Faith?* (New York: MacMillan, 1925), 195.

9. Philip Edgcumbe Hughes, *A Commentary on the Epistle to the Hebrews* (Grand Rapids: Eerdmans, 1977), 522.

10. See Arno C. Gaebelein, *The Gospel of John* (Neptune, NJ: Loizeaux Brothers, 1965), 56–59.

11. For more on the semantic properties of the aorist tense, see Frank Stagg, "The Abused Aorist," *Journal of Biblical Literature,* 9 (1972):222–31.

18 The Church

No Notes

19 Future Things

1. John F. Walvoord, "Posttribulationism Today," *Bibliotheca Sacra* 132 (1975):17.

2. For a brief summary of this area, see Robert G. Clouse, *The Meaning of the Millennium* (Downers Grove, IL: InterVarsity, 1977), 9–10.

3. See Charles C. Ryrie, *Dispensationalism Today* (Chicago: Moody Press, 1965); see also in ch. 2, The Nature of the Bible, on the biblical covenants.

4. See ch. 2, The Nature of the Bible, concerning Oswald Allis.

5. See, for example, Clouse, 9.

6. For a fairly recent, but variant, exposition of the posttribulational position, see Robert H. Gundry, *The Church and the Tribulation* (Grand Rapids: Zondervan, 1977).

7. See also David G. Winfrey, "The Great Tribulation: Kept 'Out of' or 'Through'?" *Grace Theological Journal* 3 (1982): 3–18; Thomas R. Edgar, "Robert H. Gundry and Revelation 3:10" in the same journal and issue, 19–49.

8. For additional discussion, see the series by John F. Walvoord, "Posttribulationism Today" in *Bibliotheca Sacra*, Jan. 1975 through Jan. 1977, or John F. Walvoord, *The Blessed Hope and the Tribulation* (Grand Rapids: Zondervan, 1976).

Index

Entries found in ch. 20, Quick-Reference Guide to Bible Study Terms, are not indexed here. The reader should consult that list first when looking for treatment of Bible study and doctrinal terms.

Aaron, 247, 260
Abba, 64
Abel, 138, 156
Abortion, 248
Abraham
  and allegorism, 78
  call of, 173
  and Christ, 34
  and Church, 29
  and covenant, 95
  and dispensations, 31
  and faith, 134
  giving of covenant, 136
  and Isaac, 100, 104, 214
  and justification, 271
  language of, 56
  and Melchizedek, 139, 153
  migration, 170
  and plan of the Bible, 145
  and promise, 173, 215
Abrahamic Covenant, 35, 95, 136. *See also* Covenants
Access
  by blood, 138–42
  in book of Rev., 121

  by Christ, 206
  and Melchizedek, 139
  and priesthood, 152, 221
  and Tabernacle, 132
Acco, 173
Adam
  and Christ, 248
  and the Church, 29
  and creation, 241–42
  and dispensations, 31
  and imputation, 238–39
Adam and Eve
  before fall, 241, 246
  and coverings, 138
  and fall, 26, 100, 138, 233–36, 325
  as rulers, 242
Adamic Covenant, 35. *See also* Covenants
Adonai, 203, 204, 343
Africa, 169, 174, 338
Agapē, 51
Agnosticism, 206–7
Agorazō, 261
Ahaz, 148, 161, 162, 215
Akkadian, 56
Akkadians, 170

Akrobustia, 61
Albanian, 59
Alexander the Great, 60, 172, 340
Alexandria, 78
Allegorism, 77–78, 106. *See also* Allegory; Interpretation
Allegory. *See also* Allegorism
    determining, 445
    as interpretation, 77–78
    and literary form, 77
    meaning of, 106, 144
    and parables, 107
Allēlouia, 331
Alliteration, 61
Allusions, 154
Ambiguities, 51
Amillennialism, 91–93, 298–300. *See also* Covenant theology
    assumptions, 299
    chart of, 300, 301
    and Church, local and universal, 299
    versus dispensationalism, 30
    and faith, 27
    and figurative interpretation, 28
    history, 298
Analogy, 142–54
    definition, 446
    in literature, 102
    prediction by, 153
    and quotation, 163
Anatolian, 59
Angel of the Lord, 214
Angels, 250–56
    in book of Rev., 124
    chart of, 253
    cherubs, 251
    classes, 253
    fallen, 251
    functions, 252–54
    intellect, 251
    and local church, 253
    personality, 251
    and revelation, 253
    as servants, 251
    and sin, 253
    will, 251
Anginoskō, 157
Animism, 247
Anointing. *See* Holy Spirit
Antichristos, 61
Anticipation, 123
Antioch, 170
Antiochus Epiphanes, 172
Antipater, 172
Apocalypse of Baruch, 112
Apocalypse of Ezra, 112
Apocalypse of Paul, 112
Apocrypha. *See* Canon

Application of Scripture, 75
Arabah, 321
Arabah, Sea of the. *See* Dead Sea
Arabian Desert, 173
Arabic, 56, 58, 59, 174
Aramaic, 56, 58
Archangel, 251
Areopagus, 344
Arianism, 208
Arius, 311
Ark of the Covenant, 251, 263
Armageddon, 404
Armenian, 58, 59
Arminius, James, 311
Asaph, 156
Ashdod, 351
Ashkelon, 351
Asia, 169
Assumption of Moses, 112
Assyria, 171, 173
Astartes, 353
Atheism, 206, 363
Atonement, 262. *See also* Propitiation
Authority of Scripture, 23–24, 182–84, 195–98
    and interpretation, 81
    and quotation, 158
    versus tradition, 39

Babylon, 141, 169, 172, 296
Babylonian captivity, 58, 171, 172
Babylonianism, 133–34, 364
Babylonians, 44, 350
Balto-Slavic, 59
Baptism, 228, 291–92. *See also* Holy Spirit
Baptisma, 61
Baptizō, 61
Barbaros, 313
Barnabas, 341
Baur, Ferdinand Christian, 90
Believer-priest, 140, 329
Bethshan, 173
Beza, Theodore, 69
Bible
    authorship, 13
    as a book, 11–14
    contrasts within, 14
    convicting power, 12
    copying, 16
    diversity within, 13
    doctrine of, 182–99
    integrity of, 95
    as literature, 42, 99–128
    nature of, 11–36
    origins, 14–15
    as revelation, 186
    supposed errors, 197
    unity, 13

Bible doctrine, 179–81
Bible study, 37–49
  asking questions, 41
  and backgrounds, 41
  and biography, 45
  and concordances, 45–46
  goals, 38
  helps, 39–40
  and illumination, 40
  and interpretation, 73
  and languages, 41
  openness, 72
  overviewing, 41–42
  passages, 43–44
  and the plan of the Bible, 40, 42–43
  preparation, 38–39
  presuppositions, 39
  records, 43
  role of the Holy Spirit, 38, 40
  and supposed errors, 23, 189
  systematic approach, 38
  and the testaments, 46–48
  and translations, 41
  using themes, 44–45
  and word studies, 48
Bibliology, 182
Biblos, 313
Black Sea, 169, 357
Boaz, 261
Body of Christ. *See also* Church, universal
  beginning, 27, 133
  and the Holy Spirit, 227–28
  and laying on of hands, 341
  as a new entity, 34
  not in O.T., 133
  unity of, 285
Brookes, James H., 4
Bublos, 11
Bultmann, Rudolph, 90
Bunyan, John, 77

Caesarea, 170, 173
Cain, 138
Calvin, John, 79, 315
Canaan, 56
Canaanite, 56
Canaanites, 170, 312, 351, 354
Canon, 19–21
  of Apocrypha, 20
  meaning of, 19
  and miracles, 22
  of N.T., 20–21
  of O.T., 20
  and revelation, 22
  Roman Catholic, 20
  standards of determining, 19
Carmel, 173

Carnality, 280
Caspian Sea, 357
Celtic, 59
Census, 63
Centuria, 315
Centurion, 341
Charis, 271
Cherub. *See also* Angels
  and book of Ezek., 46, 124, 253
  in cross references, 46
  function, 251
  Satan, 254
Christian Science, 207
Christophany, 150, 214
Christos, 212, 310, 316
Church Age, 43, 227–28, 231
Church, local, 286–94
  and angels, 253
  and balance, 229
  and baptism, 291
  definition, 286
  discipline, 293–94
  diversity in, 287–89
  and edification, 287–89
  elders, 287–89. *See also* Elder
  freedom in, 287–89
  Lord's Supper, 292
  ordinances, 291–93
  restrictions in, 287–89
  rule, 287–89
  spiritual gifts, 229
  worship, 287, 289
Church, universal, 283–85. *See also* Body of Christ
  beginning, 27, 29, 284
  as Bride of Christ, 148, 302
  foundation, 327
  versus Israel, 26–30, 93, 227, 299
  and Pentecost, 284
  and plan of God, 34, 283
  and Scripture, 78
  and Spirit baptism, 231
  and the tribulation, 93, 302
  uniqueness, 26–30
  unity, 246
Clement of Rome, 21
Colonia, 63
Colony, 341
Commentary in literature, 123
Communication, 42, 82
Concursive operation. *See* Inspiration
Context, 44, 81, 94–98
Coptic, 58
Cornelius, 284
Council of Nicaea, 311
Covenants
  and Bible study, 43
  and book of Ezek., 141

Covenants (*continued*)
  and Israel, 136
  and rainbow, 124
  and Scofield Bible, 5
  individual, 35
  unchanging, 134
Covenant theology, 298–300. *See also* Amillennialism
Creation, 226, 244
Creationism, 245, 449
Cross
  and fall, 248
  and Jesus' temptation, 222
  meaning of, 88
  plan of God, 5
  and Satan, 235
  and sin, 237
  as transaction, 132
Culture, 75, 96
Cyrus, 171–72

Damascus, 346
Danish, 59
David
  and Goliath, 173
  line of, 162
  as prophet-king, 152
  and Saul, 174
  throne of, 215
  and tragedy, 110
  as a type, 148
Davidic Covenant, 35, 116, 136, 137. *See also*
  Covenants
Day of Atonement, 156, 357
Deacon, 288
Dead Sea, 174
Dead Sea Scrolls, 174
Death of Christ
  and Christian baptism, 291
  commercial theory, 258
  governmental theory, 258
  martyr theory, 258
  moral influence theory, 258
  mystical theory, 258
  as ransom to Satan, 258
  value, 257–59
Deism, 11, 207, 335, 363
Delphi, 353
Devil, 255. *See also* Satan
Diabolos, 61, 255
Dialogue, 123
Dichotomy, 245
Didache, The, 21
Dikaioō, 51, 61, 275
Discipline, 293
Discourse, 54
Dispensation, 26, 30

Dispensationalism, 24–30. *See also* Plan of the
  Bible
  definition, 30
  distinctives, 30
  and faith, 27–28
  and interpretation, 29–30
  and premillennialism, 300
  and Scofield Bible, 5
Dispensations, 24
  chart, 32–33
  overview, 30
Docetism, 219
Doctrine, 179
Doubtful things, 281
Drama, 123
Dutch, 58, 59
Dynamic equivalence. *See* Translation

Eastern Sea. *See* Dead Sea
Ecclesiology, 227
Edenic Covenant, 35. *See also* Covenants
Egypt
  and Abraham, 170
  and the Exodus, 171
  and Israel, 169, 172, 173
  locusts, 342
  trade, 173, 174
Eis, 60
Ekron, 351
El, 203–4
El Shaddai, 204
Elder, 229, 287–89, 352
Election, 265–71
Elijah, 97, 141, 173, 265
Elisha, 97
Elohim, 203–4
Elzevir brothers, 363
Emmaus, 194
En Gedi, 174
English, 58, 59
Enoch, 141, 265
Ephraim and Assyrians, 171
Episkopē, 61
Episkopos, 349
Epistle, 111, 112
Erasmus, 69
Erech, 170
Eschatology, 227, 296–304. *See also* Prophecy
Esdraelon, 173, 338. *See also* Megiddo
Essene, 16, 174, 319
Eternal security, 63, 277–78
Eternal state, 133, 304
Ethiopia, 169
Ethiopic, 56, 58
Euphrates River, 170, 312
Europe, 169
Euroquilo, 323

Euthus, 62
Eve, 34
Evolution, 247, 449
Exegesis, 88, 444
Exodus, 171
Ezekiel, 44, 45
Ezra, 77, 350

Faith
  and Abraham, 134
  additions to, 273–74
  origin of, 272–73
  and revelation, 22
  and salvation, 271–75
  versus works, 272
Fall, 233–36
  and authority, 182
  consequences, 234–36
  coverings, 138
  and the cross, 248
  and dispensationalism, 26
  effects of, 233
  factuality of, 233
  and godliness, 236
  and image of God, 243
  and incarnation, 248
  and our nature, 238
  and Satan, 233–34
  and the sexes, 235
  and worship, 244, 246
Fertile Crescent, 170, 174
Figurative interpretation. *See* Interpretation
Figurative language, 84–85
  and amillennialism, 28–30
  inconclusiveness of, 122
  and the Lamb, 99–101
  types of, 105–9
Filling. *See* Holy Spirit
First Enoch, 112
Flagellum, 63
Foreknowledge, 266–68
French, 59

Gabbatha, 350
Gabriel, 251, 252–53
Gaebelein, Arno C., 4
Galilee, 173
Gap theory, 232–33, 449
Garden of Eden, 233–36
Gath, 351
Gaza, 351
Geena, 329, 332
Gegrammenon estin, 157
Gegraptai, 157
Ge-hinnom, 329

General revelation. *See* Revelation
Geography, 168–74
Georgian, 58
German, 59
Germanic, 59
Gezer, 174
Ghor, 174
Gifts. *See* Spiritual gifts
Gilead, 173
Giving, 95, 289–91
God, 200–208
  as Adonai, 203
  attributes, 200–203
  as Elohim, 203–4
  as El Shaddai, 204
  eternality, 201
  as Father, 205
  glory, 205
  goodness, 202
  grace, 26, 202, 271
  holiness, 201–2, 236
  image of, 242–46
  immensity, 201
  immutability, 145, 201
  indwelling, 206
  as Jehovah, 203
  love, 202
  mercy, 202, 270
  names, 203–4
  omnipotence, 201
  omnipresence, 201
  omniscience, 201
  plan of, 5
  as Potter, 270
  righteousness, 202
  self-existence, 200–201
  sovereignty of, 145, 164
  as Trinity, 204–8
  as truth, 202–3
  uniqueness, 201
  wrath of, 262, 266
  as Yahweh, 203
Gog and Magog, 404
Golgotha, 359
Goliath, 173
Gongusmos, 53
Gospel as literature, 111
Gospels in Scouse, The, 67
Gothic, 21, 58
Grace. *See* God
Graf-Wellhausen theory, 321
Grammatical meaning. *See* Meaning
Grammatico-historical interpretation. *See* Interpretation
Gray, James M., 4
Great Commission, 170
Great High Priest. *See* Jesus Christ
Greece, 169, 172

Greek, 59–63
    Attic, 59
    Corinthian, 59
    Cretan, 59
    Cyprian, 59
    features of N.T. authors, 61–63
    in first c., 63
    and Hebrew, 63
    Hellenistic, 60
    history, 60
    Ionic, 59
    Koine, 60–61, 63
    manuscripts, 69
    precision, 51
    proto-, 59
    syntax, 60
    Thessalian, 59
    and thought, 57
Greek Orthodox Church, 58
Gulf of Aqabah, 174, 340

Habakkuk, 104
Hadēs, 331, 332
Hagar, 106, 144, 173
Haifa, 173
Hamartiology, 232–39. *See also* Sin
Haran, 170
Har-megiddo, 311
Hasmonians, 343
Hazor, 174
Heaven, 132
Hebrew, 56–58
    characteristics, 56–58
    as a language, 51
    language family, 56
    roots, 57
    syntax, 57
    in Palestine, 63–64
    text, 64
    thought, 57
Hellenistic Greek. *See* Greek
Herod(s), 172, 174, 332, 362
Herodians, 172
Hilastērion, 49
Hill of Aries, 344
Hinnom Valley, 367
Historical Books, 40
Hittite, 59
Hittites, 59
Holy of holies, 263
Holy Spirit, 225–31
    anointing of, 228, 285
    as Author of Scripture, 13
    baptism of, 228, 231
    and Bible Study, 38, 40
    and the Church, 284, 285
    and Church Age, 227–28

and creation, 226
deity of, 205, 225–26
as earnest, 321
filling of, 228–29, 285
and the incarnation, 227
indwelling of, 95, 228, 252, 285
and inspiration, 226–27
and interpretation, 75
and Israel, 285
and kingdom, 228
ministries, 226–27
and Pentecost, 227
as person, 225–26
and quotation, 161
and rapture, 303
and regeneration, 276
and renewal, 230
in revelation, 186, 226
and Satan, 252
and sealing, 228, 285
spiritual gifts, 229
Homer, 109
Humanity, 240–49
    chart of features, 246
    commission, 242
    fall of, 240–49
    and image of God, 246
    kingship, 246, 249
    makeup, 242–46

Icelandic, 59
Ignatius, 310
Illumination, 38, 40, 166, 193–95
Immanuel, 162, 215
Imputation, 238–39, 405. *See also* Sin
Imputed sin. *See* Sin
Incarnation, 215–19, 248. *See also* Jesus Christ
Indo-European, 52, 59
Indo-Iranian, 59
Indwelling. *See* Holy Spirit
Inerrancy, 197–98
Infallibility, 197
Information, 74, 443
Inherited sin. *See* Sin
Inspiration
    concursive operation, 123
    extent, 190–92
    and the Holy Spirit, 226–27
    versus illumination, 194
    and interpretation, 80
    and Jesus Christ, 192–93
    meaning, 187–88
    nature of, 22–23
    of N.T., 191, 226–27
    of O.T., 189, 226–27
    process, 189–90
    and quotation, 158

versus revelation, 15
and service, 190
and textual criticism, 188
Interpretation, 73–98. *See also* Allegorism; Typology
  allegorical, 106, 144
  and context, 81
  difficulties in, 155
  figurative, 29, 86, 92
  grammatico-historical, 79
  history of, 76–80, 90
  and hypotheses, 87, 92
  Jewish, 77
  literal, 81, 82–86
  normal, 84
  and theology, 86
  typological, 78, 143
Iota, 338
Irony, 106, 123
Isaac, 95
Isaiah, 164
Ishtar, 353
Israel
  versus Church, 299
  and covenants, 136
  in dispensationalism, 30
  future, 28
  and Holy Spirit, 227
  and Kingdom, 93
  location, 172
  modern, 169
  national salvation, 34
  and plan of God, 26
  in quotation, 160–61
  as vineyard, 160
  as wife of Jehovah, 314
Issachar, 338
Italian, 59
Italic, 59

Jacob, 95, 110, 140
James, book of, 61, 111
Jefferson, Thomas, 204
Jehovah, 203, 204
Jehovah's Witnesses, 207
Jeroboam, 97
Jerusalem, 170, 174
Jesus Christ. *See also* Death of Christ
  and access to God, 206
  and Adam, 248
  anointing of, 310
  approved by the Father, 265
  birth of, 172
  blood of, 261
  body of, 265
  as brother, 249
  and the cross, 218

death, 227, 257–64
deity of, 205
empathy of, 220
eternality, 214
and the fall, 219
as firstborn, 326
as firstfruits, 326
forsaken by Father, 264
glory of, 220
as Great High Priest, 223, 333
humanity of, 219
humbling of, 217–21
and image of God, 248
as Immanuel, 215
incarnation of, 183, 215–19
and inspiration, 192–93
intercession of, 223, 278
kenosis theory, 217
and Kingdom, 25, 31, 35, 249
as ladder, 140
as Lamb, 85, 99–101, 125
and Melchizedek, 151, 260
as Messiah, 114, 161, 212
natures of, 222
obedience of, 218
omniscience, 218
and postmillennialism, 297
preexistence, 213–15
as priest, 214
priesthood of, 139, 221–23, 259–61
as prophet, 214
resurrection of, 137, 264
as a revelation, 186
roles, 214, 221–23
as sacrifice, 221, 236
and Satan, 192
and Scripture, 19–20, 47, 196
as Shepherd, 221
sinlessness, 216, 222
as a slave, 218
as Son, 114, 115
as Son of God, 124, 137, 160, 210–11
as Son of Man, 124, 211–12
subordination, 205
temptation, 221–23
titles, 209–13
as Vine, 221
as Word of God, 183
Jezebel, 173
Jezreel, 173. *See also* Megiddo
John, book of, 62
John the Baptist, 100, 337
Jokneam, 174
Joppa, 170, 174
Jordan, 340, 346
Jordan River, 173, 174, 357
Joseph, 109, 110
Joshua, 173

Judah, 44, 171
Judas, 110
Judean mountains, 173
Justification, 275–76

Kai, 62
Kaphar, 48, 49
Kenoō, 217, 339
Kenosis. *See* Jesus Christ
Kidron Valley, 329, 367
Kingdom
  abrogation of, 28
  chart of views, 302
  as culmination of the ages, 133
  form, 297–301
  interpretations of, 91
  and the Holy Spirit, 228
  Jesus' preaching of, 162
  length, 120
  literalness, 28, 86
  nature of, 93, 304
  and rebellion, 304
  and rule of God, 134–35
  and sin, 25
  and Temple, 160–61
  as a testing, 31
King James translation
  evaluation of, 68–70
  and modern speech, 55
  and Scofield Bible, 6, 41
  as a translation, 72
Kinsman-redeemer, 261
Kish, 170
Koinē, 60
Koine. *See* Greek
Koinōnia, 317
Koran, 13
Kosmos, 255
Kranion, 315, 330
Kurios, 343

Ladder of Tyre, 173
Ladd, George Eldon, 93
Lagash, 170
Lake of Gennesaret, 357
Lamb, 99–101
  in book of Rev., 125, 133
  and metaphor, 85
  in New Heaven and New Earth, 141
Language
  arbitrariness of, 53
  borrowing, 64
  change, 55, 68–69
  as code, 53, 65
  conventionality, 53
  and creation, 243

discourse, 54
duality, 54
economy, 55
family, 59
form in, 54
general features, 52–56
incompatibility across languages, 54
and information, 65–66
meaning in, 65
productivity, 54
redundancy, 55
and revelation, 12
sound, 52
spelling, 52
structure, 65
and thought, 57
universals, 53
Latin, 58, 63
Law
  and cross, 218
  and definition of sin, 236
  and faith, 134
  as ineffective, 133
  and plan of the Bible, 31
  sacrifices, 139
Lazarus, 211
Lebanon, 354
Legalism, 280–81
Letter of Aristeas, 58
Levir, 342
Levites, 139, 153, 260
Lexical meaning. *See* Meaning
Linguistic incompatibility, 54
Linguistics. *See also* Language
  diachronic, 52
  history, 52
  and interpretation, 79
  synchronic, 52
  value, 50–52
Literal interpretation. *See* Interpretation
Literature
  and allusion, 104–5
  apocalyptic, 112
  dramatization, 104
  and figurative language, 105
  narrative, 109
  nature of, 102, 444
  plot, 103
  poetry, 112
  prophetic, 117–26
  suspense, 104
  theme, 104
  tragedy, 110
  and types, 151
Living Bible, 442
Logos, 67–68
Lord's Supper, 292, 294
Lord's Table, 132

Lordship of Christ, 274
Lucifer, 254
Luke, Gospel of, 61
Luther, Martin, 78, 211
Lutroō, 261
Lydda, 170

Maccabeans, 172
Manuscripts. *See* Textual criticism
Mark, Gospel of, 62
Masada, 174
Mashiach, 212
Matthew, 156, 159, 161
Meal offering, 345
Meaning
   determining, 82
   expected, 85, 92
   grammatical, 54
   and inspiration, 191
   lexical, 54
   and messages, 74
Medes, 350
Mediterranean, 173
Medo-Persia, 171
Mē genoito, 63
Megiddo, 173, 174, 404
Melchizedek
   and access to God, 139
   and Christ, 260
   offerings, 140
   and priesthood, 151
   as a type, 146, 148, 149–54
Mene, mene, tekel, uparsin, 58
Mercy seat, 263
Merom, Mt., 173
Mesopotamia, 170, 171, 321
Messages, 74–75, 82, 448
Messiah. *See* Jesus Christ
Metaphor
   analysis of, 443
   and book of Rev., 122
   and expectation of, 85
   and interpretation, 91
   meaning of, 105
   and parables, 107
   and symbolism, 121
Metonymy, 105–6, 117
Michael, 251, 252–54
Midian, 171
Midtribulation rapture, 302
Millennium, 228, 345. *See also* Kingdom
Miracles, 22
Moabite, 56
Moody, D. L., 4
Mormonism, 207
Morphology, 52
Morse code, 53, 190

Mosaic Covenant, 35. *See also* Covenants
Moses, 14, 153, 174, 185

Nabhi, 145
Narrative, 123
Nazareth, 163
Nebo, Mt., 174
Nebuchadnezzar, 171
Nebuchadrezzar. *See* Nebuchadnezzar
Negev, 170, 173
New American Standard Bible, 72
New Covenant, 35, 134, 151. *See also* Covenants
New English Bible, 66, 70, 71
New Heaven and New Earth, 141
New International Version, 6, 72
New Jerusalem, 133
New Scofield Reference Bible, 5–7
Nicodemus, 97, 238, 276
Nineveh, 171
Nippur, 170
Noah, 31, 124, 139, 140
Noahic Covenant, 35, 139. *See also* Covenants
Nondispensational premillennialism. *See* Premillennialism
Northwest Semitic, 56
Norwegian, 59

Oikonomia, 26
Old Church Slavic, 58
Olives, Mt., 329
Onomatopoeia, 53
Ordinances, 291–93
Orgē, 262
Origen, 78
Oxford NIV Scofield Study Bible, 7, 41, 72

Paleography. *See* Textual criticism
Palestine, 169–70
   centrality, 172–73
   and Edomites, 321
   and Israel, 34, 447
   languages, 63–64
   and Roman rule, 172
Palestinian Covenant, 35. *See also* Covenants
Pantheism
   and Christian Science, 236
   and immanence, 335
   and Stoicism, 361
   and the Trinity, 207
   and worship, 247
Pantokratōr, 309
Papyrus, 16
Parables, 107–9, 144, 445
Parnassus, Mt., 353
Partial rapture, 302

Pascha, 64
Paul
  and Athens, 322
  and authorship, 83–84, 90
  and Corinthians, 274
  imprisonment, 81
  and inspiration, 192
  language of, 63
  and the O.T., 144
Penalty offering, 364
Pentateuch, 14, 31, 40, 321
Pentecost
  and the Holy Spirit, 227, 228
  meaning of, 80
  and nature of Church, 284, 285
Peripoieō, 261
Persia, 169
Persian Gulf, 169, 170
Persians, 353
Personal sin. *See* Sin
Personification, 106, 123, 158
Peter, 192
Peter, book of (First), 61
Petra, 346
Pettingill, William L., 4
Pharaoh, 171, 185, 269–70, 337
Pharisees, 97, 195
Phasael, 172
Philadelphia College of Bible, 4, 6
Philemon, book of, 112
Philippi, 317
Philippians, book of, 94–95
Philistines, 171
Phillips, J. B., 70
Philo, 78
Phoenician, 56
Phonology, 52
Pisteuō, 61
Pithom and Rameses, 171
Plain of Dor, 174
Plain of Philistia, 174
Plain of Sharon, 174
Plan of God, 34
Plan of the Bible, 24–35, 42–43. *See also*
  Bible study
  and Bible study, 40
  and the Church, 26–28
  and dispensationalism, 30
  and God's goal, 24–26
  and the law, 31
  and the N.T., 34
  and the O.T., 30–31, 34
  and responsibilities, 26
  and sin, 25
Pneumatology, 227
Poetry, 112–17
Polycarp, 310
Polytheism, 204, 207, 363

Pompey, 172
Pontius Pilate, 352
Portuguese, 59
Postmillennialism, 91, 297–98
Posttribulation rapture, 302
Premillennialism, 300–301
  chart, 300, 301
  and dispensationalism, 300
  history of, 300
  and the Holy Spirit, 227
  and kingdom, 91
  nondispensational, 28, 30, 93, 300
  and Scofield Bible, 5
Presbuteros, 349
Presuppositions
  and amillennialism, 29–30
  and Bible study, 39, 76
  and theology, 89, 444
  in translation, 71
  warning against, 90–91
Pretribulation rapture, 301
Priesthood, 151, 221–23, 259–61, 289
Proginōskō, 267
Progressive revelation. *See* Revelation
Prophecy, 296–304. *See also* Eschatology
  definition, 144–45
  and literature, 117–26
  and Melchizedek, 150
  and types, 143, 147–48
Propitiation, 48, 262, 264
Psalms, book of, 113
Pseudepigrapha, 322

Qumran, 16, 174
Quotation
  and accuracy of Scripture, 158
  and analogy, 163
  and authority of Scripture, 158
  change in, 159–61
  and divine agency, 158
  formulas, 157–59
  fulfillment in life, 163–64
  and the Holy Spirit, 161
  and illumination, 166
  and inspiration, 158
  reasons, 162–64
  of Septuagint, 161
  sources, 156, 166
  and sovereignty of God, 164
  and types, 165

Rabboni, 353
Rapture, 14, 22, 300, 301–3
Ras Shamra, 56
Reconciliation, 263–64

Redemption, 232, 261–62, 264
Red Sea, 171
Reformation, 29
Reformers, 78
Regeneration, 238, 276–77
Register, 84
Rehoboam, 97
Relations between the testaments, 129–67
    allusions, 404
    analogical, 142–54
    and Bible study, 46–48
    continuity, 134–35
    contrastive and completive, 131
    contrasts, 26
    and covenants, 134
    quotational, 47, 154–67, 404–6
    structural, 130–35
    themes, 133
    theological, 135–42
Repentance, 274
Repetition, 123
Resurrection, 96, 137, 235, 264
Reticence in literature, 123
Revelation
    and angels, 253
    as disclosure, 14–15
    and faith, 22
    general, 183–85
    and the Holy Spirit, 186, 226
    and interpretation, 80
    and language, 12
    nature of, 21–22
    and plan of the Bible, 34
    progressive, 80, 145, 130–31
    and sin, 15
    special, 12, 15, 183, 185–87
    termination of, 22
    unity of, 146
Revelation, book of, 62, 118–26, 132, 141
Righteousness, 239
Roman Catholic Church, 20
Romance languages, 59
Roman Empire, 170, 172, 296
Romanian, 59
Rome, 169, 170
Ruth, 261

Sabellianism, 205
Sadducees, 97
Salt Sea. *See* Dead Sea
Salvation, 271–78
Samaria, 97, 171
Samson, 173
Sanctification, 278–81
Sanhedrin, 356
Sanskrit, 59
Sapir-Whorf hypothesis, 441

Sarah, 106, 144, 173
Sardinian, 59
Satan
    activities, 254
    attractiveness, 254
    and Bible study, 38
    in book of Rev., 122
    as cherub, 232, 254
    and the cross, 235
    defeat, 249
    defense against, 256
    as the Devil, 320
    as dragon, 255
    eternal confinement, 304
    and the fall, 34
    his fall, 232–33, 254
    his fall, 227
    and Jesus Christ, 227
    and the kingdom, 25, 304
    names, 251, 254–55
    pressures from, 255
    pride, 138, 236
    and Scripture, 39, 255
    and the serpent, 233
    strategies, 255
    his system, 255
    temptations, 192
    and the tribulation, 120
    worshipped, 252
Saul, 174, 341
Schleiermacher, Friedrich, 183
Scientific method, 86
Scofield Bible, 3–7
    and dispensationalism, 24
    helps, 44
    history, 439
    and nature of Church, 285
    and premillennialism, 93
    and revision, 6
    sections, 40
    and types, 148
    and word studies, 48
Scofield, Cyrus Ingerson, 3–4
Scythians, 169
Sealing. *See* Holy Spirit
Sea of Chinnereth, 357. *See also* Sea of Galilee
Sea of Galilee, 169, 174
Sea of Reeds. *See* Red Sea
Sea of the Arabah. *See* Dead Sea
Sea of Tiberius, 357. *See also* Sea of Galilee
Second advent, 125, 300
Semantics, 52
Semitic, 56, 59
Semitisms, 64, 66
Sensus plenior, 445
Septuagint, 58–59
    and *Koine,* 60
    and N.T., 64
    origins, 58

Septuagint (*continued*)
  and propitiation, 49
  and quotation, 47, 161, 446
  and textual criticism, 17
  and translations, 58
  use, 58
Seraph, 124
Seventy weeks of Daniel, 228, 303
Shaddai, 309
Shalom, 152
Shephelah, 173
Shinar, 170
Sidon, 351
Simile, 105
Sin, 232–39
  and angels, 253
  imputed, 238–39
  inherited, 237–38
  nature of, 236–37
  origin, 233
  and pantheism, 236
  personal, 237
  and redemption, 232
  revelation, 15
  and suppressing truth, 15
  unpardonable, 227
Sin nature, 237–38
Sinai (region), 170, 171, 173, 346
Sinai, Mt., 362
Skia, 149
Slavic, 21
Solomon, 169, 174
Song of Ascents, 359
Son of God. *See* Jesus Christ
Son of Man. *See* Jesus Christ
Soothing aroma, 351
Source language. *See* Translation
Spain, 169
Spanish, 59
Special revelation. *See* Revelation
Spiritual gifts, 229–31, 288
Spirituality, 279–81
Stone Pavement, 350
Strong believer, 281. *See also* Legalism
Subjectivism, 196
Substitution, 259–61
Sumer, 169, 170
Sumerians, 170
Suspense, 123
Swedish, 59
Sweet-savor offerings, 351
Symbolism, 121, 146
Synoptic Gospels, 197
Syntax, 52
Syria, 172, 173, 174, 340

Taanach, 174
Tabernacle, 132–33, 145, 146

Talmud, 331
Ta pneumatika, 229. *See also* Spiritual gifts
Target language. *See* Translation
Tartaroō, 332, 362
Taylor, Kenneth, 442
Tehillim, 353
Teleō, 157
Temple, 85, 140, 171, 346
Temptation, 221–23
Textual criticism, 16–19
  and authority, 188
  dittography, 18
  examples, 18–19
  external evidence, 18
  haplography, 18
  harmonization, 18
  homoeoteleuton, 18
  and inspiration, 188
  internal evidence, 18
  manuscripts, 16–18, 21, 23, 69
  paleography, 16
  parchment, 366
  purpose, 16
  variant reading, 16
  vellum, 366
Textus Receptus, 69
Theology
  and Bible study, 75
  biblical, 180
  exegetical, 180
  historical, 180
  and interpretation, 86–98
  meaning, 179
  practical, 180
  and scientific method, 86
  systematic, 180, 444
Theology proper, 180
Theophany, 150, 214
Theos, 203–4
Thomas, 96
Thumos, 262
Tigris River, 170
Tocharian, 59
Tongues, 230–31. *See also* Spiritual gifts
Torah, 350
Total depravity, 219, 238
Traditionalism, 196
Traducianism, 245
Translation, 64–72
  and accuracy, 69–70
  and audience, 67
  concordant, 67, 68
  and culture, 66
  and dynamic equivalence, 67
  and implicit information, 68
  of John's Gospel, 62
  and language change, 68–69
  literal, 84

and manuscripts, 69
and original languages, 69, 71
and paraphrase, 67
and presuppositions, 71
principles of, 64–68
and problems in, 66–68
requirements, 70
and the Septuagint, 58
source language, 64
style in, 70–71
target language, 65, 67
and theology, 67, 71
and understanding, 75
word count type, 67
Translations, 64–72
and Bible study, 41
choosing, 70
early, 21
evaluating, 68
utilizing, 72
Tree of life, 133
Tribulation, The
and the Church, 93, 302
dispensationalism, 34
events, 303–4
and the Holy Spirit, 228
and sin, 120
views of, 301–3
Trichotomy, 245
Trinity, 204–8, 225–26
errors concerning, 206–8
indwelling of, 226
and interpretation, 87, 89
and progressive revelation, 135
and Ps. 2, 117
and theology proper, 180
Tupikōs, 149
Tupos, 149
Tyndale, William, 64
Types, 143–54
extent of, 148

and Melchizedek, 150
and prophecy, 143, 147–48
quotation, 165
vertical, 446
Typology, 78, 143
Tyre, 173, 351

Ugarit, 56
Ugaritic, 56
United Bible Societies, 64
Unpardonable sin, 227
Upper Room Discourse, 96, 226
Ur, 170, 173

Variant reading. *See* Textual criticism
Vellum, 16
Verbal aspect, 62
Virgin birth, 162, 215–17
Vulgate, 341

Weak believer, 281. *See also* Legalism
Wisdom literature, 111
Worship, 140, 244, 246
Wrath. *See* God
Wycliffe Bible Translators, 64

Yahweh, 203, 204, 343
Yam Suph. *See* Red Sea
Yetzer, 77
Yod, 338

Zechariah, 156
Zedek, 152
Zerubbabel, 362
Zōopoieō, 277

Selective Index of Scripture Passages Discussed

Genesis

1–2	241–42
2:7	77
3	233–36
3:15	34
3:21	100, 138
4:1–15	138
4:4	100
6:4	252
8:20	139
10:4	18
12:3	133
14	139, 149–53
15:1–6	272
18:1–33	214
22	104
22:8	100
28:10–22	140

Exodus

3	203
3:6	95–96
3:19ff	269–70

Deuteronomy

6:4	201, 204
21:22–23	97

2 Samuel

7:12–16	116
7:16	136

2 Kings

18:17–37	58

Ezra

7:6, 11	77

Psalms

2	114–17
2:4–9	120
2:7	137
19:7–9	81
22	126–27, 148, 264–65
33:6	80
69:21	164
110:4	150, 151
139:7–12	201

Isaiah

5:1–2	160
7:14	148, 161, 162, 215–16
14:12–17	233, 254

28:11–12   160, 230
55:3   116, 137
62:11   156

Jeremiah
1:5   267

Ezekiel
1   44–46, 124, 141
28:11–19   233, 254

Daniel
9   128
9:24–27   302, 303
12:4   122

Hosea
11:1   156, 160

Habakkuk
2:4   104, 134, 163, 405

Zechariah
9:9   156
12:10   34–35
13:7   130–31

Malachi
3:1   131
3:6   201

Matthew
1:10   131
1:23   161, 162
2:15   156, 160
2:23   163
4:4, 6, 10 192–93
4:15–16   162
5:17–20   193
5:18   19–20
5:45   184
12   107–8
12:28   220
13   107–8
13:35   159
18:15ff   293–94
21:1–11   163
21:4–5   156

21:33–46   160
21:42   157
22:29   39
24:15–31   157
26:36–38   220, 222
27:46   127

Mark
1:29   62
12:18–23   195
14:27   130

Luke
1:1–3   14, 61
1:32–33   136
11:50–51   156
18:31   157
19:11–27   108
20:27–38   95–96
24:13–27   129
24:13–45   194

John
1:13   71
1:14   67
1:18   216
1:23   163
1:26   64
1:29   100
1:51   140
2:6   97
3:1–17   276
3:10   97
4:9–10   97
5:17–23   210
6:45   160
7:30   62
10:28–29   278
10:34   195
12:38–40   164
12:38–41   158
13–17   96–97
14:26   191–92
15:1–8   278
15:25   165
16:13–15   166
17:12   64
19:28   157, 164
19:30   62, 127
19:31   97
20:30–31   96

Acts

1:5	27, 284
1:6	28
2	41, 227
2:38	273, 274–75
3:22–33	156
4:27	116
7:56	141
8:21	68
13:32–34	116
13:32–35	137
13:47	158
20:7	292
20:20	38
28:31	28

Romans

1:3	137
1:16–17	104
1:17	134, 163
3:10–12	238
3:21–26	202, 263
3:21–28	275
3:25	48–49
4	134, 271, 272
4:25	265
5:1–11	278
5:6–11	263–64
5:12–21	63, 238–39
5:14	105
6	292
6:1–14	280
8:28–39	278
8:29	243
8:29–30	266–68
8:31–39	63, 268
9	268–71
9:1–3	63, 188
10:9	273
10:18	159
10:19–20	158
11:2	267
12:1	40
12:1–2	280
15:3	162

1 Corinthians

1:19	163
2:10–14	193–94
2:11–12	75
2:15	279
3:1–4	280
6:19–20	262
9:26	38
9:27	278
10:4	134

11:2	291
11:23–26	292
11:27–28	293
11:30	294
12:13	27
12–14	142
13	63
14:21	160
14:21–22	230
14:26	289
14:29	71
16:1–2	290

2 Corinthians

3:6	78
6:16–18	160–61
7:10	274
8:1–9:15	290

Galatians

4:21–31	144

Ephesians

1:10	26
1:13	228
1:13–14	278
1:22–23	27
2:1–3	238
2:1–5	63
2:4	202
2:5	277
2:20	231
3:2	26
3:3–6	133
3:6	27
3:9	26
4:11	229
4:11–16	287, 289
4:16	284
4:24	243
5:9	19
5:25–32	147
6:10–20	280

Philippians

2:1–11	217–18
2:5–8	205
2:12–13	95
4:18–19	289
4:19	81

Colossians

1:17	184
1:25	26
3:1ff	279

1 Thessalonians
  1:10   302
  5:4–8   303
  5:21   71

2 Thessalonians
  3:14–15   294

1 Timothy
  2:11–15   235
  2:14   289
  3:11–13   288
  5:19–20   294

2 Timothy
  2:15–17   75, 76
  3:16   80
  3:16–17   189–90
  4:1ff   190

Titus
  1:5   287

Hebrews
  1:1   185
  1:1–2   130
  1:14   251
  2:5–18   249
  6:4–6   278
  7   149–53
  7:25   223, 278
  8:5   132
  9:9–10   133
  13:15–16   289
  13:17   288

1 Peter
  1:3   276–77
  1:10–12   27–28, 147

  1:19–20   267
  1:23–24   276–77
  2:6–8   156
  3:1   62
  4:10–11   288
  5:4   61–62
  5:12   62

2 Peter
  1:19–21   95, 190

1 John
  2:20   194
  2:27   95, 128, 194
  3:11   138

Jude
  3   80
  5   134

Revelation
  1:7   119, 132
  1:19   118–19
  2–3   119–20
  3:10   302–3
  4:1   141
  4:7   46
  4–5   123–26
  5:5–6   101
  6:2–8   122
  7   93
  9   132
  9:1–12   120
  9:20–27   120
  16:17–21   120
  18:13   133
  19   132
  20:1–7   92–93, 120
  20:4   86
  21, 22   133